THE EXPANSION OF
ELIZABETHAN ENGLAND

THE EXPANSION OF ELIZABETHAN ENGLAND

by

A. L. ROWSE

FELLOW OF ALL SOULS COLLEGE, OXFORD

Si oblitus fuero tui Jerusalem, oblivioni detur dextera mea.
PSALM. CXXXVI

CHARLES SCRIBNER'S SONS
NEW YORK

A-8.72[C]

Printed in the United States of America
Library of Congress Catalog Card Number 72-1186
SBN 684-13063-7 (paper, SL)

To
T. S. ELIOT
who gave me my first introduction
to the world of letters

PREFACE

I N *The England of Elizabeth* I attempted a portrait of English
society in the Elizabethan age, from the point of view of
structure and government, rather than social life. The subject
of this volume is the expansion of that society, both by the state
and by individual enterprise, first into the margin of backward
societies at home—Cornwall, Wales, the Borders, with the sweep
of a sickle on the map : into Ireland, where the process involved
conquest and colonisation; then across the oceans, to our first
contacts with Russia, the Canadian North—the tenacious
search for a North-East or a North-West Passage to the riches of
Eastern trade—our emergence into the Pacific, the search for
Terra Australis (the ultimate discovery of Australia may be seen
as a distant product of the Elizabethan age), the opening up of
trade with India and the Far East, from which so much has
followed for us. Then come the first projects and attempts at
the colonisation of North America : their ultimate result Bismarck
thought the decisive fact in the modern world—as it is. As a
consequence, there comes the twenty-year-long struggle with
Spain by sea and land, which filled the Elizabethan age proper
with heroic endeavour, courage and confidence, sometimes with
set-backs and depression, disillusionment and achievement.

It is a wonderful theme : in it one sees in embryo the whole
subsequent history of our people—or, I should say, peoples—
and their astonishing fate and fortune in the world. I cannot
hope to have done justice to it : I have merely done the best I can.
After this portrayal of the expansive energies of our people in
action will come, I hope, its companion account of those of the
mind and spirit, to which the former provide the key and the door.
Those are intended to form the subject of my concluding volume :
The Elizabethan Age.

The marked western bias of this volume is unavoidable : the
whole book, like Elizabethan England, has wheeled to the west.
And this to an extent which I had not at first fully visualised :
the theme developed its own dynamic movement. But it not
only reflects, it reveals, *how* much this country owed its fortune to
the Elizabethan drive across the Atlantic to the New World ; and

vii

if the discovery of the New World made the fortune of this island, it was most markedly advantageous to the West—particularly the South-West—which, from being for so long the back-door, became the front-door. (The most striking illustration is the rise of Plymouth : a first-class history of that town could be a superb book.) So perhaps, after all, I do not have to apologise for my western bias here—though certainly I hope in my last volume, if not to correct it, at least to compensate it. And that should be appropriate when I come to deal with the flowering of the mind ; for the eastern counties contributed more, culturally and intellect-ually : they were much richer and more settled (culture depends on wealth, suitably modulated), and were more closely bound up with London, which was overwhelmingly important in this respect.

This book is intended as a contribution to knowledge rather than opinion. But I am anxious that there should be no misunder-standing about my attitude with regard to the main conflict in that age, any more than in this. It is not, as seems to be thought, that of a simple anti-Puritanism. My attitude towards extremists on both sides—Counter-Reformation fanatics abroad, Puritan fanatics at home—is : a plague on both your houses. I have grown to detest the fanatic believers on both sides, who make life intolerable for sensible people in the middle. My sympathies are not with the Calvins and Cartwrights, especially not with the Philip II's and Father Parsonses, who sent so many people to their deaths, but with intelligent sceptics like Montaigne and Shakespeare, or, for that matter, with *politiques* like Elizabeth and William the Silent. My position is one of scepticism, par-ticularly with regard to the doctrinal (or ideological) certainties for which some human beings will all too readily consign others to death. It is a recurrent theme in history, a recurrent disgrace to the human record : I feel about it as Acton did—the tragedy of history. But there is no inherent reason why it should be so : I isolate this element as the most detestable trait in human nature, only too cruelly in evidence in our own century, as in the sixteenth.

In that sense, this book is a contemporary book and consciously reflects the contemporary situation. Sectarian historians have had their fling, particularly in the nineteenth century, when the consequences of sectarian conflict were not so much in evidence in ruins around them. A sceptical, Laodicean point of view, which sees the case of the moderates against the extremists on both flanks, seems rarer in historical writing—though why people should find it hard to understand defeats me. Nevertheless, though a rational attitude may be an unfashionable one just now,

Preface

I cannot complain of the response of the *public* to what I write.

On the other hand, we do not have to be too sceptical as to the possibility of historical knowledge. Even those who are most doubtful of the process of historical transmission must perceive the advantage of quoting largely from original sources : these are the very words of the actors, their emotions and thoughts that they are expressing or disguising, the very rhythms of their inner natures that all words betray. Then, too, *their* words are so fresh, so shining and full of life, where ours are worn down, defaced or deadened by use. I make no apology for quoting so much : the more Elizabethan English the better. In a book on this scale, the bulk of the material must come from what are known, professionally, as secondary sources. But, in fact, a good deal of primary material has gone into it too; in each chapter I have been able to add something new, at one point or another, from unpublished sources.

It is a great pleasure to acknowledge the hospitality and kind encouragement of my hosts at various Elizabethan houses, and their generosity with their papers: the Dowager Duchess of Devonshire at Hardwick, the Duke and Duchess of Buccleuch at Boughton, the Marquis and Marchioness of Salisbury at Hatfield, Lord and Lady De L'Isle and Dudley at Penshurst, Captain and Mrs. Meyrick at Sheafhayne. The late Duke of Alba was most kind, not only in sending me copies of his historical publications, but in entertaining me in Madrid and showing me his fascinating collections. They have all been a great help to the historian who wants to reconstruct in his mind the life of the age *as a whole*.

It has been a happiness to me to have received so much help from my fellow-scholars, and I record my indebtedness to them with warm gratitude. Sir Edmund Craster has helped me with suggestions, and by his own work, in regard to his own Border country. I have been most generously aided by Welsh scholars : both Professor A. H. Dodd of Bangor and Professor T. Jones Pierce of Aberystwyth very kindly gave me off-prints of all their articles and made the way easier for me ; Professor Idris Foster of Oxford answered many questions and has been a constant guide in conversation. I have been much honoured by the Principal and Council of the University College of Aberystwyth in inviting me to give the Gregynog Lectures, based on the early chapters of this book. Professor Cyril Falls has helped me over both Irish and military matters. Professor D. B. Quinn of Swansea has been most generous in lending me the proofs of his forthcoming, definitive work on *The Roanoke Voyages* (Hakluyt Society), in sending me rare off-prints and answering troublesome queries. Professor Richard Pares, then of Edinburgh, gave me guidance on an important point; I deeply appreciate the stimulus of his conversation on his return to All Souls.

I cannot sufficiently express what this book owes to Professor Jack Simmons of Leicester, for the care with which he read my proofs, the valuable constructive suggestions he made and for his scholarly severity. He has saved this work from several blemishes, particularly in the expression of opinion; for those that remain I am obstinately responsible. To Mr. Norman Scarfe of Leicester I am most grateful, not only for his expert proof-reading and for several historical improvements to the text, but for kindly conducting me round Ireland in pursuit of Elizabethan associations and relics in the interests of the book. Mr. G. F. Hudson and Mr. John Bowle have helped me greatly with proofs : I appreciate their goodness.

I have been much helped by patient officials at the Bodleian and Codrington libraries, and at the Public Record Office and British Museum. In America, I have greatly profited from the generosity of the Huntington Library and the Rockefeller Foundation, which made it possible for me to study at the Huntington. Nowhere in the world is there a kindlier or more propitious atmosphere for work. I was enormously helped there by the constant care and friendship of Mr. and Mrs. Godfrey Davies, and by Mr. Tyrus Harmsen. And I stand much indebted to Mr. Edward F. D'Arms of the Rockefeller Foundation. During my brief visit to the Folger Library in Washington, Mr. Louis B. Wright and Dr. Giles Dawson were kind; the latter sent me a transcript of a rare Drake document. It is a pleasure to record what I owe to the guidance of Professor Francis R. Johnson, our leading authority on Elizabethan science, at Stanford, at Oxford and in Cornwall.

A constant obligation is to All Souls College, without which I might not have been able to tackle so large a book, still unfinished : certainly it would have taken me even longer. But perhaps it may be thought that the production of works of scholarship is not all that such institutions are for.

A. L. ROWSE

Trenarren, St. Austell
Passion Sunday, 1955

x

CONTENTS

THE EXPANSION OF
ELIZABETHAN ENGLAND

CHAPTER I

THE BORDERLANDS:
THE SCOTTISH BORDERS AND CORNWALL

W E have seen in a previous volume something of the structure and organisation, we have traced the working and the growth, of the most taut and vigorous national society in Europe.[1] We must now follow its expansion.

For, by a singular chance, the expansion of that small society from Elizabethan times onward became increasingly identified with the central movement in the history of the modern world. No mere book can hope to do justice to the theme: it is written in the lives of men, in their works and arts, in the creations of their minds, in science and industry, in the busy tracks of the ocean, upon the landscape and on the face of the outer world. It was an extraordinary, an unimaginable, fate that befell the island people. Wherever we look in the world, or in modern history, we come upon evidences of the contributions they have made. Whether it is at sea, in the arts of navigation or maritime warfare from Drake to Nelson and our own time ; whether it is in voyages of discovery from the Cabots to Cook and Scott of the Antarctic, in methods of planting and colonisation from Humphrey Gilbert and Ralegh, Captain John Smith and the founders of New England to Gibbon Wakefield and Cecil Rhodes ; or in industry, trade, finance ; whether it is in the experience of self-government, laid open for all to see, or in the essential traditions of the free world—personal freedom for the citizen, liberty of opinion and speech, the sanctity of individual life (the arcana of civilised society) ; or in the example of an instinctive and generalised morality of common sense and toleration, with its precious message of individual responsibility ; whether it is in the gradual unfolding of the resources of industrial

[1] Cf. *The England of Elizabeth*, 1951. I say ' national society' because I should regard the Netherlands as perhaps the most vigorous society in Europe until its set-back with the religious strife and the struggle with Philip II.

and mechanical power (the basis of modern industrial civilisation, worked out in this island), with its subsequent developments in atomic energy and in the air ; or in the unceasing proliferation of its genius at once for literature and for science—the experience of the island people has been more and more closely bound up with the essential achievements of the modern world, the most significant and certainly the most fruitful movements of the human spirit in modern history.

This strange fate—not envisaged by the Elizabethans, though some of them (like Ralegh and Bacon, perhaps even Drake) had their intimations along with their ambitions—began to open out for a small and rather backward people on the margin of Europe in the second half of the sixteenth century, contemporaneously with the rule of a very remarkable woman, who thus gave her name, never more appropriately, to the age.

Now that we have reached the point at which that history, as a separate stream, has ceased to have its old importance and has become mingled with the main stream of the West, with its children on the other side of the Atlantic moving naturally in course of time into the leading place, now is perhaps the moment to attempt to seize something of the achievement of the age that set that astonishing dynamic movement going—even if it suggests a little an epitaph on our history for ourselves.

We have already seen something of the expansive spirit of the time at work in economic matters, developing the industries and resources of the country ; in government and politics, in the greater efficiency of administration, in the growing claims of the Commons for a share in power ; in education and even in religion.[1] We shall now have to trace the theme outwards into the backward areas of the borderlands—the Scottish Borders, Wales and Cornwall, Ireland ; then overseas, to the opening up of the new English world in North America ; finally, in the realm of the spirit, in literature, the wonderful outburst of the drama, the arts ; in science and knowledge, where Bacon, William Gilbert and Camden were spirits as representative as Spenser and Marlowe, Drake and Ralegh were in other spheres.

Expansion is the natural and instinctive impulse of any

[1] *The England of Elizabeth, v.* especially cc. iii, iv, vii, viii, xii.

healthy society. It was certainly not peculiar to the England of Elizabeth—though that which it set in motion came to have greater significance for the world than any other. In that age by far the grandest example of expansive energy was Spain, which has left a mark second only in importance to the English upon the face of the world. We followed, after an interval, in their footsteps and across them.

But first comes a more *gründlich* phase of expansion at home. Here also we were not alone.

All round the ultimate rim of North-Western Europe were the fascinating fringes of a twilit Celtic world—fascinating, if in various stages of deliquescence, decay and regeneration, partly for internal reasons of their own, partly under the impetus of the new efficiency of the Renaissance state.[1] What more natural and indeed inevitable—for here we may for once use the word legitimately of an historical process—than that so thrusting a society as Elizabethan England should push outwards into the margin of Celtic societies, yielding or resentful or resistant? The movement has an impersonal quality about it : it could not but have happened, almost apart from whether some wanted a forward move, others not.[2] People do not much understand the movements, the convolutions, in which they are caught in history ; though one can observe the motives at work—the desire for greater order, for better administration ; opportunities for gain, for adventure ; the defensive motive of forestalling an enemy, closing a back-door to possible intervention, protecting one's communications ; power or just moving in, like any natural force, into a vacuum.

We may watch some or all of these motives at work in the various comparable movements of the time. Sixteenth-century France annexed Celtic Brittany. The forced marriage of the Duchess Anne to Charles VIII in 1491—in the château at Langeais that looks out little changed upon the sandy, willow-fringed and many-islanded Loire—brought it about.[3] All her life the little Duchess fought against the absorption of her duchy into the kingdom of France, to preserve its independent entity ;

---

[1] This theme was first presented to us by Dr. David Mathew in his original book, *The Celtic Peoples and Renaissance Europe*, 1933.

[2] Naturally sceptics about human action would not ; Montaigne's disapprobation of the European irruption into the New World is a famous case. But to what point ? One might as well quarrel with Niagara.

[3] Cf. E. Durtelle de Saint-Sauveur, *Histoire de Bretagne*, I. 390 foll.

but she could not prevail against the tide. Gradually, throughout the reign of Francis I, Breton independence was whittled away, until with the reign of Henry II the process of union with the French crown was complete and the king did not bother even to describe himself as duke in his Celtic duchy any more.

At the other end of the Celtic world, a similar process was taking place in the Western Isles and Highlands of Scotland. Two years after the annexing of Brittany to the French crown, in 1493 the Macdonald lordship of the Isles was extinguished : the unrest that resulted, the incursions of Macdonalds into Ireland, made a strand in the kaleidoscopic politics of Celtic Ulster. It was not until James VI was ruling in England that the last effort of the Macdonalds to recover their hereditary land sputtered out.[1] Meanwhile, before coming to the English throne, James had suppressed the Clan Gregor and driven the Macleods out of their island of Lewis, planting it with a company of Adventurers, adopting—as a Scottish Nationalist historian charmingly says—" the method of the English in Ireland ".[2] The point is that the methods were everywhere the same. Even the weak central government in Edinburgh—so much less strong than that in London—was making its impact on Celtic chaos ; and in 1609 James made a decisive and lasting change in the history of the Western Isles, hitherto Catholic, by annexing them to the Reformed religion of the Scottish state.

By the middle of the sixteenth century England had been decisively checked in the continental obsessions that had wasted her resources as late as the reign of Henry VIII, with his last pointless, fruitless and vastly expensive French war. Then, with the loss of Calais—open door to the Continent—the English were forced to concentrate on their insular and maritime resources. It was the most fortunate defeat in our history.

The early Tudors, especially Henry VIII, had got forward with the job of absorbing Wales and Cornwall into the pattern of English government and life. These still retained their different inflection and remained different, for they were in a less advanced stage of development than progressive English agrarian society already being energised by commerce and industry : they were poor, and they were backward. Still ruder, more backward and

---

[1] P. Hume Brown, *History of Scotland*, II. 252 foll.
[2] Agnes Mure Mackenzie, *The Scotland of Queen Mary and the Religious Wars*, 295.

more of a problem were the Scottish Borders ; and, most of all, Ireland.

There a whole country, almost as large as England, presented a curious and—by all counts—deplorable spectacle of a Celtic civilisation in part medieval, in part pre-medieval, pastoral in its economy, tribal in organisation, nomadic and unsettled in habits, and of itself in a stage of rapid social decomposition— even apart from its exposure to the vital dynamic of an England pulsating with life and adventure. To this was added the dis- organisation caused by the Reformation, which the Irish never absorbed, the difference of language, of racial characteristics, of the whole outlook and experience of life. Hence the clash and conflict at every point : there was no point of agree- ment. Resistance was sometimes partial, sometimes almost general, often overt, almost always latent—even though there were considerable areas of support, and nuclei of sympathy and aid to the English and their government in their inevitable, their heart-breaking and often heartless task.

The whole thing is very complex and this is not the place to go into it ; we can, however, distinguish two main stages. Henry VIII's government, which had accomplished the essential work of the Union with Wales and its welding into the kingdom, also undertook the first stage in the extension of its authority over Ireland—a much bigger job. " The Tudor monarchy could not for ever tolerate the existence of a half-subdued dependency which, if not controlled by England, might soon be controlled by England's enemies." [1] With the energy generated by the Reformation—after the black years of upset and confusion were over—and the increased coherence and momentum of govern- ment that came with Elizabeth's rule, the forward process in Ireland was renewed : " Elizabeth extended her authority over a wider area of Ireland than had been effectively controlled by any previous English sovereign ". [2] But with the growing fierceness of the struggle against the Counter-Reformation in the latter half of the century, with England locked in a struggle for her existence with Spain, she became involved in the necessity to subdue and conquer Ireland ; and by the time the Queen died, the sickening, the imperative, process was complete. Out of that very process of subjugation, the foundations of a new

[1] J. C. Beckett, *A Short History of Ireland*, 44.
[2] *Ibid.* 61.

Ireland which *could* have come into existence were achieved : an Ireland with a real integration of stocks, Celtic and Saxon, a fusion like that which underlies the creative fertility of the English people : an integration that might have given Ireland an altogether happier, and certainly more successful, history. But that hope was ruined by the odious, the superfluous, Civil War in England.

The most fertile legacy of the long effort the Elizabethans made in Ireland is, in consequence, not to be found so much there as in the experience it yielded, the stimulus it provided, the guidance it gave towards the ultimately far more fruitful task of the planting and colonisation of North America. The West Country group who were so much concerned in warfare and planting in southern Ireland—Gilbert, Ralegh and Grenville —were precisely those who carried over their ambitions and imagination into the New World.

I. The Borders

It was Camden's enthusiasm for Roman remains that led him to perambulate Cumberland and Northumberland, and when he comes to the Wall he gives free rein to it : " I have seen the tract of it over the high pitches and steep descents of hills wonderfully rising and falling ".[1] The country produced many antiquities and inscriptions for him—it was much fuller of them then than now. At one place a poor old woman dwelling in a cottage showed him an ancient altar-stone ; there was another in a place " where now women beat their bucks on it ".[2] But we remember the nomads, and Camden could not inspect the fort at Busy Gap because of the robbers there.[3] There was a tradition among the people that Roman soldiers had planted herbs to cure wounds : hence Scottish practitioners flocked there at the beginning of summer to gather simples and wound-herbs.[4] They were certainly needed : not until the end of Elizabeth's reign and the union of the two countries were the Borders securely reduced to order. They were by far the most lawless part of the country, and the lawlessness was endemic.

There was a twofold reason for it. Not only were the Borders the country most remote from government—those high fells with

---

[1] W. Camden, *Britannia* (trans. by Philemon Holland, ed. 1637), 793.
[2] *Ibid.* 800.   [3] Cf. *The England of Elizabeth*, 71.   [4] Camden, *op. cit.* 795.

the strange green northern lights at evening, the rose-coloured rocks on the west, the black basalt and purple sandstone on the east, with their trackless mosses and upland dales then inaccessible to all but those who knew them ; but it was all frontier country. That made it impossible to reduce it to satisfactory order : the two circumstances played into each other's hands. Even if the long arm of English government had been able to reduce all its elusive subjects in these parts to obedience, " the lack of a strong and settled government at Edinburgh was a more potent factor than geography in Elizabethan Border history ".[1] The feuds and conflicts among the Border nobles on the Scottish side—personal, political, religious—were far more acute and enabled disorder to run riot.[2] The Scots were more given to reiving and raiding into England ; English reprisals were apt to be organised by the authorities themselves and to inflict more damage. Sometimes there was good co-operation between the authorities on both sides, the English and Scottish Wardens who governed these ' peccant parts ', sometimes less so. That depended on the ups and downs of internal Scottish politics in this upheaved era and on the varying relations between the two countries ; for this was an international frontier with all the paraphernalia, the delays and the hocus-pocus, that go with relations between powers.

In another aspect, it was not so much the case of Scots against English as that the settled folk on both sides were victims of the Borderers. Quiet folk planted in the valleys or on the plains, cultivating the soil, might be caught and killed at plough ;[3]

[1] D. L. W. Tough, *The Last Years of a Frontier*, 28.

[2] Cf. *Salisbury Papers* (H.M.C.), VIII. 146-7. " The irreconcilable deadly feud that be in his realm, as in the North betwixt the Earls Orkney and Caithness, the Earls Atholl and Murray, and Lord Forbes against Huntly, between the Earl Crawford and Lord Glamis, and in the South betwixt the Lord Maxwell and Laird of Johnston, the Lord Ochiltree and Douglases, the Earls Eglinton and Glencarne, the Earl Mar and Lord Leviston, besides other ensuant feuds in every corner of his realm, be such as he cannot bring a thousand men to field without a thousand particular quarrels." (A memorial to the Earl of Essex.) This, if somewhat exaggerated, brings home the consequences of a weak, as against a strong, central government.

[3] Cf. the scene described by John Carey to Burghley, *Cal. Border Papers*, II. 167. Sir John Ker of Cesford came to a poor man's wife " and asked where he was ? Who showed him where her husband was, going at the plough among many others. And Sir John, asking the poor men which was Boulton ? came to the poor man himself and asked his name. Whereupon the poor man in good manner put off his hat, told his name was Boulton. Presently Sir John very valiantly drew out his sword and cut him three blows upon the head, and left the rest of his company to cut him all in pieces." No doubt Boulton had done something.

7

cattle were constantly being stolen and driven across the fords from one country into the other ; houses were burned over people's heads, mills put out of action, timber regularly cut, bridges destroyed. Well-to-do folk who ventured too near might be put to ransom ; there are still Ransomes in those parts ; they seem to have contributed the term ' black-mail ' to the language : forbearance- or protection-money. Once one of these raids got as far as Alnwick—the seat of government of the Middle Marches ; on another occasion as far as Penrith, in spite of its castle. The little townships near the waste lands lived in constant trepidation, especially when the fat time from Michaelmas to Martinmas came near and nights were lengthening. Indeed, if one looks at Penrith today with a seeing eye, it bespeaks those days and dangers : in the centre, a wide open space to hold all the cattle, with narrow defensible lanes leading to it from the town-gates. Once the hue-and-cry was up—and sleuth-hounds were sometimes employed to track the depredators—they were away and over the Border.[1]

> They ran their horse on the Langholme howm,
> And brak their spears wi' mickle main ;
> The ladies lukit frae their loft windows—
> " God bring our men weel back agen." . . .
>
> " I'll gie thee a' these milk-white steids,
> That prance and nicker at a speir ;
> And as mickle gude Inglish gilt,
> As four of their braid backs dow bear."[2]

A further convenience for such operations, and a bother for both governments, was the fact that some of these families, or rather tribes, lived on both sides of the frontier : notably the Armstrongs of Liddesdale—and these verses celebrate one of them, the ballad of " Johnie Armstrang ". So, too, with the Elliots and the Grahams : all of the Western March, where there was most trouble. The Border proverb has it : " Armstrongs and Elliotts, ride thieves all ".

There were other circumstances, too, to account for the state of things : the primitive conditions of life, a pastoral

---

[1] Cf. R. Welford, *History of Newcastle and Gateshead*, III. 109.
[2] Sir Walter Scott, *Minstrelsy of the Scottish Border* (revised and ed. by T. F. Henderson, 1902), I. 353-4.

society living mainly off cattle, and for cereals producing only oats, rye and barley ; the people desperately poor and their poverty increased by the incessant sub-division of tenements among the children, too many people in fact for subsistence—some dales were more populous then than they are now, though at times they were depopulated by fear and depredations ; the climate rainy and cheerless, too wet, the countryside comparatively unproductive. In all this, very like Wales and Ireland : one sees the famous contrast between the Highland and the Lowland Zones of Britain at its most acute.[1] The Governor of Berwick in 1600, a Willoughby accustomed to better things, wrote home : " if I were further from the tempestuousness of Cheviot hills, and were once retired from this accursed country whence the sun is so removed, I would not change my homeliest hermitage for the highest palace there ".[2] Lord Hunsdon complained to Leicester that it gave him the stone, " having I think as much gravel within me as will gravel the way between Hackney and Wansted ", *i.e.* from his house to Leicester's.[3] (This was by way of winning the favourite's sympathy for a few words to the Queen for permission for a holiday from his post. He did not get it.) The cattle of the country were small, like those in the uplands of Cornwall. The houses of the people were just cabins that could be run up or removed in a few hours, as in Ireland. Jock o' the Syde's house—a figure famous in a ballad—was described by Sussex as " a cottage not to be compared to a dog-kennel in England ".[4]

The character of their society was according. It was a Balkan society. They followed their local leader in life and death—often to death. Those are the heroes their ballads celebrate, all that is left of them now : Kinmont Willie, Ill-drowned Geordie, Curst Hobbie, Ill Hobbie of the Ramsgill, Archie Elliott of the Hill. Their life was thieving and reiving and raiding, very much given to sports, hunting and hawking, horse-racing and football ; they were riddled with feuds, up to their eyes in fighting and blood-shed ; murder was frequent. Among themselves they could be true and staunch and generous ; they made it a particular point of honour to shelter whoever was at odds with the law, a refugee from justice. So that the name of Hector Armstrong, who

[1] Cf. Sir Cyril Fox, *The Personality of Britain*, c. i.
[2] *Cal. Border Papers*, ed. J. Bain, II. 718.   [3] *Ibid*. I. 73.
[4] q. W. W. Tomlinson, *Life in Northumberland during the Sixteenth Century*, 33.

handed over the Earl of Northumberland to the Regent Morton for money, stank in Border tradition as the traitor above all. They were fierce and brave and quarrelsome ; they were not without a certain grim humour in their exploits, many of which have come down to us in ballad or tradition. They were given up to bastardy and balladry—in both, again, like Wales and Ireland. Theirs was a ballad civilisation, and it exemplified the characteristics of such societies all over Europe.[1]

For their character, we have a report of it as it was represented to the sedate Lord Burghley in the South—so unlike the domestic life of the revered recipient.[2] They are described as a people " barbarous more of will than manners, active of person and speech, stout and subtle, inclined to theft and strife, factions and seditions, full of malice and revenge, being nursed up in these vices from their ancestors, apt to quarrel rather with blood than speech, though scant of neither. . . . They turn their deadly feuds into infinite horrible murders, and this is held impossible to be reformed among them, living as they do as infidels, so as the clown makes the gentleman knave. Notwithstanding their gallantry, some will sell the blood and death of their father for money ; as they term it, for kin-bote. Contrariwise the killer will submit himself naked upon his knees, holding his own sword by the point held to his breast, yielding the handle to his enemy's hand, and so with abject humility ask forgiveness." How often we remember such scenes of Irish chieftains, the tears streaming down their faces, on their knees before the Queen's Deputy in the Council Chamber at Dublin ! For the characteristics of such social groups, the anthropologist will know how to docket and classify, though the life evaporates.

Bastardy was so much a feature of this Northern life that one notices among Durham wills that it is accepted by the leading families, and the children take their father's name along with the rest. Perhaps it is a tribute to ideal virtue that their bastardy is specified : out in the wilds no-one bothered. Trollopes, Delavals, Lilburnes, Middletons, Rokebys—all mention their progeny on both sides of the blanket.[3] Thomas Trollope pays tribute to his " good wife who hath been and is not only much comfortable to me but much profitable " ; he leaves her as a

[1] Cf. W. J. Entwhistle, *European Balladry*, 30.
[2] *Salisbury MSS.* (H.M.C.), VIII. 562-4.
[3] Cf. *Wills and Inventories*, Surtees Soc., I. 151, 174, 204, 428; II. 36.

pledge of his confidence the care of his base-begotten son. Sir John Delaval leaves " Jane Delaval, my bastard daughter £6 13s. 4d. and George Delaval my bastard son 40s. a year, for service done and to do unto my heirs " : a convenient, and quite usual, disposition. When Sir Robert Brandling, a leading citizen of Newcastle, lay on his death-bed he had not made a will. " ' They say in this town, if you had not had so many bastards you would have made your will ere now.' And he answered, ' If I have any I am able to find them.' At which word his priest, sitting by upon a form, did rise and come to the aforesaid Sir Robert, his master, and said, ' Sir, you bid me speak to Mistress Brandling to take one of the wenches called Jane ' ", etc. There was general regret that " so wise a man should make such an end ".[1]

But what of the state of affairs among the Forsters, the family of the celebrated Sir John, for most of the reign Warden of the Middle Marches, living in some state in the abbey at Alnwick, and turning the west end of Hexham Abbey into a residence, of which traces still remain ? His brother, Thomas Forster of Edderston, made his deceased son's base-begotten son Matthew his executor.[2] His own base-begotten son Hugh, with Sir John and his base-begotten son, Nicholas, were to be supervisors. Legacies are made to three more base-begotten sons of the testator, Ralph, John and George Forster ; and to Agnes Stevenson, who looks like their mother. Further bequests are made to George and Peter Forster, the base-begotten sons of his brother Roland. This will is more eloquent than pages of social disquisition : it looks as if, in the Forster family, a good time was had by all. But it is not very exceptional, except from the point of view of quantity. Again, there are circumstances to excuse the North : the huge size of the parishes, the small number of clergy, the uncertainty with regard to religion, the unsettled ways of life, the custom of hand-fasting (which consoled the heart of good Bishop Creighton).[3] But the haphazardness in these matters shocked the new Protestant Dean Horne of Durham— " such uncleanness through fleshly life, yea such horrible incests, as have not been heard of among the heathen ".[4] These things go with certain sorts of society and temperament : everyone has always noticed them among the Cornish—the moralistic Norden

[1] R. Welford, *op. cit.* II. 415.
[2] *Wills and Inventories*, II. 164.
[3] Cf. M. Creighton, *Carlisle*, 143.
[4] R. Welford, *op. cit.* II. 355.

read them a lesson on the subject in his book ;[1] the same was true of Wales and, most blatantly of all, the Celtic society of Ireland. There the quarrels and bloodshed it gave rise to among the princely families, notably the O'Neills of Ulster, provided the principal danger to their dynasties, imperilled their succession and opened the way to their enemies.

More important from the point of view of government on the Borders were offences against person and property. We get flashes of light upon the lurid scene from the comparative security of the towns—Berwick, Alnwick, Carlisle, capitals of the respective Marches, East, Middle, West—which swept like a sickle around the danger-area. When the leading luminary of the Kirk, James Melvill, was at Alnwick in 1584, thrown out by a sudden turn in the confused politics of Edinburgh, he lodged in the house of a widow " whose son-in-law, good man of the house, was lying sick of many deadly wounds given him by the Scots thieves in the Border. And yet we received never an evil countenance of them, but by the contrary were very well treated and reasonably."[2] (Hospitality was, of course, no less a feature of such a society.) We have a vivid picture of these thieves at work in a letter from Berwick : " the Scots ride as far as Morpeth as quietly as in Tividale [*i.e.* Teviotdale]. The Tividales will ride ten or twelve in a company from town to town and call men by their names and bid them rise quickly. The poor man doth ask him what he is ? The Scot saith, ' Dost not know me by my tongue ? I am Jack of the Hare Well, or Hob, or Gilchrist, or Tom of the Covis, or a Davison or a Young.' These be the rank riders. The Scot bids, ' Rise ! the great host of Scotland is coming : all your town shall be burnt. If thou wilt be my prisoner, I will save thy horse, corn and cattle.' The simple man thinketh all true that he heareth : he riseth and giveth his hand out at window, or over the door, to be a true prisoner and enter when he is called for, or else to pay such a sum of money as they agree of." If not he is spoiled or burned.[3]

---

[1] " They are soonest overcome and most have been overthrown by a home-born enemy, whereby they have been more subdued and brought under than by outward force by their voluptuous life . . . but it hath been held a venial offence, and auricular confession and verbal repentance procured so easy a pardon, as the sweetness of the sin and the colour of remission concur, that some seldom leave this sin till ability fail them to sin." J. Norden, *Description of Cornwall* (ed. 1728), 27.

[2] *The Diary of Mr. James Melvill, 1556–1601* (Edinburgh, 1829), 120.

[3] R. Welford, *op. cit.* II. 333.

Robert Delaval on a journey to London writes home to his son, keeping the house for him at Seaton, that he is glad to hear that Hob of the Nebb has been brought into the High Castle, " for he was a practiser with others to fetch my horses out of stables and brake my locks to do it." [1]   Archie Elwood has taken cattle from his son John Delaval's house at Dissington, but they have been rescued again. It is necessary to keep watch over the house in the night and " let not the gates be opened after twilight ". But the Delavals no more than others escaped the mortality that lurked behind the bushes or when day closed in. Mistress Ridley was riding homewards with Edward and William Delaval and their servants, when Edward got a fall and William rode back to help him. " And as soon as they came to the alders at the west end of Hexham green, there came . . . a man of middle stature, thick shouldered, brownish bearded, big faced, apparelled with a sad coloured cloak under which he carried a drawn sword. Which man presently stepped before William Delaval in the highway, who asked who he was. The man answered : ' Thou art no justice of the peace to examine me ; and although thou know not me, I know thee ', and presently struck at William Delaval with his sword, who instantly fell off his horseback therewith ; and then gave the said William Delaval another stroke on the hinder part of his head, and said to him, ' Thou art Delaval, and I have vowed thy death ', and then went his way into the alder bushes. Whom this examinate pursuing, he said unto her, ' Go thy way or else I will thrust my sword in thee '. And thereupon she lost sight of him, and the said William Delaval presently died of the said strokes." [2] What lay behind the murder we do not know—evidently something : it was not accidental. The Delavals were not more feud-ridden than other families ; but twenty years before, we find that Joshua Delaval, constable of the horse in garrison at Berwick, was guilty of the murder of John Dagleish in his own house. Men could wait long for their revenges.

The consequences of these quarrels and feuds are pitiful when we are led to the bedsides of the dying men and hear their last voices. Philip Green of Morpeth craves Francis Dacre and Nicholas Ridley to " see my said wife and children maintained

---

[1] *Newcastle-on-Tyne Records Committee Publications,* IX. 161-2, 165.
[2] Sir Edmund Craster, " Tynemouth Castle ", in the *History of Northumberland,* VIII. 172.

in law for reformation of this cruel murder committed upon me by George Ogle, John Ogle, sons to James Ogle of Cawsey, Patrick and Martin Ogle of Trittlington, Alexander Ogle with others whom I fully charge with my death, having no cause against me but that I compared the Dacres' blood to be as good as the Ogles ' ".[1] One sees the strength of feudal ties and affections—Green must have been a dependent of the Dacres—and the idiocy of men's passions. Three years later, in 1586, William Clavering of Norham lay on his death-bed, making his will by word of mouth for he was " very crazed and wounded in his body " :[2] he had been shot when riding across the moor beyond Morpeth in company with Sir Cuthbert Collingwood, by a band led by William Selby.[3] For there was a feud between Selbys and Collingwoods, as between Carrs and Herons, Selbys and Greys, Greys and Widdringtons. (It is curious to think of the ancestors of the pacific Sir Edward Grey involved in these *fracas*.)

Of the bitter consequences for some families—and the triviality of the occasions—we learn from Sir John Forster himself who writes of his four great-uncles : " at a hunting and riding homeward through a town called Newham, for the biting of a greyhound they and a company of Carrs fell out, and then began bloodshed and feuds which continued till there was but one Carr of the greyhound living ; during which time my grandfather and yours and another brother of theirs called Nicholas Forster, mine being twenty years old, yours seventeen years, and Nicholas a child of fourteen, being a hunting, were waited on by one of the Carrs and two of their alliance, who set upon the three brothers and thought well to have slain them at a place called Branxton, where there stands a cross yet. But the said two were slain there, insomuch that after the slaughter my grandfather fled to Redesdale in the county, because he was safe there, and yours fled into the south parts, of whom I never heard of since that time till now."[4]

For sheer unredemption of spirit it would be hard to beat Lionel Grey, the porter of Berwick, who planned the murder of John Ainsley, captain of Norham, for some offence against the

---

[1] *Wills and Inventories*, II. 82.
[2] *Ibid.* 151.
[3] For the full story, *v.* Tomlinson, *op. cit.* 121-3.
[4] *Ibid.* 119-20.

Greys : " I never in all my life was so merry as when I heard the traitor Ainsley, sitting on his knees cry mercy."[1] We see that the soldiery were not an unmixed blessing : they added feuds of their own to those they were supposed to suppress. No wonder the famous Bernard Gilpin, ' Apostle of the North ', found such a state of unregeneration on his preaching tours. When he came to Rothbury he found the church occupied by two armed bands, one in the chancel, the other in the nave, himself in the middle. It was a good strategic position, for when " a second time their weapons made a clashing sound and the one side drew nearer to the other so that they were in danger to fall to blows in the midst of the church ", he stepped down from the pulpit between them to appease the tumult.[2] In another church Gilpin saw a glove hung up high on the wall in token of challenge ; the sexton dared not take it down when bidden : it would mean accepting the challenge. " If thou wilt but bring me hither a long staff, I will take it down myself", said Gilpin. At a church in Redesdale where there was neither minister, nor bell, nor book, there *was* " a red hand put on a spear point in defiance of deadly feud ". They had never heard preaching before, and were not used to it ; when Gilpin preached against robbing and stealing, an old man of eighty shouted out, " then the deil I give my sall to, but we are all thieves ".

They were ; and it was six of one, half a dozen of the other. Many were the bills of complaints sent in : they provided the chief business for the Warden of each March to settle with his opposite number on the Scottish side on their truce-days or meetings. The trouble was that it was impossible to arrive at the truth or to apportion the blame—so many of the cattle must have changed hands so often. In 1587 commissioners from both sides met at Berwick to consider outstanding claims : a vast schedule of offences.[3] Thomas Musgrave, deputy keeper of Bewcastle, has a complaint against Walter Scott, laird of Buccleuch, for 200 kine oxen, 300 gait (goats) and sheep ; Sir Simon Musgrave, the keeper, against the laird of Mangerton, an Armstrong, the laird's Jock, Sim's Tom and their accomplices, for the burning of his barns, wheat, rye, oats, bigg (barley),

---

[1] *Ibid.* 120.
[2] q. from Carleton's *Life*, in C. S. Collingwood, *Memoirs of Bernard Gilpin*, 164-6.
[3] J. Nicolson and R. Burn, *History and Antiquities of Westmorland and Cumberland*, I. xxx-xxxvii.

and peas, worth £1000 sterling. The poor widow of Martin Taylor and others complain against the Whitaugh Armstrongs for 140 kie and oxen, 100 sheep, 20 gait and all their insight (household goods) and of the slaughter of Martin Taylor, John Dodgson, John Skelloe and Matthew Blackburn. The inhabitants of a small township complain of the murder of three of their menfolk, the taking away of ten others and holding them to ransom, and the spoil of houses, goods and cattle.

These are only a few of the complaints of the West March against Liddesdale. Liddesdale has an equal number of claims against the inhabitants of the March. There the most notorious offenders were the Grahams ; and Walter Scott of Branxholm and his tenants, with the Maxwells and the Johnstons (who also were at feud between themselves) have a long list of charges against Will Graham of the Rose-trees, Richie Graham of the Moat, Hutchin's Richie of the Bailey, Tom's Geordie Graham, Rob Graham of the Fald and many more of their name. The sum total of the charges for England were £9700 ; for Scotland £41,600.[1] What could the commissioners do about it ? Little enough, for all these bills were " fouled by the commissioners of Berwick for lack of appearance ". They did their best to take pledges on either side, but none of the complainants—who were mostly also offenders—would dream of appearing : they were very elusive in their fastnesses.

When things got too bad, or some exceptional exploit called for attention, the Wardens took matters in their own hands and meted out direct justice by an official raid of their own ; or the governments took the matter up, testily enough, with each other. At moments of crisis in the relations between the countries the raids on either side took on the proportions of small warfare— Border warfare. At the beginning of Elizabeth's reign the French were in Scotland and there was actual war. Lord Eure sent 500 foot with horse to burn the mill at Eyemouth with the French in it. " The moon did shine very light ; they mistrusted nothing, it was so light, and kept evil watch that we were at the mill door before we were descried. The Frenchman ran out at the back door and through the water. There were ten of them taken. The mill was turved and would not burn well."[2] However, the township and their corn burned very well. Such

---

[1] I think these must be Scots pounds.
[2] J. Scott, *Berwick upon Tweed*, 139.

scenes were repeated at intervals all through these years on the Border.

At the first crisis of Elizabeth's reign, after the Rising of the Northern Earls, Buccleuch and Ferniehurst made an incursion into England with the deliberate object of causing a war ; and the Earl of Westmorland in their company watched the corn and hay go up. They failed, but their attempt encouraged Leonard Dacre in his foolhardy effort to recover his family's lands by force of arms and with the promise of Scottish support. Hunsdon, Elizabeth's cousin, whom she had made Lord Warden of the Marches, caught him by surprise by a rapid night march : the rebels, who were twice his number but half-hearted, were easily overthrown and Leonard Dacre fled overseas. That summer Sussex led the English forces through Teviotdale on a campaign of reprisals, burning castles, houses, villages of the Scottish supporters of the English rebels. The Scots had " threshed their corn, fled with their cattle, and unthatched their houses ". [1] But this may be considered to come under the heading of foreign relations.

For the ordinary course of operations on the Border it so happens that we have a first-hand account in the delightful *Memoirs* of Sir Robert Carey written years after these things were over, with the accession of James to the English throne— to announce which Carey had made his famous ride to Scotland from the death-bed of the Queen. Robert was the youngest of Hunsdon's sons ; and when his brother-in-law, Lord Scrope, was made Warden of the West March he invited him to live with him in the castle at Carlisle—an opening for a career in what was almost a Carey preserve. The Queen was careful to allot the key-posts in this frontier area to her closest relations, who might be relied on to stand staunch and true in a province which John Dudley, Duke of Northumberland, had once thought to make his own. Young Carey shortly found " we had a stirring world, and few days passed over my head but I was on horse-back, either to prevent mischief, or to take malefactors, and to bring the Border in better quiet than it had been in times past ". [2] He soon learned by experience the tricky ways of the Borderers.

Not long after, his father called him to be Deputy Warden

[1] q. Tough, *op. cit.* 213.
[2] *Memoirs of Robert Cary, Earl of Monmouth*, ed. by G. H. Powell, 26.   I prefer the spelling Carey, to distinguish this family from the Devon Carys.

of the East March—actually the most northerly, running up to Berwick, his father's headquarters and where his brother Sir John was Marshal. His opposite number was Sir Robert Ker, a brave, active young man, who proceeded to put ' a brave ' on Carey. Expressing his wish to Carey's messenger to have the happiness to meet him, he filled the messenger up with drink, put him to bed and took horse with some of his men for a little village on the English side, where " he broke up a house and took out a poor fellow who (he pretended) had done him some wrong, and before the door cruelly murdered him, and so came quietly home and went to bed ".[1] Next morning he sent Carey's man back with a polite letter. Carey had, of course, to get even with Ker for this. Shortly after, a great favourite of Ker's, an old robber called Geordie Bourne, fell into Carey's hands. Carey heard his confession : " he had lived long enough to do so many villainies as he had done . . . he had lain with above forty men's wives, what in Scotland, what in England . . . he had killed seven Englishmen with his own hands, cruelly murdering them . . . he had spent his whole time in whoring, drinking, stealing and taking deep revenge for slight offences ".[2] While Ker was waiting to reclaim the old rogue, Carey had him strung up.

That winter there were three or four raids a week out of Scotland into the East March. " I had no other means left to quiet them, but still sent out the garrison horsemen of Berwick to watch in the fittest places for them, and it was their hap many times to light upon them with the stolen goods driving before them. They were no sooner brought before me, but a jury went upon them, and being found guilty, they were presently hanged. A course which had been seldom used, but I had no way to keep the country quiet but to do so."[3] The sharp hand of the Careys—Sir Robert himself terms it the ' bloody hand '—turned out, as might be expected, more effective.

In the last years of Forster's rule of the Middle March— he was a very old man and, for all his enjoyment of life, lived to be over ninety—order was relaxed and lawlessness each year grew worse. Carey was appointed to succeed him and at once made an example of two gentlemen turned highwaymen—a new form of pleasure for those parts : he got them betrayed and

---

[1] *Memoirs of Robert Cary*, 40.   [2] *Ibid.* 44-5.   [3] *Ibid.* 41-2.

sent them to Newcastle gaol, where they were hanged. But his chief trouble was with the Armstrongs of Liddesdale, one of whose name, Sim of the Cathill, had been killed by a Ridley. The whole tribe under their chief, old Sim of Whithaugh, vowed revenge and the neighbourhood took fright, threatening to fly the country. Carey determined upon an expedition, after making it all right with King James, who left it clear that he could not keep the Armstrongs in order. The Armstrongs were equally confident : in the depths of the woods and bogs of Tarras Moss " they feared not the force nor power of England nor Scotland so long as they were there ".[1] Carey recruited a number of gentlemen—volunteers for a summer outing, and " by the help of the foot of Liddesdale and Redesdale, we had soon built a pretty fort, and within it we had all cabins made to lie in, and everyone brought beds or mattresses to lie on ". Carey had the passages to Scotland secretly blocked and then gave the alarm ; the tribe were surrounded and had five of the leaders of their name taken, including Sim's eldest sons.

Sir Robert Ker who, after long unpleasantness, was now good friends with Carey, wrote to him in favour of mildness— " tempering of extremities shall be the most assured band of quietness, and the pledges' relief on both sides shall draw more benefit to the subjects than their present estate can do. . . . If punishment should gar them ken their faults, poverty compels them again to wickedness . . . many desperate that have no means how to live will be hard to be ruled."[2] When Sir Robert had been unable to produce his promised pledges and was taken for a spell into the custody of the Archbishop of York, the latter wrote to the Council, a little naïvely, " whether he may sometimes be brought to sitting to the common hall, where he may see how careful her Majesty is that the poorest subject in her kingdom may have their right, and that her people seek remedy by law and not by avenging themselves. Perhaps it may do him good as long as he liveth."[3]

The Archbishop in his simple way was right, for that was the whole point.

The population of these counties that gave so much trouble is reckoned to have been : Northumberland some 70,000

---

[1] *Ibid.* 60-66. [2] *Salisbury Papers* (H.M.C.), VIII. 87.
[3] Strype, *Annals* (ed. 1824), IV. 448.

(roughly the same as Cornwall), Cumberland 40,000, Westmorland 17,000.[1] For their governance a special code of laws had come into being—the Laws of the Marches, the specific purpose of which was to deal with thefts and feuds and the redress of injuries, with particular provisions to catch offenders crossing and recrossing the Border—for, as we have seen, " they are a people that will be Scottish when they will and English at their pleasure ".[2] These laws dealt with murder, maiming, theft, feud, the burning of houses and crops ; hunting, sowing corn, pasturing cattle and cutting down trees in the opposite realm ; receiving stolen goods and fugitives, perjury and overswearing, and the taking of pledges. The code was added to from time to time by treaty between commissioners from both sides of the Border. One observes the growth, in general, of a spirit of co-operation from the 1580s. As the great conflict in Europe draws to its height and England finds herself at war with Spain, the young king James—reaching maturity and consolidating his power intelligently among difficulties that overwhelmed his mother—falls into line and allies himself with England. Nothing could have been more reassuring than his conduct at the crisis of the Armada and as the defeated crusade wobbled round his coasts. From that time it became indubitable that the succession to the English throne would be his. James registered it, in his pawky way, with a *mot* : he would, he said, never risk the Tower of London for the town of Berwick.[3] He was a sensible man at bottom ; and sense was precisely what his mother, with all her gifts and charms, lacked.

To govern the Borders and put these laws into execution the Wardens, on the English side, had immense powers over life and death. Theirs was a direct and summary authority—though not, it must be remembered, that of martial law : the forms of justice were to be observed and juries procured. The Wardens held regular courts to hear pleas, execute justice and their ordinances, levy fines and so on. There were the defensive regulations against the Scots to administer : no-one was supposed to employ a Scot without the Warden's licence ; there were stringent regulations regarding the coming of Scots into the garrison towns, Berwick and Carlisle. Their safety and keeping were the special care of the Wardens, whose seats of power they

---

[1] Tough, *op. cit.* 27.   [2] *Cal. Border Papers*, I. 126.
[3] *Salisbury Papers* (H.M.C.), VI. 168.

were. Here their command was both military and civil and they had the powers of the Lords Lieutenant elsewhere to muster the whole man-power at their orders.

Facing Scotland, their external relations were hardly less important. They had to execute the agreed conditions of truce between themselves and their opposite numbers, and for that there were regular meetings across the Border, or ' trew-days '— when things were liable to happen. On one such July day in 1575 took place the skirmish of the Reidswire, when the argument grew so hot that, after a flight of arrows and some confused fighting, the English Warden of the Middle March— our friend, Sir John Forster, Cuthbert Collingwood and the Earl of Bedford's son were carried off prisoners into Scotland. The Scots were jubilant and celebrated it with a ballad, " The Raid of the Reidswire ", in which all the names are rehearsed. The Queen was furious at this indignity—her ambassador refused to lie comfortably in the bed of state he had been given at Edinburgh until the matter was put right—and she made the Regent send up the offending Scots Warden to York, where he was honourably entertained and dismissed. In a similar scuffle on a truce-day at Hexpeth-gate in the Cheviots in 1585 Francis Russell, now heir to the earldom, was killed. He had married a (legitimate) daughter of old Forster, through whose issue the Russell line then passed. It was on returning from such a day that Will Armstrong of Kinmont was seized by the English and carried prisoner to Carlisle, whence his rescue was organised by Buccleuch in 1596—the famous exploit of the ballad, " Kinmont Willie ".

Other, more dangerous, persons crossed those moors in the direction of Scotland. In 1582 at the beginning of the Jesuit campaign for the subversion of England and Scotland, Forster reported to Walsingham that some Jesuit had passed through the wastes and fells ; two men took from him a bag and an old portas (breviary), " certain instruments to draw forth teeth ", and a looking-glass which was found to be stuffed with letters, of which he forwarded one in cipher to be read.[1] The priest had gold on him, for he gave the men eleven rials to let him pass. " There are three or four Jesuits receipted with the Lord Seton in Scotland : one Brewerton a Cheshire man, one Shepherd that said mass in the Earl of Northumberland's castle at Warkworth "

[1] *Cal. Border Papers*, I. 85.

—a recent exploit. This was the moment at which Parsons's opposite number, the Scottish Jesuit Crichton, was practising with the French Esmé Stuart, Earl of Lennox, to bring the king over to Catholicism. Crichton travelled to Spain to submit his plans to Parsons, but later was caught by the Dutch and handed over to England, where he spent a couple of years in the Tower. There, when William Parry consulted him whether it was permissible to kill the Queen, Crichton answered no. For this civilised opinion—contrary to that held by some of his colleagues—he was liberated by the English government. He at once engaged in a conspiracy to raise a rebellion in England.

One sees the fires of the European scene reflected in these Northern parts. In 1594 the Jesuit Ingram was executed at Gateshead.[1] He had been at work in Northumberland and had a part in bringing the Eures back to the faith : persecution kept them straight. In the same year the seminary priest Edward Waterson was executed at Newcastle : we find payments in the town records for an apron to the leech, for the making of a fire, for a spade, for a string which bound the seminary's arms, for drink which a prisoner had before he executed the priest.[2] (It is like the execution scene in *Measure for Measure* : Shakespeare hardly adds to the horror.) On another occasion, two years before, we read, " paid to a Frenchman which did take forth the seminary priest's bowels after he was hanged—20s."[3] It was a large payment, and the job was left to a Frenchman. Barbarous and terrible as it was—is our age any better?—it was not reasonable on the part of the poor priest, in such circumstances, not to have conformed.

Not the least important of the duties of these officials was that of conducting an intelligence service.[4] They had to watch and report on the least movements that might be dangerous across the Border, every turn and twist in the dizzy changes of Scottish politics, the most intimate affairs and influences upon the King. Esmé Stuart was a danger : he was a Catholic and *lié* with the Guises. The young James was enamoured of him. At once the intelligence service is humming. Sir Henry Widdrington,

---

[1] R. Welford, *op. cit.* III. 86.
[2] *Ibid.* [3] *Ibid.* 70.
[4] It was convenient that for nearly twenty years, 1577–94, Robert Bowes combined the office of Treasurer at Berwick with that of Ambassador at Edinburgh.

whose informants are the ministers of the gospel in Edinburgh, writes to Walsingham :[1] " The King altogether is persuaded and led by him, for he can hardly suffer him out of his presence [the glamorous Esmé must have been a great relief after a dreary childhood in the company of Buchanan and his beatings], and is in such love with him as in the open sight of the people often he will clasp him about the neck with his arms and kiss him." The ministers were afraid that Esmé and the Earl of Arran " go about to draw the King to carnal lust " and withdraw him from the delights of sermons. Upon admonishment—which the poor young man was always receiving, though much good it did him—James asserted that " his body was clean and unpolluted ". No doubt that was true enough, in a way.

Elizabeth appointed Hunsdon Warden of the East March and Governor of Berwick in 1568 ; twenty-one years later she made him Lord Warden General of the whole Marches, with some of the temporalities of the see of Durham. She made him many grants of land and gave him the use of a royal palace, Somerset House. Though no mention of her dead mother—who had died in such a fashion—ever crossed her lips, the Queen expressed what she thought by her kindness to and care of her mother's relations. (It is said that she had a ring which opened and shut upon a miniature of her mother.) For nearly thirty years, until his death in 1596, the Queen's cousin held the postern-gate of her kingdom for her : another of those long ministries—like Burghley's, Walsingham's, Huntingdon's, even Leicester's—which made so much for the success of her government.

---

[1] *Cal. Border Papers*, I. 82-3. Widdrington was Deputy Warden of the East Marches. The sympathies of the Widdringtons were with the Presbyterian ministers. When Melvill was at Berwick, Lady Widdrington befriended him and discharged his expenses (*Diary*, 119). This, Widdrington's second wife, whom he left a young widow, was a Cornishwoman, Elizabeth Trevanion of Carhayes. Hector Widdrington, illegitimate son of Sir John, Warden of the Middle Marches, by his maid-servant Alice, made Lady Widdrington his executrix and left her his goods. The name Trevanion was given to a son of Sir Cuthbert Collingwood. (*Durham Wills and Inventories*, II. 232, 235.) She married, secondly, Sir Robert Carey. Queen Elizabeth was very indignant at his marrying her—or perhaps his marrying at all. But she made him a good wife, and won the golden opinions of Queen Anne and James for her care of the puny and rickety baby Prince Charles, who was confided to her keeping when others would not take the risk. She brought him through to a healthy boyhood, though whether this was a service to English history may be doubted. How she came to the Border from the opposite end of the country I do not know : possibly through the Careys, for Hunsdon's eldest son was granted the custody of the estates near her home in Cornwall of the Recusant, Francis Tregian (*v.* my *Tudor Cornwall*, 351-5).

There was a great contrast between the Queen's character and her cousin's. He was a bluff, simple, direct and downright man—very different from the devious Queen, the disingenuous and insincere Leicester, the subterranean Cecil. He was a soldier in his outlook, popular with soldiers ; he was a sport and a good sort. The Queen was none of that. Hunsdon's first notable service to her was his rapid quenching of Leonard Dacre's foolish rising. He received a majestic letter of formal thanks from the Queen ; then the kinswoman took up the pen and added, " I doubt much, my Harry, whether that the victory were given me more joyed me, or that you were by God appointed the instrument of my glory ; and I assure you for my country's good, the first might suffice, but for my heart's contentation, the second more pleased me. . . . Well, I can say no more, *beatus est ille servus quem, cum Dominus venerit, invenerit facientem sua mandata. . . .* I intend to make this journey somewhat to increase your livelihood, that you may not say to yourself, *perditur quod factum est ingrato.* Your loving kinswoman, Elizabeth R."[1] (Hunsdon was hardly likely to say anything to himself in Latin : it used to be said of him that his Latin and his dissimulation were both alike, *i.e.* soon seen through.)

The unpleasant task fell to him of purchasing the rebel Northumberland from the Scots ; but Hunsdon tried to get him pardoned and, when this was refused, he would not convey him beyond the bounds of his own jurisdiction at Alnwick. He was severe with thieves and described himself, with his usual exaggeration, as " more given to hanging than to hunting or hawking ".[2] He was the only one of Elizabeth's councillors to show any sympathy for the young James, or any understanding of his youth and loneliness and poverty, surrounded by a horrible gang of nobles for ever kidnapping him and by the caterwauling of the ministers. Hunsdon dared to say what he thought, if only to Burghley : " her Majesty is all in words, but when it comes to the performance he shall find nothing . . . she is still at generalities, if he want or shall have occasion to use her friendship. These be no ways nor means to win a prince that is so far alienated from her as he is, and hath so many ill instruments about him as he hath, and having so little as he hath. . . ."[3]

[1] q. in *The Letters of Queen Elizabeth*, ed. G. B. Harrison, 83.
[2] J. Scott, *Berwick*, 172.
[3] *Cal. Border Papers*, I. 310-11.

The Queen replied in kind : she kept Hunsdon, too, short of money—he complained, in his idiosyncratic way, that he was " fed on the pap that was made from the yolk of an owl's egg ".[1] He had a sense of humour rare in an Elizabethan magnate : Thomas Sutton, Master of the Ordnance, wanted to appoint someone as his deputy, " who was as fit for it as he himself was to be a bishop ".[2]

Growing older, he appreciated relief from the climate of the North : he was tormented by gout—one can see it in his pathetically shaky hand, the shakiest writing of all the Council. We found him pleading with Leicester to get him leave to come south : again he hopes " her Majesty will give me leave in time to seek some remedy for this hellish disease, which if it breed a while upon me I am afraid will be incurable ".[3] With or without leave, he overstayed himself—and an almighty row there was. Robert Carey was standing by in the presence chamber when the Queen was at cards : " she called me to her and asked me when you meant to go to Berwick ? I told her that you determined to begin your journey presently after Whitsuntide. She grew into a great rage, beginning with God's wounds ! that she would set you by the feet, and send another in your place if you dallied with her thus, for she would not be thus dallied withal.[4] I told her that with as much possible speed as might be, you would depart. . . . She answered me that you have been going from Christmas to Easter, and from Easter to Whitsunday ; but if you deferred the time any longer, she would appoint some other in your place. And this message she commanded me to send you." [5] Hunsdon went, at once.

The Queen was right : it was only by these means—rewarding good service with generous words, if she could not often with deeds, cracking down on negligence or any dereliction of duty, unceasingly keeping people up to the mark—that she made her government the most efficient in Europe. Creighton

---

[1] J. Scott, *op. cit.* 176-7.   [2] *Ibid.* 168.   [3] *Cal. Border Papers*, I. 73.
[4] The Queen at least had the habit of swearing in common with her cousin. Cf. Sir Robert Naunton, *Fragmenta Regalia* (Arber's English Reprints), 47 : "... his custom of swearing and obscenity in speaking made him seem a worse Christian than he was ". Where did they get their bad language from ? Not from Henry VIII, who was rather particular in such matters (cf. the stories in George Puttenham, *The Arte of English Poesie*, Arber's English Reprints, 274-6).
[5] Cary, *Memoirs*, 99-100.

says well of her government of the Border : she was "justified in her boast that she paid as good heed to the remote parts of her realm as she did to those near at hand . . . the result of her method was that she was better served by her officials than had been any previous ruler of England. . . . Nowhere do we see more clearly than in the history of the Border the operation of that systematic watchfulness and care for administrative detail which are really the foundation of the glory of the Elizabethan age ".[1]

For all that she had done for him, it seems that Hunsdon died a disappointed man. He wanted the earldom of Wiltshire, of his grandfather's and hers, revived for him ; the Queen would not do it—perhaps it would revive too many memories for her. At his death-bed she consented ; it was then too late : he would not accept then what he felt he had earned in his lifetime. But he left a kind memory and he has his epitaph : " As he lived in a ruffling time, so he loved sword and buckler men, and such as our fathers were wont to call men of their hands ; of which sort he had many brave gentlemen that followed him : yet not taken for a popular and dangerous person. And this is one that stood amongst the Togati, of an honest stout heart."[2]

Keeping people up to the mark included keeping the King of Scots on tenterhooks. The way the Queen gradually increased the area of order in a naughty world was by never allowing a marked breach to go unchallenged or unpunished.[3] The taking of Kinmont Willie from Carlisle Castle provides an example. He had been captured on a truce-day, and in vain Buccleuch sought to get him released. At last he took the matter in his own hands and planned a rescue from the jaws of the Queen's own castle of Carlisle. With his own folk and with the aid of the Grahams on the English side—with whom he had been in converse at his horse-racing the day before—Buccleuch put through the attempt : a dark, muffled, misty night, scaling ladders too short, a postern-gate to break down, a rush straight to where Willie was imprisoned, carrying him off, fetters and all—it is all part of proud Scots tradition. The Queen of England was furious at the insult

---

[1] Creighton, *op. cit.* 116-17, 144.   [2] Naunton, *op. cit.* 47.
[3] Cf. her disapprobation of Sir John Carey's summary execution upon John Dagleish, expressed through Burghley : her Majesty thought this " very barbarous and seldom used among the Turks " (*Cal. Border Papers*, II. 167).

to her honour. King James proposed to do nothing about it. At once all the organ-stops are out : " Was it ever seen that a prince from his cradle preserved from the slaughter, held up in royal dignity, conserved from many treasons, maintained in all sortes of kindenes, should remunerate with so harde a measure such deare desarts ? With doubt to yealde a just treaties responce to a lawfull frendes demaunde ? Ought it to be put to a question whither a king should doe another, his like, his right ? Or shoulde a councell be demaunded their pleasure what he himselfe shoulde do ? Were it in the nonage of the prince it might have some couler, but in a fathers age it seameth strange, and I dare say without example. . . . Shall any castle or habitacle of myne be assailed by a nyght-larcyn, and shall not my confederate send the offender to his due punisher ? Shall a frend sticke at that demand that he ought rather to prevent ? . . ."[1] James sent the offender to her presence—where his audacity made a favourable impression on the wonderful old virago. The Scottish king could well afford to make the concession : she was on her way out, he was on his way in.

When he succeeded to her throne he found himself following in the tracks of her policy, and—such is the usual irony of human affairs—in one respect far more harshly. The Border had grown much quieter in the last years of the Queen's reign—tribute to the effectiveness of the long rule of her Carey relations. The West March remained the most troublesome and gradually, with increasing civility, opinion turned against the Grahams— at least, the effective opinion of the Cumberland gentry. As time goes on, one finds in these special areas the desire for regular civil administration and local self-government, with the J.P.s in control on their own doorstep.[2] The Grahams handed in an interesting protest expressing their willingness to be bound to good order, answerable to her Majesty's laws at the general sessions, and their readiness to follow the Warden in seeking revenge for any offence " committed within your lordship's March by any of Scotland "—no doubt.[3] To this the gentry replied, charging the Grahams with being " the chiefest actors in the spoil and decay of our country ", and naming all their tribes with their several leaders, familiar names—Will Graham of the Rose-trees,

[1] *Letters of Queen Elizabeth and King James VI,* ed. J. Bruce (Camden Soc.), 115.
[2] Cf. *The England of Elizabeth,* 291-2.
[3] Cf. Nicolson and Burn, *op. cit.* cvi-cxxix.

Will Graham of the Fauld, Hutchin's Davy, Jock of the Lake and the rest of them.

The end of the Border was the end of the old order and a great blow to such people : they could not believe that the world had changed. On his accession James directed a special proclamation to the Borders against those " pretending ignorance of his Majesty's resolution for the union of the two realms . . . and feeding themselves with a sinister conceit and opinion that no such union shall be established and take effect ", and commanding " all his Majesty's subjects to repute, hold and esteem both the realms as presently united and as one realm and kingdom, and the subjects of both the realms as one people, brethren and members of one body ". This left no room for mutual depredations in what had become the " middle shires " of one kingdom. This the Grahams did not grasp, and the government swept down on them with a measure for transplanting them to Ireland, where James's epoch-making Plantation of Ulster was transforming the landscape. A tax was levied on Cumberland to pay for their removal, " to the intent their lands may be inhabited by others of good and honest conversation ". Three boat-loads of them left from Workington in 1606 and 1607—we recognise many of the names ; others of them were sent to garrison the cautionary towns in the Low Countries. In subsequent years some of them trickled back into their old haunts, and began " to revive their old courses of robbing, riding armed and other heinous disorders ". They were to be expelled.

The old days were indeed over. James's Proclamation of Union announced a new age for Britain : " the Isle within itself hath almost none but imaginary bounds of separation, without but one common limit or rather guard of the Ocean sea, making the whole a little world within itself, the nations an uniformity of constitutions both of body and mind, especially in martial processes, a community of language (the principal means of civil society), an unity of religion (the deepest bond of hearty union and the surest knot of lasting peace) ".[1] The landmarks were becoming obliterated : after 1603 the special system of government of the Marches came to an end, the Wardens were no more. The Borders enjoyed " a quiet and order which they had never before

---

[1] Cf. Nicolson and Burn, *op. cit.* cxxii. No doubt proclamations have to say such things, but in fact religion was the cause of the war between England and Scotland in 1639 and that led to the Civil War.

experienced ".[1] Their government came into the civilian hands of their local gentry : Lord William Howard, from the castle of the Dacres at Naworth—and for all that he was a Catholic—exercised as large an influence on the Border by suasion and civil authority as the Wardens had done with their bands. Nor must we neglect the factor of economic improvement, the steady mounting of the wave of wealth which carried the achievement of the age, the fertilising spread of pelf from the towns—witness the abounding prosperity of Newcastle—up those dales, smoothing the bitter edge of poverty and affording outlets for their hardy stock in the expansive world beyond. Above all, land became more productive and its value greatly increased.[2]

The politics, the people and their way of life have all vanished ; but the land is full of their memorials. There is the Wall that so fascinated Camden—most remarkable of Roman remains in Northern Europe—and that the Elizabethans quarried from : someone in that age had the odd idea of repairing it and fortifying it against the Scots.[3] There are the Border castles great and small, and everywhere the peel-towers that silently express the former insecurity of life. A fine example is Dacre Castle, whence the Dacres took their rise, at the head of Ullswater, looking down on the wooded policies of Dalemain and the sounding waters of the Eamont flowing by. It is no more than a peel-tower, with a ' barmkyn '—the walled enclosure to keep the cattle safe—like Spenser's Kilcolman in Ireland : the same insecurity, the same type of building. The church-towers served for defence ; the manor-houses—like beautiful Yanwath, where, they say, Mary stayed—have their strong squat towers. So have the bigger rectories—like Embleton, which one glimpses going by on the coast road from Alnwick to Bamburgh : where the historian Creighton drank in inspiration for his work.[4] The little towns reveal the past in their lay-out—the large space in the centre for the cattle and sheep, the narrow approaches. Carlisle, of which Creighton wrote the history, is visibly a frontier-city, with its English and Scotch gates, its terraced West

---

[1] q. in Tough, *op. cit.* 278.

[2] Cf. *The Household Books of Lord William Howard* (Surtees Soc.), xxxv foll. Lord William's estates more than doubled in value in his lifetime.

[3] *Cal. Border Papers*, I. 300-302.

[4] Creighton was rector of Embleton, 1875-84, and there he did much of his best work.

Walls still complete and the Castle looking out northwards over the Debatable Land—whence Mary once looked down with hope upon the Scots and English playing at football for her favour.

Or there are such places as Naworth, where Lord William Howard lived so many years in amity with his Dacre wife, whose inheritance it was. There he is portrayed in their hall, standing at a table, a deep red velvet cloth upon it, a book open : long head, auburn hair and beard, nobly arched brows above the dark eyes, the serious expression of a scholar and a pious man. There is his wife in black, with crooked walking staff and her praying beads, painted in an alcove with a tree and a robin perched in it—an old wizened lady with parchment face and shrewd north-country expression. One mounts the stone stair of the tower to Lord William's study at the top, with his library *in situ* :[1] his Chaucer and Tudor editions of Gower's *Confessio Amantis*, with his common-place books and works of Catholic devotion. From the window there is a sheer drop of near a hundred feet to the bed of the stream below ; the noise of the water is pleasant in the haunted silence, as it must have been to Lord William among his books. The road up from Naworth looks to the high fells—Cold Fell, Tyndale Fells—his broad acres. A heron rises up from the stream winging its way towards those wastes.

The most remarkable monument of all are the intact Elizabethan fortifications of Berwick : they must provide one of the finest examples of a sixteenth-century fortress in Europe. It was built to be impregnable : Camden says that " its fortifications are so strong and regular that no besiegers can hope to carry it hereafter ".[2] No-one dared even attack it. It was begun while the French were still in occupation of Edinburgh and controlling Scottish policy, while we were in fact at war. Cecil himself favoured the idea of retrenching within the medieval walls and making the smaller area vastly stronger—one sees humps of the older walls under the grass beyond. The most expert Italian military engineers, Portinari and Jacopo Concio, were called in to advise, and they produced a masterpiece.[3] There the

[1] Alas, no longer. Since I visited it, it has been dispersed, like so many of the things one cares for. For a full description of the library as it was, *v*. David Mathew's sensitive essay, " The Library at Naworth ", in *For Hilaire Belloc*, Essays ed. by D. Woodruff.

[2] Camden, *op. cit.* 816.

[3] Scott, *op. cit.* 162 foll. ; Tough, *op. cit.* 192 foll.

walls stand unbreached, with their long shallow protective bastions covering them laterally, from the casemates of which the whole area could be enfiladed with fire : each bastion a fortress in itself, with fire-places, rooms and store-places, and covered tunnels communicating with the town. Camden was charmed by the long summer nights there and the thought that the garrison could play at dice all night without a candle. As one perambulates those walls, looking out over the dried-up moat under the bent grasses, looking towards Scotland, the thought suddenly comes to one that the intention of this place— an impregnable fortress on the Scottish side of the Tweed—was not merely defensive : it was intended to overawe Edinburgh. It remains, a visible symbol of the Elizabethan rôle in Scottish affairs until the day when her king took the road south through it to his English inheritance.

The past still breathes in these parts and in the ballads that are their contribution to our literature.

> " O mony a time ", quo Kinmont Willie,
>   " I have ridden horse baith wild and wood ;
> But a rougher beast than Red Rowan
>   I ween my legs have ne'er bestrode.

> " And mony a time ", quo' Kinmont Willie,
>   " I've pricked a horse out oure the furs ;
> But since the day I backed a steed,
>   I never wore sic cumbrous spurs ! "

> .   .   .   .   .

> 'All sore astonished stood Lord Scrope,
>   He stood as still as rock of stane ;
> He scarcely dared to trew his eyes,
>   When through the water they had gane.

> " He is either himsell a devil frae hell,
>   Or else his mother a witch maun be ;
> I wadna have ridden that wan water,
>   For a' the gowd in Christentie."

II. Cornwall

At the opposite end of the country was a little land that provides just as instructive an example of our theme—the integration of these borderlands into the English state, their welding with our society at this moment of high tension. Though no more than an average English county in size, no-one can doubt Cornwall's difference, her separateness and isolation. Almost wholly surrounded by the sea, the long narrow peninsula was very much cut off from English life. Even today, crossing into Cornwall over the magnificent expanse of the Hamoaze, or down into the Tamar gorge and up the other side at Gunnislake, or over the defensive ridge upon which Launceston stands, one has the feeling of penetrating a different country.

In earlier ages, when communications by land were difficult, a comparably much greater unity of the Celtic world subsisted by sea. Cornwall's closest relations were with Brittany, and they continued to be very intimate up to the middle of the sixteenth century and the Reformation—a decisive moment in this as in so much else. This common Celtic past was still intact in Cornish life in the first half of the century ; it is not until the reign of Elizabeth, after two valiant struggles, two revealing reactions against the process of integration—the risings of 1497 and the Prayer Book Rebellion of 1549, which are to Cornishmen what the '15 and the '45 are to the Highlands—that Cornwall was brought inevitably, and profitably, into the main stream of English life.

But the Celtic past, and especially our common ancestry with Brittany, are everywhere reflected in Cornwall. We have the names of the saints who gave their names to our parishes in common ; then there were surnames, habits, customs, the formation of society, very similar and, of course, the character and temperament of the people. Naturally the Lizard peninsula— the most southerly tongue of land projecting towards Brittany— had the closest relations and remained most rooted in the past. It was from this area that the risings both in 1497 and in 1549 started.

Up to the Reformation there was a great deal of coming to and fro : the community of language made it all the easier. Numbers of Bretons found employment in Cornwall : curates serving cures—they did not hold benefices—artisans, millers, above all labourers. Much of the earlier trade of the little south coast ports was with Brittany, and there were pilgrimages to Breton shrines : Cornish people evidently took part in Breton 'pardons'. In return, our own miracle-play, *Beunans Meriasek*, is thought to have a Breton origin. What is surprising is the size of the Breton element in the Cornish population : most of the parishes of West Cornwall had a number of Bretons.[1] They kept coming over in the first half of the century, they married and settled ; the movement was definitely arrested in the second half, and they became mingled with the rest of the population.

Relations with Wales and Ireland were much less close. We find a convenient reciprocity in piratical operations between Milford Haven and the less reputable Cornish ports, Helford and St. Ives ; and Cornish copper ore was taken to Neath to be smelted. Padstow and St. Ives had more trade with Ireland, importing Irish rugs and mantles, timber and fish. At the end of the century Cornishmen were drafted in some number to the wars in Ireland ;[2] deserters and vagrants came trickling back. Sir William Godolphin made his name as a soldier fighting there. And we do not forget that when Ralegh brought Spenser back to England with him to present the *Faerie Queene* to its heroine at Court, they landed in Mounts Bay.[3]

> There did a lofty mount at first us greet,
> Which did a stately heap of stones uprear,
> That seemed amid the surges for to fleet,
> Much greater than that frame which us did bear :
> There did our ship her fruitful womb unlade,
> And put us all ashore on Cynthia's land.[4]

In the Middle Ages Cornwall—except for the tin-trade and the peculiar institution of the Duchy, both draining its wealth out of the country and keeping it poor—hardly impinged upon England or its history. The people remained wrapped up in their own inner dream of their language and the memories it carried, their legends and their traditions—of Arthur and Tristan and King Mark, of their saints and the miracles they wrought,

---

[1] Cf. T. Taylor, *The Celtic Christianity of Cornwall*, 43-7. In Constantine parish no less than 14 Breton families were resident in 1544 ; in 1558 there were still 9 Breton labourers : Charles Henderson, *A History of the Parish of Constantine*, 212. Also cf. J. H. Matthews, *A History of the Parishes of St. Ives, Lelant, Towednack and Zennor*, 115-20. At St. Ives 23 Bretons were assessed for subsidy *c.* 1523, and one Irishman.

[2] And to a lesser extent in Brittany.

[3] Though I forgot it in my *Tudor Cornwall*. Approaching the Cornish coast is described by Spenser in " Colin Clout's Come Home Again ". Cf. A. C. Judson, *The Life of Edmund Spenser*, 138.

[4] What freight the little ship carried—Ralegh, Spenser and the MS. of his unpublished *Faerie Queene* !

the stories and the lives that marked the innumerable holy wells and crosses that are still characteristic of the country. They were content within the unbroken shell of the faith, the cocoon of the Catholicism from which the world had not yet emerged. So far as external relations with England were concerned this private world was, except for the Church, unpenetrated. So typically, so truly of Celts, the Cornish held themselves withdrawn, with that instinctive turning away from the disagreeable facts of the external world. They escaped into themselves. Their awakening—for the sixteenth century saw the great awakening for all the island peoples—was all the harsher and more exciting.

They did not all like it, any more than the Borderers, or the Welsh, or the Irish all liked it ; and West Cornwall was—as it still is today—the focus of the most intense Cornish feeling. Carew is naturally the best evidence as to the contemporary attitude of the people. " One point of their former roughness some of the western people do yet still retain ; and therethrough in some measure verify that testimony which Matthew of Westminster giveth of them, together with the Welsh, their ancient countrymen. Namely, how fostering a fresh memory of their expulsion long ago by the English, they second the same with a bitter repining at their fellowship. And this the worst sort express in combining against and working them all the shrewd terms which with hope of impunity they can devise. Howbeit, it shooteth not to a like extremity in all places and persons, but rather by little and little, weareth out unto a more mild and conversable fashion." [1] One recognises the familiar symptoms —how boring they are !—of anti-English feeling ; and the traveller, John Norden, who had the advantage of seeing them from the outside, comments, less kindly : " and as they are among themselves litigious, so seem they yet to retain a kind of concealed envy against the English, whom they yet affect with a desire of revenge for their fathers' sakes, by whom their fathers received the repulse ". [2]

Of the language similarly—its stronghold was West Cornwall ; for, writes Carew, " the English speech doth still encroach upon it and hath driven the same into the uttermost skirts of the shire. Most of the inhabitants can speak no word of Cornish, but very

[1] *Carew's Survey of Cornwall* (ed. 1811), 151-2.
[2] John Norden, *op. cit.* 28.

34

few are ignorant of the English ; and yet some so affect their own as to a stranger they will not speak it ; for if meeting them by chance you inquire the way or any such matter, your answer shall be, ' Meea navidna cawza Sawzneck ', ' I can speak no Saxonage '." [1]   Norden adds that " though the husband and wife, parents and children, master and servants, do mutually communicate in their native language, yet there is none of them in manner but is able to converse with a stranger in the English tongue unless it be some obscure people that seldom confer with the better sort. But it seemeth that in few years the Cornish language will be by little and little abandoned." [2]   Carew, who lived at Antony on the extreme eastern edge of Cornwall and, moreover, belonged to the greater gentry who did not speak the language, had a somewhat exaggerated idea of its desuetude ; for there is evidence that some people were bilingual even in mid-Cornwall as late as 1600. [3] Norden was right in saying that the language would die out : it was a consequence of the very process we are describing.

The first stirrings of a new activity in Cornwall came along with the Tudors. Cornish sympathies—or at least those of the leading gentry, the Arundells, Nanfan, John Trevelyan—were, as in West Wales, Lancastrian. Sir Richard Edgcumbe was Henry Tudor's closest adviser, and most devoted supporter in the West. After Bosworth, it was Edgcumbe who was sent from Cornwall to receive the submission of Ireland and tender the oaths of allegiance to the government there. Henry made him his principal agent in his attempt to support the independence of Brittany.

From now on Cornwall was awake. When Parliament levied a heavy tax in 1497 for the defence of the Scottish Border, the Cornish took the view that that was no concern of theirs. Its levy was very much resented, especially in the west, where a rising started in the Lizard area, under the lead of a remarkable blacksmith, Michael Joseph. It spread to the whole county and at Bodmin, the county town, it recruited the leadership of a lawyer, Flamank, who provided it with an argument : that the defence of the Scottish Border was a matter for the Borders themselves, where it was provided for by Border-service, the tenure by which the lands were held there ; to tax Cornwall for the Scottish frontier was not only unjust, but illegal. The smaller

---

[1] Carew, *op. cit.* 184.   [2] Norden, *op. cit.* 26-7.   [3] Cf. *Tudor Cornwall*, 23.

gentry of Cornish name and stock fell in with the rising : not so the grander gentry of Norman stock. This has an interesting significance : it shows an element of racial feeling, a genuine Cornishry. When Perkin Warbeck heard the news of the rising, he left Scotland for Cork, whence he landed near Land's End in September 1497. Once more the Cornish marched, to Glastonbury and Wells—can they have been drawn by some instinctive memory of Arthur and his cult there, *quondam rexque futurus* ? —where they were deserted by their leader or, no doubt, they would have fought as bravely as before. Again it is the smaller gentry of Cornish name who are noteworthy, Nankivell, Trekenning, Polwhele, Polgreen, Borlase, Retallack, Rosewarne, Trevysall, Antron.

Such risings are usually a phenomenon of the first upward surge of self-consciousness among a people. The Cornish had drawn attention to their existence as a small people not yet absorbed into the nation.

The Reformation speeded up the process, as in so much else. Not that the dissolution of the monasteries was at all unpopular in Cornwall : they had outlived any usefulness they once had, and people were glad to get hold of their property. Henry VIII intended to found a Cornish bishopric at Bodmin or St. Germans, and that would have helped to win Cornishmen over to the new deal. But the money went on the French war and such evidences of the reinforced power of the state as the fortification of the south coast : two monuments of which remain in Pendennis and St. Mawes castles, guarding the entrance to the Fal—the latter a perfect and undisturbed specimen of a Henrician fort of trilobe design, both planned by a German military engineer. As a defensive measure in carrying through such an operation as the Reformation changes, Henry tried an experiment of direct government, like that of Wales and the North, by setting up a Council of the West, with Russell as Lord President. It was found not necessary.

Subsequent developments—the suppression of the chantries and the introduction of an English Prayer Book—touched the people's faith : interference in the realm of the irrational and the customary is always more dangerous, and there were disturbances in the Lizard area once more in 1548. It is symbolical in its way that it should have been the Act of *Uniformity* next year, imposing an English Prayer Book, that produced a full-scale rebellion. The Cornish objected that the new service was no better than a Christmas mumming and that they could not understand English. Protector Somerset and Archbishop Cranmer replied sensibly that there were more people in Cornwall who understood the English tongue than Latin. But rational argument never did the irrational any good, and the rebels crossed the Tamar to join forces with Devonshire insurgents who had risen simultaneously, to besiege Exeter, set the West alight and produce a dangerous crisis for Edward VI's government.

Exeter was closely besieged for a month and had a narrow escape. Lord Russell was repulsed by the rebels in east Devon and could make no headway until reinforced by Lord Grey with foreign mercenaries, Italian and German under Spinola. The rebels fought stubbornly and suffered heavy losses. The repression was correspondingly severe. Priests who had taken part in the rebellion were hanged from their church-towers. Sir Anthony Kingston, as provost-marshal, executed martial law in Cornwall and hanged people up with a grim humour that was for long remembered. For the Cornish it was a bitter experience, a harsh lesson : henceforth they gave no more trouble.

Already in the course of these events the shape things were to take in the Elizabethan age was foreshadowed. It offers a pretty symbolism that it should have been Walter Ralegh's father who was nearly lynched by the rebels outside Exeter and that it should have been by his seamen that he was rescued. For the future was with the seamen and on the sea. The leaders of the Rebellion of 1549 were all landsmen : they represented the old order and the old faith. The two chiefs were men of considerable estates : Humphrey Arundell was a grandson of a leader in the rising of 1497 and a cadet of the leading family in Cornwall, the 'great Arundells' of Lanherne ; John Winslade of Tregarrick was actually residing at Bochym at the time of the outbreak, very convenient for the ultra-Cornish Lizard area where it lies. The Arundells were deeply compromised by the Rebellion ; the leaders of the family had not taken the field against the rebels and they had had masses said. It was obvious where their sympathies lay, and both Sir John and Sir Thomas were sent to the Tower : Sir Thomas, a more important figure at the centre than his elder brother, was executed later as a supporter of Somerset against Northumberland.[1] The Lanherne Arundells remained Catholics in Elizabeth's reign; they became recusants and for decades paid the heavy fines for non-attendance at church; they maintained priests in their households, they educated the Bodmin boy of Irish parentage, John Cornelius, to become their chaplain and a martyr. They were harassed by the government and, when Cornwall became a danger area in the war with Spain, they had to leave the county; they were imprisoned and when released lived at their Chideock house in Dorset. But they never deviated; when the French Revolution brought many English communities home from the Continent, Lanherne became—as it still is—a nunnery.

The future was not with the Arundells, but with the sea-going folk, the privateers and buccaneers. The estates of Humphrey Arundell and Winslade went to the Devonshire Carews, Sir Gawen and that fascinating old tough, Sir Peter. During the pitiable interlude of Mary's reign these were the men who gave her government trouble; the sea-going men among the western gentry were in constant opposition and came out openly against the Spanish marriage. They wanted to marry Edward Courtenay, Earl of Devon, to Elizabeth and to depose Mary. Courtenays, Carews, Pollards, Tremaynes, Killigrews were all in it. When the conspiracies failed, the Carews went to the Tower; the Tremaynes and Killigrews took to the sea, basing themselves on Rouen. Mary lived out her days miserably. When Elizabeth succeeded to the throne these West Country supporters of hers came into high favour. Edmund Tremayne, who had known how to keep her secrets on the rack, became Clerk of the Privy Council; William Killigrew, groom of her chamber—he must have been in closer contact with the Queen, known her better than anyone, for more than forty years; Henry Killigrew became Burghley's brother-in-law and a most trusted and constantly employed of Elizabethan diplomatic envoys.

Within Cornwall one can catch the change of emphasis on

---

[1] Sir Thomas was the founder of the Wardour line of the Arundells. His son Sir Matthew conformed throughout his life, all through Elizabeth's reign. It was with Thomas Arundell, 1st baron (grandson of Sir Thomas, not of Sir John Arundell of Lanherne as the *D.N.B.* mistakenly says), that the Wardour branch lapsed back to Catholicism. With the marriage in 1739 of the 7th Baron Arundell of Wardour to Mary Arundell, the heiress of Lanherne, the two branches became united again after two centuries.

the wing—from inland to the coast, from families like the Lanherne Arundells and their dependants, with their horizons confined to the land and the faith, to families upon the coast whose horizons were illimitable and who were as much at home upon the sea as on land. " We are as near to heaven by sea as by land ", were Humphrey Gilbert's last words as the *Squirrel* heaved up and down in the Atlantic : there was indeed a significant link-up between Protestantism, the western gentry and the sea.

The Killigrews had been intending a voyage to Guinea under Mary. That was a Portuguese preserve and Philip upheld their embargo on the English sharing in the trade. All his life he was determined to keep the English out of the New World and the Pacific, and to maintain his monopoly. It was this that drove the seamen more and more into active hostility to Spain and produced, with the end of the Anglo-Spanish alliance, a profound change in English policy : from the Channel warfare with France that was endemic in the later Middle Ages to the oceanic struggle for access to the New World, warfare characteristic of our modern history. The transformation of Cornwall was a small part of this vast movement : one can watch its unfolding on the map of Elizabeth's reign.

The rise of Plymouth was the work of the remarkable Hawkins family. ' Old ' William Hawkins, who had married a Plymouth Trelawny, made the first English voyages to Guinea and Brazil. John Hawkins made his three famous slaving voyages to Guinea and the West Indies from Plymouth, equipped, manned, victualled from there. The second voyage returned to Padstow, 20 September 1565 ; the third, what was left of it after the Spanish attack at San Juan de Ulloa, staggered back to Mounts Bay in terrible straits, 25 January 1569.[1] Robert Barrett of Saltash, Hawkins' right-hand man, had been captured : if he had lived he might " have been one of the great Elizabethans, courageous, competent, enterprising. Hawkins always gave him the command of parties and expeditions away from the main fleet. He was more prominent than his cousin Drake in the history of the voyage, and he was only twenty-five when the bars closed on him. A sad fate for such a man to be burnt in Seville market-place."[2] Robert Barrett, like Drake and

[1] J. A. Williamson, *Sir John Hawkins*, 113, 202.
[2] J. A. Williamson, *Hawkins of Plymouth*, 150.

Hawkins and all these seamen, was a convinced Protestant.

Drake recouped himself for his losses. The voyage upon which he rifled the mule-train carrying the King of Spain's silver was made in a little boat with a Cornish name, *Pascoe*, and there were always some Cornish seamen in his ships, like Pascoe Giddy who was lost in the Pacific on the Voyage round the World, or Peter Carder of Veryan who came back and told such a pack of lies about his adventures, and was presented to the Queen by the Lord Admiral who gave him twenty angels for his pains.[1] That most famous of all English voyages set out from Plymouth, 15 November 1577, was driven by storm to take shelter in Falmouth harbour, returned to Plymouth for repairs, set forth and came home again—Drake's ship alone out of the three—3 November 1580.[2] Cavendish's voyage round the world set sail from there on a July day in 1586—we can recognise two Cornish sailors among those who lost their lives on the expedition.[3] Almost all Drake's expeditions set out from Plymouth ; the great expedition of 1589 to Lisbon—our reply to the Armada—assembled 20,000 soldiers and sailors there. The fortunes of Plymouth people, with its considerable Cornish contingent, were made by the demand for naval stores, the commercial prosperity all this gave rise to.

In the 1580s the voyages for planting a colony in America took shape. In 1583 Humphrey Gilbert assembled his ships for his voyage to Newfoundland at Cawsand bay ; the *Golden Hind* put in alone at Falmouth on Sunday 22 September.[4] Ralegh's first exploratory voyage was made by Captain Amadas, of the Launceston family, and Barlow who had served under Ralegh in Ireland ; William Grenville was with them.[5] Next year Sir Richard Grenville sailed from Plymouth 9 April, planted his colony on Roanoke Island and anchored again at Falmouth 6 September.[6] Among those who were the first English folk to spend a year in America were a Kendall, a Prideaux, a Courtenay and Anthony Rouse of Halton, Drake's friend and first executor, who brought up his stepson, John Pym, there on Tamar-side.

---

[1] *New Light on Drake*, ed. Z. Nuttall (Hakluyt Soc.), 426 ; for Peter Carder's tale, *v.* Purchas, *Pilgrims* (ed. 1625), IV. 1187-90, and G. C. Boase, *Collectanea Cornubiensia*, 128.

[2] R. Hakluyt, *Principal Navigations* (Everyman ed.), VIII. 48, 74.

[3] William Hills of Cornwall and Nicholas Hendy—a Cornish name ; *ibid.* 220, 230.

[4] *Ibid.* VI. 7, 36.   [5] *Ibid.* 132.   [6] *Ibid.* 132-9.

John Arundell of Trerice—the Protestant branch of the Arundells—was sent home to announce the news of the successful planting. Other members of Grenville's family were as active at sea as he was himself : a Captain Grenville died on Drake's military expedition to the West Indies in 1585, on which Sir Richard's cousin, James Erisey—of the pleasant old manor of that name lost in a fold of the Lizard peninsula—commanded the *White Lion*.[1] When Grenville brought round his squadron to serve under Drake against the Armada, Erisey commanded the Spanish prize Grenville had captured on his way back from Virginia.[2] The little *God Save Her* was commanded by Grenville's second son John, whom we find again at sea, after his father's death, serving under Ralegh's orders and dying on Ralegh's Guiana Voyage in 1595.[3] And some there be that have no memorial.

In the war with Spain Cornwall was in the front line, and in the 1590s the conflict was on her doorstep, with Philip's decision to intervene in Brittany, his occupation of Blavet and his sending reinforcements of troops there and of ships and galleys into the Channel. It became necessary to fortify Plymouth still more strongly, and in fact it was turned into a fortress—with the fort on the Hoe in combination with the defences of St. Nicholas' Island. Now it was an English engineer, Robert Adams, who was competent to design the works, and he went on to strengthen the fortifications of Scilly and turn it into a strong-point at the entrance to the Channel.[4] Troops were levied in Cornwall along with other western counties for the war in Brittany, and when the campaign ended they were transferred to Ireland. The withdrawal set the Spanish galleys free to prowl in the Channel ; they made a raid on Mounts Bay, burning Penzance, Newlyn and Mousehole. In 1596 a second Armada set sail from Spain, but was scattered by storms off Finisterre in which many vessels foundered and thousands of men were lost. Next year a third attempt was set going, of which the objective was Falmouth ; but it was a feebler effort and put back before the storms it met. But with each effort, we notice the reaction in Cornwall : after this one, Falmouth was fortified more strongly

[1] *Ibid.* VII. 78, 108.
[2] Cf. my *Sir Richard Grenville of the ' Revenge '*, 259.
[3] *The Discoverie of Guiana*, by Sir Walter Ralegh, ed. V. T. Harlow, 130.
[4] *Cal. S.P. Dom. 1591-4*, 346-9.

and a professional soldier, Sir Nicholas Parker, put in command of the troops now stationed there.[1]

Meanwhile, these ports at the entrance to the Channel were active bases in the privateering operations going forward. Prizes were constantly being brought in ; sometimes a valuable prize would be cast away on Cornish rocks. The privateering Earl of Cumberland and Sir John Borough were in and out of Plymouth ; or a small boat, like the *Mayflower* of St. Ives, would do a little business on her own and, when her spoil, the *Whale*, was declared not good prize at Cork, would take her round to Kinsale for better luck.[2] The grandest persons found themselves in these harbours : Essex setting out on the Islands Voyage of 1597 was so beset by storms that he was driven back to take refuge at Falmouth, when he wrote : " In haste, in passion, and yet in hope of change of fortune, I send this bearer to acquaint her Majesty with the state of her poor servant, and with as much news as I know of the fleet. . . . Believe me that all shall yet go well." Next day he came " all night post over the rugged mountains of Cornwall " to join up with Ralegh and the rest of the battered fleet.[3]

In the last years of the reign the focus of the conflict shifted to Ireland. Cornwall remained in the foreground for despatch of troops thither : there were constant embarkations from Plymouth, Falmouth and Padstow, and a regular system of fast posts was laid from Padstow to London for news and communications. The first word was brought in to Fowey of the Spanish fleet making for Kinsale, where the issue of the war was decided.[4]

Perhaps we may regard the marked increase in the number of Members of Parliament returned for Cornish boroughs—until it reached its maximum in Elizabeth's reign—as in some small part reflecting the changed position of Cornwall in the nation's affairs, from being a backwater to being very much in the foreground. But with the Parliamentary predilections of subsequent centuries its intrinsic importance has been much exaggerated. Carew thought it enough to comment that " Cornwall sendeth an equal, if not larger, number of burgesses to any shire :

---

[1] *Cal. S.P. Dom. 1595–7*, 540, 546.
[2] *Cal. S.P. Dom. 1591–4*, 138-9.
[3] W. B. Devereux, *Lives and Letters of the Devereux, Earls of Essex*, I. 432-4.
[4] S.P. 12/281, No. 46.

the boroughs so privileged, more of favour (as the case now standeth with many of them) than merit, are these following "—and he gives their names. [1] These afforded convenient seats for local families to sit for, Edgcumbes, Grenvilles, Killigrews, Trelawnys, and also occasionally such people as Drake and Ralegh ; or officials and people at court, a Mildmay, a Stanhope, a Harington, or their opponents Peter and Paul Wentworth. It is impossible to generalise much from the Cornish representation. What we can observe is a noticeably grander representation of the county in James's first Parliament : many more important persons seem anxious to secure a seat with a new king and the important new issues to be settled now that the old Queen's hand was removed. [2]

Of the defeated side curious bits of flotsam and jetsam fetch up in odd places. Sir John Arundell's son retained Winslade's grandson, Tristram, as his servant at Lanherne. At the time of the trouble over Cuthbert Mayne—the first martyr of the seminarists, caught and hounded to death by Grenville— Winslade and his father disappeared from Cornwall, no-one knew whither. Carew says that " Winslade's son led a walking life with his harp, to gentlemen's houses, wherethrough, and by his other active qualities, he was entitled Sir Tristram : neither wanted he (as some say) a ' belle Isoult ', the more aptly to resemble his pattern ". [3] When Drake captured Don Pedro de Valdes' great ship, *Nuestra Señora del Rosario*, from the Armada, Tristram Winslade was aboard. From his examination we learn what had happened to him and his father : the father had fled to Brittany, thence to Spain and Portugal, where he died at Lisbon. [4] The son had gone to Ireland, thence through France and Germany to Italy. A few weeks later Topcliffe had permission to rack him in the Tower. [5] But he survived, to die in sanctity at Douai where he was buried in the chapel 24 November 1605.

Back on the Scottish Border, another of the circle—Nicholas Roscarrock—had come safe into harbour at last with Lord William Howard and his blind harper at Naworth. He had been much in prison, had taken many risks and had some narrow

---

[1] Carew, *op. cit.* 224.
[2] Cf. *Members of Parliament*, Return Pt. I. 437.
[3] Carew, *op. cit.* 309.
[4] From Loseley MSS. in St. G. K. Hyland, *A Century of Persecution*, 194-5.
[5] *Acts of the Privy Council, 1588*, 273.

escapes.[1] In the Tower he had managed to smuggle out letters for Father Crichton. In the Fleet with the Tregians, he was watched and reported on by a Catholic spy. Now, with James on the throne, with Lord William for company and his books around him, he could give himself up in peace to his antiquarian studies. Far away, in his Border fastness, it was Cornwall that held his mind, a Cornwall he could never go home to : bit by bit, patiently, lovingly, he was piecing it together in his mind, writing down endlessly in his great folio all that he could remember, all that he could find, of the lives of the Cornish saints, of their legends, their parishes and holy wells, of the observances and rites in their honour in the days that had vanished for ever.

[1] Cf. *Tudor Cornwall*, 368-9 ; *The Household Books of Lord William Howard* (Surtees Soc.), *passim*.

CHAPTER II

THE BORDERLANDS: WALES

WALES was happy with the Tudors. And so she had reason to be; for with them she moved from the disaster of Owen Glendower's rebellion, the oppression and misery that were its consequences, the insatisfaction and deception of her hopes in the Wars of the Roses, through a period of probation under the first Tudors and Henry VIII's revolutionary new departure with the Act of Union, to an outburst of shining achievement under Elizabeth which we may legitimately speak of as a national revival. For the Welsh were a complete people, an entire society with all its articulated members, and theirs a little country of its own. As markedly as for Cornwall, but a bigger affair altogether, the Elizabethan age was for Wales a time of stirring and awakening into action. We may even say—the Welsh were so much to the fore—that they made a showing in English life out of all proportion to their numbers.

It was the more striking after the bitter experiences of the Welsh in the previous century. Owen's rebellion reached the dimensions of a national struggle and for a time it paralysed the English government. So acute and prolonged a conflict bore its natural fruit: large parts of North Wales were wasted and depopulated, and the English reacted to a dangerous national resistance with a code of penal laws which excluded the Welsh from common citizenship.[1] They might not own land in or near the towns, which were regarded as English garrisons, or hold any office under the Crown, or serve on juries or inter-marry with the English: the usual reaction to conflicts of ir-reconcilable national spirit almost everywhere. Welsh hopes of revenge and of profiting from English dissensions in the Wars of the Roses received their quietus on the field of Edgcote in 1469, when scores of Welsh gentlemen fell with the leader of Welsh hopes, the first Herbert, Earl of Pembroke.

[1] Sir John E. Lloyd, *Owen Glendower*, 56.

This greatest of battles was lost by treachery :
at Banbury dire vengeance fell upon Wales . . .

sang the bard.[1] The bards kept going a feeling of hatred for
the English : no wonder that both Edward I and Henry IV had
tried to extinguish their profession—in vain. The best revenge
was when a Welshman came to the English throne in the person
of Henry Tudor—as the best revenge for Flodden was James
VI's accession in 1603. But the Welsh *renversement* was all the
more dramatic when we realise, as we have only lately come to
do, that the Tudors of Anglesey had been the backbone of
Glendower's resistance movement.[2]

Henry was unmistakably Welsh, and came in time, though not
till he looked like winning, to attach the national sentiment of
Wales to him. Descended of a small Anglesey family, and of the
French and English royal houses, he spent the first fourteen years
of his life in South Wales, mostly at Pembroke.[3] (Did he speak
English with a Welsh accent? Likely enough, but, alas, we
shall never know.) He owed everything to his uncle Jasper's
sleepless assiduity in the Lancastrian cause. During the long
Yorkist spell, Jasper was very canny and uncatchable: from his
stronghold at Pembroke he was able to keep in touch with Ireland,
Scotland, Brittany and ultimately to escape with his nephew
—upon whom rested the last hopes of the Lancastrians. The
next fourteen years Henry spent mostly in Brittany. As England
moved in revulsion away from the king who was a murderer,
the bards—well aware of the preparations in Brittany—turned
towards Henry with their encouragements and prophecies. There
is a tradition that in Wales he was known by the magic name of
Owen. He was the Black Bull of Anglesey. " In what seas are
thy anchors, and where art thou thyself? " sang the leading
bard, Lewis Glyn Cothi. " When wilt thou, Black Bull, come to
land ; how long shall we wait ? On the feast of the Virgin, fair
Gwynedd, in her singing watched the seas."[4]

When Henry landed in Wales his appeal to Gwynedd—North
Wales—was twofold : direct through his own family connections,
indirect through the Stanleys, the family into which his mother

[1] H. T. Evans, *Wales and the Wars of the Roses*, 184.
[2] Cf. Glyn Roberts, " The Anglesey Descendants of Ednyfed Fychan in the Four-
teenth Century ", *Trans. Anglesey Antiquarian Soc., 1951*, 34 foll.
[3] David Williams, *A History of Modern Wales*, 21.
[4] W. Garmon Jones, " Welsh Nationalism and Henry Tudor ", *Trans. Hon. oc.
Cymmrodorion*, 1917–18, 18.

had married, lords of the great Lordships of Bromfield and Yale. The desertion of Richard III by the Stanleys decided the issue at Bosworth. In West Wales Henry had Jasper's faithful remnant and the formidable support of Rhys ap Thomas. The prayers of the bards were answered : the dragon of Cadwaladr, " a red fiery dragon beaten upon white and green sarcenet ", floated over his victorious army in the heart of England. When he became king, it was necessary to provide him with an illustrious descent from Cadwaladr and a commission had to be sent down to Wales for the purpose : the bards obliged.

Henry VII remained always conscious of his Welsh ancestry and obligations, and he did what he could to satisfy their aspirations. His successor on the throne was to have been an Arthur ; the young prince was given semi-regal state at Ludlow— the seat, along with Shrewsbury, of the Council of Wales— where he died. Henry took the first step in the emancipation of Wales by enfranchising the bondmen on the great Crown lord-ships ; two years before his death he extended this to the Principality.[1] He opened the boroughs to the Welsh and gave them equality with the English before the Law. It is said that on his death-bed he adjured his successor to have a special care of Wales.[2] " The Boar is cold in his grave : the world is still and envenomed feuds asleep ", sang Lewis Glyn Cothi.

A very wise and far-seeing Welshman was Henry VII, with those deep-set melancholy eyes under the high-arched Lancastrian brows : a man prudent and wary, with no confidence in life. What an experience of life he had had : he knew all the uncertainty, the treacheries that lie in wait, the smiling hidden dangers undisclosed ; a man who kept his thoughts to himself, was capable of endless self-restraint, never betrayed by any sense of security—indeed it must have been his inbred sense of insecurity from childhood that drove him on to accumulate safety in the form of money : hence his miserliness, growing on him with age ; a man of long patience and, in the end—distrusting life—a humane man. Elizabeth took after her grandfather, and in an interview with Lambarde towards the end of her life suddenly referred to " my good grandfather ".[3] For all her pride in her

---

[1] The Principality at this time means the three shires of Anglesey, Caernarvon and Merioneth in the north, with the Crown lands of Carmarthen and Cardigan in the south.

[2] Sir John E. Lloyd, ed., *A History of Carmarthenshire*, II. 87.

[3] *v. The England of Elizabeth*, 37.

father, there is no instance of her referring to Henry VIII as
" good ". Nor—although she liked to be thought so—was she
essentially like him. The clue to Henry VIII is that he was a Yorkist
and turned after *his* grandfather, Edward IV : fleshy, extravert,
athletic, an enjoyer of all good things, with the Yorkist over-
confidence in life.

In addition to a natural pride in the achievements of the
Tudors, there must have been a deep satisfaction in that the
dynasty itself was Welsh. For in a period of not much above a
half century, which saw three risings in Cornwall, the Pilgrimage
of Grace, Wyatt's Rebellion and the Rising of the Northern
Earls—besides various other stirrings—in England, never
more than a riot took place in Wales, and not a breath was
breathed against the dynasty. Throughout the small, but various,
country there was a profound contentment : the dynasty was
theirs.

Even foreigners grasped the distinction : at the beginning,
the *Italian Relation,* after mentioning the oppression of the
Welsh, says " they may now however be said to have recovered
their former independence, for the most wise and fortunate
Henry VII is a Welshman ".[1] And towards the end of their
dynasty, in setting forth " a work in honour of Wales, where your
Highness' ancestors took name ", it was surely no mere politeness
that made Thomas Churchyard report, " of truth your Highness
is no sooner named among them, but such a general rejoicing
doth arise as maketh glad any good man's heart to behold or
hear it, it proceeds of such an affectionate favour ".[2] The bards
did not lag behind the English poets in addressing the Queen
they thought of as Welsh.

Henry's victory had been a victory for Wales ; the success
of the Tudors was a triumph for the Welsh. They flocked to
London, and some of them who came out of Wales changed the
face of things in England. One of the obscurer of Henry's Welsh
following, David Cecil, came from a small Border family, something between a yeoman and a barely recognisable gentleman—
that so characteristic an element from which the greatest Tudor
achievements came. In the third generation, the great Lord
Burghley could still be greeted as kinsman by a Wogan in remote

---

[1] q. W. L. Williams, *Y Cymmrodor,* 1903, 6.
[2] Thomas Churchyard, *The Worthiness of Wales* (reprinted from the edition of
1587), 1776, vi-vii.

Pembrokeshire,[1] was still consumed by the Welsh passion for pedigrees and in the essential traits of his personality was not very dissimilar to Henry Tudor—perhaps that was what bound William Cecil so closely to Elizabeth : they shared an instinctive sympathy of outlook deeper than the conscious convictions of the intellect, though there too they agreed.

A young Morgan Williams of Glamorgan made his way to London, where he prospered in Putney and married a sister of Thomas Cromwell. Their son got a grant of Neath Abbey, took his uncle's name and became the great-great-grandfather of Oliver Cromwell. In the Tudor household there was always a Welsh element. Elizabeth's household, both as Princess and for a few years as Queen, was run by Thomas Parry as Cofferer, to whom she entrusted her most confidential secrets and missions. [2] It fell to him to defend his young mistress to her brother's Council on the awkward subject of her relations with Lord Admiral Seymour. After Parry's death, his daughter Blanche remained with the Queen all her life as chief gentlewoman of her bed-chamber : one sees her on her monument in the little church of Bacton in Herefordshire, turned in devotion to face the Queen in whose service she spent her years. David Powell got his copy of Stradling's tract on " The Winning of the Lordship of Glamorgan "—which he printed in the *Historie of Cambria*—from Blanche Parry, " a singular well-willer and furtherer of the weal public of that country ".[3] Dr. Dee called her cousin, and she kept his reputation sweet with the Queen. [4] William Cecil, head of the family remaining at the old home, Alterennis—who was in the habit of writing with some familiarity to cousin Robert to recommend this or that Welshman for a job—presses an acquaintance for a place in the Queen's guard : " he is strong and active and attended my very good friend, Mistress Blanche Parry, when he was a youth, if God had pleased, she would have preferred him to a better room ". Even more to the point, " her Majesty, lately taking the air in Islington Fields, noted this bearer then there being a-shooting and of her goodness said he was a feat man to attend her service ".[5] The Queen's apothecary was Welsh, Hugh Morgan. [6] They were a clan around her.

[1] *v. Hist. Soc. West Wales*, VI. 203.
[2] Cf. *Salisbury MSS.* (H.M.C.), I. 73, 232-3.　　　[3] Bodl. MS. e Mus. 63.
[4] *The Private Diary of Dr. John Dee*, ed. J. O. Halliwell (Camden Soc.), 6.
[5] *Salisbury MSS.* (H.M.C.), VII. 180.
[6] *v. Nat. Library of Wales Journal*, I. 112-14.

And what are we to think of the extraordinary family of the Herberts, with their variegated abilities and accomplishments, in both the illegitimate and legitimate lines ? The first Herbert earl had been a Yorkist, but the fortune of the (illegitimate) line had been made anew by Henry VIII and he settled them at Wilton. The second earl of this second creation succeeded his father-in-law, Sir Henry Sidney, as Lord President of Wales and made Ludlow a vice-regal court, the political and social capital, from 1586 to 1601. Talent, gifts, distinction proliferated from them in many directions : Sir William, of the legitimate line, Irish undertaker, scholar and writer ; George Herbert, divine and poet ; Lord Herbert of Cherbury, philosopher and historian ; William, the third earl and his handsome brother Philip, Earl of Montgomery, with their equal interests in women and the colonisation of America, " the incomparable pair of brethren " to whom Shakespeare's plays were dedicated. For the Herberts and the Sidneys together formed the most discriminating and generous circle of patrons of the age. Samuel Daniel was a tutor in the family, William Browne lived at Wilton, Massinger's father was steward there ; Ben Jonson and Chapman partook of their bounty. William, the third earl, sent the young Inigo Jones to Italy at this very time, with its incalculable consequences in transmitting the effective Renaissance impulse in the arts, the propulsion to classicism. Pembroke's mother, Mary Sidney, and her brother Philip were famous for the encouragement they gave to other writers as well as for what he wrote and she inspired.

Nor were the Welsh less to the fore in other spheres. There is the brilliant mind of William Thomas, who had much influence with the young Edward VI and might have had importance in the state if Edward had lived and if himself could have taken a leaf out of his colleague Cecil's book and restrained his own " hot, fiery spirit ". Well acquainted with Italy, he was too much of a Machiavellian—or rather, allowed people to perceive too plainly that he was. However, young as he was when Mary took his head off, he left us the first Italian grammar and dictionary in English, besides his *History of Italy* and much else of interest.[1] Among the soldiers, Sir Roger Williams was one of the foremost ; a writing man—oddly enough for such a rough character—his book, *A Brief Discourse of War*, is a chief authority

---

[1] For his career, *v.* E. R. Adair, " William Thomas, Clerk to the Privy Council ", in *Tudor Studies Presented to A. F. Pollard.*

on the warfare of the age. His companion in arms, Sir Thomas Morgan, of whom Williams wrote that he "had never any great ambition in him although fortune presented fair unto him often ", was an able commander, but un-Welsh in one respect, for he was "unfurnished of language ". The leading seamen combined sea-faring with poetry. Captain William Middleton, who bore the news of the approaching Spanish fleet to Howard and Grenville in the Azores, completed his translation of the Psalms into Welsh "apud Scutum insulam occidentalium Indorum ". Captain Tomas Prys, who fought in Ireland, Scotland and France, took to buccaneering and saw the inside of several prisons, wrote widely and satirically on the wild life of a Welsh gentleman in London, on missing prizes at sea and on his brother bards missing prizes at home. In the end, he came back to Wales and built himself a house out of the ruined monastery on Bardsey Island, "a wild westward facing place where the wind carried sea-spray to his mouth every day ".[1]

At Oxford a Welsh college was founded, Jesus College ; and from All Souls came a contingent of Welsh lawyers who— significantly—made the leading careers in the civil-law courts. Notably Dr. David Lewis of Abergavenny, Judge of the High Court of Admiralty, and Dr. William Aubrey, a master in Chancery and in the Court of Requests, who used to go home to Brecknock to "make merry with his friends ", where he built up that admirable patrimony which his "maggoty-headed " grand-son lost, letting his affairs run " skim-skam ". Among the poets there is Donne, in whom we cannot but recognise an intellectual voluptuousness and intensity of temperament more Welsh than English ; or Sir John Davies, the exquisite poet of " Orchestra " and " Nosce Teipsum " and hot-head of the scuffle in the Temple. In science, Robert Recorde of Tenby was the leading mathematician of the first half of the century, the first to write on arithmetic, algebra and geometry in English—under somewhat rhetorical titles ; John Dee, admirable mathematician and geographer, was the son of a sewer in the household of Henry VIII. He became more popular—or rather unpopular[2]—as an astrologer, and indeed there was something of the visionary,

---

[1] Gwyn Williams, *An Introduction to Welsh Poetry*, 198 foll.
[2] The mob broke into his house and wrecked his library at Mortlake. Sir William Herbert had gone there to live to be near him.

hieratic seer in his personality like that portrayed so wonderfully in Shakespeare's Glendower.

In commerce there were the Myddeltons of Denbigh, a prolific family. Sir Thomas was a Grocer and Lord Mayor of London ; he took an active interest in American colonisation and was a Virginia adventurer. His brother, Sir Hugh, Goldsmith and projector, was the imaginative entrepreneur who brought the New River into London—a prodigious effort which strained his resources. That took four years, from 1609 to 1613 ; but what a change it marks that London should have owed its water to the Welsh !

It was Henry VIII who revolutionised Welsh affairs and integrated Wales into the English state—gave it that foundation upon which it has subsisted ever since. There could be no more classic, no more successful, example of the Renaissance state cleaving its way through the tangle of outworn medieval survivals, tidying up the mess and imposing uniformity and simplicity in the interests of good government. The previous pattern of Principality and shire-ground and Palatinate of Chester, of counties (like Pembroke and Glamorgan) and Marcher lordships (most of which had fallen in to the Crown, paving the way to union, though some remained dividing the Crown lands of West Wales from those of the North) is too complex to explain—even the Act of Union got a good many things wrong. The kaleidoscope of privileges, claims, counter-claims made good government impossible, justice often not to be obtained ; murders, felonies, cattle-stealing went unpunished, for, as on the Scottish Borders, it was difficult to get juries to return a verdict. There was a growing demand for the intervention of the state.

A series of Acts transformed the situation.[1] In 1536 the Reformation Parliament, which had changed so much in England, passed an Act applying the English system of government to Wales, making the two countries one. The intention may be read in the preamble : " because in the same country [Wales] divers rights, usages, laws and customs be far discrepant from the laws and customs of the realm and also because the people do

---

[1] It is absurd that in a standard collection like J. R. Tanner's *Tudor Constitutional Documents*, these Acts should not be given ; nor is there a single section devoted to Wales. In R. B. Merriman's *Life and Letters of Thomas Cromwell* one small paragraph is devoted to the subject.

daily use a speech nothing like nor consonant to the mother-tongue used within this realm—the country of Wales shall forever, from henceforth, be united and annexed to and with this realm of England ".[1] Wales was reorganised : the Marcher lordships were grouped to make five new shires, Brecon, Monmouth, Radnor, Denbigh, Montgomery. Other lordships and feudal enclaves went to increase the old Welsh shires and neighbouring English ones. The administration of Wales was to be similar to that in England ; English law to take the place of Welsh, and English to be the official language. All land in Wales was " henceforth to be after the English tenure nor after the form of any Welsh law or custom ". On the other hand, Wales was admitted to complete equality of citizenship and to be represented fully in Parliament, one member for each county and one for the borough in each county.

Here were the principles of a sweeping new deal. When it came to implementing them, there was doubt and some opposition. An Act of 1535 had sanctioned the appointment of J.P.s in the old Welsh shires. But there was opposition from the North on the ground that they would use their new powers to maintain their causes at law and back up their feuds ; and from Bishop Rowland Lee, who had spent years in suppressing cattle-thieving and commented that there were " very few above Brecknock who have £10 in land and their discretion is less than their land ". Henry decided to press on with his policy and to trust the Welsh gentry to develop the capacity for self-government. Another important Act in 1542 filled in the details and made the scheme operative. The system of J.P.s and sheriffs was applied all through Wales, as in England : the Welsh gentry were to be responsible for local government and administration. The Council of Wales was given statutory authority to supervise them at it. A new system of courts was established throughout the country, independent of Westminster, the Courts of Great Sessions. There were to be local chanceries and exchequers for the various districts. In fact the model of government provided by the old shires of the Principality had the effect of giving the courts more of a Welsh character throughout than previously was the case in the feudal lordships. A strong local inflexion was preserved throughout the administration, especially with the long period of rule of Sidney and Pembroke

[1] q. W. Rees, " The Union of England and Wales ", *T.S.C.*, 1937, 27 foll.

—with their Welsh connexions—covering most of Elizabeth's reign.

Wales now had a constitution and she had equality—and what a success she went forward to make of it !

All this reflected the economic changes taking place on the face of the countryside, the transformation Welsh society was undergoing : medieval tribal society was in dissolution ; in the break-up, opportunities opened out to the hardy and hard-working, the avaricious and the intelligent, to add field to field, acre to acre and build up concentrated holdings in place of the dispersed holdings of the *gwely* (kin) ; from this came the rise of a class of independent farmers, a yeomanry merging into small and greater gentry. As in England, increasing differentiation of class meant agricultural progress, greater production for increasing population, more prosperity. Only in Wales the process was even more striking, because the tempo of change was quicker, the gentry had further to go from, Wales had been so poor. We may take the political transformation as crystallising, confirming and fixing the transformation of Welsh society. Such as it was to become by the end of Elizabeth's reign, it remained essentially unchanged for the two centuries and a half up to the Industrial Revolution. In our period the consequences were all yet to be worked out.

We can watch the process, as through a microscope, especially in North Wales where tribal society held out longest : from communities of small holders, with tribal rights and scattered holdings, to little and then larger estates with their consolidated and more efficient demesne.[1] The absurdly scattered fragments are gradually, carefully, sensibly brought together, the stony pieces cleared bit by bit up the climbing hillsides. A tribal family of more enterprise than others raised itself out of the morass in this way over three generations, to emerge in Elizabeth's reign as the Maurices of Clenennau, whose Hall was the most important residence in South Caernarvonshire by 1600. A year or two later, in James's reign, Sir William Maurice was the most persistent advocate of a united kingdom of Great Britain : naturally the accent for him was all on expansion and integration.

A Lancashire family had come to Conway after Glendower's

---

[1] The microscope is Professor T. Jones Pierce's ; *v.* his valuable Introduction to the *Clenennau Letters and Papers* (*Nat. Library of Wales Journal, Supplement*, Series IV, Part I), and other articles.

Rebellion, made money in trade and gradually bought up scores of small holdings in the countryside, building up a large estate which passed into the possession of the Bulkeleys, who became the leading family in Anglesey from then on. Other town families were buying up properties in their rural hinterland, changing the look of the landscape and the social equilibrium. But many rural clansmen held their own and advanced by frugality, marriage or hardihood, " emerging in the sixteenth century as yeomen freeholders and a few, like the families of Maes-y-castell and Caerhun, took their place alongside Baron Hill [the home of the Bulkeleys] in the peculiarly native pattern of *county* life evolved in Wales during the Tudor age ".[1]

Everything contributed to this movement. Henry VII's emancipation of the bondmen helped the freeing of tenures.[2] Gavelkind had been the rule of descent until undermined by the simpler, more certain English tenures ; the gentry were increasingly opposed to it—it was an obstacle to building up an estate—and they had their way when it was abolished in 1541. Primogeniture meant that there were more younger sons on the road to London and achievement there. The first modern leases in the English fashion come in at the same time ; they were binding on the Crown as well as on the tenant, and proved a protection to the rights of the people.[3] Indeed the people everywhere encroached on the rights of the Crown. In almost every commote in the North, there was Crown land for people to squat on, annex and then refuse to pay the rent for.[4] (I have observed the same process at work on the Duchy lands in Cornwall.) A loss to the Crown, it was good business for local people. When Leicester was given a grant of all the encroached land in the Principality in 1569, all North Wales—at any rate, the smaller squires and freeholders—combined to obstruct him. As usual, the authorities at Westminster had difficulty in enforcing any decisions unless the people on the spot were with them. Meanwhile, they were prospering : up the hillsides cultivation advanced, large numbers of new tenants were placed at handsome profits to the fermors of lands.

[1] T. Jones Pierce, " The *Gafael* in Bangor MS. 1939 ", *T.S.C.*, 1944, 158 foll.
[2] A. N. Palmer and E. Owen, *A History of Ancient Tenures of Land in North Wales and the Marches*, 39 foll.
[3] *Ibid.* 210.
[4] Cf. T. Jones Pierce, " Notes on the History of Rural Caernarvonshire in the reign of Elizabeth ", *Trans. Caernarvon Hist. Soc.*, 1940, 39 foll.

What is it one is observing ? The increase of cultivation and population ; under the lead of social energies released from the constriction of the tribal and the customary, internal colonisation following upon security and order. In rock-bottom terms, feeding more people better.

The population of Wales at the time of the Union is estimated (I include Monmouth) at some 280,000.[1] By 1570 it had risen to 325,000, by 1600 to 375,000 : if these figures are reliable, a very high rate of increase, proportionately much higher than England. Even if we allow for a fair margin of error, the increase is remarkable and the fact speaks for itself. Monmouth, Glamorgan and Carmarthen were the populous counties in the south, Brecon was middling, the rest thinly inhabited.[2] In the north, Denbigh and especially Anglesey were populous, Montgomery and Caernarvon, though mountainous, were in parts fertile and fairly inhabited, Flint and Merioneth poorly. George Owen tells us that in every county except Pembroke, Anglesey, Caernarvon, Merioneth, and perhaps Denbigh and Flint, theft abounded. Monmouth was very fertile, though the ways were foul ; it was well governed, but there were many thefts. Glamorgan was mostly fertile and had the greatest number of prosperous gentry, with troops of retainers following them. (In general, Welsh gentry were small gentry.) Glamorgan people were given to feuds and frequent outrages. In Brecon there were too many retainers. Radnor people were given to idle lives and excessive gaming : " much theft and little thrift ". Carmarthen was a great shire with good land ; but there was much brawling and disorder. Pembroke and Cardigan were largely barren, unenclosed champion country ; both were quiet in government, but Cardigan abounded in theft. Denbigh was good, but given to quarrelling and lawsuits ; Flint very civil and the gentry discreet. So, too, Anglesey and Caernarvon ; virtuous Merioneth hated theft. Montgomery was unruly and there was much trouble among themselves—which probably refers to the feuds between Herberts and Vaughans. The towns were mostly mean and poor : Carmarthen was the largest,

[1] David Williams, " A Note on the Population of Wales, 1536–1801 ", *Bulletin Board of Celtic Studies*, VIII. 361.
[2] This paragraph is based on George Owen's " Description of Wales ", pub. in *The Gentleman's Magazine*, 1785, Part II, 16, 108-9, 406-9, 511-14, 597-600.

Cardiff the fairest (though not the richest) ; Abergavenny was wealthy and thriving, Brecon a big town, but evil for entertainment of travellers. Wrexham and Denbigh were prosperous, Ruthin fair, Caernarvon and Conway fine little towns. We see that this was very much a J.P.'s view of it all.

The real capital of Wales was, of course, Shrewsbury ; Chester in the north and Bristol in the south irradiated the influences of commerce and of a money economy. Camden tells us that all the commodities of North Wales flowed to Shrewsbury : it was the common mart for both nations and spoke both languages.[1] The Drapers Hall there had the monopoly of the marketing of Welsh cloth, the manufacture of which was now beginning to prosper in Denbigh, Merioneth and Montgomery ; Shrewsbury employed 600 shearmen on the finishing processes.[2] In 1571 the Shearmen made a demand of the Lord President, Sidney, to have his help against the Drapers who had " cozened an Act for buying of Welsh cloth to be at liberty ".[3] Thither came the Welsh, pouring over Welsh Bridge into the town, to make money in trade, to broil and quarrel, or to see the shows of the capital. Owens and Lloyds were much to the fore in the life of the town. Richard Owen made a handsome Armada contribution of £25 in 1588 ;[4] his fine mansion of black and white timber, with pretty figures on top of the gables, built four years later, may still be seen. So, too, Ireland's mansion of the same date—though the Irelands are now in America ; the house that was an inn half-way down Wyle Cop, the steep curving street down to English Bridge and the road into England—where Henry stayed on his way to Bosworth ; or the Market Hall in the main square, built in the year of the capture of Cadiz, always now kept gay with flowers ; or the gateway to the Lord President's lodgings, with its decorative woodwork of 1610, and, within the cobbled courtyard, the Elizabethan porch deep in nasturtium and snapdragon, fuchsia and cotoneaster.

Here came the Lord President to keep his Garter feast in St. Chad's on St. George's day, when divine service was " sung by note ".[5] On May day the masters of the School gave him a banquet in the garden, and next day 360 scholars mustered

---

[1] Camden, *Britannia* (trans. by Philemon Holland, ed. 1637), 596 foll.
[2] A. H. Dodd, *The Industrial Revolution in North Wales*, 12.
[3] H. Owen and J. B. Blakeway, *A History of Shrewsbury*, I. 355.
[4] *Ibid.* 389.   [5] *Ibid.* 371, 380, 390.

before him. A week later he left the town by river, with a water-pageant to lament his departure. Young Philip Sidney, coming to town, was regaled with wine and cakes ; and for Essex, at eighteen, there was wine, hypocras, cakes and sugar, and the scholars in battle array " at his passing through the Castle gate : he rejoiced at the sight of them, giving them great rewards with hearty thanks ". The Lord President coming from London was received with a " royalty "—eighteen chamber-pieces shot off at Wyle Cop ; orations by a scholar or two, the trumpeter blowing joyfully to see. In New Year 1589, there was a broil when Francis Newport's trumpeter blew against the house in which Vaughan and his men were lodging. Newport's sister had married a Herbert ; that is sufficient explanation : it was the Herberts against the Vaughans. The town-bailiffs were forced to ring the common bell, the townsmen rushed to help, pates were broken and swords put up. Vaughan and his men were kept confined in the house, or there would have been bloodshed.

Shrewsbury is a town in which the memories walk visible.

We have seen Camden's sympathy for Wales and his response to the landscape. (He employed a Welsh servant to help him with Welsh words in his antiquarian studies.[1]) He pays tribute to the courage of the Silures, notable in their descendants : he was conscious of the continuity of characteristics back to Roman days.[2] He comments on the type of thatched cottage in Radnorshire, the fertility of the valleys in North Wales ; on the new church Leicester had built at Denbigh, the addiction of the Welsh to prophecies and their credulity. From St. David's Head on a clear day a man may see Ireland : somebody was evidently pulling the great man's leg. But all observers were agreed that the Welsh were idle and lazy about cultivation—natural enough in a country, like the Scottish Borders, mainly given to cattle-raising, a pastoral society. There was fertile ground enough, Churchyard says (he was born and educated at Shrewsbury, and knew the country), " if the people there would be laborous ".[3]

But most of Wales likes better ease and rest.

---

[1] A. H. Dodd, "Wales and Brittany", *Proc. Llandudno, Colwyn Bay and District Field Club,* 1949, 8.

[2] Camden, *op. cit.* 616 foll.   [3] Churchyard, *op. cit.* 51.

George Owen, in his *Description of Pembrokeshire*, frequently harps on this : the Welsh there preferred cattle-breeding ; around St. David's, where there was good land, the husbandry was negligent ; where they did cultivate, they would not manure the ground ; because they were worse husbandmen, they grew oats, where the English inhabitants grew corn and exported some to Ireland and North Wales.[1] However, the Welsh were improving, though it was hard to change custom. Owen judged that there was twice as much wool shorn in Pembrokeshire now as there had been forty years before ; all the same it was sent out of the shire raw to be wrought into manufactures elsewhere, in North Wales and around Bristol. Their slates were as good as the highly-commended Cornish slates, and were exported by water— the Royal Exchange was roofed with Pembrokeshire slates. Pit coals were increasingly dug, and there were coal fires in kitchens and in some halls. Anthracite was smokeless : it had been brought to Burghley's attention to show that it excelled Newcastle coal for London use, but carriage was costly, the passage tedious. Fish were a commodity of Carmarthen, especially salmon " of such greatness and plenty as no place is better furnished ".[2] To the salmon of Usk, Churchyard paid a deserved tribute—

So fresh, so sweet, so red, so crimp withal.[3]

Fishing was a chief occupation of Cardigan Bay, and shipping from the little ports along the south coast from Cardiff to Tenby. There were wire-works at Tintern, copper-smelting at Neath— what an expansion this was to receive in the distant future ![4] Mining operations were set on foot by the Myddeltons in North Wales, for copper in Anglesey and for coal in Denbigh.[5] Sir John Wynne was also concerned in copper, in encouraging the manufacture of friezes by immigrant Irish and in reclaiming land on the Caernarvon coast. One sees the Welsh gentry pushing along the same course of enterprise and fruitful avarice as their English brothers. In woollens as in agriculture, " Wales remained till the very eve of the Industrial Revolution in the stage of economic

---

[1] *The Description of Pembrokeshire by George Owen*, ed. by H. Owen, 54 foll., 80, 87, 148 ; and cf. *The England of Elizabeth*, 76-7.

[2] T. H. Lewis, " Carmarthenshire under the Tudors ", *Hist. Soc. West Wales*, VIII. 1 foll.

[3] Churchyard, *op. cit.* 19.   [4] Cf. *Cal. S.P. Dom. 1581-90*, 10, 189.

[5] Sir John Wynne, *The History of the Gwydir Family*, vii-viii.

development they had reached under the Tudors ".[1] In short, the sixteenth century was the age of heroic achievement for Wales, until we come to the nineteenth ; as in England, the first half of the century saw the most rapid changes, the second half saw their consolidation and exploitation, the harvest and the reward.

Such was the land the Welsh gentry had to make the most of at home. If it offered new opportunities, there were also new responsibilities : they learnt not only government, but self-government. " For they could not go on dispensing the laws they so often broke—still less study them at the Inns of Court . . . without coming in course of time to think habitually in terms of the underlying political assumptions ; they could not go on collecting, however corruptly, the contributions to the national exchequer which were the price of legal equality . . . without reflecting on the policies these exactions helped to finance ; they could not go on mustering troops for home defence or for expeditions overseas without becoming acutely conscious of the external perils. . . . Gradually it became a matter of local prestige to vie with other counties in forwardness over measures for public defence, and a matter of family pride . . . to add to length of lineage a string of civic offices."[2]   Many of them shared too in the notable Elizabethan movement for the preservation of the Welsh language, literature and antiquities—country gentlemen like Sir John Wynne of Gwydir, Sir John Salusbury of Llewenny, George Owen of Henllys, Sir Edward and Sir John Stradling of St. Donat's, bishops and scholars like Bishops Davies and Morgan, William Salisbury the translator, Humphrey Llwyd, John David Rhys. These sympathies were shared by Catholic exiles like Griffith Roberts. Love of antiquities was sometimes stronger than differences of doctrine.

" Never had Welsh grammar, Welsh prosody, Welsh antiquities received greater attention than during the century that witnessed the Anglicising policy of the Act of Union ; and that at the hands of the very men who were most receptive of the wider influences of the age ."[3]   Naturally—for it was they who were awakening to full consciousness. For that blissful moment

---

[1] A. H. Dodd, *op. cit.* 12.
[2] A. H. Dodd, " The Pattern of Politics in Stuart Wales ", *T.S.C.*, 1948, 11.
[3] F. Jones, " An Approach to Welsh Genealogy ", *T.S.C.*, 1948, 205.

of equilibrium that the Elizabethan age was for them no less than for the English, the Welsh gentry could enter into the cultural life of England without losing touch with the traditional life of their own people ; indeed they were leaders of it in every sense, language and all. " Sir John Wynne of Gwydir might marry his sons to English wives, but he expected those wives to learn Welsh ; and if the enrichment of his family took first place in his thoughts, Welsh antiquities took second ". His feeling for lineage, his passion for pedigrees were very Welsh and we all know his conviction that " a great temporal blessing it is, and a great heart's ease to a man to find that he is well descended ".[1] As for the people, they had not emerged from the cocoon : " the interest of the *gwerin* [folk] in politics . . . did not dawn until the nineteenth century. . . . Their attitude towards politics was essentially that of the loyal tribesman pursuing his chieftain's feuds."[2]

Two fairly contemporary books give us a picture of what this feud-ridden society had been like : Sir John Wynne's *History of the Gwydir Family* for the north, the *Autobiography* of Lord Herbert of Cherbury for the south. Wynne describes the feud in Chirkland and the neighbourhood of Oswestry between the Trevors and the Kyffins for the sovereignty of the country. " They had their alliances, partisans and friends in all the countries round thereabouts, to whom, as the manner of the time was, they sent such of their followers as committed murder or manslaughter, which were safely kept as very precious jewels ; and they received the like from their friends. . . . It was the manner in those days that the murderer only and he that gave the death's wound should fly, which was called in Welsh a *llawrudd*, which is a *redhand*, because he had blooded his hand : the accessories and abettors to the murderers were never harkened after."[3] Indeed in the Marcher lordships the offender's friends got him off for a fine of £5 to the lord : " a damnable custom used in those days in the lordships marches, which was used also in Mawddwy, until the new Ordinance of Wales made in the seven and twentieth year of Henry VIII ". Wynne's book is full of stories and vivid flashes of such life : of a kinswoman washing her man's eyes with white wine when they were bloodshot with long

[1] Wynne, *op. cit.* 57.
[2] A. H. Dodd, " Wales and the Scottish Succession, 1570–1605 ", *T.S.C.*, 1937, 201.   [3] Wynne, *op. cit.* 61 foll.

watching for a man he was on the look-out for ; of outlaws coming to assault a house and the mistress standing by the fire watching a maid boiling worts to make metheglin and throwing the boiling stuff in the faces of the assailants ; of murders being committed in the moonlight and the murderer going off to drink and wench all night ; of a mother warding off a deadly stroke on her son's head and having half her hand and three of her fingers cut off at the blow ; of coming to a house and finding the head of it laid in his bed " and his wounded men in great number lying in a *cocherie*, above the degree near the high table, all in breadth of his hall, all gored and wallowing in their own blood ". Because of a feud in his own family Meredith ap Evan was forced to leave his own inheritance in Evioneth, " where there was nothing but killing and fighting ", and lease the castle of Dolwyddelan in the Conway valley, then swarming with thieves and bondmen, saying that he would rather fight with outlaws and thieves than with his own blood and kindred, " for if I live in mine house in Evioneth, I must either kill mine own kinsmen or be killed by them ".

The stories with which Lord Herbert begins are well known : how his father was attacked by a gang of ruffians in the church-yard of Llanerfyl, one of whom struck him from behind with a forest-bill. " Notwithstanding his skull was cut through to the *pia mater* of the brain, he saw his adversaries flee away, and after walked home to his house at Llyssyn, where, after he was cured, he offered a single combat to the chief of the family by whose procurement the mischief was committed." [1] The assailant fled to Ireland and never returned. The enemies were the Vaughans ; in Herbert's own generation his sister married one of them, " by which match some former differences betwixt our house and that were appeased and reconciled ". [2]

The picture of Welsh society presented by these two idio-syncratic books is well known ; what is not realised is that the picture relates to two generations before, the Wales of before the Union. Indeed the whole implication of Wynne's book is that this was the kind of thing that went on in his grandfather's time —Henry VII's reign—and now, behold the change ! [3] The implied moral was a just one : there had been an enormous improvement. Of course feuds continued in many counties in

---

[1] *Autobiography of Lord Herbert of Cherbury*, ed. Sidney L. Lee, 4.
[2] *Ibid.* 28.   [3] He wrote his book in 1607.

Elizabeth's reign—in that Wales did not differ from England—but they were not bloody ones. In Pembrokeshire Sir John Perrot was an overbearing, over-mighty subject, presuming on his rumoured paternity ; supported by the Wogans, he was opposed by the Phillippses of Picton, the Barlows of Slebech and our friend George Owen, the antiquary.[1] There was a deal of fuss and fuming, but nothing worse than Sir John descending on Henllys, ransacking Owen's papers and consigning him to gaol. In Glamorgan the Stradlings were against the Herberts ; in Denbigh, the Salusburys at variance with the Trevors. In the neighbourhood of Cardiff it was the Lewises against the Mathews.[2] As Elizabeth's reign progressed and the Welsh gentry came to set more store by a seat in Parliament, these rivalries became canalised into conflicts at elections, for offices and such things. They were acute enough and sometimes threatening, but it was a more civilised way of fighting them.[3] Rival factions naturally attached themselves to rival factions at the centre ; but only once—in the case of Essex, who had large estates in Wales and a considerable Welsh following—did this affect the state, and then it was a transitory matter.[4]

We can watch the gentry, in north and south alike, becoming more expert, public-spirited and responsible in their job of governing. Sir John Perrot's methods had been very haphazard and personal. His way with pirates was usually to share the swag, though sometimes he would swear that he would hang the lot, frighten an old servant into cutting his throat, or offer the government that he would clear the seas and gain £2000—less doubt about the latter.[5] In the later 1570s the western seas

<hr/>

[1] J. Phillips, " Glimpses of Elizabethan Pembrokeshire ", *Archaeologia Cambrensis*, Series V, XIV, 308 foll. ; J. Phillips, *The History of Pembrokeshire*, 435 foll.

[2] In 1596 the Lewises, marching through Llandaff in warlike array, were routed by the Mathews—this had been asking for trouble, for it was the Mathews' home-town. George Lewis, their leader, had to fly for his life over Llandaff bridge : the rumour was that he was slain, he was so beset by enemies, but he was rescued by Sir Edward Stradling. The return match was played on Lewis's home-ground, when they attacked the head of the Mathews in his Cardiff house. Next year saw a flood of lawsuits between these idiots. *Records of the County Borough of Cardiff*, ed. J. H. Mathews, 309.

[3] Cf. J. E. Neale, " Three Elizabethan Elections ", *English Historical Review*, 1931, 209 foll. ; J. E. Neale, " More Elizabethan Elections ", *E.H.R.*, 1946, 18 foll.

[4] Cf. A. H. Dodd, " North Wales in the Essex Revolt of 1601 ", *E.H.R.*, 1944, 348 foll.

[5] Cf. J. Phillips, *loc. cit.* and *Arch. Cambr.* XV ; for Callice's career, *v.* C. L'Estrange Ewen, *The Golden Chalice* (Paignton, 1939) ; for Hicks, my *Tudor Cornwall*, 390-92.

were swarming with privateers and pirates—it was sometimes difficult to tell which was which. The two most notorious pirates were Captain Callice, born at Tintern, and Captain Hicks, a Saltash man, I regret to say. In 1577 one of Perrot's retainers took a Dutch ship with a nice cargo of salt. At an interview in Carew Castle—the fine eastern front of which, with its ranges of tall mullioned windows, Perrot built—he fixed it that he should make a fake attack on the pirates. He got half the cargo of salt, and bought the ship's cable and anchors for nothing. Perrot had a vessel of his own lying off Laugharne ; when the port-reeve, who was no friend, tried to inspect it, he was warned off by " ten men with calivers ready with fire on the cock ". Essex's uncle, residing at Lamphey, had frequent dealings with the pirates : a ton of Gascon wine from a ship captured by one of Perrot's old servants made the Pembroke winter brighter. He bought corn from Captain Hicks and transported it to Galicia. Everyone took part in such traffic ; no-one took any notice of Vaughan, the Vice-Admiral. Three mayors of Sir John's own town of Haverfordwest were up to their neck in the trade ; and Cardiff and Penarth were no better than Milford. Hicks paid his Welsh helpers in kind : a bushel of rye for some smith's work wrought for him ; a barrel of rye for " keeping one of his company which was hurt aboard him " ; three pecks of rye for a feast of nice Milford oysters. Hicks and Callice chummed up and joined forces to attack a much bigger Danish ship. When Callice was in trouble, we have a charming letter of comradely solicitude from Hicks. Then Hicks was caught and hanged— which Callice never was. The difference between them seems to have been that the Welshman had friends, where the Cornish-man had none.

Ten years later we find John Wynne and his cousin William Maurice, deputy lieutenants for Caernarvon, working away at local administration as conscientiously as any J.P.s in England.[1] A trifle more consciously perhaps : Wynne is very much aware of the malice of those " seeking to work division between us and thereby to make us a pageant to laugh at ". Then he has spent all day hammering at a certificate of musters to get it into the required form, but it is impossible to follow the strict letter of this pattern—one sympathises : like Income Tax returns. So

[1] Cf. *Clenennau Letters and Papers*, ed. T. Jones Pierce, 3, 5, 14, and *passim* ; and *Calendar of Wynne Papers*, 6-44.

many commissions have come down from London and there is so much other business that he cannot spare time to come to Quarter Sessions : would Maurice do duty for them both ? He " would rather flay hogs than deal with the multitude which begins to repine ". This was at the increasing burdens of the war. There were subsidies to be paid, soldiers to be raised, mustered, trained, supplied and clothed.[1] In the last two decades of the reign a quota of 1000 men a year was raised on average from Wales—the same proportion as from Somerset, Devon and Cornwall. Most of the Welsh contingents were sent to serve in Ireland. One of the muster-masters, Captain Owen, was killed while training his men near Conway. The burden of the Irish war at the end was so great that the government bore the whole charge of the levies and relieved the counties of their proportion.

With the increasing responsibilities of the war people like Wynne and Maurice became more expert—professional adminis-trators, for all that they were amateurs and had difficulties with their tempers : Wynne learned to " bridle my choler, where-unto I was much subject ".[2] When their tempers were too much for them and open quarrels broke out among them, they received a rebuke from the Lord President : " for how can your minds be united in public defence, when they are divided by private quarrels ? And what hope of succour in the field may any man have from him who is his professed enemy at home ? Or how shall her Majesty's service in this time of danger go forwards if one of you cross the same because the dealing therein is committed to another ? All men cannot be deputy-lieutenants : some must govern, some must obey."[3] Five years later, Pembroke was appealing for them to support the big enterprise set forth by Essex and the Lord Admiral that ended in the capture of Cadiz. " If these noblemen do think it their duties to spend their goods and hazard their own persons in so honourable and behoveful an action, I think it should prejudice your credits according to your abilities you should show yourselves worse affected. . . . You have ever been forward in *comorthas* [demands] for your own private gains, wherefore I conceive you will be

---

[1] In 1578 Flint was fined for its delay in returning its certificate of musters. *Cal. S.P. Dom. 1547–80*, 596.

[2] Wynne, *op. cit.* 70.

[3] *Clenennau Letters and Papers*, 15.

much more forward in this *comortha* for the public good of the whole state."[1] He did not appeal in vain : hundreds of Welshmen took part in the most brilliant exploit of its kind in the age.

Pembroke had immense influence with his countrymen ; and justly so, for he felt along with them : the dazzling eminence, the lofty distinction, of Wilton had not lost touch with Wales : his heart was still there. Twenty years earlier, in the feud between his cousin Carne and Sir Edward Stradling, he wrote to Stradling : " Rather than you should continue in this boiling hatred, I will purposely, if otherwise it cannot be brought to pass, make a journey into the country to set you at unity, if my coming may do good ".[2] The Stradling correspondence is of a more social character and lets us see that side of life, the mutual courtesies and amenities. What is striking is the close intercourse between people across the Bristol Channel : a large number of the Devon and Cornish gentry called the Stradlings cousins, the Raleghs, Gilberts, Grenvilles, Champernownes, Bassets, Arundells, Cavells and even dear William Carnsew. In 1573 Humphrey Gilbert purposed to sup with Stradling and " do intend, God willing, to embark myself towards Devonshire in the morning. Wherefore I pray you to give order that the best boat which is in the passage may be stayed for me only."[3] How like Gilbert ! When he fell sick, Lady Stradling had nursed him : " I can never forget it, nor will during life be found unthankful for the same ; and if you will entrain yourself in coparcenary to be a sharer, I will never bring a writ to disprove your title ". Grenville writes on behalf of some Barnstaple merchants coming from St. James's fair at Bristol whose goods had been taken by a pirate and received in Wales.[4] Blanche Parry asks her cousin to help a kinsman of hers to enter upon the gaolership of Glamorgan.[5] Sir Arthur Basset requests the services of Stradling's harper, whom he had recommended to Sir Philip Sidney, who wants the man to attend on him at Salisbury where there will be " an honourable assembly and receipt of many gentlemen of good calling ".[6] Pembroke asks that his brother-in-law Robert Sidney might be chosen knight of the shire, " for the which he shall demand no charges of the country at all ".[7] Welsh M.P.s were apt to expect payment of their wages ; the distance to London

[1] *Clenennau Letters and Papers*, 31.
[2] *Stradling Correspondence*, ed. J. M. Traherne, 66. [3] *Ibid.* 155-9.
[4] *Ibid.* 179.   [5] *Ibid.* 234.   [6] *Ibid.* 240.   [7] *Ibid.* 77.

was great, so were their expenses there, and they were poor. By the end of the reign they were setting great store by Parliament, and a regular Welsh interest had grown up in the Commons.[1]

The Earl of Thomond, head of the O'Brien clan, is wind-bound in Barry and desires to become acquainted with Stradling, " and so much the rather because that you, being of the borders of Wales and I the said Earl of Thomond of the borders of Ireland, I do not doubt but we should talk more at large, if it be our fortune to meet ".[2] The antiquarian interests of the Stradlings are well represented. A friend sends Sir Edward Guicciardini, " a story worth the reading, which you may use at your pleasure ".[3] Stradling had supported, at Oxford, John David Rhys who became a distinguished scholar in Italy. Sir Edward paid for the publication of Rhys's Welsh Grammar in Latin, which introduced the language to the learned world of Europe. In his will he left fifty bound copies to Rhys and " the rest to be bestowed on such gentlemen and others as my cousin think fit for advancement of the British tongue ".[4]

All this high-mindedness did not prevent the Stradlings from quarrelling with the Herberts, one episode of which was formed by the struggle over the Lower Burrows at Merthyrmawr, where Sir Edward tried to stop the encroaching sand and asserted his rights. The story was entertainingly written up by his nephew and successor, with all its ins and outs and divagations.[5] An opponent was a young man, Edmund Van, who was waiting on his master, the Earl of Pembroke, at the Grand Christmas kept at Ludlow in 1596. " He was at that feast squire of the body to one of King Arthur's knights (Sir Gawen, I trow, was his name) from the estimation of which superficial advancement, distilled into his head such a superficial humour of vain self-weening and ambition, that unneth [*i.e.* scarcely] xvi oz. of the purest tobacco received in at his nares by artificial fumigation might stop the course thereof."[6] It is pleasant to see the Arthurian cult at Pembroke's court at Ludlow ; I omit the affray at the

---

[1] A. H. Dodd, " The Pattern of Politics in Stuart Wales ", *T.S.C.*, 1949, 21-2 ; and " Wales's Parliamentary Apprenticeship, 1536–1625 ", *T.S.C.*, 1942, 8 foll.

[2] *Stradling Correspondence*, 337.   [3] *Ibid.* 335.

[4] *Ibid.* 314. Actually his heir and successor was his nephew, Sir John Stradling ; Elizabethans used the word " cousin " more widely and inclusively than we do.

[5] John Stradling, *The Storie of the Lower Borowes of Merthyrmawr*, ed. by H. J. Randall and W. Rees (South Wales and Monmouth Record Society).

[6] *Ibid.* 74, 86.

church-stile at Llantwit. " I tell you that in a Canterbury tale devised by old friars to drive away long winter nights you shall often hear more strange accidents . . . but very seldom in a matter of truth and certainty."

Nor were women behindhand in their proper sphere in this society. There is the astonishing matrimonial career of Katherine of Berain, a parallel to Bess of Hardwick.[1] Her four marriages connected her with nearly all the families of North Wales ; her progeny made her a veritable Mam Gwalia, the subject of popular legends and tales to this day. While in Brittany Henry Tudor had begotten a son by a Breton lady, Sir Roland Vielville, who was later made Constable of Beaumaris and had half the Tudor property in Anglesey settled on him. Katherine was his daughter and heiress. She had the high-arched eyebrows of her grandfather ; for the rest a squarer, more Welsh face, with high cheek-bones. She inherited a forceful personality ; she had her bards, who sang her praises, no less than her cousin the Queen. Katherine was a ward of the Queen, whose gift to her of embroidered slippers is still in existence. She married, first, the heir to Llewenny, who left her with two sons, Thomas and John Salusbury. Next she married the rich financier, Sir Richard Clough, who was just then building his house, Plâs Clough, which still remains in Denbigh. On his death she married Maurice Wynne, father of Sir John ; a weak character, Maurice was completely under her thumb.

As happens in such cases there was trouble. Katherine and her first mother-in-law, Lady Salusbury, agreed to marry Thomas, the little son and heir, when no more than a boy, to a daughter of Maurice Wynne. The boy was always unwilling and came to hate it. But the women pushed it on : the aim was to defraud Leicester of the wardship. There was a great festive gathering at Gwydir to celebrate the sealing of the agreement— the boy's wishes were ignored : it must have been an element in the tragedy that overwhelmed him. We next learn from Leicester that " the boy hath utterly dissented from the match ". On his grandfather's death-bed, Sir John Salusbury under the influence of his wife said that he wanted the match to go forward, that he meant to deliver the boy to Maurice Wynne. It seems that the menfolk did not want the match : they appreciated its dangers. John Wynne, Katherine's step-son, wrote from the

[1] J. Ballinger, " Katherine of Berain ", *Y Cymmrodor*, 1929, 1 foll.

Inns of Court where he was serving his apprenticeship : " *they* so rule my father that he ratifieth what they think fit to be done. I would to God my father's eyes were also opened to see the same, which I doubt not might be compassed if he were once from the sirens which enchant him, I mean his own wife and my lady the boy's grandmother." The women maintained their control : the match went forward, to the boy's great unhappiness.

When Katherine was in trouble we find her beseeching her step-son, John Wynne's, help. " These are to signify unto you that, for revenge of our enemies, I am now very like to receive . . . such a foil (for your sake) as I shall never claw off, unless your wisdom and foresight be my shield and strength in my greatest necessity." A kinsman and retainer of hers had had the misfortune to kill a man ; of course it was in self-defence, but the Salusburys had written to Leicester to make matters worse against him, so that he was likely to lose his lands in escheat. (Leicester was lord of Denbigh : they would escheat to him.) No doubt the lands were the rub, but it was the heart-strings that were played on. " And my poor son and your brother-in-law, little Thomas Salusbury, is filled with great perplexity for he, poor child, hath great care of him because he was his father's man and mine, and one whom he tenderly loveth. I am but a woman foolish and fond. I cannot direct you aright in this matter ; your father is not willing to deal for some respects, knowing how little affiance he hath in Denbighshire men. You are wise and discreet and conversant with what is best to be done. I therefore require you to be faithful and vigilant in this matter, otherwise the poor man shall run into utter ruin, and I and mine in perpetual obloquy and slander for ever." The point of the letter was to get John Wynne to stir up his friends to " make my lord conceive the matter aright ", *i.e.* as she wished him to. We see the true picture of Katherine of Berain, the subject of so many foolish popular misconceptions : a scheming, plausible, passionate woman, whose plans the better judgment of her menfolk cannot approve.

Married against his will, psychologically in conflict, young Thomas Salusbury went on to Oxford where he fell for the glamorous Anthony Babington's circle of young men. Involved in conspiracy, the heir to Llewenny was executed in 1586. A shudder passed through the leading families of North Wales : for the first time under the Tudors the shadow of treason had fallen on them. Katherine hurried on the marriage of her second son, John Salusbury. She herself was now married a fourth time, to Edward Thelwall. That Christmas there was a masque at Berain, with posies for her son's marriage to an illegitimate daughter of the Earl of Derby :

> Dame Venus, dear, you may rejoice
> At your son Cupid's happy choice . . . etc.

All his life John Salusbury laboured to wipe out the stain of treason from the family, in the end with success : he was knighted for his part in rounding up the Essex faction in North Wales. His house at Llewenny—now a fragment of a ruin—was the chief meeting-ground for Welsh and English culture. He was a writer of English verse and a patron of Welsh bards, on sufficient terms with Ben Jonson and Shakespeare to invite their contributions to a book in honour of his happy married life, under the symbols of the phoenix and the turtle.[1] By then Henry VII's granddaughter had been ten years in her grave in Llanefydd church : no-one even to raise her a monument.

This past is much in mind and has its memorials still as one walks the Wynne country from Bettws-y-Coed down the valley of their salmon-river to Conway ; or crosses the mountains into Lleyn to the boyhood haunts of Maurice Clynnog and Hugh Owen ; or passes the Menai Strait to seek the source of the Tudors at Penmynnedd. It is a little place to be the fountain-spring of such a fortune. Everything in Anglesey is on a small scale, and the " head of the mountain " is but a slope looking down on a fold of the hills where the spring rushes out. The diminutive old hall is left with its fine wide fireplace of 1576. All round the homestead, the wind-breaking beeches, the tiny drive bright with escallonia, hydrangeas, a sprig of winter jasmine —as it might be Cornwall. The family built outbuildings and stables under James and under the Commonwealth : there are the dates 1618 and 1653, with their arms, three helmets and the lions rampant and the initials of those names that disturb the imagination—Richard Owen Theodore (*i.e.* Tudor). The body of the later house bears a no less symbolic date : 1776.

Conway is the Middle Ages, with its superb Edwardine castle

[1] Cf. Carleton Brown, *Poems by Sir John Salusbury and Robert Chester* (Bryn Mawr Monographs).

and town-walls speaking of Savoy and the Mediterranean world of the south. But just below is the little " Black Lion " of 1589 which, though altered, suggests the life of the age. At the cross-roads is another sixteenth-century house, hipped up on struts, upper story projecting with stone steps outside up to the main floor. Below, the water-gate gives on to the quay : across the water Orme's Head, where the Recusant Mrs. Pugh, harbourer of priests, lived then. Turn up this street and there is the fine great house, Plâs Mawr, that Robert Wynne built himself in 1577 : the elaborate stepped gables, the two courtyards, the E-shape climbing up the hill. (Where did he get the money to build so very large a house ? Nobody seems to know. Perhaps, I suggest, from trade, the town quay convenient below.) Enter the house, and one sees everywhere the rustic work of country plasterers in a remote place early in the age ; all the same, done with a spirit and a slightly exotic touch that bespeaks the Welsh imagination, for among the conventional R.W.s and E.R.s, the very rampant lions and sapient owls, the Tudor roses and lions' masks, are, surprisingly, ostriches and elephants. (Did Robert Wynne trade with Africa, one wonders ?)

And so up the valley that is full of the memories of them and their exploits to Gwydir, their ancestral home : recognisable still, in the midst of the valley with hanging woods all round and the mountains to be seen from the windows. There is the small gate-house on the road, the main block with its E-projecting bay behind as at Plâs Mawr. Inside, in spite of the devastation of fires, one recognises the same spirited plasterer at work—the lions' masks, ostriches, deer of the native mountain side. Up there on the steep slopes is their old chapel in the woods. In their parish church at Llanrwst beside the sounding Conway they lie in their chapel on the south side, with the tablet to say that it was built by Sir Richard Wynne. Though Gwydir and Plâs Mawr know them no longer, the churches here and at Conway are full of them : in the latter our Robert, the builder of Plâs Mawr, buried 30 November 1598 in the chancel among his crowded kith and kin under the grey stone slabs.

The Elizabethan Church in Wales has been much mis-represented and its bishops popularly and unjustly maligned. It must be said *tout court* that the Reformation was a success there : the people followed the dynasty and gave no trouble.

There was hardly any recusancy even, for the first two decades. But with the aggressive campaign of the Counter-Reformation and the sending of seminary priests into the country some ground was recovered, particularly round Oswestry and Wrexham and in the county of Flint, where the influence of obstinate Lancashire may have counted for something and some of the gentry, like the Mostyns and Conways, returned to the fold.[1] Naturally, as in all backward areas—like Cornwall and the North—old customs, the old folk-lore, lingered longer. In Carmarthen people knelt and knocked their breasts at communion—the poor souls did not recognise the difference from mass : this was shocking.[2] The priest broke the Host—so evidently he did not know any better either. The dead were buried with dirge and candles. William Salisbury, the translator, wrote to Archbishop Parker : " one trick of antiquity that hath overlong continued in the Church and is not like to discontinue unless your Grace help to abolish it, I mean the old custom of offering over dead corpses at burials ".[3] (What could poor Parker do about it ? He had enough nonsense on his hands for a lifetime.) The Welsh, like the Cornish and the Irish, were addicted to pilgrimages to holy wells—St. Winifred's Well continued to be a holy haunt of surreptitious Catholic devotion—and watchings in chapels in lonely places.

But the Welsh Church got its fundamental work done early and in time : it got the Prayer Book and the Bible translated and thereby attached the people to its chariot—in other words, it more or less satisfied their spiritual needs. The earliest religious book printed in Welsh was a Primer of 1546.[4] William Salisbury produced a book of Welsh proverbs and then compiled a Welsh-English dictionary, " necessary to Welshmen who will speedily learn the English tongue ". (" Will " has the sense here of " desire to " ; and there was a great desire to learn English.) In 1551 he translated the Epistles and Gospels for the whole year. So that the Welsh had a vernacular service at about the same time as the English : they did not lag behind, except so far as the Bible was concerned. In 1563 Parliament ordained

[1] E. Gwynne Jones, " Catholic Recusancy in the Counties of Denbigh, Flint and Montgomery, 1581–1625 ", *T.S.C.*, 1945, 114 foll.
[2] q. A. G. Edwards, *Landmarks in the History of the Welsh Church*, 97.
[3] Robin Flower, " William Salisbury, Richard Davies and Archbishop Parker ", *Nat. Library of Wales Journal*, Vol. II, No. 1, 10.
[4] Edwards, *op. cit.* 146.

that Prayer Book and Bible should be translated and in every Welsh church before 1 March 1567 ; the four Welsh bishops with the bishop of Hereford were to undertake it and to be fined £40 if not.[1] But who was to do the formidable job ? Only Bishop Davies of St. David's was capable of it ; a bard himself, pupil of the famed Griffith Hiraethog, and a patron of bards, he was an admirable vernacular scholar. But he was a hard-pressed administrator with an enormous diocese to get into order ; he was exemplary in his attendance in the Lords, in performing his duties as J.P., constantly called upon by the government to serve on all sorts of commissions—his service on that on piracy earned him the hostility of Perrot. Davies was an energetic, hard-working, capable, warm-hearted man—a big man ; in his palace at Abergwili he kept open house, and he was very hospitable. Of course he was given to nepotism and appointed his sons to prebends when hardly more than boys. But how else could he live ?—the Welsh sees had been stripped of their revenues. The average was now about £150 and it was recognised that their occupants could only subsist with the aid of commendams. Bishop Davies helped himself : they all had to.

Davies recruited William Salisbury to the work, and for part of the time had him to live with him. Together they translated the Prayer Book with the Psalms ; meanwhile Salisbury achieved most of the New Testament himself, Davies having time only for two or three of the shorter Epistles, and his crony, precentor Huett, the Book of Revelation. Sir John Wynne's story of their quarrelling and parting over the meaning of one word has a certain symbolic truth ; for it seems that Salisbury, who was a rare scholar, had very odd ideas about etymology and a pedant's desire to wrest the language out of its proper bed and impose classical forms on it ; while the bishop, who was more responsive to life, was also more responsive to language, and was in sympathy with its idiom and its genius. " Oh ! how my heart doth warm by recording the memory of so worthy a man! " Wynne writes. " He died poor, having never had regard to riches "—very unlike Sir John, we may say.[2]

The result was that the work had to be done over again twenty years later by William Morgan. His father had been no more than a copyhold tenant of Gwydir ; his grandparents,

---

[1] F. O. White, *Lives of the Elizabethan Bishops*, 123.
[2] Wynne, *op. cit.* 94.

before Henry VII's emancipation, bondmen. Richard Davies was a poor priest's son of Roman days and therefore illegitimate.[1] (Why not a married clergy?) So much for increasing social opportunity : the Church was performing its age-long task of providing chances for the clever boys of poor parents. Morgan's mother used to say that something good would come of her boy, he was so careful to say his paternosters at the creed-stones—the crosses by the wayside as in Cornwall.[2] He was sent to Cambridge, by the help of the Gwydir family, who were his patrons. While vicar of Llanrhaiadr he undertook the translation of the whole Bible, revising Salisbury's New Testament, pruning it of its oddities and restoring the idiom, and translating the Old Testament anew. It was a tremendous task for one man—after all, the Authorised Version took a whole committee. Whitgift encouraged the work and made him his chaplain to help him. In 1587 he was in London seeing it through the press ; Dean Goodman of Westminster, who was a Ruthin man, saw the proofs through with him. In that year of wonders, 1588, twenty years before the Authorised Version, the Welsh Bible appeared— with a preface in which it referred to the Armada and stated the case against those who did not want official countenance given to a vestigial tongue. The contemporary prejudice was all against the language as a barbarous survival ; and the difficulty of expressing abstract thought in it had challenged all the resources of even William Salisbury. The excitable Puritan Penry complained that he could not utter his mind in Welsh— perhaps that was as well—he needed to borrow the words from Latin : he had a strong antipathy to the use of his own language.[3] If it had not been for the translation of Bible and Prayer Book, Welsh would have declined to the status of Breton—a peasant *patois* ; though it would never, like Cornish, have entirely disappeared. Morgan's version of the Bible had even more influence in fixing the diction of the language than Shakespeare's contemporaneously for English. The work of Bishop Davies, William Salisbury and Bishop Morgan together conquered new territory for it and ensured its survival as a fully articulated language, a complete medium for a fully articulated society.

Elizabeth and Whitgift rewarded Morgan by making him a

---

[1] Glanmor Williams, " Richard Davies, Bishop of St. David's, 1561–81 ", *T.S.C.*, 1948, 147 foll.
[2] White, *op. cit.* 343. [3] Edwards, *op. cit.* 149.

bishop : they made the appointment for the good of Wales. And, as usual, they were justified in their man. Though a poor man, he refused commendams for himself ; arriving at St. Asaph to find the chancel unroofed, he repaired it at his own expense ; he established a regular course of sermons in the cathedral ; he defended the Church's property as well as he could, like a faithful pastor of his flock. Sir John Wynne thought that the elevation of a protégé of his family should be for the good of the patron. He pressed for the renewal of the lease of the fat rectory of Llanrwst at the old rent, very much below its value. He received a very sour raspberry : " in granting it ", the bishop wrote, " I should prove myself an unhonest, unconscionable and irreligious man ; yea, a sacrilegious robber of my church, a perfidious spoiler of my diocese, and an unnatural hinderer of preachers and good scholars—the consideration whereof would be a continual terror and torment to my conscience ".[1] Sir John was not a bit abashed. He thought himself hardly treated, and proceeded to preach the bishop an eloquent sermon : " *Hominibus ingratis loquimini, lapides.* The sower went out to sow, and some of his seed fell in stony ground where it withered, because it could take no root. The seed was good, but the land naught. I may justly say so by you. I have in all showed myself your friend, in so much as if I had not pointed you the way with my finger you had been still vicar of Llanraiadr." And so on, very much vexed. It is not the first time that an aristocratic patron has experienced a sense of deception at the poor protégé showing a mind of his own. Sir John wrote round to his friends to ease his wronged mind. " No grief to the grief of unkindness : they rewarded me ill for good to the great discomfort of my soul." After all, was not Llanrwst his own parish ? It was humiliating. The good bishop got a rather wry notice in Sir John's *Memoirs*.

The poverty of the Welsh gentry made them voracious for pickings from the Church. The dissolution of the monasteries— no-one in Wales regretted them—threw many manors and impropriated rectories on the market. The bishops, too, were squeezed of many of their best manors—the manor and palace of Lamphey, which had belonged to St. David's, had been granted to the Devereux, for example : hence Essex's residence

[1] For the rude correspondence, *v.* P. Yorke, *The Royal Tribes of Wales* (1799), 137 foll.

there as a young man, where he made the disastrous acquaintance of Gelly Meyrick, son of a Welsh bishop. Up to a point, it was reasonable to reduce bishops from the status of nobles to that of the gentry ; but in Wales, except for St. David's, it went beyond that point, and Welsh bishops were hard put to it—they could barely live on the depleted revenues of their sees alone. Hence, as at Exeter, they were allowed to hold livings *in commendam.* Acquisitive yeomen, small and bigger gentry, floated up on this tide ; tithes from impropriated rectories became an indispensable part of the finances of the Elizabethan gentry. Nowhere so much as in Wales, precisely because Wales was poor. That again impoverished the Church and drove the bishops to desperation : their correspondence, their reports on the condition of their dioceses, always come back to this ground-bass. The gentry took the produce of the rectorial tithes, paying a starveling curate a bare pittance to perform the vicarial services. Bishop Davies wrote, " the fermors [*i.e.* of benefices] will not give competent wages, but shift with a priest that shall come thither galloping from another parish, which for such pains shall have 40s. a year, £3 or £4 the best ".[1]

Naturally in each county the gentry invested in the Church lands and tithes most convenient to them. The Catholic earls of Worcester got the lands of Tintern : they remained an important part of their wealth.[2] Sir Edward Carne, Mary's ambassador at Rome, obtained Ewenny Priory. On Elizabeth's accession he performed a neat operation : he arranged to be " detained " in Rome against his will till his demise, so as to keep his sacrilegious possessions : Ewenny remained in the family for centuries. Property, after all, is more important than opinions. The ancestor of Oliver Cromwell, we have seen, got Neath Abbey : Catholics or Protestants, it was all one where land was concerned. In Pembrokeshire the brother of Bishop Barlow bought the preceptory and manor of Slebech, a delightful site, where he proceeded to raise a county family. In the third generation the Barlows were Church papists and harbourers of recusants, like some other families living off Church lands : living is more important than logic.[3] Sir John Perrot tried to

---

[1] White, *op. cit.* 125.

[2] David Williams, *A History of Modern Wales*, 57.

[3] But, unlike most, George Barlow had a conscience in the matter and devoted a house in the parish, with land and tithes, to the relief of the poor by way of retribution. F. Green, " The Barlows of Slebech ", *West Wales Historical Records*, III. 138.

jockey them out of some fields they had purchased near his house ; but not for all his packing of the jury—an art well understood in Wales—could he obtain a verdict in his favour.[1] The Barlows joined the opposition. In bare Radnorshire only the Fowlers did well : hence the Commonwealth rhyme :

> Radnorshire, poor Radnorshire,
> Never a park and never a deer.
> Never a squire of five hundred a year
> But Richard Fowler of Abbey Cwmhir.[2]

The tithes of Presteign were bought by the Bradshaws, and theirs was the pretty timbered house of black and white at the town-end : in the next generation the residence of the regicide.

It was the same with impropriations as with Church lands.[3] The eminent traitor, Hugh Owen, the mainspring of so many plots and an ultramontane fanatic, purchased the tithes of Aberdaron as an investment just before going into exile : his brothers were charged with supporting him out of them.[4] Property was property, and they certainly kept him going with money until he became a regular Spanish pensioner. In Monmouth the Worcester family and the Herberts were chief investors ; it was always a good investment, for the yield kept increasing in long-term value. In Anglesey, the Bulkeleys ; in Glamorgan, Herberts ; in Pembroke, Perrot ; in Denbigh, Salusburys and Wynnes : they all figure. But not Welsh alone. We find a number of English investors : Sir Christopher Hatton was a considerable impropriator in Cardigan and Carmarthen ; we find the names of other courtiers owning small parcels, Leicester, Sir Edward Wotton, Sir Thomas Heneage, besides the squalid dealers, Tipper and Dawe, Morrice and Phillips, who specialised in this business all over England too. Occasionally a bargain was to be made by sharp practice. A Carey got a lease of Llandewi for £40 a year ; declaring it a college with the advowsons of twelve churches depending on it, he sublet it to the Vaughans of Trawscoed for £140 a year (multiply by twenty-five for comparable valuation).[5] This led to a long series of lawsuits, but

[1] J. Phillips, " Glimpses of Elizabethan Pembrokeshire ", *Arch. Cambr.*, Series V, XIV, 308 foll.

[2] q. W. H. Howse, *Radnorshire*, 49.

[3] Cf. H. Grove, *Alienated Tithes*, cxlvii foll.

[4] A. H. Dodd, " Two Welsh Catholic Émigrés discuss the Accession of James I ", *Bulletin Board of Celtic Studies*, VIII. 345 foll.

[5] A. G. Edwards, *op. cit.* 103.

he seems to have maintained his claim. He was a gentleman of the Privy Chamber : another of Hunsdon's relations doing well. But Wales itself could do better, in the person of Dr. Ellis Price, *Y Doctor Coch* (the Red Doctor), who made a small fortune out of these things.[1] His master-stroke was when, having held the lease of a rectory for sixty years and not being able to bear the idea of parting with it, he got it put into Tipper and Dawe's patent as an impropriation and had it assigned to his son and his heirs outright. It was worth £100 a year ; the vicar's stipend for serving the cure was £6 a year. It is said that by the eighteenth century, 250 of the 300 benefices in the diocese of St. David's were impropriated to lay-owners.[2] This may be an exaggeration ; but it is clear that impropriation was the haemorrhage of the Welsh Church.

We must conclude that the Reformation helped to liberate Welsh national spirit and give it ways and means of expression in the Church. Whereas in the Middle Ages the great majority of the bishoprics and much of the higher preferment went to Englishmen—who were almost always absentees—it is a striking fact that of the sixteen Elizabethan bishops thirteen were Welsh. It is an unlucky number, and hardly any of them were up to Bishop Davies or Bishop Morgan, who would have done honour to any church. Bishops were human, some of them all too human ; but neither were they as bad as has been made out. If they were pluralists and trafficked in livings which should have gone to their clergy, it was, as we have seen, because they could hardly make ends meet otherwise. Bishop Jones of Llandaff, a very middling sort of man, " carefully and diligently travelled throughout his diocese ", where he found the people very conformable in coming to church and receiving Communion ; he preached himself and put his hand in his purse to provide other preachers.[3] Bishop Bellot of Bangor helped Morgan with his work ; and if the tradition is that he was such a misogynist that he would never even have a female in his household, who can blame him for that ?

Bishop Hughes of St. Asaph had had an awkward passage at Leicester, where he gave exceeding offence by preaching that the Hell into which Christ descended was not the abode of the damned.[4] The congregation knew better and complained to his

---

[1] A. G. Edwards, *op. cit.* 104-5.   [2] David Williams, *op. cit.* 58.
[3] White, *op cit.* 178.   [4] *Ibid.* 196.

university—which was, of course, Cambridge—to Archbishop Parker and that very theological person, the Earl of Leicester. The sage Chancellor of the University, Cecil, handed down a ruling " that no manner of person there should in any sermon, open disputation or reading, move any question or doubt upon the article *De Descensu Christi ad Inferos* ". Wise man that he was —have humans always to be treated like the idiot children they are in such matters ? This was the kind of thing they were killing each other over abroad: the sort of nonsense people are so certain about when they are less certain about the multiplication table.[1] Bishop Hughes has been condemned for his pluralism, for holding sixteen benefices: a more serious matter than any opinions he held. He did not hold all these livings together, but at different times for varying periods. No doubt he held too many, and he leased the manors of his see to his family for too long terms, and he did leave the chancel of his cathedral roofless for dear Bishop Morgan to repair. By these means he accumulated a tidy fortune and his only daughter, being something of an heiress, was able to marry a Mostyn.

The only bishop who completely fell down on his assignment was a gentleman of good family, Marmaduke Middleton, who succeeded Bishop Davies.[2] By birth a Cardiganshire man—with its special connotation for the Welsh—he lived up to expectations. From Cambridge he had been sacked for adultery ; so he went to Ireland to pursue his ecclesiastical career and was consecrated bishop of Waterford. There he found the people " stiff-necked, stubborn, papistical and incorrigible ", and in a year had made the place too hot to hold him. With a fiery Celtic temperament, impatient and intemperate, he could not get on with the Irish. And, indeed, it seems that the Welsh and the Irish were mutually antipathetic : they much preferred even the English to each other. Coming back to Wales, he proceeded to find his diocese— where Bishop Davies had been at ease in Zion—nearly as bad as his Irish one. There was small popery, but a great deal of " atheism " (whatever that means in Elizabethan times), and the people " were wonderfully given over to vicious life ".[3] He

[1] I do not underrate the uncertainties of arithmetic, when a modern Cambridge man informs us at the end of a long work on the subject that there has been established not a certainty, but a strong probability, that $1+1=2$.

[2] White, *op. cit.* 253 foll. ; and *v. D.N.B.*, and *Cal. S.P. Dom. 1581-90*, 143. Middleton visited John Dee at Mortlake, 23 Jan. 1583, *Diary of Dr. John Dee*, ed. J. O. Halliwell, Camden Soc., 18.   [3] *Cal. S.P. Dom. 1581-90*, 119.

soon made himself hated, and an attempt to kill him, he said, was made " at evening prayer with candle-light ", instigated by one of his own archdeacons. After this he spent more time at his house in Kent, whence he managed to dilapidate and embezzle the property of his see. A series of charges was laid against him, from murder, the most serious, to bigamy. He does seem to have been unlucky in his matrimonial relations. The Court of High Commission found him guilty of embezzlement, the Court of Star Chamber of forging a will. He was deprived and degraded at Lambeth, and shortly after died of the disgrace.

As for the condition of the flock, no such bright light is thrown upon them as upon the unfortunate English in the strait-jacket of their ecclesiastical courts, their public penances in church and what not. The Welsh were less submissive, or more evasive ; their secret life was locked in the secrecy of their language ; there was a mutual conspiracy to keep it to themselves. Bishop Davies reported that a great many were " slow and cold in the true service of God. Some careless for any religion, and some that wish the Romish religion again "— warmer anyway.[1] The Bishop himself was charged with being too lax a disciplinarian. Bigamy and whoredom flourished, but was the Bishop responsible ? He replied that some two hundred persons had been excommunicated for their unsuitable lives ; but the sheriffs were bribed, so that his fulminations were powerless. Fabian Phillips, a member of the Council of Wales— who must have had it in for the Bishop—made a great thing of the immorality of his diocese and pointed to the notorious case of Rees Morgan and his sister, charged with incest and murder. The Bishop retorted that Phillips should have them examined himself before the Council, as the mere rumour of such crimes was not sufficient to bring them into the Consistory Court of St. David's. For himself he pointed to the number of persons doing penance " with white sheet or blanket " in his churches to show that he was not remiss.

An indication of more civilised standards, and of the recognition of their social responsibilities, was the founding of schools, benefactions to charities—though in this Wales lagged far behind England, partly because of much poorer resources, partly because of less public spirit. In medieval Wales children's education was bound up with singing, in cathedrals, monasteries, collegiate

[1] White, *op. cit.* 125 ; Glanmor Williams, *loc. cit.*

churches ; for the rest, there were the bards and those distant, but not impossible, objectives, the English universities. (Glendower had wanted to found a Welsh university.) But there were no grammar schools ; and it was precisely here that the Elizabethan age saw a great expansion. Shrewsbury School was the largest in the country, and it chiefly served the families of North Wales, along with Shropshire, Cheshire and Lancashire. It was so remarkably successful that the Dean and Chapter of Hereford petitioned Burghley for a school there " to serve as commodiously for the training of the youth of South Wales as Shrewsbury doth for the youth of North Wales ".[1] Henry VIII had hoped to achieve something with his generous re-establishment of Brecon priory as a college, with provision for a grammar master, a reader in Holy Scripture, an usher and twenty scholars ; but it was not a good centre and the results were disappointing.[2] Ludlow had an old grammar school along with other appurtenances of civilisation.

In Carmarthen the precentor of St. David's maintained a grammar school from 1543 till his death, when it lapsed.[3] In 1576 the first Earl of Essex and Bishop Davies took the lead in founding Queen Elizabeth's Grammar School. Efforts were made to found a free (*i.e.* an elementary) school, but they came to nothing much. And that was characteristic of the age : grammar schools for the upper and middle classes were founded in scores ; elementary education for the poor made no such advance : the Elizabethans were less interested in the education of the less educable. A grammar school was founded at Abergavenny in 1543, and one at Bangor in 1557.[4] Sir Edward Stradling had meant to found a grammar school at Cowbridge ; his successor accomplished it. Thomas Churchyard tells us that Mr. Morgan at Llantarnam had lately erected a free school there.[5] At Wrexham Alderman Broughton of Chester left money for the support of the grammar school which Edward Jones—executed with Thomas Salusbury for the *beaux yeux* of Anthony Babington —had hoped to found.[6] At Ruthin a grammar school was

---

[1] G. W. Fisher, *Annals of Shrewsbury School*, 7.
[2] A. F. Leach, *English Schools at the Reformation*, 316-18.
[3] Sir John E. Lloyd, ed., *A History of Carmarthenshire*, II. 126.
[4] E. G. Hardy, *Jesus College* (College Histories), 6.
[5] Churchyard, *op. cit.* 22.
[6] A. H. Dodd, " Welsh and English in East Denbighshire ", *T.S.C.*, 1940, 34 foll.

founded ; and at Holywell the lay rector (*i.e.* the impropriator of tithe) gave £600 to found a free school : a unique example. [1] Bishop Thomas Davies of St. Asaph founded a scholarship to Cambridge. [2]

There were other benefactions, many small bequests to charities and regularly to the poor as in contemporary England : it was the thing in that believing age—promptings of conscience. Dean Goodman made a handsome benefaction to his native town of Ruthin, where he founded Christ's Hospital for a warden, ten brethren and two sisters ; he purchased an empty cloister and built twelve almshouses. Sir John Wynne did the like at Llanrwst and he endowed his almshouses with rectorial tithe he purchased—perhaps a tribute to the shade of Bishop Morgan. [3] Even Perrot made a munificent benefaction to Haverfordwest, which keeps his memory sweet in the town he tyrannised over in life.

In the grammar schools Welsh was supposed not to be spoken ; as in England, the pupils were to converse in Latin. (As if they did !) The smaller boys might, however, speak English. There was a great desire on the part of Welsh parents that their children —those who were promising—should speak good English, as we can see from Father Baker's memoirs of his childhood in Abergavenny : " as for better learning of language, viz. of the English, the which he could learn but very imperfectly, especially as to right pronunciation of it in the said town . . . since Wales, especially the nearest part of it . . . have great relation to England, it concerneth much everyone that is intended to be brought to any capacity for preferment . . . to have the natural, readiest and best pronunciation of the English tongue . . . the which they will never . . . attain to if they be not brought in their younger age in those places of England where good English is spoken ". [4] We observe that Father Baker did not attain to writing good English. He was sent to Christ's Hospital, which had a regular Welsh connection at this time, through the schoolmaster's wife being a Monmouthshire woman. The Herberts were equally anxious that their offspring should learn Welsh, and Lord Herbert of Cherbury at the age of nine was to be sent to Denbigh-

---

[1] D. R. Thomas, *History of the Diocese of St. Asaph*, 447, 480.
[2] White, *op. cit.* 171.
[3] Wynne, *op. cit.* 7.
[4] *Memorials of Father Augustine Baker*, ed. J. McCann and H. Connolly (Cath. Record Soc.), 30.

shire to learn it with Edward Thelwall—Katherine of Berain's
last husband (who had survived) : " my parents . . . believing
it necessary to enable me to treat with those of my friends and
tenants who understood no other language ".[1]

Young Herbert fell ill, so that he learnt no Welsh, nor could
he ever imitate Thelwall's " rare temper in governing his choler ".
(No doubt he had had plenty of practice, or was it his remote
English blood ?) " When occasion of offence was given him, I
have seen him redden in the face, and after remain for a while
silent ; but when he spake, his words were so calm and gentle
that I found he had digested his choler." He himself could never
attain to that perfection, and even his saintly brother, George
Herbert, was " not exempt from passion and choler, being
infirmities to which all our race is subject ".[2] So, too, Sir John
Wynne, though we find him trying to bridle his choler, " where-
unto I was much subject " : a step in the direction of self-
government.   Perrot never even tried : " by nature very
choleric ", he was " unable to brook any crosses nor dissemble
the least injuries, although offered by the greatest personages ".[3]
When Shakespeare portrays his comic Welsh curate, Sir Hugh
Evans, it is his choler that comes out : " Pless my soul, how full
of chollors I am, and trempling of mind ! " To the Elizabethans,
choler was as much a Welsh characteristic as roasted cheese or
leeks on St. David's day.

There had always been Welsh students at Oxford in the
Middle Ages, playing an excitable part in the life of the university.
But the foundation of Jesus College in 1571 marked a stage : it
came in time to mean a great deal for Wales, the education of
Welshmen and the recruitment of the Church. At first it had
hardly any endowment and led rather a notional existence ;
within fifty years James Howell could justly refer to it as the
' national college '.[4]   Hugh Price of Brecon started it with a
bequest of £600. From the first it had the closest association
with All Souls and the group of Welsh civil lawyers there, four
of whom became the first Principals of Jesus in succession :
David Lewis and John Lloyd, both Admiralty Judges, Francis
Bevans and John Williams. Other All Souls men were among
its Fellows : William Aubrey, Robert Lougher and David

[1] *Autobiography of Lord Herbert of Cherbury*, 37-8.   [2] *Ibid.* 22.
[3] Glanmor Williams, *loc. cit.* 152.
[4] E. G. Hardy, *op. cit.* 1.

Powell, the antiquary. Hugh Price's foundation bequest was even deposited with All Souls for safety, at 7 per cent. Welshmen entirely predominated in the college, especially from South Wales ; but the funds did not come in. In 1616 a national appeal was made to the Welsh gentry, and £764 : 5 : 6 was raised. That set the college firmly on its legs and enabled buildings to be erected. For thirty years a protégé of the Perrots, Griffith Powell, was the backbone of the college and saw it through to success. Perrot's illegitimate son, Sir James—who inherited, along with Haroldstone, more of his father's personality than the legitimate son—was a member : he travelled on the Continent and wrote one or two interesting books, including an unpublished Life of Philip Sidney. Another member was Sir William Vaughan, planter of a Welsh colony in Newfoundland : Cambriol.[1] Horizons were indeed opening.

Welshmen were introducing their country, and themselves, to the notice of Europe. Their scholars not only studied in, and caught the inspiration of, Renaissance Italy, but were capable of cutting a figure there. Griffith Roberts published his Welsh grammar, in Latin, at Milan, where he was a canon of the cathedral and confessor to the great Archbishop, Saint Charles Borromeo. The saint died in the arms of another Welshman, Owen Lewis, his right-hand man and vicar-general of his diocese. Owen Lewis was a man of remarkable ability and had an important ecclesiastical career abroad ; he was highly thought of in Rome, where he was employed by both Gregory XIII and Sixtus V and ended up as Bishop of Cassano, with the approbation of both the Pope and Philip II. John David Rhys became public moderator of the school at Pistoia, and published a book in Italian on the Latin language and a Latin treatise on Italian. (After many years he came home to settle at the foot of the Brecon mountains.) Such linguistic works are hardly conceivable for an Englishman of the time. It was the Welsh gift for languages, and their linguistic consciousness, that made them so eminently employable abroad. We have noticed their contributions to Welsh antiquities, their interest in Celtic origins ; but it was left for a Highland Scot, Buchanan—the best classical scholar in Britain—to discern the true relationship of the Celtic languages.

Welshmen fought in the wars of the Counter-Reformation,

[1] *v.* E. Roland Williams, *Some Studies of Elizabethan Wales*, ch. xiv.

almost all of them against it, whether in the Low Countries, Ireland or on the coast of Spain. When it came to fighting, they were with the English. The merchant and financier, Sir Richard Clough, lived much of his life abroad, immersed in the multifarious transactions of the exchanges, at Antwerp and then at Hamburg, where he died, still quite young, and was mourned at home by the bards of his family. Of the Owen brothers of Plâs Du, Robert became a canon of Mantes.[1] It was partly his brother Hugh's fluency in Spanish that gave him so much influence with the Spaniards in the Netherlands over decades— that and his talent for intrigue and intelligence work. Philip II, Parma and the Archduke Albert all listened to him : he was their expert on English affairs—so much the worse for them. For, of course, his judgment of them was utterly warped by his undying grievance, the bitterness of an irreconcilable, the perspective of a fanatic with all the characteristics of the *émigré* mentality. For ever scheming, for long sanguine, thick in the cobweb of intrigue and plotting and espionage that centred upon his lodgings below the image of Saint Michel in the Cheese-market at Brussels, even he became disillusioned at last, as the decades wore away and nothing happened to upset the Tudor Queen or disturb the quiet succession of Mary Stuart's son. He had a hand in most of the plots from Ridolfi in 1571, for his part in which he had fled discreetly into exile, to Gunpowder in 1605 : a wonderful run, and a somewhat fabulous career. He and the great Father Robert and the distinguished Cornish Jesuit, Father Baldwin, were the triumvirate that had the ear of the Spaniards on English affairs and stood for an ultramontane pro-Spanish policy among the exiles. No love was lost between them and the moderates.

Amid all his feverish hopes and as constant deceptions, Hugh Owen did not forget Wales. We find him writing politely, if disingenuously—he was a politician—to Sir Robert Sidney, commanding English forces in the Netherlands, to claim kinship with Sidney by the latter's marriage and offering every service in his power, reserving his duty to his master, the King of Spain. He " leaves the unkindness between their superiors to be decided by the Almighty " ! He did all he could to interest Ortelius

[1] A. H. Dodd, " Correspondence of the Owens of Plâs Du, 1573–1604 ", *Trans. Caernarvonshire Hist. Soc.*, 1939, 47 foll. ; " A Spy's Report, 1604 ", *Bull. Board of Celtic Studies*, IX, pt. 2, 154 foll. ; " The Spanish Treason, Gunpowder Plot and the Catholic Refugees ", *E.H.R.*, 1938, 627 foll.

in the work of Humphrey Lluyd and begged him to take care of his literary remains. Owen's nephew, Roger Gwynne, was the young Jesuit who was captured off the Cornish coast on his way to Wales in 1601 and died in the Tower in the fatal year 1605. In his correspondence with his brother, after thirty years of exile, Owen drops familiarly into Welsh. In the flats of the Low Countries he must often have seen in his mind's eye the green hills of the Lleyn, the triple peaks of the Rivals as they appear across the farmlands of the home he could never come back to, hear the beat of the sea upon those sands, the roar of the wind in the hall-roof that remains there at Plâs Du. After Gunpowder plot, Robert Cecil managed, with much difficulty and after long persistent pressure, to get the old traitor expelled from the Netherlands : the Spaniards would not surrender him. Having sent many less virtuous men to their deaths, he departed for Rome, where he died peacefully in the odour of holiness.

The chief sphere for Welsh external activity, apart from England, was Ireland. A close bond between the two countries was established at the top by the common careers of Sidney and Perrot, Essex and his father, the first earl ; the bond was essentially governmental : after all, were they not both in a sense, from the point of view of the government away in Westminster, colonial territories ? Sir Henry Sidney began his distinguished career as a colonial administrator in Ireland in 1556, in Mary's reign. In 1559 he was made Lord President of Wales, an office which he retained till his death in 1586. From 1565 to 1580 he combined it with that of Lord Deputy of Ireland, and during most of these years he was away in Ireland—tribute to the order established in Wales. Sidney had a way of getting on with Celts—an instinctive sympathy—and was popular in both countries. So was Perrot, all the more because of his bluff, rough, bullying, warm-hearted ways and his rude language : he was a personality. What neither the Welsh nor the Irish could stand, or understand, was the cold, collected, competent English official, with his inhuman demand for justice, order, objectivity. Perrot himself, who was president of Munster 1570–73 and Lord Deputy 1584–8, was maddened by his officials : they ultimately broke him. But when he left Ireland, he was seen off at the quayside by Turlough O'Neill with the tears streaming down his face.[1]

Ireland was fatal to both Earls of Essex. The first earl under-

---

[1] *v.* Cyril Falls, *Elizabeth's Irish Wars*, 161.

took to colonise Clandeboye, ruined his health and strength in the attempt—and very nearly his fortunes—and was brought home to be buried at Carmarthen. His son, Robert, lost everything by his Irish fiasco. He took over with him his faithful Welsh following : Gelly Meyrick as master of his horse ; the Catholic swordsmen, Peter Wynne, Owen and John Salisbury who had followed Sir William Stanley in the surrender of Deventer to the Spaniards and attempted a similar treason at Ostend, with the password in Welsh. Lloyd of Bodidris and Sackville Trevor had been with Essex at Cadiz. More respectable Welsh soldiers served in Ireland before and after : the Morgans, for example ; and serving under Mountjoy were Sir Matthew Morgan as Colonel, with Captains Vaughan, Floyd, Thomas Williams and Mostyn. In 1597 Burghley sent over Maurice Kyffin—" a downright, capable and courageous official "—to bring order out of the financial chaos the army was in. [1] He was an Exchequer official, who had served as vice-treasurer to the army in Normandy in 1592. One of Dr. Dee's circle, perhaps starting in his service, he combined literary interests with officialdom. In 1587 he published an excellent laudatory poem, *The Blessedness of Britain,* reflecting on the late conspiracy in which two Welshmen were involved. He translated Bishop Jewel's *Apology* into Welsh, and would have done more, but Ireland was too much for him : he died after two years of it.

Two generations before, we saw, the neighbourhood of Oswestry had been kept in constant turmoil by the feuds between Kyffins and Trevors. Sir William Herbert was a most successful undertaker : taking over 13,000 acres of Desmond lands after the rebellion, he threw himself into the work of planting, treating the Irish with consideration and understanding, though he—like everybody else—wanted them to become civilised, to end tanistry, drop their mantles and concealed weapons, and settle down. He had the Creed and Commandments translated and directed the services in his district to be read in Irish. His residence in Castle Island he hoped to make " a little England, after the example of Pembrokeshire in times past ". Archbishop Magrath said that six people like him would win people's hearts better than 6000 soldiers. Lawyers, too, were among the Welsh who went over, like the poet Sir John Davies who spent his best years as Attorney-General there. The connection is brought home to one as one

[1] *Ibid.* 201.

walks round, say, Chester Cathedral and notices a Renaissance tablet to Sir William Gerrard, Lord Chancellor of Ireland, one of the Council of Wales, Justice of Assize for Glamorgan, Brecon and Radnor, Recorder of Chester : he spent a lifetime bringing the benefits of English law into the Celtic borderlands.

Wales certainly made her impact upon the English imagination, at the very end of our period producing a couple of undying, because recognisably authentic, portraits out of the mind of their greatest dramatist. Shakespeare makes Fluellen not only gallant and brave—nobody ever doubted the fighting qualities of the Welsh—but also chivalrous:

> "Kill the poys and the luggage! 'tis expressly against the laws of arms : 'tis as arrant a piece of knavery, mark you now, as can be offer't ; in your conscience, now, is it not?"

He, too, is choleric and makes the cowardly Pistol eat his leek all right ; and we love him for his local patriotism about Monmouth. And Glendower is as we know him to have been, with his bards, his vaticinations and his prophecies :

> At my nativity
> The front of heaven was full of fiery shapes,
> Of burning cressets ; and at my birth
> The frame and huge foundation of the earth
> Shaked like a coward.

This kind of thing—the egoism, the boasting, the vision—is as eternally boring to the Englishman as it was to Hotspur. And yet Shakespeare, with the justice of his universal imagination, shows us that Hotspur was not right to despise the Welshman, that Glendower was no more of a fool than Hotspur. Or, we might say, no less.

At the end of our period it is profitable to notice the contrast with Brittany. " The medieval Welshman had been emphatically a social, but hardly a political, animal ; Welsh law itself, a highly developed system in rapid decay when the Tudors came, was a code of social rather than of political behaviour. It is the settlement embodied in the Acts of Union, and the corporate tasks thrust on the Welsh gentry by their membership of a wider community, that made the sense of common political obligation something like a normal habit of mind instead of a fitful response to strong emotional appeals. In essence the process was one of transition from personal to territorial loyalty—in brief, the replacement of a sentiment of tribal by one of national solidarity."[1] Contrast Brittany, which was left far greater autonomy in 1528, but was also left to her own devices. The French monarchy attracted the Breton nobility to Paris, which became the centre of their lives, while shutting them out from local administration or national policy. Hence Breton culture became a purely peasant affair ; neither the language nor the literature developed. The Welsh national spirit reached a " much higher degree of cohesion and resilience than this before the *pays légal* . . . fell apart from the *vrai pays* of yeomen, farmers and peasants ".[2] *There* is the explanation of the later resurgence of Welsh popular life.

In truth, the Tudor experience saw not only an expansion of the English state into Wales but a real integration of Welsh society in itself. Wales offers the first example of the English genius for coaxing self-government out of other peoples—the cardinal contribution of the English in the realm of politics. The Welsh in accepting the assumptions of society throughout the country, leaping to their opportunities, went forward to manage their own affairs : a contrast with Ireland.

[1] A. H. Dodd, " The Pattern of Politics in Stuart Wales ", *T.S.C.*, 1948, 9.
[2] *Ibid.* 88-9.

CHAPTER III

IRELAND: A CELTIC SOCIETY IN DECLINE

CELTIC society in Ireland was, if not (as some think) in plain dissolution, at any rate in decadence and decay, in flux and change to no-one can say what : in the process breaking down into chaos, without any foundation of political unity, without the capacity to form a state. What it might have evolved of itself, left on its own, we do not know : the might-have-beens of history are not a very profitable subject of study. For, of course, it did not exist in a world of its own—though all Celts, in revolt against the facts of life, cherish the dream that it might be so. Here in the full flood of Renaissance, Reformation and Counter-Reformation and, ultimately more important, of the discovery and planting of America—in the fairway to America, or not far off it, the island lay—was this anachronistic society : in some respects medieval, in others pre-medieval, in any event thoroughly out of date, enjoying the amenities and outlook of an Anglo-Saxon heptarchy, the ultimate outpost of a vanishing Celtic world. As Bacon wrote at the end of our period, " the last of the daughters of Europe " to be " reclaimed from desolation and a desert (in many parts) to population and plantation ; and from savage and barbarous customs to humanity and civility ".[1]

It is not conceivable that such a society, occupying such a position, could remain unaffected by the influences, the conflicts, the forces at large in the sixteenth century. We have seen that neither Brittany nor Cornwall, the Scottish Borders nor Wales were : nor could Ireland be anything but drawn into the whirl-pool of the age. The whole process was far more forceful and disturbing, more profound and cataclysmic, than a merely personal one ; and we have to see the personal actions and responsibilities in relation to these ineluctable forces, movements which operate through men but of which men are as much victims as agents : the clash of two civilisations, one hopelessly out of date,

[1] J. Spedding, *Life and Letters of Francis Bacon*, VI. 207.

breaking up and on the way out, the other the most efficient in Europe, abounding in energy, expansive and explosive, on the march and on the make, the future with it. It might be possible to admire the tenacious, the heroic, the hopeless, rearguard action of the Celts in Ireland—the futile bravery of it all—if there were much purpose in admiring the defence of causes lost before they began to be defended. But it is in history as it is in life : men do not know what they let themselves in for. If they were more percipient, or more sceptical, the processes of history would have so much the less matter to grind, might even be arrested—as with the civilisation of China for so long, as against the dynamism of the West ; certainly men would be less ground down by them in action. Neither the English nor the Irish in the Elizabethan age knew what they were in for ; but men can neither reflect, nor stop short : they act—and suffer.

It was in the logic of events, it was to be expected, it was only natural that once England had mastered her own destiny with the Reformation, and tremendously geared up her energies with the Dissolution, she should bring them to bear, seek outlet for their employment in the world around. Particularly in Ireland, where there had been a humiliating recession of English power in the last two centuries, especially with the Wars of the Roses, and where it was dangerous to leave a vacuum. The strategic point was brought home to Henry VIII, in the midst of his difficulties over the Divorce and the Reformation, by Chapuys' report to the Emperor that if he wanted to hurt Henry the way to hit home was through Ireland ;[1] and by the contacts of the Geraldines in rebellion with Henry's enemies abroad. For the last century or more the English government had been forced by its own debility to leave the government of Ireland in the hands of the Kildare Geraldines, who maintained a preponderance of power in their own favour among the Irish septs—a rough alliance of both Geraldines of Kildare and Desmond, with the O'Neills of Ulster, against the Butlers—and for the rest left the septs very much to their own vices. The Kildare ascendancy— they had been Yorkists in English politics against the Lancastrian Butlers—culminated in the long rule of Garret Mór, the great Earl of Kildare, who, from his stronghold at Maynooth, where

---

[1] *v.* R. Dudley Edwards, *Church and State in Tudor Ireland*, 4.

he kept the state of a Renaissance prince, with his library and his treasures, was all but king of Ireland.[1]

This was not a tolerable, or even safe, state of affairs for any English government at a time of danger in its relations with the Continent. And in the reconstruction of government emerging from the brilliant mind of Thomas Cromwell, laying the foundations of the modern English state, careful note was taken. His was statesmanship of a kind like Lenin's, very clear, cutting and uncompromising, ruthless and of an intellectual absolutism that we have come to think of as very un-English—but had he not Welsh affiliations and received his education as an adventurer in Renaissance Italy? The policy of union and cohesion that had been applied to Wales—where it was to issue in such success— was now to be applied to Ireland : the aim to make one polity.

It was a big, and even generous, conception : like everything about Thomas Cromwell and Henry VIII, powerful and ambitious, not small-minded. All through the Middle Ages the relations between the English and Irish had been like those between English and Welsh : division of race, legislation in favour of the ascendant people, keeping the inferior Celts beyond the Pale. By this time, the facts in Ireland, even more flagrantly than in Wales, contradicted the medieval theory. The recession of English civilisation had left Ireland an almost completely Celtic country. The Gaelic language had once more overflown even the English Pale. Only the towns, and of them mainly the old seaport towns, remained as outposts of English civilisation and, as needs must, of sympathy. Though even in such an old centre of English settlement as Wexford they were now talking a gallimaufry, a mingle-mangle, of English and Irish.[2] And one can follow, in the town records of Galway, the difficulty that such an independent town—practically a little city-state on its own, conducting its own maritime and commercial relations—had in protecting and preserving its character, an island amid a sea of Irish, lapping like lake-water up to its walls.[3] The Anglo-Norman nobles, the Geraldines of Desmond, the Burkes of Connaught and many lesser families, had gone almost completely Irish, out of a natural instinct of self-preservation. When Henry's legislation, setting the new course for Ireland, came to

[1] Cf. E. Curtis, *A History of Ireland*, 146 foll.
[2] E. Hogan, ed., *The Description of Ireland in 1598*, 55.
[3] H.M.C. *Report X*, App. 5, 380 foll.

be explained in the Dublin Parliament, James Butler, head of his clan, Earl of Ossory and Ormonde and, what was more advantageous, cousin of the Boleyns, had to translate the matter for the benefit of his fellow-peers : not one of them understood English. (In any case, the transition for them would have been from Norman-French to Gaelic : the English strain in them was varying, but subordinate.) Some of these Norman families went more Irish than the Irish and became more determined enemies of the English : whenever rebellion was going ahead, the Lacies were always out ; Captain Tyrrell, of a family of the Pale, a most intrepid and elusive leader of horsemen, was the most dangerous enemy of any but Tyrone himself in the last Irish war—I do not know what accounts for his irreconcilable and vindictive hatred of the English, unless it were for the sake of religion. [1]

Now all was to be changed, a new course set : the Middle Ages definitely over, the modern era begun. Henry took the title of King of Ireland : no longer the indirect and intermittent overlordship with which the medieval kings had been content. A consistent policy of Surrender and Re-grant was carried through. The Irish princes and chiefs were prevailed upon to surrender their independent tenure of their lands, and receive them back as grantees of the Crown : in other words, the settled English system of land-tenure, evolved from feudal origins, was to take the place of the antiquated Celtic custom with its complex and uncertain mesh of rights and obligations.

There was in this a fundamental misconception, which became one of the deepest sources of trouble for the next century. Henrician Englishmen were not anthropologists and could hardly be expected to realise that they were up against the land-system of a different civilisation, or at any rate of a different stage of civilisation—as different from theirs, and as remote, as that of pre-Conquest England. The fact was that, under the Celtic system, the land was not the private property of the chief to grant away in this manner. The chiefs were willing enough, to begin with, for the royal policy assured the lands to them as their personal possessions, like those of English nobles. But Celtic custom gave them but a life-tenure : the clan or sept itself was the ultimate holder of its lands—the chief's direct holding was confined to his immediate demesne lands. English law simply could not define the situation in its own terms, and there was

[1] But *v.* below, pp. 420-1.

a genuine misconception. As time went on, this produced a fearful harvest of misunderstanding, mutual accusations and betrayals. For the chiefs could not deliver the goods : they depended for their position on the good-will of their septs— there was the real source of their strength. But the septs understood very well what was the effect of granting away their lands. And very early on they were mistrustful, as they were apprehensive, of their chiefs taking English titles in return and becoming the King's earl or baron or knight. At the end of the century Mountjoy observed that English titles were a source of weakness rather than of any strength to the Irish chiefs.[1]

Again and again we observe in the course of Elizabeth's reign the tragic dilemma of an Irish chief between the obligations that have been accepted towards the English Crown and the real strength of his position that depends on the support of his own people. It was his inability to maintain himself between the two, wavering weakly to and fro, unable to control the situation, that drove the greatest prince of the South, the Earl of Desmond, into an ambiguous course, then rebellion and his miserable death at the hand of one of his own kerne in the wilds of Glenageenty in 1583. I do not believe that the great Tyrone ever wished to be a rebel to the English Crown—he knew, intelligent man that he was, what it involved ; but, in the last resort, his position, his power and perhaps the preservation of his life depended on his being the O'Neill, with all the devotion of his clan, the sanctity of his person, that Celtic custom conferred on him.[2] On the other hand, if the English did not know what they were up against in the strength of Celtic custom, of a whole alien civilisation, the Irish certainly did not know what *they* were up against—the unity and cohesion, the persistence, of the modern state.[3]

For the moment, under Henry, things went through with a deceptive ease. No-one, or hardly anyone, could have foreseen the long sequel of misunderstanding, conflict, bloodshed. The

---

[1] Fynes Morison, *Itinerary* (Maclehose edn.), III. 294.

[2] Cf. Mountjoy : " No subjects have a more dreadful awe to lay violent hands on their lawful prince than these people have to touch the person of their O'Neills ". Fynes Morison, *op. cit.* II. 172.

[3] It is interesting to note that, by the end of the century, Fynes Morison uses the word ' state ' regularly : *e.g.* the Irish lords " readily came to the State ", etc., and he has an almost modern personification of ' Queen and State ', *op. cit.* II. 181, 237, 264, 271.

Kildare power had collapsed with surprising suddenness before the forces of the Crown. Artillery reduced the stronghold of Maynooth ; the castle was razed. The young Earl, taken off to the Tower, was hanged with his five uncles at Tyburn. The great family was laid low : that was signal enough of the end of the old order, of the state depending upon its own vassal. At the same time, the new policy was inaugurated : instead of being held at arm's length as enemies and proscribed, the Irish were to be regarded as common subjects of the Crown along with the English.[1] When, at the end of the Elizabethan age, Sir John Davies came to consider in his *Discovery of the True Causes why Ireland was never entirely subdued nor brought under Obedience of the Crown of England*, as a Celt himself he seized upon this point. " This, then, I note as a great defect in the civil policy of this kingdom, in that, for the space of 350 years at least after the conquest first attempted, the English laws were not communicated to the Irish, nor the benefit and protection thereof allowed unto them. . . . As long as they were out of the protection of the law . . . how was it possible they should be other than outlaws and enemies to the Crown of England ? . . . If the English magistrates would not rule them by the law which doth punish treason and murder and theft with death, but leave them to be ruled by their own lords and laws, why should they not embrace their own Brehon law, which punisheth no offence but with a fine or erick ? If the Irish be not permitted to purchase estates of freeholds or inheritance, which might descend to their children, according to the course of our Common Law, must they not continue their custom of tanistry, which makes all their possessions uncertain, and brings confusion, barbarism and incivility ? In a word, if the English would neither in peace govern them by the law, nor could in war root them out by the sword, must they not needs be pricks in their eyes and thorns in their sides till the world's end, and so the conquest never be brought to perfection ? "[2]

There is plenty of sympathy with the Irish point of view in this statement of an Elizabethan, who was Attorney–General of Ireland. It states the recurring dilemma of English government in relation to Ireland over the next three centuries : the dichotomy between conquest and conciliation. It is fair to say that, in spite of the barbaric and beastly happenings of the time—

---

[1] C. Maxwell, ed., *Irish History from Contemporary Sources, 1509–1610*, 23.
[2] Printed in *Ireland under Elizabeth and James I*, ed. H. Morley, 268-9.

perhaps because of it—no Tudor government contemplated the conquest of Ireland. They all hoped for conciliation on the sensible and proved English basis. Elizabeth's government was, in the end, driven by events into conquest—greatly against the Queen's will. Nor had her father's wish been any different, in spite of the brutality of his ways. Oddly enough, Henry VIII, contrary to appearances, was a moderate and a conciliator : only those who cannot see below the surface can fail to perceive that. Here is Henry's view, expressed to his Deputy, the Earl of Surrey : " We and our Council think and verily believe that in case circumspect and politic ways be used, ye shall not only bring them to further obedience, for the observance of our laws and governing themselves according to the same, but also following justice, to forbear to detain rebelliously such lands and dominions as to us in right appertaineth ; which thing must as yet be practised by sober ways, politic drifts and amiable persuasions, founded in law and reason, than by rigorous dealing, comminations or any other enforcement by strength or violence ". [1] The Lord Deputy's reply was, " After my poor opinion, this land shall never be brought to good order and due subjection but only by conquest ". [2] The Deputy had the advantage of knowing Ireland and the Irish ; the King had not.

For the moment, as so often subsequently in Irish history, all went deceptively well. The Irish chiefs submitted and received English titles : Con O'Neill surrendered the title of O'Neill and became Earl of Tyrone, the O'Brien became Earl of Thomond, the MacWilliam (Burke) Earl of Clanricarde ; the O'Donnell, whom Henry was ready to make Earl of Tyrconnell, promised to hold his lands of the King and send his sons to Court to be reared in English ways. (These Irish earldoms were following the model of the Anglo-Irish—or perhaps, we should say, Norman-Irish—models : the head of the Kildare Geraldines was Earl of Kildare, of the Munster Geraldines Earl of Desmond, of the Butlers Earl of Ormonde.) Con O'Neill made his appearance at the English Court, creating as much astonishment there as the contemporary caciques from Brazil, an emissary from a world almost as strange and unknown. Neither the Irish chieftains nor the bishops made any bones about abjuring the Pope and accepting the Royal Supremacy, nor in accepting and

---

[1] q. Maxwell, *op. cit.* 103-4. [2] *Ibid.* 89.

enjoying the fruits of the Dissolution : the Irish chieftains gladly accepted abbey-lands. Nor was there much opposition to the liturgical changes ; only with Archbishop Browne's unwise destruction of images and relics—the things that really mattered, objects of the people's veneration—did the Reformation changes begin to incur unpopularity. For the rest, not a martyr, hardly a victim : a pointed contrast with England. The explanation seems to be, partly the moribund condition of the Irish Church, far more lax and corrupt than the English—actually much more in need of reform—but perhaps still more, that the gulf between English and Irish was so deep that these measures made hardly any serious impact upon the Irish mind, wrapped up in their own language and culture, their own traditions and customs, living in a different world.

No historian has brought home *how* different a world Ireland was. We are apt to see it through the spectacles of subsequent history, through the wrong end of the telescope, and to think of Ireland as a modern society comparable to England—which it only became as the result of the heroic (and drastic) efforts of the Elizabethans. In their early days it was largely *terra incognita*, almost as unknown as the coast of America. The great Lord Deputy Chichester—who now lies sleeping in his tomb in the church hard by his castle at Carrickfergus—wrote of Ulster that " before these last wars it was as inaccessible to strangers as the Kingdom of China " ;[1] and the Maguire forbade anyone wearing hat or cloak in the English fashion from penetrating into his country (*i.e.* Fermanagh).[2] Ulster in especial—the most un-alleviatedly Celtic part of the country—was a world of its own, cut off as it had always been from prehistoric times from the rest of Ireland behind its barrier of lakes, bogs and rivers.[3] Its contacts were with the Scottish Isles and the Highlands. As we look across those narrow, coloured seas to the Scottish coast, to Cantyre, to Rathlin Island lying in the offing, scene of the first Essex's ghastly massacre of Scots, or at the ruined walls of Sorley Boy MacDonell's astonishing stronghold at Dunluce, one with the cliffs, we see how it all was. And, in fact, the obscure and bloody politics of Ulster, that were for the most part a closed book to the respectable and amazed officials in London, were all bound up with the Isles : Scottish marriages

---

[1] q. Maxwell, *op. cit.* 274-5.   [2] Hogan, *op. cit.* 25.
[3] Cf. E. Estyn Evans, *Irish Heritage*, 19.

for the chieftains, MacDonalds or Campbells, with their dowries in fighting gallowglass, Scottish galleys landing at the mouth of the glens of Antrim, reinforcements summoned over by fires lighted upon the cliffs, mutual murders and massacres, the constant infiltration of Scots thrown out by the over-population of the Isles or their own intestine feuds and upheavals.

The English Pale itself had become contracted to a strip of some twenty miles to the west and north of Dublin, for immediately to the south were the mountains, from the inaccessible fastnesses of which issued the O'Byrnes and O'Tooles, whenever the English forces were elsewhere—as they very often had to be—to burn and spoil and prey. They once very nearly caught Archbishop Loftus at his house at Rathfarnham, the dour, respectable, grasping Yorkshireman, who represented all that they most hated in the new incoming class of English official : they would certainly have roasted *him* if they had caught him. Farther west and south were the wild O'Mores and O'Connors of Leix and Offaly, the latter of whom levied a large " black-rent " upon the Pale—intolerable to any self-respecting government. To the north, County Louth was subject to constant raids from " the barbarous country of the Fews, part of the county of Armagh to the north, and the country of Feony ".[1] Clonbrassil, a large area of wood and bog in County Down, was the country of the O'Kellies, " given altogether to spoils and robberies " ; while in near-by Armagh Clancane was inhabited by kerne, " who live for the most part in time of peace upon stealth and robberies "—it may be imagined what they were capable of in time of war.[2]

Such were the neighbours of the Pale, the richest, most settled and civilised part of the country, consisting essentially of the counties of Dublin, Louth and Meath. Farther afield, the Butler province of Kilkenny " hath the most show of civility of any other of the border counties ", though the Butlers had their hereditary enemies in the O'Carrolls who, like all the Irish septs, had a ghastly record of killing among themselves—apart from their relations with the English.[3] Murder never seems to have been rated very high in the Irish catalogue of crimes. Leinster was the most civilised of the provinces, particularly Wexford, the oldest area of English settlement ; but even here, out of the woods came the Kavanaghs, with their special record

[1] Hogan, 3.   [2] *Ibid.* 9, 20.   [3] *Ibid.* 65.

of savagery. In Munster lay the Butlers' immense palatinate of Tipperary, which they governed as they pleased, not admitting the Crown officials or a Queen's sheriff. The wilds of Kerry formed another palatinate in the hands of the Earl of Desmond, who dominated much of Cork also. This vast area of mountain and forest, ruled equivocally by the Anglo-Irish Fitzgeralds— caught between their feudal obligations to the Crown and the exigencies of their position in relation to the septs—was in fact an entire province of Gaeldom with the town of Cork keeping apprehensive watch upon the enemy, like Berwick upon the Scottish Borders, its Protestant bishop somewhat stranded, as Bishop Henson described himself among the Durham miners, " like a whale upon the sea-coast of Patagonia ". Connaught again was wholly Gaelic, except for one or two towns, above all Galway, which looked out from its respectable municipal tradition upon a sea of troubles ; even so, it paid tribute to a settlement of marauding Scots upon the Aran Islands in the bay for protection and defence.[1] The dominant family of the Burkes were as much given to murder and rebellion as the princely O'Neills themselves, though they were without the remarkable strain of ability that distinguished the latter house. The head of the Burkes, the Earl of Clanricarde, was consistently loyal, but his numerous offspring, legitimate and illegitimate—for he had several concubines and Celtic custom did not attach so much importance to legitimacy (hence innumerable conflicts with regard to the succession, with the frequent concomitant of murder)—were often out in rebellion, or fighting against each other.

One observes as a familiar feature the division within these families in relation to the government : Ormonde was always loyal, the chief pillar of his cousin the Queen's government among the Irish : but that did not prevent the younger Butlers from taking the field now and again against her. The Earl of Thomond was loyal, but the junior O'Briens were frequently not. Perhaps it was all part of the game to the Irish, or else family reinsurance ; it was certainly in the regular pattern of Irish life. As for the relations between these semi-independent states, the complicated dynastic approaches and quarrels, the English intelligence service (the best in Europe), which had every Spanish move registered, was in this Celtic world at sea :

---

[1] Cf. H.M.C. *Report X*, App. 5, 424 foll.

information filtered through as from remote Indian states in the eighteenth century or African in the nineteenth. But it improved with time, for the Elizabethans sent their ablest men to Ireland.

What did they see there ? What were the characteristics that chiefly struck them ?—for we want to see Ireland as the Elizabethans saw it.

The Elizabethans were shocked and horrified by the spectacle: by the backwardness, the confusion, the inefficiency and laziness and oppression, the primitiveness, what they all called the barbarism, the incivility, they found in Ireland. They had no notion of evolution and they could not console themselves with the thought that here was an interesting specimen of the stage of society, in many respects, that the English had passed through under the Heptarchy. For what was so extraordinary about Irish society was its state of arrested development : it was pre-feudal—Ireland had indeed been left behind by a world that had gone on without her.[1] It was a primitive world of incessant fighting on a small scale ; they fought with battle-axes that had been the latest thing in the Norse period—their gallowglass were by origin Hebridean mercenaries, who were axe-men ; their native kerne fought with short-bows, round shields and darts, and no armour at all. Celtic literature had stood still for the past three hundred years : what could be said was only what had been sayable three hundred years before, for the arrested forms remained the same.[2] The entries in the Annals, the obituaries of the chiefs, have the tone of the Anglo-Saxon chronicle or Icelandic saga. For it was a similar world : an heroic world, the world of epic, but run down and come to a standstill. That is not to say that there was no development at all : the trend on foot was to the increase of the power (and oppressions) of the leading chieftains—O'Neills, O'Donnells, Ormonde, Desmond and such—against the smaller septs and their chiefs. Whether this would have led in time to the concentration of power in one house and thence unity, who can say ? The probability is all the other way : as power got concentrated in

[1] Cf. G. V. Jourdan, in *History of the Church of Ireland*, ed. W. A. Phillips, II. 172.
[2] " For three centuries after the Norman Conquest Ireland produced nothing in art, literature or scholarship even faintly comparable to what she had achieved before." Douglas Hyde, *Literary History of Ireland*, 453. And cf. T. F. O'Rahilly, *Dánta Grádha*, xxi.

the hands of fewer houses, the more intense the conflict. Tyrone himself—greatest of the O'Neills and the only opponent worthy of Elizabeth herself—realised that the old Celtic world, with its tribal divisions and internecine particularism, was no basis for a modern state : he tried all in all for unity. He was defeated, as much by his own people as by the English. Since the Irish were incapable of forming a state out of their primitive society, the country had to go through the fiery furnace of its Elizabethan experience.

The Elizabethans were shocked ; and yet there was nothing they would not tackle. Here, they reflected, was a fair country with excellent natural resources in pastures, arable, woodland, rivers and harbours : how it could be made to prosper, if only it could be licked into shape ! This is the constant refrain of observer after observer, decade after decade. And then they grow discouraged with the climate, the difficulties of the task, the inadequacy of the resources allotted them by the Crown, the impossibility of the Irish, the heart-breaking impossibility of the situation between the English government and its representatives in Ireland, between the Lord Deputy and the entrenched and immovable class of English officials, between these and the Anglo-Irish lords and the chaotic world of Celtic chieftains. If only these obsolete chieftainries with their " cuttings " and exactions upon their people might be removed, if there might be a settling of their restless tribesmen into the ordered ways of English village life, holding their lands by recognisable tenures yielding proper rents to the lord and dues to the Crown to pay for the expenses of government (that constant theme in Anglo-Irish history), with a stiffening of English society introduced for the purpose, transplanting the proven social scheme of gentry, tenantry, peasants with their well-tried institutions—then what a pleasant prospect for Ireland there would be !

Such was the dream at the back of the incessant attempts at planting that defeated the hopes of so many men—Essex's father, the son's follower Captain Thomas Lee, the Chattertons and Smiths, St. Legers, Grenvilles, Carews, Ralegh himself. The reality was otherwise : abortive settlements from which the colonists were driven out and the Irish returned, in Leix and Offaly, in the Ards, in Munster ; and more often than not, a grave. A current saying in Cheshire—base for military reinforce-ments—was : " Better be hanged at home than die like dogs in

Ireland ".[1] And yet, at the end of it all, the Elizabethans *had*
subdued Ireland, in spite of everything. In the first half of the
seventeenth century the way was open to that integrated society,
that fusion of peoples, which the best minds of the Elizabethan
age had envisaged. Then came the English Civil War—which
ought never to have taken place—and with it the hopes of an
integrated Irish people vanished. Perhaps the religious division
made it hopeless anyway ; or perhaps the religious division only
expressed a difference of race, an antipathy too elemental to be
bridged. Yet, after the subsequent centuries with their hideous
story of mutual failure and broken promises, the oppression, the
offence of endemic absenteeism, in spite of renewed rebellion,
murder campaigns, war and civil war, with the very achievement
of political independence—the only Celtic people to achieve an
independent state—in the end, by the irony of history, it is the
Elizabethan concept of a modernised society that has ultimately
emerged in the descendants of the people upon whom this had
to be imposed.

For the Earl of Surrey proved right, as against the English
government which never contemplated it—least of all the Queen,
who hated the necessity : it had to be by conquest. Attorney-
General Davies tells us what the word meant to the Elizabethans
in Ireland and justifies our title : " For that I call a perfect
conquest which doth reduce all people thereof to the condition
of subjects ; and those I call subjects which are governed by the
ordinary laws and magistrates of the sovereign. For though the
Prince doth bear the title of sovereign lord of an entire country,
as our kings did of all Ireland, yet if there be two-third parts of that
country wherein he cannot punish treasons, murders or thefts
unless he send an army to do it ; if the jurisdiction of his ordinary
courts of justice doth not extend into those parts to protect
the people from wrong and oppression ; if he have no certain
revenue, no escheats or forfeitures out of the same, I cannot
justly say that such a country is wholly conquered."[2] A modern
Irish historian allows that " Elizabeth extended her authority
over a wider area of Ireland than had been effectively controlled
by any previous sovereign ".[3]   In the end she conquered it ;
as she lay dying, Tyrone—the last hope of Irish resistance—was

[1] *Cal. S.P. Ireland, 1592–6*, xxvii.
[2] *Loc. cit.* 219.
[3] J. C. Beckett, *A Short History of Ireland*, 61.

on his way to surrender. Another Irish historian concludes : " the vigour, the ingenuity, the empiricism, the hesitancy and the weaknesses of English rule in Ireland illustrate very well the capacities and the limitations of the newly consolidated national monarchies. Ireland in the later sixteenth century was the severest testing-ground for an England on the way to empire." [1] The reduction of the outer fringes, the integration of the other island peoples into one polity, were the first essential steps along that road.

But we must look at Ireland through the eyes of the Eliza- bethans. Only Spenser, with the imagination of both poet and scholar, and Davies who was a poet as well as a lawyer, took any sympathetic interest in Celtic society as such ; and they were filled with disapprobation at many things they saw. We must regret that Spenser never wrote his intended book on Irish antiquities ; but his famous *View of the Present State of Ireland,* written on his second visit to England in 1596, represents over sixteen years' experience of Irish affairs. [2] The first thing that Spenser notices is that Ireland was " a nation ever acquainted with wars, though but amongst themselves, and in their own kind of military discipline trained up ever from their youths ". [3] Nothing could restrain the fury of Irish broils : " whensoever they make head, no laws, no penalties, can restrain, but that they do in the violence of that fury tread down and trample underfoot all, both divine and human, things ". [4] He praised the gallantry and horsemanship of their fighting men, riding with no stirrups, though he could not approve. All their rebellions were begun by their lords, not by the people, who were constrained to follow. The fact was that the chieftains were essentially fighting leaders and the septs organised for endemic wars among them- selves. Spenser's often-quoted passage about the famine and desolation in Munster after the Desmond rebellion can be paralleled by Sir Henry Sidney's description of similar suffering wrought by Desmond's own oppression of a subordinate sept ; or there is O'Rourke's wiping-out of the MacCoys. Then there were the " cuttings " and exactions of the chiefs, the customary coign and livery and other obligations upon the poor churls

---

[1] D. B. Quinn, "Agenda for Irish History", in *Irish Historical Studies,* IV. 260.
[2] Cf. W. L. Renwick, ed., *A View of the Present State of Ireland,* 223.
[3] Printed in Morley, *ed. cit.* 39.
[4] *Ibid.* 47.

that kept them miserable and poor. "There are two sorts of people in Ireland to be considered of : the one called the Kerne, the other the Churls. The Kerne bred up in idleness and naturally inclined to mischiefs and wickedness, the Churl willing to labour and take pains, if he might peaceably enjoy the fruits thereof." All the Elizabethans conceived their efforts as being to help and advance the interests of the churls, the simple people at the bottom ; and they would have achieved this, if only they could have got across the barriers made by race, language and religion.

The manners and customs were those of a pastoral society much on the move, particularly in summer when the whole community with their cattle moved up into the mountains or into the wilds. (Hence the summer-time neglect of agriculture in Ireland today, these rhythms are so set in a people's way of life.) But these shifting habits were conducive to thieving : it was a life meet for outlaws, as on the Borders or in Wales. In Ireland all was still more primitive and raw. The habit of wearing glibs—a thick mass of hair over their eyes—made disguise easy, detection difficult : hence the constant legislation against the wearing of glibs and long Irish mantles (in which weapons were easily concealed) and the efforts to enforce English dress. In the intensely Celtic North it was the habit to draw the blood of living animals and make meat of it, as the pastoral Scythians did of old. The custom of fostering was so strong that the Irish were often more attached to their foster-children or to their foster-brothers than to their own.[1] "At the execution of a notable traitor at Limerick ", Spenser says, " I saw an old woman, which was his foster-mother, take up his head whilst he was quartered and suck up all the blood that ran thereout, saying that the earth was not worthy to drink it, and therewith also steeped her face and breast and tore her hair, crying out and shrieking most terribly."[2] What a land ! What a people !— the manners of the Dark Ages : a point which Spenser was the only person to grasp—" at what time England was very like to Ireland as now it stands ".

To the Elizabethan English it was a beastly manner of life,

[1] Cf. Fynes Morison: " The Earl of Kildare, with his troop of horse, served valiantly upon the rebels and took the death of his foster-brothers so to heart (after the education of the Irish) as shortly after he died ". q. Hogan, 46.
[2] *Ed. cit.* 101.

and they said so : their dwellings were " rather swine-sties than houses . . . the chiefest cause of his so beastly manner of life and savage condition, lying and living together with his beast in one house, in one room, in one bed ".[1] Barnabe Rich was still more outspoken about Irish husbandry and manners. The Irish would " rather still retain themselves in their sluttishness, in their uncleanliness, in their rudeness . . . than they would take any example from the English, either of civility, humanity or any manner of decency ".[2] All over Ireland people " had no other means to draw the plough but every ox by his own tail " ; when the hair of the tail was rubbed so short it could no longer be tied, the plough stood still. Even about Dublin the hay-harvest was left over till the corn-harvest, with the result that much of it was ruined by rain. If the parts now waste were industriously occupied, and the rest better manured, Ireland would sustain more people by two parts. All the Elizabethans were agreed about this, and no doubt Rich was right : if the Irish were not so lazy and cultivated their land better, it would sustain a much higher population. There was room for plenty of English to come in and improve things, but the natives would rather keep things as they were and occupy themselves in preying upon the audacious improvers.

The Irish held it unlucky to keep their milking vessels clean, so that they were most filthily kept. " I myself have seen that vessel which they hold under the cow . . . to be furred half an inch thick with filth." Dublin was served with the loathsome butter. Irish washing was worse, and smelt worse. " I will not speak of those affairs belonging to child-bearing women, that are no less uncivil than uncleanly in many their demeanours belonging to those businesses." And how unhandsomely they grind their oats Rich had often observed : " myself have seen a woman sitting with a mustard quern between her bare thighs grinding of oatmeal, I think a man would have little list to eat of the bread. But of this meal as ill in complexion to look upon as a little dirt under a man's feet they make their cakes, for other bread they have none and it is but seldom when they have this." (Anyone who knows Irish cooking today will find this convincing enough four hundred years ago : cooking is not a strong point with any of the Celts.) Rich concluded that " the

---

[1] *Ibid.* 122.
[2] Barnabe Rich, *A New Description of Ireland*.

farmers of Ireland are far to seek in many points of husbandry and the women (for the most part) have as little skill of housewifery ".

On the other hand, there was a plethora of charms, spells, enchantments, enchanted girdles so that no sword or weapon might hurt ; a universal addiction to fasting on fast-days, to holy wells, relics, pilgrimages. On St. Patrick's day the water in his well is more holy—or the inhabitants of Dublin more foolish, commented the rational Englishman. One observes the gulf that yawns between them. On saints' eves, especially May even and Midsummer eve, those high points of the Celtic year, " what watching, what rattling, what tinkling upon pans and candlesticks, what strewing of herbs, what clamours . . . and not only in the country but in Dublin itself ". And then, " our holy, holy brood of Jesuits, seminaries, friars and such other do perform strange things, but specially for the increase and propagation of children, not a barren woman in an house where they be lodged ". In this remark two hostile conceptions of life confront each other ; in fact, the imputation was unjust or at least out of date. Celts are apt to be sensual people, and before the victory of the Counter-Reformation over their natural impulses, the Irish were notoriously lascivious and promiscuous ; all observers noted the looseness with which the marriage-tie was regarded, concubinage was rife : a gay time was had by all— though the laxity in the princely houses, for example, the O'Neills and Burkes, was directly responsible for the family feuds and murders. Attorney-General Davies comments in James I's reign : " I omit their common repudiation of their wives ; their promiscuous generation of children ; their neglect of lawful matrimony ; their uncleanness in apparel, diet and lodging [Celts are still apt to be unwashed] ; and their contempt and scorn of all things necessary for the civil life of man ".[1] But already the Counter-Reformation was on its way to victory ; where the English could not but fail, the Roman Church was to succeed in licking them into shape and making them the most tediously puritan of all European peoples.

On the other hand, to provoke the English the more, there were the natural gifts of the Irish, their wit and conversation. All were agreed that they were a good-looking people, especially the women, and commented on their comely stature and agility

[1] Davies, *ed. cit.* 297.

of body. There was the beauty of the landscape : Spenser wrote
of Munster that broke his heart, that it was a most sweet and
beautiful country, and his poems reflect his pleasure in the
environs of Kilcolman, the streams of Buttevant, the bathing
places where the nymphs dwelt, the whispering alders. There
was the bravery of the individual Irishman, his impulsive
generosity : strong attachments could be formed between Irishman and Englishman, there was all the camaraderie of fighting
together, and, if many Englishmen lost their lives in the fighting,
many owed them to the generosity of their opponents or the
devotion of their Irish followers. Sir Henry Sidney was on
terms of special affection with McGillapatrick, Baron of Upper
Ossory, with whom he seems to have been brought up—" my
particular sworn brother, was the faithfullest man for martial
action that ever I found of that country. He followed O'More
with great skill and cunning and with much or more courage
assailed him and made the best fight with him that ever I heard
of between Irishmen."[1] Ormonde had a personality of singular
attractiveness, of great sway always with the Queen, while
Tyrone could be irresistible. It was this that made the murder
of Henry Davells, the respectable old Devonshireman who was
sheriff of Cork, by Desmond's brother, Sir John, such a scandal.
For it was said that Davells looked on him as a son and addressed
him as such when he came into the room at the inn at Tralee
where Davells was asleep after his hard day's journeying. " No
son of thine ", said Sir John, hacking the old man with his sword.
It is true that Sir John afterwards disclaimed any affection having
been between him and the old sheriff, but that did not prevent
him from coming to a horrid end in his turn : shot in the throat
by a former servant, his body hung in chains at Cork, his head
sent as a New Year's gift to the Lord Deputy.[2] Similarly with
the end of his brother, the Earl, in the woods of Glenageenty,
after terrible privations and miseries, at the hand of one of his
own kerne. When Desmond, lord of so many lordships, chieftain
over half Munster, begged for mercy, the kerne replied, " Thou
hast killed thyself long ago ".[3] There were friendships and
enmities, bonds and betrayals, on both sides, cutting across race
and kin.

Spenser, Davies and indeed all the Elizabethans who knew

[1] q. Hogan, 76.
[2] R. Bagwell, *Ireland under the Tudors*, III. 94.   [3] *Ibid.* 112.

the situation at first hand were agreed in their diagnosis and very largely as to the measures they thought necessary. Spenser advocated the carrying forward of Sidney's policy of reducing Ulster to shire-ground : this was a cause of Tyrone's rebellion, and could not be carried out until its suppression. Spenser wished to see the extinction of the sept-names and the adoption of surnames—the process going forward at this moment in Celtic Wales and Cornwall. Every parish should have its schoolmaster ; the kerne and horse-boys be driven to labour ; loose wandering persons be taken up. Among these, their fellow-poet would no doubt include the bards, who were as much a feature of Celtic society in Ireland as in Wales or Scotland. They had a strong footing, with a definite allocation of sept-lands for their support ; and we hear of Scottish bards going to Ireland to complete their training. No-one among the English loved them : they were held responsible for inciting patriotic and tribal fervour, and for pushing the chieftains into their silly actions. Many statutes, proclamations and prohibitions were issued against them, quite in vain. Spenser commented that all cattle should be marked and sold in the open market : one sees the note of the cattle-raiding, cattle-thieving society, as on the Borders. Cows were the chief currency : a chieftain's wealth depended on the number of cattle he could command, his strength on the number of men ; rents were paid in cows, fines and obligations exacted in them. There was little money anywhere in Ireland ; the fact is brought home vividly when one finds a mortgage in Galway being effected in ducats of good Spanish rials of plate.[1] Rather surprisingly, Spenser did not favour sharp penalties for religion. A characteristic comment—no-one else makes it—is that, of all ways of life, " the realm of Ireland wanteth the most principal of them, that is, the intellectual ".[2] The end and aim of all was the generously conceived one of a mingling and fusion of the two peoples, beginning at the bottom. Spenser was ready to make the Irishman the tithing-man in the parish, " whereby he shall take the less exception to partiality, and yet be the more tied thereby . . . and now, since Ireland is full of her own nation that ought not to be rooted out, and somewhat stored with English already and more to be, I think it best, by an union of manners and conformity of minds, to bring them to be one people ".[3]

[1] M. J. Blake, *Blake Family Record, 1300–1600*, 117.
[2] Spenser, *loc. cit.* 197.   [3] *Ibid.* 193.

And that intermingling, which was the objective of the Elizabethans, is in fact what essentially came about.

In Spenser's time the gulf between a modern European society
and the primitive Celtic world was too great : " a strong antipathy existed between the two cultures because there was
scarcely a point of contact between their traditions, their ideals,
their art, their jurisprudence or their social life ".[1] Davies, as
a lawyer, saw the rooted and entangled mass of Celtic custom,
particularly as to the chieftainries and land-tenures, as the main
obstacle.   " For, if we consider the nature of the Irish customs,
we shall find that the people which doth use them must of
necessity be rebels to all good government, destroy the commonwealth wherein they live, and bring barbarism and desolation
upon the richest and most fruitful land of the world."[2] He cited
the effect of Brehon law. The Brehons were not so much judges
as arbitrators, very much at the disposition of the chiefs and able
only to allot a fine for the worst offences. " Whereas by the
laws of all other well-governed kingdoms and commonweals,
murder, manslaughter, rape, robbery and theft are punished
with death, by the Irish custom or Brehon law, the highest of
these offences was punished only by fine." This certainly goes
some way to explain the Irish complaisance towards murder.
However, Ireland today is governed, not by Celtic custom, but
by English Common Law : whatever anyone may say, Ireland
exemplifies essentially an English society.

The custom of tanistry—the election by the sept of the senior
and stronger leader from within the ruling family—may have
meant the survival of the fittest, but it certainly led to many
struggles for survival. These were rendered more bloody by the
freedom of Irish marital ways. In his later years Con O'Neill had
recognised an illegitimate son, Matthew, as his heir, and Henry
VIII's government, in ignorance or accommodation, followed
suit ; when Con was made Earl, Matthew was created Baron of
Dungannon. Con's eldest legitimate son, Shane, always maintained that Matthew was no O'Neill at all : he was certainly the
son of a smith's wife at Dundalk, who, when the boy was sixteen
and a promising youth, presented him to Con as his son. " My
father being a gentleman ", said Shane, " always recognised any
son laid by the mother at his door, and he had many more."

[1] Cyril Falls, *Elizabeth's Irish Wars*, 17.
[2] Davies, *loc. cit.* 290.

The tribe supported Shane against his father and the English government ; but to make his position sure, Shane drove out his father and contrived Matthew's murder. Shane himself came to a similar end : he had captured O'Donnell by the connivance of his wife, whom Shane then took as his mistress and treated shamefully. Later, defeated by O'Donnell, he took refuge with Sorley Boy's Scots, who had a long score against him : they murdered him and sent his head to the Captain of Carrickfergus, who sent it, preserved in salt, to the Lord Deputy.

Shane's tanist and successor was a cousin, Turlough Luineach ;[1] the English government could not but in decency uphold the rights of Matthew's children, Brian and Hugh. Before Shane died, Turlough managed to get Brian, the young Baron of Dungannon, killed. Hugh, the younger, succeeded in the eyes of the English government : it is ironical that their most dangerous opponent should have owed his position to the English, for in the eyes of Celtic custom he had none to begin with. When he got the power, he disposed of the MacShanes— Shane's mostly illegitimate progeny. He kept some of them in prison, the most popular, Hugh Gavelagh, he hanged on a thorn-tree ; it was reported all over Ireland that the Earl had to do the business himself. The Earl excused himself as being " bound to do justice upon thieves and murderers ; otherwise, if I be restrained from such-like executions, and liberty left to O'Neill, O'Donnell, and others to use their ancient customs, then should I not be able to defend my country from their violence and wrongs ".[2] This, if disingenuous, was—like everything of Tyrone's—hard to answer.

At the crisis of his, and Ireland's, fate later on, at the battle of Kinsale,[3] Tyrone had to pay for his ill-treatment of the MacShanes : their friends in the Isles, the Macleans and Campbells, would not hire out their men to serve him. And he had alienated the MacDonalds, by repudiating Sorley Boy's niece whom he had kept as his mistress and then sent back to the Isles. And so, at the hour of need, he had only a few hundred Scots gallowglass in place of the many he had had before at his command.

The O'Donnells, the other great house of Ulster, had similar

---

[1] From the fact that he had been fostered with the O'Looneys.
[2] Bagwell, *op. cit.* III. 219.
[3] *v.* below pp. 433-5.

trouble through the women. Hugh Manus had married Ineen Dubh—one sees the dark, passionate creature—daughter of James MacDonald of the Isles and Lady Agnes Campbell, later wife and tartar to Turlough. Both these women of the Isles were ambitious, domineering, dangerous persons to have there. Hugh had an illegitimate son, Donnell, who was inconveniently popular with the sept ; Ineen had him murdered, in the interests of her own son, Hugh Roe. It is like the murder of Edward the Martyr by his stepmother at the gates of Corfe Castle : the manners of the Heptarchy again. No wonder the respectable Yorkshireman, Fitzwilliam, lamented his fate as a banished man, wearing himself out among unkind people, a people most accursed, who lusted after every sin. (He made a good thing out of it : he and his fellow-Yorkshireman, Loftus, were among the few who did.) Murder and incest were everyday matters, and a lying spirit brooded over all the land. It was difficult to make out any man's pedigree or title ; for heraldry was discountenanced, records destroyed and everyone greedy for the reputation conferred by rhymers, whose trade was to set forth " the most beastliest and odious parts of men's doings ".[1] Nor was Sidney's judgment any different, though he was popular among the Irish—Harry of the big Beer—as Fitzwilliam was not :[2] " Surely there was never people that lived in more misery than they do, nor as it should seem of worse minds, for matrimony among them is no more regarded in effect than conjunction between un-reasonable beasts. Perjury, robbery and murder counted allowable. Finally, I cannot find that they make any conscience of sin, and I doubt whether they christen their children or no ; for neither find I place where it should be done, nor any person able to instruct them in the rules of a Christian ; or if they were taught I see no grace in them to follow it ; and when they die I cannot see they make any account of the world to come."[3] From which we see that civilised Elizabethans did not much like the ways of a primitive heroic world when propelled into it.

It is important to bear in mind, what has been too little realised, that the feuds of the Irish among themselves often

[1] Bagwell, *op. cit.* II. 43-4.
[2] " Never man went from Ireland of his calling with more money and less love." q. in G. A. Hayes-McCoy, *Scots Mercenary Forces in Ireland, 1565–1603*, 221.
[3] A. Collins, *Letters and Memorials of State*, I. 24-5.

explain their attitude to the English government. (It is like Sorel's[1] famous principle of the relations between European states : friendship and alliance with the next neighbour but one.) All through Elizabeth's reign her cousin Ormonde was a chief prop to her government. Therefore Desmond and the Geraldines of the South were constantly disloyal and frequently in rebellion. Therefore, as long as the Desmond power remained intact, the MacCarthys were apt to be loyal ; for they had been the dominant power in the far south-west until the Norman Fitzgeralds took away their ascendancy. So Florence MacCarthy served loyally with the government forces throughout the Desmond Rebellion.[2] When the Fitzgeralds were crushed and their lands confiscated, MacCarthy aspired to take their place : he became the MacCarthy Mór and spent the rest of his life in conspiracy and opposition— most of it in the Tower. So long as he was on the side of the government, his neighbour Lord Barry was out. When MacCarthy lapsed, Lord Barry came in on the side of the government and remained faithful for the rest of his life. In Ulster the O'Donnells, who were under pressure from the O'Neills, were faithful to the government during most of the century. Until Ineen Dubh impregnated her son, Hugh Roe, with her irreconcilable hatred of the English, and Perrot, as a precautionary measure, had the young Hugh abducted and taken into protective custody in Dublin Castle. That, along with a double marriage, gave Tyrone his opportunity for a *renversement* in Ulster, which drew together the two great houses against the English. Even so, there remained cadet branches of both houses which gave the English faithful support.[3]

It is obvious that however much the Irish wanted to get rid of the English from their country—and by no means all of them did—it was not possible anyway for the Irish themselves to erect a state on such a basis. The English provided the only possible foundations for a state, even in Ireland.

---

[1] Albert, of course, not Georges: *v. L'Europe et la Révolution française*, vol. I, i.

[2] D. MacCarthy, *Life of Florence MacCarthy Mór*, 6 foll.

[3] For example, Neil Garve O'Donnell, who gave the government invaluable support in the last stages of the Irish War, and upon whom the hateful Ineen Dubh got her revenge, charging him with responsibility for Sir Cahir O'Dogherty's rising later, for which Neil Garve was ruined. Among the O'Neills, Shane's grandson, Henry Oge, and Tyrone's half-brother, Sir Turlough MacHenry, sided with the government and were rewarded. These people, of course, had their motives.

Ireland : A Celtic Society in Decline

The part played in all this mêlée, this frightful mess, by the mercenaries from the Scottish Western Isles has only recently been fully illuminated for us.[1] That too was part of the break-up and degeneration of Celtic society on both sides of the Irish Sea. We have noticed something of the effect of the end of the MacDonald lordship of the Isles. There was now endemic unrest in the islands: chronic feuds between MacDonalds and Macleans on Islay, where the latter were forcing the former out and, it would seem, over-population ; for there were thousands of fighting men available for service every year in Ireland. This process, the recruitment of mercenaries from the Highlands by the Irish chiefs to fight their battles, had been going on increasingly through the fifteenth century into the sixteenth : it was the main factor enabling the chiefs to become more autocratic and necessitating greater exactions from the poor churls to support the mercenaries. The wealthier and more powerful the chief, the more gallowglass he could hire and support : this threw power more and more into the hands of the greater chiefs—O'Neills and O'Donnells—at the expense of the lesser, their urraghts, or subordinates, as they claimed. Hence, too, the Scottish marriages of O'Neill and O'Donnell : those designing women brought their dowries in hefty Redshanks.

We must distinguish between gallowglass and Redshanks.[2] The gallowglass had been arriving in Ireland for generations ; they had spread from the North, being hired by the chiefs, right down through the country, into Munster and even into Leinster. They were now settled on the land—had their portions of land allotted them, like the Church and the bards. The two dominant tribes of them were MacDonalds and MacSweeneys ; but they recruited native Irish into their calling, contrary to the government's ordinances, and the profession became hereditary. Barnabe Rich says, "if the father hath been a gallowglass, the son will be a gallowglass ". They had had a mixed Norse and Celtic origin in the Isles ; the heavy battle-axe they carried was of Norse derivation, and they wore armour. So that they became a sort of heavy infantry against the light (very light) infantry that the unarmoured kerne made.[3] The English government hated the whole system, for indeed it was "sufficient to keep

---

[1] Cf. G. A. Hayes-McCoy, *op. cit.*
[2] Cf. *ibid.* 13 foll.
[3] Cf. review of Hayes-McCoy in *Times Literary Supplement*, 24 July 1937.

any country in a ferment of unrest " and it was the foundation of the independence of the chiefs. Hence it was the necessary and constant aim of the government to cut off the chieftains from their independent military resources. But by now the whole system was inextricably rooted in Irish society, and the government, much against its will, was—as so often in Ireland—forced to follow suit, to compromise, to take them into its service upon a composition. The custom of billeting them out as " bonnaughts " upon the country degenerated into coign and livery, arbitrary exactions for their upkeep ; the government, incapable of stamping out the system, imitated it with its imposition of cess for the upkeep of its forces. Unhappy countryside that was a prey to both ! Every grandee had his gallowglass : Ormonde and Desmond as well as the Celtic chieftains of the North and West. And since the system could not be brought to an end, until Ireland was brought fully under English rule, the Queen was forced to follow in its ways with "her Majesty's gallowglass".

The Redshanks were the unsettled mercenaries who were hired every season and passed to and fro those coasts in their galleys at their pleasure. The government learned, as the years passed, that until Ulster was conquered they could not be kept out of Ireland. When Turlough Luineach O'Neill married Lady Agnes Campbell, with her dowry he could command 3000 mercenaries : there was something for the government to worry about. The marriage was celebrated with great feasting on Rathlin Island. Essex's father, the first Earl, driven to desperation by the impossibilities of the task he had undertaken, massacred 600 Scots, men, women and children, on that island. But nothing could keep them out. The Queen began with the optimistic policy of excluding the marauding Islemen from Ireland. She ultimately found that the only thing possible was to allow some of them to settle in order to keep more out. Sorley Boy MacDonald submitted or, rather, came to terms with the government and was very well treated : in return for keeping order in his country —the constant preoccupation of the English—he was allotted all the territory between the Bush and the Bann. Angus MacDonald was allowed to settle permanently and hold the glens of Antrim from the Queen. Scots MacDonalds became Irish MacDonells.

Old Sorley Boy, safe in his stronghold at Dunluce, safer still in his submission to government, was almost the only member of his family to die in his bed. Of his brothers three were killed ; of his sons the eldest, Donald, was killed before his father's submission, and Alexander at the hand of Captain Merriman's band in 1585. Two nephews also fell to Merriman, three more to Bingham at Ardnarea and another at Sligo. What a human wastage it all was ! Then, too, there were tribal feuds among the gallowglass : in 1570 some of the Clan Donald of Tyrone treacherously set upon and slew a band of MacSweeneys. In the same year, in action against the Burkes of Mayo, separate septs of the Clan Donald were fighting on opposite sides. It was only the reinforcement of Scottish mercenaries that enabled the chiefs to keep up the struggle against the government. During the years 1581–5 Connaught was being at last subjugated and brought into order by Sir Richard Bingham, a harsh, severe, but just, man. It was a struggle "on the part of the natives to maintain and on that of the government to overthrow this system ".[1] When the Scots were at length driven out, " South Connaught acquiesced in the English settlement from this time forward ". It was followed by the Composition of Connaught : an effective and successful change to English order, by which all the irregular exactions of the chiefs and the government cess were both compounded for an annual revenue to the Crown, and the chiefs became its collectors. Once more, next year, the Scots returned, penetrating Connaught from Tyrconnell. Bingham caught them at Ardnarea and massacred every man, woman and child of them—just over 1000. An English captain wrote that never had he been so " weary with killing of men, for I protest to God, as fast as I could I did but hough and paunch them ".[2] That settled their hash, however : henceforward there was comparative peace in Connaught.

In spite of everything—climate, foreign intervention, the distraction and strain of war abroad, the constant threat of invasion, the changes of course in policy and person, the hesitations on the part of the government, the compromises of the Queen, the discouragements, the disgust of everybody sooner or later with Ireland (except for Richard Boyle, who made a fortune out of other people's disgust)—the expansion of English power went on. Only the power of an ordered state, whatever its temporary recessions and retreats, was irresistible. There was no possibility of an ordered state in Ireland—and little enough

[1] Hayes-McCoy, *op. cit.* 143-4.   [2] Bagwell, III. 155.

in Scotland—except the English state. In Elizabeth's reign we can watch the momentum of the process out of which the United Kingdom was forged, as at no other time—except for the brief interval of Cromwell's Commonwealth. At the beginning of the reign the government had little knowledge and less grasp of the kaleidoscopic politics of this Celtic world. One has to see the scene to imagine it : from the Ulster coast there is Rathlin Island, there is the Mull of Cantyre withdrawing in the haze, from Antrim or the Ards peninsula there is the Scottish mainland. The seaways gave that fluidity and quickness of movement that so much exasperated the Queen's government, at the end of the long line across England and the Irish Channel and up the coast to the frontiers of inviolate Ulster. To begin with, they could get no prise on the situation : representations to James's government in Edinburgh were of little use, since he was unable to control the Western Isles : Scotland herself was not yet a modern state and she had a Celtic hinterland larger than her own Lowland kingdom, not fully brought into our polity until the eighteenth century. Elizabeth found that she had to enter into direct negotiation with the clansmen : Killigrew recommended that a pension to Argyll would be far more effective in controlling them than any amount of negotiation. And so she found. As her reign approached its term and the prospect of his succession enabled James to consolidate his rule in Scotland, the Queen found him more and more ready to co-operate over Ireland. Nothing, save his own accession, could stop the supplies of gunpowder and ammunition from the Lowland ports, especially from the Clyde, that sustained Tyrone : here, too, 1603 would bring a unified direction of policy. Already, before succeeding to the English crown, James had proclaimed Tyrone's rebellion as a danger " als weill to the libertie of the trew religioun as of the crownis and estait of this haill Ile of Britane, quhairof Ireland is a proper dependance ".[1] There indeed is a pointer to the future : the three kingdoms united in the hands of a Scottish king after the lifetime's labour of an Anglo-Welsh queen.

The state of the Church was in keeping : it was not immune from the decay of Celtic society, but reflected it. Ireland was no longer the island of saints, of holy men with their cult of

[1] Hayes-McCoy, 330.

extreme austerities, of schools of learning sending forth scholars
to illumine the darkness of Europe, of those wonderful manuscripts
with their elaborate linear decorations and the Celtic sense of
colour, like the landscape, green and brown and purple. All
that had been in the Dark Ages, centuries ago ; and since then
time had rather stood still for Ireland, as it is apt to do for
Celts. Irish religion had lost its vitality, as elsewhere on the eve
of the Reformation, and become very much a matter of external
observances and superstitions. Here was another source of shock,
a well-spring of contempt, for Elizabethans, who had only just
emerged, after a severe struggle, from such things. Barnabe
Rich remarks of the kerne that " there is not so notable a wretch
to be found that will not observe his fasting days ", and that it
was the same with the loosest women of the Dublin ale-houses.[1]
Sir Henry Sidney comments that, in spite of the neglect of the
elements of a Christian life, there was " yet sufferance of most
detestable idolatry ", as that at Holy Cross in Tipperary,
" whereunto there is no small confluence of people daily
resorting ".[2] Nor were the people's minds disturbed by the
Reformation measures until Archbishop Browne's unfortunate
campaign against images and relics.

As English influence had weakened in the last two centuries,
the Irish Church came to depend for temporal support on the
chieftains, members of whose families usually got the sees, for
what they were worth. (They were worth very little : the combined incomes of all Irish sees were not equal to that of
Winchester.[3]) Of the bishops, on the eve of the Reformation,
those of Meath and Leighlin never visited their dioceses ; the
Bishop of Ardagh ruled his as a lay chieftain—his cathedral
was mostly on the ground ; there was often no bishop at all at
Dromore, while the diocese of Clogher was so wasted by its wars
that it could not provide a living for one ; the diocese of Kilmore,
on the other hand, had been distracted by the simultaneous
claims of two.[4] A previous bishop of Leighlin had been murdered
by his archdeacon, a Kavanagh, who was the illegitimate son of
the abbot of Duske and wanted the see for himself.[5] Since the
archdeacon was a Butler connection, Kildare had had him

[1] Barnabe Rich, *op. cit.* 10.
[2] Collins, *op. cit.* I. 20.
[3] R. Dudley Edwards, *Church and State in Tudor Ireland*, xxxviii.
[4] G. V. Jourdan in Phillips, *op. cit.* 185.
[5] *Ibid.* 181-2.

crucified without compunction. Of episcopal celibacy, it is sufficient to note that Hugh Brady, the Elizabethan Bishop of Meath, was the descendant of at least three pre-Reformation bishops.[1] The cathedral chapter of Armagh could not be called together to elect the Archbishop at the beginning of Elizabeth's reign, for they were mostly horsemen away with Shane O'Neill—which did not prevent him from burning down the cathedral when he was crossed.[2] Of the learning of these chapters we are pleasantly reminded by a chief item among the manuscripts of the see of Ossory, a Latin treatise on the virtues of *aqua vitae* : we learn that, among other virtues, *valet sterilitati de causa frigida*.[3] Either the whisky was very potent or Irish clerics did not have much to complain of on this score.

It is not surprising that there was nothing of the settled parochial order of England : the poverty of the Church was such that there was little for the priests to live upon, except the alms of the people. Hence it was that their spiritual wants were most effectively provided for by the begging friars, especially by the Franciscans ; it was they who had the people's special devotion, until the rise of the Jesuits with the Counter-Reformation. And the Jesuits in turn easily fitted into the same pattern : an ubiquitous order working in a mobile society in a state of flux and conflict. Wherever one goes in Ireland it is the ruined Franciscan " abbeys " that stand out as the relics of ancient popular devotion : such places as Muckross by Killarney, or Mellifont in its pleasant dell by the stream, or the " Abbey of the Four Masters " in Donegal by its sullen grey lough. We have seen that there was virtually no opposition to Henry's Reformation measures ; no difficulty in accepting the Royal Supremacy, or the Dissolution of the Monasteries. Actually, in the early part of the sixteenth century, the Pope had little power or interest in Ireland : one can imagine how remote such a realm was from the Rome of Julius II or Leo X. It was the Counter-Reformation that made the difference.

The total value of monastic revenues did not exceed £400 p.a. and this came mostly into the hands of lay impropriators, the chiefs and neighbouring gentlemen, most of whom were Catholics. Hence the hopeless impoverishment of the parishes,

---

[1] J. Healy, *History of the Diocese of Meath*, I. 192.
[2] *v.* Article on Adam Loftus, *D.N.B.*
[3] H.M.C. *Report X*, App. 5, 255.

to which the Elizabethans could find no answer at all. Sidney reported of the diocese of Meath, the richest and most civilised —or, rather, the least impoverished and barbarous : out of 224 parishes only 52 were served and their vicars maintained ; another 52 were in the hands of various lords and gentry. Of the remainder, 105 were leased out to farmers, *i.e.* of the benefices : " no parson or vicar resident upon any of them, and a very simple or sorry curate for the most part appointed to serve them ; among which number of curates only eighteen were found able to speak English ; the rest, Irish priests or rather Irish rogues, having very little Latin, less learning or civility. All these live upon the bare altarages (as they term them), which God knoweth are very small, and are wont to live upon the gain of masses, dirges, shrivings and such-like trumpery, godly abolished by your Majesty : no one house standing for any of them to dwell in. In many places the very walls of the churches down ; very few chancels covered, windows and doors ruined or spoiled. . . . If this be the estate of the Church in the best peopled diocese and best governed country of this your realm (as troth it is), easy it is for your Majesty to conjecture in what case the rest is, where little or no reformation either of religion or manners hath yet been planted. . . . Upon the face of the earth, where Christ is professed, there is not a Church in so miserable a case." [1]

Only the Roman Church had an answer : for the clergy, celibacy and the religious orders ; for the people, their necessary (and eleemosynary) superstitions.

Here is the greatest failure of the Elizabethans in Ireland, and here is in part the explanation. The Reformation never made any real impression on the Irish people. At the beginning it looked as if it might make headway : no opposition, no martyrs, no persecutions ; a certain amount of excitement was aroused by the novelty of the preaching in the towns. Under the progressive Reform of Edward VI only three Irish bishops withdrew : the rest went on. The Protestants were the first to set up a printing press in Dublin, to print the Prayer Book, in 1551. In 1559 a considerable number of bibles were sent over and were disposed of in two years. [2] Many of the leading figures, even among the

---

[1] Collins, *op. cit.* I. 112.
[2] Jourdan in Phillips, *op. cit.* II. 310. The figure given, from Ware's *Annals of Ireland*, is 7000 ; but I do not credit it : it is an impossible number.

chiefs, conformed—indeed they were no fanatics : they left that to the people.

But what could the government do, with such an intractable situation and no resources to deal with it ? Sidney's Dublin Parliament passed bills for founding free schools in every shire and for the repair of churches. Not a penny was raised for either purpose ; the Anglo-Irish lords and Irish chiefs had a rooted objection to raising money—indeed there was very little in the country to raise ; the government's good intentions remained a blue-print. A similar proposal to found a university, out of the revenues of St. Patrick's Cathedral, came to nothing. It was not until the end of the reign that Trinity College was founded : it should have come into being fifty years earlier, with the first impulse of the Reformation : there might then have been some hope. Similarly with the language difficulty. The bishops were bidden to preach in English : what was the use of that in a country nine-tenths of which was Irish-speaking ? Only the Pale and the corporate towns spoke English. And, in marked contrast with Wales, it was not till the beginning of James's reign that the Prayer Book was translated into Irish. By then it was too late : the Counter-Reformation offensive had settled the issue. Even so, the government played its cards badly. Some of the leading Irish clergy conformed : Dean Danyell of Armagh, of an important Irish family with influential connections, for one : he should have been made Primate. Once and again the Queen, with her unfailing political sense, nominated him ; but somehow he never got through the embattled Castle officials, pivoting upon Archbishop Loftus.

This Cambridge Puritan—he was a friend of Cartwright— was a tough type. Appointed early to the see of Armagh, he could neither be elected, for his chapter were away with O'Neill's horse, nor reside, for his see lay in hostile territory. However, he was consecrated by Archbishop Curwen and other bishops : it is nice to think—for there has been a considerable literature on the silly subject—that the episcopal succession was thus preserved for the Church of Ireland, an inestimable boon. As he had no revenues from his hostile see, he held the deanery of St. Patrick's *in commendam*, on condition that he should resign it, if St. Patrick's were converted to a college. He saw to it that it was not. It was over this subject that he became a mortal enemy to Perrot, when Lord Deputy, and the Archbishop managed to ruin him—aided by his own lack of self-control and his unwieldy Celtic temperament. Becoming Archbishop of Dublin, Loftus combined the office with that of Lord Keeper, until the arrival of Gerard from the borders of Wales. In the absence of Deputies from Dublin he was several times Lord Justice, in control of government : a permanent member of the Irish Privy Council, he was always there. He was an indefatigable preacher, and it does not seem that his sermons fatigued his audience ; indeed only he, Bishop Jones of Meath and the Bishop of Down were preachers at all. He was pious and conscientious. In 1583 he managed to lay by the heels—for he was not a *politique*, an indifferentist—a Roman Archbishop O'Hurley. O'Hurley had been an inquisitor : that was all right with his co-religionists. Since there was no rack in Dublin Castle, his feet were toasted in hot boots and he was executed : that was all right with Loftus's co-religionists.

But the effect of his piety was a little spoiled by his too evident attention to his family interests. Of course he had a large establishment to provide for—some twenty children, who needed provender ; and he had only some £400 a year. (Multiply by forty for Ireland.) So that by 1590 he was able to purchase the estate of Rathfarnham from Viscount Buttevant and build himself a stately castle. Of his sons who grew up, Edward died at the siege of Kinsale, Adam was killed in O'Byrne's country, in the Dublin Mountains. They paid their price for the tough old father. No doubt they were brave young men. The Archbishop had brought over a hopeful nephew, upon whom he bestowed a prebend, a profitable lease and made him archdeacon (he was an ecclesiastical lawyer). This Loftus became the first Viscount and the founder of a noble family.

Bishop Jones was another Cambridge lad who came to Ireland to make a career : he did so by marrying Loftus's sister-in-law, a lady of good Irish family left a widow. (Widows were great assets in the Elizabethan age and held an advantage in the marriage-mart.) Jones succeeded his brother-in-law as Dean of St. Patrick's and, after twenty years as Bishop of Meath, as Archbishop of Dublin. He, too, was an active preacher and equally active in making long profitable leases—one remembers Swift on the rascal, his predecessor, and the knaves and fools of his chapter. But Swift went too far : Bishop Jones did good works : he re-edified his cathedral and made extensive repairs to

Christ Church. He was buried in St. Patrick's ; Dean Swift made his descendant repair his tomb. Loftus, too, was not incapable of a good work, within reason : he became genuinely keen on a university for Dublin and induced the corporation to grant the site of the priory of All Hallows. He even subscribed £100 towards the founding of Trinity—a lot for a careful Yorkshireman with so many claims on him. It was due largely to him that the inception of Trinity was such a Cambridge affair, with a Puritan, or ex-Puritan, flavour. One sees his venerable appearance with the potent white beard and capacious bald head looking down from the walls there.

The Reformation in Ireland being abortive, the English government was thrown back upon another line : a temporising, waiting policy that kept the penal legislation against Catholics largely in suspense—indeed it could not be executed—and amounted to a very wide degree of toleration. In the event, there was a great contrast between the treatment of Catholics in Ireland and in England itself. People like Loftus and his friends, the Dublin officials, wanted the execution of the law, and they had this argument on their side, that the Roman Church was the government's open and most dangerous enemy, that the friars were emissaries of Papal propaganda ; the Jesuits the active agents of the Counter-Reformation and Spain. Wherever there was rebellion, the Faith was always at the back of it : James Fitzmaurice of Desmond, the irreconcilable enemy, who forced on the Desmond rebellion, was a complete Counter-Reformation fanatic, who was accompanied by an English irreconcilable, Nicholas Sanders, the Papal Nuncio. The agents and emissaries going to and from Spain and Rome, serving as liaison officers and secretaries with the chiefs, were always priests. To that extent the Protestant officials were right : *there* was the enemy. Nor was there any doubt in their minds that a full union of the peoples could not come about while this residual element was unreduced ; nor that, once Ireland was subject to their control, the religious legislation should be fully applied.

But the government in London and its direct representatives, the Lords Deputy, the Queen herself, saw the situation differently. The dilemma for the government was, to this extent, the same in Ireland as in England. The Papacy was a declared and unscrupulous enemy ; but the great majority of English Catholics were loyal, and so were large numbers in Ireland. The chief

seaport towns, for example—the essential bases of English rule—
were overwhelmingly, and increasingly openly, Catholic ; yet
they were all on the whole loyal. There was the certainty of
creating enemies superfluously, by attempting to force the
religious legislation upon them. Every Lord Deputy from the
first—with the exception of the least successful of them, Spenser's
hero, Lord Grey—was a moderate on the religious issue. " Go
to, go to ", said St. Leger to Archbishop Browne at the Council
table, " your matters of religion will mar all."[1] At the end, there
was Mountjoy protesting, " If you did but walk up and down
in the cold with us, you would not be so warm in your religion ".[2]
Even the stern Chichester, once the war was over and he was
Deputy, was anxious to see justice for the Catholic subjects no
less than the Protestant. Behind them were Ormonde and the
Queen. Ormonde's father, who had been a Protestant, thought
" nothing more necessary to induce the people to good civility
than sincerely and truly to set forth the Word of God to the
people here ";[3] the son constantly pressed for moderation and
tolerance, and, though brought up a Protestant, became a
Catholic some years before he died. The Queen exerted a constant
influence on the side of lenity with regard to religion, dissuading
from applying the laws with any rigour, though she could not,
of course, end them.

All the intelligent people on both sides were *politiques* and
trimmers—even Tyrone. He had to lay claim to fanaticism to
keep the people attached to the cause ; for that is the way fools
—or, to use a more polite word, the faithful—are got : to their
own suffering and destruction. More and more, as his rebellion
progressed, Tyrone had to pull out the Catholic stop, for that
provided the one ground-bass for a united national rising. The
" freedom of conscience " Tyrone demanded of Elizabeth's
government became, in writing to Spain, the " extirpation of
heresy ".[4] When Cecil read Tyrone's " terms "—Ireland to be
reconciled to Rome and the churches restored to Catholicism,
no restrictions upon priests, no Englishman to be preferred to
any living in Ireland, a Catholic university to be founded, etc.—
the little man took up his pen and wrote " Eutopia ".[5] For,
indeed, they were not possible ; they were just politics. The

---

[1] q. Jourdan in Phillips, *op. cit.* II. 259.   [2] *Ibid.* 491.
[3] E. Edwards, *op. cit.* 34.   [4] *Cal. Carew MSS., 1589–1600*, 350.
[5] Jourdan in Phillips, *op. cit.* II. 474.

Queen's comment was that he well knew she had never restrained him in matters of religion ; and that, he had to admit, was true. On his surrender no mention was made of toleration ; as usual in human affairs, the very bitterness of the struggle made toleration impossible.

Before the struggle with Spain and the Counter-Reformation became intense and poisoned humaner feelings, the situation was obscure, complex and not without its friendlier paradoxes. Rome, with its absolute claims and its absolutist logic, opposed the Crown appointments to bishoprics by appointing its own succession, wherever feasible—almost everywhere, except for Dublin ; so that there gradually grew up a double succession, Protestant and Catholic. On the other hand, the government seems to have recognised the older bishops who had been papally appointed, provided they made no bones about their temporal allegiance. For the most part, the papal bishops lay low in the country, not attracting the attentions of the government. It was impossible for the government to pay no attention to the claims and activities of a papal Primate : so Creaigh was arrested and held in prison till his death. So, too, with the Jesuit Nuncio, Wolfe, who took note of the military stores and munitions in the country : he spent five years in prison before his release. More agreeable is the case of Myler MacGrath, who is ill-spoken of by both sides as a time-server. Nominated by the Pope as Bishop of Down, he fell into the hands of the English and sensibly apostatized : he became Archbishop of Cashel and seems to have done his job. The world would be a pleasanter place—Elizabethan Ireland far more so—for a few more such : humans take their absurd convictions too seriously.

They took them more and more seriously as the conflict grew fiercer, and they killed each other more and more savagely. Unmistakably, as the Counter-Reformation impulse generated its full power, Ireland was won back to Catholicism. In a sense, it had never been lost—certainly not to Protestantism. Even the small ground made in the Anglicised towns was swallowed up under the inflowing tide. In Cork, the bishop complained, his congregations had dwindled to nothing ; where there had been a thousand, there were now not five ; the women, above all, had gone back to the old faith. [1] The Prayer Book service was termed the devil's service and the people crossed themselves when they met a

[1] E. Edwards, 298.

Protestant. (What powerful, subliminal, atavistic forces had been brought into play here!) This bishop, William Lyon, was a good man and had built churches and schools, provided service books and school-books and appointed schoolmasters : all to no avail. It was the same story in Galway, " once the paradise of Ireland in number and zeal of professors of the Gospel . . . so now very few of their men, and not of the chiefest, will be seen to frequent the same [the Church] ".[1] So, too, at Waterford, where the mayor and aldermen had been in the habit of at least attending church ; now they were loyal as ever, but they would not go.

The game, in this sector, was lost, and this was to have lasting importance. It has often been wondered whether the Irish were anti-English because they were Catholics, or whether they remained Catholic because they were anti-English. I think it may be concluded that the religious division both reflected and expressed a deep-reaching difference of temperament and character between the two peoples. For the Elizabethan English, Protestantism provided an ideology of activist enterprise, forward-looking and dynamic. It is only just to admit that Catholicism not only better suited the nature of Irish society—such as we have seen it to be—but that it agreed with the backward-looking Celtic temperament, with its nostalgic urge to return to the womb, its refusal to come to terms with the facts of the external world, its deepest desire to withdraw into itself.

We may say that out of the squalid, blood-infested struggle between these two—so superfluous if only humans were capable of reason—there came anew the devotion, the heroism, the sanctity that had been somewhat lost to Irish Catholicism : in the deplorable human way higher standards could only come through conflict and suffering, inflicted and borne.

[1] Phillips, *op. cit.* 617 foll., App., " The Religious Condition of Connaught in 1591".

CHAPTER IV

IRELAND: COLONISATION AND CONQUEST

SUCH was the Ireland with which the Elizabethans had to deal ; or rather, such were its leading characteristics.

How did they deal with it ? There was no question of avoiding the responsibility. For all that many Elizabethans oftentimes, like the Lord Deputy Sussex, had reason to wish the island sunk in the sea, and the Queen herself " grew weary with reading the Irish dispatches ", they could not evade the task. All the circumstances of the age bore them on. For one thing, strategic considerations, defence against the foreign enemy : Ireland was more vital to us than the Netherlands were to Spain. Then there was their own impulse and drive, their surplus energy seeking expansion. It was unthinkable that they should not go forward. And, in fact, contrary to popular belief, the Elizabethans showed ability as well as energy in dealing with the intractable problem, that taxed the limited resources of a small country. These resources would have been sufficient if, in the first place, conquest had been intended ; or secondly, if the English state had been able to concentrate them on the target. But, by the 1580s, we were engaged in a European struggle, on the ocean, in the Netherlands, in Normandy and Brittany, in attacks on Spain herself.

First, and last, the Elizabethans sent many of their ablest and most gifted men to Ireland, both administrators and soldiers. Sussex, Fitzwilliam, Russell, Bagenal, Chichester were all men of ability ; Sir John Perrot and Sir Peter Carew were remarkable, if rumbustious, figures ; Sidney was, if the anachronism of the phrase be permitted, the best colonial administrator of his time. Though Essex failed there, he was the Queen's—and the people's —darling, the prime star in the firmament. Of the soldiers, " Mountjoy . . . may perhaps be ranked as the greatest English soldier of the period . . . Sir William Pelham and Sir George Carew were most capable fighting men. Sir Richard Bingham, that fierce flail of Connaught, saw half a century of service. . . . The Norris brothers, Sir John, Sir Thomas and Sir Henry, were renowned warriors, and John's exploits on the Continent were world-famous."[1] Even poets and intellectuals were involved in the adventure : such men as Ludovic Briskett, Barnabe Rich and Barnabe Googe, Geoffrey Fenton and Sir John Davies ; while the friendship of Spenser and Ralegh, made in Ireland, has left an imperishable memory, since it is wrought into the work of two men of genius. The *Faerie Queene* was largely written in Ireland and bears evidence of it in many places. Perhaps most important in their ultimate flowering were the colonial experiments of St. Leger, Grenville, Ralegh, with the career of Humphrey Gilbert as Colonel in Munster, for it was from that group that sprang the colonising of America.

The two main ways of tackling the situation were through the efforts of individual persons in colonisation, and the extension of the area of direct control by government. For government, the choice was between direct and indirect control ; and the choice was largely dependent on financial considerations. Indirect control—leaving O'Neill, O'Donnell, Desmond and the rest to rule their tribesmen—was cheaper, and this appealed to the Queen, who could not bear the thought that Ireland, so far from paying for itself or contributing to the revenue, always cost money from the English treasury, even in peace-time. This was contrary to the views of her Deputies, in touch with the situation on the spot—in particular, to Sidney's policy : it was a subject of contention between them and led her to treat him with unmerited coldness. In spite of their relationship to Leicester, the Queen does not seem to have much liked the Sidneys. Her leaning on Ormonde in Irish affairs made Sidney sympathetic to Desmond, in so far as it was possible to be sympathetic to such a zany. She was jealous, too, of Sidney's possessing the two great administrative posts of the kind, both Wales and Ireland. Sidney longed to see Ulster reduced to shire-ground and placed under direct rule. The Queen handed it back to Shane O'Neill, after his celebrated visit to London, thereby missing a grand opportunity and storing up a peck of troubles. Sir John Davies as Speaker of the first Parliament containing representatives from all Ireland, including Ulster, exclaimed—" How glad would Sir Henry Sidney have been to

[1] Cyril Falls, *op. cit.* 7-8.

have seen this day—he that so much desired to reduce Ulster, but could never perfectly perform it ! "[1] In this respect, as in some others, the Queen held up Sidney's forward policy, though nothing—short of defeat in war—could arrest the momentum of the process as a whole.

Throughout this work tribute has been paid to the sagacity and success of the Queen's financial policy. The great exception to this is in relation to Ireland : I am bound to say that her tightness here was responsible for one of the two chief failures in her astonishing record as a ruler. If she had been prepared to lay out more money on Ireland in the middle decades of her reign, it is possible that she would not have had to pour out the large sums necessary in the end to conquer the country. While her character as a moderate and a compromiser, her opportunism and tactics of delay, brought her untold rewards in her policy as a whole, it is probable that they were disadvantageous in the circumstances of Ireland. On the other hand, it is equally probable that if she could have been in touch with the Irish scene at first hand for herself, she would have been a good deal more downright and decisive.

For financial reasons, then, the Queen was wholly in favour of planting and settlement being carried out by private individuals, the brunt falling on them, in their lives and fortunes. In truth, it could not be successfully carried through on a purely private basis, though many were the sacrifices and the lives spent. Colonisation and the extension of direct rule went forward together, and the circumstances of Ireland made them take a military mould. One sees vividly the insecurity, the danger, of settlement brought home in the bawns that remain, the fortified farmhouses with their high walls : Kilcolman, or such a one as that off the road between Kilroot (Swift's first curacy) and Carrickfergus—from which one sees the mountains behind Belfast, whence the tribesmen would descend upon the strip of cultivated plain. One sees it in a line in the *Faerie Queene*— written at the moment Spenser took up its composition again in Ireland :

> They found the gates fast barred long ere night,
> And every loup fast lockt, as fearing foes despight.

And when he looked out, this was what he saw :

[1] *v.* H. Morley, *op. cit.* 405.

Thus as he spoke, loe ! with outragious cry
A thousand villeins rownd about them swarmd
Out of the rockes and caves adjoyning nye ;
Vile caitive wretches, ragged, rude, deformd,
All threatning death, all in straunge manner armd ;
Some with unweldy clubs, some with long speares,
Some rusty knifes, some staves in fier warmd :
Sterne was their looke ; like wild amazed steares,
Staring with hollow eies, and stiffe upstanding heares.

The process of plantation had been set in motion before
Elizabeth came to the throne, the tide turning against Gaelic
Ireland. The Pale had been incessantly spoiled by the O'Mores
of Leix and the O'Connors of Offaly, that wild, inaccessible,
boggy country to the south-west. But their intransigence went
farther : Brian O'Connor's reply to Henry VIII's kingship was
that he would hear " no more name of the King of England in
Ireland than of the King of Spain ".[1] When, after the Geraldines,
Leix and Offaly went into revolt, they were laid waste and their
settlement with English taken in hand. Under Edward VI a
project was put forward for granting leases of twenty-one years
to gentlemen of the Pale and loyal Irish : they knew better than
to take it on.[2] Mary's government carried forward the process
by establishing a fort, Maryborough, in the heart of Leix, and
Philipstown on the site of O'Connor's stronghold in Offaly :
the areas around these were made shire-ground, and King's and
Queen's Counties came into being. Early in Elizabeth's reign,
a number of grants of some three or four hundred acres were
made at moderate rents, to undertakers mostly from the Pale,
whose hinterland it was. This led to incessant strife, almost
continual guerilla warfare, on the confines of the Pale throughout
the reign. " The spoilers of the Pale ", writes the Lord Deputy
in 1572, " are named Rory Oge with the O'Mores . . . Fiach
MacHugh with the O'Connors . . . the manner of their coming is
by daylight with bagpipes, by night with torchlight."[3] It has
been calculated that eighteen several times these septs attempted
to recover their independence and their lands, each time losing
ground. But so, in these conditions, were the planters : by the
end of the century not a single one of the original grantees

[1] Maxwell, *op. cit.* 48.
[2] Cf. R. Dunlop, in *Cam. Mod. Hist.*, III. 587.
[3] Maxwell, 49.

remained. It may be imagined what a waste this country immediately on the Border became and what savageries the warfare gave rise to. During Tyrone's Rebellion, the Irish War, all the natives came back again, and Mountjoy was driven to starving them out by cutting their green corn with the sword. Both chiefs, Rory and his son Owny, were killed : " Owny, being mortally wounded and fearing his head should come into the Lord Deputy's hands, had willed it to be cut off and buried after his death ".[1] What remained of the septs after this war of mutual extermination were transplanted to the remotest districts of Kerry : not until James's reign did the English plantation go forward.

Such was the background to the revealing case of the freebooting Captain Thomas Lee, whose career may be taken as not untypical, though his freedom with his pen gives him a special interest. He seems to have come to Ireland as an undertaker in the following of Essex's father.[2] After that abortive effort came to an end, Lee was employed in suppressing the rebellion of the Eustaces under Lord Grey and succeeded in capturing Baltinglas's brother. He then married a Eustace widow with property in Kildare. But he came into conflict with Ormonde, no friend to English undertakers, and he developed a complex against him and his ally Fitzwilliam, to which he was unwise enough to give unbridled expression. This was a very unsuccessful state of mind, and he became embittered and unbalanced, a desperate man : like many such, a recruit for Essex. Given command of a band of horse, in the Queen's pay, he did good, if rough, service. He was able to buy the castle of Reban, from which he went out against the O'Mores. When his band was discharged, Lee went sour, constantly petitioning the government for its restitution. Fenton wrote, " he is not without his portion of that common and secret envy which biteth most of us that serve here ".[3] In 1595 he fell into disgrace for the killing of MacPhelim Reagh, who

---

[1] Hogan, *op. cit.* 77.

[2] B. G. MacCarthy, in " The Riddle of Rose O'Toole " (*Féilscríbhinn Torna, Essays and Studies Presented to Professor Tadhg Ua Donnchadha*, ed. S. Pender), says, p. 179—I do not know on what evidence—that Lee was a native of Athy and regards him as an Irishman. But he was certainly of English stock, a cousin of Sir Henry Lee : which accounts for his access to the Queen. She regarded him with distrust from the first : the furious zeal of his father for Queen Mary's cause much distempered him with her Majesty, Sir Henry Lee writes (*Salisbury MSS.*, X. 306 ; and cf. *ibid.* 12, 180, 428). She was right, as usual ; for Lee was a double-dealer.

[3] q. in *D.N.B.*, *sub.* Thomas Lee.

was a protected person, and Lee was imprisoned in Dublin Castle. Let out, he brought in the heads of seventeen rebels ; and in May 1597 commanded the band that killed the notorious Fiach MacHugh.[1] Pleased with himself, and going beyond himself, he sent the head to the Queen, to remind her of his services. To that civilised lady such a reminder was totally unacceptable and the Council was instructed to administer a reproof : " We do find that it would have pleased her Majesty much better that the same should have been kept there, and bestowed away with other like fragments of the heads and carcases of such rebels, than to be sent over into this realm ". Torn between their instructions from on high, and their desire not to discourage good service, their lordships added lamely, " nevertheless, because the meaning was good, the error was the less. The best and most easy amendment thereof is to send the head back again by the same messenger." [2]

But the head that had been so troublesome in life was not to be disposed of so easily. Since Lee was a follower of Essex, the messenger had been instructed to take it to him, who referred the messenger to Secretary Cecil for his reward. (One sees the relations subsisting between Essex and Cecil even in such a matter.) Since the head-money had been already paid to Lee in Ireland, the disappointed messenger, having no further use for the object, tried to leave it with an acquaintance in Enfield Chase, who would not have it nor let him bury it in his garden. So he gave it to his boy to bury in the forest, who instead put it on a tree, where it was found by two boys fetching their cattle, and the matter (though not, we hope, the head) came back once more to the Council.[3] We find Cecil writing, " Her Majesty is surely not well contented that the head of such a base Robin Hood is brought so solemnly to England. It is no such trophy of a notorious victory, and yet of it his friends here make great advantage." [4] In other words, Fiach MacHugh's poor head had become a football between Cecil and Essex in contention.

Soon Lee was in Dublin Castle again on a more serious charge, that of communing with Tyrone. And, indeed, a

---

[1] Fiach MacHugh was the leader of the junior branch of the O'Byrnes, an inveterate enemy of the English and O'Neill's chief ally and support in Leinster. But it is interesting that the senior branch of the sept were loyal to the English, from whom they held their lands.

[2] E. Edwards, *Life of Sir Walter Ralegh*, I. 105.

[3] *Salisbury MSS.*, VIII. 395.   [4] E. K. Chambers, *Sir Henry Lee*, 193.

disappointed man himself, he was a covert supporter of the grand rebel : he asked to be sent to Tyrone who, he was sanguine enough to think, would be reformed, " for he hath only one little cub of an English priest, by whom he is seduced for want of his friends' access to him. . . . I know his valour and am persuaded he will perform it. . . . Being often his bedfellow, he hath divers times bemoaned himself with tears in his eyes."[1] These were politic tears, and Lee's words were those of a desperate gambler. When he got to Tyrone, Lee found him " quite changed from his former disposition and possessed with insolency and arrogancy ".

Such communings between an Essex supporter and Tyrone were very suspicious ; we shall never know all that passed between Tyrone and Essex at the ford, nor what understanding there was between them, nor what party James was to it all. All we know is that the old Queen would not accept Tyrone's submission on terms : nothing but unconditional surrender would do. We are at liberty to surmise that they were willing to force her hand. When Essex decamped from Ireland, Lee went with him. After Essex's attempted *coup d'état,* Lee tried to rescue him and Southampton from prison by force. He made no defence : he was desperate and said only that he " had lived in misery and cared not to live, his enemies were so many and so great ". He was hanged at Tyburn, dying very Christianly.

Lee left behind him two tracts, one unpublished, the other published—*A Brief Declaration of the Government of Ireland.* They are the work of a disgruntled man ; their value consists precisely in that : they are very outspoken, and quite unbalanced. Because he was embittered, he is sympathetic—in spite of his black deeds—to the Irish. The *Brief Declaration* is an attack on Fitzwilliam's administration. One sees the motive. Fitzwilliam, on arriving, had intended to remove from the command of bands well-provided officers at the Council-board who were unable to lead men and follow the fury of the wars, and give it to those who could. But he had thought better of it so as not to make enemies ; he preferred to make a good thing out of his six years as Deputy.[2] He did. Lee launched out against Dublin Castle, specifically defending O'Donnell, Maguire, Brian Oge, O'Rourke and MacMahon. He made a general charge of 300 or 400

---

[1] T. Lee, "A Brief Declaration of the Government of Ireland", in J. Lodge, *Desiderata Curiosa Hibernica,* I. 87 foll.

[2] *i.e.* 1588–94.

Irishmen under protection being summoned under colour of doing her Majesty service, " where your garrison soldiers were appointed to be, who have there most dishonestly put them all to the sword. . . . If this be a good course to draw these savage people to the state, to do your Majesty service, and not rather to enforce them to stand upon their guard, I humbly leave to your Majesty." Rebels who had been pardoned and afterwards lived dutifully and done good service had yet been arraigned for accompanying traitors, condemned for treason and executed. No doubt there were such hard cases in the circumstances of Irish warfare. Others were pardoned—and yet there were secret commissions for murdering them. (How like the Black and Tans and the Irish murder campaign : and how much the twentieth century approximates to the sixteenth !)

Lee addressed his tract, very audaciously, to the Queen and did not hesitate to make his suggestions as to her government public—" because it pleased your Highness (many years since) to impart unto me how much you abhorred to have your people there dealt withal by any practice but only upright justice, by your Majesty's laws and forces ". His tract evidently gave much offence, since the second, " The Discovery and Recovery of Ireland with the Author's Apology ", never saw the light of publication.[1] He refers to the " bad success of my former labours bestowed by her Majesty's express commandment and delivered in a book to her Highness at my being in England ".

Incorrigible man that he was, his second tract was an even more bitter attack on Ormonde than his first had been on Fitzwilliam. He charges Ormonde with half-heartedness in prosecuting the Irish war, with pulling his punches in the pursuit of the rebels when he could have extinguished them. No doubt there was something in this ; but there was a defence. Ormonde always had been a moderate, and he was an Irishman : perhaps, too, he was now ageing and going soft. He was certainly a subtle customer : the only Irishman who was a match for Tyrone. But, then, he was inclined to meet Tyrone half-way ; besides, had not Ormonde married a daughter to Tyrone's son?[2] Lee complained that Ormonde had allowed the English plantation in Leix to be destroyed, and that he would not let any of his own lands to the English, he could not abide to have them dwelling

---

[1] Brit. Museum, Add. MS. 33,743.
[2] If so, these must be illegitimate progeny.

near him. There was something in this, too, for Ormonde's was an Irish point of view, if that of an Anglo-Irish lord. It had its personal advantages, for, as Lee noticed, Ormonde's own lands were never ravaged by the rebels, while those of his English neighbours were. And when he had the chance of pursuing and finishing them, he desisted. He had, for example, invited Fiach MacHugh to feast with him—that was all his revenge upon the old traitor. Next Christmas Tyrone was his visitor, with Lee and other gentlemen, and Tyrone and Ormonde had had secret conference together. Lee insinuates that Rose O'Toole, widow of Roe O'Toole and wife of Fiach MacHugh, was Ormonde's mistress :[1] she was certainly his go-between with the rebels in the mountains and " bears herself so bold on his favours " as to pray for Tyrone, not for the Queen, who had twice pardoned her life. But Ormonde carried everything off by his wit, " which doth as far pass that of Machiavelli as English St. Paul's passeth Irish St. Patrick's ".

Lee may be glancing at Ormonde and Tyrone when he says that it was the regular policy before entering into rebellion for the father to marry his son to the daughter of some great man seeming a good subject, and pass his lands to him, the son pretending to dislike his father's proceedings. For example, the White Knight, Edmund MacGibbon, who married his son to Lord Dunboyne's daughter. When Lord Cahir was a traitor his second brother and heir stood in ; when Lord Roche was a traitor his eldest son stood in and spoke sharply to his father. No doubt there were all these tricks. Lord Roche and Patrick Condon went out purposely to be revenged upon some of the undertakers who contended with them in law for their lands—Spenser was one of these ; their purpose effected, their friends made means to bring them in. Again, one observes the hostility of the old Anglo-Irish to the new English : a constant factor in later Irish history and one that was ultimately to ruin them both. Doubtless it was the small men and the simple who suffered in all this : the great knew how to protect themselves. And, indeed, as was pointed out in defence of the government at the time, in all the warfare, the fighting, the treasons and

---

[1] B. G. MacCarthy, *loc. cit.*, regards this as an unwarranted aspersion on Rose O'Toole. She was a remarkable personality, employed as a go-between in more important negotiations (*e.g.* between Norris and O'Neill) in this complex and treacherous background. In her beauty, her passion for politics and her red-gold hair, she seems to have been a Maud Gonne of the sixteenth century.

betrayals, only one noble house, that of Desmond, was struck down.

Lee defends his own contacts with Tyrone : his journey to him was " not without the knowledge and licence of a commander in good place, the Marshal that then was ". That was, however, Sir Christopher Blount, Essex's step-father, executed for his share in Essex's plot. After Sir Conyers Clifford's defeat, Tyrone had made Lee many offers, but " his discourses were so base and to so vile purpose as I was vexed at my heart to hear them and cursed myself that ever I had known him. . . . But that which most of all grieved me were three things wherewith he acquainted me, lying in bed with him, and a fourth thing which he showed me in the morning after we were up." This was that nothing was determined against him in England but he had notice thereof as soon as the Lord Deputy, and the like intelligence what passed at the Council table in Ireland. Here was a clear accusation of treason against Ormonde, for only he was a member of both Councils.

Lee's tracts give one a first-hand insight into the intrigue within intrigue, treason within treason, rebellion and bogus-rebellion, the pursuit of rebels in inverted commas, the atmo-sphere of make-believe, the unreality and then the ghastly realities, the bogs where there should be solid ground, the obstinate resistance where there should have been common sense and agreement—all the indescribable complexities (and perplexities) that dogged English government in Ireland. No wonder the Queen was wearied reading the despatches !

We may watch the twofold drive of English expansion—private colonisation and the extension of direct government—from the moment of Sidney's return to Ireland as Lord Deputy in 1565. Though the two were different aspects of the same impulse, let us look at the campaign for colonising first. The decade 1565–75 was characterised by marked colonial activity in Ireland ; there were several important colonial ventures pressed forward by private individuals with the encouragement of the government, which would not, however, undertake the expense itself. The point was put by Sidney to Cecil, who was as actively interested in this as in all other concerns of government. " Now for the main of Ulster, too true it is that the charges will be intolerable for her Majesty, as I fear either to defend that province with soldiers or to plant it with people at her own charges ; and yet one of these two ways must needs be taken before reformation or revenue can be looked for. And therefore, in my opinion, persuasion should be used amongst the nobility and principal gentlemen of England that there might, at sundry men's charges, without exhausting of the Prince's particular purse, be induced here some colony. If it were to the number of 2000 men or more, here were room enough for them ; but they must be so furnished with money, apparel, victuals and means to till the ground and seed for the same, as if they should imagine to find nothing here but earth. And, indeed, little else shall they find saving only flesh, and some beasts for earing of the ground."[1] That is to say, the country in mind was not cultivated; it was given up in the usual lazy Celtic fashion to herds of poor cattle.[2]

This was the moment to tackle the variegated mess that was Ireland. Elizabeth's government, after surmounting the initial dangers of the change-over from Mary's bankrupt régime, was now firm in the saddle ; the Reformation impulse could go forward with no restrictions or inhibitions upon its achievements in the material world. The Elizabethans themselves, as usual, were perfectly conscious of the moment and its opportunity. " England was never that can be heard of fuller of people than it is at this day."[3] And they were aware of what this owed to the ending of monasticism : " such younger brothers as were wont to be thrust into abbeys there to live an idle life, since that is now taken from them, must now seek some other place to live in ". The dynamism of modern society was beginning to operate upon the more essentially static character of medieval life.

These early colonial ventures in Ireland all came to nothing much ; but they have their significance, not only in what they foreshadowed for Ireland—the substitution of English society for Celtic in that island—but, what was vastly more important for the world, in pointing the way to the English colonisation of America. These efforts in Ireland in the sixties and seventies

---

[1] D. B. Quinn, " Sir Thomas Smith (1513–77) and the Beginnings of English Colonial Theory ", *Proc. Amer. Phil. Soc.*, vol. 89, 544.

[2] Cf. George Owen on the Welsh part of Pembrokeshire, *The England of Elizabeth*, 76-7.

[3] Quinn, *loc. cit.* 552.

were the immediate precursors of the efforts across the Atlantic
in the eighties. Ireland was on the way to America.

And what is fascinating to observe is that the colonising efforts
in America were due to the very same West Country group
that had gained its hard-won experience, and not been put off
by its rebuffs, in Ireland :[1] Humphrey Gilbert, Grenville and
the St. Legers, Ralegh—Philip Sidney wanted to go on an
American voyage—with Drake hovering on and off in the haze
at sea.

It is not generally realised that Gilbert wrote his famous
Discourse on the North-West Passage to Cathay in Ireland. It
was natural for someone with West Country and Irish perspect-
ives to advocate the Atlantic route to the Far East, as against
the Londoners of the Muscovy Company with their hopes of a
Siberian coast route. Sidney had gone to Ireland with a scheme
to set up a Presidency in Munster and Connaught, *i.e.* direct
government, instead of relying on the Anglo-Irish earls to manage
the provinces ; and he had an ardent desire to see Ulster divided
into shires and governed accordingly. In November 1566 he
sent Gilbert back to report to the Council on the state of Ulster.[2]
While in England Gilbert was in touch with his West Country
relations who were interested in the idea of planting Ulster ;
the Queen sent him back in July 1567 with power to negotiate
with the Lord Deputy, on behalf of " certain gentlemen of the
West parts of England ", about the plantation.[3] Shortly after,
Sir Arthur Champernowne, head of the family at Dartington,
repaired to Ireland to confer with Gilbert about it.[4] Now
Champernowne was the uncle of the three Gilberts and Ralegh,
and cousin of the Grenvilles and St. Legers. The Queen's
cousin and Vice-Chamberlain, Knollys, wanted Gilbert made
President of Ulster. But the government opted, on Shane
O'Neill's death, for indirect rule and supported the quieter and
more co-operative Turlough's succession. Meanwhile the West
Country's—and Gilbert's—interest had shifted to Munster.

---

[1] This does not appear to me to be sufficiently brought out in Professor Quinn's
valuable essay on Sir Thomas Smith. It is not realised at all by Professor Howard
Mumford Jones, in his " Origins of the Colonial Idea in England ", *Proc. Amer.
Phil. Soc.*, vol. 85, 488 foll., which omits the career of Grenville, the obvious and
unmistakable link between Irish and American colonisation. It is true that these
two interesting essays are dealing with theory ; but it is the practice that matters.

[2] *Cal. S.P. Ireland, 1509–73*, 318.

[3] *Ibid.* 340.   [4] *Ibid.* 342.

Sir Warham St. Leger was the son of Henry VIII's Lord Deputy and had continued his father's association with Ireland.[1] He was on friendly terms with Desmond ; indeed, so friendly that he incurred the hostility of Ormonde at Court, who stopped him from ever being made President of Munster, which it was his aim to be. St. Leger had lent Desmond considerable sums of money, and in return Desmond had mortgaged to him several large estates around Cork, the castle of Carrigaline, the abbey of Traghton and the whole district of Kerrycurrihy. Observe that the West Country undertakers in Munster gained their first entry in this peaceful way and not by conquest. St. Leger brought into partnership with him young Richard Grenville, just back from fighting in the plains of Hungary, who had married a St. Leger cousin. Grenville took over a small number of Devon men in a " tall ship " of his. He and St. Leger were engaged in settling their lands and breaking them in when James Fitzmaurice and the MacCarthy Mór broke into open rebellion, spoiled all the inhabitants of Kerrycurrihy and put all the men in Traghton Abbey to the sword. Gilbert was put in command of the forces sent south, with the new title of Colonel of the army in Munster. He crushed Fitzmaurice's rising with much severity, and there made his reputation ; but he did not become President of Munster. Elizabeth did not often make her swordsmen governors. This, however, was the end of St. Leger's and Grenville's first effort : they had put energy and capital into it ; they had lost it all and they had lost men's lives. It was symbolic of all such efforts in Ireland.

On the borders of Ulster several ventures were undertaken, of which the most interesting was that of Sir Thomas Smith, Secretary of State, scholar and projector.[2] His ideas were somewhat influenced by his classical reading on the subject of colonisation. He got a grant from the Crown of the most eligible district of Ulster—the Ards peninsula, that undulating, cultivable country between Belfast Lough and Strangford Lough afterwards so successfully planted from Scotland. The colony was to be led by Smith's son, Thomas, and through a propaganda drive (complete with promoters' literature, anticipating the advance across the Middle West to California) over seven hundred men

---

[1] The above paragraph is summarised from the fuller account in my *Sir Richard Grenville of the ' Revenge '*, 64-70.

[2] Cf. Quinn, *loc. cit.*

were assembled at Liverpool by May 1572. The government in Dublin was alarmed by threats of rebellion among the Irish of the territory ; the expedition was held back, supplies were exhausted and Smith landed in late summer with only a hundred men. Characteristic ! He was met with armed opposition by Sir Brian MacPhelim O'Neill, lord of the country, and the Irish destroyed all the stone buildings of any size, chiefly abbeys and churches, which could give the colonists shelter through the winter. Nevertheless, in spite of much hardship, a nucleus of them lasted through the winter at Newcastle Comber, though the reinforcements sent in the spring never reached them. That summer the natives in Smith's employment suddenly attacked his household and murdered him. A rising followed and the colonists were driven out, to take refuge with the old Anglo-Irish Savages in the Lower Ards.

Already a much more ambitious scheme had taken shape : that of the first Earl of Essex for the conquest and settlement of the territories of Antrim, a sort of no-man's-land disputed between Irish and Scots, and of the frontier country between the Pale and Ulster. In Walter Devereux we can trace the lineaments of his more famous son : they were those of an Elizabethan romantic adventurer : a careless, generous nobility of bearing, a certain glamour, the appeal of pathos somewhere in the personality, for the element of overstrain upon a sensitive nervous system led to defeat and suffering—and then, the neurotic rift, the undependable streak leading to irresponsible actions. The first Essex, like his son, wanted to win renown by noble deeds : he was prepared to sacrifice life and fortune to achieve it. He put up a scheme on a large scale, for a private individual : he was to contribute 200 horse and 400 foot, the Queen a like number ; he pledged his whole patrimony and drew in a considerable following.[1] There was the rich Lord Rich, the remarkable old buccaneer Sir Peter Carew, a number of other Devon men— Sir Arthur Champernowne, Henry Sydenham, Francis Kellaway, with a number of Welsh followers like William Morgan of Pen-y-coed. The Council—Burghley, Sussex, Leicester, usually so divided—were at one in supporting the scheme ; only the Queen was doubtful. Sir Thomas Smith wrote to Burghley, who had contributed handsomely to Smith's own project : " Her Majesty remaineth in one opinion for my Lord of Essex. I trust

---

[1] Cf. Bagwell, II. 240 foll.

it will continue, and his lordship had needs make much haste. The time draweth away, and winds be changeable, and minds."[1] She had been persuaded against her better judgment.

Landed in Ireland, Essex at once ran into difficulties which his temperament was ill-fitted to subdue. There was the fundamental trouble, in Elizabethan conditions—that which accounted for the failure of all colonial enterprises—of ensuring a steady and continuous stream of supplies. There was disease— and Essex had particular ill-luck in running into plague. His men died around him like flies. He slept out among them to give them encouragement ; it only undermined his health. The Queen wrote to thank him for his services, " acknowledging the same to have been grounded not upon gain, but upon honour, an argument of true nobility ".[2] She saw that the venture was failing : Essex for all his efforts could get no leverage on the situation ; he could not get into contact with the O'Neills, let alone force them to come to terms with him : they saw that his effort was failing and that they need not take him seriously. Distracted and despairing, Essex fell back upon a piece of desperate treachery against Sir Brian MacPhelim. It is true that the latter was an enemy and had wrecked the Smiths' settlement in the Ards. But he came to Belfast with his wife and half-brother as the Earl's guests, and Essex had them whisked away and executed. This breach of the conventions of hospitality redoubled the offence in Celtic eyes. Nor did Essex's expedition against the Scots on Rathlin Island—with young Francis Drake, captain of the *Falcon*, in the offing—achieve anything except a massacre and a disgrace : it did not stop the Scots from coming in.

Nothing could stop them except the conquest of Ulster ; and this could only be achieved by the power and the forces of the Lord Deputy. Here, in Sidney's absence, while Fitzwilliam was Deputy, Essex found obstruction rather than help : the usual tale. Failing, he appealed to the Queen : he wished for the authority and powers of the office. But Elizabeth would never confer the office upon someone already in possession of a territorial appanage, as Essex was of Antrim. Discouraged, he returned to England. The Queen consoled him with majestic words, as only she knew how : " for by the decay of those things that are subject to corruption and mortality, you have, as

---

[1] Cf. Bagwell, II. 241.　　　　　　　　　[2] *Ibid.* 271.

it were, invested yourself with immortal renown, the true mark that every honourable mind ought to shoot at ".[1] That meant that she had made up her mind to abandon the scheme, but she gave Essex generous compensation—a barony in Monaghan, Island Magee and the office of Earl Marshal in Ireland for life. His life was not long : shortly after his return to duty, Essex died of dysentery, bequeathing to the Queen the care of his son.

Nor did anything come of smaller attempts in these years to make military settlements in the frontier districts : the grants to Captains Malby and Chatterton of land in the Fews, the exposed country, all wood and bog, that was the frontier between the Pale and Armagh.[2] Sidney, on his return in 1575, found that these efforts too had come to nothing : the natives on the soil were so many, the English inhabitants so few. The two Chattertons had been pertinacious in disaster " to wrastle and work and go to the worst ". It was all pitiful, " for they be tall and honest gentlemen and have lost in that enterprise all that ever they have and all that anybody else would trust them with, and their blood and limbs too ". Next year their grant was revoked.

These Celts, who were no good at cultivating their own land, were very good at breeding, and driving out those who could have made a good job of it. In the end, a good job was made ; but the conquest of Ulster had to come first.

In the 1580s the suppression of the Desmond Rebellion in Munster provided the biggest opportunity, so far, for planting ; for some half a million acres were declared forfeit by the Earl's treason. The Rebellion was over by 1583, but Munster was left in a terrible plight: the memory of it remained with Spenser the rest of his days. Here was one difficulty in the way of settlement ; the second was in the delays imposed by the size and complexity of the operation. In 1584 a commission was appointed to survey the immense area ; in 1585 a plan for peopling Munster was drawn up ; in 1586 it was amended. Meanwhile the Irish came seeping back and were as good as anybody else at taking advantage of the intricacies of the law to pursue their claims : no doubt it was hard to find anybody who had taken part in the Rebellion or were involved in Desmond's treason. The claims were so

[1] *Ibid.* 325.
[2] Cf. R. Dunlop, "Sixteenth Century Schemes for the Plantation of Ulster", *Scottish Hist. Rev.*, XXII. 118.

complicated that it was necessary to employ a whole posse of lawyers, headed by no less a person than Chief Justice Anderson. In the event, the land was allotted in estates of 12,000, 8000 and 4000 acres, with the usual promoter's boost : " You may keep a better house in Ireland for £50 a year than in England for £200 a year ".[1] No doubt—provided you could keep it at all. Among those at Court who did their duty and took up lands on a large scale were Hatton and Ralegh. Among those who had West Country associations were Sir Warham St. Leger, who returned to his last, Sir William Courtenay, Francis Berkeley, Sir George Bourchier, Sir William Herbert. One sees what an appropriate field for West Country enterprise when one looks at those wonderful harbours and estuaries, Waterford, Youghal, Kinsale, Cork, yawning towards Devon. Among the undertakers in Cork was Edmund Spenser, Deputy Clerk to the Council of Munster, his fortunes irretrievably committed to the country he came, like Swift, to detest. He took up some 3000 acres at an initial rent of £8 : 13 : 9, which was doubled as he improved the land.[2] He seated himself in what had been a small castle of the Desmonds. The trouble made for him by his Anglo-Irish neighbour, Lord Roche, was symptomatic of the feeling of the old settlers for the new undertakers. Spenser had reason to lament

My luckless lot
That banished had myself, like wight forlore,
Into that waste, where I was quite forgot.

Worse was to come. If there was one thing that was worse than to be forgotten in Ireland, it was to be remembered.

For a year or two after the Armada, Ralegh and Grenville—who could not now, in the circumstances of the war with Spain, carry their efforts to plant a colony in America to completion —reverted to Ireland and were the most active and energetic of the undertakers in Munster. Ralegh took up some 12,000 acres to begin with, started to bring over West Country settlers, set to work with his usual energy to repair and rebuild Lismore Castle[3]—finished, like so many of his enterprises, by another hand : it became the magnificent residence of the most magnificent of undertakers, Richard Boyle, first Earl of Cork. There

---

[1] q. Maxwell, 245.   [2] Bagwell, III. 199.
[3] E. Edwards, *Life of Sir Walter Ralegh*, I. 96.

it remains, singularly untouched, high up on its ridge above the park in the river-valley below—the only great house of its kind and period comparable to the many in England, as it might be Levens or Powys, Skipton or Appleby. Ralegh directed his enterprises from the College hard by the churchyard at Youghal, oozing with damp and melancholy, green with luxuriant vegetation, fern and foliage : in the garden here he is said to have introduced the root so fatal to Ireland.

Grenville took up again his partnership with St. Leger ; by May 1589 he had brought over 99 settlers, St. Leger 46.[1] A number of Grenville's family circle accompanied him : his second son, John ; his half-brother, John Arundell, who had made a Virginia voyage with him ; two brothers-in-law, John Bellew and Thomas Stukeley ; Christopher Harris, who became his son-in-law. Grenville spent the winter of 1588–9, most of 1589 and 1590 in Munster, working hard at the plantation he had undertaken : one-half of the barony of Kinallmeky, in addition to his former possessions in Kerrycurrihy. This made the Grenville interests at this moment the largest in Munster, and Grenville intended to stay there and make a success of them : " whereas I, having settled my mind to follow the planting of the seignory that I have undertaken, am for some years to make my abode in that country. . . ."[2] He built himself a house out of Gilly Abbey—reminiscent of Buckland, the house in Devon he made out of the abbey church. Like all the undertakers, he had much trouble and endless delays in getting his patents through. No sooner had he got them settled than he was called away to the service that ended at Flores and that " immortal renown " of which the Queen had written to Essex. With Ralegh's disgrace and his rustication to the West Country, he could no longer be on the spot to direct his operations and interests in Munster. In the end, both Ralegh's and Grenville's grants fell into the maw of Richard Boyle, who did well with them ; but that was not until the fate of Ireland had been settled at Kinsale.

With Grenville and Ralegh gone, the two most forward spirits were withdrawn from the hopeful plantation. The rest were nothing like so active : a commission of 1592 found that of fifty-eight undertakers only thirteen were resident, and that there

---

[1] Cf. for a full account, my *Sir Richard Grenville*, c. xv.
[2] *Ibid.* 281.

were only 245 English families settled on the land.[1] Instead of letting the lands to English tenants, building up a yeomanry as the intention was, transplanting the strength and solidity of the English social scheme, the lands were being let to the native Irish, who were prepared to pay more to return to their own. It was this that constituted the fatal danger to the plantation and accounted for the suddenness of its overthrow, when Tyrone's victory at the Yellow Ford in 1598 threatened the whole of English rule in Ireland. " The Munster Rebellion broke out like a lightning, for in one month's space almost all the Irish were in rebellious arms, and the English were murdered, or stripped and banished. . . . And to speak truth, Munster undertakers above mentioned, were in great part cause of this defection, and of their own fatal miseries. For whereas they should have built castles and brought over colonies of English, and have admitted no Irish tenant, but only English, these and like covenants were in no part performed by them. . . . All entertained Irish servants and tenants, which were now the first to betray them." [2]   The sudden horror is brought home to us in a flash in the familiar story of Spenser's flight from Kilcolman, the firing of the castle, the burning of a child in the flames, the death of England's foremost poet from the shock and the privations with which his life in Ireland had come to an end.

Let us turn now to the other, and more potent, aspect of English expansion : the extension of direct rule, a process that went forward inevitably, with halts and recessions, until it was completed by a Scottish king ruling in Elizabeth's place. Of the inner governing circle at Elizabeth's accession both Sussex and Sidney had had experience of Irish affairs. Sidney may be regarded as a key-figure in the unfolding process, the Deputy who set the pattern that was not always followed and that yet ultimately prevailed. We have an insight into the Queen's mind in a remarkable letter she wrote him about composing the quarrel between Ormonde and Desmond in the interest of good government—her archaic spellings matching her sententious idiosyncratic style are themselves a revelation of that extraordinary young woman (she was now thirty-one) : they were deliberate and must have been what she considered appropriate to her

[1] J. C. Beckett, *A Short History of Ireland*, 60.
[2] q. Maxwell, 249-50.

royal person. "Harry, If our partial slendar Managing of the
contentious Quarrell betwine the two Irische Irells, did not make
the Way to cause thes Lines to passe my Hande, this Gebourest
[gibberish] shuld hardly have cumbered your Yees ; but,
warned by my former Fault, and dreading worsar Hap to come,
I rede you [=counsel you], take good hede that the good Subjects
lost State be so revenged, that I here not the rest be won to
a right By-way to brede more Traytors Stoks, and so the Gole is
gone. Make some Difference betwixt tried, just, and false Frinde.
Let the good Servis of well Desarvers be never rewarded with
Los. Let ther Thank be suche as may incorege mo Strivars for
the like." This was a hint to favour Ormonde against Desmond,
whom Elizabeth always distrusted and detested : she could not
like a man who combined physical debility with instability of
character and mind : a pathetic creature in a princely place.
"Prometheus let me be, and Prometheus hathe bine myne to
long. I pray God your olde strainge Shepe late (as you say)
retorned in to Fold, wore not her wolly Garment upon her
wolvy Bak. You knowe a Kingdom knowes no Kindered, *Si
violandum jus regnandi causa*. A Strength to harme is perilous, in
the Hande of an ambitious Hed. Wher Myght is mixt with Wit,
ther is to good an Accord in a Government. Essayes be oft
dangerous, specially whan the Cupberar hathe receved suche a
Presarvatif, as, what met so ever betide the Drinkars Draught,
the Carier takes no Baine therby. . . . If I had not espied, thogh
very late, *Leger de main*, used in thes Cases, I had never plaid my
Part. No, if I did not se the Balances holde awry, I had never
my selfe come into the Wayhous. I hope I shall have so good a
Coustumer of you, that all under Officers shall do ther Duty
amonge you. If aught have bine amys at Home, I wyll pache,
thogh I cannot hole it. . . . Let this Memoriall be only committed
to Vulcanes base Keping. Without any longer Abode, than the
Leasure of the Reding therof, yea, and with no Mention made
therof to any other Wight. I charge you, as I may comande
you. Seme not to have had but Secretaries Letters from me.
Your lovinge Maistres, Elizabeth R." [1]

Herein we may read the Queen's secret mind ; thus did she
encourage her faithful servants and inspire their service.

In the early months of 1567 Sidney made a state journey
through southern Ireland to look into things for himself and pull

[1] Collins, *op. cit.* I. 7-8.

government, so far as possible, together. On his return he rendered a remarkable report to the Queen. Disputes between the Irish lords for the captainries of countries were endemic ; they were particularly rife on the borders of the great lordships— for example, the attacks of the younger MacGillapatricks upon Ormonde's country of Kilkenny. Sidney had consigned two of them to prison, " but surely it will never be throughly well, till the same be made shire-ground and your Highness' writ current there as in your other counties ".[1] This was Sidney's constant theme, the insufficiency of the officers under the chiefs to govern and the necessity to replace them with sheriffs and regular English administration : " if you will have that country free from the annoyance of their neighbours, your Majesty must plant (as I have often written) justice to be resident in those quarters ". The lesser lords, who suffered from the depredations and encroachments of the greater, were at this stage in favour of the extension of the Queen's rule : the gentlemen of Cork, MacCarthys, Lords Barry and Roche, and others " with open mouth and held-up hands to heaven cried out for justice and that it might please your Majesty to cause your name to be known amongst them, with reverence and your laws obeyed ; offering to submit themselves, life, lands and goods, to the same. Besides all these lords' and gentlemen's possessions, the Earl of Desmond enjoyeth under his rule, or rather tyranny, the third part of this great county, which, I assure your Majesty, to be greater than all Yorkshire. In all which his limits, neither is your name reverenced, nor your laws obeyed. Neither dare any sheriff execute any part of his office therein."[2]

Instead, Desmond ruled as he willed, a more absolute ruler in his province than the Queen was in England. And Sidney found him recalcitrant : " from this time forward, nor never since, found I any willingness in the Earl of Desmond to come to any conformity or good order, but always wayward and unwilling to do anything at my appointment that might further the weal of the country or your Majesty's service : your name no more reverenced, nor letters of commandment obeyed, than it would be in the kingdom of France ". This was the root of the trouble : the extension of direct rule meant the end of the independence of the Irish princes, and those who were strong enough—or thought themselves so—to resist were in the end driven to do so :

[1] Collins, *op. cit.* I. 18.　　　　　　　　[2] *Ibid.* 23.

first Desmond, then O'Neill and O'Donnell. It is possible that if the Queen had been willing wholly to back Sidney in a more thorough-going policy at this stage, they might have been able to drive a wedge between these princes and the lesser lords, and attach the latter to the government. That was always the argument of the Deputies on the spot. But they were over-ruled : it was the line of least resistance, it was less expensive, to go on mistrustfully giving half-confidence to the great houses. The Irish princes had their supporters or sympathisers at court ; financial stringency, the Queen's conservatism—she never wanted a great house overthrown—pointed the same way. Here, it turned out, she was wrong : subsequent history showed that half-measures were never any good in Ireland. But, as usual, she was not wholly wrong : the policy worked perfectly well with Ormonde and, after a fashion, with Turlough O'Neill. Desmond was incapable of governing ; Tyrone, on the other hand, was very capable, either by Irish, or even English, standards.[1]

The results in Munster were shocking : " like as I never was in a more pleasant country in all my life, so never saw I a more waste and desolate land, no, not in the confines of other countries where actual war hath continually been kept by the greatest princes of Christendom. And there heard I such lamentable cries and doleful complaints made by that small remain of poor people which yet are left. Who, hardly escaping the fury of the sword and fire of their outrageous neighbours, or the famine with the same, which their extortious lords hath driven them unto, either by taking their goods from them, or by spending the same by their extort taking of coign and livery, make demonstration of the miserable estate of that country. Besides this, such horrible and lamentable spectacles there are to behold as the burning of villages, the ruin of churches, the wasting of such as have been good towns and castles ; yea, the view of the bones and skulls of the dead subjects, who, partly

---

[1] Everyone pays tribute to Tyrone's ability. Spenser calls him " very subtle-headed " and Camden says : " a strong body he had, able to endure labour, watching and hunger ; his industry was great, his mind great and able for the greatest businesses ; much knowledge he had in military skill and a mind most profound to dissemble, insomuch as some did then foretell that he was born to the very great good or hurt of Ireland ".

What a pity it was that his stock could not have married with the Stuarts, so that an Irish dynasty, after a Welsh and Scottish, upon the English throne might have completed the unity of these islands !

by murder, partly by famine, have died in the fields ; as, in truth, any Christian with dry eyes could behold. Not long before my arrival there . . . a principal servant of the Earl of Desmond, after that he had burnt sundry villages and destroyed a great piece of a country, there were certain poor women sought to have been preserved ; but too late. Yet so soon after the horrible fact committed as their children were felt and seen to stir in the bodies of their dead mothers. And yet did the same Earl lodge and banquet in the house of the same murderer his servant, after the fact committed."[1] Such was the Earl of Desmond's justice and order of government in his own country in time of peace.

" I found the like of the whole county of Limerick and the country of Thomond (through which I travelled) as well for desolation, waste and ruins of the country, as also for the lack of reverence to your name, obedience to your laws and evil disposition of the people. . . . From thence I went to your Highness' town of Galway, the state whereof I found rather to resemble a town of war, frontiering upon an enemy, than a civil town in a country under one sovereign. They watch their walls nightly and guard their gates daily with armed men."[2] Sidney concluded, " if I have any judgment, your Majesty may easily perceive there is no way for reformation of these two provinces but by planting justice by Presidents and Councils in each of them ".[3] Now was the time : he pleaded with the Queen to go through with it.

Sidney's plea was answered and Presidencies—*i.e.* direct governments—were set up for Munster and Connaught. He had wanted St. Leger for Munster, but a Devonshireman, Sir John Pollard, was appointed, who never arrived. Edmund Tremayne, Clerk of the Council (and Grenville's brother-in-law), was sent over to explain and to report.[4] In the interval James Fitzmaurice's rebellion had broken out and Munster was aflame. Perrot was given the job and he did not despair. Wales and the North had been reduced to order by direct rule, and why not Munster ? " Came it to perfection elsewhere in one year ? No, not in seven."[5] Perrot's actions were less philosophical : he soon was able to report that he had killed or hanged eight

---

[1] Collins, *op. cit.* I. 24.   [2] *Ibid.* 25, 28.
[3] *Ibid.* 29.   [4] *Cal. S.P. Ireland, 1509–73*, 412.
[5] *v.* Bagwell, *op. cit.* II. 221.

hundred persons with the loss of only eighteen Englishmen, but of course this was war (and the numbers certainly exaggerated).[1] The odd thing is that Perrot, in spite of his severity, his downrightness, was never unpopular with the Irish, either as President of Munster (1570–76) in which office he gained his reputation and was successful, or as Lord Deputy, an office which ultimately cost him his life : what the Irish liked was personality—and Perrot was intensely personal. Sir Edward Fitton, who was appointed President of Connaught, had no such personality and therefore no such success.[2] At first, he was more or less shut up in Galway, as one besieged, while the Burkes raged outside. Their father, the Earl—after a spell in Dublin Castle to encourage him—was more effective : " after being set at liberty, I did within one twelve-month hang my own son, my brother's son, and one of the captains of my gallowglass, besides fifty of my own followers that bare armour and weapons ; which the Archbishop of Tuam, the Bishop of Clonfert and the whole corporation of Galway may witness ".[3] Fitton was made for a quieter life : he has it now in the long silences of the church hard by the mere and his manor-house at Gawsworth : he was another of the band from the western perimeter of the country, from Cheshire through Wales to Cornwall, who took to colonial administration in Ireland.

Perrot recommended a President for Ulster, so that the Lord Deputy might be freed from the *corvée* of having to keep perpetual watch upon the confines of that province. The Queen would not hear of further expense : she thought Sidney's Presidencies already sufficiently expensive ; she detested the fact that Ireland was a constant drain upon her treasury and sought ways and means to make it pay for itself. Before James Fitzmaurice's rebellion was well over she cut down the army and cut short its supplies—so that the rising flickered on. Sidney was in despair ; and indeed these differences had wrecked the good understanding between them. In 1571 he returned from his second spell of rule in Ireland and enjoyed four years' intermission before his last spell, 1575–7.

---

[1] We should be careful always of accepting these too rough and ready figures, especially in Ireland, especially with people of Perrot's temperament.

[2] From his son's plaint to Cecil, we see something of the Elizabethan wastage in Ireland : " where I have buried my father, mother, three brethren and great part of my fortune ". *Salisbury MSS.* X. 18.

[3] *Ibid.* 218.

For the Queen it may be said that there was the chronic difficulty of knowing what or whom to believe : sooner or later everybody quarrelled and it was hard to learn the truth. In 1573 Tremayne was sent over again to make direct contact.[1] In Sidney's absence, Fitzwilliam, who had taken his place, was quarrelling with Fitton ; Tremayne advised Burghley to speak to them. The Queen spoke to them both. Tremayne commended Perrot's administration of Munster : " Law can take no place without the assistance of the sword ". Perrot had been accused of demanding ransom of a Portuguese ship : likely enough, up to his Pembrokeshire tricks. The Queen's instruments, unlike herself, were fallible. The Lord President procured a testimonial from the obliging Portuguese and the mayor of Cork to say that he had not. " This nation," he opined, " witty in taking hold of any occasion which may serve their purpose, are utterly unwise in finding their own good."[2]

Tremayne's " Discourse whether it be better to govern Ireland after the Irish manner or reduce it to the English government " is a whole-hearted plea for direct rule.[3] As a diagnosis of Irish ills, it is in line with most English opinion on the subject ; but the official, the embryo civil servant, isolates the irresponsible rule of the great lords as the intolerable thing, *fons et origo malorum.*[4] With his horsemen, gallowglass and kerne the great lord uses inferior people at his will and pleasure, without any means to withstand him, as an absolute king. By Brehon law he has a judge of his own making, and he can take revenge at his pleasure : " so as in short terms a many see the Irish rule is such a government as the mightiest do what they list against the inferiors ". As for the Anglo-Irish—" the sweetness and gain of this Irish government hath been such as it hath rather drawn our nation to become Irish than any way wrought the reformation of the Irishry to reduce them to English laws ". So, too, with land-tenure : the English there will "rather inhabit his land with the Irish of whom he may exact than with the English by whom he may be strengthened ". Even in the

---

[1] *Cal. S.P. Ireland, 1509–73*, 509, 510, 511, 515.
[2] *Ibid.* 516.
[3] British Museum, Titus B.XII, 358.
[4] Cf. St. Leger : " It is death to all the lords and chieftains of both factions to have English government come among them, for they know that if English government be established here, their Irish exactions is laid aground ; the which to forego, they had as lief die ". Bagwell, III. 105.

English Pale there is no law between lord and tenant other than the lord's will—hardly any makes leases for lives or years but turns the tenant out at pleasure, whereby the Pale is marvellously weakened, " and tenants neither build nor repair their houses, make neither gardens, orchards nor meadows, use no enclosures, nor in effect do anything else that may be to the bettering of their tenements ".

A whole world of difference is expressed in that sentence : the chasm between a pastoral society and a settled farming community. One sees the ordered life of the English countryside at the back of Tremayne's mind. The chief aim being to remove the exactions and tyrannies of the great lords, they should be brought to declare the limits of their territories, their tenants, who free and otherwise, and to arrive at a composition by which it is certainly known what the lord should receive and the tenant pay. Thus the lords should have no cause to complain of the taking away of coign and livery, while the poor tenants and farmers, " which be in effect the very nurses that give food to the land shall be marvellously eased and comforted when they may say unto themselves, ' This is ours, this is the lord's, during thus many years or thus many lives, without such exactions as hath been used aforetime '."

In 1585 a composition was arrived at for Connaught, the chief constructive achievement of Perrot's embarrassed (and embarrassing) term as Lord Deputy (1583–8). The leading figures of the province were all on the commission, the Earls of Clanricarde and Thomond, O'Connor Sligo, O'Rourke, O'Flaherty, etc., under the lead of Bingham as governor. They agreed to bring the old Irish system of tenure to an end and to go over to the English : in consideration that " her Majesty doth graciously mind the benefit and advancement of every good subject according to his degree by reducing of their uncertain and unlawful manner of taking from others to a certain and more beneficial state of living for them and their heirs than their said pretensed titles and claims did or could hitherto afford them . . .".[1] Each landholder was confirmed in his estate and given a new title good in English law. It was agreed that the old Irish exactions from the tenants should come to an end and that a quit-rent of 10s. for every quarter (*i.e.* 120 acres) should be paid to the Crown. Altogether the Crown achieved a revenue of less than £4000

---

[1] A. M. Freeman (ed.), *The Composition Book of Connaught*, 17.

a year from the province. The scheme worked out well for the Irish ; Connaught avoided a plantation policy, and a population overwhelmingly Celtic obtained security of tenure. All the same, it was upon an English basis : the antique Gaelic way of life was on the way out and plenty of people did not like it.

O'Rourke of Leitrim, for example, who had been generously treated and whose head was turned with pride, went into rebellion, thinking that his mountainous country was inaccessible. Four companies of English soldiers proved him wrong and the lesser chieftains who groaned under him were glad to be rid of him. He escaped to Scotland, where James surrendered him, and he ended, still offensively stiff-necked, at Tyburn. He had told the Council : " I have always thought that a great distance separated you from God and the saints, whose images alone I am accustomed to venerate ". Now he was to have an opportunity to verify that. Henceforth the freeholders of O'Rourke's country and their tenants were to enjoy their lands in succession according to the laws of England, no longer at the caprice of the native lord. That there were a great many of the simple people ready to respond to the English conception may be witnessed by the popularity of Perrot's declaration that he wished to suppress " the name of a churl and crushing of a churl " and to substitute husbandman, franklin or yeoman—an expression " carried from hand to hand throughout the whole realm in less time than might be thought credible ".[1] In the end, it was the English conception that prevailed.

There remained Ulster, the *ultima Thule* of Gaeldom, its most impenetrable stronghold. It was the desire to maintain their position as quasi-independent princes, and the fear of the creeping encroachments of the state, that drew Tyrone and Hugh Roe O'Donnell into the last and greatest of the rebellions —an Irish war proper—which consumed the Queen's last years, her energies and her treasure. This war cost her £1 million in itself ; it is said that Ireland cost her treasury not less than £2 millions all told. To do her duty the Queen sold lands right and left, Church lands that had come to the Crown by the Dissolution, and even manors of the royal Duchies that had to be recovered in James's reign. As the famous old woman lay dying, Tyrone was on his way to surrender, at last—after a

[1] Bagwell, III. 124.

tremendous resistance—to her representative. Mountjoy sent
his Cornish friend (an admirable fighting soldier), Sir William
Godolphin, to hasten the Earl, for he had had private word
that the Queen was already dead. However, at Mellifont Abbey—
in that pretty, secluded valley by the sounding stream—Tyrone
made humble submission to the representative who was no
longer the Queen's representative : the fox was foxed at last.
When the great man learned the truth, he shed bitter tears—it
was said by hostile observers, tears of rage. Perhaps so. But
at such moments men are torn by conflicting emotions ; and
might there not have been elements of genuine regret and
sorrow for all the years of misery and bloodshed, of sympathy
even for the woman locked in her duty, now dead at her task,
for all the fatality and pathos of the human condition ? Perhaps
he wept for her, as well as for himself.

On his way through Wales, Tyrone was pelted by women-
folk who had lost their husbands, sons and brothers in Ireland.
But at Court the Ulster princes were well received and treated
generously : their vast estates were in the main restored and
they went back to a splendid patrimony. They were, however,
no longer independent princes and they could not accustom
themselves to it : with every year that passed they felt themselves
being hemmed in, their power undermined. Hugh Roe O'Donnell
had left Ireland for Spain after the disaster of Kinsale and died
there—it is said, of poison ; he was succeeded by his brother,
who was made Earl of Tyrconnell. One September day in 1607,
a French ship put into Lough Swilly, close by Rathmullen, where
one sees by the shore an abbey church transformed into a
Jacobean house—all one ruin now. Next day there came aboard
the two earls, Tyrone's sons and his nephew, Tyrconnell's
brother and his family, Cuconnaught Maguire—almost all the
native nobility of Ulster and their seed, who were leaving
Ireland for ever. It was 3 September, the birthday of the Queen
who, from her grave, had impelled them to go. It was a moment
that must appeal to the imagination, as it has done to that of
the Irish ever since.

The flight of the Earls opened the way to the plantation of
Ulster : their treason was assumed and the immense area over
which they had exercised lordship declared forfeit to the Crown.
The way this worked out was rather different from, and much
more complex than, popularly supposed. It did not mean a

transplantation of the native population : there was room both for them and for incoming settlers by better cultivation of the land. It did mean general changes in its ownership, though these differed from county to county. And, as a result, the way was clear to bring in English and, still more, Scottish settlers to cultivate the land properly and form agricultural communities, nuclei of a more efficient civilisation. It was this that was to change the character of Ulster and make much of it different from the rest of Ireland : this and the Protestantism the settlers brought in with them.

Lord Deputy Chichester made a journey through Ulster to see for himself the state of affairs and lay the foundations of English county government. He selected the places for the establishment of market and corporate towns and for the erection of free schools. He reserved to himself the ultimate decision as to the ownership of land, the lists of freeholders, et cetera. He was accompanied by the Lord Chancellor and Attorney-General Davies who held sessions of gaol delivery in every county, and instructed and admonished the justices of the peace. Davies described it all in a letter to Robert Cecil, now Earl of Salisbury, noting with some astonishment that their train was only some 50 or 60 horse and 120 foot, where hitherto no Lord Deputy had ever ventured with less than an army of 800 or 1000 men. The wildness of it may be imagined from what he says of Fermanagh : " the building of a gaol and sessions-house was likewise respited until my Lord Deputy had resolved of a fit place for a market and a corporate town, for the habitations of this people are so wild and transitory as there is not one fixed village in all this county ".[1] Cavan had two bishoprics in the hand of one bishop ; " but there is no divine service or sermon to be heard within either of his dioceses ".

This journey was followed by a series of commissions to survey the available lands in the counties, to hold inquisitions, allot those that were for native holders and apportion what was to be offered to incoming settlers. The counties of Down and Antrim were not essentially changed : in the latter the Scots from the isles remained undisturbed in the possessions the Queen had recognised to them : there they remained, a Gaelic and Catholic element, amid the Scottish Lowlanders arriving—the

[1] Cf. Morley, *op. cit.* 374, 378.

new factor in the situation, which the union of the crowns had made possible. Monaghan was left to its native owners ; with the result that when the rest of Ulster was, by the time of the Civil War, " full of persons of quality of British birth and of civilly educated Irish, who are even sheriffs, justices of the peace etc. . . . to this day the county is the most barbarous, poor and despicable in the kingdom ".[1] It would be. We find Chichester pleading the case of the natives of Tyrone, Armagh and Coleraine (Londonderry) as having come off less well than the inhabitants of Donegal, Fermanagh and Cavan, though they had " reformed themselves in their habit and course of life beyond others, and the common expectation held of them, for all that were able had put on English apparel and promised to live in townreds (townships) and to leave their creaghting ".[2] Chichester had managed, against the persuasions of their priests, to clear some six hundred of Tyrone's swordsmen off to Sweden, to fight to their hearts' content in Swedish wars. Some took themselves off into native Connaught ; others remained in the forest and bog-country, waiting for their revenge in 1641. The worst atrocities then were committed by precisely the people who had been most generously treated : the inhabitants of Monaghan and the Maguires.[3]

Clearance having been effected, the available lands were offered in lots of 1000, 1500 and 2000 acres. Lessons had been learned from the failure of previous attempts at plantation : this was to be a success. The mainstay of its success were the Lowland Scots, whom nothing could daunt. In came Montgomerys, Alexanders and, later, Cunninghams : whose descendants were to show themselves worthy of the tough stock they came from and to give transcendent service to the state. Mrs. Montgomery was able to write that the king had bestowed on her husband three Irish bishoprics, " the names of them I cannot remember, they are so strange, except one, which is Derry : I pray God it may make us all merry ".[4] Next year she was able to report : " We are settled in the Derry, in a very pretty little house, builded after the English fashion, but some- what with the least for our company ; but we will make it

[1] q. Maxwell, *op. cit.* 298.
[2] *Ibid.* 275. Creaghting meant the habit of moving about the country in a body along with their cattle—appropriate to a pastoral society.
[3] Cf. Falls, *The Birth of Ulster*, 106, 234.
[4] *Trevelyan Papers* (Camden Soc.), III. 79, 99-102.

bigger if you and Peggy will promise to come and dwell with us ". Not all fashions were English : " the most that I do mislike is that the Irish doth often trouble our house, and many times they doth lend to us a louse, which makes me many times remember my daughter Jane, which told me that if I went into Ireland I should be full of lice ".

No doubt there were other amenities to sweeten life in Ireland and make it more agreeable to English settlers or exiles. For one thing we know it was always cheaper. We find the young Fulke Greville with Captain Bingham in 1580 climbing " a crag to fetch an eagle from its nest ", and entertaining Sir Nicholas White, Master of the Rolls in Ireland, in Greville's cabin, " full of books and charts ". We have a delightful description, in a Latin poem by Captain Josias Bodley—the military engineer, who was governor of Newry—of his keeping Christmas with Sir Richard Moryson at Lecale and of the entertainments there : the maskers coming in after dinner with ivy leaves sewn on their shirts, with masks of dog-skin and paper-noses ; dice and skewer-the-goose were played, opponents sitting on the floor with elbows and knees locked by a wooden bar and aiming at rolling each other over.[1] At a prosperous town, like Waterford (but there were very few), good entertainment could be had : Sidney reported that there he was " in such honorable manner received and entertained as might better have been thought worthy gracious acceptation if it had been done to your most princely Majesty, than to be looked for of so mean a subject as I am ".[2] On a higher plane, we have the intellectual discourse at Ludovic Brisket's cottage just outside Dublin, where the company included Dr. Long, Archbishop of Armagh (he had plenty of leisure, no doubt), Sir Robert Dillon, Dr. Dormer, the Queen's Solicitor, Captain Christopher Carlisle, Captain Thomas Norris, Captain Warham St. Leger (all these were to make their names), and Lord Deputy Grey's secretary, Edmund Spenser. To them Spenser imparted that he had undertaken a work in heroical verse " to represent all the virtues, assigning to every virtue a knight to be the patron and defender of the same ", in short, the plan of the *Faerie Queene* ; and all the company " showed an extreme longing after his work of the *Faerie Queene*, whereof some parcels had been by some of them

[1] Cf. E. M. Hinton, *Ireland through Tudor Eyes*, 63 foll.
[2] Collins, *op. cit.* I. 21.

seen ".[1] We have noticed that very few of the English were interested in Irish antiquities and customs, they found them so barbarous ; only Spenser was sufficiently interested in Irish poetry as to " have caused divers of them to be translated unto me, that I might understand them. And surely they savoured of sweet wit and good invention, but skilled not of the goodly ornaments of poetry ; yet were they sprinkled with some pretty flowers of their natural device which gave good grace and comeliness unto them."[2]

What opportunities of fruitful intermingling, of that crossing of cultures from which such good things come, were lost ! What a contrast with the Welsh, who, accepting the assumptions of an efficient modern society, were going forward to manage their own affairs. The Irish could not, or would not—so they had it imposed on them. Perhaps the gap between Irish and English was too great to be bridged. All the same, the forcing of it—the necessity to force it even—makes a miserable story.

---

[1] But Briskett refers in his Preface to " this barbarous country of Ireland . . . where almost no trace of learning is to be seen and where the doctors of philosophy are the more needful because they are so geason [*i.e.* scarce] ". *v.* his *Discourse of Civil Life* (ed. 1606), 3, 26.

[2] Cf. Morley, *op. cit.* 114.

CHAPTER V

OCEANIC VOYAGES

NOTHING—with the exception perhaps of our literature—illustrates more clearly and decisively than our sea-history a leading theme of this book : the backwardness, in the first half of the sixteenth century, of this country left behind by the new discoveries, impulses, experiences of the Renaissance in Europe, and the sudden catching up with a swoop of the national spirit, the soaring, dizzy ascent during the two or three decades at the turn of the century. That is the Elizabethan age we think of as such, and this is the clue to its achievement. During that short time more experience crowded in upon the mind of the English people, on land and at sea, in the opening up of contacts with new peoples all over the world, in the life of the imagination and spirit, than at any time before or since. Hence the unique importance of those decades in that memory of a people which is history. Everything happened to them new then, as if for the first time.

The English were the most backward of the significant peoples along the Atlantic littoral on the fairway to the New World. They did not follow up effectively such feelers as they put out : the fifteenth-century voyages from the port of Bristol in search of the fabled Atlantic island of Brazil (the Wars of the Roses were of more pressing importance), Cabot's voyages to Newfoundland with the backing of Henry VII. The Cornish Rebellions distracted the King's attention, and Cabot brought back neither gold nor spices. Perhaps England might have been more active if she had been in a lower latitude. As it was, for sixty years after the discovery of the New World not a single work of geographical importance was published here to witness to any English interest in the new age or its characteristic science.[1] Then with Edward VI's reign, the future of the country upon the seas, the importance of its gaining a stake in the outer world, engaged the attention of the leading spirit in the government,

[1] G. B. Parks, *Richard Hakluyt and the English Voyages*, 4-5.

Northumberland—whose significance in this regard has been little appreciated. After the hiatus of Mary, whose mind was elsewhere, the Edwardian impulse was carried forward, and immensely strengthened and accelerated in the leading circle round the Queen—with Elizabeth herself taking a very active, a sometimes disingenuous but always effective, hand. As has been said by an American scholar of the younger Hakluyt, " the span of his life, from 1552 to 1616, paralleled the rise of a larger England, an England stretching fingers of empire to East and West ".[1]

Nothing is more untrue than the Victorian saying that that empire came into being in a fit of absence of mind : nothing much is apt to come into being that way. It was the result rather of a conscious, deliberate and tenacious campaign—in face of constant disappointments, and confronting undreamed-of hazards—on the part of the elect spirits of the nation. It is true that the great majority of the nation were not interested by the spectacle or the prospects of a New World opening up beyond their ken ; nor in France any more than here. In this, as in other respects, it was the leaders that mattered ; fortunately the sea-coasts, the fisheries, provided plenty of mariners to follow—though they did not always follow : sometimes their spirit failing, the flesh weak, they turned back. Not so with their leaders, except a very occasional one like Edward Fenton, or Thomas Doughty : that rather intellectual type, clever and carping, and essentially destructive, got what he asked for, at the hands of Drake, at Port St. Julian in 1578. Many of the leading spirits of the age were concerned : the Queen herself ; Burghley, though less so ; Leicester inherited his father's interest and passed it on to his (illegitimate) son, Robert Dudley, who described himself as " having ever since I could conceive of anything been delighted with the discoveries of navigation " and who, during his later life in Italy, wrote an important work on geography ; Walsingham was even more interested, the patron of all the seamen : it was a Protestant activity. Courtiers like Hatton and Dyer were no less engaged : Drake changed the name of the *Pelican* to the *Golden Hind*, off the Straits of Magellan, in honour of Hatton whose crest it was ; Hakluyt owed a great deal to the early support of Sir Edward Dyer. That is to say nothing of the still more active spirits who took to the sea themselves. Then there were the intellects engaged, scientists,

[1] *Ibid.* 56.

geographers, mathematicians, navigators—such as John Dee, the Hakluyts, Hariot, Edward Wright ; or the sea-captains, whose names are legion. Nor must we forget the merchants, Garrards, Chesters, Duckets, Osbornes, men of imagination like Sanderson or Sir Thomas Smythe, despatching Anthony Jenkinson to Russia and Persia, Harborne to Constantinople, Ralph Fitch and Newberry to Persia and on to India, Thomas Roe to the court of the great Mogul at Agra. And all in the course of these few decades !

The truth is that it gradually became a national venture, even though few were conscious of the seismic change going on under the waters ; for a nation is as its leaders are. With the turn of the century and the approaching end of the war with Spain, public interest was aroused, as never before, by the Virginia enterprise, the whole question of planting English stock upon the coast of North America : people felt, not obscurely, that the future of the nation was involved—as indeed it was. Even the imagination of that quiet countryman, William Shakespeare—the least " engaged " writer that ever was—was touched. We know from one of the witches in *Macbeth* that he had read his Hakluyt :

> Her husband's to Aleppo gone, master of the ' Tiger ' ;

or from Othello's

> travel's history ;
> Wherein of antres vast and desarts idle,
> Rough quarries, rocks and hills whose heads touch heaven . . .
> And of the Cannibals that each other eat,
> The Anthropophagi and men whose heads
> Do grow beneath their shoulders.

The shipwreck of Sir George Somers' relief expedition to Virginia upon the Bermudas in 1609 struck Shakespeare's imagination, and out of it came *The Tempest*.

Underneath, bearing it all up, carrying the movement forward, was the prosaic fact of material economic expansion. The Dissolution of the Monasteries and the profitable dispersal of Church lands generated energy in the economic sphere as the Reformation did in the psychological—perhaps we may even say, the spiritual. That stimulus to energy was, however, general in operation ; it is only in the exceptional case of a Grenville that we can note a direct affiliation : he prepared his plans for a voyage to find Terra Australis from Buckland Abbey. More directly, the funds for the voyages came from commerce— as from the Hawkinses at Plymouth, from Sir Andrew Judde and William Chester, from the Levant merchants and such great entrepreneurs as Sir Lionel Ducket, Sanderson and Sir Thomas Smythe. (We have an appealing example of the closeness of contact in Sanderson's calling three of his sons after Ralegh, Drake and Cavendish.) Then, too, the courtiers themselves backed the voyages as best they could from their resources, somewhat frayed by the demands of conspicuous consumption. It is known that Ralegh spent more than £40,000 on his enterprises. The Queen herself was the greatest investor ; she was sometimes hard put to it to see that she got priority in the returns.

We have illustrated the internal expansion going on within the body of the society ; we have followed the expansion of society and the state into the backward borderlands. We have now to trace the widening rings of that impetus in expansion overseas, and later its concurrent evidences and consequences in the realms of the mind. The sudden upsurge, reaching out into all the oceans, is witnessed precisely by Hakluyt in his Epistle Dedicatory to Walsingham of the first edition of his marvellous book, *The Principal Navigations, Traffics and Discoveries of the English Nation.* Observe the significant date of its appearance : all through Armada Year Hakluyt was slaving at seeing the bulky volume through the press. It appeared the next year, with the frontal attack on Lisbon : another announcement that a naval power of the first rank had arrived. During his five years' residence in Paris, Hakluyt had " both heard in speech and read in books other nations miraculously extolled for their discoveries and notable enterprises by sea, but the English of all others for their sluggish security and continual neglect of the like attempts . . . either ignominiously reported or exceedingly condemned ".[1] But now he was able to claim, with the same clamorous emphasis of the newly arrived that rings through all the age—in Marlowe, Shakespeare, Ben Jonson, in Spenser, Ralegh and Bacon—that the English nation " in searching the most opposite corners and quarters of the world and, to speak plainly, in compassing the vast globe of the earth more than once, have excelled all the nations and peoples of the earth.

[1] R. Hakluyt, *The Principal Navigations* (Everyman edn.), I. 2.

For which of the kings of this land before her Majesty had their banners ever seen in the Caspian Sea ? Which of them hath ever dealt with the Emperor of Persia, as her Majesty hath done, and obtained for her merchants large and loving privileges ? Who ever saw before this regimen an English lieger in the stately porch of the Grand Signior at Constantinople ? Who ever found English consuls and agents at Tripolis in Syria, at Aleppo, at Babylon, at Basra and, which is more, who ever heard of Englishmen at Goa before now ? What English ships did heretofore ever anchor in the mighty river of Plate ? Pass and repass the unpassable (in former opinion) strait of Magellan, range along the coast of Chile, Peru and all the backside of Nova Hispania, further than any Christian ever passed, traverse the mighty breadth of the South Sea, land upon the Luçones [Philippines] in despite of the enemy, enter into alliance, amity and traffic with the princes of the Moluccas and the Isle of Java, double the famous Cape of Bona Speranza, arrive at the Isle of St. Helena, and last of all return home most richly laden with the commodities of China, as the subjects of this now flourishing monarchy have done ? "[1]

It is the authentic voice of the age. He pays the usual fervent tribute to the Queen, "whom I fear not to pronounce to have received the same heroical spirit and most honourable disposition, as an inheritance from her famous father" and to her "peerless government".[2] The Elizabethans meant that, and they had good reason.

But what lee-way they had to make up !

While the English were still obsessed by the entanglements of the Hundred Years' War with France, Portugal, under the inspired leadership of Prince Henry, had been planting the Atlantic islands and reaching out along the coast of Africa with the aim of reaching the East. Portugal owed her ultimate empire to the fixed idea, the constancy, the tenacity of this visionary, living out there alone by the Cape at Sagres, with his little court of astrologers, cosmographers, merchants, mariners. There ran in him that strain of chaste dedication that appeared elsewhere in the House of Lancaster : his cousin, Henry V, had it too. As one looks at the portrait of the Infante in Nuno Gonçalves's

[1] R. Hakluyt, *The Principal Navigations* (Everyman edn.), I. 3-4.   [2] *Ibid.* 4-5.

"Veneration of St. Vincent" at Lisbon, one sees an English face, honest, stubborn, self-controlled, with the mark of asceticism on the celibate features ; for his eyes are elsewhere, his will, as a contemporary said of him, " directed to some certain end not known to men ".[1]

The results of that life, of the impulse he fixed and directed, were astonishing : a small people of just over a million discovered half the world in the century following. With the acceptance of Columbus's offer, Castile followed, even more powerfully, with a larger population and resources, in the wake of Portugal and out-passed her : the lion's share of the New World fell to Spain. While the young Henry VIII was cavorting in France, Albuquerque was capturing Goa and the Moluccas and founding the Portuguese Empire in the East ; Balboa was advancing to his first sight of the Pacific for Spain. While Henry was showing off at the Field of the Cloth of Gold and Wolsey displaying "immense ability in achieving results that were not worth having ",[2] Cortés was conquering Mexico and his fellow-countrymen reaching the Philippines. During the years in which Henry was involved mainly in Anne Boleyn, Pizarro was conquering Peru and the conquistadors reaching out across South America, down the coast to Chile, along the Orinoco, over the cordilleras and the pampas to the River Plate. Early in the 1560s Urdaneta opened the regular Spanish route across the Pacific. But by now the English were themselves getting going. That decade had seen the liquidation of our last commit-ment on the Continent, and the defeat of our attempt to recover it. As continental historians see more clearly perhaps than we, the fact that we were thrown back on ourselves freed us from hampering preoccupations : we were so much the freer to launch out overseas.[3]

With France we see how her continental interests, and her internal conflicts, ruined the fair promise of her early Atlantic ventures.[4] For she was effectively in this field earlier than we were. Her hardy Breton and Norman fishermen were among the first in force off the Banks of Newfoundland. They went in for wet-fishing—*i.e.* taking their catch home to dry, where the

---

[1] Cf. E. Prestage, *The Portuguese Pioneers*, 158.

[2] J. A. Williamson, *The Tudor Age*, 100.

[3] Cf. Lucien Romier, *History of France* (trans. Rowse), 143-4.

[4] The following two paragraphs are based on Ch. A. Julien, *Les Voyages de découverte et les premiers établissements XVᵉ–XVIᵉ siècles*, a first-class work of scholarship.

West Country fishermen were addicted to dry-fishing : they went on shore to dry their fish on the spot. That led in turn to occupation, and so Newfoundland became the oldest of the dominions of the Crown. From the Italian colony at Rouen Verrazano set sail on his remarkable voyage coasting the whole of North America from Florida to Newfoundland. It was a pity for France that Francis I found caracoling in Italy more attractive. Breton boats made an early settlement on the coast of Brazil, and for long French seamen contested with Portugal for the establishment of a colony there. Coligny did what he could ; but the miserable Valois never gave any support. It must have been from the contacts of Plymouth across the Channel that " old " William Hawkins learned about the trade to Guinea and on to Brazil. Later, we find his son, John, closely *lié* with the Huguenot privateering activities based on La Rochelle. Huguenot corsairs were ravaging the West Indies, in their warfare with Spaniards and Portuguese claiming the monopoly of the New World, while Drake was yet a child. In the 1530s Jacques Cartier of St.-Malo was exploring the St. Lawrence and taking possession of Canada for the hardly appreciative French kings.

The Treaty of Câteau-Cambrésis conceded the Portuguese monopoly in the South Atlantic, in the interests of Catholic unity. There remained North America, and Coligny gave all the support he could to the project of a colony in Florida. Three expeditions were sent out under Jean Ribault, who had been in England and made contact with Northumberland. Philip replied by founding the fort of St. Augustine and sending an expedition under Menéndez, who got the French to surrender on his promise and then massacred every man of them. Philip approved the massacre and gave the word to hang all " pirates ". There was profound resentment in France and it was a shock to opinion in England, which also maintained the view expressed by the Huguenot poet :

> Que toute ceste terre est commune aux vaillans,
> Comme aux poissons glissans les campagnes des eaux,
> Et les plaines de l'air sont libres aux oiseaux.

Philip passionately desired Coligny's overthrow, and with his assassination there disappeared the one French leader who understood the crucial importance of expansion for the future. We may contrast the Valois, holding on the whole to a Catholic course, with occasional deviations like the senseless and disastrous Strozzi expedition to the Azores, with Elizabeth's constant and unwavering, though sometimes surreptitious, support of her seamen, occasionally lying valiantly on their behalf. At the Treaty of Vervins (1598), at the end of a century of it all, Philip yielded nothing of his claim to monopoly. This contrasts with the Anglo-Spanish treaty of 1604—after all, England had fought Spain to a standstill—where nothing was said on the subject : the English interpreted this to mean that trade to the East Indies was free and North America open to them. In the end, France kept none of the territories she had explored or occupied.

Meanwhile the English record was not without attempts, but they were rather short of breath and without much effect. John Cabot's voyage of 1497—upon which he made a landfall near Cape Breton, explored the coast of Nova Scotia and sighted Newfoundland—has the importance that it was the first actual discovery of the mainland ; and upon that priority the Elizabethans, those of them who grasped its significance, did not hesitate to found their claim to primacy in Northern and Arctic waters as the English sphere. John Dee based on this an argument to prove the Queen's title to North America, Greenland and the other Arctic regions not possessed by Russia. Next year Cabot coasted along North America perhaps as far as Chesapeake Bay ; but the voyage was a dead failure. No spices, no China or Japan : no interest in the New World. Two more voyages followed in 1501 and 1502 : Henry VII, who was more far-seeing than his son, made a handsome present to " the merchants of Bristol that have been in the new found land ". A couple of Esquimaux, brought back as trophies, walked the streets of Westminster. A voyage farther south brought back wild cats and parrots for the King : " they meant more in that dawn of a new world than they can ever mean to the jaded omniscience of today ".[1] In 1508–9 Cabot's son, Sebastian, made a voyage upon which he is now thought to have discovered Hudson's Strait ; for, all his life, that somewhat mysterious man nursed a secret : he believed that he had discovered the North-West Passage, the short-cut to the riches of the East. But nobody else believed him ; discouraged, he entered Spanish service and spent most of his life in it.

An abortive voyage of John Rastell's in 1517 had an interesting

[1] J. A. Williamson, *The Voyages of the Cabots and the Discovery of North America*, 213.

literary sequel ; for, in his " Interlude of the Nature of the Four Elements ", he wrote the first English description of America :

> Within this XX yere
> Westwarde he founde new landes
> That we never harde tell of before this
> By wrytynge nor other meanys
> Yet many nowe have ben there
> And that contrey is so large of rome
> Muche lerger than all Christendome . . .

and then, with a spurt of national spirit :

> If that they that be Englyshe men
> Myght have ben the first of all
> That there shulde have take possessyon
> And made first buyldynge and habytacion
> A memory perpetuall
> And also what an honorable thynge
> Both to the realme and to the kynge
> To have had his domynyon extendynge
> There into so farre a grounde
> Whiche the noble kynge of late memory
> The most wyse prynce the VII Henry
> Causyd first for to be founde. . . .[1]

John Rastell was Sir Thomas More's brother-in-law ; we must not forget the part of the New World in the inspiration of *Utopia*.

In the years from 1530 to 1540 took place the voyages of William Hawkins from Plymouth to the Guinea coast, where they traded for ivory, and on to Brazil, whence they brought back Brazil wood and popinjays. On the second voyage they left Martin Cockeram, a Plymouth man, a hostage with the natives for their chief who wished to behold the delights of civilisation. He gave as much pleasure as he received, for at Whitehall " the King and all the nobility did not a little marvel, and not without cause ; for in his cheeks were holes . . . and therein small bones were planted, standing an inch out from the said holes, which in his own country was reputed for a great bravery. He had also another hole in his nether lip, wherein was set a precious stone about the bigness of a pea ; all his apparel, behaviour and gesture were very strange to the beholders."[2] Unfortunately, on the way back the chief died ;

---

[1] Cf. J. A. Williamson, *ibid.* 89-90.
[2] *The Hawkins' Voyages*, ed. C. R. Markham (Hakluyt Society), 4.

but such was the trust of the natives that they returned Martin Cockeram without any harm, to end his days, after such an exotic adventure, in the familiar surroundings of Sutton Pool.

These voyages point to the later primacy of Plymouth in the American and oceanic enterprises ; but actually the first impulses came from Bristol. At this port two fertilising currents of trade and information crossed : that from Iceland, which may have brought the tradition of the early Viking voyages across the Atlantic, and that from Spain, the Canaries and Madeira, in touch with the New World. A group of Bristol merchants, Thornes, Barlows, Framptons, were influential at Seville : later they had trouble with the Inquisition, and they brought their information home to England. Englishmen had taken part in the conquest of the Canaries for Spain ; an Englishman, a Bristol man, was the gunner on board Magellan's ship. Later, the English were to be working for themselves. The Thornes had their trading agents in the Canaries, and one as far afield as the West Indies. Barlow was an early voyager to Santa Cruz (Agadir), the most southerly of the Portuguese outposts along the Morocco coast. He was the first of our people to set foot on the vast pampas of the Argentine ; but what he most wished was to voyage across the Pacific with an English pilot to learn all about the route. Robert Thorne was consumed by a similar idea : he had a fixation upon the northern route across the Pole as the shortest cut to the East, and an all-English route under our control. He put forward a proposal to Henry VIII, his life-long ambition being " to attempt if our seas north-ward be navigable to the Pole or no ".[1] Barlow supported the idea in his *Briefe Summe of Geographie*, which lay unpublished till our own day ; in it he argued that the shortest route, the northern, had been reserved by Divine Providence for England. Nothing came of it : Henry had other things to think about. With the increasing awkwardness for the English in Spain, occasioned by the breach with Rome, these men came back to useful purpose at home : Thorne devoted all his wealth to founding Bristol Grammar School and other charities ;[2] we have already observed the Barlows comfortably settled upon Church property, at Slebech upon the Pembrokeshire coast ;[3] Frampton in his

---

[1] *A Brief Summe of Geographie*, ed. E. G. R. Taylor (Hakluyt Soc.), xxiv.
[2] Cf. C. P. Hill, *The History of Bristol Grammar School*, c. 1.
[3] Cf. above, p. 76.

retirement turned to a series of translations ·in the interest of English expansion.[1]

After the discouraging attempts towards the North-West, it is not surprising that, when the impulse revived with the Edwardians, they should have begun with the untried North-East. Sebastian Cabot, now back from Spain, was brought in, made Governor of the Muscovy Company and, out of his long experience, drew up the instructions for the voyage. There is a certain historic propriety that it should be he who, after half a century, links the new forward move with the first tentative beginnings. For, though " superficially the first fifty years of English oceanic history are a record of failure and disappointment, of chimerical projects and promising openings not followed up, in reality they provided a necessary apprenticeship for the more solid undertakings of the next generation ".[2] Now, one sees the English, after long hesitation, take wings and sail across the oceans in one continuous spreading impulse. In May 1553 Willoughby and Chancellor's ships set sail from the Thames. As they passed Greenwich " the courtiers came running out, and the common ·people flocked together, standing very thick upon the shore ; the Privy Council, they looked out at the windows of the Court, and the rest ran up to the tops of the towers ".[3] The ships shot off their ordnance, the sailors kept up a merry noise. Only one was absent, for whom principally all this was prepared : within the palace the boy-King was dying.

Off the coast of Lapland that winter Willoughby's ship was caught in the ice and all on board perished. But Chancellor managed to get through and across the White Sea to the mouth of the Dvina, whence he made his way to Moscow, and even into the Kremlin, where he was very well received by the Tsar. Chancellor was much impressed by the Byzantine ostentation of the Court and the insecurity of property. If a man had too much, the ruler might say, " Friend [or comrade], you have too much living . . . less will serve you ; whereupon immediately his living shall be taken away from him, and he may not once repine thereat ".[4] He must answer that " he hath nothing but it is

[1] Cf. *The Original Writings and Correspondence of the Two Richard Hakluyts*, ed. E. G. R. Taylor (Hakluyt Soc.), I. 75.

[2] J. A. Williamson, *A Short History of British Expansion : the Old Colonial Empire*, 77.

[3] Hakluyt, *Navigations (ed. cit.)*, I. 271.

[4] *Ibid.* 260-61.

God's and the Duke's Grace's, and cannot say, as we the common people in England say, if we have anything, that it is God's and our own ". The Englishman was also struck by the barbarity of the punishments meted out and the way the ruler was nevertheless abused and deceived ; by the contrast between the severity of the fasts observed and the licentiousness that followed—" for whoredom and drunkenness there be none such living ". But he returned well contented with himself, for he had made the first direct contacts with Russia and opened up a new trade which was to expand notably.

In this expansion the key-figure was a remarkable man, Anthony Jenkinson. In his youth he was employed in the Levant trade, and there he gained a wide experience of the countries of the eastern Mediterranean and Near East. Now he was called upon to take charge of the new field opening up in Russia, and an extraordinary success he made of it. He won the personal confidence of the Tsar, who gave him backing for a journey into Persia and entrusted Jenkinson with trade on his behalf, as well as the Company's. During the three years 1557–60 Jenkinson reached Moscow, went down the Volga to Astrakhan, crossed the Caspian—where " we set up the red cross of St. George in our flags, which I suppose was never seen in the Caspian Sea before " —and, joining a caravan of a thousand camels, reached Bokhara, where he hoped to link up with the overland trade with China.[1] The trade itself we are not concerned with here, though it was, of course, the breath of life and the main motive force of the expansion.

His observations have the sharpness of most of his contemporaries, whose accounts were collected by Hakluyt : it is somehow affecting to see these new worlds of experience opening up for our ancestors with the freshness with which they saw them for the first time, the strange peoples and their still stranger habits, the camaraderie and mutual help of travellers and seamen as well as the bloody conflicts and the barbarities. There was the great rock at the entry to the bay of St. Nicholas, " to which the barks that passed thereby were wont to make offerings of butter, meal and other victuals, thinking that unless they did so, their vessels should there perish, as it hath been oftentimes seen ; and there it is very dark and misty ".[2] Some days after, they passed the spot where Willoughby and all his

[1] *Ibid.* 461. [2] *Ibid.* 411.

company perished. In Moscow they observed the ceremonial breaking open of the ice on Twelfth Day, and the blessing of the Moskwa—which went on up to 1917. The marriage customs of the Russians were somewhat odd : they all drank till they were drunk, and then two naked men who led the bride from the church " danced naked a long time before all the company ".[1] The country was " full of diseases, divers and evil ", particularly venereal : the chief remedy for everything being to sweat themselves in their hot-houses, which did, however, also serve other purposes. When Jenkinson got into the Moslem world around the Caspian, he found pleasures more variegated : " every Khan or Sultan hath at the least four or five wives, besides young maidens and boys, living most viciously ".[2] It was a new experience for Jenkinson on his second voyage, when he penetrated into Persia, to find himself regarded as unclean, being a Christian. " ' Doest thou believe so ' ? said the Sophy unto me. ' Yea, that I do ', said I. ' Oh, thou unbeliever ', said he, ' we have no need to have friendship with the unbelievers ', and so willed me to depart." Departing, he was followed by a man with a basin of sand, " sifting all the way that I had gone within the said palace, even from the said Sophy's sight unto the court gate ".[3] He was succeeded by Richard Johnson, who, let us hope, was more successful with the Persians, for he was seduced by their vices and set a worse example even than the Russians. These new contacts were enlarging the experience of the backward English.

On Jenkinson's second journey, 1561–3, the Tsar charged him with a mission concerning his relations with the (Christian) Circassian states. On his return to England Jenkinson offered in 1565—at what time he was deep in discussion with Humphrey Gilbert concerning the problem—to lead an attempt to find the North-East Passage.[4] But next year he was sent back to Russia, where he succeeded in obtaining a large and generous grant : the full monopoly of all the trade in and out of Russia by the northern route, and licence to trade into Persia duty-free.[5] Nothing could have been more satisfactory : it was due to Jenkinson's ability and energy, and the confidence he aroused

---

[1] Hakluyt, *Navigations (ed. cit.)*, I. 435-7.
[2] *Ibid.* 450.   [3] *Ibid.* II. 22.
[4] The arguments he advanced may be found set out in *Cal. S.P. Col., East Indies, 1513–1616*, 4-5.
[5] Cf. *ibid.* 73-7.

in the Tsar. The agreement was implemented by a full-scale
ambassador, Thomas Randolph, who observed nothing so much
as the vast number of whales engendering together in the White
Sea, the " spermacetae which we might plainly see swimming
upon the sea " and the abominable vices of Kholmogori.[1] At
the Kremlin he found that the autocrat did business by night ;
but the Tsar was in genial mood and " I obtained at his hands
my whole demands for large privileges in general, together with
all the rest my particular requests ".[2]

By 1571 the accord had broken and there were mutual
recriminations. The Tsar wanted a defensive alliance ; he also
wanted to marry a kinswoman of the blood royal—apparently
Lady Mary Hastings was thought of for promotion to the bed of
Ivan the Terrible. She was not having any, and Queen Elizabeth
was not the woman to force such a consummation upon any lady.
This aroused the suspicions of the age-long Russian inferiority
complex in regard to the West. Nor was it helped by the fact
that the English factors in Russia were misconducting themselves,
it seems over-reaching themselves. The Tsar annulled all the
privileges so hardly won and so willingly granted. Only
Jenkinson could repair the breach.

He returned to Russia a last time, 1571–2. English artisans
were now not allowed to leave the country ; an Englishman
who had gone over to the Russians had been stirring up trouble ;
Jenkinson was told that the Tsar would have his head. He
waited patiently, and, when at last he was accorded an interview,
the Tsar made a dignified and impressive statement of his
grievances : " Anthony, the last time thou wast with us here, we
did commit unto thee our trusty and secret message, to be
declared unto the Queen's Majesty herself ", etc.[3] It seemed
that the official translater, Ralph Rutter, had been responsible
for a good deal of trouble, " a rebel to the Queen's Majesty and
an enemy to his country ".[4] The negotiations were labyrinthine
and difficult, but the good understanding between the Tsar and
Jenkinson brought them through to success. Jenkinson enjoyed
an immensely long retirement, " being weary and growing old,
I am content to take my rest in mine own house, chiefly com-
forting myself in that my service hath been honourably accepted
and rewarded of her Majesty and the rest by whom I have been

---

[1] *Ibid.* 81-2.   [2] *Ibid.* 85.
[3] *Ibid.* 138.   [4] *Ibid.* 147.

employed ".[1] He had deserved well of them. He married a cousin of Sir Thomas Gresham's, and was granted a coat of arms with the stars of the Muscovy Company, with a sea-horse for crest. Of no birth himself, his descendant was for long Prime Minister of Great Britain.

Meanwhile, the search along the coast for an outlet to the East continued. In April 1556 Stephen Burrough took the little *Searchthrift* on the quest—the "good old gentleman Master Cabota" coming on board to bid them farewell.[2] In July they were off Nova Zembla and landing in Samoyed country, where they saw a heap of idols, "the worst and the most unartificial work that ever I saw : the eyes and mouths of sundry of them were bloody, they had the shape of men, women and children, very grossly wrought and that which they had made for other parts, was also sprinkled with blood ".[3] Farther along the coast they went, making towards the river Ob, until they were among the Vaigatz Islands ; the nights waxed dark, winter was drawing on with its storms, the pack-ice was closing in, the north-east winds grew more terrible. They could get no farther. Nor did anyone get much farther. In 1580 Pet and Jackman got a little beyond Vaigatz. They found the coast beyond " a very fair coast, and even and plain, and not full of mountains nor rocks " ; but the sea was largely frozen, and they made their way with great difficulty through the packs : " the *William* being encumbered with ice, and perceiving that she did little good, took in all her sails, and made herself fast to a piece of ice ", and so they continued, mooring their ships to the ice as they went along.[4] They were forced to turn back. But the *William* would not give up : she wintered in Norway and, early in the New Year, going north once more, she was never heard of again.

The southward trade-route to the Atlantic coast of Morocco was also set going by the Edwardian impulse. This raised a serious problem of policy ; for it meant an incursion into the sphere of Portuguese-Spanish monopoly, confirmed by Papal grant. Papal confirmation had no validity, however, for the Protestant English : another of the imponderable, inestimable benefits of the Reformation. Thomas Windham, with Cabot

---

[1] *Cal. S.P. Col., East Indies, 1513–1616*, 158.   [2] Hakluyt, I. 334.
[3] *Ibid.* 347.   [4] *Ibid.* II. 233, 235.

lending aid in the background, led two voyages there in 1551 and 1552 ; and these established the Barbary trade, mainly in sugar and fruits, for good. In 1553 he went on to the fever-stricken Gold Coast, to get gold, pepper and ivory. Most of the pioneers on these voyages died : on the first, among others, Sir John Luttrell—of the remarkable votive picture by Eworth which portrays this handsome man in the sea, naked torso and arm held high above the waves, his ship in the background. On the last voyage Windham himself died and two-thirds of his crew. One sees him in his portrait, bluff and brawny, a rather brutal type, with out-thrust paunch and his sea-captain's whistle. Such was the other side to oceanic enterprise—the fearful mortality ; for few enough were the commanders who understood the elements of hygiene and their ships were almost always over-manned, partly to offset the expected mortality.

" The Portugals were much offended with this our new trade into Barbary . . . and gave out that if they took us in those parts, they would use us as their mortal enemies."[1] They were fortifying the coast against interlopers ; they " think to be Lords of half the world, envying that others should enjoy the commodities which they themselves cannot wholly possess ".[2] Such was the English point of view. Everybody took the same attitude towards interlopers in the sixteenth century. The English took the same line about the Dutch who intruded into the northern trade with Russia at the end of the century. People think what suits them : one never has to have any respect for the intellectual positions human beings take up : there is seldom any objectivity or disinterest—as Montaigne so sadly understood. All the same, the English did not set about the Dutch in the northern seas—as the Dutch massacred the English factors at Amboyna in 1623. The simple truth is that the English have a humaner record than other peoples.

They are not the less tough for that. When Philip married Mary, and the Catholic point of view was supposed to prevail, the trade was prohibited. But the English ships going to the Gold Coast did not stop. With Elizabeth's accession there was nothing in their way. Three embassies were sent to her to protest. To the first two, while her hand was not yet a strong one, she replied accommodatingly ; to the third, she refused outright to forbid the trade, while Cecil took the occasion to tell the Spanish

[1] *Ibid.* IV. 35.   [2] *Ibid.* 36.

ambassador that England did not recognise the distribution of territories by Papal grants. Henceforth English doctrine gave free rein to English enterprise : only effective occupation of territory was recognised, the seas were open to all.

The voyages of John Hawkins, 1562–9, brought the conflict of principle between England and Spain to a crisis and led to the turning-point in their relations. Hawkins succeeded to his father's interests in the Canaries trade, whence he learned too about the prospects and needs of the West Indies. The latter needed, above all, labour ; and from early years they had been buying negro slaves from Africa. But they could not .be got in sufficient quantity. Hardly anyone, except possibly Montaigne, saw anything wrong in the slave trade. There always had been slaves and indeed many negroes had a better prospect of life, as such, than if they had remained at home with their bloody tribal wars and their cannibalistic practices. Hawkins made his first round voyage from the Guinea coast with some 300 negroes, whom he sold to the Spanish colonists in the West Indies, and then out through the Florida Channel catching the south-westerlies home. It had been a very profitable voyage ; but much more than profit was involved in it.

We now know that the point of Hawkins's voyages was that they were a considered, if bold, attempt to try out whether the King of Spain would not see the advantages of permitting Hawkins to serve the known needs of the colonists on a regular and agreed basis. (Perhaps something like the *asiento* of the Treaty of Utrecht would have met the case—but the Spaniards would not agree even to that, until a century and a half of incessant attacks had brought about the attrition of their Empire.) Hawkins was known to Philip and everywhere declared himself, as he had been, a servitor of the King's. But the word went out that on no account were the colonists to trade with him : monopoly was the fixed and inflexible rule of the Spanish Empire. In Hawkins's second voyage the Queen herself invested a large, if somewhat moribund, ship, the *Jesus* of Lübeck. Hawkins everywhere made the point that " he was in an armado of the Queen's Majesty's of England "—in other words, that his voyage had official sanction.[1] But the colonists had had their orders and were afraid to trade openly, though they badly needed the slaves ; so by various subterfuges and making a pretence of

[1] *The Hawkins' Voyages* (Hakluyt Soc.), ed. C. R. Markham, 38.

being forced, they engaged in a secret trade. This voyage, too, was a great success : we have a delightful account of it from John Spark the younger, of Plymouth, full of vivid, natural and naïf observations, particularly of West Indian habits and customs. On his way home Hawkins coasted along the whole of Florida, looking for good harbours and aiding the French colony there with victuals. It was shortly after extinguished. Spark was much impressed by the green fertility of the country and the rate of increase of cattle there ; Hakluyt duly pointed the moral in the margin : " Measure to reap a sufficient profit in Florida and Virginia ".[1]

On his third voyage Hawkins had ten ships, big and small, including two ships of the Queen's, the *Jesus* and the *Minion*. He made a successful trading voyage, the colonists again being only too glad to trade with him by connivance, against the commands of their remote master. Hawkins was ready to return, when gales sprang up and the leaky hulk of the *Jesus* nearly foundered. She was in urgent need of repair, if she was ever to get home, and the only harbour was the port of Mexico, San Juan de Ulloa. While the English were in harbour, the new Viceroy arrived with a large fleet. Hawkins, with his superior gun-power, could have kept him out. But that would have been an open declaration of war, and Hawkins was the Queen's representative. With misgivings in his heart, he made way and made room. Don Martín Enríquez gave his written word that all should be well— and then seized the opportunity, with overwhelming man-power, to board the English ships. It was an act of simple and black treachery which was never forgotten or forgiven by any of the Elizabethan seamen—though it was in keeping with much else that the Spaniards did in this high noonday of their power, like Menéndez's promise to the French garrison in Florida and, then, slaughtering them.

The immediate consequences for the English were terrible. The *Jesus*, the occasion of the disaster, was left there disabled. Such of her crew as survived the sudden onslaught leaped into the *Minion*, which got away—with 200 men on board and hardly any victuals or water. The little *Judith*, whose captain was the young Drake, " forsook us in our great misery ".[2] (Drake was one to look out for himself ; but, indeed, what could he have done ?) Half of Hawkins's men, unable to endure any more, insisted on

[1] *Ibid.* 62.   [2] *Ibid.* 79.

being landed to surrender at the mercy of the Spaniards. The remainder nearly all died on their ghastly journey home across the Atlantic ; it is said that only some fifteen were alive to handle the *Minion* when she at length crawled into Mounts Bay in January 1569.[1] It was the end of Hawkins's experiment. It was also the end of a great deal more than that : the end of the Anglo-Spanish friendship that had endured since the early days of Henry VII. Henceforth, Spain had a vigorous and clever and tenacious enemy to deal with.

We know now, hundreds of years afterwards, who these men were that fell into the hands of Spain and exactly what they suffered. The colonists were kind and friendly, did what they could and gave them food and clothing. But when the heretics came into the hands of the Inquisition—we cannot recite all their fates, but here are a few : John Moon, of Looe, aged twenty-six, seaman, 200 lashes and six years in the galleys ; John Williams, of Cornwall, twenty-eight, 200 lashes and eight years in the galleys ; Robert Plympton, of Plymouth, thirty, 200 lashes and eight years in the galleys ; George Ribley, of Gravesend, thirty, seaman, to be burnt at the stake, but first strangled.[2] This was the more merciful custom of the Mexican Inquisition. Robert Barrett of Saltash, master of the *Jesus*, graced a more august spectacle. If he had lived he " might have been one of the great Elizabethans, courageous, competent, enterprising. Hawkins always gave him the command of parties and expeditions away from the main fleet. He was more prominent than his cousin Drake in the history of the voyage, and he was only twenty-five when the bars closed on him. A sad fate for such a man to be burnt in Seville market-place."[3] The place is not much changed when one goes there to remember him : there is the Renaissance palace of the *Contratación* House ; there is the sumptuous pile of the Cathedral in all its majesty and pride ; between them is the blood-soaked and bone-huddled spot where so many people were frazzled for the Faith.

The ultimate consequences for Spain were more grave and far-reaching. One must not—in the rational quietude, the sceptical disbelief, of a later age—underestimate the force of the hatred for Spain all this piled up among the Protestants of

---

[1] J. A. Williamson, *Sir Francis Drake*, 24.
[2] Cf. J. A. Williamson, *Hawkins of Plymouth*, 154.
[3] *Ibid.* 150.

Europe. It was unrelenting, undying, ubiquitous among them :
as such it was an historic force of momentous consequence. The
Spanish Inquisition made the Calvinists right—alas that the
maniac extremes on either side made life miserable for sensible
people in the middle, almost unbearable for sensitive ones.
Hawkins asked the Queen's leave to attack the treasure fleets
and recoup his losses. She refused : she had her own subtler
resources and, moreover, was not yet ready to challenge Philip's
empire. However, in that year 1569, the treasure he had borrowed
from his bankers to pay his troops in the Netherlands was, while
on its way up Channel, " borrowed " by the Queen. Drake set
out on his private war of revenge against Philip : the proceeds
of the Peru raid went mainly on keeping the Netherlands'
resistance going for years—until it ultimately added a new nation
to the community of Europe. The conjunction of San Juan de
Ulloa with the occupation of Antwerp by Alva brought about
a re-alignment of English policy, which coincided with, and
released, England's oceanic development. Decidedly, Philip
would have done better to consider Hawkins's approaches : it
might have led to a great development of American trade, the
shoring-up of the Anglo-Spanish alliance and a very doughty
addition, on terms, to the defence of Spanish America. Spain
could not have lost more than she did anyway by her inflexibility
and (increasingly undermined) insistence on monopoly.

For the next eight years the West Indies were kept in a
ferment of reprisals and irregular warfare by the privateers :
the English had penetrated into the Caribbean, " and in one
capacity or another they have been there ever since ".[1] The
key-figure in this phase is the young Drake. With his early career
we enter the realm of the romantic—it is like *Treasure Island*
translated back into history—as, with his later, we enter the region
of the palpably heroic. We must not, however, with the
sophistication of a later age, flinch from this, or in any way dis-
consider it : that would be to commit an historical solecism. For
those characteristics in Drake's unique career were of the essence
of the age—as we can see from the way it took Drake to its heart
and made of him the most famous Englishman of his day. Along
with many other incidents and gestures of the time, flashes of
Drake's personality, images of him at revealing moments, have
become part of the myth of the English people. Drake was one

[1] J. A. Williamson, *The Ocean in English History*, 41.

of those rare persons in history who had a magic about him : he possessed an aura, along with a charmed life. There is no doubt about it : Spaniards bore witness to the quality in their most dangerous enemy, no less than the English. The simple inhabitants of the coasts he visited thought of him as something more than human, a demon ; instructed Spaniards could not withhold their admiration from the combination of fighting courage with humanity, of a natural force—like a thunderbolt coming out of the blue—with debonair good manners that charmed all those he captured. Lope de Vega, who devoted a whole epic to recounting his misdeeds, could not forbear a tribute to the man. And Juan de Castellanos, who witnessed the havoc Drake made in the Indies in 1585, wrote a narrative poem that bears witness to the nobility that was in the Spanish nature no less than in the subject of the poem :

> Cresçió con el un alto pensamiento,
> grandes y superbíssimos conceptos,
> no sin fatiga del entendimiento . . .[1]

and there follows a description of how he looked at that moment :

> Hes hombre rojo de gracioso gesto,
> menos en estatura que mediano ;
> mas en sus proporciones bien compriesto
> y en plática, medido cortesano,
> respuestas vivas, un ingenio presto
> en todas quantas cosas pone mano,
> en negoçios mayormente de guerra
> muy pocas o ningunas veces yerra.[2]

The English have so many moments of him imprinted on their mind : of the early August Sunday in 1573, about sermon time, when the news ran over the town at Plymouth that the Captain was back from Nombre de Dios, and all the congregation poured out of St. Andrew's, their minds were so surpassed " with desire and delight to see him that very few or none remained with the preacher ".[3] Or perhaps it is at Nombre de Dios itself, outside the King's treasure-house, and Drake telling his men

---

[1] Joan de Castellanos, *Discurso de el capitán Francisco Draque*, 2.

[2] *Ibid.* 55. Drake was evidently one of the small great men of history, like Napoleon and Wellington ; but he was broad-shouldered and strong.

[3] Cf. J. S. Corbett, *Drake and the Tudor Navy*, I. 189.

that he had brought them to the mouth of the treasure-house of all the world ; or climbing that tree from which he first saw the Pacific and praying, if God would give him life and leave, that he might sail an English ship once upon those waters ; or listening in the silent night for the sound of mule-bells outside Venta de las Cruces ; or, at the end, taking a gold quoit out of his doublet, " Thank God, our voyage is made ". Or we think of him on the voyage round the world, discovering that there was sea to the south of the American continent, going out to the uttermost point of land, flinging himself on the ground and reaching out over as far as he could go ; or preaching his sermon to the quarrelling ship's company, " I must have the gentleman to haul and draw with the mariner, and the mariner with the gentleman ". Or hovering in the haze behind St. Nicholas's Island—that is now called after his name—on his return, with his first question, " Is the Queen alive or dead ? " ; and the scene on board the *Golden Hind* with the Queen threatening to cut off his head and handing the sword to the French ambassador to knight him—by way of inculpating France a little. Or we think of the sad last voyage, ending where he had begun in those familiar, coloured, hurricane-visited seas and, checkmated and dying, rising out of delirium to put on his armour and " meet death like a soldier ". His body was committed to the sea there, but his spirit can never be far away from Plymouth Hoe. Or we may think of him in the end as the first governor in Newfoundland, when a boy at home in Devon, remembered seeing him

> As he was walking up Totnes' long street :
> He asked me whose I was ? I answered him.
> He asked me if his good friend were within ?
> A fair red orange in his hand he had ;
> He gave it me, whereof I was right glad,
> Takes and kissed me, and prays God bless my boy.[1]

We recall that he had no children of his own.

His children were his exploits. They were the fruit of careful planning and preparation. The Hawkins brothers sent Drake out in the winter of 1570–71 as a first step towards recouping their losses : he despoiled Venta de las Cruces. Later in 1571, in the

[1] From R. H.–*Q(uodlibets)*, 1628. I owe this rare reference to Professor Jack Simmons. This little book by Robert Hayman must be the first book of English verse to come from the New World.

25-ton *Swan*, he made a rapid reconnaissance voyage on which he burnt a ship in Cartagena and brought the owner back to Plymouth for ransom. Next year, 1572–3, with the *Swan* and the *Pasco* of 70 tons, he carried out the campaign he planned, for which he had gathered information and made his preparations.[1] It involved more than campaigning : it necessitated first-class seamanship : " the crews of those days included carpenters, smiths and sail-makers, who could do wonders of shipbuilding on desolate beaches, all with the tools and materials they carried with them ".[2] They took back some £40,000 in treasure : multiply by thirty, but divide by two, for half went to the syndicate's French partners. Hawkins had financed the venture ; the returns can hardly have met his losses at San Juan, but they were something towards it.

Nor was Drake the only venturer into the forbidden preserve : the Spanish envoys in England complained that ships were continually sailing for the Caribbean and with Hawkins's backing. In 1574 John Noble took a ship there with a crew of twenty-eight : they were all killed except two boys who were sent to the galleys for life.[3] In 1574–5 Gilbert Horsley appeared off the coast attacked the coast-wise shipping, collected a handsome profit and made off home again. In 1576 Andrew Barker, a Bristol merchant who had had a ship and cargo confiscated in the Canaries on the ground of his heresy—accused *in absentia* by the Inquisition—sought his own redress in the Caribbean : he made a valuable haul, but mutineers made off with it : their skiff capsized in a storm, while the Spaniards got Barker's head. John Oxenham's venture of 1576–7 was much more important : it had no less than the strategic intention of seizing the Isthmus and holding it against the Spaniards with the aid of the rebellious Cimaroons. These were a cross-breed of natives and negroes, who held much of the interior of the Isthmus : they hated the Spaniards and had worked in league with Drake, as they were to do with Oxenham.

Oxenham was another Plymouth man, a few years Drake's senior—" a man of grave demeanour, much feared and respected

---

[1] I follow here Miss E. G. R. Taylor's summary, *E.H.R.*, 1934, 361-2, of the new information from Spanish sources in Miss I. A. Wright, *Documents Concerning English Voyages to the Spanish Main, 1569–80* (Hakluyt Soc.).
[2] J. A. Williamson, *Sir Francis Drake*, 31.
[3] Cf. J. A. Williamson, *The Age of Drake*, 129-44.

and obeyed by his soldiers "—and had been with Drake in 1572–3 when they vowed they would sail in the Pacific. Oxenham was now attempting the Isthmus with only fifty men, and he might have brought it off, at least temporarily, if circumstances had not been against him. The Spaniards discovered the hiding-place of his ships while he was absent and captured all his stores. Still he was at large, until the English habit of releasing prisoners led to the discovery of his whereabouts, and the convergence of overwhelming forces from Panama got him. For long Oxenham's fate was not known ; when Drake was coming up the coast of Peru in 1579, he was still in the dark, and it may be that the plan of a joint attack on the Isthmus was the undescried secret between Drake and the Queen, in the planning of the voyage. When he entered the harbour of Callao, Drake learned the truth : all the common seamen had been hanged, Oxenham and the ships' officers were in prison at Lima awaiting a grander fate : in 1580 they were " reconciled " to the Church, paraded round at an *auto da fé* and then hanged.[1]

Meanwhile, at home, schemes for long-range discovery and overseas settlement were beginning to take shape. By far the most important was Grenville's carefully planned, and very nearly made ready, project for such a voyage into the Pacific, the first of its kind.[2] He gathered round him the backing of his friends and relations—Edgcumbe, Basset, Edmund Tremayne, William Hawkins : they were an entirely West Country group, based on Plymouth. The two problems of the Pacific that exercised the keenest minds at the time were that of the existence of *Terra Australis*, a great continent in the southern hemisphere to balance the land-mass of Europe and Asia in the northern ; and that of the whereabouts of a supposed Strait of Anian leading from the Pacific end to the North-West Passage into the Atlantic. The main object of the voyage was to discover this continent, open up trade with it and plant settlements there. It was argued in the promoters' literature that such a continent should yield results to England comparable with those of Spain from America and of Portugal from the East. Here was a fourth sphere of the world reserved " by God's providence " for the English. (We remember that the North had also been reserved to them " by God's providence " : the interchangeable term

---

[1] Cf. Z. Nuttall, *New Light on Drake* (Hakluyt Soc.), 1-4.
[2] Cf. my *Sir Richard Grenville of the ' Revenge '*, c. v.

may be omitted : common form.) The benefits were the usual ones in view : increase of shipping and God's word, a market for manufactured goods, discovery of gold, above all settlement, for—as Oxenham told his Spanish captors—England had many inhabitants and little land. " In sum, the projectors were setting forth the complete programme of a colonial empire." [1]

It is the emphasis on settlement that is so interesting, and particularly that it should come from Grenville. When one considers the actual work he did in planting settlements in Ireland and in Virginia, along with this first Australian project, Grenville emerges as a leading figure in the origins of the Empire, though his career has been little appreciated as such.

We learn from Oxenham's examination before the Inquisition that Grenville had bought two ships for the purpose and was going to buy others ; that Oxenham had discussed the idea with Drake, who often said that if the Queen would grant him licence he would enter the Pacific and found settlements there in some good country. [2]   In 1574 circumstances were not propitious for such a challenge to the Spanish Empire, and the Queen refused to grant Grenville a licence. Three years later they had changed : she was willing to grant to the upstart young captain what she had refused to an aristocratic Grenville. According to Drake, she had said, " Drake ! So it is that I would gladly be revenged on the King of Spain for divers injuries that I have received." To the Spanish ambassador she said, " The gentleman careth not if I disavow him ". In fact, Drake's voyage took on a weightier character : it was backed by no mere private West Country group, but by Leicester, Walsingham, Hatton, the Lord Admiral, Hawkins and the Queen herself : " the business was as fully a state undertaking, although capable of disguise, as Hawkins's West Indian expeditions had been ". [3]

It was only this fact and the authority it gave him that enabled Drake to surmount the critical difficulties of a venture " which becomes ever more astonishing as we learn more about it ". [4]   At home the Queen did her best for him, writing herself to lull Philip at the moment of Drake's departure : " We beg very affectionately that all suspicions may be banished from between us, if any such have been raised by the acts of wicked men with

---

[1] J. A. Williamson, *The Age of Drake,* 151.
[2] Z. Nuttall, *op. cit.* 9-10.
[3] J. A. Williamson, *op. cit.* 169.   [4] *Ibid.* 145.

the object of destroying the close friendship which we enjoyed in our earlier years. . . ."[1]   The strain of the voyage was tremendous, and not merely physical.   There was the latent opposition of Doughty, coming gradually into the open and issuing in disloyalty and disaffection that might well have wrecked the voyage, as similar divisions wrecked so many others.   The objectives had been kept absolutely secret : when they were revealed at the equator, those who objected to the course (they had been told they were going to Alexandria) provided a party in support of Doughty—mainly the landsmen on board against the seamen, who were with Drake.   None of them had crossed the equator before, and nerves were on edge in the equatorial calms in which they made no progress ; the baffling winds and calms off the coast of Brazil the men put down to Doughty's conjuring ; the furious storms they met with once they were through the Strait and in the belt of Brave West Winds threatened to drive them back on to the coast or into the Strait again for shelter—from which Winter in the *Elizabeth* could not emerge, though he tried again and again.   Drake in the *Golden Hind* had had his usual luck and made the exceedingly dangerous navigation of the passage in sixteen days—the shortest record of the century. (Magellan had taken thirty-seven days, Cavendish and Richard Hawkins were to take forty-nine and forty-six : they were repeatedly blown back at the exit by the head wind from the west.)

Once through into the Pacific—" as a pelican alone in the wilderness "—Drake made a lunge westward to find the coast of *Terra Australis*, but the winds were dead against.   It was then, too, that he discovered that there was a sea-passage around the southernmost tip of the American continent ; but he made nothing of it : perhaps because he did not want the Spaniards to get hold of his discovery.   Off Panama, his voyage was " made " by the capture of the richly laden treasure-ship the *Cacafuego* : " we found in her great riches, as jewels and precious stones, thirteen chests full of reals of plate, four score pound weight of gold, and six and twenty ton of silver ".[2]   Drake's young cousin, John—they were often painting together in Drake's cabin—was the first to catch sight of her from the top and so to earn Drake's

---

[1] Cf. Taylor, *The Original Writings and Correspondence of the Two Richard Hakluyts*, I. 115.
[2] Hakluyt, VIII. 60.

gold chain. This lad was wrecked on the Plate coast a few years later ; made prisoner by the Inquisition, he was reconciled to the Church, married safely in the country and lived the rest of his life there—so Drake blood is there still. [1]

We can now see the famous voyage from the Spanish side, from the subsequent evidence of the prisoners whom Drake invariably released, after little acts of courtesy and kindness that conquered their hearts. They all spoke well of the English corsair who apologised as he took a cross of emerald from one or some porcelain and silks from another—but we must not call him a " corsair ", for that made him angry : he insisted to all and sundry that he was the Queen's officer holding her commission. And he told his captives exactly how he viewed things and what was the ground of dispute : if the King would not permit trade in the Atlantic, then he would suffer depredations in both oceans ; he himself intended to go on until he recovered the two millions his cousin had lost at San Juan de Ulloa. He meant to plant settlements. [2] Don Francisco de Zarate was sailing along in the moonlight just before dawn, off Acapulco, when he found the *Golden Hind* beside him : this gentleman was a cousin of the Duke of Medina Sidonia—Drake was to become well known to the family. [3] There was no resistance and, when Don Francisco was brought on board, Drake was walking up and down on deck. " He received me with a show of kindness and took me to his cabin, where he bade me be seated and said, ' I am a friend of those who tell me the truth, but with those who do not I get out of humour '." Drake asked if there were any gold or silver, or anything belonging to Don Martín Enríquez, on board. On being told that there was not, he said, " Well, it would give me greater joy to come across him than all the gold and silver in the Indies. You would see how the words of gentlemen should be kept." [4] At dinner, " he ordered me to sit next to him and began giving me food from his own plate, telling me not to grieve, that my life and property were safe. I kissed his hands for this. . . . Of that which belonged to me he took but little. Indeed he was quite courteous about it. Certain trifles of mine having taken his fancy, he had them brought to his ship

---

[1] For his story *v.* Nuttall, *op. cit.* 18 foll.
[2] *Ibid.* xxxix, xlv.   [3] *Ibid.* 199-210.
[4] An unkind scribe here inserted in the margin, "¡ Ojo ! a Don Martín Enríquez".

and gave me, in exchange for them, a falchion [a broad-sword] and a small brazier of silver, and I can assure your Excellency that he lost nothing by the bargain. On his return to his vessel he asked me to pardon him for taking the trifles, but that they were for his wife."

To each of the Spanish sailors and of the poor among the passengers Drake gave a handful of reals—which we may contrast with the Spanish treatment of the French in Florida, or the English at Lima. Zarate gives us the most intimate view into the *Golden Hind* that we have : Drake's men were under strict discipline—the clue to his success where so many others broke down ; " when our ship was sacked, no man dared take anything without his orders : he shows them great favour, but punishes the least-fault. . . . Each one takes particular pains to keep his arquebus clean. He also carries painters who paint for him pictures of the coast in exact colours. He carries trained carpenters and artisans, so as to be able to careen the ship at any time. . . . He is served on silver dishes with gold borders and gilded garlands, in which are his arms. He carries all possible dainties and perfumed waters : he said that many of these had been given him by the Queen. He dines and sups to the music of viols." There was always music and musicians on board these ships— singing and dancing were a chief solace of the sailors : on Cavendish's voyage round the world " they played and danced all the forenoon among the negroes " on shore (who can think of sailors dancing without a leap of the heart ?).[1] After Drake's death there was taken from his ship " a chest of instruments of music . . . lute, oboes, sackbuts, cornets and orpharions, bandora and suchlike ".[2] But that was happily twenty years on. When Don Francisco managed to ascertain " whether the General was well liked, all said that they adored him ".

And so on up the Pacific coast beyond California into higher latitudes—to the coast of present-day British Columbia—until the weather grew rough and cold : possibly Drake was looking for the Strait of Anian through which to come direct home. Turning back again, he found a good anchorage near modern San Francisco where to give the ship a refit before crossing the Pacific. Here the white men were worshipped as gods by the local Indians—embarrassing for a rather devout Protestant like

---

[1] Hakluyt, VIII. 208.
[2] D. B. Quinn, *The Roanoke Voyages* (Hakluyt Soc.), II. 741.

Drake, who took Foxe's *Book of Martyrs* with him (as other ships did), and pointed out victims of the Inquisition to insufficiently inquisitive Spaniards. At this spot Drake raised a monument with an inscription proclaiming California one of the Queen's dominions under the name of New Albion. Thence he made a prosperous passage across the Pacific to the Moluccas, crossed the Indian Ocean and so back to Plymouth Sound.

The voyage had reverberating effects in every direction. It was a sudden and brilliant demonstration that a new power had arrived on the oceans. Drake was not only the first Englishman to sail the Pacific, but the first to cross the Indian Ocean—familiar to the Portuguese since Vasco da Gama. That showed how backward the English had been—and also with what a sudden swoop they were now catching up : for Drake had accomplished in one voyage what Diaz, da Gama and Magellan had done separately over years. It enormously raised the prestige of England in Europe and the confidence of England in herself, on the threshold of the 'eighties that were to see the country not afraid to come to grips with the world-empire. Spain's enemies were everywhere encouraged. It was for the Queen to face the music ; and that she must have done with some amusement, for she had taken an artist's pleasure in the performance from the first. To Spanish protests she turned a brazen face.

The immediate consequences of the voyage were to set going further ventures to follow up the openings Drake had made. He had made a verbal agreement with the Sultan of Ternate which allowed the English to break into the Portuguese monopoly of the spice trade. On his return a voyage was set on foot to exploit this. It was an important venture : our first attempt to get a footing in the East Indies and to penetrate to China. Fenton, the commander, was instructed to leave an agent behind in China to learn the language and condition of the people, and act as factor for trade with them. Leicester invested largely, £2200 ; Drake, 1000 marks and a bark, the *Francis* ; all the leading Court figures had smaller investments, except the prescient Queen : she lost nothing. There were two large ships, the galleon *Leicester* and the *Edward Bonaventure*, " deeply laden " with goods for trade, the bark *Francis* and a pinnace, *Elizabeth.*

It so happens that this voyage is extremely well documented, so that we can follow everything that happened.[1] A young Fellow of All Souls, Richard Madox, was appointed chaplain to Leicester's ship by his recommendation; the diary he kept gives us an insight into the company and conversation of the people at Court and in the City who were so closely concerned with overseas expansion.[2] There were the dinners at Muscovy House, with Alderman Barnes and Sheriff Martin, supper with Mr. Towerson in Tower Street, who had been to Guinea in Queen Mary's days and could tell how the storks would eat men. At the Dean of Westminster's talk was of the great and bloody meteor seen streaming from north-west to south-west; Sir Francis Drake, Mr. Fenton and the sea-captains were commended as "great favourers of scholars, but better acquainted with Cambridge than Oxford men". Mr. Ashley, who made playing cards, was making beads and other gewgaws for Red Indians for Sir Humphrey Gilbert's new voyage preparing for America; Ashley expected to see a letter, dated at London, 1 May, delivered at China before the following midsummer, for the Indians had report of a suitable passage over America between 43° and 46°, through which Sir Francis Drake had returned from the Moluccas. We know what to think of that. But it is a fascinating glimpse of the talk, the optimism, the expectations of the time.

The realities, as so often with these voyages, were sadly different. From the first there was dissension in the company, and Fenton could not control the expedition. Its whole story proves how right Drake had been to deal with Doughty and insist on his single authority; shows how valuable it was to have the Queen's commission behind one; shows up the difference between commanders of the first rank who could maintain their authority and unity of command—a Drake or Hawkins, Frobisher, John Davis, or Cavendish at his best—and those who could not. In the event, this most promising of ventures was utterly overthrown. The promoters would have done better to make Frobisher its captain; but the Muscovy Company was against him on account of his North-Western voyages, and anyway he was always jealous of Drake. So, it turned out, was Fenton—like many other people who fancied

[1] Cf. *Cal. S.P. Col., E. Indies, 1513–1616,* 72 foll.; in addition to the account in Hakluyt, VIII. 99-132.
[2] *Ibid.* 85-7.

themselves in the same class with Drake, but were not. At sea Fenton said angrily to William Hawkins, his second-in-command, that Sir Francis Drake had played the pirate and thief, and added, " I know how to make my voyage without any . . . advices ".[1] The result showed that he did not. Quarrelling, they hung about off the coast of Guinea, while men died of fever. They stood over to the coast of Brazil, and then could not agree whether to round the Cape of Good Hope or to make for the Plate. Sickness increased and over a score of men died. It was now too late to cross to the Cape. William Hawkins was in favour of following Drake's course through the Strait into the Pacific. That Fenton would not do, and, too late for either, decided to come back having achieved nothing. This was too much for spirited young John Drake, who made off on his own with the *Francis* : we know his fate. Fenton was of good family : there was no-one to call him over the coals—as there would have been had Drake failed. This was a set-back to prospects of trade with the East Indies for over a decade.

There followed a series of attempts to repeat Drake's success in the Pacific, of which only one came off. That was the voyage round the world of Thomas Cavendish of Trimley in Suffolk— the site of the house where he lived may be seen among the fields down by the Orwell, off the high road to Felixstowe ; the pleasant account of it was written by his neighbour, Francis Pretty of Eye.[2] The Orwell estuary, Ipswich and the neighbouring coast made a secondary centre to London and the West Country in all this maritime activity. After all, there was Hakluyt beneficed near by, at Wetheringsett ; he married a Cavendish ; his prebend at Bristol and canonry at Westminster provided him with convenient access to all three centres and made him an invaluable, an incomparable, link. (If only he could have been vicar of St. Andrew's at Plymouth too !) Cavendish made a prosperous voyage, 1586–8, capturing the Manila galleon, the *Santa Anna*, with a rich cargo. On his way back from the Cape, following Drake's course, he was the first Englishman to land on St. Helena, of which Pretty gives us a pretty description. They arrived back at Plymouth 9 September 1588, crossing the Armada remnants' homeward course, to hear the news of its shattering defeat. Cavendish wrote an account

---

[1] Cf. *Cal. S.P. Col., E. Indies, 1513–1616*, 91.
[2] Hakluyt, VIII. 206-55.

of his doings at once to Hunsdon, the Lord Chamberlain : " all which services with my self I humbly prostrate at her Majesty's feet . . . for at this day she is the most famous and victorious prince that liveth in the world ".[1]

Next year there set sail from Plymouth a West Country venture of John Chidley and Andrew Meyrick, three tall ships which came to utter disaster. It must have ruined the Chidley family, for one does not hear much of them again. In the Straits they came upon a solitary survivor of the Spanish garrison posted there in 1582 and left without succour to starve and be killed off by the Stone-age Patagonians. But the ships could not get through the Straits ; time and again they were driven back from the exit, " forced back as much in two hours as we were getting up in eight hours ".[2] For six weeks they tried, losing men and tackle and anchors, consuming their provisions. The two larger ships foundered with all hands ; Meyrick's ship, the *Delight*, was left with only six men when they were wrecked off Cherbourg : four Englishmen out of over three hundred were all that came back.

Cavendish's second venture, sailing from Plymouth in August 1591, with John Davis as second-in-command, suffered similar abortiveness and even worse horrors.[3] To these were added the desolation of a complete breach between the two commanders, mutual recriminations and accusations of desertion. The young Cavendish was a changed man since the first voyage : the strain of such a life was too much, and the frustration of his voyage seems to have driven him off his head ; on the way homeward he died, no-one knows where. All kinds of miseries overtook them, graphically recorded by John Jane, " a man of good observation, employed in the same and many other voyages " : he was a Cornishman, viewing matters from Davis's point of view, " with whom and for whose sake I went this voyage ". The weather was exceedingly stormy, men died of famine, " and all the sick men in the galleon were most uncharitably put ashore into the woods in the snow, rain and cold, where they ended their lives in the highest degree of misery, Master Cavendish all this while being aboard the *Desire* ". Cavendish turned back, while Davis was for still pressing on : all his life Davis was consumed by the idea of finding the North-West Passage, and he had joined

[1] *Ibid.* 280.

[2] *Ibid.* 284.　　　　[3] *Ibid.* 289-95.

Cavendish on the understanding that from California he might part company and search for the Passage. But the ship was now rotten and could not go forward ; the men were dying of famine, " their sinews were stiff and their flesh dead, and many of them were so eaten with lice, as that in their flesh did lie clusters of lice as big as peason, yea and some as big as beans. . . . Divers grew raging mad and some died in most loathsome and furious pain. It were incredible to write our misery as it was : there was no man in perfect health but the captain and one boy. . . . To be short, all our men died except sixteen [out of ninety-one], of which there were five able to move." These got the ship to Berehaven in Ireland, whence they passed over in a fisher-boat to Padstow. Such was the price the Elizabethans paid.

The last of the Elizabethans to penetrate into the Pacific bore a famous name, that with which these southward voyages began : Richard Hawkins, son of Sir John, grandson of ' old ' William. He wrote it all up in his admirable *Observations*, " the best detailed description of the passage, with . . . the hardships, difficulties and reverses incident to what was then the most exacting piece of pilotage in the world ".[1] It also has an exciting account of the battle in the Bay of Atacames against the squadron that rounded him up. For things had changed in the Pacific and the West Indies since the early days of his father and Drake— as they were both yet to find. The Spaniards had been forced to fortify their coasts and arm their ships. The good days were over. No doubt the Spaniards thought it poetic justice that they should end with the young sprig of a Hawkins laid by the heels : in spite of the promises of his captor, they kept him in prison in Spain a good many years. But Don Beltran de Castro was a gentleman and did not cease his efforts to get him out : Richard Hawkins came home a middle-aged man, to end his days at Plymouth, the last of the remarkable dynasty through whom the town grew to maturity and fame.

Informed opinion for long favoured the northern routes for outward expansion and to reach the East. It may be wondered why no-one favoured the route that became the classic highway of the Empire in time to come—that via the Cape to India. Not

[1] Williamson, *The Age of Drake*, 347. The work has been edited, with an introduction, by Williamson, Argonaut Press, 1933.

until all others had been tried and found impracticable were the Elizabethans, towards the end of the century, driven to this conclusion. They thought it far too long, the navigation dangerous —the difficulty of rounding the Cape was greatly exaggerated— and, moreover, at the other end the Portuguese were entrenched in force. As late as the 1580s we find the arguments advanced that a North-West route would be only half the distance, that the Straits of Magellan route was some 9800 miles compared with a North-West one of 3800 miles, " and no manner of danger of any foreign princes or pirate ".[1]

Among those who urged that the North-West Passage was preferable to the North-East it seems now that Humphrey Gilbert was a key-figure. At the time of Anthony Jenkinson's proposal to lead a Siberian voyage, Gilbert debated the issue with him, the respective merits of the routes, before the Queen and some of her councillors. He petitioned for a grant of the monopoly of the Passage to himself and his heirs, with the government of the territories discovered and various trading privileges.[2] He seems to have brought over Jenkinson to his point of view and they made a joint petition ; while Jenkinson was away in Russia Gilbert was to prepare the voyage " against my return "—at the same time Jenkinson was anxious that he should share in any privileges granted to Gilbert. (Gilbert had the advantage of being a courtier, well known to the Queen, in whose household he had been brought up from his youth.) Then the Muscovy Company took a hand : they regarded Gilbert's demands as contrary to their monopoly of the Northern routes : they would welcome his advice and assistance, but any dominion or trading monopoly in the North would be derogatory to their privileges. That ended the matter for the present, though the project was duly reported to Philip. Gilbert went off to fight in Ireland.

In these years he wrote a " Discourse to prove a passage by the North-West to Cathay and the East Indies ", which circulated in manuscript and played its part in turning minds in that direction. Ten years later, when the Muscovy Company— discouraged by the fruitless attempts towards the Siberian coast —was ready to permit ventures North-West, Gilbert's *Discourse* was published as part of the propaganda for Frobisher's voyages

[1] *Cal. S.P. Col., East Indies, 1513–1616*, 94.
[2] *Ibid.* 6-8 ; cf. also D. B. Quinn, *The Voyages and Colonising Enterprises of Sir Humphrey Gilbert* (Hakluyt Soc.), I. 6-11.

thither, 1576–8. It is a characteristic Elizabethan mingle-mangle of sense and nonsense, of the critical and the credulous, of deductive argumentations from classical authorities with interesting inferences from current expérience. It is the last that has most interest for us : the rumours of a great sea that Jacques Cartier picked up at his farthest penetration into Canada (evidently of the Great Lakes), of Sebastian Cabot's description of the Passage in his charts hanging in the Queen's Privy Gallery at Whitehall—these must have been a constant stimulus to an imaginative young attendant upon her.[1] And Gilbert was certainly imaginative : his was the originating mind in the business of peopling America. As early as this we find him advocating " that we might inhabit some part of those countries and settle there such needy people of our country, which now trouble the commonwealth . . . through want here at home ". There were the current rumours that Urdaneta had returned through the Passage. The conception Gilbert had of it was a south-western transit from about Hudson's Bay to about the Columbia River in the far west—though no-one had any conception of the vast land-breadth of North America. He argued, correctly enough, that the distance to China was less by half than that by the Siberian coast ; moreover, the winds were propitious as against the easterly winds off Siberia. And it was very doubtful " whether we should long enjoy that trade by the North-East . . . the commodities thereof once known to the Muscovite ". There, perhaps, he had a good point. We can catch a remote reflection from the interest aroused by Gilbert's book by our old friend Carnsew's reading it while on a visit to Lord Mountjoy in Somerset at the end of September 1576.[2] But, then, Carnsew was a fairly close acquaintance of Adrian Gilbert, with whom he co-operated over West Country mineral matters and whom he visited at his house by the Dart.

In June Frobisher had been sent off on his first voyage to search for the Passage, with two small barks and a pinnace. His backers were almost equally from the Court and from the

---

[1] We find Leonard Fryer, Serjeant-Painter 1598–1605, paid 52s. "for laying clear colouring, gilding and varnishing of five great frames for maps in the gallery". E. Auerbach, *Tudor Artists*, 118. Alas, that these things should have disappeared, along with such treasures as the Journal of Drake's Voyage round the World, which he gave to the Queen—either lost in the deplorable Civil War, which destroyed so much, or perhaps in the Whitehall fire.

[2] S.P. 46/16.

City—young Philip Sidney among them for £25.[1] Outside the palace at Greenwich they dressed ship and shot off their ordnance, while the Queen waved her hand to them from a window ; she sent one of her gentlemen aboard to give them her good wishes and, later, her secretary Woolley with her instructions to the company to obey their officers in all things.[2] She had not subscribed : there was no money in it. But Frobisher certainly added to geographical knowledge : he rounded the southern point of Greenland, sailed up the coast and crossed over to Baffin Island, where he took one of the westward-looking openings for the Passage. He observed the Tartar-featured Esquimaux, and lost a boat with five men among them in Five Men's Sound : probably eaten, for next year they found that the natives were " rather anthropophagi, or devourers of man's flesh than otherwise : for that there is no flesh or fish which they find dead (smell it never so filthy) but they will eat it as they find it, without any other dressing. A loathsome thing, either to the beholders or hearers." [3] They also found an old shirt, a doublet, a girdle and shoes : these were presumably inedible.

Frobisher brought home a piece of an unknown black ore, and the idea got about that it contained gold. There was no difficulty in financing the next voyage : the courtiers doubled their subscriptions, the Queen subscribed £500 and furnished a ship, the *Aid*.[4] This time Frobisher made no further search for the Passage : he formally annexed the country, could not get to grips with the shy and very fly Esquimaux and contented himself with lading 200 tons of the ore. His return led to a boom that was the first Elizabethan experience of such things. Burchard Cranich, the German mining expert, declared his expectations of a good yield from the ore. People rushed to invest : the Queen subscribed £1350 (probably of a promised £2000), the unwise young Earl of Oxford £2000, his prudent father-in-law, the sage Burghley, £100. Altogether some fifteen ships set sail in 1578, among them John Rashleigh's ship, the *Francis of Fowey*, and forty-one miners were taken on board at Plymouth. This time there was no chance of discovery, though Frobisher penetrated into Hudson Strait and thought he had found the Passage. The ships were engaged in lading ore—the

[1] *Cal. S.P. Col., E. Indies*, 11.
[2] Hakluyt, V. 131-7. [3] *Ibid.* 151.
[4] *Cal. S.P. Col. cit.*, 17-37 ; and cf. Hakluyt, V. 154-65.

little *Francis* alone carried 140 tons. Great efforts were made in testing the stuff, " for that her Majesty hath very great expectation of the same ".[1] Fenton was sent down to Cornwall to get specimens of various ores to mix with it : all to no avail : it was useless.[2] The Queen, for once, had burnt her fingers ; but so had a good many other people : Oxford had lost a lot of money, the promoter, Michael Lok, was ruined by it and in prison, Frobisher's wife and children in want. This fiasco put people off the North-West Passage for a few years.

But the Gilberts were not going to allow the matter to drop. When Humphrey Gilbert's fertile mind moved on to the more promising field of the American mainland, Adrian took over the North-Western projects, and in 1585 obtained the patent for discovery and trade that his brother had petitioned for twenty years before. The Gilberts were neighbours of John Davis at Sandridge on the Dart, to whom they entrusted the command of the three voyages to the North-West in 1585, 1586 and 1587 from Dartmouth. We may take Davis as the type of the best Elizabethan navigator—for Drake had genius, which puts him into a class by himself. Davis was a " scientific navigator, who clearly advanced the practice of his science, a commander of steady purpose who never faltered in the utmost disaster, and a humane and honest man with none of the common piratical background "[3]—though, strange to say, he came to an end at the hands of Japanese pirates in the Far East : a scene out of Conrad. He was a humorous, kindly, well-educated man, who wrote *The World's Hydrographical Description*, to prove the existence of the Passage, and *The Seaman's Secrets*, the first practical work on navigation by an Englishman (1594) ; hitherto we had been dependent on Spanish manuals. By then he was able not only to applaud the excellence of English map-making and ship-building, but to declare that as navigators and seamen " we are not to be matched by any nation of the earth ". The Elizabethans had seen that come true in their own lifetime, nor has their achievement ever been lost since. Nothing mean or even questionable has ever been recorded of John Davis : as one sits in a pew he might have occupied in the church at Stoke Gabriel where he worshipped, the tide coming up the Dart

[1] *Cal. S.P. Col. cit.*, 43.
[2] *Ibid.* 46.
[3] Williamson, *The Age of Drake*, 250.

below the churchyard outside, one remembers him for a good man.

In these years the Gilberts were in close touch with the learned, the hieratic, the mysterious Dr. Dee, who had direct access to the Queen—to whom, in 1577, he had declared her title to Greenland, Eastotiland (Labrador) and Friseland (the Canadian lands farther north). In January 1583 Walsingham and Adrian Gilbert came to discuss North-Western discovery with Dee; and on 24 January " I, Mr. Adrian Gilbert and John Davis went by appointment to Mr. Secretary Beale his house, where only we four were secret, and we made Mr. Secretary privy of the North West Passage, and all charts and rutters were agreed upon in general ".[1] Davis's first voyage—written up by John Jane, who was Sanderson's nephew, employed by him, the chief backer of these attempts—got as far up as Baffin Land in 66° and found Cumberland Sound, north of Frobisher's Strait, which he thought might give passage. There were the usual sparring entertainments with the Esquimaux : " the people of the country having espied us, made a lamentable noise, as we thought, with great outcries and screechings : we hearing them thought it had been the howling of wolves. . . . When they came unto us, we caused our musicians to play, ourselves dancing and making many signs of friendship."[2] " The cliffs were all of such ore as M. Frobisher brought from Meta Incognita."[3]

Next year Davis went again with the two little barks, the *Sunshine* and the *Moonshine*. The weather was not favourable for farther penetration northwards, but they loaded a cargo of seal-skins and observed the ways of the Esquimaux, who turned out to be as good wrestlers as the West Countrymen. They had witches and " have many kinds of enchantments, which they often used, but to small purpose, thanks be to God." [4] They also turned out to be great thieves, especially of anything made of iron, which they " could in no wise forbear stealing : which when I perceived [this is Davis himself writing], it did but minister unto me an occasion of laughter, to see their simplicity, and I willed that in no case they should be any more hardly used ". On the third voyage Davis reached the record latitude of 73°, and found the sea still extending clear north-westward. That farthest point on the Greenland coast he named

[1] *The Private Diary of Dr. John Dee*, ed. J. O. Halliwell (Camden Soc.), 18.
[2] Hakluyt, V. 285.   [3] *Ibid.* 287.   [4] *Ibid.* 295.

Sanderson his Hope ; but the wind came north and he crossed over to the opposite shore. His voyages had established the correct nature of the relation between Greenland and America. When he came back he reported : " I have been in 73 degrees, finding the sea all open and forty leagues between land and land. The passage is most probable, the execution easy."[1] But he was never to fulfil his passion to go north once more : when he sailed from Dartmouth again it was to fight the Armada.

Out of the struggle with Spain the Dutch were emerging a first-class sea-power ; and it was to forestall their competition that a new cycle of Arctic exploration was set in motion by the London merchants, led by Sir Thomas Smythe.[2] In a series of voyages Hudson scoured the Arctic region. He first tried out Robert Thorne's idea of eighty years before, going up the east coast of Greenland and following the ice-pack along to Spitzbergen, where the Muscovy Company now had a profitable whaling fishery. Like his predecessors, he could not get beyond Vaigatz to the Siberian coast. On a later attempt, for the Dutch East India Company, his Dutch crew refused to go on any farther ; so he stretched back across the North Atlantic to the American coast, exploring its bays, and went up the Hudson River as far as Albany. On his last voyage he got through Hudson's Strait into the bay, explored it and established its true nature ; and wintered in the southern inlet, James Bay, where they were frozen in. Next spring, after the hardships of the winter, the crew mutinied and this fine navigator was cast adrift in the boat's shallop to die.[3]

Sir Thomas Smythe did not relax his efforts and sent out voyages piloted by William Baffin. In 1615 he passed up Fox Channel and in 1616 he got farther north than any had reached, into Davis Strait, 78°. He held the view that if there were a passage it would be along this route. The promoters had to content themselves with that : the North-West Passage had defeated a century's efforts and geographical information remained roughly there until the nineteenth century, when the passage along the Arctic coast was at length made. Baffin, like Davis, was haunted by the desire to make it ; and, like him, took

---

[1] Hakluyt, V. 317.
[2] Cf. G. B. Parks, *Richard Hakluyt and the English Voyages*, 208.
[3] *Purchas, his Pilgrims* (Maclehose edn.), XIII. 398-9. For Hudson's voyages, *v.* *ibid.* 294-412.

service in the East, hoping one day to make an attempt from north of Japan. And in the East, like Davis, he died : by one of those proprieties of history, in aiding the Shah of Persia to drive the Portuguese out of Ormuz, the stronghold from which they had long dominated the Gulf route to India.[1]

The first direct voyages to the East via the Cape were enough to corroborate the worst fears of the Elizabethans : on the immensely long journey disasters overtook the ships and there was a fearful mortality among the inexperienced English. The Portuguese had found by long experience that their carracks of over 1000 tons (more than double the size of the bigger English merchant ships) answered their purposes best. And the Dutch, at the turn of the century, introduced such improvements in navigation and hygiene as to give them the lead in the East Indies. They also put the main effort of the nation into it. It looks as if the English here, too, were backward ; though, when they got through into the eastern seas, they gave a good account of themselves, for their gun-power was greater and their gunnery better. Ships like the *Hector* and the *Edward Bonaventure* were as much armed privateers as merchant-ships and had done their bit against the Armada. But if it had not been for the resolution of a few of the leading City merchants, especially Sir Thomas Smythe, the determination of captains like Lancaster and John Davis, and the example of the Dutch, the English might have still held back. The indomitable will of an ageing woman urged them on : on 5 November 1601 the East India Company received a tart reminder of " Her Majesty's mislike of the slackness of the Company in the seconding of their former voyage to the East Indies by the Cape of Bona Speranza ; propounding unto them the example of the Dutch, who do prosecute their voyages with a more honorable resolution ".[2]

Actually, the English were now already, in these same wonderful 1570s, in India by the overland route. Shakespeare's ship, the *Tiger*, bound for Aleppo—had he perchance seen her depart ?—carried on board those excellent honest merchants, John Newbery and Ralph Fitch. The Queen wrote her letters on their behalf to " the most invincible and most mighty prince,

---

[1] Cf. *D.N.B.*, *sub* William Baffin.

[2] *The Voyage of Sir Henry Middleton to the Moluccas*, ed. Sir W. Foster (Hakluyt Soc.), xiii.

Lord Zelabdim Echebar, King of Cambaya ", signifying " the great affection which our subjects have to visit the most distant places of the world, not without good will and intention to introduce the trade of merchandise of all nations whatsoever they can " ; and to the King of China hoping that " to your people it will bring some profit ".[1] The Son of Heaven was above such a consideration—though hardly anybody else in the wide world was. John Newbery, however, did not penetrate into China.

But an extraordinary journey he did make of it. The *Tiger* was driven back into Falmouth by bad weather, and thence to Syria without once anchoring. At both Tripolis and Aleppo he had made earnest enquiry for the Cosmography of Abilfada Ismael for his friend Hakluyt, " but by no means can hear of it : some say that possibly it may be had in Persia, but notwithstanding I will not fail to make enquiry for it, both in Babylon and in Basra ".[2] Hakluyt had given Newbery a letter to Father Thomas Stevens, a Wiltshireman who was the first of our nation to live his life in India : a priest of the order of St. Paul, he worked with the Portuguese at Goa ; but he had not forgotten his native country and gave Newbery and his fellows valuable help when they were imprisoned there. For, of course, the Portuguese were very jealous of this incursion into their sphere.

Newbery and his company made a profitable journey as far as Ormuz—and later Fitch wrote it all up, with an account of India which is none the less fascinating for being derived in part from an Italian source. They crossed the Syrian desert in a camel-caravan, and thence went down the Euphrates to Babylon, observing the ruins of the Tower of Babel not far from it. Two days farther on was " a strange thing to see : a mouth that doth continually throw forth against the air boiling pitch with a filthy smoke : which pitch doth run abroad into a great field which is always full thereof. The Moors say that it is the mouth of Hell." [3] (Some may think, observing the consequences oil has had for civilisation, that it has proved to be.) Arrived at Ormuz, they were arrested on the excuse that Drake had fired two shots at a galleon of the King of Portugal in the Moluccas : " and so perceiving that this did greatly grieve them, I asked if they would be revenged of me for that which Master Drake had done ? To the which he [the Aveador] answered,

[1] Hakluyt, III. 269-70.   [2] *Ibid.* 271.   [3] *Ibid.* 283.

No, although his meaning was to the contrary."[1]   But Newbery had been at Ormuz before—no doubt in the Portuguese trade— and he had a friend in the Captain of the fort, who had been well sweetened by presents and allowed them to go on by sea to Goa, on the western coast of India, the chief link in the chain of Portuguese stations that controlled the trade along these coasts all the way to Macao in China.

At Goa they were thrown into prison again : " if these troubles had not chanced, I had been in possibility to have made as good a voyage as ever any man made with so much money ".[2]   Those cold, blue, all-seeing eyes in the Escorial caught up with their doings : Philip wrote once and again, in fact four times, ordering their retention and extradition.   But, as usual, he was too late : the birds had flown.   " We presently determined rather to seek our liberties than to be in danger for ever to be slaves in the country, for it was told us we should have the strapado.   Whereupon presently, 5 April 1585, in the morning we ran from thence."[3]   They made south for Golconda, apparently to investigate the possibilities of trade in precious stones : one of the company, Leeds, was a jeweller.   Then they made north-west to the court of the Great Mogul, at Agra and Fatipur, " two very great cities, either of them much greater than London and very populous ".[4]   Here they separated : Newbery was anxious to get home to report on the possibilities and arrange a new venture, evidently to come by sea via the Cape to Bengal, for he directed Fitch thither " and did promise me, if it pleased God, to meet me in Bengal within two years with a ship out of England ".[5]   On the overland route back, Newbery died, it is " unknown how or where ".   " A pioneer in the exploration of Mesopotamia and Southern Persia, his crowning achievement had been to lead the first English commercial expedition to reach India."[6]   Leeds the jeweller remained behind with the Mogul in Fatipur, " who did entertain him very well and gave him an house and five slaves, an horse and every day six shillings in money ".[7]   Fitch proceeded on his yet more wonderful travels, down the Ganges to Hugli, up into Kutch Bihar and the foothills of the Himalayas, by ship to Pegu (Burma) and thence into Siam ; then along the Malay coast to

[1] *Ibid.* 277.   [2] *Ibid.* 278.   [3] *Ibid.* 287.
[4] *Ibid.* 289.   [5] *Ibid.* 290.
[6] Sir W. Foster, *England's Quest of Eastern Trade*, 287.   [7] Hakluyt, III. 290.

Malacca, noting the possibilities of the trade with China. In March 1588 he began his journey back by sea via Colombo and Goa to Ormuz, where he managed to conceal his identity. He arrived back in London in 1591, eight years after he had set out, to find that he had been deemed dead and his goods divided. He lived on to become a member of the East India Company and give them valuable advice and, after his long wanderings, was happily buried in the church of St. Katherine Cree.

In the same year that Fitch returned—in response to a petition of the London merchants to the Queen, after the defeat of the Armada, now to penetrate to the East Indies via the Cape—the first reconnaissance was made, with three fighting merchant ships, the *Penelope, Merchant Royal* and *Edward Bonaventure*, with Lancaster in the last.[1] Lancaster had lived for many years in Portugal as merchant and as soldier ; after Philip's annexation of the country he had come away with bitterness in his heart—it is probable that, like Hawkins, he had been given reason to repine and get his own back. On the way out, there was so heavy a mortality from scurvy that from Table Bay the *Merchant Royal* was sent back and the rest of her company distributed between the other two ships ; shortly after leaving the Cape the *Penelope* went down with all hands in a storm ; Lancaster was alone in the Indian Ocean, with a very inadequate idea of its navigation. He managed, after he had given up hope, to pass Cape Comorin and get round Ceylon, then to make for Malaya and the Malacca Strait to prey on Portuguese shipping. His men were very sick and insisted on returning home. Rounding the Cape he wished to make for Brazil, to catch, in addition to whatever else was going, the homeward winds. The ship's company, knowing better, insisted on a direct course home and naturally got into the Doldrums, where they were becalmed and sickness increased. The only thing left was to make for the West Indies in the hope of picking up victuals, which were at an end. Getting out of the Caribbean by the Florida Channel, the ship was blown back upon the Bermudas—the first English ship there ; but food was utterly spent and with great difficulty, the men ready to mutiny, they got back to their old anchorage off the island of Mona. Here Lancaster and eighteen men landed to search for provisions ; those aboard, five men and a boy, left him marooned and went

---

[1] *The Voyages of Sir James Lancaster,* ed. Sir W. Foster (Hakluyt Soc.), xii. foll.

off with the ship, which was—fools that they were—shortly afterwards cast away on the coast. Lancaster and his remnant were brought back by a French ship. But what a voyage !—all that the *Merchant Royal* had returned with was a cargo of sick men : it serves to illustrate the hardships and discouragements of these early Cape voyages to the East.

Meanwhile, provoking evidence of the incomparable wealth of the eastern trade accumulated. In 1587 Drake had captured the first East Indies carrack, the *San Felipe* : she was worth £108,000. (Multiply !) In 1592 the *Madre de Dios* was taken : " an instance of God's great favour towards our nation, who, by putting this purchase into our hands, hath manifestly discovered those secret trades and Indian riches, which hitherto lay strangely hidden and cunningly concealed from us ".[1] It seemed that " the will of God for our good is (if our weakness could apprehend it) to have us communicate with them in those East Indian treasures, and by the erection of a lawful traffic to better our means to advance true religion and His holy service ". A very useful treasure taken was a complete account of China, its resources and the riches of its trade, a volume " enclosed in a case of sweet cedar wood and lapped up almost an hundred fold in fine Calicut cloth, as though it had been some incomparable jewel ".[2] The *Madre de Dios* was worth £140,000 ; the *Cinco Llagas* (Five Wounds), which put up a strong resistance and was burnt to the water's edge in the Azores, was said to have been worth even more.

In 1596 Sir Robert Dudley equipped three ships to go out after these treasures. There is something touching about their names, that no-one has observed : the *Bear*, the *Bear's Whelp*, the *Benjamin*. The bear was the family crest of the dead Leicester ; the bear's whelp was Dudley, Leicester's son, his Benjamin, who could never be recognised, though it was he who carried in his blood the ability and the passionate interest in the country's maritime expansion of his father and his grandfather.[3] Beating

[1] Hakluyt, V. 66. [2] q. Foster, *op. cit.* 137.

[3] Sir Robert Dudley was Leicester's son by Lady Douglas Sheffield, who subsequently married Sir Edward Stafford : they were patrons of Hakluyt, whom Stafford took as his chaplain when he went as ambassador to Paris. We have an illustration of Leicester's keen interest in a letter of 1574 about a new voyage being set forth by the Muscovy Company : " I am fully persuaded it will fall out the best voyage that ever was made out of this realm, Drake or any. . . . I assure you that if I had had £10,000 in my purse I would have adventured it every penny myself." E. Lodge, *Illustrations of British History*, II. 125.

in vain against the walls of law and convention, Dudley left England and lived the life of an exile : in their own country the Dudleys had no successors.

The voyage met with utter disaster. The little *Benjamin* was lost off the Cape. Sickness reduced the men until there were only sufficient to work the *Bear*. On the Malay coast the *Whelp* was emptied and burnt ; then the *Bear* was lost somewhere in the Indian Ocean. One survivor, a Frenchman, was taken off Mauritius twenty months later : a French Robinson Crusoe, for the island was then uninhabited. Not a single Englishman survived of them all.

Such were the beginnings of English enterprise in the Indies. To provoke the faithful the more, the first Dutch voyage, 1595–7, was a modest success and three out of its four ships returned to prove that it could be done. There was immense enthusiasm in Holland and in 1598 no less than twenty-two ships left for the East. On Houtman's second voyage John Davis went as pilot-major of the fleet, to learn the route for his country. Spurred on by emulation of the Dutch, Lancaster was organising an expedition of the four best merchant ships in the kingdom, under the flag of the powerful privateer named by the old-fashioned, sententious Queen the *Scourge of Malice*. (That was very like her, but it was too much for other people, who renamed the ship the *Red Dragon*.) On the outward voyage there was the usual amount of sickness—one quarter of the men died—though not on Lancaster's ship, for he dosed his men with lime-juice. They made a successful voyage and laded pepper at Achin in Sumatra. At Bantam, in Java, Lancaster established the first English " factory " —destined, in spite of its pestilential climate, to be for long the centre of our trade in the East. Better still, he captured a carrack, which " made " the voyage ; the scene closes with the King of Achin and his nobles singing one of the Psalms of David, to which Lancaster and his companions responded with another.[1] Lancaster's safe return with all four ships may be taken to have established the trade via the Cape to the East Indies ; though it was left to Middleton, who headed the voyage urged by the Queen in 1601, to get to the Moluccas. Thenceforward the English had to contend with the intense opposition of the Dutch who were fighting to capture the Portuguese monopoly of the trade and had, in the struggle, not only the backing of the young

[1] *Voyages of Sir James Lancaster*, xxx.

state but its concentrated resources. By the time Lancaster got back, in September 1603, the Queen was dead ; himself a bachelor, he was able to leave his fortune for charitable purposes in his native town of Basingstoke and so to continue his name.[1]

The position the Dutch won in the Spice Islands forced the English back upon India, and the long tenuous tentacles began to reach the peninsula. In 1600 there came overland from Aleppo a Levant merchant, John Mildenhall—accompanied part way by a cleric, John Cartwright, who was simply out to see the world—who arrived at Agra and presented himself to the great Akbar, from whom he received trading privileges on behalf of the East India Company, in spite of the opposition and intrigues of the Portuguese and the Jesuits. Mildenhall came back to India once more, where he died a Catholic : his tomb still exists in the cemetery at Agra.[2] The Company directed its third voyage (1607) to the west coast and William Hawkins arrived òff Surat, where he established the "factory" that became subsequently so famous in the Company's history. He, too, travelled to Agra, where he was kindly received by Akbar's son, Jahangir ; but he was obstructed in his demands for a permanent footing for trade. Succeeding voyages met with armed interference from the Portuguese ; there was a series of fights in which the English were victorious, and this inclined the Court to listen to their petitions for more favour. Downton's victory over the Goa squadron clinched the matter : English gunnery was more effective than arguments.

At the same time Sir Thomas Smythe proposed to the Company to send a special ambassador to obtain a permanent footing for our trade from the Mogul. Sir Thomas Roe was sent, in proper state and equipped with suitable presents. He was both able and good-looking : he had been an Esquire of the Body to Queen Elizabeth, with whom good looks in such a position were a *sine qua non*. An extravagant young man, he had depleted his patrimony and now undertook the journey to India to recoup himself, as so many were to do later. He bore a letter from King James emphasising the naval strength of the English, " which maketh us ever a terror to all other nations ".[3] The ambassador determined to take a high line from the first :

---

[1] Cf. Bacon's dictum, *The England of Elizabeth*, 497.
[2] Foster, *England's Quest of Eastern Trade*, 173 foll.
[3] *The Embassy of Sir Thomas Roe to India*, ed. W. Foster (Hakluyt Soc.), I. viii.

hitherto the English had not asserted their dignity but had been suppliants for trade. Roe's line paid. The Portuguese were pressing for the exclusion of the English. Jahangir was impressed by Roe's demeanour ; but what impressed him more, perhaps, was the English naval victory off Goa. Roe secured his grant of a permanent footing for trade : his scarlet liveries in the streets of Agra were prophetic of future empire.

From Surat the English factors on the western coast opened up regular trade with the Persian Gulf, and took part in the reduction of Ormuz, which marked the end of the Portuguese domination for the past century. From 1608 the Company, under Smythe's inspired leadership, resolved to send out ships annually. On the east coast the establishment of a " factory " at Masulipatam was the first move that foreshadowed expansion south to Madras and north to Bengal. In 1612 the English entered Siam and penetrated into the Shan States. Next year the English ship *Clove* arrived on the coast of Japan, where Will Adams, the Gillingham pilot, was living his protected, favoured life. He had arrived there in 1600 in terrible straits, after a desperate Dutch voyage across the Pacific. This excellent seaman and shipbuilder had won the favour of the Shogun, the able Iyéyasu, by building ships on western lines for him and giving him some elementary instruction in geometry and mathematics. In return, Adams was given an estate with many servants and a wife (he had a wife and family in England) ; but he was never allowed to return until, when at last the *Clove* arrived to initiate trade with Japan, he no longer wished to go back. It seems that he, too, was bitten with the desire to discover the outlet of the North-West Passage and that the Shogun had promised his aid. But Adams, like all the other Elizabethan navigators, died with his desire unfulfilled, his dream unrealised : his memory has always been held in honour in Japan; his tomb still remains on the hill overlooking the harbour of Yokusuka.

In all these movements that we have traced we see the tremendous energy that had been generated in the southern half of the small island in the northern seas—lunging out northeast towards Siberia, in an arc around the Arctic ice-pack to Greenland and the broken lands and passages north of Canada ; down the African coast, into the Caribbean and southward along the Brazil coast through the Straits of Magellan, into and across the Pacific ; and, lastly, tackling the long direct voyage round the Cape and across the Indian Ocean to the Far East. It was a tremendous outburst of human energy to take shape within a few decades : Portugal and Spain had been over most of the area before (always excepting the Arctic North), but they had taken more than a century about it. It was an essential part of that sweep of mind, body and spirit that gave the Elizabethan age its uniqueness. As with the modest beginnings of the Industrial Revolution, we can see something of the shape things were to take for the English peoples foreshadowed in these early efforts and achievements : the Gold Coast, the Cape, the Gulf, India, Burma, the Malay peninsula, the route to China ; the West Indies, Trinidad, the Plate Coast, Cape Horn, the Pacific islands, the quest for *Terra Australis* ; the northern waters off Spitzbergen, the White Sea, Iceland, Greenland, Labrador, Newfoundland : what future reverberations these voyages were to have in English ears !

CHAPTER VI

AMERICAN COLONISATION

THE obstacle that blocked the way to the riches of the East was a whole New World : we have seen the energy the Elizabethans displayed in getting round it. In the end they were forced to tackle the problem of the obstacle itself. In the process—in the usual human way, without quite grasping what was happening—they gradually unveiled the unexpected truth : that the discovery of the New World was much the greatest event in the history of the Old.

Only a few elect spirits glimpsed the significance that America might come to hold for England herself ; but among these were the most characteristic Elizabethans. We owe the direction of English interest into planting North America, the expansion of our society across the Atlantic, to two groups essentially : on the side of action, that of Humphrey Gilbert, Ralegh, Grenville and their friends ; on the intellectual and propaganda side, Dee, the Hakluyts, Adrian Gilbert. These groups were closely linked and had common affiliations ; they were in intimate contact with the Queen, who was interested in everything that concerned America, while Walsingham exercised a constant supervision in the matter and encouraged the projects all he possibly could. It is fascinating to observe that of these two forward-marching groups one came from the West Country, the other from the Welsh Border. We have already noticed that it is the West Country group, up to the hilt in Irish colonisation, that took the lead in planting North America : the same impulse to expansion drove them forward—we may say relentlessly, for it led Gilbert, Grenville and Ralegh each to his death—to make a much longer leap across the Atlantic. While the Hakluyts and John Dee, like the Cecils, the Parrys and the Devereux, came from the Border country of Hereford. May it not be that belonging to a borderland generates some special self-consciousness that makes for expansion ?

The English needed prodding : they were as backward in this sphere as we find them in others. It is not until the beginning of Elizabeth's reign that we encounter the first projects for settling in North America, and then in imitation of, or in association with, the French Huguenots. Even so, these remained but projects. After his return from his first Florida colony in 1562, Jean Ribault came to England.[1] The translation of his report of it—the first detailed account of a visit to North America to appear in English—stimulated interest, and plans were made for a joint Anglo-French enterprise under Ribault and the unsatisfactory Stukeley to carry on the French colony. This fell through, as did another scheme that Hawkins should establish a colony there. Meanwhile, Laudonnière had replanted it, and Hawkins paid it a friendly visit on his way home, in 1565, before the Spaniards extinguished it by fire and sword.

By this time Gilbert's interest was already alight. In his *Discourse* he suggested a settlement as a trading base half-way to Asia " about Sierra Nevada " (*i.e.* California), and went on to advocate, the first to do so, colonisation in America for its own sake, to settle there " such needy people of our country which now trouble the commonwealth ".[2] As early as 1567 he was considering a voyage to America. His experience in Ireland broadened his conception of the purposes of colonisation : the transplanting and reproduction of English society on American soil, territorial wealth and power for its promoters.

Adrian Gilbert was a close neighbour of the elder Hakluyt in the Middle Temple, and it was to the latter's chamber there that his young cousin came, when a boy at Westminster, and found, in the books of cosmography and the world-map lying open upon the board, his vocation. Never was a vocation more tenaciously pursued, and few have been more influential. At Christ Church the younger Hakluyt laid the foundation of his unique knowledge of voyages of discovery by reading all that had been printed on the subject in the modern as well as the ancient tongues ; he equipped himself to lecture, a new departure, on mathematics and geography, " the eye of history ". At Oxford he was friendly with the most

[1] D. B. Quinn, *Voyages and Colonising Enterprises of Sir Humphrey Gilbert* (Hakluyt Soc.), I. 5-6.
[2] q. *ibid.* 9.

promising young mathematicians, Hariot and Thomas Warner ; the Hungarian scholar, Stephen Parmenius—drowned in Gilbert's Newfoundland voyage—was his bed-fellow. The five years he spent as chaplain to the ambassador in Paris, 1583–8, gave him the opportunity, of which he made the fullest use, to make contact with continental scholarship.

We see how the threads draw together on the threshold of the marvellous 1580s. English progress towards the exploration and settlement of America had been slow ; when it came, like everything else it came with a rush. Hakluyt's propaganda was brought forth by Gilbert's projects for a series of voyages for discovery and planting along the North American coast—the fruit of the fertilising, experimenting 1570s. English fishermen, long after their Breton and Basque rivals, were upon the Banks and in Newfoundland in force. Anthony Parkhurst, who worked with the Bristol merchants, had made several private voyages to the Gulf of St. Lawrence and advocated a permanent settlement on Newfoundland for the benefit and protection of the fisheries, which had expanded from thirty sail to fifty in the past four years.[1] Moreover, the English ships were better armed, so that they were " commonly lords of the harbours where they fish "—the advantage of which was brought home on the outbreak of war with Spain, when the whole of the Spaniards' fishing fleet was rounded up and captured by Bernard Drake. In 1578 Gilbert managed to get together his first expedition to plant a colony, it would seem on the coast of Florida ; but the enterprise broke up in the Atlantic and little is known of it, except that Ralegh was in command of his own ship and had some hard fighting to get back. But Gilbert was not going to give up : next year he sent a tiny frigate of eight tons[2] to reconnoitre the coast : it crossed the Atlantic safely and landed the men—no-one knows where, probably in the latitude of New England.[3]

Along with Gilbert's voyages the propaganda for American planting was getting rapidly under way : in letter upon letter, pamphlet after pamphlet, book after book, the younger Hakluyt directed attention to the most important area for expansion,

[1] E. G. R. Taylor, *Writings and Correspondence of the Two Richard Hakluyts* (Hakluyt Soc.), I. 14-15, 128.

[2] Probably in modern tonnage nearer sixteen.

[3] Quinn, *op. cit.* I. 50.

upon which the future destiny of the nation was mainly to depend. The whole emphasis was upon " Western Planting " as against Eastern voyages. We may say that the focusing of the nation's interest upon America, the priority of the American school in thought and action, was largely due to the life's work of the younger Hakluyt : it has been given to few men to fertilise the history of their country so prodigiously. No effort was too laborious for him to undertake : he journeyed two hundred miles simply to get the story of the last survivor of a Newfoundland voyage.[1] He made himself the prime organiser of geographical publishing ; the smallest part of his work, that of translation alone, was enough to fill a big volume. The successive editions of his great book did not exhaust the immense amount of material he accumulated : what was left over formed the foundation of Purchas's monstrous edifice. To Hakluyt we owe the survival of nearly everything we know of the American voyages.[2] He was the one continuing figure that linked the two waves of Virginia enterprise, the successive attempts of the 1580s and those that gained a permanent footing after Elizabeth's death. And, like an Elizabethan, he did not hesitate to tell his readers " what restless nights, what painful days, what heat, what cold I have endured ; how many famous libraries I have researched into ; what variety of ancient and modern writers I have perused ; what a number of old records, patents, privileges, letters, etc. I have redeemed from obscurity and perishing ; into how manifold acquaintance I have entered ; what expenses I have not spared ; and yet what fair opportunities of private gain, preferment and ease I have neglected ".[3] A complaint characteristic of so insatiable an age : in fact he was well rewarded by the Queen in preferment, still more in the estimation of the leading spirits of the time and by posterity.

There is a great difference to be observed between the elder and the younger Hakluyts : a difference not only of temper and interest, but a difference between generations. As the international tension increased with Spain's power, with her growing pressure upon and interference with other countries in Europe, and with her resistance to their expansion beyond, the spirit of the younger generation in England became more

[1] G. B. Parks, *Richard Hakluyt and the English Voyages*, 126.
[2] D. B. Quinn, *The Roanoke Voyages* (Hakluyt Soc.), I. 9.
[3] Taylor, II. 433.

aggressive and intense. It can be heard in the younger Hakluyt's earliest writing, on the threshold of the annexation of the Portuguese Empire to the crown of Spain : " the peril that may ensue to all the princes of Europe if the King of Spain be suffered to enjoy Portugal with the East Indies is such as is not on sudden to be set down, but is a matter of great and grave consideration ".[1] It led him to propose the occupation of the Straits of Magellan. The elder Hakluyt was primarily interested in the economic aspects of overseas trade, in new commodities and techniques for industry, in opening up markets for our products and, as a consequence, in planting unemployed and " the offals of our people " overseas. The mind of the younger Hakluyt grasped the strategic issue of the struggle with Spain for a place in the outer world. His publication of the *Divers Voyages* to the North-West, in 1582, was intended to stake out the English claim to North America as unoccupied by the Spaniards ; and in his Preface to Philip Sidney, who was a sub-grantee under Gilbert for an immense tract of land there, Hakluyt says : " I marvel not a little that since the first discovery of America (which is now full fourscore and ten years) after so great conquest and plantings of the Spaniards and the Portingales there, that we of England could never have the grace to set fast footing in such fertile and temperate places as are left as yet unpossessed by them. But again when I consider that there is a time for all men, and see the Portingales' time to be out of date and that the nakedness of the Spaniards and their long-hidden secrets are now at length espied . . . I conceive great hope that the time approacheth and now is that we of England may share and part stakes (if we will ourselves) both with the Spaniard and the Portingale in part of America and other regions as yet undiscovered."[2]

He was instinctively and prophetically right. The marvellous outpouring of the Peninsular peoples that had affected so much of the outer world was nearing the end of its impulse. The wave of Spanish conquest in America had in the main spent itself.[3] The Empire had achieved its form. The Spaniards and Portuguese had checkmated the French—or rather, as Hakluyt pointed out, their own internal dissensions had done ; and

---

[1] Taylor, I. 139.
[2] *Ibid.* 175.
[3] F. A. Kirkpatrick, *The Spanish Conquistadores*, 328.

he added that if it had not been for the wars, the Low Countries would have undertaken the discovery of America. The opportunity was England's for the taking. Nor did he fear any more than his friends, the seamen, the challenge it involved to Spanish power : he thought Spain's real strength over-estimated, the resources and man-power of the Peninsula inadequate to support such a structure ; that the structure was maintained by prestige and American supplies of treasure. " I mean first to begin with the West Indies as there to lay a chief foundation for his over-throw. . . . Philip rather governeth in the West Indies by opinion than might. For the small manred of Spain itself being always at the best slenderly peopled was never able to rule so many regions, or to keep in subjection such worlds of people as be there."[1]

In 1578 Gilbert had got his Letters Patent to discover and occupy lands not possessed by any Christian prince ; he and his heirs were granted the lands they should settle in perpetuity, with the power to sub-grant such lands and to expel any intruders within 200 leagues.[2] Gilbert was to exercise all jurisdiction and make laws for the colony, " agreeable to the form of the laws and policies of England ". In other words, he had power to found a new England beyond the seas, and in this high endeavour he spent himself and his own and his wife's fortunes. A group of Catholics, headed by Sir George Peckham and Sir Thomas Gerrard, were interested in the prospect of finding an outlet for their co-religionists, where they might have toleration for their worship. But the Spanish ambassador, Mendoza, had his eye on the preparations and warned them through their priests that they would immediately have their throats cut if they went there, as Jean Ribault's men had had.[3] He also warned them that they would be imperilling their consciences by going contrary to the interests of His Holiness. Though Peckham continued to support Gilbert, the Catholics took no active part. Mendoza did : he had a spy on board Gilbert's expedition of 1578 to report the whole course of the action.[4] One sees the intolerable conflict of conscience Catholics were pressed into, and how Protestantism was identified with the interest of the nation.

Gilbert's patent gave him six years in which to get going,

[1] Taylor, II. 246-7.
[2] Quinn, I. 188-94.
[3] *Ibid.* II. 278-9.
[4] *Ibid.* I. 199.

and in 1582 he " brought his last and most elaborate project
to light : it branches into a maze of individual and corporate
enterprises for the . . . settlement of North America and . . .
led to the first plantation of Virginia less than a year after his
death ".[1]   Gilbert got together five small ships, of which the
largest was set forth by his half-brother Ralegh, now enjoying
the ticklish delights of the Queen's first favour.   At the last
moment she desired Gilbert not to go, as " a man noted of not
good hap by sea " : as usual, not wrong.[2]   Then she relented,
and sent him a token by Ralegh, " an anchor guided by a Lady ".
It did not mitigate his ill-luck.

The somewhat boring godliness of Edward Hayes's famous
account of the voyage does not disguise a critical attitude to
Gilbert's failings : the rash intemperateness, the bad judgment,
the rages, the sadistic streak in him.   On the other hand, there
was the sense of high purpose, the dedication, and Gilbert had
imagination and a certain bedraggled nobility.   Gilbert was
" the first of our nation that carried people to erect an habita-
tion in those northerly countries of America ".[3]   It was indeed
time, for was not this the last age of the world when the time
was complete for receiving those Gentiles into His mercy ?
(Poor creatures—when one thinks what was to happen to them
in the process ! But only sceptics like Montaigne had any
perception of that.)   It seemed probable " by event of prece-
dent attempts made by the Spaniards and French sundry times,
that the countries lying north of Florida God hath reserved
the same to be reduced unto Christian civility by the English
nation ".

" We were in number in all about 260 men : among whom
we had of every faculty good choice, as shipwrights, masons,
carpenters, smiths and such-like requisites to such an action ;
also mineral men and refiners.   Besides, for solace of our people
and allurement of the savages, we were provided of music in
good variety, not omitting the least toys, as morris dancers,
hobby horses and May-like conceits to delight the savage people,
whom we intended to win by all fair means possible."[4]   Arrived
in the harbour of St. Johns in Newfoundland, Gilbert took
possession of it " and 200 leagues every way, invested the Queen's

---

[1] Quinn, I. 55.   [2] *Ibid.* 82-3.
[3] Hakluyt, *Principal Navigations* (Everyman edn.), VI. 3-5.
[4] *Ibid.* 12.

Majesty with the title and dignity thereof, had delivered unto him (after the custom of England) a rod and a turf of the same soil, entering possession also for him his heirs and assigns for ever. . . . And afterwards were erected not far from that place the arms of England engraven in lead and enfixed upon a pillar of wood."[1] So Newfoundland became the first and oldest dominion of the Crown overseas.

When Gilbert left the Newfoundland coast for the mainland, he sailed into a void : Spaniards and Portuguese had navigated the coast before, but they were careful to keep their soundings secret. The regular course was to sail northward from Florida with the winds : Gilbert was to try the opposite and sail southward along the unknown coast—the way Cabot had been lost. One Wednesday night, " like the swan that singeth before her death, they in the Admiral, or *Delight*, continued in sounding of trumpets with drums and fifes, also winding the cornets, oboes, and in the end of their jollity left with the battle and ringing of doleful knells ".[2] Next day, keeping very ill watch, she struck upon a shoal and foundered. It meant the overthrow of the voyage, for a hundred men were drowned and most of the stores and equipment for planting was lost with her. Nothing for it but to turn back. Gilbert professed himself encouraged by what he had seen of these northern parts, " affirming that this voyage had won his heart from the South, and that he was now become a Northern man altogether ".[3] He determined to return next spring. On his way back through the tempestuous seas of that summer he refused to move from the tiny *Squirrel* of 10 tons, in which he was last seen reading a book before she too foundered. The fact was that he was afraid to be thought afraid of the sea and incurred the fate of such as " prefer the wind of a vain report to the weight of his own life ".[4]

Ralegh, who was closely in touch with his half-brother's originating ideas and the nearest to him in temerarious imagination, at once undertook to carry them forward. He obtained a new charter with even fuller powers and had it confirmed by Parliament. Such time as he could spare from intimate attendance upon the Queen—these early days were the spring-time of their excited interest in each other—he spent in preparing a voyage : his unexpected fortune in finding favour in those calculating

---

[1] *Ibid.* 18.   [2] *Ibid.* 28.
[3] *Ibid.* 34.   [4] *Ibid.* 35.

eyes gave him the resources. The Hakluyts were called in to write the promoters' literature : the elder in his "Inducements to the Liking of the Voyage" concentrated on the complementary character of the southern region in view, with a climate like that of the Mediterranean offering, it was hoped, similar possibilities—vines, olives, mulberries, sugar.[1] The younger Hakluyt wrote an important tract, the *Discourse of Western Planting*, intended only for the eye of the Queen (and not published until our time), advocating the view that North American colonisation was a matter for the enterprise and resources of the state, rather than of private persons.[2] This was not the Queen's view. To render service to the country was what she expected of those to whom she opened the treasures of her favour. To the Virginia voyages—conscious, as ever, of her maiden-state—she contributed precisely the name Virginia. However, we must allow, more generously, that without her favour Ralegh would hardly have had the wherewithal.

Immediately upon the issue of his charter, in 1584, Ralegh sent out a couple of West Country barks to the southern region, approaching it via the West Indies and up the coast of Florida. Here among the low sandy islands and fish-swarming sounds of the North Carolina coast, they reported an earthly Paradise : "the soil is the most plentiful, sweet, fruitful and wholesome of all the world. . . . We found the people most gentle, loving and faithful, void of all guile and treason, and such as live after the manner of the golden age."[3] Ralegh's sea-captains brought back two leading young Indians, Manteo and Wanchese, who play an important part in the story of these voyages, a symbolic one in the history of the contacts between races.

Next year the expedition set sail : three ships of between 100 and 150 tons, one of fifty, a small bark and two pinnaces. Ralegh was ardently anxious to lead it, but the Queen could not forgo his fascinating company : his cousin Grenville took his place and successfully planted the first colony of Englishmen in America on Roanoke Island in Pamlico Sound.[4] Impossible to exaggerate the importance of this first colony, though it remained there only a year : from it everything else sprang,

---

[1] Taylor, *Hakluyts*, II. 327 foll.
[2] *Ibid.* 211 foll.
[3] Hakluyt, *ed. cit.* VI. 128.
[4] *v.* for the story in full, my *Sir Richard Grenville*, c. xi.

attempt after attempt, until at length the English took permanent root. It bore a very representative company to the new England that was to rise on the other side of the Atlantic : Ralph Lane, one of the Queen's equerries and one of those who got their first colonial experience in Ireland ; the young Cavendish, who followed in Drake's footsteps in circumnavigating the globe. Two experts have left us a brilliant record of the colony—which would have made an even stronger impression on posterity if their papers had survived more fully. A number of John White's maps of the area and drawings illustrating Indian ways of life have survived to give him a name as the first of English water-colourists ;[1] for long after his own day his maps remained the authority for this part of the sea-board : they were the only ones based on survey from the ground. His drawings were used for the engravings in de Bry's famous book on America, which announced to Europe that a new colonial power had entered the world. Hariot's *Brief and True Report* is a model of scientific and anthropological observation, the first classic contribution of the English to knowledge of America.[2] For a century his observations were cited as authoritative by European botanists ; the impact of a first-class scientific mind would have been all the more marked if his papers had not disappeared.

Grenville's expedition, like the succeeding ones, had a strong West Country contingent, since it was largely set forth from there : on this first were an Arundell, a Gorges, a Kendall, a Prideaux, a Rouse. Grenville landed his colony safely, with the livestock he had collected in the West Indies, explored the country to the south and sailed back to England to bring reinforcements and supplies next year. He left under Lane a colony of over a hundred men to make good. They made Roanoke their headquarters, whence they explored north towards Chesapeake Bay. This was the area, favoured by Hakluyt, where permanent settlement ultimately took root : what became the colony and state of Virginia proper. It had the indispensable advantage of deep-water harbours on the Bay, while Roanoke was in the midst of the dangerous shoals and shallows of the North Carolina sounds, exposed to hurricanes and with no anchorage. The colony came up against the funda-mental difficulty of all early settlements, Spanish too, that of

[1] Cf. Laurence Binyon, *English Water Colours*, 1-4.
[2] Hakluyt, VI. 164 foll.

food supplies : with their primitive cultivation there was not enough for both Indians and Europeans. Mutual mistrust and suspicion spread, after the early welcome, and led to conflict in which, Hariot says, " some of our company towards the end of the year showed themselves too fierce in slaying some of the people in some towns, upon causes that on our part might easily enough have been borne withal ".[1] It was an Irishman who brought in the head of Pemisapan, leader of the " conspiracy " against the colonists : Ireland over again. Some of the Indians, impressed by the English having no˙women with them and not relishing theirs, thought that the visitants were not born of women and therefore not mortal, but had put on immortality. Others " would likewise seem to prophesy that there were more of our generation yet to come to kill theirs and take their places, as some thought the purpose was by that which was already done ".[2] Here they were not wrong.

Lane wrote to Walsingham from " Port Ferdinando in Virginia " that he was " comforted chiefly hereunto with an assurance of her Majesty's greatness hereby to grow by the addition of such a kingdom as this is to the rest of her dominions ",[3] and to Hakluyt that they had discovered the mainland to be " the goodliest and most pleasing territory of the world, for the soil is of a huge unknown greatness . . . and the climate˙ so wholesome that we have not had one sick. . . . If Virginia had but horses and kine in some reasonable proportion, I dare assure myself, being inhabited with English no realm in Christendom were comparable to it."[4] To Sir Philip Sidney he wrote that they had discovered the nakedness of the Spaniards in the islands of Hispaniola and Puerto Rico and advocated his leading a small force to take possession of them.[5] Drake was, at this moment of the entry into open war, ravaging the West Indies : we see how these enterprises fit together strategically in the attack on the life-line of the Spanish Empire in Central America. A base so near Florida would be a constant threat to the shipping passing out by the Florida Channel.

On his way home Drake anchored off the coast and offered the colonists a boat and further supplies, since Grenville was long

[1] Hakluyt, VI. 193.
[2] *Ibid.* 192.
[3] q. Quinn, ed., *The Roanoke Voyages, 1584–90* (Hakluyt Soc.), I. 203.
[4] *Ibid.* 208.   [5] *Ibid.* 205.

overdue : spirits were flagging, nerves frayed by the novel ordeal, moreover, Lane mistrusted and detested Grenville. A sudden hurricane arose and Drake had to put to sea. The thought of their succour vanishing over the horizon was too much for the mercurial Elizabethans : they opted, before it was too late, to return with him. Shortly after, there arrived a fast bark, which Ralegh had " freighted with all manner of things in most plentiful manner for the supply and relief of his colony ".[1] Not finding the colonists, the ship returned with all its provisions to England. A fortnight later Grenville appeared on the scene—somewhat delayed by his propensity for looking out for prizes on the way— with a substantial reinforcement in the *Roebuck* and the *Tiger*. Surprised to hear no news of the colony, he travelled up into the country looking for them. He was " unwilling to lose the possession of the country which Englishmen had so long held " and decided to leave fifteen men on Roanoke Island with supplies for a couple of years, until he could come out and re-found the colony.[2]

It must have been a bitter disappointment to Ralegh and Grenville, and it is not a little ironical that the whole sequence of planting should have been thrown out of gear by Drake, of all people. Nor was it the first time that he had crossed Grenville.

In 1587, " intending to persevere in the planting of his country of Virginia ", Ralegh sent out a new colony, some hundred men and seventeen women, under John White as governor.[3] They were directed to search for the survivors at Roanoke and then to move on and plant their settlement on Chesapeake Bay. This the ship's crew refused to do, and the colonists showed themselves insubordinate and undisciplined—a way to deserve the fate that overtook them. Landing on Roanoke at sunset, they found the bones of one of the fifteen ; the fort had been razed, " but all the houses standing intact, saving that the nether rooms of them were overgrown with melons of divers sorts and deer within them feeding on those melons : so we returned to our company, without hope of ever seeing any of the fifteen men living ". Nor did they. On Croatoan Island, inhabited by the faithful Manteo's kindred, they heard the story of how Wanchese, leading their enemies, had caught the colonists off their guard and driven them out of Roanoke. For

---

[1] Hakluyt, VI. 162. [2] *Ibid.* 164. [3] *Ibid.* 196 foll.

his faithful service Manteo was named lord of the island and rewarded with the inestimable benefit of christening. On 18 August a daughter was born to Eleanor, John White's daughter, wife of Ananias Dare—the first English child born in America. They named her Virginia.

The idea of the 1587 colony was some vague sort of self-government, with the colonists themselves investing their all : each volunteer was to have 500 acres, with Ralegh as a mere overlord in the background. Such democratic conceptions were to put too much of a strain upon Elizabethan nature ; the colonists first sent the Governor home for supplies and then went their own way to perdition—how, no-one has ever discovered. It has become known to history as the Lost Colony, when really it had more promising prospects of survival, since they had some women with them to breed from and continue the stock.

It must have been evident to Ralegh that what was needed was the force and authority of a Grenville ; and they both exerted themselves to put forth their biggest effort. But it was now the year 1588 : the supreme moment was drawing near : all that they could do was contingent upon events. Preparations went forward at Bideford, Grenville's home port ; meanwhile, White begged some speedy relief for the colony and two little pinnaces, the *Brave* and the *Roe*, were despatched. But they never got across the Atlantic : in the disturbed conditions at sea that summer they were continually chased and giving chase, and came back to Bideford considerably mauled. When Grenville was ready to leave, with a strong little fleet of three ships and some pinnaces, the news came that the Armada was ready to sail : his voyage was countermanded and he was ordered to take his ships round to Plymouth to serve under Drake.

Both Ralegh and Grenville were discouraged : nothing to show for all their efforts and all the money poured out. As we have seen, they transferred their attention to the more promising prospects in Ireland ; Grenville spent the greater part of the next two years working at his plantation there. In 1587 Ralegh, occupied with so much else, had transferred control of the colony to a Governor and twelve assistants ; now in 1589 he handed over his powers to a company of London merchants, principal among them being Sanderson and Thomas Smythe.

Not until 1590 did they manage to send John White away with three ships.[1]   Arrived at Roanoke, they found the agreed sign CRO, signifying that the colonists had gone to Croatoan, without any sign of distress.   But they found pieces of the colonists' guns, evidently overthrown by the Indians ; and in one place White found " five chests that had been carefully hidden of the planters, and of the same chests three were my own, and about the place many of my things spoiled and broken and my books torn from the covers, the frames of some of my pictures and maps rotten and spoiled with rain, and my armour almost eaten through with rust ".   He concluded that this had been done by enemy Indians on the departure of the colony for friendly Croatoan. `Unforgivably, White never went to Croatoan to see what had happened to them.   A sudden storm blew up and the ships had to put to sea out of those shallow sounds for safety.   Some think that remnants of the colony were lost in the forest trying to make their way to Chesapeake Bay : there is a tradition that white blood flowed in the veins of some of the tribes.   No doubt : the colonists must have been scalped and eaten.

When Bacon came to write his essay " Of Plantations ", he wrote the epitaph on this one :   " It is the sinfullest thing in the world to forsake or destitute a plantation once in forwardness ; for besides the dishonour, it is the guiltiness of blood of many commiserable persons ".[2]   It was the end of English colonising ventures in America for more than a decade.

More humane, less terrible than the Spaniards to the Indians —indeed not terrible at all—the English were in consequence unsuccessful.   The original intentions of English colonisation betray an embryo conception of humanitarian trusteeship to which the British Empire—any more than any other—has been unable wholly to adhere.   And yet there is a curious consistency of ideal that must be true to the English nature.   John Hooker, in his dedication of his Irish history to Ralegh, wrote :   " what can be more honourable to princes than to enlarge the bounds of their kingdoms without injury, wrong and bloodshed ;   and to frame them from a savage life to a civil government, neither of which the Spaniards in their government have performed ? "[3]

---

[1] Hakluyt, VI. 213 foll.
[2] *The Works of Francis Bacon* (ed. Spedding), VI. 459.
[3] q. Quinn, *op. cit.*, I. 491.

The English felt themselves morally superior to the Spaniards, " who because with all cruel inhumanity, contrary to all natural humanity, they subdued a naked and yielding people, whom they sought for gain and not for any religion or plantation of a commonwealth . . . did most cruelly tyrannize and against the course of all human nature did scorch and roast them to death, as by their own histories doth appear ".

However, Cortés and Pizarro had succeeded where the English, though understandably, had so far failed.

The more the English came to appreciate the difficulties of colonising, the more they were prepared to pay tribute to the Spaniards, who, after all, were the fountain-head of colonial experience and exploration, and had already explored more of North America than is generally realised.[1] When Virginia was at length under way, Michael Lock wrote : " consider the industry, travails of the Spaniard, their exceeding charge in furnishing so many ships . . . their continual supplies to further their attempts and their active and undaunted spirits in executing matters of that quality and difficulty, and lastly their constant resolution of plantation ".[2] Ralegh himself in the *History of the World* paid a noble tribute to the courage and constancy of the people he at once admired and detested as the tyrants of Europe : " I cannot forbear to commend the patient virtue of the Spaniards. We seldom or never find that any nation hath endured so many misadventures and miseries as the Spaniards have done in their Indian discoveries ; yet persisting in their enterprises with invincible constancy, they have annexed to their kingdom so many goodly provinces as bury the remembrance of all dangers past."[3]

Certainly Spain was determined to deny as much of North America as she could to other powers.[4] The order went forth for the creation of a series of posts along the coast of Florida. As early as 1572 the Spaniards were scouting in Chesapeake Bay, though they kept it quiet to themselves. When they heard of the English colony in *their* Florida,[5] they gave orders that

---

[1] Cf. J. B. Brebner, *The Explorers of North America, 1492–1806*, cc. v., vi.

[2] q. Quinn, *op. cit.* II. 717.

[3] q. F. A. Kirkpatrick, *The Spanish Conquistadores*, 346-7.

[4] Cf. Quinn, " Some Spanish Reactions to Elizabethan Colonial Enterprises ", *Trans. R. Hist. Soc.*, 1951.

[5] We must keep in mind that to the Spaniards North America was " Florida ", to the English " Virginia ".

it should be wiped out as the French colonies had been. In 1588 Pedro Menéndez Marquéus sent a bark along the coast as far as Chesapeake without finding any trace of the English. The intention was to build a strong fort on the Chesapeake : the failure of the English rendered it unnecessary. Menéndez urged Philip to conquer North America soon, for " if some other nations go to settle it, forming a friendship—as they will—with the local Indians, it will thereafter be most difficult to conquer and rule it ".[1]

In the curious way in which, for the English, defeats sometimes turn out advantageous, it may have been as well that those early colonies did not take root. The Spaniards would have tracked them down, and that might have led to the Spanish occupation of the coast up to Chesapeake Bay, where Jamestown was to be founded. The war in Europe brought about a recession of efforts on both sides in North America—and that left it open for the future to decide. The English preoccupation in home waters led to a temporary abandonment of colonial efforts : we have seen how the threat of the Armada frustrated Grenville's last endeavour. Later, the defeat of the Hawkins–Drake attack on the Caribbean in 1595–6 marked the turn of the crisis for Spain in Central America. But the long struggle had exhausted her. Menéndez tried in vain to revive Spanish interest in Florida ; henceforth there was recession, an ebbing of vitality and power : the wonderful century was over. Spain was ready to withdraw from Florida just when, towards the end of the war, the English were sending out expeditions again to look for new sites for permanent settlement.

There remained the possibilities of the Caribbean area—the islands not possessed by Spain, and Guiana, the vast unexplored country between the Orinoco and the Amazon. " Their time had not yet come, for, as long as the wars endured, true colonisation had to wait upon raiding and privateering."[2] The legend spread that up in the mountains of Guiana, beyond the gorges and the rapids that made it inaccessible, was the country of El Dorado, the gilded king, where gold was to be got in abundance. This fixation inspired the extraordinary career of Berrio, an old

[1] q. Quinn, *The Roanoke Voyages*, II. 772.
[2] J. A. Williamson, *The Age of Drake*, 361.

soldier of Charles V, last and most appealing of the conquistadors. An old man in his sixties, he three times attempted to penetrate to this country of gold, coming over the mountains from New Granada, performing astonishing feats of endurance, undergoing terrible privations and losses of men. At last he made up his mind that the only possible approach was from the coast, up the rivers and the rapids.

Ralegh was *au fait* with the subject ; and, himself disappointed with Virginia, in the fifteen-nineties it fell in with his needs and provided him with a new, an urgent, objective. For he had fallen into disgrace with the Queen. After years of protesting single-hearted devotion to the exacting royal spinster, devotion that had been well rewarded, Ralegh fell in love with one of her maids-of-honour, sullied the honour and had to marry her. It was an unforgivable offence : Elizabeth could not bear to think of the handsome men, who found favour in her eyes, finding pleasure in the arms of others. Ralegh and his wife were disgraced and kept away from Court for years. In Guiana, in finding the country of El Dorado, lay the one chance of a striking exploit—like Drake's Voyage—which might win back the Queen's lost favour. As he wrote in the poem he was thinking of in these years, but, like Virginia, could never complete :

> To seek new worlds, for gold, for praise, for glory,
> To try desire, to try love severed far,
> When I was gone she sent her memory
> More strong than were ten thousand ships of war.[1]

Ralegh got together an expedition, recruited from his West Country following—Grenville's son, John (who was killed on it), Ralegh's nephew, John Gilbert, a Gorges, a Thynne, a Whiddon, a Connock—and sailed from Plymouth early in 1595. The first thing that happened was highly dramatic : Berrio, who was waiting all unsuspecting in Trinidad for orders from Spain, was captured by Ralegh. It was hard on Berrio and a stroke of luck for Ralegh : henceforth he had the leading source of information on the subject at his disposal. Berrio did not minimise the difficulties of the task. Two other English expeditions were reconnoitring in these waters : Sir Robert Dudley sent a boat up the Orinoco, and George Somers was raiding the Main ;

[1] From " The Book of the to Ocean Cynthia ", *The Poems of Sir Walter Ralegh*, ed. Agnes Latham, 27.

but neither would co-operate with Ralegh. Ralegh made the most of Berrio's information and followed his plan of campaign : Guiana, too, had become a race between the Spaniards and the English. He made for the delta of the Orinoco, successfully surmounted its difficulties, struck the right channel and rowed upstream to the confluence with the Caroni, that led direct into the mountains. All the way along he made friends with the Indians, impressed upon them the greatness of the Queen, Ezrabeta Cassipuna Aquerewana—the subject uppermost in his mind, whom all these ardours were designed to impress—and made a firm impression upon them himself, for he had faithful followers among them to the end of his life. He told them that she was the great Cacique of the North and a virgin, an enemy to the Spaniards " in respect of their tyranny and oppression, and that she delivered all such nations about her as were by them oppressed, and having freed all the coast of the northern world from their servitude had sent me to free them also and withal to defend the country of Guiana from their invasion and conquest. I showed them her Majesty's picture. . . ."[1] The natives were suitably moved, and ready to bow down and worship.

And perhaps this was Ralegh's most solid service : to lay the foundations of good feeling between English and Indians, who detested the Spaniards and longed for deliverance from their oppression. For when he reached the Caroni the river was in flood and it was impossible to get the boats up the cataracts. A long and difficult march was necessary, carrying all provisions, and with its attendant toils and fevers. This would not have daunted a Berrio, but the truth was that Ralegh was, after years at Court, no conquistador. He contented himself, like Frobisher, with taking back what he took to be samples of auriferous ore from what Captain Keymis took to be a gold-mine, and dropped down the rivers again to his ships, hoping to return another day. On his way he generously released Berrio. The moment Ralegh turned his back, his face homewards to the Queen, the old hero got together a force, went up to the Caroni confluence and there founded the fortified post of San Thomé : which frustrated Ralegh's design twenty-two years later, brought his last voyage to a tragic fiasco and him to destruction.

The Queen was not impressed. It took Ralegh a year or

[1] *The Discovery of Guiana*, by Sir Walter Ralegh, ed. V. T. Harlow, 15.

two more—and the misconduct of his rival, Essex, with other maids-of-honour—to work his passage back into the royal virgin's favour. (What a fragile glass-house she ruled, to be sure, and what a razor-edge she herself walked to the end !) Others, jealous of Ralegh's glittering talents, the superiority of his gifts (not till he was a prisoner for life did they pardon them in him), said that he had never been on the voyage at all, but had lain hid in Cornwall. Ralegh could never refrain from answering fools, and to that we owe a masterpiece of his prose, *The Discovery of the Large, Rich, and Beautiful Empire of Guiana.*

Ralegh's description of his own experiences in this is accurate enough, and it incorporates a great deal of information both from Berrio and from his own observation. He advocated, as Hakluyt had done for Virginia, that Guiana should be undertaken as an enterprise of state, since it was too much for a private person's resources. He saw it as a means of checking Spain's power in the heart of the Spanish Main, and an inexhaustible source of wealth for this country. We see the disadvantages that attach to so imaginative a mind in the realm of politics. " Guiana is a country that yet hath her maidenhead, never sacked, turned nor wrought, the face of the earth hath not been torn, nor the virtue and salt of the soil spent by manurance, the graves have not been opened for gold, the mines not broken with sledges, nor their images pulled down out of their temples."[1] But this was not a practical possibility. In Ralegh's mind Guiana was to be our Peru : it was a mirage, an hallucination that possessed him for the rest of his life. " If there were but a small army afoot in Guiana, marching towards Manoa the chief city of the Inca, he would yield her Majesty so many hundred thousand pounds yearly, as should both defend all enemies abroad and defray all expenses at home."[2] After all, the Spaniards had achieved as much ; and " after the first or second year I doubt not but to see in London a *Contratación* house of more receipt for Guiana, than there is now in Seville for the West Indies ". Ralegh saw himself as another Cortés—if he might not prevail at Court, then Viceroy of Guiana. The trouble with him as a man of action was that—suitably enough for a poet— ideas went to his head.

The work of settlement and colonisation in these waters was

---

[1] *The Discovery of Guiana*, by Sir Walter Ralegh, ed. V. T. Harlow, 73.
[2] *Ibid.* 75.

carried forward by soberer minds, more prosaic persons.[1] Captain
Leigh planned a settlement in 1602, and tried out tobacco
planting from 1604–6 in eastern (now French) Guiana. Reinforcements and supplies were sent out in 1605 ; but the *Olive
Plant*, owned by Sir Oliph Leigh, was swept past by the winds
and currents and managed to effect a lodgment on St. Lucia
in the Windward Islands, which was shortly scuppered by the
horrid Caribs. A second attempt to settle was made, in 1609,
on Grenada : with the same result. In the same year, Robert
Harcourt, perhaps inspired by Ralegh, initiated a more ambitious
colonising project upon the coastlands of Guiana.[2] He sent
exploring parties into the interior and formally annexed the whole
of Guiana between Orinoco and Amazon in the name of King
James. His patent was closely similar to the Virginia charter
of 1612 ; but he failed to attract capital enough to work it :
he seems to have spent most of his life in a vain attempt to
make a success of it and may have died there. Ralegh sent out
boats in 1596 to keep some sort of contact, before his final
desperate venture in 1617. Thomas Roe explored the Amazon
and spent a year or so upon the coast in 1610–11. By now the
Dutch were equally interested : they and the English have
been there ever since.

" I shall yet live to see it an English nation ", wrote Ralegh
of Virginia. In the event he did. He witnessed the founding
of the settlement of Jamestown, in the way that so often happens
with such men, in the name of the king he detested and despised,
and under the aegis of others. He did something to keep contact :
in 1602 he sent out a bark under a Weymouth mariner to find
John White's lost colony of 1587. The account in Purchas
defends Ralegh's efforts : " to whose succour he hath sent five
several times at his own charges. The parties by him set forth
performed nothing ; some of them following their own profit
elsewhere ; others returning with frivolous allegations."[3] So
also with this effort. On Gosnold's voyage of this year there was
a Gilbert, and a report on the prospects was made to Ralegh.

---

[1] Cf. A. P. Newton, "The Beginnings of English Colonisation", in *Cambridge
Hist. of the British Empire*, I. 86 foll.
[2] Cf. Robert Harcourt, *A Relation of a Voyage to Guiana* (Hakluyt Soc.), ed. Sir
Alexander Harris.
[3] *Purchas, his Pilgrims* (Maclehose edn.), XVIII. 321.

This voyage set in motion a new series of Virginia expeditions and the account of it reawakened the excited interest of twenty years before. Of the leading spirits of that glad spring-time—Gilbert, Ralegh, Grenville—only Hakluyt remained effective, no longer young, ageing but indomitable. He was responsible for persuading the Bristol merchants to follow up Gosnold with a couple of small ships next year under Pring. In 1600 he had brought his mighty book up to date with its last edition ; but he went on gathering material, most of which Purchas made use of. The magnet of his practical interests had always been America ; now that the long war was drawing to an end and English energies were gathering for a renewed response to the challenge of Virginia, Hakluyt was there ready with counsel and encouragement, as he had been at the beginning. Along with the military commanders who sued for the charter of 1606 he appears, the only civilian, the only survivor. It was proposed to add to his other preferments the living of Jamestown, at £500 a year.[1] Elizabethans were nothing if not sanguine.

Gosnold had coasted down from the north by Newfoundland, naming Cape Cod and Martha's Vineyard on his way, landing at one or two places, making acquaintance with the country and the Indians, when " began some of our company that before vowed to stay, to make revolt : whereupon the planters diminishing, all was given over ".[2] Several ships went out in quick succession to reconnoitre : in 1603 Bartholomew Gilbert, who had been with Gosnold, succeeded in fetching Chesapeake Bay, which he " so much thirsted after, to seek out the people for Sir Walter Ralegh left near those parts in the year 1587 ".[3] His thirst was quenched for ever : landing there he was killed by the Indians. In 1605 the Earl of Southampton sent out a ship under George Weymouth, who made an excellent landfall : " as we passed with a gentle wind up with our ship in this river, any man may conceive with what admiration we all consented in joy. . . . Some that were with Sir Walter Ralegh in his voyage to Guiana in the discovery of the river Orinoco, which echoed fame to the world's ears, gave reasons why it was not to be compared with this."[4] Others preferred it to the famous rivers of France ; but " I will not prefer it before our river of Thames, because it is *natale solum*, England's richest treasure ".

[1] Parks, *op. cit.* 205. [2] Purchas, *loc. cit.* 313.
[3] *Ibid.* 334. [4] *Ibid.* 351.

The ground was now prepared for the planting of Virginia. In the negotiations with Spain in 1600 the English had stipulated for the recognition of the doctrine that only effective occupation could give a valid title to new lands—the rest were open and free. This the Spaniards would never agree to, and the Queen, as stubborn as they in defence of her country's interests, ended the negotiations. On her death the peace was made without mentioning the issue, and the English interpreted this as leaving North America, unoccupied by Spain, open to colonisation. Two leading groups were actively engaged in promoting it. There were the London merchants interested in the East India, Levant and Muscovy Companies, chief instruments in the country's commercial expansion, whose leader was Customer Smythe's son, Sir Thomas : his contribution surpassed all others. And there were the West Country interests, chiefly concerned with fur trade and fisheries, with whom the leadership was taken by Sir Ferdinando Gorges, governor of Plymouth. From the one group, we may say roughly, sprang Virginia and all that followed her ; from the other, ultimately, grew New England.

The national interest was engaged as never before and it was felt that the honour of the nation was involved in the success of the project. The Crown was therefore brought directly into the government of the colony, as it had not been under Gilbert and Ralegh's charters : a royal Council for Virginia was created to have general control over the whole area, which was regarded as one : a clear warning to Spain not to interfere. " From the beginning the colonists carried with them overseas into land of the Crown not only their allegiance, but also their English law and their indefeasible rights as Englishmen."[1] The Instructions drawn up later for the management of the colony represented the best thought of the time on colonisation, carefully prepared in consultation with Hakluyt.

For the voyage Drayton wrote his famous Ode, from which we may see to what point the poets read their *Principal Navigations* :

> You brave heroic minds,
> Worthy your country's name,
> That honour still pursue,
> Go and subdue,
> Whilst loitering hinds
> Lurk here at home with shame.

---

[1] A. P. Newton in *Camb. Hist. Brit. Empire*, I. 79.

                        And cheerfully at sea
                        Success you still entice
                              To get the pearl and gold
                              And ours to hold,
                        Virginia,
                        Earth's only paradise.

We observe how the very phrases of the voyagers had entered
into the mind of the stay-at-home poet : where

                              the ambitious vine
                        Crowns with his purple mass,
                              The cedar reaching high
                              To kiss the sky
                        The cypress, pine
                        And useful sassafras.

                        When as the luscious smell
                        Of that delicious land,
                              Above the sea that flows,
                              The clear wind throws,
                        Your hearts to swell
                        Approaching the dear strand . . .

The realities were grimmer than ever before. The fleet of
three ships—the *Susan Constant, Godspeed* and *Discovery*—arrived
in Chesapeake Bay, naming Cape Henry and Cape Comfort.
On 14 May " we landed all our men, which were set to work
about the fortification " : Jamestown was planted on the first site
it occupied.[1] The number of planters was the usual hundred, as
with Grenville's colony and White's. Those colonies had at least
been remarkably healthy ; but at Jamestown a fearful mortality
began : day by day the men died. " Our men were destroyed
with cruel diseases as swellings, fluxes, burning fevers and by
wars, and some departed suddenly, but for the most part they
died of mere famine."[2] At their last gasp the colonists were
relieved by the Indians with ample provisions, " otherwise we
had all perished ". Among those who died was Bartholomew
Gosnold. Meanwhile a second colony was planted farther north
by the Plymouth group ; it returned to England after a very
short time. The West Country interest had not the resources to
send regular supplies—indispensable to success in the first stage
of plantation—and henceforth concentrated on profitable trading

[1] Purchas, *loc. cit.* 412.   [2] *Ibid.* 418-19.

228

voyages for fish and fur in their area, North Virginia : subsequently New England.

In 1609 the most powerful reinforcement that had yet been sent to Virginia sailed under Sir Thomas Gates and Sir George Somers ; but a tempest separated their ships and Somers was wrecked upon Bermuda. We have a most eloquent description of it all from William Strachey :[1] " the clouds gathering thick upon us and the winds singing and whistling most unusually ". . . . day turned into night, the blackness of the heaven, the distraction of the company, the strange light that appeared upon the mainmast, shooting from shroud to shroud ; all the pumps continually going and the ship having to be run ashore upon the islands commonly called " the Devil's Islands, feared and avoided of all sea travellers alive, above any other place in the world ".[2] The islands were supposed to be enchanted and were full of noises ; yet there were many fair anchorages, where " the argosies of Venice may ride there with water enough and safe land-locked ". There Somers made a garden and set up a memorial cross out of the timbers of the ship ; two children were born and christened Bermuda and Bermudas ; there were attempts at mutiny and in the end a couple of pinnaces were built, in which they carried some of their scanty supplies to the rescue of Virginia, which was within four days of starving—so near a thing it was to being abandoned, before Lord de la Warr arrived to save it.

That the colony survived at all was due to the toughness and resilience of a natural leader who came to the fore among the colonists and took command of the situation when it was critical. This was Captain John Smith, whose humorous jaunty character is displayed with much verve and piquancy—he had a double dose of life—in his book, *The General History of Virginia, New England and the Summer Isles*, the first classic of English America. He had no mind to starve there (" the President whom no persuasions could persuade to starve "),[3] so he made the Indians hand over food in return for services, goods and trifles ; while among the colonists he enforced the principle that those who

---

[1] He was the first secretary and recorder to the Virginia colony. We may note that his descendant Lytton Strachey's last work was a study of *The Tempest*. For William Strachey and his likely acquaintance with Shakespeare—two of whose friends, Southampton and Sir Thomas Russell, were interested in Virginia—*v.* C. R. Sanders, *The Strachey Family, 1558–1932*, c. ii.

[2] Purchas, XIX. 6 foll.

[3] Captain John Smith, *The General History of Virginia*, etc. (Maclehose edn.), I. 153.

would not work should not eat, grappling bravely with the indiscipline and sheer laziness that brought all the early colonies in peril. Only so did he carry the planters through the winter of 1608–9. Of course it brought him into danger with both Indians and colonists. We all know the story of how he fell into the power of the chief Powhatan, who intended to kill him, when his life was saved by the chief's daughter, Pocohontas : it is part of the folk-memory of the English no less than of the Americans. But it is not so well known that the colonists' greatest danger arose from the duplicity and treachery of the Germans among them, who handed over weapons to the hostile Indians and planned to surprise the camp along with them. A characteristic part they played—but, as usual, it did them no good : when their treachery was discovered they came to an end at the hands of English and Indians alike. Powhatan had the brains of his brace of Germans beaten out. [1]

One of the chief dangers was the weakening of the corporate strength of the colony by bartering away goods for private gain : " there was ten times more care to maintain their damnable and private trade than to provide for the colony things that were necessary ". [2] So early in the history of the Empire do we find this constant theme. A neat exploit in capturing a hostile chief was performed by Captain Madison—a surname to be famous in Virginia's later annals. [3] But the dangers and troubles were varied by entertainments. The Indian maidens laid on a kind of masque with dancing and singing, coming naked out of the woods ; and " having re-accommodated themselves, they solemnly invited him to their lodgings, where he was no sooner within the house but all these nymphs more tormented him than ever, most tediously crying, ' Love you not me ? Love you not me ? ' " [4] The Indians had difficulty in understanding this reluctance, for the custom of the country was to provide a traveller " at night where his lodging is appointed " with " a woman fresh painted red with pocones and oil to be his bed-fellow ". [5]

However, Smith had pulled the colony round at its lowest point and left an amusing account of it all to our literature. It is pretty certain that the rôle of the great commercial magnate, Sir Thomas Smythe, who never left London, was more important

---

[1] Cf. for the story, Smith, *op. cit.* 157, 163, 175, 184, 197.
[2] *Ibid.* 146.   [3] *Ibid.* 303.   [4] *Ibid.* 141.   [5] *Ibid.* 71.

in keeping the colony afloat and making it a going concern. He was the only man with the experience and ability, and with the command of capital, to see this costly experiment through to success. For thirty years he was involved in the main colonial activities of the time, the gathering momentum of the avalanche set in motion by the Elizabethans. It soon became evident that fortunes were to be lost, not made, in Virginia : it was no Peru, not even a Mexico. English colonisation there was to be a long and arduous process of disappointment and self-sacrifice, patient heroism which put a premium upon the Puritan virtues.

On his return to England Smith turned his attention to the prospects farther north, to North Virginia. In 1614 he was employed on an expedition to the coast, which gave him an opportunity for exploring and looking for a suitable site for a colony. Like Gilbert, he too became a " Northern man ". He hit upon the name New England for this region and wrote a book which excited so much interest that the name took on at once. He made himself the chief propagandist for the north : " of all the four parts of the world that I have yet seen not inhabited, could I have means to transport a colony, I would rather live there than anywhere. . . . New England is great enough to make many kingdoms and countries, were it all inhabited."[1] And on the size of North America he has an eloquent passage, for no-one yet appreciated the immensity of its spaces : " as for the goodness and fine substance of the land, we are for the most part yet altogether ignorant of them, but only here and there where we have touched or seen a little, the edges of those large dominions which do stretch themselves into the main, God doth know how many thousand miles ".[2]

Smith's propaganda promoted the interest in the New England fishery and helped to revive colonial activity in the West Country, in whose sphere New England lay. The London merchants had the money, the Western men were " most proper for fishing ". Smith urged that " it is near as much trouble, but much more danger, to sail from London to Plymouth than from Plymouth to New England ", so that the colony should be set forth from Plymouth.[3] In 1615 he went out again to reconnoitre Cape Cod for a plantation. He had much difficulty in bringing London and the West Country together, since the latter hung back : he spent the summer of 1616—the year of

---

[1] Smith, *op. cit.* II. 14. [2] *Ibid.* 10. [3] *Ibid.* 38 foll.

Hakluyt's death—in visiting all the sea-port towns of the West Country and " the most of the gentry in Cornwall and Devon, giving them books and maps, showing how in six months the most of those ships had made their voyages " and collecting promises of support.[1] In the event, mainly by the unceasing efforts of Gorges from Plymouth,[2] a colony was sent out four years later and New Plymouth was founded, with Governor Bradford, Captain Miles Standish and all. Supplies were sent out with the usual difficulty, but the colony was not really secure and vigorous until " about some hundred of your Brownists of England, Amsterdam and Leyden went to New England, whose humorous ignorances caused them for more than a year to endure a wonderful deal of misery with an infinite patience ".[3] People's absurd convictions are perhaps to be judged not so much in themselves as for their survival-value to the community. All one can say is that as one looks at the simple fragments of those early days—a Bible or a crock, a table or a rude cradle[4]—one is brought close to the heroic simplicity of those earlier Englishmen, the first Americans, and to the hardships they endured. As one draws near over the waste of waters to the low-lying rim of those coasts, their promised land, one is very near to tears for all that it meant for them, their hopes and trials, the bravery of it all, the end of the old world, of the old life, the entry into the wilderness, into the unknown.

We have brought this story to the point at which the future can be configured. Before the close of the sixteenth century the rival colonising powers had laid down the general lines of their expansion in succeeding centuries. By the time of Hakluyt's death the English were permanently planted in North America— but with what difficulty, after what trials and failures, what endurances and what frustrations ! That is the moral of the story : what most strikes one is the difficulty they had in accomplishing it—so much more faltering and hesitant than the direct and brutal assault of Cortés and Pizarro. There is a clear

[1] Smith, *op. cit.* 53.

[2] For Gorges' long continued efforts, resulting ultimately in the foundation of his province of Maine, *v.* R. A. Preston, *Gorges of Plymouth Fort*, and J. P. Baxter, *Sir Ferdinando Gorges and his Province of Maine*.

[3] Smith, *op. cit.* 182.

[4] Such as one sees, for example, in the admirable historical museum at Plymouth, Massachusetts.

contrast between Spanish and English methods : the Spaniards conquered the natives and made them subjects of Spain ; the English treated the Indians as independent peoples, with whom relations were difficult, complex and variously unsatisfactory. Northern stocks have always been less good at miscegenation than the Mediterranean peoples.

In the wave of expansion of the English stocks across the Atlantic that was now gathering force—the most momentous impulse in their history since their first crossing the North Sea —the Elizabethan was the heroic age when they fought for a free hand and the future. The long struggle with Spain ended by leaving North America open to them. But the French were now in Canada and making south towards New England. The English had not fought Spain for that result, and in 1613 the Virginia Company expelled the French settlements from Acadia : it was to become Nova Scotia. Thus was the long colonial struggle between England and France for North America foreshadowed.

Already the New World was making its impact upon the life and mind of Englishmen. The date and channel by which the potato was introduced have been much disputed. But it looks as if it was probably brought home by Hariot, on board Drake's ship, from the sojourn of the first Virginia colony upon Roanoke.[1] And it seems that the tenacious tradition that Ralegh introduced the potato into Ireland is probably true. Tobacco had reached this country earlier, about the beginning of the reign. Apparently the first English description of its uses comes from Hawkins' second voyage, of 1565.[2] The most striking feature in its conquest of the Old World is the rapidity of it ; and yet perhaps one should not be surprised considering the strength of the addiction once acquired. The Elizabethans thought it as useful medically as pleasurable. By the end of the reign it had conquered the English upper class, at any rate the menfolk at Court and among nobility and gentry. (Too expensive for others !) Again, it was Ralegh who was chiefly responsible for introducing the habit and patronising the cult—another score against him in the mind of King James, who detested it : " it seems a miracle to me how a custom springing from so vile a ground and brought in by a father so generally hated should be welcomed upon so slender a warrant ".[3]

---

[1] R. N. Salaman, *The History and Social Influence of the Potato*, 146-7.
[2] C. M. MacInnes, *The Early English Tobacco Trade*, 27-8.   [3] q. *ibid.* 32.

We have seen something of the place taken by America in the practical intellectual interests of the time, but the leaven was beginning to work in the imagination of the poets. As More's *Utopia* is the first work of genius to reflect the impact of the New World upon the early Tudor mind, so we may take *The Tempest*, a century later, as the latest at the end of it all. It is not only that the imagination of the dramatist was set off by the circumstance of Somers's wreck on the Bermudas, that the details—the cries, the howling, the island inhabited by devils, St. Elmo's fire flaming along the mast and yards—come straight from Strachey's account, but that the whole atmosphere of the play is drenched in the voyages ; or we may say that it distils them into a magical transparency. The conception of Caliban (=cannibal) comes from reading about the New World—though Shakespeare could write of nothing without that divine inner sympathy, so that we see the pathos of the poor creature : after all, the land was his :

> This island's mine, by Sycorax my mother,
> Which thou takest from me. When thou camest first,
> Thou strok'dst me and mad'st much of me, would'st give me
> Water with berries in't, and teach me how
> To name the bigger light, and how the less,
> That burn by day and night : and then I loved thee

—which was what John Smith was doing, to the marvel of the savages in Virginia, a year or two before the play was written.[1] Montaigne's sympathy with primitive society we know ; Gonzalo's wish for a Utopian commonwealth comes straight out of Montaigne :

> I' the commonwealth I would by contraries
> Execute all things ; for no kind of traffic
> Would I admit ; no name of magistrate :
> Letters should not be known ; riches, poverty,
> And use of service, none : contract, succession,
> Bourn, bound of land, tilth, vineyard, none ;
> No use of metal, corn, or wine, or oil ;
> No occupation : all men idle, all ;
> And women too, but innocent and pure. . . .

[1] Cf. Smith, *op. cit.* I. 97 : " he demonstrated . . . the roundness of the earth and skies, the sphere of the sun, moon and stars, and how the sun did chase the night round about the world continually. . . . They all stood as amazed with admiration."

There is, indeed, a kind of innocence, as of a world newly
ravished, underneath Prospero's knowledge and disenchantment.
All the action moves to the sound of music and the sea :
Prospero's

> Ye elves of hills, brooks, standing lakes and groves,
> And ye that on the sands with printless foot
> Do chase the ebbing Neptune and do fly him
> When he comes back . . .
> > by whose aid,
> Weak masters though ye be, I have bedimm'd
> The noontide sun, call'd forth the mutinous winds,
> And twixt the green sea and the azured vault
> Set roaring war . . .
> > the strong-based promontory
> Have I made shake and by the spurs pluck'd up
> The pine and cedar . . .

(Those pines and cedars of the Carolina coast, that appear in
Hakluyt, lodged in the poets' minds : Drayton remembered
them too.) Or Ariel's

> Come unto these yellow sands,
> And then take hands :
> Courtsied when you have and kissed
> The wild waves whist . . .

It may not be fanciful to see something of the influence in
Timon, too : the spendthrift who, ruined, took to the woods ; there,
like the Virginia colonists, digging for roots, he came upon
gold, as they did not. When Timon prepares his grave, it is

> Lie where the light foam of the sea may beat
> Thy grave-stone daily.

It was an Elizabethan situation, frequent enough, to voyage
into the wilderness to avoid creditors and escape from debt.
It was the motive of the novelist Lodge's joining Cavendish
on his last journey to the Straits of Magellan.[1]   When he
published his novel, *A Margaret of America*, he pretended that
" some four years since, being at sea with Master Cavendish . . .
it was my chance in the library of the Jesuits in Santos to find
this history in the Spanish tongue. . . . The place where I began
my work was a ship." [2]

[1] *Thomas Lodge and other Elizabethans*, ed. C. J. Sisson, 106-7.
[2] Greene's *Menaphon*, Lodge's *A Margaret of America*, ed. G. B. Harrison, 113.

Already Spenser, first of the poets to respond to the new impulses, had written :

> Who ever heard of the Indian Peru ?
> Or who in venturous vessel measured
> The Amazons' huge river, now found true ?
> Or fruitfullest Virginia who did ever view ?

> Yet all these were when no man did them know ;
> Yet have from wisest ages hidden been ;
> And later times things more unknown shall show.

In the Sidney circle Daniel responded imaginatively to the challenge of the New World in his *Musophilus*, as Philip Sidney had to the lure and promise of the voyages. In Ralegh's circle Chapman hailed his voyage to Guiana with a long poem, *De Guiana, Carmen Epicum*, and addressed better verses to Hariot. It is probable that the scenes in *Eastward Hoe* dealing with a projected Virginia voyage that comes to grief in the Thames were by Chapman.[1] Ralegh's imagination was evidently engaged :

> My hopes clean out of sight, with forced wind
> To kingdoms strange, to lands far-off addressed . . .

> On highest mountains where those cedars grew,
> Against whose banks the troubled ocean beat,

> And wear the marks to find thy hoped port,
> Into a soil far-off themselves remove . . .

It was Donne into the passion of whose mind the excitement and inspiration of a New World most intimately entered. A follower of Essex, he was a voyager himself, to Cadiz in 1596 and on the Islands Voyage in 1597. From the latter he has left two famous verse-letters, describing " the Storm " at the beginning and " the Calm " that followed. But it is the images and metaphors that spring up in that heated Celtic mind that reveal how much he was touched by the influence :

> Let sea-discoverers to new worlds have gone,
> Let maps to others worlds on worlds have shown,
> Let us possess one world, each hath one, and is one.

---

[1] Cf. Seagull, " Come, boys, Virginia longs till we share the rest of her maidenhead ", Act III, Sc. 1. We recall Ralegh's phrase about Guiana, above, p. 224.

American Colonisation

In addressing his mistress, going to bed, he rhapsodises :

> O my America ! my new-found-land,
> My kingdom, safeliest when with one man manned,
> My mine of precious stones, my empery,
> How blest am I in this discovering thee !

Everywhere in Donne there are these extraordinary images and suggestions, revealing how much his mind was fired by thoughts of geography and the sea, continents and planets ; sun and moon, and the new worlds of knowledge opening up :

> That unripe side of earth, that heavy clime
> That gives us man up now, like Adam's time
> Before he ate ; man's shape, that would yet be
> (Knew they not it, and feared beasts' company)
> So naked at this day, as though man there
> From Paradise so great a distance were . . .

Perhaps we may, in the end, turn back to the hopes of our stock and of our name, expressed by the Elizabethan poet in his " Ode to the Virginian Voyage ", which have not been without reverberation and fulfilment in our own time :

> And in regions far
> Such heroes bring ye forth,
> As those from whom we came,
> And plant our name,
> Under that star
> Not known unto our north.

CHAPTER VII

THE SEA-STRUGGLE WITH SPAIN

THE consequence of this turning towards the ocean was the prolonged war with Spain. The conflict, we may say, was inevitable, since Spain was determined to keep all others out of the New World and the English were equally determined to break out of bounds and expand. It is the function of war to resolve by force these *impasses* in human society, since it is too much to expect rational accommodation of human beings—at least, so history seems to show.

The later sixteenth century, like most centuries except the fortunate and humane nineteenth, was an age of war. Indeed, a characteristic spirit among the later Elizabethans, Ralegh, tells us that " the ordinary theme and argument of history is war ".[1] He might well think so, for all his days were nurtured in war or the rumour of it : reared in his young years in the civil and religious wars in France, then fighting in Ireland and at sea, his mind in later years fixed on the struggle with Spain. Over great parts of Europe the conflict raged, for this was the heyday of the struggle between Counter-Reformation and Protestantism, and, where faith was involved, there were the usual accompaniments of ferocity and devastation.

For nearly a quarter of a century the Queen's sedate and prudent government kept this country out of foreign war, during which time its resources were nourished and increased, grew to demand outlet. So that the Elizabethans who were growing up then thought of it as a blissful time of peace and security. That is the argument of my first volume, which portrays the peaceful aspects of the reign—most evident in a picture of the internal structure of a society. But here is its outward face : energies demanding outlet, conflict, aggression and defence, war : for the rest of the reign—and very much contrary to the wishes of the lady who reigned and who was often to be found seeking

[1] Ralegh's *Works*, ed. Oldys and Birch, VIII. 253.

peace while her fleets knocked at the gates of Spain—it was a society at war.

We must not think of war as the totalitarian affair of modern societies : it was apt to absorb the surplus energies of a society rather than to bleed it white, and it occupied mainly those who liked it rather than those who did not. Nor was it continuous : it flared up and died down, especially at sea ; there were intervals when nothing much happened. On land, armies folded themselves up in winter, went into winter quarters ; and though there were privation and disease as constant companions, there was a great deal of jollity too, of the sort we can see reflected in the Sidney papers or the correspondence of the Veres, or as we see it depicted a little later in the paintings of Franz Hals, the " Night-Watch " of Rembrandt.

That gave breathing-spaces for recruitment of strength, when the waging of war was conditioned by such very limited resources. At every point in Elizabethan warfare we have to re-imagine the extent, the variety of ways in which physical conditions determined action—true at all times, but vastly more so then, particularly at sea : where all depended on wind and weather, and good seamanship told all the more effectively.

But the conditions of war were being revolutionised—like so much else—and modern warfare, dependent on fire-power in small arms, artillery, ships of battle, was coming into being. The local wars of the fifteenth century were merging into one wide complex,[1] extended by the new energy the Counter-Reformation called up, with the crusading zeal of Spain as its strong right arm reaching out across the Mediterranean, across Atlantic and Pacific, through Italy up into the Netherlands and round into North-Western Europe :

> un Monarca, un Imperio y una Espada :
>   Ya el orbe de la tierra siente en parte
> y espera en todo vuestra monarquía
> conquistada por vos en justa guerra,
> que a quien ha dado Christo su estandarte,
> dará el segundo más dichoso día
> en que vencido el mar, venza la tierra.[2]

The poet announces the universal monarchy of Philip II, and with the fifteen-eighties it looked not impossible. Philip's

---

[1] Cf. Sir Charles Oman, *History of the Art of War in the Sixteenth Century*, 5.
[2] Hernando de Acuña, " Al rey nuestro señor ", *Oxford Book of Spanish Verse*, 104.

world-wide dominions were unchallengeably under his control ; with the annexation of Portugal, Spain acquired not only the Portuguese empire in the East but an ocean-going fleet : at one blow she became a first-class naval power. Meanwhile France was divided by civil war and could be counted out ; the revolted Netherlands were failing and Parma was advising Philip that the war would soon end ; England was untried.

The struggle with England must be primarily at sea ; it was in the course of it that the secular shift of power from the Mediterranean to the Atlantic and the North-West was revealed : 1588 brought it home to a surprised Europe. The English, as the danger they had done so much to provoke came nearer, could not afford to allow the Netherlands to go under, their independence extinguished, to pass completely into the control of Spain : trade, religion, strategy, everything was involved : we had to intervene. As Philip's aggressions and self-imposed obligations for the Faith advanced after 1580, his tentacles crept up to the Channel coast of France : he occupied a base in Brittany, ordered Parma to close in on Henry IV from Picardy, supported the League in occupation of Paris. Elizabeth was drawn in at one time or another, and usually with reluctance, along the whole Channel littoral from Brittany and Normandy to Flanders, Zealand and Holland. It was war on land as well as at sea.

The fascination, and the importance, of the war to the student of politics lie in its being the first of our modern wars, that which set the classic model of our policy in subsequent centuries : of a free association of smaller threatened powers against an over-whelmingly powerful aggressor—after Philip II, Louis XIV and Napoleon, the Germany of Bismarck and Hitler.[1] Burghley and Robert Cecil were as aware of this as the younger Pitt or Churchill. Bacon expressed it : " the policy of Spain hath trodden more bloody steps than any state of Christendom " ; her ambition was the empire of Christendom and all Christian princes were opposed to the design.[2]

The agglomeration of power in Philip's hands, in Europe and the world outside, military and now naval too, was something new :[3] it upset the whole balance and, identifying itself with the

---

[1] Cf. my essay on " The Historical Tradition of British Policy ", in *The English Spirit*.
[2] Bacon's *Letters and Life*, ed. Spedding, VII. 26.
[3] Cf. J. R. Seeley, *The Growth of British Policy*, I. 10.

strength and resources of the Counter-Reformation, was a far more aggressive danger to the liberties of Europe than Charles V's Empire. Of this the Elizabethans had a dawning consciousness : one hears the note of surprise at the revolution that had taken place in his time when old Burghley writes in 1589 : " the state of the world is marvellously changed when we true Englishmen have cause for our own quietness to wish good success to a French king and a king of Scots ; but seeing both are enemies to our enemies we have cause to join with them in their actions against our enemies ".[1] It is like Churchill's speech welcoming the Russians as allies against Hitler in 1941. At the outbreak of war in 1585—war was never declared—in the government's appeal to the public opinion of Europe on their action in going to the help of the Low Countries, the Queen still refers to Philip as her " ally " ; but the operative motive for her intervention may be read in the sentence, after referring to the Spanish occupation of Naples and other countries, " we did manifestly see in what danger ourselves, our countries and people might shortly be, if in convenient time we did not speedily otherwise regard to prevent or stay the same ".[2] And throughout this *Declaration* one sees, as against the supra-nationalism of the Habsburgs and the universalism of Philip, the nationalist assumption, which was the air the English breathed, that the Low Countries should govern themselves and not be held down by foreigners.

As for England's national interest, confronting the greatest monarchy in the world, it is Burghley again who sums up the perils on either hand and concludes : " Although her Majesty should thereby enter into a war presently [*i.e.* immediately], yet were she better to do it now, while she may make the same out of her realm, having the help of the people of Holland and before the King of Spain shall have consummated his conquests in these countries, whereby he shall be so provoked with pride, solicited by the Pope and tempted by the Queen's own subjects, and shall be so strong by sea and so free from all other actions and quarrels, yea, shall be so formidable to all the rest of Christendom, as that her Majesty shall no wise be able with her own power, nor with the aid of any other, neither by sea nor land, to withstand his attempts, but shall be forced to give place

---

[1] E. Lodge, *Illustrations of British History*, II. 400.
[2] *A Declaration of the Causes moving the Queen of England to give Aid to the Defence of the People afflicted and oppressed in the Low Countries* (1585), 11.

to his insatiable malice, which is most terrible to be thought of, but most miserable to suffer ".[1]

One sees that in the ultimate issues of policy Burghley was the Queen's prime minister and one understands how it was that he merited her life-long confidence by the undeflectable straightness of his judgment, going warily, wisely to the heart of the issue, influenced by no partial or personal considerations where the well-being of the state was concerned. How well he deserved Sussex's tribute to " the continual trouble which you have of long time taken for the benefit of the commonwealth ; and the upright course which ye have always taken, respecting the matter and not the person, in all causes ".[2] Of them all, only the Queen herself and Burghley's son achieved such standards ; but happy was the country that had these to guide them.

Perhaps we may draw attention to something else in this remarkable *Declaration*, standing as it does at the beginning of the long tradition of our policy in the defence of the liberties of Europe—the tone of moderation, of indefeasible reason, the appeal to the common interest. No wonder it became the " Common Cause " : here is the first hesitant foreshadowing of its later and classic formulation. There is the wise limitation of objectives : the intercourse between England and the Low Countries is so close and intimate, has continued so long, that it is like a work of nature, as of husband and wife. The Spaniards are strangers there, " men more exercised in wars than in peaceable government and some of them notably delighted in blood, as hath appeared by their actions " :[3] these are they who have " broken the ancient laws and liberties of all the countries, and in a tyrannous sort have banished, killed and destroyed without order of law within the space of a few months, many of the most ancient and principal persons of the natural nobility that were most worthy of government ".[4] In the name of the Catholic religion ? But no-one was more devoted to it than Egmont, " the very glory of that country, who neither for

[1] q. Conyers Read, *Mr. Secretary Walsingham*, III. 82-3. I see no reason why this memorandum should lay Burghley open to the charge " that he was badly infected by the same germ of indecision that possessed his mistress ". This sort of reflection shows how easily and censoriously professors judge matters that agonise statesmen. Elizabeth and Burghley were confronting a momentous decision ; they were right to take their time, but they did decide and decide rightly.

[2] Lodge, *op. cit.* II. 229.

[3] This, of course, referred specially to Alva.

[4] *Loc. cit.* 5-6.

his singular victories in the service of the King of Spain can be forgotten in the true histories, nor yet for the cruelty used for his destruction to be but for ever lamented in the hearts of the natural people of that country ". The King of France would have accepted the sovereignty but for the house of Guise ; the Queen of England is sending aid " to the natural people of those countries, only to defend them and their towns from sacking and desolation, and thereby to procure them safety . . . and to enjoy their ancient liberties for them and their posterity ".[1]

The language employed towards Philip is respectful throughout ; the Queen willingly acknowledges that she was beholden to him in the time of her sister. And in reply to a malicious slander that the Queen had entertained a plot to kill Parma, the pamphlet ends with a notable and generous tribute to him, " of whom we have ever had an honourable conceit, in respect of those singular rare parts we have always noted in him, which hath won unto him as great reputation as any man this day living carrieth of his degree and quality . . . and who hath dealt in a more honourable and gracious sort in the charge committed unto him than any other that hath ever gone before him, or is likely to succeed after him."[2] There speaks the Queen herself, who admired greatness in a man : generous, and at the same time astute, for it was gall and wormwood to Philip to hear Parma praised.

How much higher a standard of decency and of a good conscience this appeal to European opinion sets than Philip, with his murder of Escobedo, his deliberate incitement to assassinate William the Silent ! The language itself in its reasonableness and moderation may be contrasted with that of Spain's greatest poet, Góngora, speeding the Armada against the heretic island :

> Agora condenada á infamia eterna
> Por la que te gobierna
> Con la mano ocupada
> Del huso en vez del cetro y de la espada,
> Mujer de muchos, y de muchos nuera !
> ¡ Oh reina infame ; reina no, mas loba
> Libidinosa y fiera ![3]

---

[1] *Ibid.* 18. [2] *An Addition to the Declaration*, 4.
[3] Luis de Góngora, " A la armada que el rey Felipe II nuestro señor envió contra Inglaterra ", q. C. F. Duro, *La armada invencible*, I. 238.

It is not without significance that English standards in international relations go back to this formative period of a woman's rule, cautious, civilised and humane.

Elizabeth's government was as aware as subsequent English governments up to our time have been of the political advantage of a good cause, a just case. Hatton's speech to the Commons early in the war was directed to opinion at home, especially to the commercial classes : it was not meet that a neighbour should grow too strong, the recovery of the Netherlands would be good for our trade.[1] When the Queen herself spoke, in 1593, she brought out her strongest plea, which was not the less effective for being true : " All this time of my reign I have not sought to advance my territories and enlarge my dominions ", yet she had had plenty of opportunity.[2] (Had she not been offered the sovereignty of the Netherlands ?) She put down her renunciation to her being a woman—probably truly enough. " My mind was never to invade my neighbours or to usurp over any. I am contented to reign over mine own and to rule as a just prince. Yet the King of Spain doth challenge me to be the quarreller and the beginner of all these wars. He doth me the greatest wrong that can be, for my conscience doth not accuse my thoughts wherein I have done him the least injury." Her conscience, like everyone's in high place, was an elastic one ; but there is no doubt that she regarded her blows against Philip as retaliations for injuries received.

The war dragged on and on, with its burdens. Nobody wished for peace more than the Queen did ; but she insisted on the practical independence of the Netherlands as a *sine qua non*, and a recognition of the open door to America and the East. These Philip would not concede. In 1597 the Lord Keeper spoke for her to her people who " could not but see, and the wisest but admire their happiness therein, the whole realm enjoying peace in all security [*i.e.* internal peace] wherein our neighbour countries have been torn in pieces and tormented continually with cruel and bloody wars. . . . But there is no cause at all to fear ; for this war is just, it is in defence of the religion of God, of our most gracious sovereign and of our natural country, of our wives, our children, our liberties, lands, lives and whatsoever we have."[3] The point was that the war was

---

[1] D'Ewes, *Journal*, 408.
[2] *Ibid.* 466.   [3] *Ibid.* 524-5.

becoming increasingly burdensome : the Queen had long been having to sell Crown lands, and the country was obliged to tax itself more heavily. Philip did not need so much to appeal to public opinion in his country : he financed his wars by American treasure : only American treasure, as the English did not fail to point out, enabled him to maintain his various tyrannies, in Italy, Portugal, the Low Countries, and to interfere all over Western Europe.

It has been the English case throughout modern history that if foreign governments had to depend on their peoples, they would not be so ready to wage war : it was Marlborough's argument for a constitutional monarchy in France, Gladstone's for parliamentary government in Germany ; it has not changed in our time in face of more barbarous challenges to freedom and peace.

The Elizabethans did not make the mistake of under-estimating the grandest monarchy in the world—the only one, after St.-Quentin and Lepanto, to attach to itself an aura of universal glory. (Hubris, as often in history, was largely responsible for its decline : like Louis XIV, Napoleon, Hitler, it overstrained its people's resources.) *Un Monarca, un Imperio y una Espada* : one sees it all expressed in stone in the Escorial which Philip was raising on the bare mountain-side of the Guadarama at this time, impressing the stamp of the unity, the homogeneity, the monotony of his rule upon the natural variousness and spontaneity, the fissiparousness and chaotic anarchism of Spaniards. He himself was hardly a Spaniard at all : flaxen-haired and blue-eyed, with the fixed look of the fanatic, he had the bureaucratism, the liking for *gleichschaltung*, of a German. It was a tragedy that the one thing he got above all from Spain was a further reinforcement of his fanaticism. Then there was his sense of inferiority to his father, a man made on a big scale, an extravert, in touch with life on all sides ; where Philip, an introvert, undersized, no man of action, could only keep the upper hand by withdrawing from the harsh, enriching contacts with life, into that pure mountain air, that fastness dedicated to power and penance and prayer. It is an inspired situation, for Philip was an aesthete and had inherited the taste of the Burgundian line : the enormous palace-monastery high up on a half-moon spur of the hills, hard sunlight upon stone by day, the shadows becoming more intensely blue—blue of the sea he could not subdue—with evening, the light pale gold in the chapel of the monks of St. Laurence and the dark figure, almost always in black, taking his place quietly along with them in his stall for vespers, some intermission from the affairs of this world, his mind now fixed upon the next, where his heart already was. Perhaps the next world would not fail him as this did ? " This bare mountain-side ", he wrote, " whence I rule the affairs of half the world " ; unfortunately the affairs of this world are not so readily at one's disposal as one's fantasies about the next.

It is probable that the Elizabethans were over-impressed by the spectacle of Spain's greatness at the beginning of the war. Only the seamen had taken the measure of her deficiencies at sea ; but some of these were made up as the war progressed. On land there was, of course, no comparison : Spain was the greatest power in the world and remained so until well into the next century. If Parma had once been able to land his *tercios* in England, the Armada to disgorge its seasoned troops, it is unlikely that they would have encountered an effective military resistance, any more than the Germans would have done in 1940. Everything for us depended on what happened at sea.

But there were certain factors that gave England greater strength than anyone realised at the time—certainly than her size and population warranted—and that made the struggle more even than anyone judging by appearances could have supposed. Some of these, the geographical for instance, have been continuing factors. The south coast controlled the busiest thoroughfare of world traffic and the character of its harbours offered a decided advantage ; deep water, in close proximity to centres of trade, made admirable bases. [1] Then there was the length of coast-line, the ease and cheapness of water transport. Land-powers have hardly any conception of the advantage here in speed of communications, flexibility and movement of resources to the required point. Anyone who knows Spain will appreciate the slowness and delays that hampered Philip's preparations, the difficulty of concentration : his resources could hardly ever be fully brought to bear, except in 1588, and then only after long delays and much loss. English mobilisation was so rapid and efficient that the Queen needed to keep only a small portion of her fleet in being : it could always be expanded at short notice, and that meant great saving in cost, in disturbance

[1] Cf. A. T. Mahan, *The Influence of Sea-Power upon History*, 25, 29, 32, 43.

of the economy, in the strain upon the country. There was the character of the population, the large number available from all round the coasts to man the fleets. Here the Queen's government reaped its reward for its steadfast and strenuous measures to nurse the fisheries.[1] The country had a large and constantly increasing shipping to operate with, both commercial and naval ; the big armed merchant ships could give as good an account of themselves as most ships of war—indeed, they were ships of war. The nation's shipping could sustain blows without being checked, could take them in its stride, for it was growing all the time.

Such were some of the specific advantages of sea-power, but its imponderable potential for war was still greater. As Bacon saw at the end of the war, " he that commands the sea is at great liberty and may take as much and as little of the war as he will. Whereas those that be strongest by land are many times nevertheless in great straits."[2] The Huguenot Sully wrote, with some exaggeration, that " Spain was one of those states whose legs and arms are strong and powerful, but the heart infinitely weak and feeble ".[3] The real point is that insularity enabled England to concentrate her resources, with a unity of aim that more than doubled them, against the disperal of Spain's strength upon so many different objectives strung out across Europe. There were also the factors of morale. Bacon saw that taxation by consent, as in England and the Low Countries, discouraged people less and gave them a stake in their country's effort, an incentive to success. They each enjoyed a much larger middle sort of people than Spain : Bacon thought them a solider foundation for war. Though Spain had the fanaticism of the Counter-Reformation fighting for her, and England the Protestant zeal of her seamen, Philip aroused against himself the strongest of all such forces we can see at work in the modern world—nationalism, acute and aflame in Elizabethan England : nor have we lost ever since the inspiration it gave us then. The strength of Elizabeth's government was that it was in fullest accord with the impulses and desires, the native strength, of the people. Nor did she commit them to open war until it was recognised to be unavoidable.

At the end of it England emerged far stronger than at the

[1] Cf. *The England of Elizabeth*, 139-42.
[2] Bacon, *Works, ed. cit.*, VI. 451.
[3] q. Mahan, *op. cit.* 41.

beginning, Spain much weaker, though still the most considerable military power. The shift of gravity to the North-West was evident. With James's accession the island was united, England had become Great Britain, a power henceforth of the first rank. Ireland had been reduced and Bacon was able to point out that the King was more powerful than any of his ancestors.[1] Our footing in France had been a source of trouble rather than of strength. The Dutch, whose state had come into being under the Queen's protection, now independent and the most powerful nation at sea, were in close relations with us : the junction of our navies could blockade both Spain and the Indies. With Spain the root was too narrow for the tops, her kingdoms too distant to concentrate her forces. While the future was to bear out the truth of Bacon's words in his essay " Of the True Greatness of Kingdoms and Estates " : " some that have but a small dimension of stem [are] yet apt to be the foundation of great monarchies ".[2]

The compass of the reign saw the ending of an old cycle in our wars and the opening of a new. The Treaty of Edinburgh drove the French out of Scotland ; the fortification of Berwick clinched it : henceforth the island was, for all foreign purposes, virtually one. Elizabeth's intervention in the first French war of religion was a mistake[3]—there were not many ; but the temptation to win a gage for Calais, and to triumph over the dead Mary, recovering what she had lost, was irresistible. It was the last example of the purely cross-Channel warfare characteristic of the Middle Ages ; thenceforward, from the gathering conflict with Spain, our sea warfare became oceanic : the modern pattern was set.

As for our preparedness, the character of our equipment for the new age, Elizabethan England showed a marked difference of step at sea from on land : which has appeared also at intervals throughout our history, an uneven rhythm such as only the security of an island sea-power could permit to a state. We were in the van as a naval power, working out new types of ship, setting new standards of seamanship, suited to the transition from the Mediterranean to the Atlantic and northern waters.

---

[1] Bacon, *Works*, VI. 445.

[2] *Ibid*. VII. 22 foll.

[3] A. F. Pollard says, " perhaps the greatest blunder of the reign ", *Political History of England, 1547–1603*, 248.

On land we were again backward and behind as in so many fields : half-way through the Queen's reign, in a Europe dominated by the new fire-arms and military organisation, English musters were still armed with bows and bills. The English had to learn in the school of continental warfare.

These themes must now receive their illustration in more detail.

The history of the Royal Navy as a continuous force begins with the Tudors.[1] In this development, as in the secular impulse to our society with the liquidation of the monasteries and chantries, the relegation of religion to its proper place, Henry VIII was the prime mover. He built the most powerful navy of his time, and it was that more than anything else that made it impossible for foreign powers to take advantage of the internal weakness of the state during the middle of the century. He laid down two new dockyards, that remained active to the last days of wooden ships, and organised the administration that lasted in essence till yesterday : the Navy Board that came into being at the end of his reign continued up to 1832. Northumberland was very conscious of sea-power, and under his government we see the beginnings of the dockyard at Chatham, the constitution of a separate Victualling Department. Mary did not seriously let down the navy : for that and the protection of the route to the Netherlands Philip married her. But she allowed the ships to get into disrepair : she cared more for Corpus Christi processions and, incomprehensibly, preferred priests to sailors. They did not stand her in such good stead : by that Calais was lost. Upon Elizabeth's accession the Abbey of Grace on Tower Hill was taken over for the Victualling Department : à symbolic change.

The shift from the Mediterranean to the Atlantic meant a shift from galleys to sail, with the ultimate result of an English naval supremacy that lasted throughout the whole epoch of sail, the developments from Lepanto onwards that culminated in Trafalgar.[2] The first steps in these developments were slow. The new type of man-of-war seems to have been evolved, reasonably enough, from the tried and tested merchantmen used

[1] Cf. J. A. Williamson, *Hawkins of Plymouth*, 231.
[2] We may add that the Industrial Revolution enabled that supremacy to be continued throughout a second epoch, that of steam—a fortunate dispensation for this island, an exceptional fate in history for one people.

to all waters. The English navy included merchant ships along with the king's ships ; indeed, the former were the greater part of it and we have seen what doughty fighters they became under Elizabeth. The fleet that came out against the Armada was three-quarters of it mercantile : 1588 was very much in the tradition. In the sum-total of English naval power commerce was a most important factor, and a hard-hitting one.

The change-over from medieval to modern in naval power is marked by the emergence of the galleon. Contrary to popular belief, this was not a Spanish development but—like everything in the Renaissance of the arts and sciences—Italian.[1] The conception may have reached us, in the usual way, via France ; what was characteristic of the model was an average length of about three times its beam. Henry VIII revolutionised the fleet by his construction along these lines, but he also retained galleys as a subordinate weapon : they could be used in a calm, or in shallow water, and were not wholly superseded in the Channel at the end of the century.[2] On the basis of the Italian model, the English made developments which probably arose in close conjunction with the extension of commerce and maritime experience into the Atlantic. For the two men who were most closely associated with the adoption of the type of ship that fought the Armada were, primarily, Hawkins and, secondarily, Drake. With these ships, on the threshold of the 1580s, there was a sudden increase in the range of action of our naval power : it too spread its wings and became oceanic.

Some of the improvements that are listed by Ralegh came, also, from the Mediterranean. " Whosoever were the inventors, we find that every age had added somewhat to ships . . . and in my own time the shape of our English ships hath been greatly bettered. It is not long since the striking of the top-mast (a wonderful ease to great ships, both at sea and harbour) hath been devised, together with the chain-pump, which takes up twice as much water as the ordinary did."[3] Then there was the lengthening of cable that enabled ships to ride out stronger winds, the weighing of anchors by capstan, the new varieties of sail, though there were still no fore and aft sails. All these things

---

[1] Cf. Sir Julian Corbett, *Drake and the Tudor Navy*, I. 24.

[2] Cf. E. R. Adair, " English Galleys in the Sixteenth Century ", *E.H.R.* 1920, 497 foll.

[3] " A Discourse of the Invention of Ships, etc.", Ralegh's *Works, ed. cit.,* VIII. 323.

increased sea-endurance, of primary importance when conditions became oceanic. And, in fact, Elizabethan ships kept the seas : only two lesser ships of the Queen's were wrecked in the whole age.[1]

From the 1570s we see the new type of warship being laid down : English ideas were coming into their own in this sphere earlier than in literature or the arts. In 1575–7 the *Revenge* was built, a middle-sized ship of 500 tons, which Drake thought the perfect galleon of his time and chose for his flagship in 1588. She became the type for Hawkins' rebuilding of the fleet when he became Treasurer of the Navy in 1577, with Sir William Winter, Drake and the ship-designers, Matthew Baker and Peter Pett, on the Board. The big ships—the *Elizabeth Jonas, Victory, Merehonour, Triumph* and *White Bear*—fell out of favour ; Ralegh tells us why. " We find by experience that the greatest ships are least serviceable, go very deep to water and of marvellous charge . . . besides, they are less nimble, less mainable and very seldom employed. *Grande navio grande fatiga*, saith the Spaniard ; a ship of 600 tons will carry as good ordnance as a ship of 1200 tons and . . . the lesser will turn her broadsides twice before the greater can wind once."[2] In the event the big ships (from 800 to 1000 tons) were only turned out when the fleet was in full strength, *i.e.* very rarely ; the middle-sized galleons, like the *Revenge, Defiance, Vanguard, Rainbow*, were the mainstay of the fleet upon which its regular work depended. They were wonderfully manoeuvrable. They were armed increasingly with culverin instead of cannon : those were lighter to carry, with less recoil, much quicker in firing and had the advantage of a longer range. The English had a monopoly of iron ordnance, cheaper than brass, which Ralegh regarded as " a jewel of great value . . . no other could ever attain unto it although they have assayed it with great charge ". Moreover, the English were accounted valiant gunners in action, if less scientific in theory : " they are hardy or without fear about their ordnance, but for the knowledge in it other nations and countries have tasted better thereof ".[3] In ordnance the Elizabethans were now reaping the reward of the early providence of Burghley :[4]

---

[1] M. Oppenheim, *History of the Administration of the Royal Navy, 1509–1660*, 123.
[2] " Observations concerning the Royal Navy ", Ralegh's *Works*, VIII. 337.
[3] William Bourne, q. in A. R. Hall, *Ballistics in the Seventeenth Century*, 29.
[4] Cf. *The England of Elizabeth*, 124-5.

English guns were the best in Europe, the Netherlands were provided with them and the government had difficulty in stopping the export to Spain. Then, too, there was a further advantage in the large number of light pinnaces Hawkins built ; in 1588 the fleet had eighteen ocean-going ones. English naval intelligence was as efficient as Walsingham's political intelligence service : the Navy never took its eyes off the coast of Spain, every movement was at once reported. (The notable exception is, of course, the actual approach of the Armada in 1588, which achieved a tactical surprise : all the more exciting.)

As for conditions at sea, it is no use anachronistically comparing the life of the seamen then with that of today : it is four centuries ago and the whole conditions of society were different, harsher, more brutal and barbarous. We can compare the state of things relatively to other countries at the time, and, as we should expect, English seamen were better paid and looked after—as the people in general were better fed and provided for all through our modern history. Nothing like the thousands of galley-slaves whom the King of Spain got at a cheap rate from the Emperor, and who died like flies. Hawkins brought in reforms in manning the ships and managed to get the seaman's wage increased to 10s. a month—good relatively to other wages—shortly before the Armada. English discipline on board was purely maritime, with far more freedom, flexibility and individual responsibility, reflecting the society, where Spanish discipline was military, even at sea : the seamen took second place, were told off and given their orders.[1] Where soldiers were concerned Spanish discipline was much superior, far harder and more rigid. All soldiers and sailors in that age were apt to run away when they had had too much, or even before they had had anything ; the boot was not always on one leg, nor were all the advantages with the officers : it was the regular thing for impressed men to take their commanders' money and then give them the slip. Often they were rounded up in the taverns : slyer types easily escaped through the wide meshes of the net.[2]

The worst side of Elizabethan naval and military life was the victualling and provisioning : here we see the inefficiency of an earlier society at its most flagrant : they had not the means,

---

[1] Corbett, *op. cit.* I. 386.
[2] Cf. the vivacious paragraph in Sir Richard Hawkins, *Observations*, ed. J. A. Williamson, 20.

the resources nor the organisation to ensure regularity of supplies in any respect as we have. They were at the mercy not only of wind and weather, but of dearth and disease, of endemic peculation and irrepressible dishonesty. Victuallers consistently supplied bad ships' biscuit, mouldy and worm-eaten, along with the good. They provided putrid salt beef along with the rest, and beer that was sour. Good victual was thieved, the bad passed on to the men ; even if it started good, it went bad before it got to them. There were constant hold-ups in transport ; ships having to keep the seas for unwontedly long periods, as in the stormy summer of 1588, exhausted their supplies and it was a slow job revictualling them—which was precisely what happened when the Armada came. In consequence the death-rate from disease, chiefly scurvy, was very high : Richard Hawkins tells us that 10,000 sailors died of it in these two decades. (At the same time we must remember the regular ravages of plague on land.)

It is a popular misconception, repeated by generations of historians, that the government did nothing for its sick and wounded soldiers and sailors. This is quite untrue : in fact it did as much as could be expected in sixteenth-century conditions. Acts of Parliament were passed instituting compulsory collections in the parishes for maintenance and help for such persons.[1] Small places, jobs and pensions were provided for many ; still more, as was usual throughout that society, depended on charity. The government regularly issued licences to beg to deserving cases ; and that, in those days, was a privilege. Shortly after the Armada, Hawkins and Drake took the initiative in setting up the Chatham Chest, a fund for the relief of sick and aged mariners, which functioned well to begin with but afterwards fell victim to the corruption of the succeeding age.[2]

Everything of the Queen's in those days was fair game : if she had not been the woman she was, her government would have been bankrupt and she could not have sustained the war. Hawkins reported that since 1570 the Queen had paid £9000 for timber and plank, and not £4000 worth had her service

---

[1] Oppenheim, *op. cit.* 135.

[2] Cf. Williamson, *Hawkins of Plymouth*, 316. The seamen had agreed to advance a proportion of their pay to the relief of their fellows in distress. Hawkins at his own cost founded an almshouse for poor decayed mariners and shipwrights, endowing it with £66 a year in land. In 1609 it was supporting ten pensioners at 2s. a week. Hasted's *Kent* (ed. 1798), IV. 218.

got out of it.[1] Of Sir William Winter's own ships, the *Edward* had been wholly, the *Mary Fortune* mainly, built out of government timber. The timber for the first of the new medium-sized galleons, the *Foresight*, was already largely provided, yet the Queen paid for it all again. Queen and people paid about twice as much as they should have done for the ships that were theirs. In every other respect it was the same story : captains took bribes to let men off service, kept back arms and wages ; pursers stole provisions and made false entries, cooks sold victuals, boatswains removed rigging and cordage—everybody according to his sphere.[2] The pursuit of the Armada was held up by the exhaustion of powder and ammunition ; but the master-gunner of the *Ark Royal*[3] was able to store away in his house four barrels by his account, though a neighbour offered to prove that " after the fight there came to his house forty barrels, which was to her Majesty in that fight great hindrance ".[4] Even if this is an exaggeration, in the kind way that neighbours have, we see how things were all through. George Cary of Cockington spoke true when he said, " I find all these sea-goods are mixed with bird-lime ; for no man can lay his hand of them, but is limed and must bring away somewhat. Watch and look never so narrowly, they will steal and pilfer."[5] The Queen has been constantly abused by ignorant historians for her niggardliness in these matters. Let us hope that henceforward we shall hear no more of it.

These were the pretty ways of the age. In spite of them, and also by means of them, the Queen's fleet was built and rebuilt—altogether some 29 new ships of war were built during her reign, the rest re-modelled, the high upper works and decks cut down, the ships made lower according to the new designs emerging from the leading shipwrights, Pett and Baker, founders of dynasties in those yards. By the time of the Armada there were some 25 middle-sized and big galleons to fight it, and 150 merchant ships that could give an account of themselves.[6] The ships must have been beautiful in their vivid colours, in full rig with all their sails and pennons. The *White Bear* was painted red, the

---

[1] Williamson, *op. cit.* 252.   [2] Oppenheim, 146.
[3] The Lord Admiral's flagship.   [4] Oppenheim, 158-9.
[5] J. K. Laughton, ed. *The Defeat of the Spanish Armada*, II. 187.
[6] Cf. the fight put up by five London ships, headed by *The Merchant Royal*, against eleven galleys and two frigates off Pantelleria, 13 July 1586. Hakluyt, *Principal Navigations*, III. 359-68.

Bonaventure black and white, the *Lion* " timber-colour ", the *Revenge*
and *Scout* green and white. They all had figureheads, dragons,
lions, unicorns, tigers.[1] When the *White Bear* was rebuilt she
bore a carved " image of Jupiter sitting upon an eagle with the
clouds before the head of the ship, side-boards for the head with
compartments and badges and fruitages . . . the great piece of
Neptune and the nymphs about him for the upright of the stern ".
Here was the Renaissance, with the English, going to sea.

We can tell how proud Hawkins was of his ships—after the
complaints that had been made against him too—from the way
his brother William writes to him from Plymouth in the early
spring of 1588, working day and night to get them in trim :
" the ships sit aground so strongly and are so staunch as if they
were made of a whole tree ".[2] Still, " the doing of it is very
chargeable, for that it is done by torchlights and cressets, and
in an extreme gale of wind, which consumes pitch, tallow and
furze abundantly. . . . The *Hope* and *Nonpareil* are both graved,
tallowed and this tide into the road again ; and the *Revenge*, now
aground, I hope she shall likewise go into the road also tomorrow.
We have, and do, trim one side of every ship by night and the
other side by day, so that we end the three great ships in three
days this spring." It is pleasant to think that the flags they
carried had been made by Mrs. Hawkins and her maids, green
and white, the Queen's own colours. Safely ensconced in Rome,
Cardinal Allen could assure Philip that the rot in the fleet
was such that only four ships were fit for sea.[3] Nothing like the
rot he thought. However, Philip did not depend for his naval intelligence on the illusions of an émigré, and he was taking no
chances.

The changes taking place in the relations of the powers, the
growth of Anglo-Spanish rivalry in place of the old friendship,
the ranging of Catholics against Protestants in France and the
Netherlands, are reflected in the growing disorder, the hostilities,
at sea leading to open war. The turning point may be seen in
the critical years 1569–72 : the Papal excommunication of the
Queen, the Ridolfi Plot against her, Philip's support of Mary
Stuart, his prohibition of trade with America, the disaster of

[1] Oppenheim, 130-1.
[2] J. K. Laughton, *The Defeat of the Spanish Armada*, I. 73.
[3] Cf. Williamson, *op. cit.* 290.

San Juan de Ulloa, Elizabeth's effective arrest of the treasure going up-Channel to pay Alva's troops, revolt in the Netherlands. Highway robbery had always been endemic at sea as on land. The English were past masters at it, their chief hunting-ground the western approaches to the Channel. Now their activities were given a tremendous impetus and a varying sanction. The distinction between piracy and privateering is in theory simple : privateering means depredations upon the trade of an enemy power by licence of lawful authority, under letters of marque ; piracy is plain robbery. But the two ran inextricably into each other. Were the letters of marque conferred by the Huguenot leaders, Condé, the King of Navarre, the Prince of Orange, to be recognised ? Many Englishmen, whether they had a score against Spaniards or not, sheltered behind them and were not discouraged by the government when it had its own grievances to repay against Philip. In the 1570s the Channel and the western seas were filled with indiscriminate scuffling and disorder, in which the English seamen had the upper hand.

It was a school of sea-warfare, as we see from Frobisher's early career.[1] From 1563 to 1573 he was associated with the Hawkinses, Killigrews and Eriseys in constant privateering activities. In May 1563 he brought into Plymouth five French prizes. Next, we find him in association with Thomas Cobham, who captured a ship, the *Catherine*, which had tapestries for Philip himself on board. The Council arrested the goods and sent Frobisher to Launceston gaol. (He married a Launceston girl.) He was soon out and cruising in the *Mary Flower* in 1565. In 1566 he gave security not to go to sea without a licence. At once he got a commission from Cardinal Châtillon, the Huguenot leader, to capture French enemy ships. In 1569 he sailed under the Prince of Orange's commission, and was arrested and sent to the Marshalsea over a French prize. The ship was taken over by Lady Clinton, wife of the Lord Admiral. She was the poet Surrey's Geraldine : a remarkable business head, much occupied with Admiralty matters, especially wreck or pirates' goods or the Lord Admiral's perquisites, and in high favour with the Queen. We next find Frobisher in the Queen's service : " I hear you do conceive well of him of late ", someone writes to Burghley. Frobisher was employed in 1572 against the rebels in Ireland.

[1] Cf. R. G. Marsden, " The Early Career of Sir Martin Frobisher ", *E.H.R.*, July 1906.

Next year Philip was sounding him to engage his services, and he was still hoping for them in 1575, as he had been for those of Hawkins earlier. But Philip was too late : an indispensable condition was to admit the English to share in the trade with the New World. That he never would grant. Hence the English seamen carried on their private war with him, until it merged into the greater struggle.

One observes the common Protestant front coming into being at sea before it did on land, and—to anticipate—we may say that the Protestant powers owed their survival and their victory, as they did their strength, to sea-power. There was the closest association between La Rochelle, an almost independent Huguenot city-state, and Plymouth.[1] The Queen did not hesitate to help La Rochelle against Catholic pressure ; the links of Killigrews and Tremaynes, Hawkins and Drake, Champernowne and Ralegh, with Huguenot France were very close. La Rochelle and Plymouth fought Dieppe and Rouen, made depredations together upon the trade through the Channel. Their hand stretched out to the Dutch Sea-Beggars at the other end of it. Plymouth became quite an emporium for goods taken at sea, often on account of Hawkins and his partners recouping themselves for their losses in the West Indies.

Their activities extended into the Atlantic and across it, as we have seen : a state of warfare in the Caribbean—since legitimate trade was prohibited—which never ceased and in the seventeenth century was largely responsible for the decay of the Spanish Empire.[2] Out of it grew Drake's strategic intention to cut the waist-line of the Empire at the Isthmus. In the Channel there were such exploits as Philip Budockshide's capture of the Barbary hulks in Plymouth Sound, a pretty stratagem, or the achievements of the well-named and well-armed *Castle of Comfort*, in which Hawkins held a share with Grenville.[3] In 1572 the Dutch rovers, ordered away from Dover, took possession of Brille, later to become for decades a cautionary town in English possession ;

---

[1] On this *v.* J. A. Williamson, *Sir John Hawkins*, esp. Bk. II, cc. i and iii.

[2] In that century—the really bad time for Spain—English, French and Dutch smashed up everything that could be got at from the coast, almost destroyed the trade between the provinces, drove large sections of the population to piracy by making any other livelihood impossible, and helped to make the traders from Spain to America so few and far between. It was an almighty revenge for Spain's rôle in the sixteenth century. I owe this point to the kindness of Professor R. Pares.

[3] For these *v.* my *Sir Richard Grenville*, cc. iv and vi.

shortly after, the second, Flushing—key to Zealand—fell to the rebels and Gilbert led a contingent over to their aid. After that, the Netherlands war was never extinguished until it led to their independence.[1]

As one turns over the musty, fat paper books of the Court of Admiralty, often bound in the parchment of some medieval scholastic manuscript—a nice epitome of the changed state of affairs—some sense of those Channel excitements in the 'seventies comes back to one. There are the rough sea-captains and the mariners giving their evidence as to their dubious doings; there is Mr. Doctor Lewis or Mr. Doctor Caesar, Judges of the Admiralty Court, the scratching of their pens taking down the details—" Thomas Lucas servaunt to Mr. Roger Parker clarke of the Admiraltie writt this ".[2] The *Galleon Lombardo* was captured by Michael Roscarrock's ship, called after himself, and brought into Padstow, his home port.[3] A Padstow seaman deposes that " when the company of the *Michael Roscarrock* came aboard, [the *Galleon Lombardo*] had all her upper deck above the main-mast broken up, and her forecastle blown up with the powder, and the ship otherwise in such case that without the help of God and the great labour and industry of the captain and company of the *Michael Roscarrock*, it was impossible she could have been saved, for she was in such danger that they were forced to frap her about with cables to hold her together, otherwise he certainly knoweth she would have sunk ".[4] As often as not—or so they made out—the boot was on the other leg : the bark *Greyhound* was chased into Mounts Bay by the *Brave* of Conquet and spoiled of £530 in Spanish reals of four and eight in six canvas bags, belonging to a merchant of Exeter.[5] When the *Minion* was hammered by three Flushingers thwart of Start Point, " they searched with candlelight every corner of the same ship and left not the same night nor day until they came thwart of Flushing. And as they passed from one ship to another the reals of plate shed and dropped out of their sleeves. This examinant

---

[1] Cf. P. Geyl, *The Revolt of the Netherlands*, 120 : " It all began with the capture of the Brille ".

[2] H.C.A. 13/16.

[3] The two youngest sons of this Protestant family became Catholic devotees, lifelong recusants, *v.* my " Nicholas Roscarrock and his Lives of the Saints ", in *Essays Presented to G. M. Trevelyan.*

[4] H.C.A. 13/26.

[5] H.C.A. 13/21.

also saw the mariners of the said ships, which were left on board the *Minion* to keep the same there, to play at dice and cards for Spanish reals of four and two the piece, being of the money gotten in the said ship."[1] Several times in these years, when the situation became too intolerable, the government sent out a squadron under one or the other of the Winters to clear the seas of the pirates and/or privateers.[2] William Batts of Saltash, sailing in the *William Bonaventure* under letters of marque from the King of Navarre, had taken two French boats, one with a cargo of 3000 Newfoundland fish and another with 22 pipes of Guinea grains and 600 elephants' tusks, meaning to take the goods to La Rochelle—or so he said—when " he fell into the lap of her Majesty's ships under the charge of George Winter, esquire ".[3]

Such were the doings at the entrance to the Channel in these years.[4]

Don Antonio's attempt to gain possession of the Azores (where he had more support than in Portugal itself), with the aid of Catherine de Medici and French contingents serving with Strozzi, was utterly destroyed by Santa Cruz in a naval battle off Terceira in 1583.[5] Most of the French slunk off without fighting, but those crews that were captured were massacred in the Spanish fashion : the action put France out as a naval power for a generation. In the exaltation of victory Santa Cruz wrote to Philip proposing the enterprise of England next year : it was already in mind.[6] Alva's strategic sense had always been against a war with England : he held that the King could undertake any enemies, provided he remained on friendly terms with England. But the time for that was over. Philip replied to Santa Cruz that matters were not yet ripe : " pues dependen del tiempo y ocasiones que han de dar la regla despues ".[7] But he

---

[1] H.C.A. 13/22.

[2] Lansdowne, 142, f. 83, gives a brief note of pirates executed : 1561 : 13 ; 1567 : 11 ; 1570 : 20 ; 1573 : 28 ; 1575 : 4 ; 1577 : 16 ; 1579 : 14 ; 1580 : 6.

[3] H.C.A. 1/40.

[4] The above are only a few illustrations. Most of the files of Indictments for the reign have been lost, so that only a fraction of the cases have come down to us.

[5] Don Antonio, Prior of Crato, was the illegitimate son of a previous Portuguese king and Pretender to the throne. Elizabeth had refused him her support at this point ; the French gave him unofficial support. When war broke out he naturally entered into English plans, came to England and was on friendly terms with Drake and the seamen.

[6] Cf. C. F. Duro, *La armada invencible*, I. 241-3.

[7] *Ibid.* 244.

added that Santa Cruz was to go on collecting provisions of ships' biscuit from Italy and to press forward the construction of the Biscayan galleons. (On his accession to the crown of Portugal and the acquisition of at least twelve first-class galleons, Philip had ordered nine more to be laid down in the Biscay ports.)

Philip's slowly maturing, contingent preparations went forward. Two years later, on a failure of the corn crops in Spain, he gave special inducements to English merchants to send over supplies ; immediately the corn-ships in considerable number were in Spanish harbours he declared an embargo, arrested ships and cargoes and imprisoned the crews. There was a tremendous outburst of anger in England : it provided just the spark of righteous indignation to touch off the war. And indeed the war is usually considered, in England, to have begun with that. At once measures of retaliation were ordered—though, a little later, Philip released the ships. General letters of reprisal were issued to all and sundry : from henceforth the seas were alive with English privateers against Spain.[1] Anything Spanish on the high seas was fair prey. The ordinances then issued remained in force for the rest of the reign, with the proviso of formal condemnation in prize-court added in 1589. Later, contraband was defined and lists issued. All powers asserted the right to seize contraband of war ; the only difference was that the English were in a strong position to exert it and did : hence the outcry. It led to a complex and dangerous issue in subsequent years with our Dutch allies, as they grew rich by trading with the enemy. Their case was that they could not finance the war without it ; and indeed the English themselves, on a much smaller scale, traded war supplies to Spain, chiefly guns and grain. The Queen complained that Spain would not have been able to sustain the war in Brittany but for Dutch supplies—and the Dutch prospered exceedingly by it. One observes the lunacy of human affairs and also how it foreshadows the sense of our later wars : blockade, seizure of contraband were indispensable weapons to a naval power ; the classic formulation of policy, the system of courts, the refinement of rules—it all goes back to the Elizabethan age.

Two specific measures of retaliation were swiftly decided on. In June 1585 Bernard Drake of Ashe was ordered to Newfoundland to round up all the Spanish fishing fleet and bring it into

[1] Cheyney, *op. cit.* I. 469 foll.

West Country ports : a useful diminution to the potential food supplies of the Enterprise of England.[1] Francis Drake was at this moment assembling a powerful expedition to the Far East : it would have followed in the wake of his great Voyage, stripped the coast of Peru and probably ante-dated the East India Company by fifteen years. Now he was sent to the West Indies as the Queen's Vice-Admiral in command of a small fleet and a small army : the time of subterfuges was past, this was a direct attack upon the centre of Spanish colonial power. It meant that the Queen was prepared to fight Philip in America, while still not committing herself to an all-out war in Europe.

Drake's conquering expedition to the West Indies, in which he captured two colonial capitals, San Domingo and Cartagena, is—like everything he did—very famous. We can now, centuries afterwards, see the story from the Spanish side.[2] He began by sailing into Vigo, occupying it and brazenly using it, as he might Plymouth, to complete his preparations for crossing the Atlantic : one can see it all from the Guia, the high point he seized looking down the long narrow sleeve of water to the islands at the mouth. Philip could do nothing about it : Drake finished and sailed away : very good for morale and prestige. But at the Cape Verdes he took fever on board and three hundred men died. When he arrived off San Domingo the Spaniards expected a frontal assault : the harbour entrance was narrow and defended by batteries. No care was taken of the approach to the town from the rear, where there was a strip of shingle between the rocks and the sea. Here Drake landed his men by night and the town was his with hardly a struggle. No wonder the surprised Spaniards paid tribute to his prudence as much as to his daring : both were present in his make-up, as in the Queen's : " a cautious commander ", they say, " equal to any undertaking ".[3] The oldest of Spanish colonial cities was pillaged and then ransomed. We have a close-up of Drake as he appeared to the Spaniards against the background of their sacked city : " a man of medium stature, blonde, rather heavy than slender, merry, careful. He

[1] S.P. 12/179, 21. Bernard Drake was the head of the county family of that name —from which the Churchills are descended. There is no evidence that Francis Drake belonged to it, though a remote relationship is usually assumed : perhaps he belonged to the clan.

[2] From the documents assembled by Miss I. A. Wright in her *Further English Voyages to Spanish America, 1583–1594* (Hakluyt Soc.).

[3] *Ibid.* 36.

commands and governs imperiously. . . . Sharp, restless, well-spoken, inclined to liberality and to ambition, vainglorious, boastful, not very cruel."[1] Indeed, humane : a Spaniard, who had been taken prisoner and escaped, reported that "in San Domingo and throughout Hispaniola, Drake behaved with such humanity to the Indians and negroes that they all love him and their houses were open to all English ".[2]

Thence he sailed off to attack Cartagena, the most important city on the Spanish Main, in a strong natural situation. It had received warning from San Domingo, but that only served to demoralise the defenders. Here Drake made the assault by night—tribute to the discipline of his force—against all the risks of a *mêlée*. The town fell at a first onrush, though the fort held out a little longer. We have a glimpse of Drake, while waiting for its ransom to be collected, showing the townsmen the guns of his flag-ship, no doubt with special intention.[3] What he had at heart was a raid on Panama, but that was not possible with his men wasted by fever and Philip's fleet likely to appear. Nor was it possible to hold Cartagena, as some have argued : Drake had no authority from the Queen for that—it would have meant constant reinforcement and regular war, to which she did not regard herself even yet as committed.

The effects of the campaign were of the first importance. The inadequacy of Spanish defences in the West Indies was exposed : no naval forces were stationed there, San Domingo had no garrison, its defences were poor, colonial morale low. Philip was forced to fortify the colonies and provide forces, ships and garrisons, for their defence, thus distracting his energies and dispersing his resources—the key to the weakening of Spain's power.[4] Meanwhile, Drake had gone off with 240 guns, a severe loss to a power which did not manufacture but had to import them. Philip was seriously set back in the plans he was revolving for the war which *he* regarded as inevitable, and, in what had become the first round of it, he had sustained a damaging blow, encouraging to all his enemies.

The reaction of Santa Cruz was to return to the charge with

[1] Wright, *op. cit.* 225. I suspect that the words ' sharp, restless, well-spoken ' would be better rendered as ' acute, tireless, amiable '.

[2] *Cal. S.P. Venetian, 1581–91*, 155.

[3] Wright, *op. cit.* 44.

[4] We can follow Philip's reaction in his correspondence with Santa Cruz, *v.* V. Fernández Asis, *Epistolario de Felipe II sobre asuntos de mar*, 161-2.

Philip and propose a vast Armada to overwhelm England : he demanded 77,000 tons of shipping, 30,000 mariners and 60,000 soldiers.[1] This was quite beyond Philip's resources and he headed him off by ordering him to the West Indies to repair the damage Drake had done. But the General of the Ocean Sea was too busy with his preparations at Lisbon. His conception of the Enterprise was a seaman's : first defeat the English at sea, then invade, and he saw that for this to succeed something overwhelming would be necessary. Like a practical politician, Philip adopted a compromise solution : an Armada powerful enough to keep the English fleet at bay, to land its troops and ferry across Parma's army in the Netherlands. It is fascinating to observe the reluctance of Elizabeth and Philip to come to grips, for meanwhile the Queen did nothing in 1586 to follow up Drake's blow in 1585 or to impede the preparations centred on Lisbon. She ordered Hawkins merely " to ply up and down " the Channel : a useless proceeding that reflected her uncertainty before the final decision, and only resulted in his missing both the East Indian carracks and the plate-fleet. She was reluctant to take the last step into the unknown hazards of war : she was a politician and she was involved in incessant negotiation with Parma. We now know the reason for her marked politeness to him : she was trying to tempt him away with the offer of an independent sovereignty in the Netherlands. And that would have been an admirable solution to the inextricable tangle there, the bloody war consuming so many lives, which was to go on for years. Only, like so many admirable solutions in human affairs, it was not possible.

The seamen sensed what the Queen was up to better than subsequent unimaginative historians ; and they were much more patient than might have been expected—tribute to the discipline she commanded in the state—for indeed it constantly held up their operations and made them more difficult to conduct. *There* is the interest of the war, which has perhaps not been hitherto quite realised : the unprecedented nature of the operations, the difficulty of co-ordinating them, the inability of the combatants to come completely to grips, the incompleteness and unsatisfactoriness of so many of the actions and hence its long-drawn-out, interminable character.

[1] The correspondence between Philip and Santa Cruz is given in Duro, *op. cit.* I. 244 foll.

But Philip had made his resolve and could not turn back : no amount of negotiation could now shake him. At Lisbon the galleons were gathering and being armed : one hears the sound of hammering and welding still coming up those smiling terraced slopes to the castle of St. George[1] on guard above the sunlit waters of the lagoon. At last, in 1587, alarmed by the noise of the preparations, the Council let loose Drake to impede them. Some evidence of the doubts and divisions of opinion remains in a draft among the State papers to the effect that " he is to forbear offering any violence to his [Philip's] towns or shipping within harbours and confine himself to Spanish shipping at sea " ![2] Something of Drake's spirit we may catch from his letter to his fellow Protestant, Walsingham, from on board the *Elizabeth Bonaventure* : " there was never more likely in any fleet of a more loving agreement than we hope the one of the other, I thank God. I find no man but as all members of one body to stand for our gracious Queen and country against Anti-Christ and his members. . . . If your honour did now see the fleet under sail and knew with what resolution men's minds do enter into this action, so you would judge a small force would not divide them. . . . Each wind commands me away, our ship is under sail, God grant we may so live in his fear as the enemy may have cause to say that God doth fight for her Majesty, as well abroad as at home, and give her long and happy life and ever victory against God's enemies and her Majesty's."[3] At last he could spread wings from Plymouth Sound : he was off on the famous exploit of the " Singeing of the King of Spain's Beard ".

On the coast of Spain he learnt and saw for himself : " the like preparation was never heard of nor known as the King of Spain hath and daily maketh to invade England ".[4] It seems that Drake had no authority to attack Lisbon, and to penetrate that narrow, heavily defended entrance was a hazard that only total destruction of the Armada within could warrant : here, again, Drake's caution matched his daring. Hearing of a secondary concentration of shipping at Cadiz, he determined to penetrate the harbour, in spite of the galley-squadron and the shore batteries defending it, and against the protest of his second in command, an old experienced naval officer. The risk he took was justified

---

[1] The medieval English had played a considerable part in the reconquest of Lisbon from the Muslims.
[2] S.P. 12/200, 17.   [3] *Ibid.* No. 2.   [4] *Ibid.* No. 46.

by 100 per cent success : he destroyed the great bulk of the shipping in harbour, a big Biscayan of 1200 tons, Santa Cruz' own ship of 1500 tons and thirty-one other vessels, big and small.[1] On his way back, off Lisbon, he sent in taunting messages to the Marquis to come out and fight. This was much disapproved of by Lord Burghley as impolite : the wonderful old statesman had no liking for Drake : he was never one to overplay *his* hand.

Off the Azores Drake had the luck to capture the big carrack, *San Felipe* : the fantastic riches of her cargo more than twice paid the costs of the whole expedition.[2] In the absence of an English Peru to pay for the war, this was a good way of financing it. And it pointed up Hawkins's conception of the strategy to be pursued : he seems to have been the only person to put forward a consistent plan of operations.[3] A professional seaman, born and bred to the sea, he was against any foreign entanglements on land " but of mere necessity " ; he proposed a constant blockade of the coast of Spain by relays of the Queen's ships. (It was a conception that was to receive its development on an ever-growing scale in our later history.) For the present, Philip's plans were sufficiently disarrayed. It was pure pleasure to the boastful Englishman to find that the lading of the *San Felipe* was mostly Philip's own : he had come to think of the war, as a good many others did, as a duel between himself and the King. Philip ordered Santa Cruz to the Azores to safeguard the remaining carracks on their way home ; by the time he returned it was too late for the Armada to set sail for England that year. Drake's campaign had completely dislocated the plan. The King was urgent : supplies were being eaten up, his credit undermined, Parma's army running down. But the Armada was in no condition to move. By next spring Santa Cruz was dead.

---

[1] These are Drake's own figures, *ibid.*

[2] Philip was so chagrined at the loss of the *San Felipe*, which was largely laden with luxury goods for him, that he hoped some ships might be spared to intercept her off Ushant. *v. Epistolario, ed. cit.* 162-3. But nothing could be done about it.

[3] Cf. Laughton, *op. cit.* I. 58-62.

CHAPTER VIII

THE ARMADA AND AFTER

IN spite of these two brilliant examples Drake had given to the contrary—the early years of the war were Drake's—the advantages in sixteenth-century warfare were largely with the defensive : people were so much more at the mercy of wind and weather, of difficulties with regard to supply and man-power. Nothing brings this home more clearly than the two cases of the Armada offensive and our reply to it with the Lisbon expedition in 1589 : the one a disaster, the other a fiasco. It was fortunate that underneath the many offences she had given Philip, the Queen's mind, when it came to the point, was instinctively with the defensive.

Two contrary effects resulted from Drake's blows. In England the seamen now tended to underestimate Spain's fighting power—and the Armada, when it came, surprised them. In Spain Philip did his best to apply the lessons so hardly learned : he increased the weight of metal on his ships, gathering all the guns he could, so that the Armada had a superiority in heavy cannon, medium and short-range, and in ammunition. The English were caught short of supplies ; but then the conditions of conflict, between two ocean-going fleets, were unprecedented in history.

We owe to the excellent Venetian news service our impression of the mood of the moment. In Rome the Pope, grown garrulous, —who often sang the praises of his erring daughter, the Queen of England—now turned with admiration to Drake. To the Venetian ambassador : " Have you heard how Drake with his fleet has offered battle to the Armada ? With what courage ! Do you think he showed any fear ? "—going on to recount Drake's exploits at San Domingo and Cadiz, the fleets he had captured, the riches he had acquired *to his great glory*.[1] In the Escorial

---

[1] *Cal. S.P. Venetian, 1581–91*, 383.

Philip rose from the council table in anger at hearing that he was made the butt of comedies on the public stage.[1] (So like Napoleon and Hitler.) As the day drew near, the King spent two or three hours on his knees every day before the sacrament (the Queen was more profitably employed) ; but he did not neglect more elementary precautions. It was his will-power that drove on the immense preparations, for the mood in Spain was one of apprehension and discouragement. They feared " the machinations of that most cunning woman ", and the general opinion was that the English were of a different quality from the Spaniards at sea : " they bore a name above all the West for being expert and enterprising in all maritime affairs, and the finest fighters upon the sea ".[2] The Venetian opinion was that they would win ; French opinion, less generous, that they would hold off their enemies at sea.[3]

On Santa Cruz' death the Duke of Medina Sidonia protested his incapacity for the command which the king laid upon him, and solemnly urged Philip to make peace.[4] The Queen had a powerful embassy to Parma in the Netherlands at this moment, but she would never make peace without guarantees of their liberty.[5] Perhaps the Duke was the best choice Philip could make for the command : he had been second to Santa Cruz in the hierarchy of the preparations, he had the requisite rank to command the sea-officers and he had a council of them to advise him. Camden's contemporary figures for the equipment are well attested : altogether 130 ships, carrying 19,290 soldiers on board, 8350 sailors, 2080 galley slaves, and 2630 great ordnance —an immense quantity.[6]

As the day drew near, the mood became one of prayer and religious exaltation. There were constant services in the churches, processions and acts of propitiation.[7] The soldiers and sailors of the Crusade for the conversion of England were all to be confessed and communicated—it was the Middle Ages against the modern world. Everyone hoped that " the greater the difficulties, humanly speaking, the greater the favour of God ". The blessing of the Duke's standard was performed with much

[1] Cf. E. Armstrong, " Venetian Dispatches on the Armada and its Results ", *E.H.R.*, Oct. 1897, 664.

[2] q. Corbett, *op. cit.* II. 153.

[3] *Ibid.* I. 347.

[4] Duro, *op. cit.* I. 414-17.

[5] Camden, *History* (ed. 1675), 407.

[6] *Ibid.* 410.

[7] *Cal. S.P. Venetian, 1581–91*, 350.

pomp off Belem—the great Jeronymite votive church raised by the water-side by King Manuel in honour of Vasco da Gama's voyage to the East Indies. The Duke, whom the King would not release from his duty, gave out his orders that since the reason for the crusade was the service of God and the restoration of a people to his Church, the Armada was to be highly moral : there were to be no harlots on board, no feuds or quarrels, no swearing.[1] The comment on this of Spain's greatest dramatist, Lope de Vega, who was there with the rest, was to pay his visits to a young courtesan in the town, maintained by a mercenary old woman.[2] Lope had fled to Lisbon from an amorous escapade in Madrid ; such time as he could spare from these delights he spent in writing poetry, in which we see reflected the hour, the ships, the sea :

> De pechos sobre una torre
> que la mar combate y cerca,
> mirando las fuertes naves
> que se van a Inglaterra . . .

> Famosa armada de estandartes llena,
> partidos todas de la roja estola,
> árboles de la fe, donde tremola
> tanta flámula blanca en cada entena.

And what was the purpose of it all ?—

> selva del mar, a nuestra vista amena,
> que del cristiano Ulises la fe sola
> te saca de la margen española
> contra la falsedad de una sirena.

Meanwhile, in England, the Siren's blandishments were a cause of alarm to her seamen : these were all in favour of the offensive. Howard, who, as a member of the Council, had appreciated the purpose of them, on arriving at Plymouth, where the fleet was concentrating, went over to the point of view of his sea-officers. "The opinion of Sir Francis Drake, Mr. Hawkins, Mr. Frobisher and others that be men of greatest judgment and experience is that the surest way to meet with the Spanish fleet is upon their coast, or in any harbour of their own, and there to defeat them. . . . I confess my error at that

---

[1] *Cal. S.P. Venetian, 1581–91*, 356.
[2] Cf. L. A. Marín, *Vida azarosa de Lope de Vega*, 97 foll.

time, which was otherwise ; but I did and will yield ever unto
them of greater experience."[1] It seems that the Queen herself
leaned rather to this view ; but there were others who held back,
notably Burghley, and whatever he thought weighed with her.
Certainly she was bombarded by letters from Drake : 13 April,
" if your Majesty will give present order for our proceeding to
the sea and send to the strengthening of this fleet here four more
of your Majesty's good ships and those sixteen sail of ships with
their pinnaces which are preparing in London . . . I assure
your Majesty I have not in my lifetime known better men and
possessed with gallanter minds than your Majesty's people are
which are here gathered together voluntarily to put their hands
and hearts to the finishing of this good piece of work, wherein
we are all persuaded that God, the giver of all victories, will in
mercy look upon your most excellent Majesty and us your poor
subjects, who for the defence of your Majesty, our religion and
natural country have resolutely vowed the hazard of our lives."[2]
" The advantage of time and place in all martial actions is half a
victory, which being lost is irrecoverable ; wherefore if your
Majesty will command me away, with those ships that are here
already and the rest to follow with all possible expedition." . . .
28 April : " if a good peace for your Majesty be not forthwith
concluded (which I as much as any man desireth) then these
great preparations of the Spaniard may be speedily prevented
as much as in your Majesty lieth, by sending your forces to encounter theirs, somewhat far off and more near their own coast,
which will be the better cheap for your Majesty and people,
and much the dearer for the enemy ".[3] It would be interesting
to know the effect of these adjurations on that clever equivo-
cating mind : she was not one to take her politics from Francis
Drake.

All that spring Drake was waiting and making ready at
Plymouth, with five of the Queen's galleons and some fifty
merchant ships of London and the West Country. Shortly he
was joined by Sir Richard Grenville, ordered to give up the
most promising expedition yet for Virginia and to take his
ships round from Bideford : he cannot have liked that, but
he submitted without a murmur. The whole country was indeed
keyed up to the height of the moment—perhaps one may for

---

[1] q. Laughton, *op. cit.* I. 200, 205.
[2] *Ibid.* 148.   [3] *Ibid.* 166.

once say that a sense of destiny inspired them, so that not even the commanders quarrelled (that came later, the tension over). On land, defence measures were directed by a Council of War, on which famous soldiers, Lord Grey, Sir John Norris, Sir Richard Bingham, Sir Roger Williams, served along with Ralegh and Drake—the whole presided over by Burghley.[1] The long and tedious work that had been put over the past decade into bringing the musters up to scratch, re-equipping them with calivers and muskets in place of bows and bills, training them and organising them, now saw its justification. In the southern counties, at any rate, a much higher level of efficiency was reached : the men were turned out in their thousands, the beacons were laid, arrangements were made for reinforcements to be moved across the counties to the place invaded.[2] The lords-lieutenant and their deputies had been hard at work surveying, reporting deficiencies, giving orders. We find men like Ralegh and Grenville sent down to their counties to make a final round of inspection. At Tilbury a camp was formed of some 20,000 men under Leicester's command to oppose Parma's landing. Another army, under Hunsdon, was formed to defend the person of the Queen. The whole country was turned out : everyone whose name we know in its public life makes his appearance at this moment : it is as if the whole life of the time, lighted up in that glow, passes before our eyes in those famous weeks. When the Armada was actually in the Channel the young men ran from Court down to the coast, hiring their own boats to get aboard the fleet : the young earls, Oxford, Cumberland, Northumberland ; Ralegh and his cousin, the poet, Arthur Gorges ; Charles Blount, the handsome boy who became famous later as Mountjoy in Ireland ; Robert Carey, Hunsdon's son, who wrote it up in his Memoirs ;[3] Burghley's son, Thomas, and young Robert Cecil—the latter at once sending back an intelligence report : he was born to be Secretary.[4] They all felt that not to be there was not to be there on Crispin's day.

The sage Burghley, at his wit's end at the ruinous expense of it all—for he had to raise the cash—was reduced to sighing : " a man would wish, if peace cannot be had, that the enemy would not longer delay, but prove, as I trust, his evil fortune ".[5]

---

[1] S.P. 12/209, 49. [2] *Ibid.* No. 51.
[3] *Memoirs of Robert Cary* (King's Classics), 8-11.
[4] Cf. Laughton, *op. cit.* I. lxxvi-lxxvii, 342-4. [5] *Ibid.* 285.

Queen and Council were willing now to take the offensive, but the storms early that summer frustrated their intentions. On 23 May Lord Admiral Howard arrived at Plymouth, with the main body of the Queen's galleons, to take command. Drake went out to meet him with full sixty sail. Howard's first words were of the good spirit in the fleet and of the need of victuals, consumed by such long waiting. To Burghley : " My good lord, there is here the gallantest company of captains, soldiers and mariners that I think ever was seen in England. It were pity they should lack meat, when they are so desirous to spend their lives in her Majesty's service." [1] He was proud of his ships : " I do thank God that they be in the estate that they be in ; and there is never a one of them that knows what a leak means ". [2] Of his own flag-ship, the *Ark Royal* : " whensoever they should come, I mean not to change out of her for any ship that ever was made ". [3] The ships needed to be strong, for " we have endured these three days an extreme continual storm. Myself, and four or five of the greatest ships, have ridden it out in the Sound, because we had no room in Cattewater, for the lesser ships that were there ; nor betwixt the shore and the island, because Sir Francis Drake, with four or five other ships, did ride there. Myself and my company do continually tarry and lie aboard in all the storm, where we may compare that we have danced as lustily as the gallantest dancers in the Court." [4] Hawkins had even more reason to be proud of his ships : " the four great ships—the *Triumph*, the *Elizabeth Jonas*, the *Bear* and the *Victory*—are in most royal and perfect estate ; and it is not seen by them, neither do they feel that they have been at sea, more than if they had ridden at Chatham ". [5]

The westerly gales not only frustrated two attempts to set out for the coast of Spain, but, while food supplies were consumed, prevented the victualling ships from getting down-Channel. One watches Howard's growing anxiety in his correspondence : " if it does not come, yet assure yourself we will not lose any opportunity, nor we will not lack ; there is good fishing in the seas ". [6] " My lords, our victuals are not yet come . . . and yet we have sent three or four pinnaces to seek them out. If they

---

[1] *Ibid.* 190.   [2] *Ibid.* 79.
[3] *Ibid.* 108. She had been built, as the *Ark Ralegh*, for Ralegh and purchased for the Crown.
[4] *Ibid.* 201.   [5] *Ibid.* 274-5.   [6] *Ibid.* 198.

come not, our extremity will be very great. . . . Many men have fallen sick, and by thousands fain to be discharged."[1] The countryside round Plymouth had been scoured for victuals for such a large fleet ; the West Country beer was sour and made the men ill. Then, his patience worn thin, to the Queen : " For the love of Jesus Christ, Madam, awake thoroughly and see the villainous treasons round about you, against your Majesty and your realm, and draw your forces round about you, like a mighty prince to defend you. Truly, Madam, if you do so, there is no cause to fear."[2] In truth, she was not afraid ; she, too, had done her duty by her country, trying for peace to the last. As Burghley said, in reproof to Walsingham, " Surely, sir, as God will be best pleased with peace, so in nothing can her Majesty content her realm better than in procuring of peace ; which, if it cannot be had, yet is she excused afore God and the world."[3] Though all depended now on the arbitrament of war, they well knew the moral advantage of having right on their side.

In these last weeks we find Howard asking touchingly that " if it please God to call me to Him in this service of her Majesty ", she would " of her goodness bestow the wardship of his boy on his wife ".[4] The Queen, indeed, was not wrong in her choice of him for Lord Admiral—by far the best man of the very unsatisfactory tribe of Howards, her cousins. Where they were devious and unreliable, he was bluff, straight and sincere, honourable and of good judgment, just the man to pull together those individualist prima donnas of the fleet. Instead of being concerned with himself—from which his rank and position excused him—we find him giving most of his thought to the well-being and feeding of his men. He well deserved Camden's commendation of him : " of whose fortunate conduct she had a very great persuasion, and whom she knew by his moderate and noble carriage to be skilful in sea-matters, wary and provident, valiant and courageous, industrious and active, of great authority and esteem amongst the seamen of her navy ".[5] When all was over and the Armada had passed, we find him writing to the Queen—and it is revealing of how her menfolk felt about her : " the great goodness of your Majesty towards me that hath so little deserved, doth make me

[1] Cf. Laughton, *op. cit.* 218. [2] *Ibid.* 225.
[3] *Ibid.* 142. [4] *Ibid.* 212.
[5] Camden, *op. cit.* 405.

in case that I know not how to write to your Majesty how much
I am bound to you for your infinite goodnesses, nor cannot be
answered by any ways but with the spend of my blood and life
in your Majesty's service, which I will be as ready and as willing
to do as ever creature that lived was for their prince ".[1]

Early in July the Armada set sail and was descried from Scilly
before it was driven back to Corunna by the gales. Howard made
out of Plymouth in the hope of cutting off the detachment that
had reached Scilly : he took up his position in mid-Channel,
Hawkins towards Scilly, Drake in the van towards Ushant.
In mid-July the wind changed for a brief spell and Howard
made towards Corunna, where the Armada was having to be
revictualled and Medina Sidonia asked once more that the
enterprise might be given up.[2] Then the winds changed and
drove the English fleet back into Plymouth, their supplies
exhausted in turn. " Such summer season saw I never the like,
what for storms and variable unsettled winds ", wrote Seymour,
in command of the squadron in the Downs watching Parma's
movements.[3] At the last moment victuals had come : they
were being taken on board when the news arrived that the
Armada was off the Lizard, 19 July. " The southerly wind that
brought us back from the coast of Spain brought them out.
God blessed us with turning us back. Sir, for the love of God
and our country, let us have with speed some great shot sent us
of all bigness ; for this service will continue long ; and some
powder with it."[4]

The Armada had, in fact, achieved a tactical surprise. The
beacons that night were spreading up the south coast of England.

It is only at this late day, nearly four centuries after the
event, that we realise fully the circumstances of the action, of
the series of actions that took place that decisive week in the
Channel :[5] the unprecedented nature of the fighting, the inexperience of both sides, each fleet engaged with the unknown,
not really coming to grips until the end, the battle off Gravelines.

[1] Laughton, *op. cit.* 138.
[2] Duro, *op. cit.* II. 134 foll.
[3] Laughton, *op. cit.* 253.
[4] *Ibid.* 288-9.
[5] Largely as the result of the series of articles on " Armada Guns " by Professor
Michael Lewis in the *Mariner's Mirror*, XXVIII and XXIX.

Then, too, there is the exhaustion of ammunition, the complaint on both sides, so much firing to no great effect—the Spaniards losing ships one by one, more by ill chance than from the enemy ; yet in the end they were demoralised, disorganised and worn down by superior seamanship. The contemporary testimony of the seamen is the best indication. Howard wrote immediately after : " all the world never saw such a force as theirs was ; and some Spaniards that were in the fight at Lepanto do say that the worst of our four fights . . . did exceed far the fight they had there . . . and that at some of our fights we had twenty times as much great shot there plied as they had there ".[1] Howard's mood was no more one of elation than Wellington's after Waterloo : " God be thanked ; it is well ".[2]

We can catch the excitement of those first hours from the letter of Hawkins's brother, William, Mayor of Plymouth that year. Sunday, 21 July : " The Spanish fleet was in view of this town yesternight and my Lord Admiral passed to the sea before our said view and was out of our sight. Since which time we have certain knowledge, both by certain pinnaces come from his lordship as also by plain view this present morning, that my Lord being to the windwards of the enemy are in fight, which we beheld. And for that we suppose that his lordship will find in this action great want of men, we have thought most meet to send such forth as the town and country will yield and in that behalf we have provided divers ships and bottoms to carry them so fast as they come."[3]

Some of Medina Sidonia's officers had urged him to attack Plymouth and catch Drake there in harbour. The four Falmouth fishermen picked up by Juan Gil[4] told them that the Admiral of England was there too and had already put to sea. What happened was this : Howard worked to windward outside the Armada, while the ships that had been still victualling worked out around the lee of Rame Head and got to windward that night. Next morning they all joined, with the Armada now to the east. " It was a feat of seamanship which revealed the sailing quality of the English galleons to the Spanish officers, who knew that their own fleet could not have done it."[5] In

[1] Laughton, *op. cit.* II. 60.
[2] *Ibid.* 55.
[3] S.P. 12/212, 81.
[4] He was among those put to death in Ireland. Laughton, II. 302.
[5] J. A. Williamson, *The Tudor Age*, 382.

short, the tactical surprise was nullified : no catching the English at a disadvantage, they now had the advantage of the wind. Medina Sidonia's Relation pays tribute to it : " the enemy recovered the wind, their ships being very nimble and of such good steerage as they did with them whatever they desired ".[1]

On meeting, that Sunday morning, Howard sent his pinnace, the *Disdain*, to give the Duke defiance ; the Duke ran up the royal standard of Spain at his foremast. There was a short brush of a couple of hours, in which the flag-ship of Portugal sustained some damage, and Philip's treasure-ship, the *San Salvador*, was badly damaged by an explosion—sabotage by a Flemish gunner on board. In the flurry of re-forming its order that evening, the big galleon of Pedro de Valdes, *Nuestra Señora del Rosario*, was involved in collision, lost her bowsprit and foremast and in the night was left behind. She surrendered to Drake next day and was taken into Dartmouth. The damaged *San Salvador* was captured and taken into Weymouth. Not much impression had yet been made on the Armada, which went slowly up-Channel to its appointed *rendez-vous*. It was considerably superior to Howard in fighting galleons, upon which most of the serious work of fighting fell : the Duke had over thirty of them, the rest hulks and troopships ; Howard had some sixteen with him, Seymour's squadron of five were waiting in the Downs ; but, as we have seen, some of the merchant ships were good fighters and were mentioned by Howard for their work.[2] That night the Duke despatched the ensign-bearer, Juan Gil, with a message to Parma to be ready.

On the third day, 23 July, there was a good deal of fighting. The fleets were now off Portland Bill when the wind veered round and gave the Armada the advantage. Philip's instructions were : " above all it must be borne in mind that the enemy's object will be to fight at long distance, in consequence of his advantage in artillery. The aim of our men on the contrary must be to bring him to close quarters and grapple with him."[3] Frobisher in the *Triumph*, with his squadron of five merchant ships, was near the land and separated from the fleet ; the Spaniards bore down on them and attempted to close. The squadron resisted

[1] q. in Laughton, II. 357.
[2] Cf. the tribute to the *Mayflower* of London, Laughton, I. 11-12.
[3] q. M. Lewis in the *Mariner's Mirror*, XXIX. 12.

stoutly for an hour and a half, until Howard came to their rescue. Medina Sidonia moved out of the throng of his fleet with sixteen of his best galleons and there developed a general engagement between the biggest ships, the *Ark*, the *Elizabeth Jonas*, the *Galleon Leicester*, the *Golden Lion*, the *Victory*, the *Mary Rose*, the *Dreadnought* and the *Swallow* going in in that order. Then the wind went round to south-west, enabling Hawkins and Drake outside to get into action, and Medina Sidonia broke off. The Armada sailed, less majestically but still unbroken, on its way.

The situation was now critical ; for all the English could see, the Armada was well on its way to reaching its objective, the junction with Parma. And in all the fighting of the 23rd Howard had practically exhausted his ammunition : only enough for one more general action was left, and that had to be decisive. But, unknown to the English, the Spaniards were in no good shape : they, too, were suffering from an extreme shortage of shot, their ships had suffered far more damage than the English. No fighting on the 24th ; but on the 25th two ships that lagged in the rear, a Portuguese galleon and Recalde's flag-ship, *Santa Ana*, were mauled ; the latter so badly that in the night she drifted over to the French coast and became a total wreck, the third of the big galleons to be lost. On the 25th, the 26th and the 27th the Duke sent messages to Parma, each more urgent than the last, to come out without delay, to send him powder and shot. Meanwhile, as they moved on, the English were receiving reinforcements from the ports and castles along the coast. The balance was unobtrusively moving in their favour. On the 26th Howard knighted Lord Thomas Howard, Lord Sheffield and those hard-working professionals, John Hawkins and Martin Frobisher—at last—on board the *Ark*. " All this day and Saturday, being the 27th of July, the Spaniards went always before the English army like sheep."[1] But on the Saturday evening the flock arrived safely off Calais, there to await Parma. At the same time, Seymour's squadron—the Spaniards thought they were Hawkins'—joined Howard. The decisive moment had come.

At midnight on Sunday Howard let loose eight fire-ships, with the wind and tide driving straight on to the Armada at its anchorage. The direct damage they did was little, the indirect

[1] Laughton, I. 14.

irreparable ; for the Spaniards, fearing explosions, cut their cables and drifted off in utter confusion. In the *mêlée* the admiral of the galleasses was in collision and later ran aground. Next day the Duke collected his fleet together off Dunkirk, only just managing to sheer off the banks, upon which the Armada was driving and where there might have been a total disaster. That day, with the balance that had been strongly with the Armada off Plymouth now shifted against it, the whole English fleet went in to the attack.

Monday, 29 July : the battle of Gravelines. The fighting began at daybreak and continued all day. The greater part of the English fleet, say the Spaniards, " assaulted our flag-ship, with great shooting of ordnance, approaching within musket-shot or even arquebus-shot ".[1] They went in much closer than before, but not so as to give the Spaniards an opportunity of boarding. Howard resisted the advice to grapple with them, arguing (like Jellicoe at Jutland) that " if he were vanquished he should very much endanger all England ; and if he were conqueror he should only gain a little honour for overthrowing the fleet ".[2] But this day English gunnery wrought havoc among the Armada, as we can see from the Spanish Relation : " Don Alonso de Leyva and Juan Martínez de Recalde and the *capitana* [flag-ship] of Oquendo, and all the ships of the camp-masters, as well Castilians as Portuguese, and the *capitana* of Diego Flórez and that of Bertendona, and the galleon *San Juan* of Sicily . . . sustained the assault of the enemy as stoutly as was possible, so as all these ships were very much spoiled and almost unable to make further resistance, and the greater part of them without shot for their ordnance."[3] Other ships in the rear were very hard pressed, their rigging and tackle cut to pieces and many men killed and wounded. That night the English claimed a galleon sunk ; two more, *San Mateo* and *San Felipe*, driven on to the coast of Zealand where they were taken and carried into Flushing, besides other ships sunk. That evening Howard reported to Walsingham : " I will not write unto her Majesty before more be done. Their force is wonderful great and strong ; and yet we pluck their feathers by little and little."[4] He had not yet realised that the Armada was beaten : it could not fight again. In addition to losing eight of its finest ships, a good deal of

[1] q. Laughton, II. 365. [2] Camden, *op. cit.* 413.
[3] q. Laughton, II. 366. [4] *Ibid.* I. 341.

damage had been done to many others. It is astonishing that not one English ship suffered any serious harm : best tribute to their skill.

Meanwhile, Parma, blockaded by Dutch and English and with the wind now blowing hard from the North-West, was unable to move. It is untrue that Parma had made no effort, though he had no belief in the enterprise. He had dug waterways to bring vessels from Sluys to Nieuport, where he concentrated some 16,000 men. And once or twice he began embarking them, though his ships were not gunned nor had they sails. Perhaps it was lucky for him that he could not put to sea, though the Spaniards blamed him none the less.[1] The Armada could not return through the Channel ; it was being blown upon the shoals of the Flemish coast : " men of experience of that coast told the Duke at this time that it was not possible to save a single ship of the Armada ".[2] *Solo Dios lo podía remediar*, sighed the Duke : it was a favourite phrase with him : he excused himself to Philip with it. But St. Lawrence did not desert Spain ; on the eve of the saint's day, " God ", according to the Duke, " was pleased to change the wind to W S W ", by which means they slipped away from the dangerous proximity of the shoals into the North Sea, bound upon their terrible journey back to Spain. For the ships were, many of them, in a bad way from the hammering they had received, and all of them were short of food and water.

The English fleet, too, had no powder and shot left, so they " put on a brag countenance " to pursue them up the coast and see them off the premises. Drake wrote on 31 July, with his usual ebullience and with a West Country phrase : " We have the army of Spain before us and mind . . . to wrestle a pull with him. There was never anything pleased me better than the seeing the enemy flying with a southerly wind to the north-wards. . . . I doubt it not but ere it be long so to handle the matter with the Duke of Sidonia as he shall wish himself at St. Mary Port among his orange trees."[3] But it was another who was to have the pleasure of encountering him there. Howard saw the Armada safely past the Firth of Forth and then returned to clear up the mess.

[1] L. van der Essen, *Alexandre Farnèse, Prince de Parme, 1545–92*, V. 220, 225.
[2] *Ibid.* II. 368.
[3] Laughton, I. 364.

Seymour had been ordered to remain behind with his squadron to watch Parma's movements ; he obeyed " much against his will " he informed the Queen, signing himself " Your Majesty's most bounden and faithful fisherman ".[1] She, who showed herself " not a whit dismayed " all through the crisis, now came out from London for the famous review of the army at Tilbury.[2] While the Armada was lumbering around the north of Scotland in increasing straits, the government sent a squadron out under Grenville to watch the western seas in case of its return.[3] Howard came back from the Forth in no mood for jubilation : " sickness and mortality begins wonderfully to grow amongst us ; and it is a most pitiful sight to see, here at Margate, how the men, having no place to receive them into here, die in the streets. I am driven myself, of force, to come a-land, to see them bestowed in some lodging ; and the best I can get is barns and outhouses. It would grieve any man's heart to see them that have served so valiantly to die so miserably."[4] The men were dying, not of any wounds—there were not a hundred casualties all told on the English side—but of scurvy and typhus, the usual diseases that ravaged sailors.

In September the Queen went through the City in state to a solemn service of thanksgiving—*afflavit Deus et dissipati sunt*—at St. Paul's, where the flags, very many of them, taken from the Armada were laid up. Everywhere the Queen was received with joyful acclaim : it was like her coronation over again, all the streets hung with blue stammel, the City companies standing in their order. But she, too, was in little mood for jubilation. On his way back to Kenilworth from Tilbury, Leicester had paused at Rycote—where, when they were young and the world was at their feet, they had been happy together[5]—to write her a letter inquiring after her health, " the chiefest thing in this world I pray for ". Worn out with his exertions he was dying ; he dated it " from your old lodging at Rycote ". When she received the letter he was already dead ; taking up her pen she wrote on it, " His last letter ", folded it up and put it away.

The death of Leicester in no way diminished the public rejoicing—he had never been liked ; though it was observed

---

[1] *Ibid.* II. 2-3.   [2] *v.* below, pp. 362-5.
[3] Cf. my *Sir Richard Grenville*, 264-5.   [4] Laughton, II. 96.
[5] Cf. my " Elizabeth at Rycote " in *The English Spirit*.

that the Queen took it much to heart. The country's affairs had no place for the private grief of the woman.

And then the terrible, savagely jubilant news came in from Ireland : nearly half the galleons wrecked in the storms of that autumn on those coasts. (It seemed that God was a Protestant after all.) The English ambassador in Paris was able to inform the Venetian of nineteen sunk with at least 4000 men[1]—Sir Richard Bingham, on the spot, said 6000 or 7000, of whom 700 or 800 had been put to the sword.[2] When the Queen received the news there were tears of joy in her eyes : it had been an almighty deliverance.

No place here to go in detail into those savage doings in Ireland ; we may content ourselves with a new touch or two from a best-selling pamphlet rushed out by Richard Field, Shakespeare's fellow-townsman, friend and publisher, and read to pieces by the public.[3] The King of Spain's illegitimate son, the Prince of Ascoli, it appears, was among the drowned. We have a description of how he looked—evidently rather like his father—from a captured Spaniard : " The Prince of Ascoli was a slender-made man and of a reasonable [*i.e.* moderate] stature, of twenty-eight years of age, his hair of an auburn colour, stroked upward, of a high forehead, a very little beard marquesotted, whitely faced with some little red in the cheeks. He was drowned in apparel of white satin ; for his doublet and breeches after the Spanish fashion cut, with russet silk stockings. When this prince came into their ship at Calais, he was apparelled in black raised velvet laid on with broad gold lace." The Prince served as a volunteer on board the Duke's flagship, *San Martin*, and went in a little shallop from ship to ship giving the Duke's orders. (In those days there was no system of flag-signalling.) He must have changed ship. A Portuguese gave evidence of the losses off Calais : in addition to those we know, a Biscayan of 500 tons and a Castilian of 400 tons were sunk. He illuminates for us the mood of the men serving in the Armada : " they were

---

[1] *C.S.P. Venetian, 1581–91*, 404.

[2] Laughton, II. 239.

[3] *Certain Advertisements out of Ireland concerning the Losses and Distresses happened to the Spanish Navy upon the West Coasts of Ireland.* Published for Richard Field, 1588. I am indebted to the present representative of Drake's family, Captain R. A. Meyrick, of Sheafhayne Manor, Devon, for showing me this pamphlet. It is exciting to read it, in what may very well have been Drake's own copy, perhaps picked up that autumn in passing through Paul's churchyard.

in great fear of the English fleet and doubted much of boarding. Those in the ship that he is in do say that they will rather
go into the ground themselves than come in such a journey
again for England. The best that be in the Admiral's ship are
scarce able to stand ; if they tarry where they are any time
they will all perish. For himself he would not pass into Portugal
again if he might choose, for he would not be constrained to
such another journey." I do not suppose, poor fellow, he had
the choice : he must have been put to the sword like all the
others.

Nor need we go into the privations and sufferings of the
survivors on the way home. Only half of the King's galleons
got back, and less than half his men—they died like flies, of fever
and thirst. The Duke was ill when he reached Spain and could
not journey to Court. Two of the finest fighting leaders in the
Armada died shortly after their return, worn out by their
experiences : Oquendo in September, Recalde in October. It
had been a terrible disaster, without mitigation or consolation.
For all Philip's philosophical calm or constitutional impassivity
(" It is the Lord's will ", etc.), he fell ill himself for a bit : the
papers piled up unanswered on his table.

Meanwhile, an astonished Europe hardly grasped the full
significance of the event : symbol of the shift of power from
Mediterranean to North-West. But the effects were seen at once :
it raised the Queen to a dazzling pinnacle of prestige all over
Europe ; Spain's enemies were everywhere encouraged ; even
the Dutch, in their enthusiasm, were ready to tax themselves for
the war. In Spain the reaction was at first one of consternation.
Then anger supervened, anger at the insolent, heretic nation
(odd that a more philosophical reflection should not have
occurred to it ; but peoples, like people, are incorrigible).
Pride was injured—pride was the dominant characteristic of
this nation in its golden age, and the source of its disasters.
The cities volunteered Philip money to retrieve the nation's
humiliation. He could not bear to have it said that the Queen
would be able to defend herself against the forces he would
next gather against her.[1] Recovering, he said one evening,
sitting at table : " We will sell these candlesticks if no other
way of raising money can be found ".[2] (It is like Louis XIV

---

[1] *C.S.P. Venetian, 1581–91*, 406.
[2] *Ibid.* 410.

in 1709.) He was prepared even to plead for funds from the Cortes.[1]

The war was to go on.

What was our reply to the Armada to be? The Queen characteristically pressed for an attack at once on the treasure-fleet from the Indies. But it was impossible to fit out ships, all of which had been engaged in action, in time for such an expedition. Hawkins again put forward his plan for a regular and continual blockade, with small squadrons succeeding each other upon the Azores station. We had not the forces or the organisation for that : a very professional conception, it was a century and a half before its time. There remained the idea of a direct offensive against the centre of the enemy's power : Drake's favourite idea and that with which his name was associated in the public mind—not only in this country either. For this the government had not the money ; the Queen and Burghley were at their wits' end for cash : the Armada campaign had cost the extraordinary sum of £160,000 and the war-chest of some £300,000, amassed by the prudent Treasurer by the beginning of the war, was now empty.

Meanwhile, the remains of the Armada had taken refuge in the Biscayan ports, some forty ships altogether at Santander and a dozen at San Sebastián. They were in a helpless state, but protected by land-batteries and even more by the difficulty there was from the winds in approaching and getting away from that awkward corner of the Bay of Biscay. There they presented a favourable opportunity to smash Spain's naval power.

Since the government could not afford to undertake it itself, the answer to the problem was one of those half-government, half-private ventures which had often been successful before. And for its command the obvious candidate was Drake. He had stood out in the public mind as the hero of the struggle with the Armada—rather unjustly as usual. He had had the luck of having Pedro de Valdes surrender to him personally. Other people had borne more of the brunt of the fighting, Frobisher for example, who was furious at the disparity in their rewards.[2] Seymour went so far as to say that if Howard came into the

---

[1] E. Armstrong, " Venetian Despatches on the Armada and its Results ", *E.H.R.*, Oct. 1897, 664.
[2] Cf. Laughton, II. 102-4.

Channel—Seymour's command—with Drake as his Vice-Admiral he would refuse to serve under him. [1] Howard's official *Relation* did not omit to pass stricture on Drake for leaving the watch, which he was to set on the night of 21 July off Plymouth, to pursue five Flemish hulks on his own. [2] No doubt Drake thought they would make good prize, and he was always an incorrigible individualist. At the decision that Drake was to have the command the Lord Admiral himself blew up : incoherent with indignation he wrote, " I think he liveth not that in any age that any man was seen in this realm where any landing of men was, but it did ever belong to the Admiral of England . . . yea, and by admirals of my name ". [3]

Other objectives now were grafted on to that which was the primary one in the government's eye. Don Antonio had been hanging about in England for some time now, very thick with Drake and the West Countrymen, and, like all exiles, very large with his promises as to the results of a landing in Portugal : capture Lisbon and the country would rise in his favour. To create another Netherlands for Philip in Portugal would demand a military effort on a large scale—and here Sir John Norris came in with his experience of fighting in the Netherlands. The Dutch were ready to get in a blow at their oppressors, and Norris was made joint-General with Drake to command the military forces. Thirdly, there was the longest-standing objective : to capture one or other of the Azores. From the divided command and the divided objectives came the troubles of the expedition and its ultimate frustration : for it failed in all three. [4]

The Queen was to contribute six of her ships, victuals for four months and arms for the troops, £20,000 in cash ; Drake and Norris undertook to raise £20,000 more, besides ships and men of their own following ; the Dutch were to make a contribution of six men-of-war—which were not forthcoming. It must be noticed that as against the exhausting effort that the Armada had been for Spain, years in preparation, the reply to it represented a very small proportion of the national energy : perhaps a fourth of the Queen's galleons, 115

---

[1] *Ibid.* 108.   [2] *Ibid.* I. 8.   [3] Corbett, *op. cit.* II. 296.

[4] For the proper interpretation of the expedition we have had to wait for the article of R. B. Wernham, " Queen Elizabeth and the Portugal Expedition of 1589 ", *E.H.R.*, April 1951. This supersedes previous accounts, such as Corbett's and Williamson's chapter in his *Sir Francis Drake*. Extraordinary as it seems now, the naval historians have all blamed the failure on to the Queen.

companies of troops grouped for the first time in this country into regiments. The island was beginning to show an unexpected aptitude for war, a resilient potential that spoke well for the future.

The news of the venture, under two such popular captains, raised public enthusiasm to unwonted heights. Crowds of volunteers flocked down to Plymouth : Drake and Norris wrote that " the army has doubly increased by reason of the gentlemen offering to serve, whom by no means we can refuse to entertain ".[1] The result was that the provisioning of the forces went hopelessly out of gear : the sea-stores were consumed by the landsmen and would soon be at an end. There was not enough shipping for the numbers. Then Drake made a *coup* : he pressed into service sixty Dutch fly-boats on their way to do contraband trade with Spain. Now the weather took a hand : it blew such gales that the expedition was detained in harbour consuming its supplies. Drake was driven in desperation to sue to Burghley : " I did never write to your Lordship with so discontented a mind as I do now ".[2] The West Country was scoured for provisions, but it could not meet the needs of so large an army.[3] The Queen, unwilling that the expedition should be prejudiced, generously revictualled both fleet and army. But that she had reason to distrust the intentions of the commanders we shall shortly see ; nor, in the circumstances, could she wholly command their obedience.

When the expedition sailed it carried, in addition to 3200 English and 900 Dutch mariners, 20,000 men—far too many.[4] Among those whom Drake and Norris found they could by no means refuse to entertain appeared at the last moment the young Earl of Essex, Leicester's stepson, who had replaced Leicester in the Queen's lonely affections—run away from Court to join the *Swiftsure*. Norris and Drake's apologies reveal connivance : they had sent their letters after the said Earl, " if it should fall out he were there ", but " the pinnace not being able to weather the point next the harbour . . . was forced to come in again that night ", etc.[5] Weather always provided a convenient excuse for the seamen : Essex joined them on the coast of Spain. The Queen drafted a letter censuring Norris and Drake, and ordering them to discharge Sir Roger Williams for " departing from the

---

[1] S.P. 12/223, 59.   [2] *Ibid.* 70.   [3] Cf. *ibid.* 224, 7.
[4] Drake's own estimate, S.P. 12/223, 61.   [5] *Ibid.* 68.

fleet with one of our principal ships . . . as ye will answer to the
contrary at your perils, for as we have authority to rule, so we
look to be obeyed ".[1] It was not a good omen. Everything
points to the difficulty of ensuring discipline in sixteenth-century
warfare.

At the end of April the fleet arrived at Corunna and at once
the lower town was captured by a night-assault, five hundred
Spanish soldiers cut off in the confusion being put to the sword.
The bulk of their forces retreated to the fortress of the higher
town, which the English were unable to capture for the want of
a siege-train : they had been promised it, but it had not
materialised. The Spaniards set fire to the one galleon in
harbour and abandoned the rest of the shipping ; the stores fell
into the hands of the English, enough meal to provision the fleet,
if they had not also got hold of a storehouse of wine, on which
they drank themselves silly and started the disease which ravaged
the expedition and helped to bring it to naught. Outside the
town they drove back the forces marching to its relief. They
were now ready to make off with the spoil, some sixty pieces of
ordnance.

But they were not ready to proceed with what, in the Queen's
eyes, was the main purpose of the show : the elimination
of Spain's navy. They had their excuses : Drake said that
he could not destroy the shipping unless the land-batteries
were taken ; Norris said that he could not take the batteries
without artillery ; Drake said that the winds were not fair
for such a move so deep into the Bay. No doubt there was
something in this, but also there was no spoil to be got from
doing what the Queen wished. They decided to make next
for Lisbon.

Her mistrust was justified : she sent her agent, Sir Anthony
Ashley, with the reminder that " before your departure hence
you did, at sundry times, so far forth promise as with oaths to
assure us and some of our Council that your first and principal
action should be to take and distress the King of Spain's navy
and ships where they lay ; which if ye did not, ye affirmed that
ye were content to be reputed as traitors ".[2] Windebank reported
to Walsingham, Drake's protector and friend, an irate conversation with her :[3] she said that " they had left two places where

[1] S.P. 12/224, 10.   [2] q. Wernham, *loc. cit.* 202.
[3] S.P. 12/224, 50.

they should have done greater service in taking and burning the ships, for, said she, they had eight days fair winds to have gone to those two places before they had come to the Groyne. [*i.e.* Corunna.] Whereat I answered that I thought her Majesty was misinformed. . . . She then replied that they went to places more for profit than for service." Windebank besought her to suspend judgment, but " I do most plainly perceive how strangely she is informed ". On the contrary, she was correctly informed. We have a draft of a letter from her, upbraiding Norris and Drake for neglecting the main object, "the Groyne being of little importance ".[1] She expected them to proceed to destroy the fleet and then to restore Don Antonio in Portugal. "And so to draw to an end, we must put you in mind that you suffer not yourselves to be transported with an haviour of vainglory which will obfuscate the eyes of your judgment." Whether it was vainglory or, even more, the desire for spoil, obfuscate their judgment—it is a key-word with the Queen—it certainly did.

From Corunna a number of ships with some 2000 men made off home with what they had got. On the way to Lisbon Essex in the *Swiftsure*—which had made some catches of its own— met Drake and Norris. It was decided, without waiting to get to the Tagus, to land the army immediately at Peniche, a little place forty or fifty miles to the north-west of Lisbon and to march overland. This was crazy—and Norris and Don Antonio were responsible for it, not Drake. It gave Lisbon more time to prepare its defence and made it far more difficult to synchronise the military and naval sides of the operation. The sensible thing would have been to use the army to mask St. Julian's castle that guarded the difficult entrance to the Tagus, while Drake battered his way in. As it was, when he arrived at the entrance and the wind was fair, he hesitated to push past the land defences without the army's support.

Meanwhile the army lumbered across difficult country in torrid heat, the men falling out in hundreds from the sickness, probably dysentery, raking the ranks. Not a Portuguese rose at the magic name of Don Antonio. During these days Philip's deputy, the Cardinal-Archduke Albert, terrorised the inhabitants of Lisbon : all conceivable supporters of the Pretender were imprisoned, a number strung up : no-one made a move. The

[1] S.P. 12/224, 53.

English army took possession of the suburbs, but in deference to Antonio no plundering was allowed or " we had been the richest army that ever went out of England ".[1] They were now down to 9000 in number, of whom only two-thirds were fit ; but with no demonstration on behalf of the Pretender within and no artillery to force a way in, there was nothing for it but to retreat. After the first day the wind turned foul for entering the Tagus ; when at length it turned fair and Drake was on the point of making the attempt, he heard that the army was in full retreat upon Cascaes. That was the end ; and the beginning of a great deal of acrimony—according to the usual pattern in combined operations that fail to combine—between the two services. Norris maintained that Drake should have entered the harbour at the same moment as the army approached the city. The fault, of course, was in landing at Peniche—not redeemed by the silly gallantry of young Essex, the childish gesture that so much appealed to the age : " the Earl of Essex was the first that landed, who by reason the billows were high, waded to the shoulder to come on shore."[2] It must have spoiled a splendid suit.

At the last moment a stroke of good luck happened for Drake. A large fleet of some sixty Hanseatic hulks arrived, bringing corn and other contraband : possible supplies for a new Armada. Very well aware of the English attitude, they had gone round the north of Scotland and so eluded Frobisher's Channel squadron. Drake now scuppered the lot—and gained corn supplies to continue with the third objective. But the weather was contrary and kept him on the coast of Spain. Peremptory orders arrived for Essex to return and the young man, having won " honour ", was content to go back to his sovereign's side. Drake filled in time by putting in at Vigo, burning the city and wasting the country round. Only some 2000 effectives were left now ; with these and a nucleus of his ships he tried to make for the Azores. A great gale beat down on them, the ships were separated, the *Revenge* sprang a leak and was with difficulty kept afloat on the way back to Plymouth.

Thus, futilely, ended the grand *riposte* to the Armada.

Of course, it had not been entirely without results : it had inflicted further damage on Philip, especially in forcing the destruction of the Lisbon granaries with their corn supplies for

---

[1] q. Corbett, II. 325.   [2] S.P. 12/224, 86.

the next Armada. It had brought back 150 brass ordnance ; the prizes sold for £30,000. Philip's prestige suffered from the way the English descended at will on his coasts : the news from Corunna was suppressed in Madrid to protect the prestige of the Crown.[1] Norris defended himself to Walsingham against the expectation that her Majesty would " dislike of the event of our journey : if the enemy had done so much upon us, his party would have made bonfires in most parts of Christendom ".[2] True enough. But it was nothing compared with what might have been achieved. If all the resources had been concentrated first upon Santander and San Sebastián, the naval power of Spain might have been completely wiped out. A Nelson would have seen to that : therein lies the difference between the aesthetic perfection of the professionalism of a Nelson and the marvellously lucky, but haphazard, individualism of Drake. In a way, it reflects strikingly two periods in the sea-history of the English state : the inspiring but erratic beginnings and the flawless execution of maturity. The upshot of the Lisbon expedition certainly reflected the difficulty the youthful state had in encompassing combined operations—though it succeeded in accomplishing a brilliant example at Cadiz in 1596.

The Venetian news service gives us some clues : it tells us that it was a strong disappointment to the English that Lisbon did not rise on behalf of Don Antonio, and that the city owed its salvation to the days wasted at Corunna, which gave time for rigorous measures to keep the city firm.[3] Such, too, was the Queen's opinion, though no expression of her disappointment reached the public. In public : " We cannot but acknowledge ourselves infinitely bound unto Almighty God in that it hath pleased him in his great goodness and mercy to bless your attempt " ; assuring Norris and Drake " for both your comforts that we do most thankfully accept of your service and do acknowledge that there hath been as much performed by you as true valour and good conduction could yield ".[4] She asked them to express her thanks to " the colonels and captains as also to the inferior sort of soldiers and mariners that had showed under you as great valour as ever nation did ". The Queen had a great deal to put up with from the foolery of human beings, but she knew on the other hand how to recognise the service

---

[1] *C.S.P. Venetian, 1581–91*, 442.   [2] S.P. 12/225, 5.

[3] *C.S.P. Venetian, 1581–91*, 445, 453.   [4] S.P. 12/225, 15.

they gave according to their restricted abilities. Few of them realised as she did that this meant that the war would go on and on. That summer the treasure-fleet came.home to Philip safe and sound ; he was able to re-equip the ships in the Biscay ports at leisure ; there was now a Spanish fleet in being again ; the English would have to fight their way in the waters round the Azores—the nodal point of Spanish sea communications—as Richard Grenville in Drake's *Revenge* found in 1591. What the Queen thought was to be seen better from her actions : at the height of his powers, Drake was laid aside; he was not employed again until the last year of his life, when he was called out of retirement to make one more expedition with Hawkins, their last, to the West Indies.

Any chance there might have been of ending the war quickly had now gone ; and, in spite of the disaster of 1588, even more tempting prospects for Philip opened up in France with the assassination of Henry III. The succession of Navarre, head of the Protestants, as Henry IV was disputed by half the country ; in the Catholic League Philip had a formidable weapon to hand ; the civil war burned more fiercely than ever. Philip was not without hope of placing his daughter, whom he greatly loved—the Infanta Isabella, daughter of his favourite wife, Elizabeth of Valois, who looks out at us with her mother's charm from so many pictures—upon the throne of France. So men are led on by the will-o'-the-wisps of faith, pride, love, family devotion, to disaster.

With declining, and overtaxed, resources Spain made a greater effort than ever. What is characteristic of the 1590s is her revival as a naval power—essential to her to protect her communications or the Empire would have foundered. The revival began in the West Indies, where the key-points were strongly fortified and Pedro Menéndez Marqués developed a type of fast frigate (origin perhaps of the cruiser) which could fight anything of its own size and could outsail anything bigger: the *gallezabra*. The life-blood of American treasure was to be carried in them. Terceira, the focal point in the Azores upon which both treasure-fleets and the East Indies carracks converged, was fortified so powerfully that it was unassailable and ships could not be cut out under the batteries commanding the roads. Philip's answer to the privateers, the commerce-raiding upon an ever increasing scale, was the same as ours in the Napoleonic and the German wars of 1914 and 1939 : convoys. The Indian guard across the Atlantic was greatly strengthened. The war became harder : gone were the glad romantic days.

At home Philip did all he could to apply the lessons he had learned from the English :[1] he was not an unintelligent man. Twelve new galleons on the English model were to be built in Biscay, nine on the Portuguese in Lisbon. He adopted Elizabeth's system of auxiliary squadrons of fighting merchant ships. Fast *avisos*—ocean-going pinnaces—were built to speed news ; naval intelligence much improved. By 1592 Philip had some forty galleons under construction : far more than the Queen had, though she, too, was building a small number of our favourite *Revenges*. By these means it is not generally realised that Philip was able to send a second Armada against us in 1596, a third in 1597, and there would have been a fourth, if the Dutch had not disorganised it, in 1599. The great difference between the two powers remained that to us sea-power was natural, based on our own resources, while Philip was wholly dependent on other countries to equip his fleets :[2] timber, spars, pitch, cordage from the Baltic ; corn and fish from the Hanse and the Dutch ; ordnance and shipping from Italy. Only American silver enabled him to keep his war-effort going, his fleets to sail, his armies to move.

In these circumstances the English went in for commerce-raiding on the grand scale ; and, in fact, during the next phase of the war—from the fiasco of 1589 to Drake and Hawkins' last voyage in 1595—it became the chief form our naval warfare took. Innumerable expeditions, large and small, left these shores; small men and local gentry, leading London merchants and great courtiers, the Queen herself, had money in privateering ventures ; Plymouth became an emporium for captured goods, prize and otherwise. At the same time, this was the moment of the formulation of our modern attitude towards contraband trade and the freedom of the seas—themes that have had so long a reverberation in our subsequent history. The Queen would never

---

[1] Cf. Corbett, II. 336-40.

[2] Cf. M. Oppenheim, who puts the point much too strongly : " The difference was that Philip had no real navy and would have had to construct from the foundation both in shipping and in organisation ; that his subjects were not naturally seamen, were accustomed to summer navigations and used to precise galley actions, were more or less ignorant of ship fighting ; and that strategically his position was radically weak." *The Naval Tracts of Sir William Monson*, I. 13-14.

recognise the New World as vested in Spain: she always stated the claim to the freedom of the seas and of traffic thither. In 1589 the Council issued a formal decree justifying the confiscation of ships carrying munitions of war and victual to the enemy. After all, the Armada had been largely equipped with food and naval stores from Hanseatic ports. To stop this, so far as it could, was essential to the waging of war by a naval power; in these years the policy was " asserted, enforced, defined and defended, and during the whole remainder of Elizabeth's reign was an established part of the policy of her government ".[1]

All vessels passing through the Channel were liable to be stayed, unless they could show a pass from the Lord Admiral. Through the winter a squadron was posted in the Downs to supervise the traffic. It led to the troubles we became so familiar with later in our diplomatic relations : protests poured in from the Hanse, Denmark, Poland, the Empire, the Dutch. In the end there was the threat of something like an Armed Neutrality fomented against us by Spain, through her interest with the Empire. But though our policy had to fluctuate with circumstances, it remained unchanged and firm on this issue. In the famous flurry of extempore Latin which the surprised Queen poured out upon the handsome Polish ambassador, who was sent to protest when she expected compliments, she did not fail (in Latin !) to make a correct statement of the government's position.[2] In 1600 the French ambassador protested that his government could no longer endure their ships being searched by the Queen's.[3] Yet, while appearing more conciliatory with the dying down of the war, the government never relaxed its claims. At the end of its long struggle, in 1602, it restated its position, less aggressively but with the same arguments.[4] " Thus

---

[1] E. P. Cheyney, " International Law under Queen Elizabeth ", *E.H.R.* 1905, 665.

[2] This was in 1596 and it made a fine impression. Cecil wrote off an account of the Queen's exploit to Essex engaged in his upon Cadiz.

[3] One whole volume of Sir Julius Caesar's papers, Add. MS. 5664—he was Judge of the Admiralty Court—is largely taken up by the letters and protests of one French Ambassador, the Vicomte de Beaumont.

[4] " Her Majesty thinketh and knoweth it by the rules of the law as well of nature as of men, and specially by the law civil, that whenever any doth directly help her enemy with succours of any victual, armour or any kind of munition to enable his ships to maintain themselves, she may lawfully interrupt the same ; and this agreeth with the law of God, the law of nature, the law of nations, and hath been in all times practised and in all countries betwixt prince and prince, and country and country." Cheyney, *loc. cit.* 664.

during the last twenty three years of the reign of Elizabeth . . . her government asserted consistently two important claims in the field of international law : first, that during the progress of a war goods carried by merchants of a nation not engaged in the war, which might aid one party, may justly be confiscated by the other ; secondly, that the sea is free, in the sense that no nation may exclude others from any large stretch of it, nor place arbitrary restrictions upon them when navigating it."[1]

Of all the privateers the most brilliant figure was made by one of the greatest nobles in the realm, George Clifford, Earl of Cumberland—one can always recognise him in his portraits by the glove he carries in his hat, one that the Queen dropped, which he had mounted with jewels and carried ever after as a favour, regarding himself as her champion. (She had many : those who did not respond need expect no favour from her.) Of the good relations that usually subsisted between them we have evidence in a charming letter she wrote him when he was away on a privateering voyage in 1591. " Right trusty and well-beloved cousin, we greet you well. It may seem strange to you that we should once vouchsafe to trouble our thoughts with any care for any person of roguish condition, being always disposed rather to command others to chasten men of that profession.[2] But such is our pleasure at this time . . . as we are well content to take occasion by our letters to express our great desire to hear of your well-doing . . . hoping well of good success in the action now you have in hand. . . . Provided always you do not requite this our good meaning with bewraying our extraordinary care of you to our Knight Marshal here, who may by this our partiality to you abroad grow bold hereafter in favouring them at home whom we would not have him suffer to pass uncorrected for divers their misdemeanours. And so do we for this time (with this aforesaid caution) make an end, assuring you of our most princely care for your safety and daily wishes of your safe return, whereof we shall be right glad as any friend you have. Dated at our Court at Bishop's Waltham, whither we are returned from our progress where we have spent some part of this summer in viewing our fortifications at Portsmouth and other our principal towns along

---

[1] Cheyney, *loq. cit.* 671. Of course when our interests changed, our doctrine changed with them, political and economic doctrine having no substantive independence of its own.

[2] Remember the legislation against rogues and vagrants.

the sea coast." The letter has the superscription : " Your very loving Sovereign, Elizabeth R."[1]

The joke of the letter, caricaturing (only half-seriously) her usual style, consists in the fact that the Queen was a partner with the Earl in this voyage : he sailed in one of her ships, the *Garland*, one of the new *Revenges* to be built. There were seven other ships of his and his partners, but as it happened this expedition had no luck and must have made a considerable loss. The only thing it achieved was to warn Lord Thomas Howard off Flores of the approach of the large Spanish fleet that captured the *Revenge* : Grenville could not get away in time. The Queen was a partner in some other of his expeditions ; in 1597 Robert Cecil writes to Essex : " Lord Cumberland is a suitor to go a royal journey in October. The plot is very secret between her Majesty and him ; it is to be wished that his spirit which loves action should be well cherished. Tell Sir Walter Ralegh I think he will venture the *Roebuck* with him instead of my *True Love*, which I will adventure if I hear her speak at her return : if you meet her, let us have no searching of Admiral Bredgate nor borrowing our sugar loaves."[2] We see the terms of partnership on which the leading figures at Court stood in regard to privateering, with Cecil himself taking a hand—unthinkable for his father.

The greatest prize to be captured was taken next year, 1592, by ships of Ralegh and his brother, Carew Ralegh, the Queen and some of the City, aided by others of Cumberland's, who had found the Queen's prohibition on laying her ships alongside Spaniards in boarding, for fear of both being fired, somewhat of a drawback. This prize was the carrack, *Madre de Dios*, captured off the Azores with a cargo worth £150,000.[3] Her principal wares were, first, jewels ; then spices, *i.e.* " pepper, cloves, maces, nutmegs, cinnamon, green ginger. The drugs were benjamin, frankincense, galingale, mirabolans, zocotrine and camphor. The silks : damasks, taffetas, sarcanets, altobassos, that is counterfeit cloth of gold, unwrought China silk, sleeved silks, white twisted silk, curled cypress. The calicoes were book calicoes, calico lawns, broad white calicoes, fine starched calicoes, coarse white calicoes,

---

[1] q. in G. C. Williamson, *George, Third Earl of Cumberland, 1558–1605*, 78–9.
[2] *Ibid.* 174.
[3] For an account of her capture *v. The Naval Tracts of Sir William Monson*, ed. M. Oppenheim, I. 280–96.

brown broad calicoes, brown coarse calicoes. There were also canopies and coarse diaper towels, quilts of coarse sarcanet and of calico, carpets like those of Turkey, whereunto are to be added the pearl, musk, civet and ambergris." [1] Besides " elephants' teeth, porcelain, vessels of China, coconuts, hides, ebony wood as black as jet, bedsteads of the same ; cloth of the rinds of trees, very strange for the matter and artificial in workmanship ". No wonder English and Dutch mouths watered for the riches of the East Indian trade !

As soon as this rich prey was taken there was a regular scuttle of the ships that had captured her into West Country ports with all that they could scoop. Ralegh had to be released from imprisonment over Elizabeth Throgmorton to go down and attempt to recover some of the losses : " If I meet any of them coming up, if it be upon the wildest heath in all the way I mean to strip them as naked as ever they were born. For it is infinite that her Majesty hath been robbed and that of the most rare things." [2] The London jewellers had their agents there before the government, buying up the jewels dirt cheap. One man had " 320 sparks of diamond, a collar of a threefold roll of pearl with six tags of crystal garnished with gold, a small string of pearl with a pelican of gold, a small round pearl garnished with gold, two chains of two-fold pearl with buttons of gold and two small jewels hanging unto the ends thereof, also three silver hafts for knives and a silver fork ". [3] Another had " a chain of pearls orient, two rests of gold, four very big pearls of the bigness of a fair pea, four forks of crystal and four spoons of crystal set with gold and stones and two cods of musk ". And so on. (These riches must have been not without an enriching effect upon the mind, and ultimately the art, of the privateering nation.)

Cecil had to be sent down to recover the spoil. " Everyone I met within seven miles of Exeter that either had anything in a cloak, bag or malle which did but smell of the prizes either at Dartmouth or Plymouth (for I could well smell them also such had been the spoils of ambergris and musk among them) I did (though he had little about him) return him with me to the town of Exeter." [4] The West Country townsmen, fearing to

---

[1] q. G. C. Williamson, *op. cit.* 87.
[2] E. Edwards, *The Life of Sir Walter Ralegh*, II. 70-71.
[3] G. C. Williamson, 98-9.
[4] S.P. 12/243, 16.

be balked, turned stubborn and Cecil sent a couple of innkeepers to gaol : a week before, that would have saved the Queen £20,000. " I found already in a shop a bag of seed pearl, pieces of damask, cypress and calico, a very great pot of musk, certain tassels of pearl and divers other things." Sailors were selling magnificent porcelain dishes at sixpence the piece. Then Ralegh turned up : " I am still the Queen of England's poor captive ", he announced with his usual self-dramatisation. He was received with enthusiasm by his followers, " and all the mariners came to him with shouts of joy. I never saw a man more troubled to quiet them ; but his heart is broken, as he is extremely pensive, unless he is busied, in which he can toil terribly."[1] The heavy goods, silks, calicoes, spices, when brought together at Leadenhall, totalled £141,200 in value. In sharing out, the Queen received by far the largest share ; Cumberland was very generously treated : he had adventured £19,000 and was awarded £36,000. Ralegh, who had adventured with Hawkins' £34,000, received along with him only £36,000. He was treated badly in the share-out ; but then, had he not Elizabeth Throgmorton ?

Cumberland had bad luck with the voyage he set forth two years later, in 1594, which fought but failed to take two carracks, both larger and richer than the *Madre de Dios*. The *Cinco Llagas* (Five Wounds) was attacked all day by three London ships, " like three good English mastiffs upon the Spanish wild bull "—the *Mayflower* which we have met before, the *Sampson* and the *Royal Exchange*.[2] They succeeded in firing her, but she fought back bravely and would not surrender. The *Mayflower* herself caught fire from the carrack, which burned to the water's edge with " multitudes of the enemy which here for themselves soon enough (if not too late for us) leaped into the sea. . . . In which burning and sinking of this carrack as also drowning of many hundreds of the passengers, soldiers and sailors also very many of their bravest Spanish gallants, men and women, goodly personages gorgeously apparelled, yea and decked with rich chains of gold, jewels, pearls and precious stones of great price, stripping themselves of all this (with so strange a stratagem seldom seen) all naked upon a sudden desperately cast themselves into the sea." The English from their decks saw one Spaniard go up to the

---

[1] *Ibid.* 17.
[2] Cf. the account of this voyage by Robinson given in G. C. Williamson, 128-36.

captain and protest vehemently against his refusal to surrender. The captain of the *Mayflower*, a valiant Cornishman, was himself killed. A fortnight later they encountered the *San Felipe*—which had taken the place of Drake's captured carrack : she had the richest lading of any ship that sailed from the East Indies, worth two million ducats. She fought off her assailants all day, and to a demand for surrender her captain replied, " I was at the taking and burning of the *Revenge*, the Queen's of England : Let him [the English commander] do as much as he can for his Queen, I will do as much as I can for my King ". In the night she got away. One sees the war hardening. There were only a few prisoners to show for the voyage.

The Earl spent in all some £100,000 on his voyages, and on balance he was very much down. Clearly he hoped that something like the *Madre de Dios* would turn up every year around the corner. It never did again for him, and he died very much indebted—though not wrecked, for his estates came through intact to his daughter, the celebrated Lady Anne Clifford, who adored his memory and wrote of his " applying himself to the sea and to navigation, especially towards the West Indies and those new found lands, wherein he became the most knowing and eminent man, of a lord, in his time ".[1]

As usual it was the professionals, not the amateurs, who profited.[2] Gentlemen amateurs sometimes, like Sir Thomas Shirley, ruined themselves. Gentlemen captains were more successful, with the steady flow of merchants' resources behind them. Over these years we watch the development of privateering from a promiscuous, free-for-all scrimmage of an individualist character into a regular business with syndicates and large capital involved, a constituent part of the war, but also inextricably bound up with trade and commerce. When the war ended, privateering did not end : the last days of the Elizabethan rovers became the first of the Buccaneers.[3] Before the war privateering was conducted chiefly by small vessels, owned by seamen or gentlemen mainly from the western seaways. They made short trips for modest returns, rarely more than £200. As the war progressed, London rose to a dominating position in

[1] q. *Ibid.* 10-11.
[2] For most of the substance of this paragraph I am indebted to the summary of a thesis by K. R. Andrews on Elizabethan Privateering, *Bulletin Inst. Hist. Research*, May 1952.
[3] J. S. Corbett, *The Successors of Drake*, 403.

the business ; the West Country share fell first to a quarter, then (in 1598) to one-eighth, of the ships. A dozen of Bristol's leading merchants set forth most of the port's twenty-four privateers during 1589–91—largely as a substitute for Bristol's trade with Spain, ruined by the war. The medium-sized privateer of 100-200 tons made the best profit ; the best hunting-ground was the Spanish-American trade, the chief commodities hides and sugar. With the increase in the number and size of ships the London merchants came to combine trade with privateering. Some twenty or thirty Londoners—we find the familiar names frequently associated with Cumberland and Ralegh[1]—with a handful of provincial merchants dominated the show : they set forth half the ships and raked in more than half the prize goods (from £150,000 to £300,000 a year). Where these activities had been injurious to the exporting cloth-trade before the war, they became immensely profitable to importers of hides and sugars, spices and luxury goods during the war. Sugar valued at £100,000 was captured during 1589–91, where the annual import before was worth only £18,000. Some of the greatest merchants engaged in privateering, like Sir Thomas Myddleton, developed sugar-refining ; and thus in the course of the war England achieved a virtual monopoly of the European sugar supply. Shipbuilding and the luxury trades boomed along with it. These same merchants were the leaders in the trade to the Levant, Morocco and West Africa ; from their privateering experience, in developing the market for luxury goods and tropical raw materials, they laid the basis for the East Indian trade which, by the war, was being wrested from Portugal and Spain into the hands of English and Dutch. So privateering, along with its function in waging war, became a further weapon in the drive for oceanic expansion.

It would be possible to illustrate this subject at length from all kinds of material published and unpublished—the state papers are full of it, both domestic and foreign, the Acts of the Privy Council (for the Council was constantly concerned), the correspondence of ambassadors and envoys, the official papers of Sir Julius Caesar, which happen to remain. Space forbids. It is all very much of a character with the pre-war privateering,

---

[1] Such men as Paul Banning, Leonard Holliday, John Moore, Thomas Cordell, William Garraway, James Lancaster, Sir John Hart, Sir Thomas Myddleton, above all, Alderman Watts.

which we have touched on before. It has the same features, grisly or endearing ; the West Country is as much to the fore as ever, for it was in the front-line of action ; Frobisher continues a characteristic figure, respectable now—Sir Martin indeed, the old buccaneer—carrying his flag in Drake's *Revenge*. (Drake cannot have liked that, kept at home as he was, supervising the fortification of Plymouth, bringing water into the town, cultivating his garden, while others took his place at sea.) We follow Frobisher's track into Plymouth with his prize—cargoes of cochineal and anneal, Rouen cloth, hides and sugar,[1] or the *Sparke* of Plymouth's catch of 365 cwt. of ginger, 1300 India hides, 32 chests of sugar from the *Corpo Santo*.[2] A fine prize of Lord Cumberland's is lost in December weather upon the Lizard, " in a hellish place, rightly called in our Cornish language, Halseffern, in English Hell Cliff ", writes Sir Francis Godolphin, with doubtful etymology.[3] " I compounded with the unruly multitude of country people there assembled to grant them of the hides the fourth part, for saving and bringing them unto the top of the high cliff, and 10 or 12s for each chest of cochineal. . . . And for the treasure in the sea lying, I will direct them for recovery and saving the same as sufficiently as I am able. . . . Some hides and other things were embezzled before my repair ; and when men do the best they may, evil people will filch partly by day, but chiefly these long dark nights." It is pleasant to find a cargo of nuts and almonds brought into Scilly in time for Christmas in 1603.[4]

But it is more important to indicate the successive phases of the war—even so, far more briefly than the opening ones.

Philip's struggle for the control of France, the greatest prize of all to be dangled before his obsessive eyes, necessitated our intervention in both Normandy and Brittany : the war on land became more urgent in these years, the military effort took precedence, the soldiers came to the fore and became increasingly professional : at last English troops could hold their own with Spanish veterans. What is interesting in the later phase of the

[1] Lansdowne MS. 62, 11, 12, 14.
[2] John Sparke of Plymouth and his company received a licence for reprisal for the loss of one ship and cargo to the value of £3720. Lansdowne MS. 115, 73.
[3] Lansdowne MS. 145, 104.
[4] Add. MS. 5664, f. 403.

war is to observe the increasing interdependence of land and sea operations. Philip's seizure of a base at Blavet[1] in Brittany (1590) and the fall of Calais to him (1596) enabled him to reinforce his armies at both ends of the Channel, if somewhat hazardously, by sea, and both alarmed the English government, bringing the war right on to our doorstep. But it was with the Irish war, that dominated the last phase for us, that we see the perfect interlocking of land and sea strategy, the mature use of sea-power to decide the operations on land. Though Spain had the advantage of the prevailing winds in regard to Ireland, English sea-power, at last properly deployed and constantly exerted, decided the issue or, rather, sustained the conditions in which Mountjoy could bring the war to a conclusion.

In 1590 Hawkins and Frobisher were sent to sea to intercept the West Indian treasure-fleet. The idea was a sort of inner and outer screen, Hawkins watching the coast of Spain, Frobisher the Azores. In the West Indies a ship of Watts captured two of the richest vessels of the *flota* ; and Philip in alarm ordered it to winter there and not to attempt to cross the Atlantic. This extreme measure precipitated a further shock to Philip's credit and made it difficult for him to raise money in Europe—in the end he failed to meet his obligations to his Italian bankers, to their ruin ; it impeded his construction of a new Armada and, worst of all, paralysed Parma's movements in the Netherlands for want of pay for his starving troops. Henry IV won the battle of Ivry— turning-point for his cause—and could lay siege to his own recalcitrant, Leaguer-infested capital. One sees the remote effects of the pressure of sea-power.

Next year, 1591, a small squadron of six of the Queen's galleons was sent, under Lord Thomas Howard and Grenville, to lie in wait at the Azores for the *flota*. They had been at sea three or four months, with sickness raging in the ships and many of their men on land at Flores, when the King's main fleet of over twenty galleons, on its way to escort the *flota* home, bore down on them from the east. Everyone knows the famous action that resulted, the last fight of the *Revenge* : part of English legend.[2] Grenville was the last to get his men on board ; Howard with the rest of the ships managed to sheer away from

[1] Near the place where the naval base of Lorient was later developed.

[2] In my *Sir Richard Grenville of the ' Revenge '*, c. xvii, I was able to tell the full story, for the first time, from the Spanish documents.

overwhelming forces. It seems that there was just a chance that Grenville might have done so too, but instead—so like his over-bearing, dare-devil, unpleasant nature—he determined to cut his way right through the two Spanish squadrons. He had passed their leading ships, when he was becalmed under the lee of the towering *San Felipe*, largest of the new Apostles, and was at once grappled on either side and by the stern. The battle raged from the sun going down far into the night; with the daylight she had to surrender—nothing but a locked mass of sputtering ships around the *Revenge* heaving up and down with the sea. She had done tremendous damage: two Spanish ships were sunk; her crew was at the end of its resources (only 100 able men at the beginning). Grenville was mortally wounded, but would not surrender; with a Viking resolve, he ordered the ship to be blown up, but was overborne. He died on board the Spanish flag-ship.

Within the next few days a tremendous cyclone swept the Azores. It is said that of the Spanish fleets concentrating there—both *flotas* and Bazan's fleet—over 120 in all, some 70 ships perished. Linschoten, the Dutch East Indiaman, tells us that off Terceira alone twelve ships were cast away, on every side nothing but crying and lamenting and, for twenty days after the storm, the drowned men driving continually ashore. Among the ships dashed in pieces upon the coast was the *Revenge*. Ralegh writes her epitaph in words that do not fail to move us still, when we think of all that she had been through : " So it pleased them to honour the burial of that renowned ship the *Revenge*, not suffering her to perish alone, for the great honour she achieved in her life-time ".

The Spaniards and Portuguese in Terceira thought, as they well might, that God fought on the side of the heretics; that Grenville, like Drake, had command over the spirits and raised them from the deep to revenge him. Fighting spirit was rising on both sides :[1] we have seen the pride the Spaniards took in the capture of the *Revenge*—it was the only galleon of the Queen's they ever did take. The marvellous story of her fight gave no pleasure to the Queen : useless displays of heroism moved her less than

---

[1] Cf. the fine fight put up this year by the *Centurion*, a London merchantman, which fought off a squadron of five galleys near Gibraltar ; her consort, the little *Dolphin*, blew herself up with every man on board rather than surrender. Cf. Hakluyt, *Principal Navigations*, Everyman ed., IV. 383-6.

anyone. Ralegh's famous pamphlet was an apology, a defence of his dead cousin.

Drake and Hawkins' last voyage, 1595–6, achieved even less. The famous townsmen were given a send-off by Plymouth from the Hoe : the waits, cheering, the firing of guns. The beloved town can hardly have thought that neither of the familiar figures would walk their streets again. They had the usual small squadron of half a dozen of the Queen's galleons, with some supporting ships : nothing like enough to tackle the *flota* and its guard nowadays. In that lay the misconception that underlay the half-measures of these years—" half-doings " as Walsingham had called them.[1] And it is clear that Drake and Hawkins, now in the decline of their powers and out of date, had no idea of the transformation that Philip had wrought in Spain's naval power and in the fortification of the key-points of his empire : he, too, had his heroism. There was discordance between the old partners : Hawkins, true to his nature, had made careful preparations in equipment and victuals ; Drake, true to his, had taken on more men again than he could feed, and trusted to luck. But luck was against them throughout. They missed the treasure-fleet—though that may have been a good thing, for it was convoyed by twelve galleons. Worse, five fast frigates got ahead of them to take away the treasure at Puerto Rico and alert the West Indies. One sees that throughout sixteenth-century sea-warfare both achievements and losses were rather more due to chance and circumstance than they were the results of deliberate action—at least, the latter come second.

Arrived in the West Indies, Hawkins, full of presentiment of failure, died ; his last act was to beg the Queen to accept a legacy of £2000 as amends for his having urged her to undertake the voyage. Drake's night attack on Puerto Rico was repulsed : gone were the days of his happy assaults on San Domingo and Cartagena. (Cartagena had been surrounded by a girdle of massive walls and turrets since his last visit : they remain in all their grandeur and mellow beauty today.) Drake was not his old—or, rather, young—self : he had lost decision, but not his old weakness for boasting : " I will bring you to twenty places far more wealthy and easier to be gotten ".[2] But they had none of the advantage of surprise now, and though Santa Marta and

---

[1] Laughton, *op. cit.* II. 69.
[2] q. Corbett, II. 396.

Nombre de Dios were occupied nothing was found. Moreover, a fleet of twenty-three fine galleons from Spain were on Drake's track. In haste, an attack was made on the Isthmus—Drake's old idea of cutting the waist-line, though it could never have been held now. The troops under Baskerville found the routes to Panama held by strong-points and they had to retreat, badly cut up, to the ships. Drake recognised that this was the end of his hopes : " since our return from Panama he never carried mirth nor joy in his face ".[1] Shortly after he went down with dysentery, which was raging in the fleet, and began to keep his cabin. On the day he died, in delirium, he raved, with the usual Elizabethan persecution-mania, against traitors ; he rose and put on his armour, saying that he would meet death like a soldier, and then, carried to his bed, died quietly enough. He was buried solemnly at sea—Captain William Parker, another Plymouth man, who carried out a dashing raid five years later, tells us where : off Porto Bello on the mainland, " somewhat to the eastward of the castle of St. Philip, where Sir Francis Drake's coffin was thrown overboard ".[2]

It was clear that the war would not be decided this way, and all the men of action thought so. Ralegh summed up their feeling later : " if the late Queen would have believed her men of war as she did her scribes, we had in her time beaten that great empire to pieces, and made their kings kings of figs and oranges, as in old times ".[3] This was, so like him, going too far. But there is something in what he went on to say : " her Majesty did all things by halves, and by petty invasions taught the Spaniard how to defend himself . . . which, till our attempts taught him, was hardly known to himself ". We have seen that she was not at all to blame for the failure in the grand opportunity of 1589. The conclusion she drew from that was not to put out her neck again. And here we may perhaps offer our second main criticism of her record :[4] her conduct of the war, especially in these years, 1589–95, when our chief weapon, sea-power, was only half deployed. We have to remember in fairness to her government that there was no guarantee, with the lack of ability to exert full control over her commanders, that that power would

---

[1] q. Corbett, II. 398.
[2] *Purchas,.his Pilgrims* (Maclehose edn.), XVI. 297.
[3] E. Edwards, *Life of Sir Walter Ralegh*, I. 245.
[4] For the first, in relation to her policy in Ireland, *v.* above, p. 128.

be properly employed when she entrusted it to them—witness Drake in 1589, Essex in 1597. We must remember, too, that finance was the limiting factor and that she could not have done much more without straining her country's resources, as Philip was exhausting his, and that anyway the war on land was taking priority in these years.

But we may, perhaps, legitimately criticise her for not imposing her will on the war, as she did on foreign policy and diplomacy, internal government and Church affairs—to the country's immense profit. Much of the war took place at sea— and the Queen had never been to sea. Out of her element in war, for she had not the advantage here of being a man (nor the dangers), she had not the self-confidence she felt in almost every other field of government to impose a judgment that was in essence superior to everyone else's, even Burghley's, as he readily recognised. She was not the less wonderful a ruler for not having her heart in the war. A consummate politician, like the younger Pitt, like him she had not the instinctive grasp of military strategy—though her individual judgments were often sound—of a Chatham or a Churchill. It was too much to expect of a lady. She did not like war ; it is difficult for people to be supreme in what they do not like.

She wanted peace : she was a pacific, humane woman, to whom compromise was the essence of her subtle, difficult, precariously poised nature. All through the war she was looking through her fingers for a chance to make peace. But she would never give way on the fundamental interests of the country or the crown : on the Netherlands, on the open door in North America, freedom of the seas or of trade to the East ; Ireland she regarded as her sole province, subject to her crown. There she was obstinate and unwavering : she would accept nothing but surrender. The result was that she followed the war, rather than imposed an initiative, doing her best with the instruments at hand—they often broke or let her down ; working hard, *au fait* with everything, to an extraordinary degree : she saw to it that she was informed of everything. Her knowledge of affairs astonishes one, as it astonished people at the time ; to the last limit of her will-power she was bent on her duty as ruler : keeping people up to the mark. We see her, with the eyes of sympathy and understanding, an ageing woman still hard at work on state business, one day at the end of January 1597 :

" her Majesty and the Lords closed up in the Privy Chamber till candlelight ".[1] Since then, tired out, " she is at rest attended by my Lady Scrope ". A few days later, " I left the Queen at six very quiet and, as I guess, will not stir till it be very late ; but I will attend the time and present it [more business, from the Secretary of State] if she do but breathe a little while afore her going to bed ".[2]

The government was coming to the conclusion that a campaign on a much larger scale was necessary : a national effort— what was then called a " royal " enterprise—deploying our sea-power on a full scale. For 1596 there was planned the biggest show since 1589, and in several respects it marks a notable contrast with that : in the speed and effectiveness of the preparations, the training and discipline of the troops, the surprise achieved, the shattering success upon the target. The English were becoming vastly more professional at waging war. Even Burghley was in favour of the offensive and delivered an opinion backing the project : " To the Queen's Majesty's only most fair hands, from a simple weak head ". (The old man, within two years of his death, was reduced to the prevailing language of gallantry too.) Vere's professional opinion was for an enterprise " more royally set forward as well in regard to the upholding of her Majesty's reputation as for the main proceeding of this war, which cannot prosper with us if in time we bring it not nearer to them ".[3] It was to be a combined naval and military assault upon Cadiz ; absolute secrecy was maintained as to the objective, a chief condition of its triumph.

At the last moment, in April, a frightful blow fell : Calais was captured by the Spaniards and there was a panic in London. Its fall was due to the game of double-bluff played by the Queen and Henry IV as to who should bear the burden of its rescue ; but the latter told the truth when he said that he would rather see the Spaniards there than the English. From his point of view, rightly : at the peace the Spaniards would give it back, the English never. It would have been too spectacular a triumph over her sister for even the Queen to resist : all through Elizabeth's reign the English held on to the hope of recovering

[1] *Salisbury MSS.* (H.M.C.), VII. 41.
[2] *Ibid.* 55.
[3] J. S. Corbett, *The Successors of Drake*, 39.

Calais some day. Now the loss was irretrievable; Essex made frantic efforts to come to its rescue, but it was all too late. It is to the Queen's credit that the disaster did not deflect her from the main strategical objective. But one sees the wear and tear on her nerves from the difficulties she began to make, as usual, when some risky undertaking was just about to take off: " the Queen wrangles with our action for no cause but because it is in hand ".[1] It was her way of steeling her resolution. Back came formal protests from the commanders down at Plymouth; this was what she was waiting for, the last propulsion over the edge. She composed a prayer for the expedition, explaining to the Almighty her reasons for undertaking it; then, " these being the grounds, Thou that diddest inspire the mind, we humbly beseech with bended knees prosper the work, and with the best forewinds guide the journey, speed the victory and make the return the advancement of Thy fame and surety to the realm, with the least loss of English blood." That was what she cared most about.

On 3 June Sir Ferdinando Gorges wrote from Plymouth that the fleet had sailed that morning " and are now out of sight ".[2] It must have been a splendid spectacle: an Armada of some 110 or 120 ships, of which forty-seven were ships of war—seventeen of the Queen's galleons and armed merchantmen—the rest transports, victuallers, flyboats and pinnaces. The Lord Admiral and Essex as Earl Marshal were in command of what was the fleet and army of England. The fleet sailed in four squadrons, of which Howard and Essex commanded the first two, Lord Thomas Howard the third and Ralegh the fourth: this was to be their revenge for the *Revenge*. A fifth squadron consisted of Dutch ships, under their own Admiral, for our junior allies were now in a position to contribute contingents to our major enterprises, in addition to their own operations: Dutch sea-power was growing so fast that after the Queen's death it would outstrip ours. The troops provided the chief contrast with the amateurishness of 1589: 2000 veterans from the Netherlands, under the most experienced captains—Sir Francis Vere, Sir Matthew Morgan, Sir Conyers Clifford, Lord Burgh—made a stiffening for the county levies.[3] The time of waiting at Plymouth had been well employed in training and exercising them, so that their

[1] q. Corbett, *op. cit.* 46.
[2] *Salisbury MSS.*, VI. 208. [3] *Ibid.* 205-6.

discipline and order in marching provided another shock for the Spaniards at Cadiz. In the wake of Essex there was a great turn-out of the younger generation among the volunteers : courtiers like Sir Anthony Ashley, Thomas Egerton and Sir Edward Hoby ; scholars like Henry Wotton and Henry Cuffe ; divines and poets such as Edward Reynolds and William Alabaster, and among them, it is fairly certain, John Donne, some of whose Epigrams refer to episodes in the action :[1]

> Under an undermined and shot-bruised wall
> A too-bold captain perished by the fall,
> Whose brave misfortune happiest men envied
> That had a town for tomb, his bones to hide.

The surprise of Cadiz on that Sunday morning of June was complete.[2] The church bells jangled the alarm at two o'clock, and with the dawn there appeared what even the Spaniards could not help thinking *una hermosísima vista.*[3] The West Indian *flota* that Drake had missed was fitting out in harbour for the return journey, but its guard of galleons was away at San Lucar. The President of the *Contratación* house was himself in the town. The Duke of Medina Sidonia, whose province this was, was somewhere on the other side of the bay : lucky for him that he was too late to cross by boat to take command of the city, or he would have fetched a prince's ransom. Ill as he was, he sat up writing letters in all directions and succeeded in throwing a couple of infantry companies and some cavalry into the city, to be caught there. There was some delay while the English changed their plan of attack. They had arrived off the little headland that juts out into those crystalline waters under the grey walls of the fort of San Sebastián, with its pepper-pot turrets unchanged today. Essex was bent on making a landing here at once, but, with a south-westerly freshening, the surf was rising and making it dangerous. Fortunately the seamen over-bore him and the fleet went round the point into the sheltered

---

[1] H. J. C. Grierson regards the series of five, "Fall of a Wall ", "A Burnt Ship ", "A Lame Beggar ", "Cales and Guiana " and "Sir John Wingfield ", as all having been composed during the Cadiz expedition. *The Poems of John Donne*, II. 59.

[2] The capture of Cadiz has usually been described from the English side. We are enabled to see it from the Spanish from the relations and documents brought together in a rare Spanish book, A. de Castro, ed. *Historia del saqueo de Cádiz* (Cadiz, 1866).

[3] *Ibid.* 2.

water of the outer harbour. The Spanish ships had retreated into the inner harbour, where the four Apostles moored themselves end to end across the channel at its narrowest to block it, presenting their broadsides to the attack. They were supported by a couple of Portuguese galleons, the big Levanters and three frigates. Meanwhile the merchant vessels of the *flota* were trying to take refuge in the shallow waters of the innermost bay. It fell to Ralegh to lead the attack—there was acute competition for the honour and some jostling of ships for the post—and it was not long before the line was broken. Two of the Apostles were captured and two sunk, the soldiers tumbling into the sea " so thick as if coals had been poured out of a sack in many ports at once, some drowned, some sticking in the mud. . . . The spectacle was very lamentable on their side ; for many drowned themselves ; many, half-burnt, leaped into the water ; very many hanging by the ropes' ends by the ships' sides even to the lips ; many swimming with grievous wounds, strucken out of water and put out of their pain."[1] There was no further resistance ; the squadron of galleys managed to make their escape by the almost impassably shallow inlet between the island of León and the mainland.

The city lay open to attack ; clearly the Spaniards were completely demoralised by the suddenness of the blow. Cadiz was seized by panic ; there was utter disorder and, in the end, very little resistance—in spite of the friars rushing up and down with crucifixes trying to put heart into the people. Thousands of them crowded into the churches, three thousand into the chief church of San Francisco, where they spent their time confessing, and some, more usefully, in stowing valuables away into tombs— over which the English, characteristically, were cheated, since they generously agreed not to search the churches. Everything else in the city was fair game ; by the recognised rules of warfare a conquered town was given over to spoil. It was not long before it was in Essex's hand ; the Spaniards were struck by the disciplined march of the troops across the difficult sand of the

[1] Ralegh's *Works* (ed. Oldys and Birch), VIII. 668. Cf. Donne : " A Burnt Ship " :

> Out of a fired ship, which by no way
> But drowning could be rescued from the flame,
> Some men leaped forth, and ever as they came
> Near the foes' ships, did by their shot decay ;
> So all were lost which in the ship were found :
> They in the sea being burnt, they in the burnt ship drowned.

peninsula upon which he had landed, and in at the town gate, to take possession of the *plaza mayor* where they carried out their manœuvres and did all things as if they were in London itself. Sir John Wingfield, one of the colonels of regiments, who was killed, was buried with full military honours in the cathedral. Donne wrote of his friend :

> Beyond the old Pillars many have travellèd
> Towards the Sun's cradle, and his throne, and bed.
> A fitter Pillar our Earl did bestow
> In that late Island ;[1] for he well did know
> Farther than Wingfield no man dares to go.

Sir George Carew could write home to the Secretary " from her Majesty's city of Cales [Cadiz], not in fancy but won and yet held by her soldiers' swords ".[2] The interest is not so much in the easy capture of the city as in the sack that followed.

Pandemonium ruled. But what surprised the Spaniards was the humanity of the English—so different from their own intentions in 1588 and their behaviour in the Netherlands and elsewhere. All their accounts of the sack pay tribute to it. Essex had given orders that friars, monks and women were not to be maltreated ; he placed barges at their disposal to evacuate 1500 of them out of harm's way.[3] His chivalry and gallantry made an extraordinary impression on the susceptible Spaniards. And it turned out to be useful : it appealed strongly to the war-weariness of the people and immensely increased their desire for peace. Not so with the Dutch : they had old scores to pay off and behaved accordingly. Ralegh tells us, " ourselves spared the lives of all after the victory ; but the Flemings, who did little or nothing in the fight, used merciless slaughter, till they were by myself and afterward by my Lord Admiral beaten off ".[4] Objects, particularly religious objects, provided a substitute : the soldiers went for images and vestments. (It is interesting to observe the Protestant feeling of superiority at not worshipping the saints.) Soldiers pranced about in the sacred vestments, pillaging right and left, dragging the images off their altars and round the streets. In the chapel of the English College at

---

[1] Cadiz is practically an island, joined by a spit of sand on to the island of León. " Late Island ", discussed by Grierson, means " in that island of the late events ".

[2] *Salisbury MSS.* VI. 229.

[3] De Castro, 116.

[4] Ralegh, *loc. cit.*

Valladolid today one sees a war casualty from Cadiz : a damaged
Virgin, the *Vulnerata,* on the altar.

One of the amusing features of the occupation was the
discussion that took place between the English scholars and
divines and the Spanish theologians. One would like to know
whether Donne was present—it would be very much to his taste ;
what is certain is that Alabaster was, for he was converted by a
Spaniard—so like the English, allowing themselves to be taken
in by the defeated. But Alabaster was rather an exception :
a silly, light-headed fellow, he went round like a weather-cock
and was converted back and forth again and again.[1] A more
ironic exchange was that between Lord Admiral Howard and
the Duke of Medina Sidonia : having been general against him
in 1588, Howard wrote, he thought he might be not wholly
unknown to him.[2] He asked the Duke to exchange the 51
Englishmen serving in the galleys for an equivalent number of
prisoners, and this was accorded.[3] No-one has ever doubted
that Medina Sidonia was a great gentleman ; but he was rather
unfortunate in his contacts with the English. His own people
treated him worse. When he returned from the Armada and
was lying ill in his palace by the sea at Puerto Santa María,
the populace had chanted outside his windows that Drake was
coming to fetch him. Now the greatest genius of Spain devoted
a satirical sonnet to him :

> Tronó la tierra, obscurecióse el cielo,
> Amenazando una total ruina ;
> Y al cabo en Cádiz, con mesura harta,
> Ido ya el Conde,[4] sin ningún recelo,
> Triunfando entró el gran Duque de Medina.[5]

But the Duke had the last word with Howard : he balked
him of the *flota.* The King's officials offered two million ducats
for its ransom ; the English asked for four. While they were
attacking the city a squadron should have been told off to take
the *flota* entire ; but all the commanders were ashore battling

---

[1] The Archbishop gave him a spell of imprisonment at Cambridge to cool his
hot head. *Salisbury MSS.* VII. 395.

[2] *Salisbury MSS.* VI. 241.

[3] *Salisbury MSS.* says 31, but this may be a misreading ; the Spanish authorities
say 51 and they are likely to know the exact number.

[4] *i.e.* Essex.

[5] Cervantes, q. Corbett, 117.

for honour, in Elizabethan fashion. Now the Duke ordered the *flota* to be fired : thirty-six merchant ships went up in flames, with their cargoes worth twelve millions, it was estimated. The Duke wrote the King the terrible news from Cadiz : one tired ailing man to another. Philip approved his action ; not so the merchants : one more wedge between the monarch and the nation. The losses at Cadiz were enormous : four of the big Apostles (two captured, two sunk), five Biscayans, two galleasses, four Levanters, three Italians laden with artillery and munitions for Flanders, the three big frigates from the West Indies and a mass of smaller ships. Among the prisoners were the President of the *Contratación* of Seville and all the prebendaries of the Cathedral—their ransoms went unpaid, in spite of the Chapter's contribution of 1500 ducats ; so they languished in prison in England, complaining of the cold and wet, until July 1603.[1] The city itself paid a ransom of 120,000 ducats. Its appearance after the sack, said the Spaniards, was as if the infernal legions had ravaged it, houses and walls down, bodies of men and horses filling the streets strewn with books and papers, the bells taken from the churches, all guns and munitions carried away ; then came a plague of flies like the plagues of Egypt—and, no doubt, disease.

The question for the English was whether to hold on to the wrecked city. Essex was strongly in favour of the attempt ; and there was an offer on the part of the Moors of Morocco to collaborate. This was rejected. The Spaniards were terrified of such a conjuncture ; their clerical emissaries appealed to the common interest of Spain and England in the true faith—a concept that does not seem to have interested them in any other connection—against the unbelievers. The Spaniards themselves said that reasonable Anglo-Dutch opinion had peace with Spain in view ; it was the King who would not make peace with heretics. One sees the division between Philip and his subjects transpiring discreetly from the Relation.[2] Cadiz opened the eyes of the English to these possibilities : Sir George Carew wrote to Cecil on the way home, " from her Majesty's good ship, the *Mary Rose* : the wiser sort of the Spaniards that are prisoners with us do confess in one voice that a greater grievance could not have been done unto him, in so much as they are of opinion that his people with their clamour will enforce him to seek for peace from her

---

[1] De Castro, 45 foll.   [2] *Ibid.* 130.

Majesty ".[1]   Carew goes on to enumerate the consequences of
the King's financial losses ; it is probable that not the least
achievement of the most brilliant exploit of the war was its effect
in undermining the Spanish people's will to resist, their confidence
in themselves.[2]

The Queen wrote her magnificent thanks : " Let the army
know I care not so much for being Queen, as that I am sovereign
of such subjects ".[3]   She was shortly to be disillusioned.   The
homeward-bound treasure-fleet from the West Indies was on
its way : now was the moment to attack it and knock Spain right
out of the war.   But the English fleet was so bent on getting home
with its pillage that it would not wait ; and this, in spite of the fact
that it was still well victualled, without disease, and could have
kept the seas.   Historians have constantly wondered at what they
call the Queen's " ingratitude ".   This was why ; this kind of
thing was always the reason of it.   We have to allow for
Elizabethan circumstances : the men themselves, soldiers and
sailors, were bent on getting back with their spoils, and the
commanders might not have been able to control them, even
if they would.   (Howard and Ralegh had no wish ; only Essex
was for staying out.)   Stallenge, the Queen's official at Plymouth,
feared as much :   " their companies having gotten so much
pillage . . . I fear will hardly be kept any longer at the seas ".[4]
On the heels of this the fleet came back to Plymouth, unexpectedly early ; Gorges was in favour of reconstituting it to
intercept the plate-fleet.   Not a hope of it :   " as a poor well-
wisher of my country's good, I do heartily wish that that of the
Indian fleet had gone forward, for without all contradiction it
was the most reasonablest and most necessariest that could have
been thought of ".[5]   It was already too late : the fleet was off
to the Thames, its leaders to Court.   No wonder they got a cool,
or rather a hot, reception : here was a chance of ending the war
at a blow lost again.

And not only that, there was the question of the spoil.   The
expedition had been a national enterprise, at the Queen's
expense : in no sense a private venture.   The Lord Admiral

---

[1] *Salisbury MSS.* VI. 250.
[2] It is an interesting indication of the fear Drake's name had inspired in Spain
that when Philip wrote to thank Medina Sidonia for the zeal he had shown at
Cadiz, he slipped into writing " el saqueo de Cádiz por *Drake* " !   *Epistolario, ed. cit.*.
268.   [3] q. Corbett, 130.
[4] *Salisbury MSS.* VI. 315.   [5] *Ibid.* 334.

and the Earl Marshal were under strict orders to allot the proceeds to offset the expenses : no less than her duty, as the Queen saw it, to spare the burden weighing on the country. Instead of that—and it is again a commentary on the immaturity of the state and the inability to enforce its discipline—Howard and Essex allowed everyone throughout navy and army to keep and get away with what he could. The Queen's officials down at Plymouth were helpless. William Killigrew, Groom of her Chamber, whom she had sent down : " in this town, for all the little stay the fleet make here, there is much landed, but in huxters' handling ".[1] Sir Ferdinando Gorges : " I do not see but that very much goods will be embezzled ".[2] William Stallenge : " all or most part of the goods landed in this place was given by the Generals to men of desert, and is by them sold to others and the money received, which will hardly be gotten from them ".[3] The Queen's own agent, Sir Anthony Ashley, who sailed with the fleet expressly to look after the interests of the Crown, betrayed them. His state of mind may be seen from the postscript of a letter to Essex's steward : " I pray conceal all for fear of the worst, nor be not known I have writ to you ".[4] He did all he could to hold on to what he had laid hold of : chests of it brought into his house, a great diamond that should have come to the Queen broken up among the London jewellers. She disgraced him, and kept him in disgrace ; but there was no getting the jewel back—correspondence about it goes on and on in the official papers.[5]

This indiscipline and inability to exert full control was one of the penalties paid for the greater individualism and liberty of action in the English state. Philip evidently had far more control over his captains and commanders. It is a remarkable tribute to his personality and method of government that he made his will prevail throughout his vast Empire.[6] But the price was more than it was worth in discouragement of spirit,

---

[1] *Salisbury MSS.* VI. 327.   [2] *Ibid.* 321.

[3] *Ibid.* 329. Among those hiding away swag from Cadiz we find the nasty Topcliffe's nasty son. *Ibid.* 370.

[4] *Ibid.* 328.

[5] Cf. *Salisbury MSS.* VI, VII, VIII *passim.*

[6] English historians have tended very much to underrate Philip. Cf. a really silly judgment by that excellent historian, Sir Julian Corbett : " In war it [the Queen's diplomacy] was disastrous, and gave away the game to one of the most tedious bunglers that ever played it for a nation's sins." *Op. cit.* 4.

suffocation of individual enterprise, hardening of arteries, in the end.

Philip's will was not yet broken, though Cadiz had ruined his prestige and credit alike. Immediately upon it he had to dishonour the whole of the bills of his Governor in the Nether-lands, to the tune of a million and a half. The result was a panic upon all the exchanges. His own loans he tried to repudiate at 45 per cent ; when his creditors asked more he refused to pay anything. Result : a great number of commercial houses in Italy, in part his own subjects, went bankrupt. One way or another Cadiz must be revenged.[1] The King was determined that the Armada which he had been building up should sail. Late as the season was, and against the Adelantado's protest, in the last week of October Philip drove the fleet to sea. He had managed to get together some hundred sail, among which there were over twenty galleons. But the ships were ill-found and Spanish ships were never good at keeping the seas in the storms of the North Atlantic. In the Bay of Biscay they were struck by an autumn gale and something between twenty and thirty of the warships foundered, among them, it seems, no less than seven galleons. An untold number of smaller craft went down ; altogether some three thousand men perished. There was nothing for it but to struggle back, dispersed and broken, as best they could. Next year, and again in 1599, plague added its terrors to the griefs of the coast towns.[2]

As in 1589 the English government was bent on eliminating the core of the Armada that had got back, laid up at Ferrol in its admirable strategic position at the extreme north-western face of the peninsula. Burghley and the Queen were as usual at one on this : " I think nothing so needful as to attempt some enterprise against the Spanish army in Ferrol ", he wrote.[3] The old man was a better strategist than any of the fighting young men : this was the proper objective. That spring the government put its best foot forth to equip a powerful fleet and army to go with it, against a background of noticeable

---

[1] Portocarrero, General of the galleys, was sent to prison for his bad service there. *Salisbury MSS.* VIII. 185.

[2] Cf. for 1599 Vicente de Colmo to Luis Vásquez, 15 August : "At Lisbon there has been a great pestilence : more than forty thousand persons dead, so that the city is almost deserted. I went there by order of the Adelantado. There was nothing like it but Cadiz after the sack." *Salisbury MSS.* IX. 273.

[3] q. Corbett, *op. cit.* 154.

war-weariness of which no-one was more conscious than Burghley. He knew only too well how burdensome the war was, particularly to the southern coastal counties, their trade and their ports. The counties were finding it difficult to raise and equip the men demanded of them—increasingly the government had to come to their help and shoulder the expenses; the ports were replying that they had not the ships to contribute. Even London, which was the greatest source of war-supplies and had always been readiest to provide them, now hung back. A Parliament was summoned to which the government could put its case and ask for help from the country—a striking contrast with the state of affairs in Spain, impoverished and suffering, yet with no means of holding up a dying fanatic. (In one of his comas this last year of his life the King kept saying over and over, "What more can Don Martín want? Will he never be ready?")

In England a fleet was fitted out: seventeen of the Queen's galleons, including the two Apostles captured at Cadiz, twenty-four transports to carry a fine fighting force of 6000 men; twenty-two Dutch men-of-war formed a fourth squadron under the same commanders as at Cadiz. The young men were in command: Essex as General, with Lord Thomas Howard and Ralegh joined with him, each commanding a squadron. What is noticeable is that the leadership in the last stage of the war is shifting away from the seamen to the soldiers; the army has become much more professional and efficient, the condition of the ships less good than it was. The objectives were clearly laid down. First, to destroy the enemy fleet at Ferrol: "with the least danger and loss of our people expedite this special service for the ruin of the enemy, especially by the destruction of his ships; which being well executed, there is no cause for us to doubt of any peril to come for a long time from him".[1] If the Adelantado's fleet had put to sea, it was to follow and engage it. When it was destroyed, then Essex might proceed to the Azores to intercept the West Indian convoy and the carracks; and there he might reduce Terceira and garrison it—provided it would not need an annual fleet to supply it. It was the plan that Drake and his Portuguese entourage had always hankered after.

The summer of 1597, like that of 1588, was very stormy. The fleet was kept waiting for weeks at Plymouth, eating up

---

[1] q. Corbett, *op. cit.* 171.

its provisions and the troops sickening ; when it got out it was driven back by a tremendous gale. Observe that, though the ships and men suffered a great deal from the buffeting—and Essex wrote to the Queen in highest strain with all the poetic extremism of his temperament—not one was lost. But, driven back to Plymouth and having lost valuable time, he decided on his own authority to disband most of the troops. That spoke for itself : the voyage was to be an essentially maritime expedition : no capturing Ferrol or Terceira without troops. What the Queen thought of this we do not know, but perhaps we may guess from Cecil's reaction to the news from Ferrol.

Arrived off Ferrol, they again had unfavourable weather and fairly serious trouble with the unseaworthy Spanish galleons, which were sent back. Essex, Howard and Ralegh made the weather the excuse for not attacking the Armada within the harbour : they assured themselves that it was incapable of moving and this justified them, in their own eyes, in leaving the Spanish coast and making for the Azores, where there was far more exciting (and remunerative) prey to catch. From this moment we can see that no great hopes of the expedition were entertained at the centre of affairs. We have a very cool estimate of the prospects from Cecil : " I hope for nothing but the keeping up of the journey's reputation, by keeping the sea as long as the time of year for the Spaniard to come out doth serve, and to lie off at the Islands to interrupt the Indian fleet ; but the fleet at Ferrol will not be burnt, the carracks are come home, the Islands cannot be taken ".[1] That tiresome Cassandra, Cecil's aunt, Lady Russell, was not wholly wrong in her ill-omened forecast : " I in no wise like of the enterprise toward. It may have good beginning, but I fear ill success in end, by lives and loss of more than the King of Spain and all his is worth."[2] The Queen expressed her disapprobation to Essex : " when we do look back to the beginning of this action which hath stirred so great expectation in the world and charged us so deeply, we cannot but be sorry to foresee already how near all our expectations and your great hopes are to a fruitless conclusion ".[3] Meanwhile the Armada at Ferrol had been given time to effect repairs and revictual, to make ready again.

[1] *Salisbury MSS.* VII. 361.
[2] *Ibid.* 282. For a portrait of this tartar, *v.* my essay on " Bisham and the Hobys " in *The English Past.*   [3] *Salisbury MSS.* VII. 433.

In the Azores Essex learned that the *flota* had not yet arrived, nor had the Adelantado sailed to meet it. Excitement ran high : here was the longed-for opportunity. The treasure-fleet had to be intercepted before it got into the safety of the Angra Road, under the shelter of the most powerful guns of the time. While waiting Essex spread his fleet about the Islands, and Ralegh performed the one exploit of the voyage—the landing on Fayal which, because of the " honour " involved, made an irreparable breach between the two. Essex altered his dispositions again and again, probably from nervous excitement and want of experience at sea. With the result that when the *flota* at length appeared, he was at the eastern end of the islands with the bulk of the fleet and the *flota* sailed straight into Angra Road. Monson with a few ships in the dark found himself in company with the tail-end of the *flota* and gave chase all night. But to no purpose : Philip's treasure was safe, was at once unloaded and taken ashore, the ships warped right up under the commanding batteries. Three hours later Essex arrived, mad with rage to see what a fool he had been : he, of course, wanted to go in at once, but that would have been fatal. Philip had had the narrowest escape from disaster : Drake had missed the treasure-fleet in 1585 by twelve hours.

Meanwhile England lay uncovered. When Philip learned that the English fleet had left the coast of Spain for the Azores he determined to stake everything on his last chance. It was a gambler's throw : with blind fixed resolve he drove on his Armada. He did everything he could to strengthen it and replenish it : an Italian squadron was added to carry three whole tercios of his Italian veterans, when Italy was on the brink of revolt. At this last crisis of his long life, so replete with cheated hopes, the treasure-ships must take their chance : the lure of catching England off guard was worth more than the treasure of the Indies. But it was a gambler's judgment—to this had his faith reduced him ; for it was no longer possible to bring it off. The Adelantado was against the attempt. At last the King was reduced to threatening he would hang him at his wife's neck if he did not sail. The Armada Philip had so painfully built up made a fine show : 136 ships, of which sixty were warships, carrying nine thousand soldiers and four thousand sailors. The Seville squadron were to follow with thirty ships and three tercios of the finest infantry in Europe. The Adelantado had a galaxy of Spain's best sea commanders under him. The plan was a complicated creaking one that looked well on paper : product, no doubt, of long night vigils at the Escorial, emanating from the small cramped room with its window looking on to the high altar of the church. It was megalomania, rather than war. The Armada was to make for Blavet and there pick up the squadron of galleys, cross to Cornwall and occupy Falmouth as a base ; the fleet to return to the Scillies to intercept the home-coming English fleet, destroy it and make up-Channel. If this programme had been adhered to, something like the conditions of 1588 might have been repeated.

Still the Adelantado delayed for a whole month ; it was not until 9 October that he set out. By this time Essex was returning home, and the two fleets, unknown to each other, were converging upon the western approaches to the Channel : in fact their paths crossed. The Adelantado arrived off Blavet when the usual autumn gale struck and dispersed his fleet. Some of his ships held on their course and were sighted off the Lizard. The alarm was totally unexpected. Parliament was meeting at West-minster and had to be prorogued : more important work to do in the localities. Essex arrived at Plymouth to find that the Adelantado was out " and the Spaniards are upon the coast ; upon which, if we do not bestir ourselves as never men did, let us be counted not worthy to serve such a Queen ", etc. ; and, with his usual asinine emotionalism, " though we eat ropes' ends and drink nothing but rain water, we will out, that we may be partly the instruments to make a final end of this proud nation that is destined to destruction ".[1] In the emergency the Earl was given full power and authority to take command at Plymouth, as Howard had done in 1588. Essex was all for pursuing the Spaniards to Ireland, whither he was certain they had gone. The Queen did not need his excited advice, nor did she fail to remind him that " already by your late leaving the coast upon an uncertain probability that no army would come forth of Ferrol till March, you have given the enemy leisure and courage to attempt us ".[2] She was not one to refrain from saying " I told you so " ; now " take heed . . . that you do not in any case, upon any probability or light advertisements, once adventure to leave our own coasts to transport our forces to Ireland, whereby our own kingdom may lie open to serious

[1] *Salisbury MSS.* VII. 445. [2] *Ibid.* 449.

dangers. . . ." Actually the emergency had already passed, for the bulk of the Armada, dispersed by the gale, raced home before it to the shelter of Spanish ports. And, what made it all the more humiliating, with no great losses this time : the failure made it flagrantly obvious that the Spanish will to war, so far as England was concerned, was broken, that Philip's subjects had ceased to believe that England could be conquered, or even defeated now. It was enough to break Philip's heart—or, what had taken the place of his heart, his pride—at last.

It is interesting to observe towards the close of the struggle the rhythms of the opening moves repeated : the victory of 1588 followed by the fiasco of 1589, the triumph of 1596 by the failure of 1597. After the Islands Voyage the Queen did not send a major expedition to sea again ; in any case the Irish war was reaching its climax and cost unprecedented sums. After the Adelantado's final failure Philip, in his last months, was prepared to recognise defeat in the main objectives of his life : the subjugation of the Netherlands, the conquest of England, their salvation from heresy, reconciliation to the Church. (Why could he not have done so before—and saved thousands of lives ? We put our finger on a major tragedy in human history : the consequences of hubris.) Now that he was dying, from that small room whence he had ruled half the world, now filled with the stench of the festering sores with which his body was covered, nursed with tender devotion by his daughter the Infanta, his eyes on the altar, Philip dictated his instructions to the son who was to succeed him. He made peace with France, restoring Calais and withdrawing from Brittany. He wished to come to terms with England : he was prepared to recognise that it would continue to be a heretic country. He would grant full liberty of trade in Spain and Italy, and even permit licence to trade in the Indies, given guarantees—which was all that Hawkins had asked for thirty years before. The English could have had peace on favourable terms for themselves, if they would leave the Dutch in the lurch. This neither Burghley nor the Queen would do. Philip sketched a possible future for the Netherlands with his plan for setting up his daughter there, marrying her to the Archduke and giving them semi-independent sovereignty. But the Dutch could never accept Spanish rule in any form again. English policy would have preferred, as throughout the ages, a strong, united Netherlands independent of anyone. But what ultimately emerged suited English interests very well : semi-independent rule in the southern Netherlands under the distant aegis of Spain, thereby averting the danger of absorption into France ; complete independence for the northern Netherlands. It followed the lines that Elizabeth would gladly have agreed upon with Parma years before.

Since Spain would not yet grant this and we would not make peace without the Dutch, the war continued after the deaths of Philip and Burghley—those old antagonists—in 1598. At sea it was no longer war on the grand scale : neither side had the will any longer to knock the other out. The Peace of Vervins changed the situation for us : a united and powerful France might become more of a danger than a defeated and exhausted Spain. Spain fought on in the Netherlands and at sea there were exciting episodes and exploits : on the Spanish side, along the line of communications thither ; on the English, along the line between Spanish America and Spain. In this same year Cumberland brought off a brilliant coup with the capture of Puerto Rico, which Drake had not been able to achieve. In 1601 Drake's fellow-townsman, Captain Parker, did even better : he captured Porto Bello and found himself in possession of the " treasure-house of the world ".[1] Unfortunately most of the treasure had just been shipped: " such treasure as was found in the King's house to the value of some nine or ten thousand ducats, I reserved to myself, which was nothing to that which we did expect ". He also captured the famous Pedro Menéndez Marqués himself, who had reorganised the treasure-trade for Philip and done more than anyone to frustrate the English attacks on it : whom " in regard that he had valiantly carried himself in making resistance until he had ten or eleven wounds upon him, I did not only at length dismiss without any penny for his ransom, but also caused my chirurgeon very carefully to dress and trim his wounds : using him and his far otherwise than Pedro Menéndez his great-uncle used John Ribault, Laudonnière and the French nation in Florida, whom they most cruelly murdered and massacred as many as they could lay any hands upon ". Being an Elizabethan, Parker would not omit to make the point (why should he ?) ; but, in fact, relations between the Spaniards and the English, after their long breach and the offences given on both sides, were becoming better.

[1] *v.* Parker's own account in *Purchas, his Pilgrims*, XVI. 292-7.

As for the treasure-fleet itself, so often lain in wait for, so often missed, the young fighting seaman, Sir Richard Leveson (one sees him erect in bronze upon his pedestal in Wolverhampton church), at length met with it between the Azores and Spain.[1] But Leveson had too few ships with him to do any good : only four galleons to the sixteen of the Indian Guard. He consoled himself with a fine exploit : the cutting out of a huge carrack that had taken refuge in Cezimbra Bay from under the land-batteries overlooking the Road and the hornets' nest of galleys (like our motor-gunboats) that surrounded her.[2]

On the Spanish side, too, a gifted commander of the younger generation performed some superb exploits : this was the brother of the famous Genoese soldier, Spinola.[3] It was, perversely, in galley-warfare that Frederico Spinola—a youthful, rather feminine type, with irresistible charm and unconquerable spirit— made his name in northern waters. He badgered the Spaniards until at last, in 1599, discouraged and without any hope, they gave him half a dozen galleys to do what he liked with them. With this little squadron which he trained himself—like our own Cornish Hitchens with his gunboats in the last war—he made a wonderful dash up-Channel and through the Straits of Dover to Sluys. In 1602 he repeated his exploit, against all the chances, for several squadrons of English and Dutch were on the lookout for him. This time he came right in behind the English ships, practically touching the coast at the South Foreland before he could give them the slip and get into Dunkirk safe with his treasure. But that kind of thing could be done once too often. Hampered by the unimaginativeness of the Spanish command and hurt by the estimation in which he was held, the sensitive Italian virtually sought his death in his last engagement with the Dutch. The end of the galleys was a symbolic thing : the last sputter of Mediterranean sea-warfare. The future was with the North and the Atlantic.

The war was dying down. But the Queen—for all that the forward party and the men of action blamed her half-heartedness —would not make peace without conditions for the Dutch or

---

[1] *v. Monson's Tracts*, II. 152.

[2] *Ibid.* 154-63.

[3] Monson pays tribute to the part he played at Cezimbra, where Spinola " followed not the example of the Marquis [of Santa Cruz, commanding the squadron], but made good the road. Which the other seeing, with shame returned." The galleys then fought bravely, but were routed.

assurances for trade with America. She died, still in that state of undeclared war which dominated the last two decades of her reign and gave it, rather against her will, its glory and renown. (She gloried more in the long internal peace she kept within the country.) With the accession of Mary Stuart's son, a scion of the most international house in Europe, the House of Lorraine, and with no inner response to the strongest force urging the English on—their flaming national feeling—the way was open to peace.

Spain needed it. Negotiations had been going on during the last three years.[1] At Boulogne in 1600 representatives from both sides met, but Spanish pride still insisted on precedence. In 1604 the Spaniards had to come to London if they wanted peace ; Cecil was there to see that nothing was given away.[2] And nothing was, though Cecil received a large Spanish pension at the conclusion of it : the custom of the time. He, too, like his father, was determined that the Dutch should suffer no loss ; and, in fact, it remained open for them to recruit volunteers to serve with their forces, and the English remained in possession of the cautionary towns to defend them. English traders in Spain were not to be questioned or interfered with by the Inquisition. No engagement whatsoever was entered into to restrict our liberty of action in America. If Spain would enter into no engagements beyond the line,[3] it would leave her colonies open to the illicit trading, the depredations, that sapped the strength of her Empire in the next century. Above all, North America was open to English colonisation, and shortly the spate began.

The war upon so many fronts, the exigencies of Philip's rule, the insatiable demands made upon Spain, impossible to fulfil—though, inspired by the faith, she made heroic efforts to fulfil them and achieve the impossible—left the country exhausted, and, along with the effects of the autocracy and the Inquisition, permanently impaired.[4] After her brief and golden flowering there shortly set in the hardening of the arteries from which

---

[1] Cf. E. P. Cheyney, *History of England from the Defeat of the Armada to the Death of Elizabeth*, II. 560.

[2] Cf. S. R. Gardiner, *History of England from the Accession of James I to the Outbreak of the Civil War*, I. 207 foll.

[3] *i.e.* beyond the line laid down by the Papal confirmation of the New World to Spain and Portugal.

[4] In Spain in this century, the generation of 1898 (*i.e.* after the Spanish-American war and the loss of Cuba) devoted a great deal of discussion to this. Cf. Menéndez Pidal, *The Spaniards in their History* (trans. by Walter Starkie).

Spain has suffered ever since. It is fitting that the spirit of Spain's *siglo de oro* at the moment of deception and defeat should have inspired the greatest masterpiece in her literature. *Don Quixote* is the most wonderful parable, of inexhaustible humanity and unfathomable profundity, on the theme of disillusionment in life. There is an edge on Cervantes's treatment of his hero that reveals the autobiographical inspiration. Cervantes, too, had had his romantic illusions about achievement in the real world of action : he had fought at Lepanto, lost the use of his hand there, been captured by the Moors on his way home with despatches recommending his promotion, spent five years as a slave in Algiers, returned home to find that nobody wanted him ; he spent the rest of his life in a grinding struggle, frustrated, unsuccessful, poor, maintaining a house full of squabbling women. Out of his frustration in the real world, as is the way with the highest art—with the *Divine Comedy, Paradise Lost,* the Ninth Symphony—he created an enduring inner world that reflects it and transcends it. Don Quixote is " the incarnation of the spirit of non-compromise. When the fit is on him he believes in his own absolute rightness and virtue, and then nothing can deflect him from the course he has chosen. We call his moral passion and inflexibility noble because it appears to override self-interest, though modern psychologists have given a different interpretation to such states of mind. And we notice that whatever he does at such times ends in failure, because it takes no account of reality." [1]

That is exactly what happened to Spain at the end of the sixteenth century.

The impact of the war on this country was in striking contrast. It was in the course of it that England achieved maturity, became a modern state, where Spain remained a medieval country with a large empire overseas. We have already noticed that England could take the war in its stride, its society flexible and resilient, and that its strength and resources grew in spite of the war. The war may be seen, in large part, as the conse-quence of the nation's growing strength, the irresistible impulse towards expansion, which Corbett sees as " the great outcome of the Elizabethan regeneration ". [2] The Elizabethan English fought for the future : they disputed the Atlantic and the New World with Spain : they won their place in it. We can watch

[1] Gerald Brenan, *The Literature of the Spanish People,* 197.
[2] Corbett, *op. cit.* 406.

in our later history the fulfilment of these chances, the flowering on the oceans and overseas, for which the Elizabethans fought.

One further reflection : the war was fought very prudently and wisely, with the least drain—so far as the Queen could help it—upon the country's resources, so far as might be " with least loss of English blood ". Throughout the war one sees the Queen's government careful to keep in touch with the nation's feeling, restraining its excesses, moderating its expectations, but always associating the people with its cause ; trying to make clear its responsibilities to them, subtly and immediately responsive to their griefs and complaints. In the last stages of the war, when the burdens grew heavy[1] and war-weariness spread, we observe the Queen's government taking care at every step to explain its case to the people, in speeches of the Queen and her ministers to Parliament, in the preambles to legislation, in messages to the long-suffering counties groaning under their burdens. The Queen spent on the war practically all the lands that had come to the Crown by the Dissolution : an immense loss to the monarchy, but none to the nation, which gained by it. The long Elizabethan war, like our recent wars in the twentieth century, had their effect, which has never been assessed and hardly realised, upon the country's social and constitutional evolution. In the last months of her life one finds the Queen, unable to meet the expense of raising a fleet for convoy duty in the Channel, appealing for contributions for an auxiliary fleet of private ships. The voice of opposition had already been heard,[2] and in the draft of the appeal " we see the old Queen sounding its exact value as Cecil pens its corrections. All his additions are designed to make it clear that the whole scheme is voluntary, that the

[1] Cf. Sir John Fortescue, Chancellor of the Exchequer, to Sir Robert Cecil, 28 June 1598. " Her Majesty's great want is such as for the present payments . . . my Lord, your father, and myself are so much aggrieved as we know not whither to turn ourselves. We have called in all customers, receivers and collectors, the receiver for the Court of Wards, and now lastly must press you [as Chancellor of the Duchy of Lancaster], praying you to cause the receiver general of the Duchy to pay into the Receipt all the money that remains in his hands, for all will be too little to supply the present necessity." *Salisbury MSS*. VIII. 236.

[2] In return for an unprecedented grant of four subsidies to the government the Commons of 1602 were permitted an unprecedented liberty in discussing affairs of state. A Mr. Peake, M.P. for Sandwich, complained that he was always hearing of her Majesty's charges, " but what ensueth or cometh of it, I never yet knew ". One recognises the phrase of a fool, but there was only one member of that Parliament to give utterance to it. Cf. Corbett, 359-60.

government is merely paternally organizing an undertaking for the benefit of the community which the community had no machinery to organize for itself. She claims no right to levy the money, nor even to administer it when levied. It is simply that she sets on foot a national insurance company governed by a national board of directors, to which she gives special privileges to ensure its success. . . . Surely no sovereign ever felt the beat of her people's heart so justly as the wizened old Queen, who, after leading them so far and so high, could still stoop patiently to listen, with one foot already in the grave."[1]

It is a just tribute from a man of action who wrote the story of her war at sea from their point of view, not hers. And it would seem that *all* the subsequent themes of our history take their rise then.

Our interest in the fact of sea-power in itself, in the sheer fascination of the story of sea-warfare, has led us to neglect its consideration as an expression of society. Perhaps we may put it in perspective by a few reflections in themselves obvious enough.

The whole history of this country has been largely determined by the fact of our inhabiting an island, by its character and geographical situation. Sea-power was therefore natural and indispensable to it : its first line of defence at all times and, when the society achieved integration and maturity, abounded with energies seeking outlet, its chief means of expansion and aggression. We must not say, however, that it was all-in-all to us, as it was to the Dutch. In our period the Dutch owed everything to it : preservation of their liberty and independence, their food, their trade and raw materials, their wealth, expansion overseas, empire. The Dutch lived by the sea and concentrated everything on it ; for half a century the new state, that had emerged as a *protégé*, took the lead of England.[2]

The English state rested on a more balanced foundation : it was primarily a sea-power, but the size and rich resources of the wonderful island gave it greater staying power. On land it was never negligible, once its resources were fully

[1] Corbett, 398-9.
[2] Cf. Ralegh's *Works, ed. cit.* VIII. 300. Though the Dutch were less apt for soldiers, their armies being strengthened by English, Scots, French and Germans, they were able by James's reign " to put forth more ships of war and mariners than all England and Scotland can do, in shorter time ", and " are become the most orderly and best disciplined men of war by sea in all Europe ".

deployed ; though, as such, history shows how easy it has been for people to underestimate the island-state.

The commonplaces of sea-power were well understood, though perhaps not all its advantages finely appreciated. A poem of the fifteenth century, *The Libel of English Policy*, is wholly devoted to the subject. In his usual way of elevating commonplace to poetry, Shakespeare expresses the heart of the matter : to us the sea is

> as a moat defensive to a house
> Against the envy of less happier lands.

The sea was England's moat : " Look to your Moat ", said the great Lord Halifax.

With us, therefore, sea-power rested on the natural basis— was a natural expression—of the sea-concerns of the island people all round the coasts : the coastal and river communications, which were cheaper and easier than those by land ; the fisheries about the coasts, in all the seas around the islands and, in our period, expanding notably across the Atlantic to Newfoundland and in northern waters ; commerce, which expanded along with it the striking power and strength of the Queen's navy.

These various aspects, as they arise out of and influence the society, are already reflected in this book, when one looks into it. There are the two main areas, balancing each other and with interesting inter-relations, London and the West Country. In the earlier part of the reign the West Country gentry—who were all adherents of the Protestant Elizabeth—were much to the fore, in operations that combined commerce with privateering, merging into piracy. Hand in glove with them were the soberer, but not less tough, merchants of the towns of Plymouth, Dartmouth, Exeter, Bristol. We have seen that as the reign went on London exerted an increasing pull, with its expanding trade, larger ships and larger capital resources. An interesting indication of the pull is the way John Hawkins leaves Plymouth for London, and transfers his interests mainly there. Drake, who continues to base himself on the West Country, comes frequently to Court, to Parliament or the City where he has many friends. The West Country group is strongly represented in Parliament and we find its members regularly serving on all committees to deal with sea matters.

The sea offered much better chances of rising in society

than services in the army did. Commanders were usually gentlemen of good family ; but Hawkins, Drake and Frobisher were not the only new men to rise by the sea. The Crosses, Fenners and Winters—and fine fighting sailors they were—rose from no particular families to command the Queen's ships. And under Drake's command[1] one finds an agreeable social mix-up : West Country gentlemen like James Erisey, John Grenville, John St. Leger, Ambrose Mannaton, commanding ships along with professionals like George Fenner and Robert Flicke, a big merchant like James Lancaster, small Plymouth merchants like James Fownes, or John Young, or men of no family like Hannibal Sharpham who commanded the *Heart's-ease*, William Coxe the *Delight*, John Grisling the *Nightingale*. It must have been a school of good comradeship and perhaps of good citizenship.

At bottom were the seamen, recruited mainly from the sailors of the ports, from the fishermen and from the Thames wherrymen. We have seen with what trouble the government encouraged and stimulated the fisheries—two fish days a week imposed by legislation and enforced—with the specific object of nursing man-power for the navy.[2] The Thames provided a useful reservoir for London ships : not less than 2000 small boats and wherries served passengers up and down London's main highway : there must have been a sailor population of not less than 6000 to draw upon.[3] There were plenty of men who went to sea of their own will ; but to man expeditions and fleets for special service impressment was the regular resort. Conditions of life, however, must await another chapter, another volume.

[1] *E.g.* in 1588, for which *v.* Laughton, *op. cit.* II. 326.
[2] Cf. my *England of Elizabeth*, 139-42.
[3] Cf. Stow's *Survey of London*, ed. Kingsford, I. 12. Stow says " whereby 3000 poor men at the least be set on work and maintained ", but this means only Thames watermen.

CHAPTER IX

WAR ON LAND: MILITARY ORGANISATION

I F this country was behindhand and needed to take tips in
shipbuilding and design from abroad, when naval power was
indispensable to its existence, how much more backward it
was in military matters and the art of war on land ! Behind its
moat it was about half a century belated in military developments : not until the country became involved in intervention
in the Low Countries, from 1572 onwards, did we begin to catch
up. If any hostile power had managed to break through the
barrier of naval power, it would have been a very serious matter—
as serious as it would have been in 1940. For, on the Continent,
a revolution in warfare was taking place and gathering momentum
as the century went forward : in the development of artillery,
but most of all in that of small firearms for infantry and cavalry,
bringing about radical changes in methods of fighting, in the
organisation of armies and the training of troops. During all
this, right up to more than half-way through Elizabeth's reign,
the main weapons of her forces, it is extraordinary to think,
were bills and bows.

The sixteenth century saw the transition—it seems impossible
to avoid the word—from medieval conditions of warfare to modern,
with the power of the state expressed in increasing organisation,
gradually taking over the functions of former feudal levies and
private armies. It is the change-over from the old inefficient
militia to regular trained army—but with how sad steps and
slow ! The key to the organisation of the modern army may be
said to be the grouping of companies into the larger unit known
as the regiment, with the emergence of the office of Colonel
as the intermediate between the General and the captains of
independent companies. This indispensable officer makes his
appearance on the Continent about 1520. It was not until fifty
years later, in 1572, that the English woke up to the necessity

of his function, when Sir Humphrey Gilbert was sent to the Netherlands with a number of companies grouped under him as Colonel.

The time-lag is equally marked whether in weapons or drill, training or organisation. Behind our sea-walls, it seems the islands went on with their out-of-date medieval warfare, variegated with some unpleasant episodes when foreign mercenaries were imported with their nasty modern methods—which did not make them any more popular with the conservative islanders. Italy was the school of war in the early sixteenth century—in which the Spaniards emerged on top—as the Netherlands became in the later decades of the century. A contingent of hired Italian musketeers contributed to the victory of Pinkie in 1547. The revolting Cornish peasants were similarly treated in 1549—and little did they fancy their treatment; while German *landsknechts* helped to subdue the Norfolk peasants. In 1560 the English came up against French musketry in their assault on Leith and were repulsed with heavy losses. It was sea-power that decided the issue in Scotland.

The Spaniards were the first to arm their infantry with large-calibred muskets.[1] (We may note as part of the charming fantasy of the age that they were called " mosquitos ", as the larger weapons with their flying projectiles were called after drakes and falcons.) The Spanish arquebusiers became the first in Europe, and for long their infantry deserved their fame as unbeatable. They owed this, as French and English agreed, not to any superiority as a fighting people, but to their discipline, strange as that may seem to us, their obedience, their good order and *esprit de corps*. The Spanish troops were good *camarades* ; the English had to unlearn their individualist ways, their enterprising insubordination, so useful to them at sea. England was the last important state to go to school in modern warfare : the advantage, and the danger, of insularity.

Similar radical changes had come about in cavalry tactics, from line to column, from shock action to missiles, from lance to pistol. The most successful mounted mercenaries were the German *reiters*, who, as might be expected of Germans, were proverbial for brutality all over Europe. Meanwhile, in the blissful island, as late as 1569 the militia, called out against the

[1] For the following paragraphs *v.* J. W. Fortescue, *History of the British Army*, I. 98 foll.

Northern Earls, had hardly any horse and only some sixty firearms among 2500 infantry.[1]

In England a standing army was unknown, and there was no effective general military organisation. The French war at the end of Mary's reign produced a statute requiring the middle and upper classes to equip themselves with armour and weapons according to their social grade and financial ability. Nothing could have been more eloquently anachronistic ; for full armour was going out of use and must have been familiar, hanging unscoured upon the wall, while the weapons prescribed were still bills and bows. The longbow continued, in good conservative fashion, to be exalted as the national weapon. It had had a famous past, at Crécy, Poitiers, Agincourt ; it was now out of date, but people would not recognise the fact. Even the military reformer, Sir John Smythe, as late as 1591 continued to defend it and sing its praises.[2] Not until 1595 was the verdict finally given in favour of the modernists against the bow, when the Privy Council ordered that not archers should be enrolled in the trained bands, but arquebusiers, caliver-men or musketeers.[3]

A second statute of Philip and Mary, "for the taking of Musters", was designed to stop evasion of national service. Captains were in the regular habit of letting men off for bribes ; they also lined their own pockets by withholding the men's pay, appropriating dead-pays, keeping the numbers of the companies as low as possible, filling them up with hired stop-gaps on muster-days and in all the little ways so well known to Sir John Falstaff, Lieutenant Bardolph, Corporal Nym and Ancient (*i.e.* Ensign) Pistol. There was a saying that a captain's company was all the freehold and riches he had.[4] A fundamental difficulty of principle was that the county levies, organised such as they were on a county basis, were not liable for service beyond their boundaries, except in case of invasion.[5] Elaborate arrangements were drawn up in 1588 and after, for county levies to move

---

[1] J. W. Fortescue, "The Army : Military Service and Equipment", in *Shakespeare's England*, I. 113.

[2] There was this to be said for the bow, among other things—as Smythe and even the technician Thomas Digges pointed out in his *Stratioticos*—that bowmen could deliver a far more rapid and concentrated fire than arquebusiers, who could only fire rank by rank then fall back to reload : complicated movements demanding time, skill and training.

[3] Cf. Sir Charles Oman, *History of the Art of War in the Sixteenth Century*, 380-4.

[4] *Salisbury MSS.* XIV. 104.

[5] C. G. Cruickshank, *Elizabeth's Army*, 6.

across the boundaries to each other's aid at selected danger-points in case of invasion ; but it was perhaps as well that they were never called upon to be operated.

Such was the creaking archaic system with which the Elizabethans confronted the demands and stresses of a new age.

I

We perceive, even more clearly on land than at sea, the fundamental change from the pattern of our medieval wars—the struggle with France across the Channel, with Scotland a back-door enemy on the Border—to that of our modern wars, the island united, the core of coalitions of the smaller states fighting for their independence against overweening tyrannies and for the independence of Europe.

Elizabeth inherited Philip and Mary's war with France and their loss of Calais. It was a bitter pill for her to swallow at the beginning of her reign and, dependent as she was on Philip at the peace negotiations, she tried all in all not to have to. New to the job and as yet inexperienced, she had the courage to upbraid her commissioners for subservience to Philip ; she refused her acquiescence—she would break off negotiations if Philip did.[1] Neither Philip nor Henry II had any intention of renewing the war for her *beaux yeux* : they were both itching to get to grips with their heretics. At length Elizabeth had to agree to the *de facto* retrocession of Calais ; but it may be said that she never gave up all hope of getting it back. Its recovery was a chief aim of her policy in the next decade or so ; and even at the end of her reign she tried hard to use Henry IV's necessities to bring pressure on him to give up Calais.

Elizabeth also confronted at her accession the hostility of the Auld Alliance in its most dangerous form. For the young Scottish Queen was married to the heir to the throne of France, and on her marriage had secretly demised her kingdom to the French Crown. She was next in hereditary succession to the English throne, too. What vast prospects this opened up, should Elizabeth die or be defeated, of a kingdom with its feet on the Mediterranean, its apex in the Orkneys ! Henry II, a simple-

[1] Cf. A. F. Pollard, *History of England, 1547–1603*, 195.

minded politician but a good soldier, could hardly ignore these tempting prospects for his son and daughter-in-law. He was engaged in pushing forward considerable reinforcements for Mary of Guise, who was ruling Scotland on her daughter's behalf and in the French interest, when he received his death-wound in a tournament. Mary Stuart, who had assumed the titles and arms of England on Mary Tudor's death, as her legitimate heir in many Catholic eyes abroad, now became Queen of France. Her ambitious Guise uncles took control of her interests and managed to send 1000 reinforcements to their sister in Scotland.

For French rule had produced a reaction in Scottish national feeling that coincided with the hot-gospelling of Knox and the spread of Calvinism against an established Catholicism more than usually effete and corrupt. The Protestant Lords of the Congregation, with English promises, a little money and even less cohesion, took to the field and active resistance to French rule. The premature attempt of Henry VIII and Somerset to force a sensible unity of the island upon Scotland had failed and produced a reaction in favour of France. Now Elizabeth had a Scottish party ready to hand, ready to co-operate with her, dependent on her support.

The problem was how to intervene by force in the affairs of another sovereign with whom she was at peace ; how to give support, without incriminating herself, to rebels against lawful authority. These difficulties have never proved insuperable to the necessary casuistry of politicians. In the last months of Elizabeth's life, when Mary Stuart's son was waiting patiently to take Elizabeth's place, Robert Cecil wrote, in a fascinating letter to his crony and agent, the Master of Gray : " trust no more than you think is wisdom for a prince to observe, for what formalities soever princes observe in these days of giving such words, I see most of them think they are bound to nothing that is evil for themselves ; wherein they say they break not as out of lack of honesty, but because as kings they are tied to do that which concurs with their commonwealths' utility, for whom they are born, and not for themselves." [1] We knew well enough that rulers acted in accordance with *raison d'état*, but never was there such a statement from one in the best position to observe : it is unique in the correspondence of Robert Cecil.

[1] *Salisbury MSS.* XIV (Addenda), 249.

The real problem, as always in politics, was to assess the relative weights of the opposing forces, the lengths to which wills would go. The country, as we have seen, was out of date in military force and equipment, dependent on foreign supplies for ordnance and ammunition, and even the navy was not up to scratch. Argument over the pros and cons of intervention swayed to and fro within the Council. Cecil's keen strategic eye saw that now was the moment : he pressed intervention on the Queen. An old Scots prophecy foretold the great change when there should be two winters in Scotland in one year. That winter Admiral Winter was sent with the fleet to lie in the Forth, but with negative instructions, merely to observe the French.[1] The Council concluded that it was too dangerous to sustain open hostility to the French. The insufferable Feria multiplied his warnings and reprehensions : the Queen had " no friends, no council, no finances, no noblemen of conduct, no captains, no soldiers, and no reputation in the world ".[2] He lectured Elizabeth's ambassador in Brussels : " What meaneth your Queen ? Is this a meet time picked forth to exasperate the French ? She rather had need by all good means to put off war. Doth she not know her own weakness and the rawness of her affairs ? Are Arran's or Throckmorton's persuasions worth such an adventure ? "[3]

It was the sense of her weakness that held the Queen back ; what no-one gauged so well as Cecil was the inherent strength of England's position, and we can watch his successive drafts getting stronger and stronger. Moreover, he was replenishing our depleted stocks of arms through Gresham in the Low Countries. Elaborate information was obtained as to the strength the Lords of the Congregation could put forth—which revealed the extreme weakness of the Scottish state as such. At length the Protestant Norfolk was sent north, still with defensive instructions. Weather came to the aid of the English : in January 1560 a strong French reinforcement under d'Elbœuf was driven back from the North Sea, with the loss of six or seven vessels.[4] Norfolk now gave Winter instructions to act on his own responsibility in regard to the French ships lying in the Forth : a blockade took shape. In February Norfolk signed the Treaty of Berwick with the Scottish Lords, assuring them of armed aid :

[1] *Cal. S.P. For. 1559–60*, 199.   [2] q. Pollard, 230.
[3] *Cal. S.P. For. 1559–60*, 170–1.   [4] *Ibid.* 287.

they needed it : they made a very poor show in the field, against the Regent's professional soldiers. Still hesitation. In March Cecil assured the Catholic Earl of Huntly : " the Queen meaneth princely and, like a good neighbour, to relieve the declination of that kingdom of Scotland ".[1] Cecil had nothing to learn in the way of diplomatic language. His subsequent Proclamation of the Causes moving the Queen to intervene placed it on an entirely defensive footing—defending Scotland from direct French intervention and England from indirect ; even so, the action was directed not against France, but against the aggression of the House of Guise.[2] This was well calculated to appeal to Catherine de Medici and all those in France who had no love for the Guises. Moreover, it was the truth—and English policy has never underrated the moral advantage of establishing a right relation with the truth.

Elizabeth and Cecil were, in time, to have lifelong practice in these equivocal situations : they came to be second nature to the Queen, and it was rarely that she was caught out. The setting was now ready for the situation to be clarified by force. The army was sent forward into Scotland, under that not very fortunate soldier the thirteenth Lord Grey. (He had been stuck through the mouth with a pike at Pinkie ; he was in command at Calais and Guisnes when they had been forced to surrender ; the ransom of 20,000 crowns he was forced to pay permanently impaired his estate.) His instructions forbade him to attack Edinburgh Castle, where the Regent lay, and which he could easily have captured. He was to attack the French in their entrenched position at Leith.

Norfolk was jubilant : " now they shall know that her Majesty will go through, either by fair or foul means. . . . There be others that cast perils, if the sky fall we shall have larks."[3] Early in April there was a hot skirmish outside Leith, in which over a hundred fell on each side. The Queen sent her commendations to the officers, like young Tremayne, who had done well.[4] But it was clear that the French, though inferior in numbers, were far better equipped and superior in fighting. On 7 May Grey ordered an assault on Leith—with scaling ladders six feet too short. The English were repulsed with serious losses, some eight hundred dead and wounded in the trenches. At once

[1] *Salisbury MSS.* I. 193.   [2] *Ibid.* 197-8.
[3] *Ibid.* 212.   [4] *Ibid.* 209, 211.

the Queen ordered new levies to reinforce her shaken army, " as the enterprise must be achieved for the honour and safety of the realm ".[1]

Sea-power and luck accomplished what the antiquated military forces could not. The fleet blockaded the French so that no supplies could get through ; on 10 July the stout-hearted Regent died in Edinburgh Castle. Cecil's diplomacy completed the rest. He hurried north and on 6 July the treaty of Edinburgh ended French rule in Scotland and the Auld Alliance for ever. It was the first resounding achievement of the reign and its implications were immeasurable. For the practical purposes of foreign policy, the island might henceforth be regarded as one : no longer the insecurity of the client-state of an enemy on the Border. The great fortress of Berwick arose to clinch the matter and overawe Edinburgh. Where her father had run into defeat by precipitating matters, Elizabeth was prepared to wait—in the event, all her life, till the union she had prepared came with the accession of her rival's son to her own throne. Though the thought gave her no pleasure at all, it was one of those things she worked for as concurring with her " commonwealth's utility ". In her first venture in war she had had great luck—in the death of Henry II, in that of Mary of Guise, as ultimately in Mary Stuart's persistence in Catholicism. It would seem that, in addition to intelligence and ability, a politician must have luck.

Elated by their triumph in Scotland, Elizabeth and Cecil were led on, at the outbreak of the first French War of Religion in 1562, to try and play the same game in France. Their aim was to get Calais back, as had been promised by the treaty of Cateau-Cambrésis ; and to this end they made a treaty with Condé, as leader of the Huguenots, permitting the English to occupy Havre until Calais should be restored. The Queen asserted that she was acting by the advice of the young Charles IX's councillors in his defence.[2] Such formulae, which were apt to shock nineteenth-century historians, we have become accustomed to in our own disagreeable century, which has so much more in common with the sixteenth than had the civilised nineteenth century.

[1] *Salisbury MSS.* I. 219-20.
[2] *Cal. S.P. For. 1562*, 364.

In October the English occupied Havre, called by them New-haven—a town of no strength and no fortification except a little earth thrown up around it.[1] Their munitions had not arrived, and the whole episode was to prove a sorry record of inexperience and incompetence, bravery and useless suffering. The forces were under the command of that rather ineffective figure Ambrose Dudley, Earl of Warwick, Leicester's elder brother. Charles IX's reply to the English seizure of Havre and Dieppe was to appeal to French national feeling : the war was not now about religion, but for the preservation of the Crown.[2] This undermined the moral position of the Huguenots—such as it was. Elizabeth replied that Francis II had usurped the title and arms of England and sent forces into Scotland ; that the treaty of Edinburgh remained unratified and the fortifications of Calais dismantled contrary to the treaty of Cateau-Cambrésis.[3] Excuses can always be found for anything anybody wants to do in politics. In the disingenuous exchanges that took place between Elizabeth and Catherine de Medici, Elizabeth got decidedly the worst of the argument : after all, Catherine replied, would not a peaceful *ambassade* be the proper way to settle these grievances ?[4]

The French political parties proceeded with their little war in the name of religion. The Huguenots did badly. Rouen fell —where Henry Killigrew was wounded and taken prisoner.[5] Guise, who had hanged a number of the English and sent English and Scots—now fighting together—to the galleys, would have put Killigrew to death if it had not been for Marshal Damville. Catherine sent for this important prisoner : he lived to become one of the most indefatigable of Elizabeth's diplomatic envoys. Condé was defeated and captured at the battle of Dreux ; he came to terms with the Queen Mother to expel the English. They were left without support, a war with France on their hands ; and, where in Scotland they had had national sentiment with them, in France they were fighting against this strongest of all political forces.

The garrison at Havre consisted of some 4535 soldiers and 229 pioneers, with a band of 50 Scots horse.[6] The English had command of the sea and were sending in reinforcements. But nothing like enough : Warwick complained that he needed

[1] *Ibid.* 354.   [2] *Ibid.* 376.
[3] *Ibid.* 397.   [4] *Ibid.* 431.
[5] *Ibid.* 442, 456.   [6] *Ibid.* 504.

2000 pioneers if he were to fortify the town adequately before the French invested it.[1] His engineering expert was Portinari —no-one in England would have been sufficiently skilled in the art of fortification at this date. And indeed, during the first half of the reign, it was Italian experts who carried out the most important works of this kind. From the Tower, which was the ordnance depôt, came supplies; but they were hopelessly deficient and antiquated : the iron pieces were unserviceable ; no axle-trees, stocks or wheels for the cannon ; rods for ramrods were short ; much of the shot was decayed, there were no bow-strings nor arrows for the archers ; the carpenters sent were ignorant of military requirements.[2] From Berwick, the chief active base in the country, came reinforcements of fighting men, a few bands of pistoliers, the only horsemen properly equipped for modern warfare on the Continent.

In May 1563, Havre was invested by the French. Early in June, plague broke out among the English in the town. By the 9th, deaths were at 20-30 a day ; by the end of the month 60 a day ; by mid-July they were 100 and towards the end even reached 120.[3] The garrison was down to only 1500 effectives. There was no point in sending any further reinforcements in such conditions. A further 1300 who were ready to go over were stayed, and on July 24 the haven was lost. Warwick kept a good spirit to the last, though complaining bitterly of want of supplies. The only thing to do was to surrender and get out. During those two terrible months, of the total force of 5500 and 2000 reinforcements sent, 2600 men died. It was the soldiers returning from Havre who brought the severe plague of 1563 into the realm.

There were naturally invasion alarms along the south coast that summer. But the French did not want war and were in no condition to wage it. Peace was made at Troyes in 1564. Throckmorton, whose Huguenot sympathies had warped his judgment and made him misjudge the situation, was very properly retired and his place as ambassador taken by the more sedate Smith. The Queen and Cecil took their lesson to heart : they would take no more chances on other people's promises : they would rely only on their own resources and take no course for

---

[1] *Cal. S.P. For. 1562*, 573.   [2] *Cal. S.P. For. 1563*, ix.
[3] *Ibid.* and cf. David Stewart, " Sickness and Mortality Rates of the English Army in the Sixteenth Century ", *Journal Roy. Army Medical Corps*, July 1948, 33.

which these were not adequate. Wary and *rusé* by nature, they had received a smarting reminder that it was well to be even more so in the game of politics.

From the technical point of view, the high rate of casualties among the horsemen is to be observed : evidence of the effectiveness of the new firearms. For examples of this and for the life of the army at this time, let us look at the brothers Nicholas and Andrew Tremayne, who were well liked and well known in their day, both killed in France that summer. They were twin sons of Edmund Tremayne, Clerk of the Privy Council : they were so much alike physically and in mind and temperament that people had difficulty in telling them apart, nor is it easy to keep them separate in mind today. Risdon tells us that " they agreed in mind and affections as much as in body ; for what one loved, the other desired ; so on the contrary the loathing of the one was the dislike of the other. Yea, such a confederation of inbred power and sympathy was in their natures that if Nicholas was sick and grieved, Andrew felt the like pain, though they were far distant and remote in their persons ; and this without any intelligence given unto either party. And what is further observable, if Andrew was merry, Nicholas was so affected, although in different places : which long they could not endure to be, for they ever desired to eat, drink, sleep and wake together. Yea, so they lived and so died." [1]

They had an exciting youth, owing to their father's support of Elizabeth when princess and of the Courtenay conspiracy against Mary. Andrew fled the country with Sir Peter Carew ; he returned, and both twins were imprisoned for their doings in the Channel, but escaped to France. Again, they were involved in Sir Anthony Kingston's plot in 1556. On Elizabeth's accession they were taken into her service—of such stuff were her supporters made. At Leith Andrew led a brilliant charge of his horse-band, while the Queen employed Nicholas in special services carrying despatches.

In May 1562 we find a charming letter from a fellow officer at Berwick, giving us a glimpse of garrison life there. [2] Nicholas is away at Court, but his lieutenant is merry, keeps his company in good order and his horses are in health, fair and fat. When he comes back, let him bring a good bowl with him : he is sure

---

[1] q. in J. Prince, *Worthies of Devon* (ed. 1810), 741.
[2] *Cal. S.P. For. 1562*, 22.

to be challenged, my Lord (*i.e.* Grey) being a doctor at it. But in December Nicholas is at Portsmouth with his band of fifty horse ; he will leave his brother Andrew to look after them till transport is ready.[1] From Havre he asks for fifty lances to furnish his band.[2]

In February 1563 Andrew spent two or three days at the Scottish Court, where the Queen and whole Court took very well to him ; he brought a ring as a token of her love from Lady Throckmorton to Marie de Béthune, one of the Queen's four Maries.[3] In April the Privy Council, which in general appointed the captains, gave Nicholas command of a hundred horse at Havre, so long as they were all English.[4] In May, in a skirmish with the Rhinegrave, Tremayne's horse drove him off with large losses.[5] On 26 May, in another encounter, he was slain with a pistolet at the left side of his head, by a chain-shot such as *reiters* use.[6] At the Court at Edinburgh the Queen expressed herself sorry for the death of " gentle Tremayne ", " no less lamented here than he is at home ".[7] By June eight or ten of the English captains had been killed—a high proportion ; but Tremayne's death had been revenged by five or six of the Rhinegrave's best captains being killed.[8]

In that month reinforcements were embarked direct from Berwick under Captains Carew and Andrew Tremayne : Andrew reports to Cecil that their bands are trained soldiers and of long service, to whom they have joined untrained men to make up the numbers to 200 apiece.[9] The keen young officer thought the Marshal of Berwick, deputy in Lord Grey's absence, unfit for the post : if it had not been for the Treasurer the troops would never have been got into order for embarkation. A month after his arrival Andrew followed his twin brother : on 18 July he was killed.[10]

In their death they were not divided. Now they may be seen, looking towards each other, portrayed upon the tomb put up in Armada year in the church at Lamerton, the parish church of the house at Collacombe, amid the green lanes and hills between Tamar and Tavy that knew them as boys.

[1] *Cal. S.P. For. 1562,* 559.   [2] *Ibid.* 573.
[3] *Cal. S.P. For. 1563,* 169, 435.   [4] *Ibid.* 293.   [5] *Ibid.* 360.
[6] *Ibid.* 371.   [7] *Ibid.* 399.   [8] *Ibid.* 390.
[9] *Ibid.* 377, 386.   [10] *Ibid.* 459.

II

For the next two decades we were at peace with foreign powers, though towards the end of the period we were being drawn increasingly into unofficial intervention in the struggle in the Netherlands : not till 1585 did we intervene openly, as an act of state.

Meanwhile, the young men who wanted to gain experience of soldiering went abroad to fight—young bloods like Richard Grenville and his companions, William Gorges, Philip Budockshide, Sir John Smythe and Henry Champernowne went off to Hungary in 1566 to fight against the Turk.[1] On their return Champernowne and Budockshide went to the French wars, taking Walter Ralegh and Francis Berkeley with them.[2] Here, too, Sir John Norris—famous " Black Norris " of later days—got his first training under Coligny. And there was always Ireland for rough fighting : that was no school of training for the new warfare.

This surplus energy got its outlet and found a focus in the war in the Netherlands, from 1572 on. For four years a sullen, sporadic resistance had been put up to the monstrous tyranny of Alva's administration ; now, in the spring of this year, a sudden popular insurrection sprang up all over the country. With no understanding of sea-power, the Spaniards had neglected to fortify Flushing, which, though then only a poor fishing town —nothing compared with what it became afterwards—yet had the strategic potentiality of becoming the key to Zealand. Greatly unsure of themselves, " without town, fort, fortress or village to friend in all that country ", its seamen and burgesses threw out their Spanish garrison, received a contingent of Walloons and Flemings from the Prince of Orange, and asked for aid from their sympathisers in London.

Sir Roger Williams gives us the gist of what happened. " At this time there was a fair muster of Londoners before the Queen's Majesty at Greenwich. Amongst the Londoners were divers captains and soldiers who had served, some in Scotland, some in Ireland, others in France. And having nothing to do,

---

[1] Camden, *History* (ed. 1675), 82.
[2] *Ibid.* 137.

with the countenance of some great men who favoured the cause and the small helps of the deputies of Flushing, Captain Thomas Morgan levied a fair company of three hundred strong ; amongst whom were divers officers which had commanded before, with many gentlemen, at the least above one hundred, amongst which myself was one."[1]

We see the picture : the large number of gentlemen-volunteers from whom officers could be made ; the beginning of the long history of the English regiments in the Low Countries until they won their independence. Fortescue, perhaps a little flamboyantly, regards that May Day review at Greenwich as the birth of the British Army.[2]

We are fortunate to have this first phase of our modern military history written by one who took part in it, in an admirable Elizabethan book. With the concise writing of this soldier, one finds oneself rushing forward to see what happens— as is not often the case with Elizabethan books, which are apt to be too wordy and to move at too slow a pace. This is not so with Roger Williams's *The Actions of the Low Countries*, whose writing deserves Hayward's commendation as his bravery did Manwood's tribute. Unfortunately, the book ends with this first phase : we may curse the ass of a servant who lost the rest of his papers : a full account of his career in the wars might well have been a masterpiece.

For Roger Williams's life was that of a full-time soldier spent wholly in the wars ; a young soldier of fortune becoming a professional : it is very characteristic. Of an old Monmouthshire family, he began life as a page to the first Earl of Pembroke and may have been with him at St.-Quentin. After the first phase of fighting under Thomas Morgan and Sir Humphrey Gilbert, 1572–4, he was returning penniless and without employment from Germany when he ran into Julián Romero, most famous of Spanish infantry commanders, whose portrait by El Greco as a penitent in the cloak of the Order of Santiago we may see in the church of the Trinidad at Toledo.[3] Williams then served with the Spaniards, under Romero, then Mondragón and in the household of Don Juan, for the next three years, learning the methods of war in the finest school in Europe, building up

[1] Sir Roger Williams, *The Actions of the Low Countries* (1618), 56.
[2] J. W. Fortescue, *History of the British Army*, I. 134.
[3] For Romero, *v.* Antonio Marichalar, Marqués de Montesa, *Julián Romero*.

that knowledge of the Spanish discipline from the inside which is the real subject of his *Brief Discourse of War*.

In 1577 he joined Norris's force in the Netherlands and for the next seven years served as his second in command. A convincing anecdote shows him scoring off the Queen on a visit to Court to press some suit. The Queen, to get rid of him and always sensitive to smell, said, " Faugh, Williams, I prithee begone : thy boots stink ". To which Williams replied, " Tut, madam, 'tis my suit that stinks ". It is characteristic, too, of the simple joke Elizabethans enjoyed. In 1586 Williams, emulating a famous exploit of Romero's, performed an astonishing *coup*, when with a company of English lances he penetrated the Spanish lines one night and got as far as Parma's tent, where he killed the secretary. By now the English were becoming more professional. But they were not the less exhibitionist. At the siege of Doesburg he was wounded : " I warned him of it ", wrote Leicester, " being in trench with me, and would need run up and down so oft out of the trench, with a great plume of feathers in his gilt morion, as so many shot coming at him he could hardly escape with so little hurt ".[1] We know from Williams that Sir Thomas Baskerville could be recognised at the defence of Sluys by his great plume of feathers, and Sir Francis Vere by his red mandilion (*i.e.* jerkin). Leicester had the highest opinion of him : " Roger Williams is worth his weight in gold, for he is no more valiant than he is wise and of judgment to govern his doings ".[2] After the action of Zutphen, not far from Arnhem, where Philip Sidney got his death-wound, Williams was knighted by Leicester.

At the time of the Armada he was serving under Leicester at Tilbury.[3] Next year he left the Low Countries for the Normandy campaign, taking part in a dashing attack at Dieppe. In 1592 he performed another exploit, and continued to serve mostly in France until his death in 1595. It was then found that he had left everything he had, gold and silver, plate, apparel, horses, to Essex—darling of all the soldiers—to whom he had dedicated his *Discourse* with his love.

Williams tells us that Morgan's troops were " the first perfect arquebusiers that were of our nation and the first troops that ·taught our nation to like the musket "—evidently they graduated

---

[1] *Leicester Correspondence*, ed. J. Bruce, Camden Soc., 407.
[2] *Ibid.* 430.   [3] *v.* below, p. 362.

quickly from one to the other. (It was Alva who introduced the musket into the Low Countries and first practised it on the unwarlike Netherlanders : no wonder he was, with inferior forces, master of the field.)

The English acquitted themselves well at their first skirmish outside Flushing : " our men so behaved themselves that the enemy lost three for one ".[1] Next day they had the vanguard and, " to make the skirmish the more honorable we sallied with our ensigns ". Morgan posted his men well, guarding a causeway and a bridge ; superior numbers forced the shot to retire, when, according to proper contemporary practice, Morgan " advanced resolutely to the push of pike " with his pikemen. It was a very hot fight : Morgan's ensign was surrounded by the enemy and bravely rescued by a band of young gentlemen. Several of these were slain, along with fifty soldiers : nearly a fifth of the whole force. The first English volunteers to fight in the Netherlands had been blooded.

Shortly after, Morgan got Sir Humphrey Gilbert to come over with some 1500 men—nine or ten companies forming the first of our regiments, with Gilbert as Colonel : which post Morgan " might easily have obtained for himself ". But, " to say troth, this captain had never any great ambition in him ; although fortune presented fair unto him often, beside this time ". Gilbert's first attempt was upon the important town of Sluys, outside which an ambush was posted : " in such sort that, at the opening of the gates (had our men known the wars as divers of them did since) we might easily have entered the town ". But " those that sent us were as ignorant as ourselves ", and the opportunity was lost. When Gilbert advanced, he was beaten back, and the governor of the town kept him several days in parley while bringing in reinforcements. Gilbert then summoned the town to surrender : he " was in great choler, swearing divers oaths that he would put all to the sword unless they would yield ". But this was not Ireland, where he had terrorised the natives. His fellow commander, the governor of Flushing, persuaded him to pocket his humiliation and retire, for superior forces were drawing near. The English retreat was so disorderly that the regiment might easily have been cut up.

Gilbert's next attempt was on Goes, on the neighbouring

---

[1] The quotations in the above paragraphs are from Williams's *Actions, passim* whose account I follow.

island of South Beveland. Here, the vanguard, with Rowland Yorke and Williams, fell into an ambush and most of them were killed : " such as escaped swam and struggled through muddy ditches ". At the first alarm Gilbert and his men halted, " and not without marvel ; for, I persuade myself, the most of them were afraid. I am to blame to judge their minds, but let me speak troth." Meanwhile, the Spaniards were withdrawing from their exposed position at Ziericksee, and Gilbert lost a fine chance to cut them off. " Sir Humphrey should have directed at least half his troops to cut betwixt them and the town. . . . Some may say perhaps there were no ways, or he knew of none." But " a commander that enters the enemy's countries ought to know the places that he doth attempt. If not, he ought to be furnished with guides. But we were so ignorant that we knew not our own estate, much less the enemy's."

A second attempt was made on Goes ; this time a direct assault by night, with " some two thousand of our best men, all in *camisados*[1] with scaling ladders, God knows like ignorant soldiers : else we would never have attempted a *scalado* on such a troop ". For the town was well defended by trained soldiers, who withheld their fire until the assailants were fully exposed and ready to enter. A murderous fire drove them back with heavy losses. " This attempt so quailed our courage that we despaired of the town." Meanwhile, Mondragón was bringing reinforcements 3000 strong and managed to get them across to the island by wading at low water. " Judge you what would have become of his troops had we been commanded by expert governors and charged them at their landing with half our numbers." As it was, their landing was unimpeached ; it was the English and Dutch who took to their ships in such disorder that many were drowned, others slain or taken prisoners. " Thus ended our ignorant poor siege."

" Our blow was so great that Sir Humphrey and most of our men, not being acquainted with such disasters, sought all means to return into England." The Prince of Orange did all he could to retain Gilbert and his regiment in his service ; but Sir Humphrey had had enough : " all would not serve to stay either Sir Humphrey or any of his troops ". They returned to England having lost many good men and accomplished absolutely

---

[1] *i.e.* shirts, usually white for night operations, to distinguish friends from enemies in the dark.

nothing. But it was all in the way of apprenticeship to modern warfare and very much in the tradition of England's fighting, paying a heavy price for pitting amateurs against professionals. Shortly after, Sir William Pelham, Lieut.-General of the Ordnance, was sent to view Flushing : he reported that " it was a place not worthy to be kept, meaning not sufficient to withstand so great an enemy any long time. If that be true, we were not very great captains at that time ; for then without fellow he was accounted our chiefest soldier." Actually Flushing was made impregnable, the strategic key to all Zealand and the base for the entry of English forces into the Low Countries.

All the same, their experience was of value in training the professionals of the future ; those first days, when they were young and green, ardent and inexperienced, had a charm upon them—as such things have—to the men, grown old in war, looking back. One discerns the accent of nostalgia in Williams. Those were the days : we were the lads ! Morgan's lieutenant, Rowland Yorke, Captain Tristan and Ambrose Duke, the Walloon, were the leading spirits : " to say troth, these three were the minions in all attempts of our troops in those days ". Time brings its corruption : Tristan was killed ; Rowland Yorke died, a traitor, in Spanish service ; only brave old Roger remained, unharmed and untarnished.

A delightful survival, a pleasant piece of flotsam and jetsam direct from that time, has washed up and come to rest in the library at All Souls.[1] It is a volume of pretty drawings of the events of just those years, 1572–4, made by Walter Morgan, one of the captains serving in the Netherlands. There, portrayed for us with naïf vivacity and life-like detail so that we can see very much what they looked like, are the famous scenes that unfold themselves again as we turn over the pages : the taking of Brill that touched it all off, the capture of Rotterdam by the Spaniards, Alva's terrible massacres after the surrenders of Naarden and Haarlem ; the sea-fight off Flushing in which thirty-two Spanish skiffs and barges were scuppered ; the manœuvres by Orange and Alva in front of Mons, its surrender and Julián Romero's famous *camisado*, described by Roger Williams. Julián penetrated the enemy lines one night with his band,

---

[1] *v.* for an account of it, Sir Charles Oman, " Walter Morgan's Illustrated Chronicle of the War in the Low Countries, 1572–4 ", in the *Archaeological Journal*, 1930.

forced the guard around the Prince's tent, killed two of his secretaries and would have caught the Prince, if he had not been awakened in time by his dog. " Ever since, until the Prince's dying day, he kept one of that dog's race ; so did many of his friends and followers. The most or all of these dogs were white little hounds with crooked noses, called camuses." One sees them sometimes in the pictures of grandees of the time.

Walter Morgan was·one of several members of his clan who fought in the Low Countries. The eldest of them, Sir William, of Pen-y-coed in Glamorgan, joined the Huguenots just after Jarnac and took service with Louis of Nassau ; most of his subsequent career was spent in Ireland. Sir Thomas, whom we have seen in action, was altogether a Netherlands man and spent most of his life there. He married there—it was thought above him—a Dutch lady, daughter of the Baron van Merode, and this displeased the Dutch ; however, after his death, she married the Prince's illegitimate son, Justinus, so perhaps this was all right. Lord Willoughby, who quarrelled with him, thought him " a very sufficient gallant gentlemen ", but—strange for a Welshman—" unfurnished of language ". He, too, left a bequest to Essex, his best rapier and dagger ; to his nephew, Sir Matthew, his gilt armour. Our Captain Walter, of whom so little is known, " returned in the dead of this late winter [1573–4] to my native soil ", where he worked up his book of drawings to present to Lord Burghley.[1] He left half the book empty to complete them in the next round. For in the spring we hear of him going over with 500 soldiers ; and we never hear of him again : he must have died there.

After the withdrawal of Gilbert and his regiment, English contingents remained fighting in the Low Countries and volunteers continued to go over. A small number of Catholic exiles fought with the Spaniards ; Hugh Owen always remained at the centre of his web of conspiracy, intrigue, diplomacy. An English contingent was badly hammered by Alva outside of

---

[1] Sir Charles Oman missed Sir Roger Williams's references to Walter Morgan and did not know therefore that he was a captain. Williams says of him before the second attempt on Goes, " Captain Walter Morgan served very well ; who was overthrown with a musket shot in the head of the armed men ". The information from a Spanish spy (Oman, p. 6) that Bingham was a crypto-Catholic and would try to win over Morgan is obviously not to be trusted. Two Binghams were killed in action with the Dutch ; the third, Richard, became the well-known soldier in Ireland, Governor of Connaught.

Haarlem, its *laager* of wagons broken into and the unit cut up.[1]
At Rotterdam we find some bands of Scots with the Orangists,
and at the siege of Alkmaar there were 400 Scots with the
defenders.[2] English and Scots were becoming used to fighting
side by side : comradeship in the long war must have been a
useful preparative to the union, after the centuries of fighting
each other. The heroic defence of Alkmaar and Alva's resounding failure before it brought about his disgrace and recall :
his reign of terror had only resulted in a people's revolt. The
splendid Renaissance statue of himself in bronze, crushing
rebellion in the persons of Orange, Egmont and Horn, which
he erected in the square at Antwerp, was somewhat premature :
all that remains of it is the design one sees today among the
Alba Collections in Madrid. All the same, Roger Williams was
clear that if Alva had been left there and given support, he
would have subjugated the Netherlands : only force could do
it. But he was too great a subject ; Philip was afraid of his
becoming too powerful and successful—as he was of Don John
and Parma later : this, too, was a factor in Philip's losing the
Netherlands.

Requesens succeeded him with a policy of moderation (1574–6).
During this period came the celebrated siege of Leyden[3]—a
turning-point in the resistance : Orange at last found himself
heading a national movement and, for the time, a national
union. The revolt of the Netherlands became the prime problem
of European diplomacy, an issue immensely complicated and
confused. We cannot go into it here, except in so far as it drew
this country increasingly into war. We can only point out
a few fundamental considerations that shaped events. Philip
would never grant freedom of conscience, which the rebels
made a condition of peace—so the war had to go on. Elizabeth's
government genuinely wanted peace between the combatants.
English interests demanded that neither Spain nor France
should subjugate the Netherlands : their independence was a
prime objective of our policy. Elizabeth's calculation of our
interests was exact, and her defence of them brilliant ; but
it went against the grain with her to have to support rebels
against constituted authority, and she never liked the Dutch.

[1] Roger Williams, *op. cit.* 98.
[2] *Ibid.* 104, 111.
[3] There were English troops aiding the defence.

She had the same reason to complain against them as Canning had, in their habit of "giving too little and asking too much". On the other hand, the sympathies of the Prince of Orange were pro-French—necessarily so : he was a *grand seigneur* in culture and outlook, his principality of Orange was at their mercy, and he did not believe that the Queen would ever bring herself to intervene. The rest of Europe did not think she would dare ; but on the Prince's assassination—at Philip's orders—she had to, or see the Netherlands go under.

The year 1575, then, was taken up with complex negotiations. Requesens wanted to renew the alliance with England and to get the Queen to permit English exiles (rebels to her) to serve for him at sea, where Spain was inferior.[1] An embassy was sent to her, but she was not falling for that. At this, Orange sent an embassy asking her to undertake the protection of the Netherlands and their sovereignty. This hazardous offer of greatness she rejected—as no mere man would have done, certainly not her father.[2] She genuinely wanted the distracting differences composed. Then followed Requesens' death, mutinies of Spanish troops all over the southern Netherlands, their ghastly sack of Antwerp in November and a temporary Union and Pacification of the Provinces. All this was very bitter to Philip ; but Don John, his half-brother, was on his way to take over the government, with secret intentions to undo the settlement and recover the position. Alert and informed as always,[3] the Queen for security's sake advanced the States £20,000 on condition that they did not change their religion or prince, or receive the French into the Netherlands, or refuse a peace on reasonable conditions—a fairly clear indication of her objectives.[4]

Next year Don John broke out of the Pacification and renewed the war, administering a shattering defeat to the Netherlanders at Gemblours. At that, the Queen made a league with the States to send them large reinforcements : they became in effect a client-state, promising to enter into no alliance without her approbation, and in case of need to put their fleet under the Admiral of England. There were the usual complex exchanges and disingenuous explanations, but the Spaniards had to accept

[1] Cf. Camden, *History*, 207.

[2] We must make an exception for her grandfather : Henry VII would have resisted it.

[3] For English information as to his intentions, cf. *Cal. S.P. For. 1577–8*, xii.

[4] Camden, *op. cit.* 215.

the situation : they were at a disadvantage, for Don John had plotted against Elizabeth to seat Mary Stuart on the throne with himself beside her. Camden sums up the situation, as a contemporary later saw it : " Thus sate she as an heroical princess and umpire betwixt the Spaniards, the French and the States ; so as she might well have used that saying of her father, *Cui adhaereo, praeest*, that is, The party to which I adhere getteth the upper hand.[1] And true it was which one hath written, that France and Spain are as it were the scales in the balance of Europe, and England the tongue or the holder of the balance."[2] The classic pattern of our future policy was taking shape.

The next phase of intervention was dominated by a more effective, a more professional, soldier than Humphrey Gilbert : John Norris, second son of Henry, Lord Norris of Rycote. Henry had been called by his father after the king whose intimate he was. It was dangerous to be an intimate of Henry VIII : Henry killed him to inculpate Anne Boleyn. Elizabeth believed him innocent and was always kind to the son and his family. His six sons all served her : of whom only one came home to rest. The other five all died in action, fighting in her wars. The eldest died on service in Ireland in 1579 ; the youngest, Maximilian, was killed in Brittany in 1593. Henry and Edward went over with John in this year to serve their apprenticeship ;[3] and with Thomas, the brothers were serving together in Ireland in 1584. Edward made his career mainly in the Low Countries, where he became governor of Ostend. Henry, after service in the Low Countries, fought in Brittany and then became Colonel-General of the infantry in Ireland. The fifth son, Thomas, began as captain of a troop of horse in Ireland and had a distinguished career wholly there, succeeding his famous brother, John, as President of Munster. Worn out with service and his old wounds, John died in his brother's arms there in 1599. The same year, Thomas, wounded with a pike-thrust below the ear, died there ; so, too, Henry, after being wounded in the leg and bearing an amputation with " extraordinary patience ". The mother and father, at home at Rycote, must have needed

[1] We may note that Henry VIII had not been able to decide the balance : the English state was growing more powerful.

[2] Camden, 223.

[3] Camden makes the purpose clear : they went, he says, " to learn the rudiments of military discipline ", *op. cit.* 226.

all the majestic words of consolation the Queen had at the end of her pen : " Mine own crow ", she wrote to Lady Norris, who was dear to her, and she recalled the last son from service to comfort his parents. He did not long survive : ill in 1601, in 1603 he too was dead.

It is interesting to watch these families of professional soldiers, Norrises, Binghams, Morgans, Yorkes, Parkers, Veres : a feature of the age. One observes, too, the price paid for its greatness.

Another feature is the number of writers the war breeds. Three who became pals went over in that first contingent of Morgan's : Churchyard, Gascoigne and Barnabe Rich. Gascoigne, with his friends Rowland Yorke and William Herle, had a narrow escape when their drunken Dutch pilot ran their boat on the coast : twenty lads were drowned. He lived to distinguish himself at the siege of Middelburg, to be rewarded by the Prince, and to write up his adventures. They were all indefatigable journalists, writing up the news in prose or verse : precursors of our war correspondents. A promising young poet, Arthur Brooke—whose poem *Romeus and Juliet* was the source of Shakespeare's play—was drowned near Rye in the *Greyhound*, with nearly everyone on board, intending to go over to Havre in March 1563.[1] George Turberville writes of him in accents that Milton echoes :

> Ay me, that time, thou crooked Dolphin, where
> Wast thou, Arion's help and only stay,
> That safely him from sea to shore didst bear ?
> When Brooke was drowned why wast thou then away ?

George Whetstone appeared in the Low Countries in 1585 and, having been present at Zutphen, wrote Sidney's life in verse.[2] He came to a sticky end. Thomas Digges, who was Muster-Master-General of the Forces, appointed Whetstone his deputy, whom he found careful, honest and just. Captains had more than once seriously wounded those who questioned their accounts, and Whetstone's challenging those of Captain Udall led to a duel in which he was killed.[3] Thomas Churchyard's book, *A True Discourse Historical of the Succeeding Governors in the Netherlands*,

---

[1] *Brooke's Romeus and Juliet*, ed. J. J. Munro, xxii-xxiii, 165-7.
[2] T. C. Izard, *George Whetstone*, 11, disproves the hitherto held view (cf. *D.N.B.*) that he went over in 1572.
[3] *Ibid.* 29-31.

reliably covers the next phase of the war, in which we may say that Norris was, deservedly, his hero.

In the summer of 1577 Norris went over with his brothers, Lord North's eldest son, Henry Cavendish and three hundred men to serve under the Prince. Next year he won distinction at the important engagement of Rymenant, where Don John and Parma had 12,000 foot and 2000 horse.[1] Norris, who had only arrived an hour before on the field, was sent with certain of the shot of his regiment, seconded by some of the Scots, to line the hedges running from the river to the Dutch entrenchments, the enemy all the time sending up successive bodies of infantry, which were beaten back. It was a very hot day and the English fought in their shirts, the tails trussed up under their thighs. Count Bossu, in command, wrote that the way the men did their duty could not have been better. " Norris, who had three horses killed under him, and Bingham, Cavendish's lieutenant-colonel, who lost two brothers, behaved so that Caesars could have done no better."

The English were learning the game, and the demonstration that the Spanish army, hitherto invincible in the open field, could be held was not lost on the Queen. She was considering coming to terms with the States, when they now made their treaty with Anjou, accepting him as their sovereign. This inclined the Queen back to the Spaniards, and Walsingham was sent to Don John proposing terms. They met, as it happened, on St. Bartholomew's day, under a fine oak in a wide plain, Don John with nearly 2000 horse with him. Walsingham was immensely taken with him and wrote home to Burghley, " surely I never saw a gentleman for personage, spirit, wit and entertainment comparable to him ".[2] The scene is worth recording : it helps to explain why Don John became the only Spaniard to enter into English myth. The bastard stock of the Emperor was made of finer stuff than the legitimate line : Philip was not up to Margaret of Parma, Don John, or the splendid soldier that Parma was. But no accommodation was possible : Don John was bent on victory. Instead, he died.

In these years we find Norris campaigning alongside of La Noue, most famous of the Huguenot captains and a very professional soldier.[3] Constantly we find Norris commended for

---

[1] *Cal. S.P. For. 1578–9*, 114-15.   [2] *Ibid.* xxiv.
[3] Cf. P. Kervyn de Volkaersbeke, *Correspondance de François de la Noue*, 186, 194.

his valour and activity. On two occasions he managed to force convoys of supplies through the enemy to relieve Steenwyk.[1] At Malines he was repulsed, though he killed with his own hand the big Spanish friar who had directed the ordnance on to the English ranks. In the retreat Norris was shot through the buttock, and had his horse killed under him. A less serious occasion was no less characteristic of the wars. One day, at Antwerp in 1580, in a fracas between his servants and a mob roused by a drunken wagoner, Norris was struck by " a great staff over his nose and one eye, wherewith his nose was beaten flat to his face and his eye somewhat bruised ".[2] He had to take to his bed : now " the eye is already well recovered, and the nose so raised up again that it will be no disfigure at all ".

That autumn Norris was manœuvring against one of the ablest of the Spanish commanders, Verdugo ; and at Northorne he was wounded again, with a bullet in his right hand. He should have been commander of all the English forces, to stop faction and constant disputes, and achieve a united discipline.[3] But Anjou would not allow him to be made General : that might make the English too powerful. As it was, the English troops, like others, were miserably underpaid ; at this time their pay was five months in arrears—we have seen what their captains were capable of : the men starved or lived on the country or sometimes, when driven desperate, went over to the enemy. (There were some English, Catholic exiles, fighting with them, too.) In 1582 there was a regular mutiny. The men thought that Norris was detaining their pay. They went on strike, and some deserted to the enemy. Norris wrote to his cousin Walsingham : " our camp is the very image of Hell, and in it none more tormented than myself ; for besides the trouble with strangers and this shameful disorder, our own chiefs will not yet suffer me to live in quiet ".[4] He was accused of having received three months' pay for the soldiers—money which he could have let out at use and profited from or simply squandered, both of which were often done by the captains ; but it seems to have been proved that he had not yet received one month's pay.[5] Money was the crying trouble of all these armies in the Low Countries and everywhere : it was often the crux of military

---

[1] Cf. Churchyard, *op. cit.* 37-42.
[2] *Cal. S.P. For. 1579–80*, 312.   [3] *Cal. S.P. For. 1578–9*, 131.
[4] *Cal. S.P. For. 1582*, 195.   [5] *Ibid.* 229.

operations, which were held up by mutinies—in the Spanish army even more than others. Both Alva and Parma's operations were on occasion nullified by them and reduced to the defensive : if either of them had been fully supported he might have conquered the Netherlands.

Norris had Anjou's opposition to put up with. When at last he and Morgan won his praise for their bravery in a skirmish near Antwerp, the Duke commended " our nation to be valiant, if they would join obedience with it ".[1] This infuriated Herle, with the spectacle of French insubordination and civil war the scandal of Europe, preventing France from taking any united action and leaving the way open for Spanish ascendancy. Herle wrote home hotly : " he neither remembers the insolence of his own people, nor the extreme poverty that might occasion our poor men to demand some relief". Norris made things worse by feasting Anjou and Orange at the English house in Antwerp : he had reasons of his own. At this great supper they had " with them their mistresses to the number of twenty four or thereabouts, noted to be the only courtesans of this most arrogant place ".[2] One sees that war has its usual consolations ; the men were furious, no doubt at not sharing them. The result, however, was a mellowing of spirits, a better understanding—and Norris was made General of the States' forces in Flanders.[3]

Then the Queen cut up badly : she could not bear her subjects taking orders from anyone else, and the situation was an equivocal one. She made trouble for Norris in undertaking the defence of the Waes at their orders, and in 1583 he returned, ostensibly to visit his parents but perhaps at her order. The Prince could ill dispense with him, but wrote a glowing testimonial to his services.[4] Before his return he made a fighting retreat upon Ghent, assailed by English in the service of Spain—Anjou and Orange, neither much good as soldiers, looking on en-couragingly from the walls. " That night the English were appointed to lie in a little island or piece of ground environed with water and had reeds to make them cabins for their succour. Then the town of Ghent sent them very great store of victuals, and Sir John Norris at his own charges sent them a pipe of Rhenish wine and three hogsheads of claret wine to make them merry withal."[5] So sometimes there were good times—and

---

[1] *Cal. S.P. For. 1582*, 237.   [2] *Ibid.* 400.   [3] *Cal. S.P. For. 1583*, 36.
[4] *Ibid.* 374.   [5] Churchyard, 49.

very necessary too, in those waterlogged, aguish low countries, where warfare was to a considerable extent amphibious. Men sickened and died, got on each other's nerves, quarrelled and killed each other. Yorke's jars with Norris were a contributory cause of his treason. Norris, like everybody else, had a quick temper and was very irascible ; he quarrelled with Morgan and challenged him. It was because the men were without pay again that Alost was betrayed for money by the English garrison, by Pigott with the aid of Captains Dalton and Taylor.[1] When a Welsh captain in Spanish service sent Norris a challenge, Roger Williams took it up and a duel followed in view of both armies.[2] The two Welshmen gave each other some fierce blows without either being hurt, and then took to a carouse together. Drink was sometimes a pacifier.

Such incidents were remembered and recounted by old warriors maundering by winter firesides, in the remote places to which they returned : how Captain Hunnings, wounded and pursued by Spaniards, tried to leap into a boat, but jumping short was weighed down by his armour and drowned ;[3] Edward Stanley scaling the rampire at Zutphen fort, seizing the enemy's pike thrust at him to lever himself up and gain the top ;[4] Norris's injured nose ; John Carew's hand blown off by a cannon-ball at the siege of Ostend, himself coming back to throw it on the table with " This is the hand that cut the pudding at dinner ", the iron hand he had made for himself that has come down in the family of the Tremaynes, a gruesome reminder of those days of the Netherlands' struggle for freedom and the memorable brave deeds of Englishmen.

III

Meanwhile at home the 1570s were, as in other fields— cosmography, voyages of discovery, literature, the drama—a period of preparation for the heroic age which was to come with the war.

The year 1572, with its revelation of internal and external

---

[1] *Cal. S.P. For. 1583–4*, 246.　　[2] Churchyard, 38.
[3] *Ibid.* 71.　　[4] *Ibid.* 93.

danger to the state and the going over of the first bands of volunteers, marked a new departure : the government realised that it must set about putting the military forces of the country in order, transforming them from disorderly levies of billmen and bowmen into modern forces, trained and equipped with firearms, organised on a national footing. It was a tremendous task. From now on one watches the increasing pressure, the unremitting energy, with which the government through all its recognised instruments strives to bring about a revolutionary change. (One jibs at the over-worked word, but it may more truly be applied to this achievement than to many others of less importance which have received more attention.) By the 1580s the transformation was taking place, and 1588 saw the high watermark of national organisation as of national spirit. In the 1590s one observes the increasing control of the central government, along with evidences of war-weariness and strain towards the end.

It was the Privy Council and the governing elements in the nation that gave the lead and provided the will-power : they were a dynamo of energy and proved themselves well worthy of the people they led, and of their place in society. The chief trouble, as usual with the English, was to arouse them out of their insular sense of comfort into a sense of danger. Not until the danger was upon them, as in 1940, would they take the matter in earnest and do their best. We find continual evidence of the struggle the authorities had to put up against conservative ways, inertia, local inefficiency and local jealousies, varying standards and resources, sheer selfishness, indifference and innumerable tricks of evasion.

We must keep in mind the overriding objective : to get adequately trained and equipped forces out of the reservoir of the nation's man-power. The trained forces were only a small proportion of the untrained numbers called upon to serve.[1] The whole manhood of the country, from sixteen to sixty, was liable and there was, theoretically, an elaborate system of pains and penalties to see that they did :[2] the nation in arms—but the arms were bills and bows. Long peace had increased the sense of security and encouraged the desuetude of the old

---

[1] C. G. Cruickshank, *Elizabeth's Army*, 8.
[2] For an account of these, *v.* E. Green, *The Preparations in Somerset against the Spanish Armada*, 15-16.

military organisation. In effect, all was to do again. The government's chief instruments were the Lords Lieutenants at the apex of the organisation, who gave their orders to the J.P.s in the counties. Eight of the members of the Privy Council were Lords Lieutenant of a considerable number of counties. As time goes on, the most active J.P.s in a county become deputy-lieutenants, who carry the burden of military affairs. In addition, the professional soldiers play an increasing part, advising the authorities, helping to carry out their instructions in the localities. Earlier, there was a great lack of trained officers to give instruction, and we were forced to bring in foreigners—as in other fields and techniques. Intervention abroad and increasing experience in the wars remedied this ; in the 1580s most counties had their muster-masters to train their forces. In every respect the system becomes more efficient with the extending control of the government.

We can trace this process step by step or, rather, from time to time, if we are not to be drowned in the ocean of papers that still remain relating to it.[1]

In March 1573 a Commission was appointed to take General Musters throughout the realm.[2] The clergy, not being liable to serve, were to furnish horses and armour : one watches the cumulative burden this threw upon the backs of those willing, hard-worked camels, the bishops. From the returns one gets a picture of unpreparedness, some idea of the leeway to be made up. Devon puts forward 10,000 as the number of men able for service, of whom 1000 might be selected for training ; the county is not able to pay the expenses of it, owing to the falling off of trade.[3] Derbyshire has 4000 able men, but training 500 is all the county can bear. (Note that the expense of training fell entirely on the counties in these earlier years ; later, the government bore an increasing share.) Dorset has chosen 500 men, Surrey 300, but the inhabitants of both are unwilling to be burdened with the expense.[4] Worcestershire delays training until after harvest, Hertfordshire is inconvenienced by the want

---

[1] There is a vast mass of material among the State Papers Domestic, Acts of the Privy Council, Historical MSS. Commission Reports, Lansdowne MSS. etc. I suggest this as a fruitful subject of research ; it would yield important data for the study of population.

[2] *Cal. S.P. Dom. 1547-80*, 459.

[3] *Ibid.* 460.

[4] *Ibid.* 465.

Oxfordshire reports 5000 ; Cambridge is a poor county and gives no satisfaction.[1] Nottingham and Derby are poor counties ; the former has 2000 able men, the latter 600 foot and forty horse.[2] Measures are beginning to be taken for coastal counties to be reinforced by neighbouring ones in case of invasion ; for example, Surrey is to send men to aid Kent, Sussex or Hampshire. Later, more elaborate instructions for mutual aid were given among counties like Dorset, Somerset, Devon and Cornwall, and for sending reinforcements to the Isle of Wight, Portsmouth, Plymouth and Falmouth.

Hertford reports an increase of horses, but they have not appointed captains, there being few expert enough for that office.[3] Huntingdon has rated the propertied class for furnishing light horse, but all show their disability for observance of the same.[4] In Warwickshire a number of persons refuse voluntarily to provide horses : the J.P.s ask for an order for their restraint.[5] The gentry of that county were much divided between Protestant and Catholic, and that led to feuds—and perhaps reflected them. The Bishop of Chester reports that many of the Lancashire gentry neglected their duty to prepare light horse for Ireland, expecting some great change would shortly take place.[6] They were Catholics—and hope springs eternal in the foolish breast.

The Council was disappointed with the number of horses returned, and suggested to the commissioners that many parties might be rated at a higher number. It would seem that this country was backward in breeding horses, too—certainly presents of horses from abroad were greatly esteemed ; scraggy parts like Wales, Anglesey and Cornwall produced no horses worth speaking of, but only nags. The fact was that a lot of people in the propertied class got out of their duty if they could, and rated themselves at a much lower rate for the provision of horse—an expensive item, for it meant not only the horse, but the horseman with arms and equipment—than their estate warranted.[7] (What was the point of being in a position to apportion the rate on

---

[1] *Cal. S.P. Dom. 1547–80*, 662, 675. Thomas Wenman of Witney Park, Oxon., refused to furnish a light horse, though he was of ability and living, *ibid.* 664.

[2] *Ibid.* 663-4. Nottingham displays a good spirit in 1598, though few trained men are left in the shires—so many are by then abroad in the Wars. *Salisbury MSS.* IX. 289, 291.

[3] *Cal. S.P. Dom. 1547–80*, 662.   [4] *Ibid.* 648.

[5] *Ibid.* 676.   [6] *Ibid.* 680.

[7] *Musters, Beacons, Subsidies, etc. in the County of Northampton*, ed. Joan Wake, lxiv.

others if you did not take the opportunity to let yourself and your friends off? This provided fuel for many enjoyable quarrels in the counties.) Her Majesty expressed her displeasure with the shires that neglected to return their certificates. So the work of government was egged and nagged along.

With the outbreak of war in 1585, matters were speeded up, the organisation tightened. Every J.P. was to find two petronels on horseback, *i.e.* horse-pistoliers.[1] Recusants were rated as heavily as bishops to support light horse. A complete system of muster masters covered the counties and endeavoured to bring them up to scratch. The trainers of companies were to have the title of corporals. Butts were set up, remote from highways, for firearm practice. To form the army that Norris was taking to the Low Countries, by the treaty with the States, levies were made in all the counties round London, and some farther afield. Norris requested that the J.P.s might have the power to impress recruits.[2] Sussex contributed 150 men, very poorly and meanly set forth in every respect—some carried their furniture and armour on their backs.[3] (This, which would not have been objected to by armies on the Continent, was contrary to English practice : we were accustomed to employ wains for the purpose.) Two Baskervilles escorted 300 men from Gloucester, and 200 men from Wiltshire.[4] From Kent 150 men embarked for Flanders in the little ship, the *Flower of Comfort* in which precious little comfort was probably to be found. The States were pressing for the 4000 foot the Queen had agreed to send to be increased to 5000. Poor old Burghley prays Walsingham to get Norris and Davison to concert how 4000 soldiers may be increased to 5000, without new levies: " scribbled, with a weary head, in my bed ".[5]

With the opening of the year 1588 the government makes strenuous efforts to bring the country up to its highest fighting efficiency. Not even the growing danger could arouse some people out of their sloth or prevent quarrels from hindering preparations. In Devon some gentlemen stood on their privilege as stannators and refused to attend the county musters.[6] Hampshire continued to get bad reports, in spite of its being an exposed area.[7] People there feared that the new increase of

[1] *Cal. S.P. Dom. 1581–90*, 249.
[2] *Ibid.* 254.
[3] *Ibid.* 261.
[4] *Ibid.* 254, 259.
[5] *Ibid.* 265.
[6] *Ibid.* 469.
[7] *Ibid.* 464, 485, 498.

charges for arms and equipment would become permanent—after all, it is the way with governments. Things were held up by differences between the Marquis of Winchester and the Earl of Sussex. When these were over, the Marquis and the Bishop quarrelled. The Bishop said that he had had himself to muster the clergy's forces under the very nose of the Marquis. The Marquis replied that though he was very well nosed, his nose was not long enough to reach or smell all the way from Tidworth to Winchester, sixteen miles. In May the muster master reported a total of 9088 men, but " many of them rawly furnished, some lacking a head-piece, some a sword, some one thing or other that is evil, unfit or unbecoming about him ". In the North the Lord President reported that the gentry would respond more willingly, after their old custom, to personal call in an emergency than to musters.[1] Their petronels were not of the sort contemplated by the Council, and the gentry objected to raising light horse : they feared the charge might become permanent. If it were to serve only against Scotland, they would not object to it. Really, at this date ! One sees, in a flash, what a different world the North was.[2]

The admirable county of Somerset continued to get good reports. In 1587 their muster master had found " beyond mine expectation and unto my great comfort the country so excellently furnished with all sorts of armour and weapons, and that very good in such perfect readiness, the men so well sorted and chosen both for able bodies and comely personages "—evidently the good types of the Somerset Light Infantry.[3] " I must needs say it is a country second unto none for serviceable men, good munition, and willing and most dutiful minds that ever I set my foot in." That year the men along the coasts were instructed as to the likely places of descent, where they were to repair to upon the alarm, and the order of firing the beacons. It must be said that no such preparations obtained in Spain, nor could Spain have achieved such an organisation of the whole country. Now,

[1] *Cal. S.P. Dom. 1581–90*, 479.

[2] In 1586 Yorkshire, *e.g.*, is required to furnish 6000 men : West Riding 2400, North Riding 2000, East Riding 1600. Cf. these numbers with the southern counties, more populous and prosperous, also more submissive. The government was careful of northern susceptibilities : they were assured that they would not be called on for foreign service. By 1589 the numbers for Yorkshire had been stepped up to 6000 trained, 4000 untrained foot ; 400 light horse, 200 more in case of invasion, to be kept private. H.M.C. *Various*, II. 98 foll., 106.

[3] Green, *op. cit.* 101-4.

in March 1588, Captain Orde finds nothing but praise for Somerset : " for the old charge of 3000 men, I find them brave and very well furnished, especially the pikes and shot, whereof there are many muskets ". The new charge of 1000 men were little inferior. " The truth is it is a most gallant country for the men, armour and readiness. They may well guard her Majesty's person if she had occasion to them."[1] It is pleasant to think that they did go up.

A guard of 4000 foot and 1000 horse was proposed for the person of the Queen. She would not consent to it : no doubt financial considerations fortified that cool courage, that collected head that never lost control. After all, she had now ruled with good success for thirty years : she could not believe it possible she might be unseated.

Norris was sent to view the eastern Channel coast, to give orders for opposing landings. He surveyed Hampshire and Dorset, but asked that someone else be appointed for Sussex and Kent—it took more time than he expected.[2] Sir Thomas Leighton was to view Essex, Suffolk and Norfolk ; while the Earl of Bath, Ralegh and Grenville were busy in the West.

The miserable counties of Bedford and Cambridge do poorly, as usual. Lord North reports that Cambridge was very badly furnished of armour and munition, and that many of the J.P.s refused to furnish petronels, for " some nice and curious reasons which might have been forborne in this time of special service ".[3] He certified the names of those who refused to the Council. For himself, he would furnish at his own charges 30 lances and 20 petronels, besides 20 petronels of his own followers and 60 shot. For now that the emergency was upon us, it was decided to form an army round the Queen and another at Tilbury. Men from the inland counties were drawn to London, the household servants of the Queen enrolled, and the nobles were to attend on her.

It is fascinating, and touching, to read their offers. Lord Morley will contribute 20 light horse, 30 muskets, 70 calivers at his own expense, though his estate is much reduced by his father's fond departure, to resist foreign attempts against this

---

[1] Orde was " now passing into Wilts to begin the musters there, being credibly informed that I shall find all things in as good sort as I have found here in this country ".

[2] *Cal. S.P. Dom. 1581–90*, 478.

[3] *Ibid.* 482.

realm, his natural and sweet country.[1] (One observes the defensive note : his father went abroad for religion.) Lord Dacre offers 10 lances, 10 light horse, 10 petronels, 40 corselets, 20 muskets and 20 calivers : he is only sorry that his long suits at law prevent him doing more.[2] Lord Sandys' embarrassed circumstances prevent him from contributing more than 10 horse from his household, but he may raise more from his tenants.[3] Lord Montague is put out in that he has not received a summons as others—perhaps because he was a Catholic.[4] The Earl of Pembroke, from his immense estates, will attend the Queen with 300 horse and 500 foot of his own followers, armed at his own costs.[5] But these large numbers with which the peers were now coming forward had the effect of cutting into and decreasing the counties' musters : it is a pretty demonstration of the conflict between the medieval idea of feudal service and the modern one of service to the state. At the centre of the hive—county levies, peers' retainers, her own household servants, alive in every nerve, not at all discomposed, still negotiating with Parma, in intelligence with all Philip's enemies throughout Europe—lay the queen-bee.

Leicester was now at Tilbury, awaiting Parma. He would send Norris to Dover, 24 July, to put the coast in arms. " There is no looking back now to any oversight that is past."[6] He asked that 1000 of the best sort be sent him from London. He complained that he was extremely ill supplied with officers to help him regulate the army. He had to see to everything himself : " I am here cook, cater and hunt " (*i.e.* caterer and huntsman).[7] He was angry with Norris and Sir Roger Williams who could not resist going down to Dover to see the Armada : " they have put me to more travail than ever I was in before ". Four thousand men from Essex arrived on him, but with no victuals : " not a barrel of beer nor a loaf of bread . . . enough after twenty miles' march to have been discouraged and to have mutinied ; but all with one voice, finding it to be due to the speediness of their coming, said they would abide more hunger than this to serve her Majesty and the country ".[8] He sent to London for

[1] *Ibid.* 495. [2] *Ibid.* 507.
[3] *Ibid.* 501. [4] *Ibid.* 510.
[5] *Ibid.* 516. [6] *Ibid.* 511, 513, 520.
[7] Laughton, *op. cit.* I. 305, 321.
[8] q. M. Christy, " Queen Elizabeth's Visit to Tilbury in 1588 ", *E.H.R.* 1919, 43 foll.

100 tuns of beer and to halt its thousand men, unless they
brought provisions with them. A number of burgonets (*i.e.*
helmets) have arrived from the Tower, but not a man will buy
one, they are ashamed to wear them. The Armoury must be
better looked to ; there is great want of powder and munition.
Somehow he got round his difficulties in time for the Queen's
visit to the camp, which he advised : " for her own person—the
most dainty and sacred thing we have in this world to care for—
he cannot consent that she should go to the confines of her
realm to meet her enemy, but advises her to go to her house at
Havering, with the army round about her there, and to spend
two or three days at the camp, and there to rest in her poor
lieutenant's cabin ; and thus far but no further can he consent
to adventure her person ".[1] By now reinforcements were arriving
from the Low Countries : Sir Thomas Morgan landed at
Margate with 800 shot, veterans of the wars.[2] We see the
advantage command of the sea gave us to move troops to and
fro across the Channel. Parma's chance was passing.

Before the crisis was over the Queen decided to pay her
visit to the camp : " good sweet Queen ", wrote Leicester,
" alter not your purpose if God give ye good health ". The camp
was pitched on the low hill on which West Tilbury church stands,
commanding a fine view up and down the river ; headquarters
(for those who appreciate continuity in such things) were within
the prehistoric encampment on the summit with its banks and
ditches.[3] On 8 August the Queen arrived in her barge at the
blockhouse by the river : cannon were discharged,

> The drums do sound, the fifes do yield their notes.

She was met by an escort of 1000 horse and 2000 foot under
Sir Roger Williams. As she passed, the guards lining the route
couched their pikes, bowed their ensigns and fell on their knees
—the Queen on foot, waving her hand, her plume of feathers
tossing. And so to Arderne Hall for the night, where her lodging
was prepared—the timber brew-house and dovecote are all that
remain now. Next day took place the formal review. The Lord
General and Lord Marshal went to meet the Queen and a
procession was formed that made its way through the camp :

---

[1] *Cal. S.P. Dom. 1581–90*, 514.
[2] *Ibid.* 526.
[3] *v.* M. Christy, *loc. cit.*

the serjeant-trumpeter with his mace, nine trumpeters in scarlet following ; the king of heralds bearing the arms of England ; the Queen's serjeants with their maces before the Lord General and the Lord Marshal. Then came the woman on whom the eyes of all Europe were turned at this moment, erect on a white charger, holding her bâton ("I myself will be your General "). Four footmen walked on either side of her horse ; then came her ladies in attendance and last the bodyguard.

She took her stand for a march past of the troops ; and after this left her ladies and her guard to ride with the General and the Marshal all round the army, wherever she appeared the pikes, the lances, the colours all lowered. So she passed, "like some Amazonian empress ", through the ranks. Then she spoke to the men, made that speech the echoes of which still reverberate among her people. She had been advised to take heed of her person, she said—with a pointed reminder of the Counter-Reformation's favourite weapon of assassination. She would do nothing of the kind : tyrants might fear to show themselves (Philip hardly emerged from the seclusion of the Escorial nowadays), but she had always placed her trust in the loyal hearts and the good-will of her people. Now she had come to show them she was resolved " to live or die amongst you all, to lay down for my God and for my kingdom and for my people, my honour and my blood, even in the dust. I know I have the body of a weak and feeble woman, but I have the heart and stomach of a king, and of a King of England too. And I think foul scorn that Parma or Spain or any prince of Europe should dare to invade the borders of my realm. To which, rather than any dishonour shall grow by me, I myself will be your General."

Camden tells us how " sometimes with a martial pace, another while gently like a woman, incredible it is how much she encouraged the hearts of her captains and soldiers by her speech to them ".[1] It can well be believed ; indeed, it has not been forgotten.

At the end of her speech the troops raised a mighty shout ; the trumpets sounded and she went to dinner in Leicester's tent at noon. During the meal despatches arrived—there had been no news since the dispersal of the Armada off Calais on 28 July—that Howard had seen it off from the Forth too battered to return. Report came, too, that Parma was determined to

[1] Camden, *op. cit.* 416.

come out this spring-tide. The Queen did not credit it, but was ready with a " conceit that in honour she could not return, in case there were any likelihood that the enemy would attempt anything. Thus your lordship seeth that this place breedeth courage "—so Walsingham from the camp to Burghley.[1] Not until late in the day did the Queen leave. A week later it was safe to break up the camp. The Queen did not omit to write her thanks to the lords lieutenant of the counties : for many of the men there that day it must have been the only time they set eyes on their famous sovereign.

We should take a glance at how all this touched the people in town and country—the receiving end. And, first, London : which the government at Westminster always dealt with respectfully, very careful of its susceptibilities and of its liberties. In 1580 Walsingham complains that they had been neglecting the training of their shot.[2] The Lord Mayor replies, not at all : the order had been put into execution, but suspended the following summer because of plague. The training ground for the city's bands, 2000 shot and 1000 pikemen, was Mile End. Shakespeare must often have watched them at it : did not Justice Shallow " remember at Mile-end Green, when I lay at Clements Inn . . . there was a little quiver fellow, and a' would manage you his piece thus ; and a' would about and about, and come you in and come you in : ' rah, tah, tah ' would a' say ; ' bounce ' would a' say ; and away again would a' go, and again would a' come : I shall ne'er see such a fellow."

That year the city has to levy 300 caliver men, not of its trained bands, for service in Ireland : 100 to serve in ships, two companies of 100 under Edward Denny and Walter Ralegh.[3] The force has a surgeon, two drummers and two fifes :

> O, farewell,
> Farewell the neighing steed and the shrill trump,
> The spirit-stirring drum, the ear-piercing fife . . .

We must not forget the noise, the colour and clamour of Elizabethan life, the feelings these things aroused : " I have known when there was no music with him but the drum and the

---

[1] Laughton, *op. cit.* II. 83.
[2] *Remembrancia, City of London, 1579–1664*, 230.
[3] *Ibid.* 232-3.

fife. . . . I have known when he would have walked ten mile afoot to see a good armour."

In London there were the usual difficulties, in addition to some peculiar to itself. Men impressed to serve on ships stole away to take service with merchants on foreign voyages. Once Norris found that no less than a hundred of the men he had pressed had managed to make off. Were freemen who lived in Surrey eligible to serve in the city or the county ? People within the various liberties refused to contribute—among them, in 1592, her Majesty's Apothecary and her Turner, men of known wealth.[1] No doubt they would have their excuse : rated elsewhere. The privileged places had become sanctuaries for all unwilling to serve. In 1592, 350 were sent to Normandy, three parts pikes, the remainder muskets ; in 1593, 300 to the Low Countries, under Vere ; in 1594, 350 under Norris to Brittany to rescue Brest, one-third pikes, one-third muskets, one-third calivers.[2] In case of invasion, in the alarms of 1588 and 1596, the city was to send 3000 men to Kent and Essex.[3] In the latter year we hear of 1000 marks' worth of its armour pawned or made away with in the county of Kent.[4]

For a country town let us look at the bustling, and characteristic, town of Stratford. In the gild-hall the corporation kept harness for four trained men and could provide it for ten in an emergency.[5] We find payments of 5s. to William the cutler for dressing it, 1d. for nails to hang it up. We hope William kept it in better order than Petruchio's on his wedding-day, who " wore an old rusty sword ta'en out of the town-armoury, with a broken hilt and chapeless " (*i.e.* the point of the scabbard missing). In 1578 every alderman was to pay 6s. 8d., every burgess 3s. 4d., towards furnishing three pikemen, two billmen and one archer : for some reason, Alderman Shakespeare was let off at a burgess's rate.[6] We notice that the town's expenses for their soldiers attending musters at Warwick are quite considerable : dressing four guns with all necessaries, gunpowder, powder-flasks, touch-boxes ; four swords with hilts, blades and handles ; four daggers, with girdles and hangers. Then Mosley's piece has to be mended at Warwick ; on St. Luke's day, half a pound of powder and match and a knife are bought for Mosley,

---

[1] *Remembrancia, City of London, 1579–1664*, 237-8.   [2] *Ibid.* 240-2.
[3] *Ibid.* 243.   [4] *Ibid.* 245.
[5] *Minutes and Accounts of Stratford-upon-Avon*, ed. E. I. Fripp, IV. xxiv.
[6] *Ibid.* III. 11, 13, 16, 45.

who proceeded to hurt himself. Two years later the vice-pin of Mosley's caliver has to be repaired at Warwick : poor Mosley, he seems always in trouble—perhaps an original of Mouldy, Wart or Bullcalf.

The town's charges in 1588 are quite large : £23 : 18s., according to the account of the constables—John Shakespeare the shoemaker, not the poet's father, and his fellows.[1] The equipment was in good shape, and not much needed doing ; but the soldiers' coats cost £8, their conduct-money £6, while their charges at Warwick were 18s. 8d. and, for Friday, Saturday and Sunday morning, 24s. 6d. One sees them that summer, making a week-end of it, under the walls of the Castle, the clear waters of the Avon, the narrow streets ; over the town-gate coming in from Stratford, Leicester's hospital (then occupied by the tiresome Cartwright, somewhat quieted down) ; the friendlier, crowded ale-houses.

We find also the Certificate of horse provided by the shire, 33 lances, 63 light horses, 4 petronels : 100 in all.[2] From this we derive a picture of the Warwickshire gentry on this 4 August 1588. There are Sir Fulke Greville, Philip Sidney's friend, the smart of his loss still recent ; Sir Thomas Lucy of Charlecote, a familiar enough figure to the young actor-poet away in London ; Sir John Harington, cousin of the courtier and wit ; Sir Henry Goodere, patron and friend of Drayton, who was brought up in his house at Polesworth ; Thomas Burdett, to whom Holinshed had been steward at Bramscote ; Ralph Sheldon, to whom we owe the first English tapestries. There are less happy names— William Somerville of Edstone, Robert Arden of Park : brother and son of two men executed for an insane scheme to kill the Queen five years before, both Catholics ; the latter, of the family to which Shakespeare's mother belonged. We see what an interesting society a small English county at that time could contain.

We may conclude, with Fortescue, as to the veracity of Shakespeare's picture of contemporary life, underneath the caricature : " Falstaff the fraudulent captain, Pistol the swaggering ensign, Bardolph the rascally corporal, Nym the impostor who affects military brevity, Parolles ' the damnable both-sides rogue ', nay, even Fluellen, a brave and honest man but a pedant, soaked in classical affectation and seeking his

[1] *Ibid.* IV. 39-40. [2] *Ibid.* 42-4.

model for everything in Pompey's camp—all these had their counterparts in every shire of England and were probably to be seen daily on the drill-ground at the Mile End."[1]

As part of the increasing preparedness of these years, we encounter an outcrop of military writings like those we have noticed on agriculture.[2] The fact was that society was vibrant with self-consciousness—at any rate its leading elements were : not, of course, Professor Tawney's beloved yokels. And it is they, the intelligent, the conscious—not the vegetative—who make a society what it is, and are therefore more properly interesting to the historian.

It is symptomatic that that rather unattractive journalist, Barnabe Rich, cashes in on the rising interest in military matters with a series of tracts. He was a soldier of sorts : writing in 1585, " it is now thirty years since I became a soldier. . . . In this mean space I have spent what my friends left me, which was something ; I have lost part of my blood, which was more ; and I have consumed my prime of youth and flourishing years, which was most." A self-taught man, brought up " in the fields among unlettered soldiers ", he wrote over thirty books—the favourite reading, according to Nashe, of Lichfield, the Cambridge barber. Rich learnt French and Italian, and from one of his tales Shakespeare took the plot of *Twelfth Night*. As early as 1574 Rich published, with a dedication to Ambrose, Earl of Warwick, *A Right Excellent and Pleasant Dialogue between Mercury and an English Soldier* : " These books are to be sold at the corner shop, at the south west door of Paul's church ".

In 1578 he produced his *Alarm to England, foreshadowing what Perils are procured where the People live without Regard of Martial Law* (*i.e.* without military discipline). From the fact that this book, printed by the Queen's Printer and dedicated to Hatton, Captain of her Gentlemen Pensioners, was " perused and allowed ", we may regard it as virtually a piece of official propaganda. It militantly attacks the pacific, civilian frame of mind after the long peace, that was as much out of accordance with the facts as our own was in the 1930s. So far from wars offending God, Rich instructs us, wars are commanded by God : " And the Lord spake unto Moses saying, ' Avenge the children of Israel

[1] J. W. Fortescue, *Hist. of the British Army*, I. 140.
[2] Cf. *The England of Elizabeth*, 98-103.

of the Midianites ' ", etc. ; and so throughout the Old Testament. Wars are sometimes more pleasing to God than peace : Rich gives instances. It is better to offend than defend. No renown is so great as that gained by martial prowess. The second part defends the trade of soldiering as honest—many merchants are less so, and lawyers worse : they pretend peace but are the authors of civil dissensions. The number of competent soldiers in England is very small, and soldiers of all others are held in least estimation. The last part deals with the decay of military preparedness, and points to Rome and other classical examples —from which all these writers draw the lessons—of the consequences in the overthrow of commonwealths. Boldness is no good without experience and training ; the greatest care should be taken in appointing captains ; obedience is the chief virtue in soldiers : the means to it, to keep them paid and punished.

The echo among the people we hear in the serving men in *Coriolanus* : " Let me have war, say I ; it exceeds peace as far as day does night ; it's spritely, waking, audible and full of vent . . . Peace is a great maker of cuckolds." " Ay," says another, " and it makes men hate one another." " Reason . . . because they then less need one another. The wars for my money." In the end, in *Pericles*, when the war is over, with that extraordinary justice of mind that might so easily be confused with sceptical indifference to human foolery, Shakespeare makes the pimp say : " What would you have me do ? Go to the wars, would you ? Where a man may serve seven years for the loss of a leg, and have not money enough in the end to buy him a wooden one ? "

With Thomas Digges we come to a technician, one of an admirable family of scientists and mathematicians, whom Leicester made Muster Master-General in the Netherlands. His book, *An Arithmetical Warlike Treatise named Stratioticos*, was published in 1579.[1] It is a practical manual of drill, teaching the science of numbers, fractions and equations, as requisite for the soldier in infantry formations—for want of which, no doubt, the Cheshire muster master got into trouble with his " pye of squares ". In addition, it adumbrates a modern system of discipline, with the laws of camps and armies, and ends with a

---

[1] It is pleasant to think that the Bodleian copy of the 1590 edition, corrected and augmented, belonged to John Aubrey, who inscribed it, " This was one of my honoured grandfather Mr. Isaac Lyte's books ".

section on artillery, promising a " Treatise of Great Artillery and Pyrotechny ".[1]

Digges's whole attitude is professional : he insists " how barbarous that common opinion is that an Englishman will be trained in a few weeks to be a perfect soldier ". The vanity of the common sort, if they have but carried arms and seen a little service, is to think themselves perfect soldiers. Digges insists, as all these writers do, on the antique perfection of Roman discipline. The model of modern discipline is that of the Spanish army, where a prince on first joining may trail a pike along with the rest. The Spaniards receive newcomers as *Camarades*, taking pleasure in teaching them their duties ; and " of all other nations there is none more obedient to their officers, for you shall see a sergeant of a private band among them to be obeyed of the best gentleman or nobleman of the band ". The implication is that with the English it is otherwise : more class-conscious, perhaps, we may say. Nor will our officers bestow as much pains in training a new soldier as on a horse : that strikes a familiar note in the English character. Above all, obedience to orders is the key to training. The conclusion seems unavoidable, from the emphasis of these writers, that the individualistic qualities of our people, their high spirits and insubordination, formed in these early days a real difficulty in making a disciplined modern army out of them.

Digges goes on to enumerate all the officers necessary in a fully organised army, from the corporal to the general, with their requisite qualities and the functions they perform. The captain is a key-figure, since he has charge of the lives of his men, and he must have good judgment in choosing his subordinate officers. He is not to beat his men, but to hand them over to the marshal or provost for punishment ; that instruction speaks volumes for what the practice was. As for the Lord General he needs to be patient and modest, temperate, sober, wise, liberal, courteous, eloquent, of good fame and reputation, learned in histories and in the sciences, especially that of fortification. Of all Elizabethan officers only Sir Francis Vere and Mountjoy came near filling this bill—and Mountjoy had the handicap

[1] This he did not achieve, or at least publish. Neither does he seem to have finished the " discourse of military robberies in musters and payments whereof before my departure from the Court at Greenwich I delivered to your lordship some two or three chapters ". Thomas Digges to Burghley, 13 Feb. 1592-3. Lansdowne MSS. 73, No. 6.

of his *liaison* with Penelope Rich. Instructions are given for the training of shot, which have now become the decisive arm, " of all other weapons in the field for all kinds of services, of especial account ". Digges's preference was for a massy battle (*i.e.* main body) of pikes, empaled with three or four ranks of musketeers, enough to cover them from the charge of lances, the musketeers to discharge kneeling on the right knee, to be the better protected by the pikes. He ridicules the soldiers' superstition that numbers in the ranks must always be odd, not even. His constant theme is that it is training that makes soldiers, and no nation is by nature always military. No message could be more encouraging for the latest arrival upon the European military scene : from now on it was to bear fruit in the formation of an unexpectedly splendid and proud tradition.

The year 1588 brought forth more books on war than ever —rather naturally. A young student of Gray's Inn, Peter Whitehorne, produced a tract, *Certain Ways for the Ordering of Soldiers in Battle Array and Setting of Battles* (*i.e.* formations), which expounded ways to bring varying numbers into order, with diagrams ; it had sections on fortification and how to make saltpetre, gunpowder, fireworks or wildfire. He also produced a new edition of his translation of Machiavelli's *Art of War*, with a didactic dedication to the Queen, boldly affirming that " of many strangers which from foreign countries have heretofore in this your Majesty's realm arrived, there is none in comparison to be preferred before this worthy Florentine and Italian " : he trusts that Machiavelli " shall deserve of all good English hearts most lovingly and friendly to be entertained, embraced and cherished ".

In 1591 there came out a posthumous book by William Garrard, who had served with the Spanish army fourteen years. It was a thorough-going criticism of the English system ; but it may be doubted whether Garrard realised how much progress had been made. His book, however, is excellent for its writing : exile had not dimmed his sense of the natural rhythm of his native tongue. " Let the pikeman march with a good grace, holding up his head gallantly, his face full of gravity and state and such as is fit for his person. . . . And every pace and motion with one accord and consent they ought to make at one instant of time. And in this sort all the ranks ought to go sometimes softly, sometimes fast, according to the stroke of the drum. . . .

So shall they go just and even with a gallant and sumptuous pace ; for by doing so they shall be esteemed, honoured and commended of the lookers on, who shall take wonderful delight to behold them."[1] It is a very Elizabethan sentiment ; note, too, that the march has got into the very rhythm of his style.

In 1590 a more important book than any of these came out from Paternoster Row : Roger Williams's *Brief Discourse of War*. It drove home the lesson of the last two decades : though there was a large element of luck in battle, and battles were sometimes won or lost by a small chance, yet long-term success in war was the result of training and expertise. How otherwise should Parma, with an army of 8000, have captured Antwerp in 1585 with a garrison of 16,000 ? What makes the Spanish discipline so famous ? Williams points out that it needs explanation, for the Spaniards of themselves are a base and cowardly people. Look at the way twice the number of Norris's army had run away from him before Lisbon in 1589 and allowed him to stay there several days and march off without interference ; or, again, outside Corunna, " where 6000 of ours overthrew 16,000 of theirs ".[2] The English record in the Low Countries, where our trained troops could beat equal numbers of them, both under Norris and since, was many times more worthy of praise than Medina Sidonia's attempt on England. Yet no army equals Parma's : how should this be ?

Williams does not point out that the Spanish army in the Netherlands—made up of Spaniards and Italians, Walloons and Germans—had become virtually a separate arm of the state. Philip would not have dared to summon it back to Spain : no wonder he had apprehensions of all its successive commanders, Alva, Don John, Parma. What Williams does point out is the long continued existence of that army since the time of Charles V : no-one had had the school of the wars unbroken but themselves. This had given them tremendous *esprit de corps* : pride in themselves ran throughout the army. " A camp continually maintained in action is like an university continually in exercises ; when

---

[1] q. Fortescue, *op. cit.* 141. The book had an Appendix by Robert Hitchcock on the English Army Rations in the Time of Queen Elizabeth, reproduced in *Social England Illustrated* (*Arber's English Garner*), 115 foll. This is a tract chiefly devoted to estimates of weights and prices. For Hitchcock's project for a national fishing fleet, *v. The England of Elizabeth*, 141. He was a Buckinghamshire gentleman, living at Caversfield.

[2] *Op. cit.* 8-9.

famous scholars die, as good or better step in their places. Especially in armies, where there be every day new inventions, stratagems of wars, change of weapons, munition and all sort of engines newly invented and corrected daily."[1] The effect was to be seen in the command : " the least of thirty commanders they had always amongst them were sufficient to command 10,000 soldiers." It is very evident how inferior the English were here.

The effects were to be seen in the field. The Spanish army had such a superior technique in fortification, the use of entrenchments, etc., that they could always conduct a siege with half their forces, leaving the rest free for *camisados*, surprise attacks like that which ruined the Prince of Orange's attempt to relieve Mons—where the defenders and William's army together, it may be added, were greatly superior in number. Sir Roger expounds the Spanish order of battle, in three sections, van, battle, rear, the order being changed every day so that each section should have its turn of the honour of leading the van. Regiments threw dice as to who should have the charge. No soldiers in the world were made so much of, so favoured or so honoured.

English and Scots were not inferior in valour and hardihood : indeed Williams thought them superior, but they could not compare with foreigners unless they took to lances and firearms. (Actually the sixteenth century followed a mistaken use of cavalry, throwing away their essential function of shock and weight—as Gustavus Adolphus and Cromwell were to prove and remedy in the next century.) Muskets were far more effective than calivers, and the Spanish fashion of firing them from the shoulder was best for recoil. Pikes were the best weapon for foot, but bills must be of good iron with a long steel pike, not like our common brown bills. Out of 5000 bowmen scarce 500 are able to make any strong shoots after three or four months' service ; 500 muskets = 1500 bowmen. But the English were learning in the only school. After the stubborn defence of Sluys (1587) and its surrender, Parma had asked to meet Baskerville and embraced him for a brave soldier. Among the English, who had detested Alva for his inhumanity, there was an immense respect for Parma's humanity, courtesy and invincible resolution : a superb soldier with whom, or rather against whom, they were proud to go to school.

[1] *Ibid.* 29.

CHAPTER X

INTERVENTION IN THE NETHERLANDS

THE assassination of William the Silent at Delft,[1] 9 July 1584, left the Dutch cause in a desperate state. One by one the national leaders who stood in the way of the Counter-Reformation had been marked down : Moray in Scotland, Coligny in France, now William—and Elizabeth would have followed, if the fanatics could have had their way. The Catholic cause was very unrespectable in its methods, nor is it sensible to regard them as ineffective : they were bitterly effective. The Protestants may perhaps be excused for regarding their survival—and ultimate victory—as providential : the usual way people have of expressing it when the strongest of instincts, that of self-preservation, wins through.

William was one of the truly great men of history. Unsurpassed as Elizabeth was as a ruler—as I hope, this book has made abundantly clear—William's was a rarer kind of statesmanship, conducted in far more difficult circumstances, and with a symbolic quality of a world that was yet to come into being. Things were simpler for the Queen : she was an anointed sovereign with indisputable authority : it was for her to rule as she well knew how. William had no such authority : he was the leader of a revolt, and to his people could never be more than the leader of a party. Surrounded by a world of enemies, his greatest difficulties came from within his own ranks, the instruments he had to make use of for the common cause. The aim of his life was to free the Netherlands from Spanish rule, while maintaining their unity. Like all the truly intelligent, he was a moderate and a *politique*. It was senseless for the Calvinist minority to persecute the Catholic majority—after all, many

---

[1] William, I need hardly say, was anything but Silent. The soubriquet ' le Taciturne ' meant that he could keep his counsel to himself : he needed to. Like Roosevelt, he was friendly and familiar, overflowing with talk ; but he kept his true thoughts to himself. His enemies meant by ' taciturne ' that he was sly ; which, of course, he was. The name so famous in history misrepresents him, and I do not care to use it ; it would be truer to call him William the Wise.

of the Catholics were patriots alike engaged in expelling the Spaniards. William's unceasing labours to keep them together in the common cause were " atheism " to the lunatic fanatics ; and again and again he had to stand by and watch them wreck their own cause.

He had, indeed, a superhuman patience in putting up with it all. Only once do we see his self-control giving way, the anguish underneath breaking through, at an emergency conference with the city council of Antwerp when they refused him the means to save Maestricht from Parma—while the Prince sat in the midst of it, his head bowed in his hands.[1] But it may be said that *he* had to put up with it—as Elizabeth never would have done : great noble as he was, he was a popular leader, his strength lay in the people, he had to depend on the people. And that is what makes him so very remarkable a phenomenon in his own time : he is a modern statesman, the only one of them all whose statecraft is exercised in modern conditions, who points the way to our world.

He had a genius for working with, and through, popular assemblies, an immense art in management of men and public opinion.[2] (He was very much the Franklin Roosevelt of his time.) Then, too, there was the irresistible combination of intellectual subtlety with simplicity of heart. Nothing he did not understand about human beings : no illusions : one hears his accents in the sad reflection on " the ingratitude inherent in men and the unbridled desire to speak ill ". " Who in this world ", he asked, " is sufficiently courageous to touch another's conscience ? "[3] (Alas, the answer is that almost any fool is.)

As time went on he was driven more and more to rely on the Calvinists, as they proved themselves the only people who would fight to the end, who would never submit. So we watch William becoming one with this people : the greatest lord in the Netherlands—who had been a member of Charles V's Council before he was twenty-one and upon whose shoulder the Emperor had leaned during the touching scene of taking his farewell of the States—now living the life of a Dutch burgher among others, having sacrificed wealth, estates, possessions, everything, to the cause. An English envoy was astonished to see one of the most

[1] Cf. C. V. Wedgwood, *William the Silent*, 202.
[2] P. Geyl, *The Revolt of the Netherlands*, 193.
[3] Blok, *History of the Netherlands*, III. 172.

famous men in Europe ill-clad in fustian, doublet unbuttoned, like the burghers who surrounded him. But the Englishman—no doubt very grandly dressed—was impressed to see, the moment he approached, the natural deference the burghers instinctively gave the Prince, the withdrawal of familiarity, before a foreigner.[1]

William wielded an incomparable moral authority in the nascent state, more important than the offices he held. He was Stadtholder of the provinces of Holland, Zealand and Utrecht, but his life was the thread that linked provincial estates, states general and council of state. Never was there a more cumbersome and dilatory mode of government : only William could hold it together. To this end he dedicated his life. As he grew older, the subtle, scheming mind became subordinated to a simpler faith, to one overriding end. The luxurious, cultivated prince of former days lived the life of a citizen, very open and familiar with all, exposed to every demand upon him, exposed to the attempts of assassins. He took on the character of a father of his people, " faithful unto death " as the " Wilhelmus " prophesied—the song of the Orange cause, the tune one now hears from many a Dutch belfry. No-one else has brought a whole people into being, nursed it into existence—and of what an achievement among the nations ! So that we must think of him as one of the greatest of men.

Now he was dead : no-one could replace him.

The situation of the northern provinces looked desperate. William had realised that they could not save themselves without external aid and he placed all his hope on French intervention —even after the bitter deception of Anjou's attempted *coup d'état*. (Anjou, when brought in, found that he was a mere cipher, expected to do what the Dutch told him : he had attempted to end the intolerable situation by capturing complete power for himself. Even after this, William went on negotiating with the French : needs must.) Philip now had the ablest of all his servants, the young Parma, in command and he was going from strength to strength. One by one he was capturing the towns of the south in preparation for a final campaign against the irreducible Holland and Zealand, behind their barrier of waterways. The submission of Termonde was followed by that of Ghent. The Calvinists of Ghent had frustrated William's

---

[1] The envoy was Sir Fulke Greville, *v. Life of Sir Philip Sidney*, 20-1.

policy by their extremism and intolerance : now they got what they deserved—two years in which to vert or go. In March 1585 Brussels capitulated and was followed by Nijmegen in its strong position, the five low hills commanding the Waal. Bruges and Malines next surrendered, without any conditions. Parma was free to invest Antwerp : a small but highly efficient army of some 8000 surrounded the city, defended by 16,000 incompetent troops. The burghers had neglected William's advice to construct strong-points to keep the Scheldt open below the city : Parma was enabled to build a boom across and seal it off.

The siege of Antwerp was a major operation of war and lasted many months. The governor was William's close friend, Marnix, lord of St. Aldegonde—intellectual leader of the cause—a man of intelligence, of the type that is driven to despair by men's folly. He entered into negotiation with Parma : two such intelligent men had a good deal of mutual sympathy. If Parma had been able to offer liberty of conscience, it is probable that the Netherlands cause would have collapsed, certainly Holland and Zealand would have been insulated. But this he could never do : it was contrary to Philip's " *sainte inclination* "[1]—the fool ! So the war went on. A final offer on the part of the States to France had to be rejected by Henry III : he was no longer his own master, his liberty of action circumscribed by the League, with Philip behind it. Neither William nor Marnix had ever believed that Elizabeth would intervene to save them. Marnix was now negotiating with Parma ; in the course of the negotiations Parma told him that Philip would always have the upper hand, thanks to the gold from the Indies. [2] This was just what his opponents said : it was their case : it was American treasure that enabled him to oppress the liberties of Europe.

The States turned to the Queen of England with an offer of the sovereignty over them : by which they meant to engage her and the resources of her people indefinitely and illimitably in their cause. The Queen's conception of the matter—and it was intensely her own—was different. Her overwhelming pre-occupation was the well-being of her own people, her prime obligation the interests of her own country. Her objectives in the Netherlands were limited. She did not want to wrest the sovereignty away from Philip, their legitimate ruler. If at any

---

[1] L. van der Essen, *Alexandre Farnèse, Prince de Parme, 1545–92*, IV. 13.
[2] *Ibid.* 114.

moment he would return to the terms of the Pacification of Ghent, granting virtual " Home-Rule " to the Netherlands, she would lay down arms. The negotiations with the burgher envoys at Greenwich were very tough and protracted. The Queen was desperately anxious to save Antwerp : Norris had 3000 foot and 200 horse ready to start for its succour. The envoys were Northerners and were much less concerned, it seemed, with the fate of the southern capital. Nothing would move the Queen from her limited conception of her intervention and, in the end, her terms had to be agreed to. These, defined by the Treaty of Greenwich on that day subsequently so famous in our history, 3 September, were very wise and prudent. She would maintain an army of 4000 foot—later raised to 5000—and 1000 horse ; the Provinces were to hand over two " cautionary " towns, Flushing and Brill, to English occupation as pledges for the repayment of the sums she advanced. These she would garrison, in addition to her other troops. She would send a person of eminent authority to take command in her name and would provide two members of their Council of State *to assist them with advice*—a conception to which she adhered through the crisis of the next two or three years : she would not take over the direct government.

It is monstrous how much the Queen has been maligned for the terms of this treaty and of her intervention in the Netherlands —and really very naïvely, by historians who do not understand how high policy necessarily works.[1] Her action is condemned as " selfish ". But, of course, policy must always provide for the interest of its own state : the ultimate question is whether that concurs with the interest of others. It has been the sheet-anchor of our security in these last centuries that our policy, more than that of any other great country, has done so. We see the

---

[1] By Motley most of all, in his classic *History of the United Netherlands*. The American Motley had the very English characteristic that anything the English did was wrong, what anybody else did was right. His book is a shocking—and famous—case of historical bias : the anti-English bias of a nineteenth-century New Englander, perhaps the specifically anti-Elizabethan bias of a New England Puritan. C. R. Markham in *The Fighting Veres* shows up instance after instance of Motley's mis-representations, *v.* 281-2, 286, 289, 292-3, 299, 302-4, 320, 328, 349, 359.

But even P. Geyl commits some injustices today in his *Revolt of the Netherlands*. Elizabeth's policy is described as " jealous and capricious ", she is held responsible for the delay by which Antwerp fell ; the woman whose action saved the Netherlands is described as unwilling to be answerable for their future, " as self-opinionated as she was incalculable " (182, 197, 198, 203). Parma's biographer knows better : he pays tribute to the cleverness and caution of the treaty, *op. cit.* IV. 82.

beginnings of this classic formation in the Elizabethan age. The practical independence of the Netherlands was our objective— but it was what the Netherlands wanted too : what was wrong with that ? The fact that the Queen defined the obligations she accepted in treaty-terms and stuck to them—with a generous interpretation, as we shall see—was no less right. Her revenues were very modest compared with those of France and Spain. She was ready to advance some £125,000 a year in support of her intervention : that is to say, two-thirds of the ordinary expenditure of her government up to this time, about a half of her total receipts.[1] She could not have afforded more : for the intervention meant open war with Spain ; she would have to provide for that, for the defence of her own country, for inter- vention in France and the aid of Henry IV later, and—most expensive of all—the war in Ireland. Contemporary rulers in Europe were much impressed by her courage in undertaking what she did : the King of Sweden regarded her as risking her own crown on the hazard of war.[2] She had, in the way charac- teristic of the English people, hesitated long before committing herself ; but, once committed—whatever people who do not understand policy have said, then or since—she did not desist till her dying day, or her people cease their effort till the Dutch were virtually free.

Before the negotiations were finished and the treaty concluded, the terrible news that Antwerp had fallen arrived : no fault of hers. The phlegmatic Philip in the Escorial was so excited by the news that he woke up his daughter, Isabella, in the middle of the night to tell her.[3] He really believed now that he need make no concessions, that Holland and Zealand would follow the way of Antwerp : hubris as usual preparing the way for its defeat. Before Parma entered, eight hundred Protestant families, of the most active and vital, left Antwerp for the North. Mean- while Dutch ships took up their stations to blockade the Scheldt : the blockade lasted two centuries—quite a price to pay for return to the bosom of the Church. It is from the capitulation of Antwerp that we may date the real division of the Netherlands, with Antwerp as the frontier city of Catholic Belgium, guarding the

---

[1] J. E. Neale, " Elizabeth and the Netherlands ", *E.H.R.* 1930, 375.
[2] J. Bruce, ed. *The Correspondence of Robert Dudley, Earl of Leicester* (Camden Soc.), xii.
[3] L. van der Essen, *op. cit.* IV. 136.

line behind which the southern provinces remain Catholic. The submission of the southern towns cut them off from the sea and trade, so that soon famine conditions began to prevail. The country had been much fought over ; its old prosperity lost, it sank into misery : one of Parma's chief difficulties : he was full of sympathy, Philip not. Meanwhile, the northern provinces were gaining strength from the sea, by trade and fisheries, by recruiting to themselves industrious and vital elements from the south. The country bears many marks of its rebirth in the course of these years : not only such a famous monument as the University of Leyden, but the old town-houses of Brill, the fine town-hall of Flushing, built under the English occupation.

The strategy of the war was largely determined by the large rivers and their mouths, constituting a series of lines running roughly from east to west : the Rhine the most northerly, then the Waal, then the Maas. Between these rivers lay the rich, disputed territories with their comic names, rustic caricatures of English : between Rhine and Waal the Betuwe, between Waal and Maas the Bommelwaart—names to become very familiar to generations of English soldiers. The land was much less drained then and far more of it was under water. Around the islands of the river-mouths there was a great deal of drowned land, that could be crossed at low water. Operations were in part amphibious and here the allies had the tremendous advantage of sea-power : they were able to use the intricate waterways much more freely than the Spaniards. Actions in these areas were much conditioned by the tides, as we see early on in Walcheren, later in the famous siege of Ostend and the battle of Nieuport. I think we may conclude that if the Netherlands had had more sense of unity and more capacity for fighting on land, the Spaniards would never have been able to bring them to such a pass. As it was, no-one can deny that the English intervention made all the difference : in the end it saved them.

The Privy Council was unanimously agreed on the necessity of intervention ; the Queen hated its necessity, but recognised it. She published her reasons for undertaking it, in what has been described, not unreasonably, as " one of the noblest state papers that was ever written ".[1] The leading figure in the kingdom was sent as her lieutenant and to command her army—Leicester.

---

[1] C. R. Markham, *The Fighting Veres*, 69. He compares it to the Declaration of Independence.

He had been the foremost advocate of intervention ; on leaving England we find him making a touching appeal to his old opponent, Burghley, to give him all the help he could. " Her Majesty, I see, my lord, oftentimes doth fall into mislike of this cause . . . but I trust that, seeing that mine and other men's poor lives and substances are adventured for her sake . . . she will fortify and maintain her own action to the full performance of that she hath agreed on. . . . Good my lord, have me thus far only in your care that in these things which her Majesty and you have all agreed and confirmed for me to do, that I be not made a metamorphosis, that I shall not know what to do." [1]

There was an ambivalence from the first in Leicester's position, though not in the Queen's mind. There may have been something more than that : a secret understanding with the Dutch to take over sovereignty, at least the " absolute government ", against her will and at her expense. We have already dealt with the personal aspects of the conflict between the Queen and her representative ; [2] here we need only note its political connotations and consequences, its effect on the war. No sooner had Leicester arrived in the Netherlands than he accepted the absolute governorship thrust upon him by the States. He did not perceive that their aim was to make him *their* Governor, *i.e.* the executive instrument of *their* aims, not the Queen's. She had a sixth sense where anything concerning her power was concerned, and the extraordinary struggle she proceeded to put up against her favourite, the States and the whole of her Council, was sustained by herself alone, we now know, and not—as they thought—supported by anyone else. To have accepted the position would have been to give away the underlying premise of the treaty, which was to leave this country to judge when it considered the just aims of the intervention to have been secured, and to make the Dutch arbiters of our action.

Leicester, blinded by the magnificence of his outward position, did not perceive this. He was invested with all the formal authority of one of Charles V's own governors : " his Excellency ", a title unknown to England, which the Queen did not relish. Nor would she allow him to be accompanied by a number of magnates to aid him : there was to be no second Court, under his sway. Leicester had come to take the place of William of

---

[1] J. Bruce, *op. cit.* 23.
[2] Cf. *The England of Elizabeth*, 273-5.

Orange, but really no-one could fill that rôle : certainly not a foreigner, ignorant of the language, the people, their obstinate traditions and acute divisions. Nor had he the character for such an intolerable position—one that required a Burghley, infinitely politic and self-controlled. Leicester was an intelligent man, but he was not wise. The Queen used to say that there " lacked a Northumberland in his place "—by which she meant, I suppose, he was not the man his father was.[1] He was Machiavellian and uncandid, personal in his reactions, vindictive to those who crossed him : he had not that impersonality, that disillusioned justice of mind necessary to those in the highest place. In consequence, he created enemies. Like Anjou, like William, he found he had a lot to put up with. After the honeymoon of his reception, he began to see that the Dutch idea was to make him their instrument ; or rather, that the very small minority that controlled the province of Holland, a burgher oligarchy run by Paul Buys and Oldenbarneveldt, had every intention of ruling affairs, contrary to the wishes of the great majority in the other provinces, particularly of the democratic artisan population of the towns, like Utrecht, centre of Leicester's partisans. Far from being the leader of a united people—not even the Prince had achieved that—Leicester became the embittered leader of a faction within it. Moreover, he did not acquire the prestige of victory : he brought with him military incompetence : Parma's victories continued, English intervention—as often in our affairs at first—proved an acute disillusionment, our prestige dwindled to its nadir in just those years.

The clue to English ill-success was, as usual, amateurishness, unprofessionalism, in the beginning. We can observe in a few years the attainment of professionalism, of military excellence, until, under the leadership of Vere, the English troops were the best in Prince Maurice's army. Leicester's correspondence is full of *cris de cœur* for aid : he has no sufficient staff to help him ; he wants Sir William Pelham, Master of the Ordnance and the most reputed soldier of experience, sent over ; now he wants Sir William Stanley, one of the best commanders in Ireland. He asks for Daniel Rogers or Thomas Bodley to aid him in his endless confabulations with the States. They were sent him— though Burghley added his own brother-in-law, Henry Killigrew, to keep an eye on what was going on. Leicester did not make

[1] J. Bruce, *op. cit.* 388.

things any easier by an open breach with Norris, by far the
ablest soldier on the spot, who was certainly better qualified to
command the army. Immediately before Leicester's arrival,
Norris rendered two pieces of good service. He captured a
sconce, *i.e.* a strong point, by Arnhem and he beat off an attack
by Parma himself with some loss on the way towards Nijmegen.[1]
The Queen wrote to congratulate him, but cautioned him that
her orders were to stand on the defensive, both from care of
her subjects' lives and because her meaning in the Netherlands,
as she had notified the world, was " principally to defend ".[2]
Norris was to have special care that " the young gentlemen of
best birth " should not undertake hazardous attempts. (One is
reminded of Nicholas I's civilised intervention to keep the
young Tolstoy out of the front-line at Sebastopol.) But, indeed, it
was a lady's conception of conducting war, and the men at the
front had reason to complain that it was not possible to fight on
such terms. The Queen's genius was not for war ; she had no
liking for it and no belief in it.

When Leicester arrived he judged that it was impossible
to meet Parma in the open field : no doubt reasonably enough,
with himself in command. He complained of the poor fighting
quality of the Dutch, of the state of his own men, of the Queen's
failure to make up the required number of horse. Actually, he
had brought over more men than the Queen had agreed to pay
for : so men went unpaid, unclothed, unfed. Among those he
brought over were some five hundred from among his tenantry :[3]
a quasi-feudal touch, which illustrates the unprofessionalism of it
all—so unlike Vere's army later. Leicester writes : " there was
no soldier yet able to buy himself a pair of hose, and it is too
too great shame to see how they go, and it kills their hearts to
show themselves among men ".[4] And again, " it is folly to speak
for [*i.e.* ask for] money, though our men be ragged and torn and
like rogues : pity to see them. Specially those of her Majesty's
pay the worst." No doubt, like Wellington's army, they were the
scum of the earth, who " saved the sum of things for [very little]
pay ". For depredations of these rogues upon Dutch citizens the
Queen had given express command that she would hold the chiefs

---

[1] T. Churchyard, *Discourses*, 71-3 ; *Cal. S.P. For. 1585–6*, 165.
[2] *Ibid.* xiii.
[3] J. Bruce, *op. cit.* 11.
[4] *Ibid.* 167, 285.

responsible. Hence Roger Williams, for some offences committed upon the island of Tertolle : " At midnight I trussed up three of the principals upon the gibbet, in addition to two who were strangled in the lodging ".[1] Digges, whom Leicester brought over as Muster Master, wrote that in the garrisons the men were " so licentiously accustomed heretofore as any due military discipline seemeth to them intolerable ".[2] The fact was that a due military discipline had not yet been achieved in the English army ; and in the absence of it, Leicester thought it better to garrison the towns, which he feared would go over to the enemy otherwise. This meant dispersing his forces, frittering away the strength of his army, as Norris saw it. A public breach opened between his Excellency and his best fighting soldier ; only an intervention by the Queen kept Norris in the Netherlands : she told him to lay aside all private passions and respects and bend his mind wholly to the service in hand.[3]

The result was to be seen in the disappointment of the extravagant hopes entertained of the first summer's campaign. Leicester began by being far too sanguine : on arrival he liked the prospects twenty times better than he had done at home ; then he liked them ten times better. In August he was confiding his discouragement to Walsingham : " if I have wanted wit, the fault is hers and yours among you for the choice and that would not better assist me. . . . Well, I must be short (I have made a great blot, through sudden drops of rain falling)."[4] We see that he was at last writing from the open field. For Parma had taken Grave, Venlo and Neuss and was securing the forward line of the Maas. Leicester was furious at the surrender of Grave, which had been well provided for : he was convinced that it was by treachery, and had the young Dutch commander hanged—which infuriated the Dutch : William had put up with such things, surrounded as he had been by treacheries all his life. And the English troops were no better : Alost had been betrayed to the enemy by its English commander, Captain Piggott, aided by Captains Dalton and Taylor, all for want of pay.[5] Now, July : " It is no marvel our men run fast away. I am ashamed to write it, there was five hundred ran away in two days, and a great many to the enemy."[6] This theme crops up again and again :

---

[1] *Cal. S.P. For. 1585–6*, 165.
[2] *Ibid.* 115.
[3] *Cal. S.P. For. 1585–7*, xxiii.
[4] J. Bruce, *op. cit.* 395.
[5] *Cal. S.P. For. 1583–4*, 246.
[6] J. Bruce, 338.

now Leicester has taken some four hundred deserters " and have executed some for example, but not many, for that in conscience they suffer overmuch ".[1] By contrast the young gentlemen of spirit, for whom the Queen was anxious, were signalising themselves by foolhardy exploits which had no real effect on the war.

Philip Sidney, Leicester's nephew and Walsingham's son-in-law, had been given the key-post of Governor of Flushing ; a representative of the other party in the Council, Burghley's elder son, Thomas Cecil, being made Governor of Brill. Now Sidney was out in the field : " Your son Philip with his bands had the leading and entering the town [Axel], which was notably handled ; for they caused thirty or forty to swim over the ditch and so get up the wall and opened the gate ".[2] They effected a surprise and captured the town, with a garrison of some six hundred beside burghers. But Parma was marching upon a much more important objective, Rheinberg—a key to the Rhine, which would open communications with Germany for his famished provinces—and Leicester dared not attack him. The best Leicester could do was to attack Doesburg, to draw him away. Here, Pelham was wounded by Leicester's side. " I being weary and ready to go to bed, the Marshal came to me and told me what beastly pioneers the Dutchmen were, and having begun their trench every shot makes them run away. . . . I, much against his will, would needs go with him. It was very dark when we set out and afterward somewhat starlight, insomuch as we found ourselves suddenly almost at the very gate of the town. The Marshal perceiving he had missed a little his way, he and I going before the rest six or seven paces, he stepped before me to see the right way, with which instant a caliver shot from the wall strake him in the belly. Thinking himself slain, he turned about speaking very cheerfully to me and thanked God it was his hap to be between me and that blow. . . . So, at his home-coming, I had Goodrowse to see his wound and it was three fingers just, with the navel on the right side, and how far the bullet entered we know not."[3] How familiar and repetitive the episodes of war are ! His Excellency's vivid description does not conceal his pride at having been in the firing-line. Pelham recovered but was fated to carry that bullet in his belly

---

[1] *Ibid.* 365.   [2] *Ibid.* 337.   [3] *Ibid.* 401.

the rest of his life, which was not long.[1]

That autumn he took part in a more celebrated exploit : the attack on the convoy going into Zutphen, not far from Arnhem—of a searching memory to our own generation—in which Philip Sidney received his death-wound. It was a piece of bravado led by Norris : the troop of 60 horse consisting almost wholly of the young gentlemen of birth the Queen had asked him to take special care of. Altogether there were some 200 horse supported by 300 foot under Sir William Stanley : " he and old Read are worth their weight in pearl ; they be two as rare captains as any prince living hath ".[2] While waiting in the early morning mist for the convoy to lumber into view, Sidney, noticing that Pelham had no cuisses (leg-armour), threw aside his own. When the mist lifted they found themselves attacking a convoy of some 1500 horse and 3000 foot. They did not desist, but went straight for them, inflicting heavy losses before they drew off. The convoy got through to Zutphen. But among the wounded was Sidney, who rode off the field, his thigh-bone broken by a musket-shot. Leicester wrote : " but for his hurt, that Thursday may run amongst any of our Thursdays, for there was never a more valiant day's service seen this hundred years by so few men against so many ".[3]

Everyone knows the story his friend Fulke Greville tells : it is part of the immemorial legend of the English people, and so much part of the age that it may not be omitted without the kind of hurt that over-sophistication does to the truth of life. " In which sad progress, passing along by the rest of the army, where his uncle the General was, and being thirsty with excess of bleeding, he called for drink. But as he was putting the bottle to his mouth, he saw a poor soldier carried along, who had eaten his last at that same feast, ghastly casting up his eyes at the bottle. Which Sir Philip perceiving, took it from his head before he drank and delivered it to the poor man with these words, ' Thy necessity is yet greater than mine '. And when he had pledged this poor soldier, he was presently carried to Arnhem."[4]

There he lingered for some weeks and was thought to be

---

[1] He came home to recuperate by drinking the waters at Bath ; next year, on his return to Flushing, he died.

[2] Leicester, in Bruce, 417.

[3] *Ibid.* 430.

[4] *Sir Fulke Greville's Life of Sir Philip Sidney* (ed. 1907), 129-30.

recovering. Leicester wrote bulletins of his progress to Walsingham : " your son and mine is well amending as ever any man hath done for so short time. He feeleth no grief now but his long lying."[1] In fact he was wasting away, " the very shoulder-bones of this delicate patient worn through his skin, with constant and obedient posturing of his body " to the doctors.[2] He was too observant to have much hope in them, willing " rather to submit his body to these artists than any further to believe in them ". No doubt they killed him. One morning, lifting up the bedclothes for greater ease, he smelt the unmistakable smell of putrefaction and knew he was lost. With Christian resignation he made all the preparations for his end, calling the ministers about him with whom he pondered the strangeness of fate and " the design of God in afflicting the children of men "[3]—as he well might, since he was a devout believer. The artist in him did not die : " this restless soul of his (changing only the air, and not the chords of her harmony) calls for music, especially that song which himself had entitled *La Cuisse rompue* ".[4] And then, at the end, taking leave of his friends : " ' Love my memory . . . But above all, govern your will and affections by the will and word of your Creator ; in me beholding the end of this world with all her vanities.' "

Philip Sidney's death made an extraordinary impression both abroad and at home. Leicester wrote to Walsingham : " Sir, the grief I have taken for the loss of my dear son and yours would not suffer me to write sooner of those ill news unto you, specially being in so good hope so very little time before of his good recovery. . . . What perfection he was grown unto and how able to serve her Majesty and his country all men here almost wondered at. For my own part, I have lost, beside the comfort of my life, a most principal stay and help in my service here and, if I may say it, I think none of all hath a greater loss than the Queen's Majesty herself."[5] The Queen had never been particularly kind to Sidney and was always quick to blame him : there was something in his personality that was uncongenial to her, perhaps the very note of perfection Leicester mentioned, the priggishness. But now she was so much affected, that in sending a bearer of a message of consolation " for the loss of her

[1] J. Bruce, 429.
[2] *Greville's Life*, 133.
[3] M. W. Wallace, *Life of Sir Philip Sidney*, 385.
[4] *Greville's Life*, 139-40.
[5] J. Bruce, 445-6.

dear servant and your lordship's dearest nephew, as she forgot to touch some things in those her letters ".[1] When she recovered herself, the old termagant reverted to her normal attitude and later would refer to "that inconsiderate fellow, Sidney " : he had thrown away his life in her service, instead of preserving it to serve her.

The world does not judge so rationally : it takes a hero to its heart. It is doubtful if the Queen of England recognised the category—except in those who were both heroic *and* successful, like Drake. And indeed, it is difficult for us to grasp all that Philip Sidney meant to his age. Leicester's word " perfection " must be the clue, an achieved goodness of heart. In a world that was brutal and violent, Sidney, though a young man of spirit, had made himself gentle ; where others were pushing and jostling in a too competitive society, he was self-sacrificing ; where people were envious and mean, he was kind and encouraging. And this in addition to his gifts of mind and taste, for he had genius : one of the first poets and prose-writers of the age, one of the prime creators of its literature. No wonder the enemy, Mendoza, " could not but lament to see Christendom deprived of so rare a light in these dark times ".[2] Those cold, all-seeing eyes in the Escorial turned aside from the report to note in the margin : " He was my godson ".

Unlike his uncle, Sidney was popular in the Netherlands. The Prince of Orange had had a high regard for him when quite young and prophesied great things of him ; if he had lived he would have had a very eminent career in the Netherlands. Now the States of Zealand asked to have him buried in their midst. But it was determined to give him a magnificent public funeral at home—which was as well, for Sidney, generous to a fault, had not left the wherewithal to bury himself. Like the Prince, he had deeply indebted himself for the cause. Early the next year his body was brought across on *The Black Pinnace* and borne in solemn pageantry, representing the whole English state, to its resting-place in St. Paul's. (Later, Sir Roger Williams was laid at his feet : no-one now knows where.) No subject had ever been accorded such a funeral : precursor of Nelson and Wellington in that spot. With Philip Sidney some ideal quality went out of the war—as with Rupert Brooke in the war of 1914 :

[1] J. Bruce, 451.
[2] q. Wallace, *op. cit.* 391.

it ceased to be amateurish and sometimes chivalrous ; it became tougher and more professional.

This miserable winter of 1586–7 saw English prestige in the Netherlands at its lowest. Leicester had ended up in open conflict with the States, which for their part were determined to reduce his power to a minimum. Leicester regarded his credit as " cracked " ever since the Queen sent Heneage with her orders to him to give up the " absolute government " ; " for indeed ", he wrote, with a kick at the Queen—in the security of his correspondence with Walsingham—" the government they seemed they had given from themselves to me stuck in their stomachs always, and but to have pleased her Majesty and satisfy the people they would never have done it. . . . For my own part, I will not endure such another year's service, with so many crosses and wants and so little assistance every way, if I were sure to gain as much as all these provinces were worth." [1] Sick of it all, disillusioned and discouraged, braved by " churls and tinkers ", he was anxious to return. Now the Queen, with greater sense of responsibility, would not allow him to come away until some order had been taken for government in his absence and for the command of her army. Though he retained his formal title and made a brief return the next year, it was the end of Leicester's effective power. Willoughby, whom the Queen would have preferred all along, succeeded him as General and did better in conditions that could not be worse.

In that first year the war had engulfed £140,000, yet many of the troops were without pay or food or clothes : that was the main reason for the desertions and the betrayals of places to the enemy. [2] Sixty per cent of the army were sick, wounded or dead. This was a higher rate of casualties than usual : it was generally estimated that at the end of six months an army would be down to fifty per cent from sickness and desertion. The simple truth is that there was indescribable corruption and confusion in the army, and Leicester, so far from dealing with it—no-one could have done that all at once—had made it worse. He began by increasing the pay of the officers, including his own ; but none of this got through to the men. He found the companies on his arrival even lower in strength than ordinary : the usual dodge, for the captains received pay for a full company :

[1] J. Bruce, 424, 429.
[2] *Cal. S.P. For. 1586–7*, xxiv.

the fewer in strength the more the captains pocketed.[1] He and the States kept engaging more forces, which they could not pay and the Queen had not contracted for.[2] However, to keep them from starving her money was diverted to pay them ; her own troops then went short. I fear that Leicester, though acute enough in matters of private finance, had no firm hold on the principles of public finance.

In June–July 1587 the Queen sent a new force of 4650 foot to make up the depleted numbers.[3] She had agreed to meet the cost of sending them ; once they were over, the States refused to pay them, though they were nominally in their pay along with some 1800 others : both remained an additional burden on her. Her own officers—as in most armies of the time—were all in the conspiracy against any adequate checks, from the General, who had his own troop of horse to make out of, down to the meanest captain. Leicester : " It is the thing the captain desireth, never to have full pay, but to run on with imprests [*i.e.* advances on account], for so shall his bands be never looked into. . . . There will be whole bands demanded for half bands and all the world cannot help it, do what man can." Whatever sums the Queen sent to answer Leicester's repeated demands for money, she could never get any account rendered, " God knows by whose default. . . . It is a sieve that spends as it receives to little purpose." She found that she could trust no-one to keep a proper watch over finance. We have seen that corruption was endemic in sixteenth-century administration ; it was at its highest in the army, where everyone was in fraud. " Only the common soldier shared the honour of being a mere victim with the Queen. . . . Elizabeth did her best for him as she did for herself." But without accounts she was helpless ; she insisted again and again, before she would send more money, that

---

[1] For the government's line in all this, cf. an undated communication in *Salisbury MSS*. XIV. 312-13 : " The Queen is not disposed to send over a new supply of treasure until your accounts are sent over. There is a proportion of £11,000 set down, which exceeds ours by £1000, and will be greatly misliked by the Queen ; whereof you will do well to put the Lord General in mind. Considering the great mortality that has happened among the soldiers, of whom about 2000 are said to be dead, and that the number of persons covenanted to be entertained is not yet full, it is looked for that the defalcations shall abate so much of the said proportion of £10,000 as that the whole allowance for the time shall not exceed £8000 a month."

[2] *Salisbury MSS*. XIII. 309.

[3] In these two paragraphs I follow, and the quotations are from, J. E. Neale, " Elizabeth and the Netherlands ", *E.H.R.* 1930, 373 foll.

accounts be rendered : " though it be continually alleged that great sums are due, yet why such sums are due or to whom they are due, and who are paid and who not paid . . . is never certified ".

She determined next year on a policy of seeing the common soldier fed, leaving the rest to suffer for their sins if they pleased. She ordered Buckhurst, whom she sent over, to allot and earmark moneys for specific purposes. Still the money went down the drain : still no proper check, no accounts for it. She refused to send more treasure. But the troops could not be allowed to starve : she sent £30,000. The Council ordered a detailed examination of the complaints of the men : they found that the captains had been paid, the men defrauded. At last the Queen went on strike : no accounts, no money. In December the accounts came : pay was fifteen months in arrear ! Professor Neale concludes : " When the history of official probity is written the Elizabethan Age will not make pleasant reading. . . . [The Queen's] financial principles were those of sound business : to pay what she owed and spend what she could afford. They were principles rare among princes in her day and explain that miracle of her age, the solvency of her government."

It was fortunate for the English that Parma was harassed by similar difficulties, and his were to increase, while the English gradually surmounted theirs. At this moment when Parma was poised for the final onslaught on the North, Philip began distracting him from his objective with demands to prepare for the invasion of England, in which Parma never believed ; he was then ordered to invade France twice in support of Philip's plans there, so that the moment passed for ever. Dispersal of effort was the clue to Philip's failure as of Louis XIV's and Napoleon's, of Germany's under William II and Hitler ; limitation of objective, of which Elizabeth gave so instinctive and tenacious an example, the clue to England's success. What added to the distrust between her and the States was that all this time she was in negotiation with Parma. It did no ultimate harm : it revealed the duplicity of the Spaniards, who spun out the negotiations until the Armada was ready ; Parma's Secretary, Richardot, made it clear that they had no real interest in peace : they expected to dictate terms on English soil. The Queen made a determined effort for peace in the spring of 1587 : now, very much against her will, she had to go on.

What roused the Dutch to fury against the English was Sir William Stanley's betrayal of Deventer to the Spaniards. " By this treason we are all grown hateful to this people, having nothing in their mouths but the treasons and disorders of the English." [1] A tremor of fear passed through the nation—the crisis was a factor in making them a nation : it precipitated a bitter determination in the Dutch oligarchy, the men of William's circle, to assume and exercise all power themselves. Elizabeth's determination to give no support to Leicester's faction played into their hands : people might say, as they often have said, that the English were sacrificing their friends to make up to their enemies. But it was the right policy : all through the crisis the Queen was doing her best to reconcile people to the States and hold things together. For treason in the English command shook confidence to its foundations. Leicester had insisted on bringing Stanley over from Ireland, where he had had a long career of able, hard service. He had served fifteen years, doing severe execution upon the O'Tooles and the Kavanaghs in 1581, stringing up three hundred rebels of Desmond's in Munster so that " a man might now travel the whole country and none molest him ". He petitioned to be made President of Connaught for his services : his petition was refused.

With Leicester in the Netherlands, they decided to recruit Irish bands as being hardier and less subject to sickness. It was against the Queen's wishes ; but Stanley went back to Ireland and recruited some 1400 of them. These were the hooligans—the word is Irish—who disgraced the capture of Doesburg, sacking the town and rifling the churches. [2] On his way through London he had been in touch with his brother, the Jesuit—he came completely under Jesuit influence at this heyday of their hopes. Stanley had been brought up a Catholic, the head actually of the senior branch of the family. He had served his apprenticeship under Alva. He fought, as always, gallantly and with resolution at Zutphen ; Leicester, as we have seen, thought him worth his weight in pearl. He now made him Governor of Deventer— against the wishes of the States. Once in command, Stanley made all the arrangements with Rowland Yorke to surrender Deventer and Zutphen sconce to the Spaniards and pass over, with practically all their officers and men, into Spanish service.

[1] *Cal. S.P. For. 1586-7*, xviii.
[2] Cf. *Cal. S.P. For. 1585-6*, xxxviii.

They did it only for religion's sake, Stanley said. The action did untold damage to the English name ; it was some years before the places were recovered and the stain wiped out. The government had not realised the obvious effect on a man of such abilities, who had rendered such services—and with his back-ground—of frustrating his proper ambitions. It is a very contemporary theme, a situation familiar in our own torn time. What added to its irony was that at this moment the Queen was about to reward his services with honours, and considering making him Lord Deputy of Ireland. She was too late : he had his moment of sweet revenge upon the people who had too long disregarded him. The rest of his life was bitter enough : he journeyed to Spain to advise on the invasion of England—and was disappointed at his reception. In 1588 he stood ready at Parma's side to join the invasion. In 1590 he was in Spain again advising on invasion and thereafter made almost yearly journeys to urge measures against the Queen : in 1595 he was reproved by the Spanish government for his violence against her. In 1600 he had the pleasure of witnessing the brilliant defeat of the Spanish infantry, at last, by Vere's English at Nieuport. He lived to be old : in 1624 he was in Madrid—his pension had been unpaid for six years. Towards the end he quarrelled with the Jesuits, who had deflected him from his duty and ruined his life, and transferred his devotion to the Carthusians. Though peace and good relations had long been restored, he never got permission to come home to England again.[1]

All through 1587 the Dutch remained suspicious, sullen and unco-operative. They dismissed most of the English troops in their pay. They brought the young Maurice, hardly more than a boy, into the open, made him governor of Holland and Zealand. Willoughby, left to clear up the *débris* of Leicester's grandeur, had a difficult time with them : " there is nothing prevaileth with these people but fear ", he wrote.[2] In spite of large reinforcements and a heartening defence, Sluys fell—which gave Philip, immersed in his fantasy of conquest, unwonted joy : a port of embarkation for England. Maurice's fleet had sailed away leaving the place to its fate.[3] We have a very

---

[1] His estates do not seem to have been confiscated : his grandson succeeded to them ; he was made a baronet at the Restoration.

[2] *Cal. S.P. For. Jan.–July 1589*, xii.

[3] *Cal. S.P. For. Jan.–June 1588*, ix.

unfavourable report of him from the young Robert Cecil from the Hague, in a letter to his father : " On my life I never saw a worse behaviour, except it were one lately come from school ".[1] Maurice had been entirely brought up in camps and in war, without the civilising influence of women—to whom, for the rest, he did not respond. The supercilious young courtier was misled, as his successors, generations later, were by the boorish manners of William of Orange : though no politician, Maurice became a great soldier. An Italian merchant had been ill-handled by English troops and held to ransom : the Queen interposed, ordered restitution and " be careful hereafter that no such barbarous act be committed ; for that such kind of proceedings cannot but render us and the cause hateful unto the world ".[2] An English troop of horse was cut to pieces by Verdugo outside the gates of Zwolle, because the burghers would not open them to let them in.[3] Robert Cecil reported re-assuringly that Parma's shipping in the Scheldt was but a scare-crow : there were no ships to speak of, only a lot of flat-bottomed boats : someone said that one of the Queen's ships " would clatter them altogether ".[4] The Zealanders kept watch on the Scheldt, an easy assignment ; but this is all the Dutch would do against the Armada. They took no part in the fighting : they left the English to fight it out themselves. After the victory the Queen did not fail to point out, against their assumption of responsibility for it, that " they had not dealt with the enemy ".[5]

In fact 1588 was the turning-point here, too : as in 1940, people realised that, underneath the shifts and changes of policy, the English were a tough, courageous people who, though they did not wish to be responsible for war, were not afraid to wage it when they had to. The Dutch saw that they were not going to be deserted. They began to perceive that the Queen's deter-mination not to wage war beyond her means[6] implied that she meant to be the ally of the United Provinces, not their sovereign. This had been *her* policy all along. The Leicester episode had

---

[1] *Cal. S.P. For. Jan.–June 1588*, ix.   [2] *Ibid.* 388.   [3] *Ibid.* xlvii.
[4] *Ibid.* 245.   [5] *Cal. S.P. For. July–Dec. 1588*, xvi.
[6] Already from 1585 to 1588 she had spent £378,000 in aiding the Netherlands. The Treasury expenses rose from £149,000 in 1583 to £367,000 in 1587 and in 1588 £420,000. This could not go on. In 1589, in spite of a large grant from Parliament, the Queen was driven to borrow £100,000 in Germany and to sell, in one year, Crown lands to the value of £125,000. *Cal. S.P. For. July–Dec. 1588*, vi.

been a false start, though perhaps it was unavoidable as an attempt to fill the vacuum after William's assassination. In an extraordinarily short time the able men around Oldenbarneveldt established their power and created a state on the basis of their oligarchy, beginning with the establishment of a financial administration that was viable, and exercising sovereign functions. By the end of 1588 the authority of the States General was firmly established throughout the United Provinces : henceforth the alliance was on a firm foundation for the rest of the war. The policy of the English government, which had in a special sense been the Queen's, had been pursued " with a persistency and realism of which many historians would hardly believe them capable "[1]—or, we may add, which the simple categories of nineteenth-century historians, Froude as much as Motley, were incapable of comprehending. The sad experience of our time enables us to do it better justice, to appreciate how fitted it was to shifting, complex, unprecedented circumstances.

Parma had been unable to move out at the crucial moment of the Armada's arrival at Calais, though he had dug waterways for his flat-bottomed boats from Sluys to Nieuport and put his men aboard them.[2] But weather, lack of preparation, the flight of the Armada into the North Sea, the tactical situation, made a move out of the question—and the Spaniards blamed the great soldier for the Armada's failure.[3] Immediately after its passing—like Napoleon's grander movement from Boulogne to Austerlitz—Parma swiftly concentrated an army of 12,000 against Bergen-op-Zoom, in English occupation and controlling the passage of the Scheldt to Antwerp. Bergen had been denuded of men to defend England. The Queen at once sent Morgan's companies back and 2000 more men under Norris.[4] Inspired by the events of that summer, the spirit was very much Roger Williams's " with God's help, he shall be fought withal on the breach and come on't what will, he never gets one of our ensigns. At the worst, I will burn them."[5] A stratagem was laid by William Grimston to encourage a premature assault : a fake offer of betrayal was made to Parma—it was hoped to catch

---

[1] *Ibid.* xlvii.   [2] L. van der Essen, *op. cit.* V. 220.

[3] Philip's increasing distrust of Parma became known in France and was counted on there from 1589. *Salisbury MSS.* XIII. 404.

[4] *Cal. S.P. For. July–Dec. 1588*, xx.

[5] *Cal. S.P. For. 1585–6*, xvi.

Stanley.[1] A large number of Spanish troops were caught in a bad position, with an incoming tide behind them in which many were drowned. Parma was so discouraged as to withdraw from the siege, with one-third of his troops put out of action, the rest exhausted. " The successful defence of Bergen against the finest army in Europe, led by the greatest captain of the age, reflected no less credit upon England's soldiers than the . . . Armada actions did upon her sailors."[2]

The circumstances of the war were changing : it was becoming regular, the state could take it in its stride ; its conduct was becoming more professional, especially in the Netherlands, that central school of warfare, where a new generation of commanders was coming to the fore. With Philip's intervention in France, the Queen was forced to send expedition after expedition in the 'nineties to oppose the Spaniards and aid Henry IV : on average in these years she had some 10,000 or 12,000 troops strung out along the Channel littoral from Brittany to Zealand.[3] In 1590 Philip sent 3000 soldiers to Brittany to aid the League there and gain a foothold at that end of the Channel. It was a move that had to be opposed and Norris was sent with a comparable force : 1500 Low Countries' veterans, 1500 new raw levies from the West Country. Henry was supposed to contribute double the number ; in fact he was at the other end of the Channel opposing Parma, who had been ordered into Picardy.[4] The French force amounted to only half the English and we had to bear the brunt of the campaign. There was an exceptionally high rate of sickness and sometimes the force was down to 1200 men ; it consumed several infusions of man-power : only half, if that, ever returned.

In 1591 the Queen was drawn into the struggle in Normandy. The young Essex knelt before her a couple of hours on three occasions to be allowed to command it : against her judgment she let him go. Under him the best equipped and most prompt of all her expeditions accomplished least : at one point he went caracoling with most of his officers, only a troop of horse,

---

[1] For full account *v.* T. Churchyard, *op. cit.* 107-9.
[2] *Cal. S.P. For. July–Dec. 1588*, xxiii.
[3] E. P. Cheyney, *A History of England*, I. 260.
[4] For the Queen's frequent protests to Henry, and for the matter in the above paragraphs *v. Correspondence of Sir Henry Unton (Roxburghe Club), passim.* It was a handicap that Unton, our ambassador, was ill most of the time and—in spite of being treated with unicorn's horn—died.

through enemy country to meet Henry IV, losing his only brother, " the half-arch of my house ". This was the kind of bravado that made Essex the darling of the London mob ; and it was the war in Normandy—always closest to English hearts —that called forth *Henry VI*, gave it its success and started the career of the most popular dramatist of the time. The objective of the campaign was the reduction of Rouen : the Queen had set her mind on it : probably as a pledge for the return of Calais. Henry knew two to that one—he consistently outplayed the Queen at her own games. He found himself too much engaged in Picardy to play his promised part in joint operations. Parma marched across country to relieve Rouen : the campaign was abortive. Our forces were down to a half from sickness : the usual rate expected after six months in the field—really much the same as during the Peninsular War, lower than that in the Crimean.[1]

All the while Elizabeth was feeding Henry with subsidies in the common cause, £60,000 in one year, " such aids as never any king hath done the like to any other ".[2] At the arrival of English bullion on one occasion, the impecunious Béarnais said he had never seen so much money at one time—likely enough ! Between 1589 and 1595 five expeditions were sent to France, a total of some 20,000 men, of whom perhaps half returned. In 1593 Henry changed the situation by making his peace with Catholicism. His return to the bosom of the true faith gave no pleasure in Spain : it threw plans quite out. Elizabeth—who took these things more sincerely than some people who made more fuss—was much upset. She wrote Henry argumentative letters, sorrowful rather than indignant ; she searched the Scriptures and the Fathers ; she had long conversations with her Archbishop and finally consoled herself with translating Boethius's *Consolation of Philosophy*. She had received a shock : we see that she was, what many have denied, a genuine Protestant, of an undogmatic kind. Henry, for his part, was quite right to vert : from being the king of a faction he now became king of the nation. The League was defeated : Philip's plans for giving France a monarch, which Parma had always seen to be a fantasy, come to nothing.[3]

[1] D. Stewart, " Sickness and Mortality Rates of the English Army in the Sixteenth Century ", *Journal R.A.M.C.*, July 1945, 27.
[2] q. Cheyney, *op. cit.* I. 217.   [3] L. van der Essen, *op. cit.* V. 302.

By 1595 a vast change had come over the situation. Henry was now a national ruler, the United Provinces much nearer national independence, the English state had proved that it could support a long war and sustain a leading rôle in Europe ; Spain was contained, her overwhelming ascendancy undermined, the country exhausted—to achieve what ? But Elizabeth was still subject to Henry's demands for support. Her constant theme in her correspondence with him was that she must conserve her people's love, that people forgot that she had another realm besides France to keep—and then, was he not allowing the Spaniards to occupy Breton ports too easily ?[1] Her acknowledged aim was to maintain the balance of Europe. To this end she formed a Triple Alliance, with France and the United Provinces, by the Treaty of Greenwich in 1596. With this country as the connecting link in the coalition, how it looks forward to our essential rôle in maintaining the balance, and the liberties of Europe, in the centuries to come ! The Queen swore to the treaty on the gospels at Greenwich : her interpretation was that each was bound not to make a separate peace—which Henry did not subsequently deny, though he made it with Spain in 1598. This, however, gave her the chance to make a new treaty with the Netherlands. They were stronger now and, through the years of war, become exceedingly prosperous : in the next decades they were to go ahead of us and become the leading sea-power—a remarkable transformation, a wonderful achievement. The States acknowledged a debt of £800,000 and at last took steps to pay it ; they would contribute to the pay of English troops in the Netherlands ; they would aid this country with ships and men in case of need. We see that they are treated as an independent state, as equal allies ; and on this basis the war was fought to a conclusion.

It is impossible to describe its later, more successful stages, on the same scale as we have its difficult unprosperous beginnings, let alone portray the war as a whole in its various theatres over twenty years.[2] This book can only proceed representatively, and since the Netherlands provided the most significant theatre, a continuous school of warfare for the rest, let us return to it,

---

[1] Cf. *Salisbury MSS.* XIII. xxv, 448.
[2] The best, though a somewhat colourless, account is to be found in Cheyney, *op. cit.*

if summarily. We can conveniently group its events around its leading figure, Sir Francis Vere.

Vere offers a striking contrast with the commanders in the earlier part of the war : where they were impulsive, chancy, amateurish, very much hit-or-miss, he was entirely professional and he never missed. He had a remarkable, an unbroken, record of success—in this like Wellington, whom as a commander he much resembled. He was, unlike most Elizabethans, a rather impersonal man, a cool, objective head, reserved and indeed secret, with an infallible eye for a position or a tactical opening. He never made a mistake—which does not mean that he was a purely defensive soldier : when the situation was prepared, when the moment he had in mind came, he never hesitated but struck hard—in this, unlike his friend, Prince Maurice, who was slower to make up his mind.[1] Vere was a complete soldier, who lived all his life in camps and hardly ever appeared at Court.[2] Unmarried himself, he was very much opposed to his officers marrying : it softened them and slackened discipline. He could not bear absenting captains. As we should expect—and so unlike his predecessors—he was a first-class organiser, who gave his mind to every aspect of military matters, discipline, supply, as much as fighting in the field. As a fighting man he was very tough and brave, often in the forefront and many times wounded : he was not old when he died, worn out by his wounds and incessant service. As a commander, he was exceedingly *rusé*, full of stratagems and surprises : his captains were apt to call him " the Fox ".[3] His attitude was a scientific one : he was skilled at entrenchments, much interested in fortifications and works ; this he had learned mainly from Maurice, whose forte it was. When we consider his all-round excellence, his long run of unbroken victories, we are justified in considering him " the first great English general in modern history ".[4]

Also, Vere had the inestimable advantage of getting on with the States. When Willoughby was withdrawn to take command in Normandy, Elizabeth made no more generals : she left the

---

[1] Cf. Vere's own judgment of Maurice, " as he is naturally slow in resolving ". *Commentaries, ed. cit.* 85.

[2] Cf. Naunton, *Fragmenta Regalia* (Arber's English Reprints), 62.

[3] Cf. Sir John Ogle's " Continuation of the Siege of Ostend ", in Vere's *Commentaries,* 157.

[4] C. R. Markham, *The Fighting Veres,* iv.

command of her troops in the Netherlands to the young Vere, who was no more than Serjeant-Major-General. We watch him gradually gaining the confidence of the States until they make him *their* General of all the English troops in their pay. Then the Queen becomes jealous of his following their service rather than hers. In the end, he is made a General and given the governorship of Brill. The States trusted him absolutely and confided some of their most difficult enterprises to him. Meteren tells us, " le Chevalier François Vere était homme fort habile, et agréable aux Provinces, plus qu'aucun autre étranger ".[1] When he retired from their service, they rewarded him unprecedentedly with a large pension. So that his name recovered in him something of the fortune squandered by his cousin, the seventeenth Earl ; where other Elizabethan commanders spent their fortunes on war, this professional—again like Wellington—made his out of it.

We are fortunate in possessing Vere's own *Commentaries* on his actions : we note the Renaissance reference to Caesar, and from the book the broad profile of Vere's personality emerges: concise, impersonal, not a redundant word, factual and trustworthy, not a touch of the usual Elizabethan *brio*.[2] Vere's first assignment was the defence of the Bommelwaart in 1589—practically an island between Waal and Maas : an immensely strong position, against which Mansfeld deployed an army of 12,000 men. Maurice had only 800, of whom 600 were Vere's Englishmen. The complicated operations lasted most of the season. They fill many pages of the State Papers ; all that Vere says of them is, " I used such industry in the entrenching of the island and planting artillery, that the enemy in the end desisted from the enterprise ".[3] In fact it was the decisive check of the offensive towards the North and with heavy losses. It was followed by the relief of Rheinberg on two successive

---

[1] q. C. R. Markham, *The Fighting Veres*, 147. Motley chooses to suggest that Vere was not on good terms with the States General. Meteren should know better —and indeed the whole evidence is clean contrary.

[2] Considering that Vere wrote his *Commentaries* several years after the events—he had no thought of publication—it is remarkably accurate, save in slightly exaggerated estimates of enemy casualties. Motley describes the work as " marked throughout by spleen, inordinate personal and national self-esteem, undisguised hostility to the Nassaus and the Hollanders, and wounded pride of opinion ". One wonders how Motley can have got this impression—the truth is so much the opposite. Cf. Markham, 302.

[3] Vere, *Commentaries*, 2.

occasions ; on the second, great slaughter was done upon the Neapolitans, " who made no great resistance. . . . The fight was begun and ended with one of the two English troops, which could not exceed four hundred men. . . . The enemy lost about eight hundred men."[1] Further pursuit was held up by " the covetousness of the soldier, whereof a good part could no longer be kept from rifling the enemy and taking horses ".

Next year the castle of Litkenhoven was relieved : the enemy fort dominating it having refused to yield, it was assaulted and, in accordance with custom, " all the men put to the sword, being in number three hundred and fifty, all chosen men, with the loss and hurting of about four score of my men ".[2] In 1591, Zutphen sconce, which had been betrayed by Rowland Yorke, was captured by a ruse : " I chose a good number of lusty and hardy young soldiers, the most of which I apparelled like the country women of those parts, the rest like the men, gave to some baskets, to other packs, with such burthens as the people usually carry to the market, with pistols and short swords and daggers ".[3] So they sat about in groups by the ferry, waiting for the town-gate to open. Next, Stanley's prize, Deventer, surrendered ; Vere had an English gentleman, presumably a Catholic exile, executed for his slanders upon the Queen, " not for his first but second offence ".[4]

While Maurice was reducing enemy positions in Friesland and Groningen, Parma invaded the Betuwe—country between Rhine and Waal. Here Vere opposed him before Knodsenborg fort and repulsed him with the loss of two or three hundred prisoners. " This defeat so troubled the Duke that . . . he retired his army thence . . . with more dishonour than in any action that he had undertaken in these wars."[5] The splendid soldier, from whom they had all learnt, was not what he had been : he was only forty-six, but he was dying. Since 1588 nothing had gone right : Philip had wrecked his chances of reconquering the Netherlands with the distractions of the Armada and intervention in France. Now it was too late for ever. Philip was already resolved upon the recall of his ablest servant. It was not necessary. The Queen of England had held a high opinion of Parma from his first appearance in the Netherlands :[6] now, she

---

[1] *Ibid.* 8-9. [2] *Ibid.* 12. [3] *Ibid.* 17.
[4] *Ibid.* 19. [5] *Ibid.* 24.
[6] *Salisbury MSS.* XIII. 139.

said, " a great man has died, who deserved to live ".[1] Henceforth, Philip had more subservient, less able, instruments.

In the ensuing years Vere was fighting under Maurice—though " along with " him would be a more exact description of their relations—engaged mainly in operations to clear the North and East of the enemy : in 1595 Groningen fell to them. In a desperate Balaclava-charge across the Lippe in this country Vere's youngest brother, Robert, was killed. The next brother, Horace, had come out in 1590, was wounded at Steenwyk and fought at Groningen : he became a distinguished soldier, succeeding to something of his brother's position and remaining with the Dutch many years after his retirement. Francis Vere left no account of these years' operations, but he gives us valuable accounts of the Cadiz and Islands expeditions. At Cadiz he was Lieut.-General under Essex ; next year that place was given to Mountjoy. The consequence was a breach between Essex, who had almost all the military men at his devotion,[2] and Vere, who passed over to Cecil's side : clever little Robert caressed him greatly and made much of this valuable recruit. The first-fruits were to be seen next year, 1598, with the lucrative governorship of Brill—not that Vere had not deserved it.

The other important governorship, Flushing, remained in the hands of the Essex party with Robert Sidney, who got it on his brother Philip's death. From his voluminous correspondence at Penshurst we derive a familiar picture of military life, especially of garrison life, its boredom variegated by occasional alarms, the " practises " of the enemy, the misdoings of the soldiers.[3] The captains club together to pay their preacher 6d. a week—it is to be hoped in addition to his regular allowance.[4] His ministrations did not prevent affrays among the officers : Ogle, a very tough soldier and a client of Vere's, was accused of setting on men to kill another captain with whom he had quarrelled.[5] Another captain had a woman clamouring in the street after him for money for his lodging, and as he went to the water-port she got hold of his cloak. " He drew his dagger

---

[1] L. van der Essen, *op. cit.* V. 373.

[2] Essex's determination to subject all the martial men to himself—*e.g.* his point-blank demand of Lord Grey whether he was a friend to him or to Cecil—was intolerable and increased the Queen's mistrust of him. *Salisbury MSS.* VIII. 269.

[3] For instructions as to the conduct of troops in garrison towns in the Netherlands, *v. Salisbury MSS.* XIV. 299.

[4] *De L'Isle and Dudley MSS.* III. 3.   [5] *Ibid.* 59-60.

and under his cloak, as he says, meant to prick her in the fingers and so to make her loose her hold, but struck her in the belly, whereof she died suddenly. Had I not told them what he was, he would have been brought to sentence next day and, as the fashion of this country is, had been buried by her he killed."[1]

Pleasanter aspects are the frequent sending over of boar-pies, for which Sidney had a great liking—boar-hunting and hawking were the two most esteemed country sports of the officers. Then there are demands for books, for Ralegh's *Discourse of Guiana*, the Scottish edition of *Arcadia*, for the new map of Ireland.[2] Sidney's agent, Rowland White, has difficulty in finding him a Spanish grammar and dictionary : " for money they are not to be had in Paul's Churchyard. But now they are in the press, with Minsheu's augmentation of 1000 words more than Percival's former : I saw sixty leaves printed. By Michaelmas it will out, and no sooner than shall your lordship have them."[3] White has had the portrait of Languet, Philip's old friend and mentor, delivered him and will send it down to Penshurst.[4] There it still is. Thoughts of " sweet Penshurst " besiege its absent owner's mind : " Sweetheart, I pray you remember to send to Jacques, the gardener, to come to Penshurst against All Hallowtide and to bring yellow peaches, apricots, cherry and plum trees to set along the wall towards the church ".[5] Robert was very fond of the heiress, his wife ; but was she not too extravagant in her housekeeping ? " For you have by your roll eleven women in the house, and, though I do not know what women's services be, yet I do assure myself that never a lady in England keeps in London so many, and four fewer might do all that they have to do : but some of your women are kept only to wait upon the rest. . . . We must not keep sixty at our house in London."[6] Robert sweetens this with twelve boar-pies and a piece of hangings for Lord Rich, and " I send you the Alchermish, which is an excellent thing against weakness of the heart or melancholy ".

Not much love was lost between the Sidneys and Vere : they were jealous of his ascendancy with the States, as to which we have direct evidence. The Veres had been brought up in

---

[1] *Ibid.* 330. [2] *Ibid.* II. 166, 182, 387.
[3] *Ibid.* 385. [4] *Ibid.* 174.
[5] *Ibid.* 164. [6] *Ibid.* 185.

the wars by a faithful old captain, William Browne, their " good father ", to whom they were " your loving sons ". Now, Sir William Browne was Sidney's deputy at Flushing and takes his colouring. Browne says that Vere's " great command is grudged at by French, Dutch and English ".[1] Valcke, treasurer of Zealand, according to Browne, " marvelled that her Majesty would not join any man with him [*i.e.* in command]. I told him that he, with the power he had gotten among them, did make her believe that he could . . . manage matters for her service as he pleased, and that he had the States at his devotion. ' So he hath indeed,' said M. Valcke ; ' and of late the matter being touched to Oldenbarneveldt of the great authority that was given M. Vere, he answered : " Que voulez-vous, nous sommes trop avant avec lui pour pouvoir à l'heure retranchir quelque chose " '. . . I told him I heard Oldenbarneveldt was lately advised not to bend so much to Sir Francis Vere, and it was his practice that so much graced Sir Francis Vere above all men else." The usual grudging of the second-rate at the superiority of the superior.

Pleasant amenities pass between English and Dutch ; the war was becoming the settled background of their lives. M. Valcke and his wife are coming to dine with Sir William at Flushing.[2] At the other end, " I will this morning go buy the best ear-rings I can find in London for Monsieur St. Aldegonde [perhaps we see them still in some portrait of him ?], and set in hand all these perfumed gloves you write for [these were for the young prince]. And will seek over all Cheapside for shag and taffeta answerable to this pattern you send me."[3] In return Rhenish wine is sent over, with pictures and tapestries for Penshurst.

Much of the correspondence is taken up with constant and necessary pressure on the government for supplies : much of this takes the form of suits to Burghley, waylaying him, badgering him, beseeching him : " old Saturnus is a melancholy and wayward planet, but yet predominant here ".[4] Sometimes he skedaddles away, shies from Rowland White's importunate presence ; he is very good at passing the buck, very difficult to nail down. What is remarkable is the invariable courtesy, the patience with which Burghley stands it all, year in, year out. When he chooses, he answers very much to the point : " this

[1] *De L'Isle and Dudley MSS.* III. 586-7.   [2] *Ibid.* 496.
[3] *Ibid.* 193.   [4] *Ibid.* 123.

day my Lord Treasurer told me that he said not I abused him, but that he conceived by me the powder was defalked from the soldiers' wages. I answered that it was, though not from his weekly poor lendings or from his apparel, but from a residue kept from the soldier. It were better, quoth he, that you fasted this month than that the Queen should be so answered."[1]

Then there are Sir Robert's suits to the Queen, for leave to come over, for the Wardenship of the Cinque Ports, the Vice-Chamberlainship of the Household, for this or that. He wants to come over, in 1595, if only for six weeks. " ' Those six weeks you speak of would be six months ', said the Queen, ' and I will not have him away when the Cardinal comes there ' "[2] (*i.e.* the Cardinal-Archduke who succeeded Parma in the government of the Netherlands). She relents when his aunt is bereaved, and gives him leave.[3] Another time he overstays it, hanging about at Margate—perhaps paying an illicit visit to Penshurst to see how the new gallery is going forward ; she has to drive him back to his charge.[4] Now he wants the Cinque Ports. Lady Scudamore, in attendance, got the Queen to read his letter. " ' Do you not know the contents of it ? ' said the Queen. ' No, Madam,' said she—when her Majesty said, ' Here is much ado about the Cinque Ports'. I demanded of my Lady Scudamore what she observed in her Majesty while she was a-reading of it : who said that she read it all over with two or three pushe " (poohs).[5]

The correspondence throws occasional light on matters of high policy and the Queen's own attitude to the war, as it died down or flared up. In May 1597, just before the Islands Voyage : " here has been much ado between the Queen and the Lords, about the preparation to sea ; she opposing it by no danger appearing anywhere, she was extremely angry with them that made such haste on it. No reason could prevail, but her Majesty commanded to stay all proceeding."[6] In the end she gave way —and the Islands expedition was a complete, and expensive, fiasco. Historians who criticise her for not prosecuting the war more aggressively, bringing it to a point, do not sufficiently realise the conditions, the fallibility of so much of Elizabethan action.

[1] *Ibid.* 174.   [2] *Ibid.* 196.
[3] *Ibid.* 203-4.   [4] *Ibid.* 351-2.
[5] *Ibid.* 254.   [6] *Ibid.* 282.

We may conclude with a really wonderful close-up of her, as she was, nearing the end, her finger still not only on the pulse of affairs, but her mind well acquainted with the detailed moves of the war. The siege of Ostend was beginning and she was anxious that Maurice should move south to threaten the Archduke and relieve the pressure upon it. Sir William Browne at last had his heart's desire and came face to face with his sovereign. It was August 1601.[1] " Very honourably on Sunday morning after prayers the Queen, walking into the garden at Sir William Clark's, after Mr. Bodley had first spoken four or five words with her Majesty, Mr. Secretary mentioned me ; she presently [*i.e.* immediately] called for me and was pleased to say I was welcome, with many good words. . . . I had no sooner kissed her sacred hands but that she presently made me stand up and spake somewhat loud and said, ' Come hither, Browne ! ' and pronounced that she held me for an old faithful servant of hers and said, ' I must give content to Browne,' or some such speeches. And then the train following her, [she] said : ' Stand, stand back ! will you not let us speak but ye will be hearers ? ' And then walked a turn or two, protesting of her most gracious opinion of myself : ' And before God, Browne,' said she, ' they do me wrong that will make so honest a servant be jealous that I should mistrust him.'

" I forgot to tell your lordship that when I first kneeled I delivered your lordship's letter, which she received, but read it not till I was gone from her quite. . . . But I must not forget to tell your lordship that, having walked a turn or two, she called for a stool, which was set under a tree, and I began to kneel, but she would not suffer me ; in so much that after two or three denials which I made to kneel, still she was pleased to say that she would not speak with me unless I stood up. Whereupon I stood up and . . . she discoursed of many things and particularly of the distaste she had of the States' armies returning. And it seems that Sir Francis Vere hath rejected all the fault upon Count Maurice ; yet I answered thus much that I heard that Count Maurice did protest that this journey was never of his plotting nor much allowed of by him. ' Tush ! Browne,' saith she, ' I know more than thou dost. When I heard that they were at the first with their army as high as Nymegen, I knew then that no good would be done ; but Maurice to serve his own turn would

[1] *De L'Isle and Dudley MSS.* III. 531-4.

in the end turn to the Grave. I looked they should have come down nearer to Ostend, or have taken some town in the part of Brabant or Flanders that might have startled the enemy. And that they promised me, or else I would not have let them have so many men, and with much discontentment to my subjects— as I know but for the love which they bear me, they would not so well disgest. And now, forsooth, Maurice is come to his weapon, to the spade—for all that he is one of the best in Christendom ' (*i.e.* he was digging himself in).

" Then she talked of the French king, [of] that he had promised them. I answered . . . that the French king rather marvelled at their foolish boldness in venturing their army so far than that he ever gave them any assurance to join with them. ' Tush ! Browne,' said she, ' do not I know that Bucenval was written to, and written to again, to move the army to go that way and that then he would help them.' ' If that were so ', said I, ' then your Majesty may think it was but a French promise.' "

To Browne's recommendation that she might do something for Zealand, she responded as we might expect, non-committally with some useful propaganda to be carried back there. " ' Alas ! poor Zealanders, I know that they love me with all their hearts.' I added that they prayed continually for her. ' Yea, Browne,' said she, ' I know it well enough, and I will tell thee one thing. Faith, here is a church of that country men in London. I protest, next after the divine Providence that governs all my well-doing, I attribute much of the happiness which befalls me to be given me of God by those men's effectual and zealous prayers, who, I know, pray with that fervency for me as none of my subjects can do more.' "

She turned to administer another injection of propaganda in a different direction : Secretary Cecil was in the offing, waiting for her attention : he was not regarded with that favour by the military men that she thought his due. " ' Dost thou see that little fellow that kneels there ? It hath been told you that he hath been an enemy to soldiers. On my faith, Browne, he is the best friend that soldiers have.' " To which Cecil, who could do no wrong now in her eyes, made antiphon that " it was from her Majesty alone from whom flowed all soldiers' good ". Faithful old Browne derived such joy from the experience " as that I shall think of it during life "—as no doubt he did.

The positive old lady in the garden, who knew all the answers and could not be told anything, had not ceased to be a marvellous politician.

The Sidney correspondence gives us detailed, sometimes daily or weekly, accounts of the long-drawn-out siege of Ostend that concluded the war for us. But for that and for its last actions, let us return to Vere, who was the central figure in them.

In the winter of 1597 an enemy army of 600 horse and 4000 foot advanced towards Breda for some enterprise. Secretly an allied army was gathered to surprise them. Sir Robert Sidney joined Vere with 300 men from his garrison. The night before was very cold, " insomuch as the Count Maurice himself going up and down the quarter, with straw and such other blazing stuff made fires with his own hands by the *corps du garde*. Sir Robert Sidney and I got us into a barn thronged with soldiers to rest, because there was no sleeping by the Count Maurice, who was disposed to watch, whence I was also called to attend him."[1] That day the English had the van ; the problem was to bring the retreating Spaniards to action. Vere insisted on pursuit, managed to capture the bridgehead held by the enemy rear and to hang on to their skirts until the allied horse came up and broke them on the open heath. It was a complete rout : 300 killed, among them the commander, the Count of Varras and his General de Ballancy, 600 prisoners, 38 ensigns taken.[2] There was rejoicing in London : at last the tables were being turned. The action was dramatised—we see the thirst of the people for bloody battles and understand the better the need the theatre met, the atmosphere that permeated it. " Two days ago the overthrow of Turnhout was acted upon a stage, and all your names used that were at it ; especially Sir Francis Vere's, and he that played the part got a beard resembling his and a watchet [*i.e.* crimson] satin doublet, with hose trimmed with silver lace. It was full of quips ; I saw it not, but I heard it was so."[3] Next day : " this afternoon I saw the overthrow of Turnhout played, and saw Sir Robert Sidney and Sir Francis Vere upon the stage, killing, slaying and overthrowing the Spaniard ". Vere complained that his despatches, in

[1] Vere, *op. cit.* 73.   [2] I follow Markham's figures, *op. cit.* 260.
[3] *De L'Isle and Dudley MSS.* II. 406, 408.

which he had mentioned Sidney, "were held back and his delivered : which art of doubleness changed the love I had so long borne him into a deep dislike, that could not be soon digested ".[1] A no less characteristic aftermath of an Elizabethan action.

In 1600 the changed posture of affairs was dramatically illustrated by the remarkable victory of Nieuport, won almost wholly, as Maurice recognised in his letter to the Queen, by Vere and his English troops. The States now felt strong enough to hazard an aggressive advance into Flanders : an army was landed on the Scheldt and marched straight through enemy territory to Nieuport, near Ostend. The Archduke followed with a large army, and at Nieuport the allies turned to give battle. Maurice had already lost two better opportunities of inflicting a defeat, through excessive caution. Now it fell to Vere to hold them up among the sand-dunes in blood-sodden Flanders. There was no time for the men to strip themselves of their clothes in crossing the haven at low tide, before taking up the positions Vere had cleverly and cautiously selected. The key to the position was two sandhills, connected by a low ridge : the exposed east hill " being steep and sandy was not easily to be mounted, and in the top so hollow that the men lay covered from the hills on the other side, and might fight from it as from a parapet ".[2] These were the forlorn hope. On the west hill he posted his Frisian musketeers, with orders to fire only to the southward, the ground along which he hoped to shepherd the enemy cavalry. Behind the ridge he placed his pikemen and shot. One is reminded of the dispositions at Waterloo, with the east hill playing the part of Hougoumont.

Vere's object was to wear down the Archduke's greatly superior—but rather tired—army, himself employing his force sparingly, feeding them in piece-meal, until Maurice with the bulk of the army in the rear could move in decisively. And so it came about. No place to go into detail here : enough to say that the English on the east hill and along the ridge bore the brunt of the Archduke's whole army : they were tried to the uttermost. Vere sent messenger after messenger to Maurice to come to their aid : they do not seem to have got through. At last the hill was taken and there was a confused *mêlée* in the bottom below into which Vere himself, though wounded, had to plunge

[1] Vere, *op. cit.* 81.   [2] *Ibid.* 89.

to encourage his men. At the critical moment Horace Vere rallied a troop of horse from the beach and charged the mass of Spanish infantry. Maurice, posted on his hill, cried joyfully, " Voyez, voyez les Anglais qui tournent à la charge ! "[1] He now ordered a series of cavalry charges—one of them led by Sir Edward Cecil—under which the Spaniards broke and fled. The Archduke did not draw rein until he reached the safety of Bruges. About a third of the Spanish army was lost, in killed and wounded. The terrible slaughter of the English shows how much it was their victory : half the force of 1600 fell in killed and wounded, " eight captains slain, the rest all but two hurt and most of my inferior officers hurt and slain ".[2] Vere permits himself to say—surely, fairly enough—" yet this victory had been as assured with less loss and touch of reproach . . . had the succours of horse or the foot I called for come sooner to us, wherein I will charge and accuse none but the messengers of their slackness ". He himself was ill for long of his wounds ; but the victory confirmed his mastery. It meant that as a modern military power we had at length attained our majority.

The increased confidence of the States was shown by the events of next year. They proposed another invasion of Flanders. Vere was sent to England to get 3000 reinforcements out of the Queen, delivering " the whole plot to her Majesty, who liked and allowed thereof, and with some difficulty (as her manner was) granted the men to be levied and transported in ten days' warning ".[3] When they arrived Sir Horace Vere was able to comment, " for the soldiers, in my time, I have not seen their like for proper men, well armed and apparelled."[4] This was, indeed, a change from former times. As a counter-move, the Archduke decided to devote the bulk of his forces to the siege of Ostend, the defences of which were weak and the garrison low. Browne thought that the States would not so disgrace themselves as to select Sir Francis Vere to defend it.[5] They did, with as large a commission as Maurice had as their general. Wonders are looked for, wrote Browne. They were forthcoming.

By June the town was surrounded within its water defences and it hardly seemed that it could long hold out. The key to it was the Sandhill, the strong-point on the north-west that

---

[1] Ogle's account of the battle in Vere, 109. [2] Vere, 104-5.
[3] *Ibid.* 119. [4] q. Markham, 315.
[5] *De L'Isle and Dudley MSS.* II. 525-6.

dominated the narrowest crossing over the haven. The haven on the west was unusable, being commanded by the Archduke's artillery. On the east of the town was another inlet, the Gueule, which Vere deepened and made usable as a haven instead. When this was interdicted by enemy artillery he made another inlet between it and the town, dominated by his own : so that Ostend went on for long comfortably receiving reinforcements. He got 2000 reinforcements in, repaired and strengthened the works and set himself to entice the Spaniards into the drowned lands of the polder south of the town, " which I knew would cause great expense, great labour and much loss and consumption of men ".[1] To provoke them the more, Vere tried out his little game on St. James's day, their patron saint : the faithful could not resist that. He overlooked nothing : Vere was full of art—as much an artist in his way as his cousin the, Earl-poet.

The finest example of this was the trap he led the Spaniards into that Christmas. The weather had held up all reinforcements and supplies and he was down to the lowest possible : 4000 men were barely enough to man the works : he had only 2000 available. There were no hospitals for the sick in Ostend : the whole town was now under pretty constant bombardment ; hardly a house was standing. The Archduke had got a vast fortified camp, an army of 20,000 men, around the beleaguered town. Vere knew that the final assault was impending. At the last moment, taking counsel with no-one, he sent his intimate, Sir John Ogle, to the Archduke to ask for some qualified person to speak with him.[2] The Spaniards naturally expected terms of surrender to be the subject of discussion. It was agreed that Ogle and Sir Charles Fairfax should remain as hostages for the Spanish intermediaries sent to Vere. When these had gone, the Archduke asked Ogle if there were any ruse intended. Ogle answered that if there were it was more than he knew— truthfully, for Vere had told him nothing : to have done so might have defeated his purpose.

On the pretext of some irregularity Vere would not receive the Spanish envoys ; he returned them for further powers—but via the east side so that they had to make a long round : a night and a day gained. Still no sign of his promised reinforcements.

---

[1] Vere, 126-7.
[2] *v.* Ogle's account of this episode, in Vere, 143 foll.

Next evening the envoys returned ; Sir Francis received them most hospitably. " My Lord smooths over the uncivil entertainment of the night past ; together they sup on Christmas Eve, till their hopes betray their judgments, the cups walk and *post epula ad lectum.*"[1] Sir Francis showed his guests to his own comfortable bed ; no talk of surrender, he showed a disposition rather to suggest that the Archduke should raise the siege. Next morning they were awakened by the batteries greeting the appearance of three ships of war, with 400 men and supplies of every kind. Vere told the Spaniards frankly that " the fashion of soldiers is to help themselves in extremity with their wits . . . now his succours were come, he could not without ruin of his honour go forward with them ".

During the truce the Archduke walked the Infanta—Philip's favourite daughter Isabella, whom he had had married to her cousin and upon them settled the Netherlands before he died—with her train of twenty ladies and gentlemen before the walls of the town : it was years before they were to enter. For the next ten days Vere was feverishly preparing for the grand assault ; he hardly slept, but toured the works incessantly, directing, urging, planning. Ruined houses were pulled down to make palisades where the ramparts had been battered—some 160,000 cannon-shot had been fired into the town. Firkins of ashes to blind the assailants, barrels of tenter-nails to pour down on them, hoops of fireworks to garland their necks, hand-grenades, ropes of pitch, clubs, stones, bricks, spars—everything was ready, in addition to the more regular implements of war. The waters of the west sluice were banked up in the town ditch. No need to describe the assault : it was very fierce, and at its fiercest at the Sandhill and at the Schottenburgh, where the defences had been weakened by the sea and where Vere stationed himself. At length the assaults were beaten off ; but when the main body of enemy troops tried to retreat across the west ditch the sluice was opened and they were drowned in hundreds. Ogle writes : " under Sandhill and all along the walls of the old town, the Porc-épic and West Ravelin, lay whole heaps of dead carcases, forty or fifty upon a heap, stark naked, goodly young men, Spaniards and Italians ".[2] Such is war.

Vere's practice was criticised by the unintelligent among the

---

[1] *De L'Isle and Dudley MSS.* II. 554.
[2] In Vere, 174.

Dutch.[1] Even Meynartson, commissary of the States General, was disposed to doubt ; even Browne felt bound to defend. " I, telling him it was a worthy stratagem of the General, ' It is true,' said he, ' it is well happened ; but there are a thousand and a thousand whose hearts it will not seek into that this was done for a stratagem, to win time to make up the works '."[2] And he raised some doubts himself. In fact, it had saved Ostend. It was a long time before the Spaniards mounted another assault. Before then, Vere had left the town to join Maurice in the open field. For the real strategic purpose of defending the town was not any value that it had in itself, but that it locked up the bulk of the Archduke's army, almost purposelessly, while Maurice went forward mopping up town after town, making secure the area that was shortly to emerge, after so long and heroic a struggle, as the new state of the United Provinces. Meanwhile, the Archduke was so engaged on the stage of Europe that he had to prosecute the siege to the end, his army worn down and exhausted by the long attrition. The siege did not come to an end till 1604. James made peace with Spain ; but all the world was reasonably sure of the independence of the Dutch and, even so, English troops continued to fight alongside of them until it was recognised.

We can now see that the ultimate consequences of the courageous gamble upon intervention in the Netherlands were more fortunate for this country than any Elizabethan could have believed. The main motive at the time was defensive. In the event, this country was covered, Spanish domination of Europe was averted, a brilliant new state came into being.

---

[1] And by the strait-laced Motley of course ; cf. Markham's note, p. 320. Motley says, " Sir Francis Vere called his principal officers together, announced his intention of proposing at once to treat and to protract the negotiations as long as possible, until the wished-for sails should be discerned in the offing ". He regards this as " a cynical trifling with the sacredness of trumpets of truce and offers of capitulation, such as in that loose age *were* [sic] deemed far from creditable ". Further on he describes the episode as " Vere's perfidy " and " gross treachery ". Markham points out that no such proposal was made by Vere to the council, and consequently that the council never " highly applauded the scheme " and again that it " never importuned the general to carry it into effect ". Nor did Vere make any offer of capitulation. Markham comments mildly that " Mr. Motley appears never to have read the narratives of Ogle and Hexham ". It is indeed difficult to account for a conscientious man perpetrating so many misrepresentations ; one can only suppose that Motley had made up his mind, taken his *parti pris*, and simply closed his eyes to the evidence. But Puritans have seldom much minded about truth in what they say of others ; and Motley was a great friend of Bismarck.

[2] *De L'Isle and Dudley MSS.* II. 555.

Beyond this, the upshot from the point of view of this country's interests and security was happy. The Netherlands as a unity came into the possession of no great power. They were divided : the south remained in the hands of Habsburgs, Spanish then Austrian, virtually independent—in any case out of the hands of France, to which it would have brought an insupportably dangerous accession of power ; the north became fully independent, first our clients, then our rivals, for the rest our allies. We see how, here too, in the structure of our position in Europe, the foundations of our secular policy, the Elizabethan age foreshadowed the shape of things to come. By the end of the Queen's reign this country had arrived upon the scene, a European power of the first rank, the foundations laid for an unimagined—and, indeed, looking back on it all now, an unimaginable—career in the world.

It remained to complete the foundations of unity within the islands.

CHAPTER XI

THE IRISH WAR

NOWHERE was the change in the technique of warfare more
marked by the end of the reign than in Ireland. We have
seen the immense disparity between English and Irish
methods of waging war that reflected the disparity between their
stages of civilisation.[1] But in the last decade of the century the
Irish suddenly, and to a considerable extent, caught up. That
they did so was mainly due to the genius of the last O'Neill, the
great Tyrone.

We must not underrate the difficulties of Irish warfare in
general. The Elizabethans did not : they sent their ablest
soldiers there ; most of the Lords Deputy were men of high
military capacity. Ireland was their North-West Frontier, and
it offered similar problems. It was essentially guerilla warfare,
and its difficulties have been conveniently summed up for us.[2]
" If it be a misapprehension to despise Irish warfare as un-
important, it is still wider of the mark to regard it as easy. It
was, in fact, more difficult than continental warfare because,
while it might occasionally include episodes of a type usual on
the Continent, it was more often of a very different nature.
The efficient commander had to be ready to fight either in the
continental style or in the Irish skirmishing style. In the latter
case his obvious difficulties were tactical, but he was also faced
by the overmastering strategic difficulty of war in such a country
that, apart from the enemy's troops, who were extremely elusive,
there was no obvious objective the loss of which would ruin the
enemy. . . . The characteristic Irish style made high demands
upon the commander's eye for country, his skill in minor tactics,
his system of intelligence and knowledge of the enemy's habits
and methods, his courage, fortitude, vigilance, speed of thought,
and ability to maintain a supply system in the field in country

[1] v. above, c. iii.
[2] In an admirable book covering the whole subject : Cyril Falls, *Elizabeth's Irish Wars.*

where it might be necessary to lay down hurdles in order to pass vehicles over heavy ground or even impossible to employ vehicles at all. Irish warfare was an art which some men who had won fame in other theatres took long to learn or never fully acquired. It was also arduous in the extreme. The fighting men lived hard, if not miserably—' all the soldiers in Christendom must give place in that to the soldier of Ireland ', said Sir William Pelham, who had plenty of experience of other wars."[1]

In short, the Irish had all the advantages of terrain, of its being their own country, their own people ; the English of technique and equipment. These last were considerable, even when Tyrone and O'Donnell had trained their men to firearms and the pike. There was the importance of horse in these conditions, to ride down and cut up a mobile and elusive enemy. Troops of horse were by far the most effective arm for the English to rely on : cavalry successes were won at enormous odds and, conversely, a disaster like that of the Yellow Ford would never have happened if Ormonde had been there with his horse. Artillery was another advantage, though not so great as might be thought : Irish warfare, unlike the Netherlands, offered few targets. But a cannon was of use in battering a castle and the Irish had no reply to it. Sea-power was, as always, a tremendous advantage ; though here the Spaniards had the benefit of the predominant south-westerly winds. They never made any use of it until the end, with the Kinsale expedition. The English often had to wait for weeks for a favouring easterly. Their greatest advantage of all was that they had an organised state behind them, regular, dependable, persistent—unbeatable, save by another state. That Tyrone would have dearly liked to build : he was capable of it, the only Irishman who was. He was too late : a lonely, grand, tragic figure.

English disadvantages, too, were considerable. The wetness of the climate made the men ill : there was a particular form of ague, or perhaps heavy incidence of it, that made people specify an " Irish ague " as such ; and tempestuous weather often held up operations. In the autumn of 1600 Mountjoy writes from the Fagher, " Since my coming to this camp, where we have been almost twenty days, there hath been weather scant fair enough to write in our tents, except some few days or hours : the opportunity whereof I have taken to be doing with our near

---

[1] Cyril Falls, *Elizabeth's Irish Wars*, 10.

neighbours, who are continually in sight of us, and whom we have well made know that not they but the extremity of the weather and waters doth arrest our passage. . . . Our tents are often blown down, and at this instant it doth rain into mine, so that I can scant write." [1] Sir Geoffrey Fenton put it down to the witches : " I think the unseasonableness of the weather [January 1601] is the chiefest hinderer of all good success there . . . in all the time of my service I have not seen so tempestuous weather so long together ; which maketh me think that, if God hath given liberty to the witches of that country (which aboundeth with witches), they are all set on work to cross the service by extraordinary unseasonable weather ". [2]

The troubles we are familiar with in England and the Netherlands were worse in Ireland : commissariat, supplies, frauds in the musters, desertions. The captains sold the men's clothes, if the soldiers had not done so themselves : they went half naked. The bad quality of the victuals, the difficulty of preserving them for any time, in addition to deliberate frauds at every point from contractor to men's mouths, made the soldiers ill. Of the newly raised body of 4000 sent over in these months only just over 1000 were fit a year after. [3] The fact was that until modern medicine discovered the causes, it was not possible to check disease : it took its course ; there was an improvement in spring and early summer, in autumn and winter it worsened again. Of 3500 sent over in 1596, by July not 1000 were left : the rest " either dead, run away or converted into Irish ". [4] No wonder the men deserted in hundreds : some went over to the Irish, many more got passage back to England—so many in fact that the western counties groaned at the incursion, and the Privy Council ordered that in Munster only the Lord President himself was to grant passports. [5] Many Irish were taken into the army : they could support the climate and feed themselves better ; but at any reverse, some, though by no means all, were liable to go over to their countrymen. Irish warfare was an Alice-in-Wonderland world in which the croquet-mallets turned into flamingoes, the hoops into hedgehogs.

The discouragements that an honest Muster Master met with in trying to raise efficiency and check frauds may be seen

---

[1] *Cal. Carew MSS., 1589–1600*, 466.   [2] *Cal. S.P. Ireland, 1600–1*, ix.
[3] David Stewart, *Journal R.A.M.C.*, July 1948, 26.   [4] *Ibid.* 35.
[5] *Pacata Hibernia* (based on Sir George Carew's Papers), ed. 1810, I. 151.

from the case of Anthony Reynolds at Derry in these months of 1601. He wished to take a muster twice a month, " by which I should have raised the check by a third and should have got to know the true strength of the companies ".[1] Captain Digges, serjeant-major-general of the army there, would not have this. " The difference in the check cannot be accounted for by the fact that men have been killed in those three weeks, for not more than six were killed during the time. In some companies I found as many as twenty men who were no soldiers but borrowed to deceive the Queen. . . . The borrowing of men by the captains from one another is not so objectionable as the hiring of sutlers and their men, horse-boys, *passe-volants* and such like." Defective numbers are due to sickness, and this " by the palpable wrong of the captain, who detains part of that poor 3s. a week which her Majesty allows the soldier, and by the unwholesome victuals sent over by those who are put in trust therewith. . . . Many hundred barrels of musty bran—I cannot call it meal, for I have seen divers barrels of them myself, two inches on the top meal, all the rest bran—have been consumed." At the end of the month the musters showed 805 persons deficient—out of a nominal force of some 4000.[2] Reynolds got on to the frauds in clothing too. " The soldier has his due and is well contented if he gets a suit each half year . . . if I distribute full suits to men who have not served for them, the soldier will not gain, but the captain. Many captains have sold much apparel of this winter's proportion, yet will they not cease to suggest that their soldiers die for want of it."[3]

Naturally the captains did not love this Nosy Parker of an official too insistently bent on doing his duty. They caught him in an awkward posture or rather invented one for him. " Captain Floyd and Captain Vaughan, knowing me to be in the preacher's house alone with the maid of the house spread scandalous reports about my having been found there accompanied with a whore, and reported it to the Governor, who jested of it to myself." The Governor, Sir Henry Docwra, an excellent soldier, did not think that his company should be checked to a man : he told Reynolds that before his time he had always had twenty men given him in muster (*i.e.* their pays allotted him) and suggested that Reynolds should do the like for him. When Reynolds refused he found himself brought before a court of the Governor

---

[1] *Cal. S.P. Ireland, 1601–3*, 59-60.   [2] *Ibid.* 102.   [3] *Ibid.* 176-8.

and his captains, accused by the preacher, " having schooled his maid to say that I had an intent to have forced her if time and place had served " ; reviled by Vaughan as " apish lecher ", " Jack " and " clerksmaw's man " ; laid by the heels by the Governor for fourteen days, " where, for anything I know, I remain his prisoner still ".[1] That stopped him from taking the musters with such disagreeable exactitude ; he was now without his statistics and could only guess the deficiencies to be around 700. How hard are the paths of the righteous ! We are not surprised to find a considerable discrepancy between the returns of the Governor and those of the prying Muster Master.[2]

But all sixteenth-century life was like this ; perhaps we may take the complaints as tribute to the desire for improvement, as evidence even that better existed and was regarded as the proper standard. Sir John Dowdall specifies some particular defects at this moment : " the soldiers do rather imitate the disarmed companies that came out of Brittany and Picardy, desiring a scald rapier before a good sword, a pike without carettes or burgeonet, a hagbutter without a morion, which hath not been accustomed in this country but of late . . . a course fitter to take blows than make a good stand ".[3] Many of the captains and gentlemen are fitter for the wars of the Low Countries and Brittany, where they were quartered upon good villages, than here on waste towns, bog or wood after long marches. The soldiers should carry calivers, not muskets which are too heavy. (In fact calivers were increasingly used in preference in Ireland.) There are the usual complaints about victual and clothing, reducing the men to beggarly ghosts, fitter for their graves than to fight a prince's battle : the report so works in men's minds that they had as lief go to the gallows as to the Irish wars. On the other hand, " why is the Irish rebel so strong, so well armed, apparelled, victualled and moneyed ? He endures no wants ; he makes booty upon all parts of the kingdom and sells it back for money. . . . There is no soldier with a good sword but some Irish merchant or townsman will buy it from him. The soldier, being poor, sells it for 10s. or 12s., and if excellent good it is commonly worth among the rebels £3 or £4. A graven morion, bought of a poor soldier for a noble or 10s., is worth among the rebels £3. The soldiers likewise, through necessity and penury, sell their powder at 12d. a pound, and the

[1] *Ibid.* 214. [2] *Ibid.* 215. [3] *Cal. Carew MSS., 1589–1600*, 353-5.

Irish merchants or townsmen collect it and sell it again to the traitors at 3s." These are familiar phenomena in all such wars.

Considering all the difficulties, " the astonishing thing is how excellent the English soldier was under competent leadership, how brave and enduring, how ready to take on the enemy, Irish, Scot or even Spaniard, at long odds, how regularly he was successful, what a mere handful of English troops normally sufficed to hold down a turbulent country where there was always some disaffection, frequent rebellion, and most men went armed ".[1] This generous tribute, from an Irishman, points out that it was an average of a mere 1000 to 1500 that kept order normally in Ireland : the numbers went up sharply in times of revolt—to 9000 during the Desmond rebellion. But it should be added that these small numbers were sufficient only because of the disparity in equipment and technique during most of the reign. This was now, with Tyrone's rebellion—the only one to reach the status of a war—to be drastically changed.

We have already observed the social and political background of it and the ambivalence of Tyrone's position, caught between two civilisations.[2] He could not hope to win in the end, as he of all men knew ; yet he was driven by the constant encroachment of English power into challenging it. Some of the English sympathised with him in his dilemma—notably Sir John Norris, who, sent as General against him, temporised and was in favour of compromise with him. For this Norris was blamed. Certainly Tyrone took advantage of this to build up a strong position before he came into the open with his challenge.

The clue to it was his training of his troops, equipping them with modern arms on a par with the English. While nominally at peace, or during the frequent truces he made to suit his convenience—for Tyrone was the soul of disingenuousness—he followed the policy of changing his men often so as to increase the number of those trained.[3] For some time the English had been complaining that the Irish were catching up : the kerne were becoming musketeers, the gallowglass, pikemen. Tyrone made use of the Irish who came over, already trained, from the English armies, and especially of an English deserter like the uncatchable Tyrrell (married to an Irish woman : perhaps there

---

[1] Falls, *op. cit.* 47.   [2] *v.* above, c. iii.
[3] Fynes Moryson, *Itinerary* (Maclehose edn.), II. 189.

lay the explanation, as with Erskine Childers) :[1] Tyrrell was the De Wet of this war—in so many respects like the Boer War. That the Irish were now wearing morions, even the rebels in Munster, we know from an ambush between Cork and Kinsale being given away by them : perhaps the sun suddenly came out, for Captain Bostock riding over a bridge " espied the morions of some of the sunk ambush in the glen ".[2] At Clontibret, Tyrone had three hundred musketeers in red coats, " like English soldiers ".[3] At the parley at which Ormonde was captured by surprise, among five hundred foot and twenty horse were three hundred bonnaughts, " the best furnished men for the war and the best appointed that we have seen in this kingdom ".[4] Only the strength of English horses enabled Thomond and Carew to escape : " our horses were strong and by that means did break through them, in tumbling down on all sides those that were before and behind us ". Tyrone got his supplies fairly regularly from Glasgow, less regularly from Spain and often enough from the enemy he was fighting—another usual feature in such wars.

Above all, Tyrone owed his success to the tactics he developed and enforced : attacking English columns on the march in unfavourable terrain, always from the shelter of wood, bog or river-bank, and usually while they were strung out thinly and out of contact in going through the " passes " of the country, *i.e.* narrow trackways through woods or overhanging hills. The moment of changing formation, with the ranks in disorder, was the moment of danger, and these opportunities Tyrone did not fail to take. Such tactics were perfectly conceived to exploit the advantages of the Irish at their maximum ; for, notice that Tyrone did not allow his men to face the English in open country—they could not stand the weight of an English charge : it was this that proved fatal in the end at Kinsale.

The English had been so used to victory on such easy terms that it took them a long time to tumble to these tactics : again and again they fell into the trap. They obstinately played into Tyrone's hands, too, by the mistaken policy of placing isolated garrisons at too long distance from each other : that had to be relieved at regular intervals by an army, which exposed itself

[1] Tyrrell married the sister of Owny MacRory O'More, who planned and carried out Ormonde's capture.

[2] *Pacata Hibernia*, I. 53.

[3] Cf. G. A. Hayes-McCoy, " Clontibret ", in *Irish Historical Studies*, June 1949, 158 foll.   [4] *Pacata Hibernia*, I. 43.

in doing so to galling attacks all along the flanks in difficult
" passes ". In this way Tyrone built up the most notable series
of victories the Irish ever gained against England. In 1594 the
relieving of Enniskillen led to defeat at the Ford of the Biscuits.
In 1595 the relief of Monaghan led to the mauling of Bagenal
at Clontibret, where the Marshal walked into the trap. Attacked
en route, Bagenal fought his way stubbornly through and delivered
his supplies ; next day he was thoroughly mauled in traversing
the Moyry : he managed to reach Newry but had to evacuate
the foot by sea. What a humiliation, that the Queen's army did
not dare show itself in the field : Elizabeth herself was furious
at it, and mourned " the loss and death of so many good soldiers
in relieving Monaghan ".[1] But the stupid Bagenal—he was a sort
of Redvers Buller—still would not learn, and went the same
way to disaster and his own destruction at the death-trap of the
Yellow Ford in 1598. This was the severest blow to English
power ; for a moment the state itself quailed and the bulk of
Ireland lay open to the rebels—or to the national cause, take your
choice. Tyrone himself began to hope : from that moment
he was lost. The unfailing pulse of an efficient state recovered
the ground.

There were three strategic keys to unreduced Gaelic Ulster :
the direct route from Dublin via Dundalk, Newry and Armagh
to the centre of Tyrone's country, west of Lough Neagh, the
prehistoric camp on the steep hill of Dungannon, where he
chiefly resided, Benburb and Tullahogue with the sacred stone
upon which the O'Neills had been inaugurated time out of mind ;
Ballyshannon, the ford across the river at the western end of
Lough Erne, the entry from Connaught into Donegal, the centre
of O'Donnell's princely power ; Derry, at the neck of Lough
Foyle, commanding the chief pass between Tyrone's and
O'Donnell's countries : this in the hands of the English would
place a stranglehold on both. To reduce Ulster the English
had to maintain pressure on all three. To command the first
route a fort—or, rather, a strong-point, walls of turf, a garrison
of 300—was made on the Blackwater beyond Armagh. In 1597
Tyrone attempted to reduce it with a strong storming party,
scaling ladders and all : bloodily repulsed by a stout-hearted
and much tried Welshman, Captain Thomas Williams. (Since
the Celts have never had any sense of unity, the English—who

[1] q. Hayes-McCoy, *loc. cit.*

had—could always use one against the other.)

Next year Tyrone, unwilling to venture on another assault after losing so many men last time, decided to blockade the fort and starve it out. Ormonde, who was Lieutenant-General, was in favour of leaving the fort to its fate : too far in enemy territory to rescue. Bagenal, who had a personal vendetta against Tyrone—Tyrone had abducted his sister, married and maltreated her—determined at the last moment to push an army through to relieve the fort : some 4000 foot, 300 horse, two regiments in the van, two in the battle (*i.e.* main body), two in the rear. Bagenal pushed forward with the van, though his place was with the main body, to the trap waiting for him : the ford —it looks harmless enough today, with its clay-coloured banks— with the whole of Tyrone's army on the left flank sheltered behind a bog, O'Donnell's on the right protected by a wood, a long deep trench before them. Galled by flanking fire, held up by a cannon's getting bogged, the head of the column was thrown into disorder ; at the moment of turning back to link up with the main battle, it was charged by the Irish and broken up in a few minutes. The battle, attempting to come to the support of the van, was partly cut up and dispersed. At this moment a powder-barrel blew up, adding to the confusion ; Irish companies began to go over to their countrymen, raw English recruits to run away. Meanwhile, the rear regiments were unaware of what was happening ; when they came up, their officers charged again and again to secure a breathing space to bring off what remnants they could and secure the ford in the rear. There were not enough cavalry to hold the Irish off. Nothing of this would have happened if Ormonde had been there with his horse. Why was he not ? It looks as if Lee's strictures were not without justification : Ormonde had gone to Leinster to look after his own.[1] Some 1300 were lost in killed and missing, and perhaps another 700 in deserters. It was a disaster, " the worst that has ever been suffered by the English in Ireland ".[2]

What made it worse was the loss of nerve that followed. There was no Lord Deputy, and the Lords Justices wrote a grovelling appeal to Tyrone to let the forces now sheltering at Armagh " go without doing them any further hurt. . . . And besides, your ancient adversary the Marshal being now taken away, we hope you will cease all further revenge towards the

[1] Cf. above, pp. 133-4.   [2] Falls, *op. cit.* 219.

rest."[1] (Does one not hear the note of archi-episcopal humbug in this, of a Loftus ageing now and rendered craven by panic? He was one of the two Lords Justices in charge.) If Tyrone could have marched on Dublin, he might have carried it; if the Spaniards had fulfilled their promises of aid he might have carried Ireland. But the moment passed : the nuclei of English power remained and, across the Channel, an embattled and victorious state. After her long record of success the Queen could not bear to be braved by a mere tribal chieftain : what displeased her most was " that it must be the Queen of England's fortune (who hath held down the greatest enemy she had) to make a base Irish kerne to be accounted so famous a rebel ".[2] To the Lords Justices she wrote : " We may not pass over this foul error to our dishonour, when you of our Council framed such a letter to the traitor, after the defeat, as never was read the like, either in form or substance, for baseness, being such as we persuade ourself, if you shall peruse it again, when you are yourselves, that you will be ashamed of your own absurdities and grieved that any fear or rashness should ever make you authors of an action so much to your Sovereign's dishonour and to the increasing of the traitor's insolency ".[3]

It would have been more to the purpose to appoint a Lord Deputy at once to take the situation in hand; but this was rendered difficult by the acute stage that party conflict had reached in the Council at home—which also points a long foreboding finger to subsequent centuries in Anglo-Irish relations. The Queen would have appointed Mountjoy, but Essex was against this—he regarded Mountjoy as too " bookish "—and he made any other appointment than himself impossible. Elizabeth had long ceased to have any confidence in him—if indeed " confidence " be the word for what she had felt for him, ever. Not until April 1599 did he reach Dublin; but he came with full powers under the exalted title of Lord Lieutenant, and never had so fine an army been assembled in Ireland, 16,000 foot, 1300 horse. Whatever the government may have felt about Essex, they did their best for him : Vere had been ordered to send over 2000 of his seasoned soldiers; other large levies had been made upon the English counties; big contracts were entered into for regular supplies; stores of equipment were sent over to plant the garrison of 3000 destined for Derry. " No army ever

[1] q. Falls, *op. cit.* 221.   [2] *Cal. Carew MSS. 1589–1600*, 315.   [3] q. Falls, 222.

established in Ireland had better prospects of being adequately maintained."[1]

Essex proceeded to accomplish nothing whatever with it. The season was too early to march into Ulster, so he made a journey into Munster, where he reduced Cahir Castle. This, the " taking of an Irish hold from a rabble of rogues ", the Queen regarded as no great matter.[2] But his strength was now down to 11,000. When he got back, instead of going straight for Tyrone, he turned aside for an expedition into Leix and Offaly. The Queen : " Before your departure no man's counsel was held sound which persuaded not presently the main prosecution in Ulster : all was nothing without that, and nothing was too much for that."[3] For this purpose alone had such efforts been made and extra reinforcements at Essex's request allowed—an additional 300 horsemen above the thousand, " which was assented to, which were only to be in pay during service in Ulster ". Then followed " a new demand of 2000 men, to which, if we would assent, you could speedily undertake what we had so often commanded. . . . If sickness of the army be the reason, why was not the action undertaken when the army was in better state ? if winter's approach, why were the summer months of July and August lost ? if the spring were too soon, and the summer that followed otherwise spent ? if the harvest that succeeded were so neglected as nothing hath been done, then surely we must conclude that none of the four quarters of the year will be in season for you and that Council to agree of Tyrone's prosecution, for which all our charge is intended. Further, we require you to consider whether we have not great cause to think that your purpose is not to end the war, when yourself have often told us that all the petty undertakings in Leix, Munster and Connaught are but loss of time, consumption of treasure and, most of all, our people, until Tyrone himself be first beaten, on whom all the rest depend. . . . How often have you told us that others that preceded you had no judgment to end the war, who often resolved us until Lough Foyle and Ballyshannon were planted, there could be no hope of doing service on the capital rebels."

With these scarifying reminders she drove him on to move against Tyrone. It was now too late : what with planting far

---

[1] *Ibid.* 232.   [2] *Cal. Carew MSS. 1589–1600*, 315.
[3] R. B. Devereux, *Lives and Letters of the Devereux, Earls of Essex*, II. 61-4.

too many garrisons in Munster and elsewhere, and sickness in the army, Essex had barely 3000 to oppose to Tyrone : Tyrone had a two-to-one superiority. But Essex put himself irretrievably in the wrong by his parley with Tyrone at the ford, alone. No-one heard what they said ; but the Queen guessed, and afterwards learned—no-one knows how—what was mentioned : the shape of things after her demise. That was what both Tyrone and Essex had their eyes on : it gave them a common bond. The accents of suspicion and contempt may be heard in the Queen's letter : " You and the traitor spoke half an hour together without anybody's hearing ; wherein, though we that trust you with a kingdom are far from mistrusting you with a traitor, yet both for comeliness, example and your own discharge, we marvel you would carry it no better ; especially having in all things since your arrival been so precise to have good testimony for your actions, as whenever anything was to be done to which our commandment tied you, it seemed sufficient warrant for you if your fellow councillors allowed better of other ways . . . to whose conduct, if we had meant that Ireland, after all the calamities in which they have wrapped it, should still have been abandoned, then it was very superfluous to have sent over such a personage as yourself ".[1]

When she wrote this letter the Queen did not know that Essex had already concluded a truce with Tyrone, and was on his way home, perhaps to force her hand. This is not the place to follow the struggle that ensued between Elizabeth and the first man in the kingdom ; though perhaps one may say that, underneath the overt conflict of wills for power, one discerns a sexual element : the desire of the woman to reduce the irreducible element of the male in him, to get her own back on the man who would not submit, perhaps on life itself that had cheated her. Ineluctably, she was driven to kill him—he asked for it ; and then she found that she had killed her own heart. But it was Ireland, with that fatal touch, that produced the last conflict—as in so many famous careers : Strafford, the younger Pitt, Peel, Parnell, Gladstone.

The winter of 1599 saw Tyrone at the apparent apogee of his power, in a position to give the law to most of Gaelic Ireland.

---

[1] R. B. Devereux, *Lives and Letters of the Devereux, Earls of Essex*, II. 73-5. Professor Falls (*op. cit.* 246) says " regarding the private conversation with Tyrone, she was indeed gentle ". I do not think that was the tone of her voice.

He left his Ulster fastness on an ostentatious pilgrimage to the relic of the Holy Cross at Tipperary. Religion, the restoration of a Catholic Ireland, had become the ground-bass of his propaganda, with the Irish people at home and for support among Catholic powers abroad. " Hang thee up ", said Essex to him at the ford, " thou carest for religion as much as my horse."[1] Of course ; but it provided the most effective unifying motive for action : without it, the idiot people would not have been so moved. His mission sanctified by the holy relic, Tyrone moved into Munster on his real purpose : arranging measures of co-operation with the leading rebels there, the Sugane (*i.e.* straw-rope) Earl of Desmond and Florence MacCarthy. O'Donnell had come down the western route to prey on the Earl of Thomond and the O'Briens for their loyalty ; Tyrone now spoiled Lord Barry for his. We see the cracks in Celtic unity, and actually the exceptional accord between O'Donnell and his father-in-law was beginning to loosen under the unnatural strain. Hugh Roe, who was a doughtier fighter than his senior partner, was beginning to think himself as good a man : which was not the case.

At last, in 1600, the right man was sent to take command of the situation : Mountjoy, a very different character from his friend Essex, cautious, reflective, systematic, persistent : just what was needed. He had not wished to go and, owing to the wastage of generals in the wars, there were very few available to choose from.[2] He was accompanied by Sir George Carew as Lord President of Munster : also a very good choice, able, politic, tough, perhaps a good sort, for he was very dear to Cecil and much liked by the Queen. We see here, too, the two parties in the state balanced in these appointments. But we find Cecil playing the part of honest broker, in the interests of the service doing good offices between the two, doing his best to make them good friends.[3] Cecil well deserved the absolute confidence of the Queen : only he and his father had this capacity of rising above their own personal affections and affiliations in the interests of the state. And clever honesty received its reward : when the crisis of Essex's outbreak came,

---

[1] Fynes Moryson, *op. cit.* II. 321. [2] *Ibid.* 273.
[3] Cf. J. Maclean ed., *Letters from Sir Robert Cecil to Sir George Carew* (Camden Society), 5, 30.

after a moment's terrible apprehension, Mountjoy passed over to Cecil's side, as Vere had done before. The circle that was to control the peaceful accession of James was forming.

We are fortunate in having an intimate portrait of Mountjoy and his doings in Ireland from the hand of his secretary, Fynes Moryson. It is an engaging character that emerges, if a somewhat cool and reserved one, with none of the *brio* of the more familiar Elizabethans : all his ardour seems to have gone into his lifelong liaison with Penelope Rich, Essex's sister : that and the study of divinity were the two passions of his life. In his youth Mountjoy had been a Catholic : the Blounts were all tinged with Catholicism. His father's exhaustion of the family fortune by his addiction to alchemy gave his son the motive, and the motto, *Ad re-aedificandam antiquam Domum*. Where in Ireland most people found the grave of their fortunes, Mountjoy made his. He needed to be careful, and he was.

Fynes Moryson describes him for us. " His forehead was broad and high ; the eyes great, black and lovely ; his nose something low and short, and a little blunt in the end ; his chin round ; his cheeks full, round and ruddy ; his countenance cheerful and as amiable as ever I beheld of any man."[1] Mountjoy was a man of delicate sensibilities and rather delicate health, of which he took care : " In Ireland he wore jerkins and round hose . . . and besides his ordinary stockings of silk, he wore under boots another pair of woollen or worsted, with a pair of high linen boot-hose, yea, three waistcoats in cold weather and a thick ruff, besides a russet scarf about his neck thrice folded under it. So as I never observed any of his age and strength to keep his body so warm. . . . In the time of the war, he used commonly to break his fast with a dry crust of bread, and in the spring time with butter and sage, with a cup of stale beer, wherewith sometimes in winter he would have sugar and nutmeg mixed." And, like Sir Winston Churchill, " he used to sleep in the afternoons, and that long, and upon his bed ". This had the advantage that he was often very wide awake at night, before others were stirring. He was an intellectual kind of man, who " delighted in study, in gardens, an house richly furnished and delectable rooms for retreat ". For " in his nature he loved private retiredness, with good fare and some few choice friends ". A close concealer of his secrets and sparing of speech, " he kept his word in public affairs

[1] Fynes Moryson, *op. cit.* II. 262 foll.

inviolably, without which he could never have been trusted of the Irish ".

Such a man was well suited to the task before him, though no-one could have guessed how well. He was a man of a cool courage, who deliberately exposed himself to danger to embolden his men. (Tyrrell told off a hundred shot to look out for him.) Several of his staff were killed beside him. Exposure to the conditions of Irish warfare, to winter weather, probably took toll of his health ; for, only a few years after the end of the war, he died, at forty-three.

His first care was to restore the morale of the army : " the hearts of the English common soldiers, broken with a current of disastrous successes, he heartened and encouraged by leading them warily, expecially in his first actions : being more careful that our men should not be foiled than that the rebels should be attempted with boldness ".[1] He built up their confidence in a series of smaller actions, gradually pressing in on Tyrone. His policy—as in similar wars later, in South Africa, for example— was to establish blockhouses containing the enemy : these were so well planted that they broke up co-operative movements among the rebels. It was all part of the policy of ceaselessly harrying the enemy and giving them no rest to recruit their strength. Hence his prosecution of winter warfare, himself in the saddle commonly five days a week at least. " This brake their hearts ; for the air being sharp and they naked, and they being driven from their lodgings into the woods bare of leaves, they had no shelter for themselves."[2] Their cattle were wasted by driving to and fro ; in spring-time they could not sow, and before harvest their corn was cut down before it was ripe. In fact, it was a war of attrition : only starving them out would make them yield. On the English side, this made the war all the more expensive : the army and the garrisons had to be provisioned from England. But commissariat had improved and supplies were regular. Cecil confided to Carew that the war was costing £300,000 a year and in the exchequer " the receipts are so short of the issue as my hair stands upright to think of it ".[3] But the government never failed to give Mountjoy and Carew support : they were determined to see the thing through now, none more so than the Queen who would not hear of accepting any less than unconditional surrender.

[1] *Ibid.* 268.   [2] *Ibid.* 270.   [3] *Letters of Sir R. Cecil to Sir G. Carew,* 148.

Then Mountjoy took the decisive step of planting Docwra, with an army of 4000, as large as his own, on Lough Foyle. In spite of a very high rate of sickness among the troops, this began to yield dividends at once. O'Donnell's cousin, Neill Garve, of the older branch—who thought himself more entitled to the chieftainship—came in with large offers, which he proceeded to fulfil. His hands were imbrued in his kinsmen's blood, so that he could not turn back. " For Neill Garve ", wrote Docwra, " I cannot compare him to anything more like than a quince. Let him be sugared and dressed with much cost and he will be good for somewhat."[1] He was good for a great deal : he made a rift in the solid support of the O'Donnells for rebellion.[2] The plantation of Derry enabled the tribe of O'Dogherty that occupied the rich cattle country of Inishowen,. the peninsula between Lough Foyle and Lough Swilly, to escape the control of O'Donnell and O'Neill. These lesser tribes found their interest often in alliance with government against the tyranny of the greater ; it was Mountjoy's consistent policy to support them and not to countenance claims to overlordship. Early in 1601 Docwra was able to report, " I doubt not of present possession of all Tyrconnell, which is almost wholly wasted already ".[3] Shortly after, he gave as his opinion that unless some foreign power intervened, the war would be finished by the summer.

But that summer rumours grew that the Spaniards were preparing to intervene. Carew was convinced that these were true and that Munster would be their objective. He had done as well as Mountjoy.[4] With an army of 3000 in list, actually down to 1700 effectives, he had at one time some 7000 rebels to hold. He had dealt with them by a skilful mixture of policy and hard blows. He made the utmost use of dissension among the rebels, exploiting the divisions within the house of Desmond and buying the support of Dermot O'Connor ; for the rest, a relentless campaign of reducing rebel castles by artillery. It was fortunate for him that by 1601 the Munster Rising of 1598, which had overthrown the Undertakers and the whole plantation, was practically extinguished, with the Sugane Earl and the light-headed Florence MacCarthy, who had such exaggerated

---

[1] *Cal. S.P. Ireland, 1600–1*, 263.
[2] For his career *v.* Cyril Falls, " Neill Garve : English Ally and Victim ", *The Irish Sword, Journal Mil. Hist. Soc. Ireland*, 1949–50.
[3] *Cal. S.P. Ireland, 1600–1*, xxi-xxii.
[4] For Carew in Munster, *v. Pacata Hibernia.*

notions of his own greatness, safe in the Tower. Carew's services well merited the recognition they received : " My faithful George, If ever more service of worth were performed in shorter space than you have done, we are deceived among many eye witnesses : we have received the fruit thereof and bid you faithfully credit that whatso wit, courage, or care may do, we truly find they have all been thoroughly acted in all your charge. And for the same believe that it shall be neither unremembered nor unrewarded, and in meanwhile believe my help nor prayers shall never fail you. Your Sovereign that best regards you, E. R."[1]

That summer, reinforcements of 2000 men were ordered for Munster. In September a Spanish fleet of some forty ships was seen off Scilly, making for Ireland. It intended, it seems, to land at Cork ; but it could not make it and was blown farther west to Kinsale. On board were some 4500 foot, some artillery, plenty of provisions and saddles for the horses the Spaniards expected the Irish to provide. A smaller detachment of the expedition, with some 800 men, got separated by bad weather off Corunna and arrived later, farther west at Castlehaven. When the news of the landing arrived Mountjoy was at Kilkenny, and at once wrote to Cecil, " If we beat them, let it not trouble you though you hear all Ireland doth revolt, for (by the grace of God) you shall have them all return presently with halters about their necks : if we do not, all providence bestowed on any other place is vain ".[2] The crisis upon which the issue of the war turned had arrived and was being met with a spirit of resolution on all sides.

At Kilkenny, Carew was able to say that he could supply the Lord Deputy's army for two or three months ; he had managed to save all his provisions for the last half-year, and much of his munitions.[3] Mountjoy, overcome by this providential frugality, rose from his chair and embraced Carew : he was able to march south immediately. Characteristically, Mountjoy was not underrating his opponents : he reminded Cecil that " the war of the Low Countries was begun and hath been maintained with few more natural Spaniards than are arrived here already, and that putting arms and discipline into this people, they are more warlike than any of his auxiliaries ".[4] In London the government levied an additional three thousand

[1] Fynes Moryson, II. 449.
[2] *Ibid.* 454.
[3] *Pacata Hibernia*, 349.
[4] Fynes Moryson, III. 10.

men, making 5000 reinforcements in all : they were taking no chances.[1] Sir Richard Leveson with a squadron of the fleet was ordered to the Munster coast : the Lord Admiral boasted that " there never was such a fleet of the Queen's ships so suddenly sent out by any Admiral before ".[2] The Queen had Mountjoy's spirited letter " read to us all in Council ", improving the occasion with some words of her own to the effect that so far from Mountjoy being a sacrifice, " she doth not doubt but you shall live to do her many more services, after you have made the province of Munster serve for a sepulchre to these new conquerors ".[3] In her own hand the old woman wrote to Mountjoy : " We doubt not but their gain will be their bane, and glory their shame. . . . Tell Our Army from Us that we make full account that every hundred of them will beat a thousand, and every thousand theirs doubled. I am the bolder to pronounce it in his name that ever hath protected my righteous cause, in which I bless them all. And putting you in the first place I end, scribbling in haste, Your loving Sovereign, E. R."

The time of decision had come : one senses it in the letters.

The clue to the operations that autumn around Kinsale was the rapidity with which Mountjoy marched upon the town, with slightly inferior forces, to besiege the Spaniards within its walls. (Nothing much of those walls remains today, only a gate-tower on the steep hill out of the town to the west to give one an idea.) One cannot but think that Don Juan de Águila, experienced soldier as he was, was rather passive to allow himself to be cooped up there by an inferior force. But he was waiting for the appearance of the Irish army of Tyrone and O'Donnell, to whom he despatched letter after letter : together they would have an overwhelming superiority over Mountjoy. Meanwhile, Mountjoy captured the two forts that commanded the approach by the river, invested the town, drawing the entrenchments—that were designed by Josiah Bodley—ever closer, beginning his bombardment of the town. As usual, the worst enemies were weather and sickness. In a winter siege the advantages were with the besieged : they had houses to live in and shelter. The weather was rainy and tempestuous ; the trenches were filled with

---

[1] Fynes Moryson, III. 20-1.   [2] q. Falls, 298.
[3] Fynes Moryson, III. 21.

water ; men died daily in dozens, hundreds of them were sick :
Mountjoy opened a hospital for them in Cork, but it was nothing
like sufficient. Many more hundreds deserted as the siege
dragged on, until numbers were down to what they had been
before the reinforcements arrived. Mountjoy wrote : " I protest
even our chief commanders (whose diligence I cannot but
mightily commend) do many of them look like spirits with toil
and watching " ; and we have a self-portrait of him from " my
house of turf . . . having been up most of this night, it groweth
now about four o'clock in the morning, at which time I nightly
choose to visit our guards myself and am now going about
that business, in a morning as cold as stone and as dark as
pitch ".[1]

Mountjoy was convinced that if he had not marched on them
immediately, but had allowed the Spaniards to be master of the
field for even a week, " all the towns of this province would
have revolted and the current of that fortune would have run
so violently through all Ireland that it would have been too
late to have stopped it ". Meanwhile, a month had passed and
there was no sign of Tyrone and O'Donnell : this was having
the worst effect on the Spaniards, who felt themselves deserted
and betrayed. At last they made a full-scale sortie, with some
2000 men, against the trenches and the fort that was being built
close up to the west gate of the town. The Spaniards captured
the fort and entered the trenches, in spite of many brave charges
by Sir William Godolphin.[2] But at length they were beaten
back with heavy losses—nearly two hundred killed ; among the
heaps of dead it was noticed that most were scarred by venereal
disease.[3] This was the end of any aggressive attempt on the
part of the Spaniards to break out : they were content to await
rescue by their dilatory allies.

O'Donnell was first to arrive, having made a rapid march,
once he started, down the west of Ireland and given Carew the
slip, who had been sent to intercept him, by a characteristically
agile move across bog and mountain. But Carew, moving on
inner lines, got back to Kinsale first. On Thomond's arrival
with reinforcements, Mountjoy formed a west camp to confront
O'Donnell's army, the forces he had brought from Ulster with
those he had raised from the far west of Munster. Now, moving
slowly and dilatorily, Tyrone arrived on the scene. He has been

[1] *Ibid.* 35-6. [2] *Ibid.* 54. [3] *Ibid.* 55.

much blamed for his slowness in coming to the rescue ; but who knows what his difficulties in Ulster were ? It seems probable that the mortal threat of the establishment on Lough Foyle held him up, and it would have been better for him had he never come.

Now Mountjoy in turn was encircled by Tyrone and O'Donnell and the Irish. It was becoming a contest of endurance, and it is probable that, for the Irish, Tyrone's Fabian tactics would have answered best, wearing the English down without risking a battle in open country. But it seems that O'Donnell and the Spaniards in combination were too much for this subtle, calculating mind. They determined on a combined assault upon the English, the Spaniards breaking out of the town at the moment of the Irish attack. Together they now had a three to two superiority at least. Mountjoy was very watchful, hardly going to bed at night ; but the Irish weakness for whisky gave away the day of the assault. One of Tyrone's commanders, running out of whisky, sent over to Carew for a bottle and rewarded him with a message to stand on guard that night.[1]

It was the morning of Christmas Eve, dark and wild, with thunder and lightning about. Mountjoy was already alert, making his dispositions : which reveal very clearly what he thought of the Irish. He took with him three or four hundred horse and under 1200 foot to confront Tyrone and O'Donnell, leaving 4000 men to watch half the number of Spaniards. Tyrone and O'Donnell were late in putting their plan into execution : they had been quarrelling as to who should have the honour of the attack.[2] So that when Mountjoy arrived on the scene their dispositions were not very firm ; indeed they were in course of withdrawal behind a bog and were caught in some confusion. The Irish army was drawn up in three divisions, Tyrone in command of the main battle, Tyrrell of the van with a reinforcement of 250 Spaniards, O'Donnell of the rear. When Mountjoy learned that there was open champion country beyond the bog—just what he wanted—he gave his orders at once : he had most of the horse with him, the foot were to be drawn up " with all expedition close together, who marched as fast as it was possible for them to keep their orders ".[3] There

[1] Fynes Moryson, III. 76.   [2] Cf. Sean O'Faolain, *The Great O'Neill*, 262.
[3] *Pacata Hibernia*, 418.

was some skirmishing at the bog-side, and a charge of horse towards Tyrone's main battle of a thousand foot, wheeling about at the last moment. Then all the English horse together charged the Irish horse and their battle in the rear : in a few minutes they broke up in disorder and streamed from the field, pursued by the English cavalry, hacking and hewing. Tyrrell attempted to bring his van to the rescue, but the Irish, in a panic at what had happened, fled, leaving the Spaniards to be cut down and most of them killed. O'Donnell in the rear, observing the rout, left the field without fighting and made for Castlehaven, whence he escaped to Spain.

That one cavalry charge on open ground saw the end of independent Gaelic Ireland.[1] There were only the fragments now to gather up.

First, the Spaniards. Águila was ready to surrender. At his first conference with Godolphin, who conducted the negotiations to Mountjoy's warm satisfaction, Águila said that he had found the Lord Deputy an honourable enemy, but " the Irish not only weak and barbarous, but (as he feared) perfidious friends ".[2] Mountjoy, in reporting the terms of the surrender to the Council, says : " The contempt and scorn in which the Spaniards hold the Irish, and the distaste which the Irish have of them, are not to be believed by any but those who are present to see their behaviours and hear their speeches ; insomuch as . . . it will be a difficult thing for the Irish hereafter to procure aids out of Spain ".[3] So much for the co-operation of Catholic Ireland with Catholic Spain.

Águila even volunteered himself to go and blast the Irish out of Dunboy Castle, which O'Sullivan Bere had taken possession of on the surrender of the Spaniards.[4] But Mountjoy was anxious to see the backs of the Spaniards : fortunate in negotiations as in war, for his own strength was much depleted by sickness, and Spain was preparing further reinforcements,

---

[1] Cf. for the Irish view, G. A. Hayes-McCoy, " The Battle of Kinsale, 1601 ", *Irish Historical Studies*, 1949. " In so far as the history of Ireland is concerned, it is *the* decisive battle. With the defeat of Tyrone and O'Donnell perished alike the organisation of Ireland as a Gaelic nation, the institutional system, the mercenary scheme—the entire gamut of Gaelic social establishments." G. A. Hayes-McCoy, *Scots Mercenary Forces in Ireland, 1565–1603*, 334.

[2] Fynes Moryson, III. 89.   [3] *Ibid.* 104.   [4] *Pacata Hibernia*, 484.

which the surrender made pointless. It remained for Carew to order the reduction of Dunboy : its defenders thought the place impregnable, that last remote peninsula in the farthest west : a quiet enough spot now beside its little bay, with the rocks where so many men were entombed, the blackened shell of a victim of later Irish warfare looking on the desolate scene. The Castle was battered in, when MacGeoghan its commander, lying mortally wounded, " raised himself from the ground, snatching a lighted candle, and staggering therewith to a barrel of powder . . . offering to cast it into the same . . . was by our men instantly killed ".[1] Next day all the prisoners were executed. " The whole number of the ward consisted of one hundred and forty three selected fighting men, being the best choice of all their forces, of the which no one man escaped, but were either slain, executed or buried in the ruins : so obstinate and resolved a defence had not been seen within this kingdom."

Tyrone's army melted away in his long flight from Kinsale back to the north : most of them deserted, many cut off and drowned in the bogs by their countrymen who had suffered their depredations. Tyrone no longer had an army, but he had the magic of his name—he was The O'Neill—and the loyalty of his people : no-one would betray him as Desmond had been betrayed. He took refuge with his following in the trackless depths of the forest of Glenconkein where no-one could pursue him. He was ready to submit upon modest conditions. His heroic effort for Gaelic Ireland was at an end : he had been irretrievably defeated, by the follies of his own side, by the hopelessness of an antiquated, chaotic society, as much as by the power and discipline of a modern state. He was no longer a danger. He could be a helpful instrument in the settlement of the north. The policy of reduction by starvation was being pursued : all good men desired an end to the miseries of the war.

It is evident from their correspondence that Cecil and Mountjoy both desired that Tyrone's offers should be accepted. It is equally evident that the obstacle was the Queen. She had been offended at her most sensitive spot : not merely her vanity, but what was more fundamental—and a key to her character— her pride. A rooted part of it was engaged : her fixed resolve, in the absence of other satisfactions, to leave a name to posterity

[1] *Pacata Hibernia,* 573-4.

as a famous and unchallengeable ruler. Beneath the careful accents of her Secretary we detect Cecil's disagreement, we perceive the difficulty he was having with the autocratic old woman he, nevertheless, so rightly admired. He confided his trouble to Mountjoy, with whom he had now achieved, in the perceptive words of Fynes Moryson, " a firm combination of love, or (at least) so firm as to such great persons is incident ".[1] The Queen had refused any authority to Mountjoy to pardon Tyrone. Cecil: " as her Majesty (in these cases) may well (out of experience of government) assume more to her royal prudence than any of her Council: so (God in Heaven doth know) that even in these great causes, she is pleased to proceed more absolutely than ever, by the rules of her own princely judgment ".[2] He refers to " the difficulty of her own nature to forgive that offender, as although in effect she had done little more than nothing before, yet she thinks any mercy to him to be much ". A month later, " I am sorry to find my Sovereign's heart so great and magnanimous (though I must confess she hath very just cause) as not to be contented to have made virtue of necessity and . . . pardon the greatest Rebel . . . where I am of opinion that if he were sure to be pardoned and live in any security, with the quality of any greatness . . . he would be made one of the best instruments in that kingdom ".[3]

A royal letter to Mountjoy recurs to the theme of the anguish the Irish war had brought her: it refers to the burden " which our Crown of England cannot endure, without the extreme diminution of the greatness and felicity thereof, and alienation of Our people's minds from Us, considering that for these only rebellions in Ireland, We have been forced to part with many of Our ancient possessions, which are part of Our flowers of Our Crown, and to draw from our subjects (a thing contrary to Our nature) those great payments . . . they would not so willingly have borne, nor We so justly could have imposed upon them ".[4]

In the month before her death, as she drew near to what she must have thought of as rendering her own account, she gave

---

[1] Fynes Moryson, III. 172.   [2] *Ibid.* 189-90.
[3] *Ibid.* 205.   [4] *Ibid.* 225.

way and authorised Mountjoy to pardon Tyrone. She had not been able to make peace with Spain, but her successor would be able to : everything was rounded up and in order for him to take over—a new and pacific reign, a more opulent and less heroic age.

INDEX

439

440

Index

Index

Frobisher, Sir Martin, 187, 191, 192-4, 195, 223, 256-7, 268, 275-6, 282, 287, 298, 299

Galway, 92, 99, 108, 125, 148, 149
Garrard, William, military writer, 371-2
Gascoigne, George, poet, 349
Gemblours (Gembloux), 347
Germans in Virginia, 230; *Reiters*, 328; Germany, 240
Gerrard, Sir William, 88, 121
Ghent, 352, 376-7; —, Pacification of, 347, 378
Gil, Juan, ensign-bearer in the Armada, 274, 275
Gilbert, Adrian, 192, 195, 207; —, Bartholomew, 226; —, Sir Humphrey, 39, 66; — and American colonisation, 1, 6, 40, 187, 194-5, 206, 207-8, 210, 211-13; — in Ireland, 127; — in Netherlands, 328, 342-3, 344; — and North-West Passage, 137-8, 170, 191-2
Gilpin, Bernard, 'Apostle of the North', 15
Glamorgan, 56, 63
Glasgow, 421
Glendower, Owen, 45, 46, 81, 88
Gloucestershire, 359
Goa, 162, 163, 198-9, 203
Goes, 342-3
Godolphin, Sir Francis, 298; —, Sir William, 33, 153, 433, 435
Góngora, Luis de, 243
Goodere, Sir Henry, 367
Goodman, Gabriel, Dean of Westminster, 74, 82
Gorges, Arthur, 270; —, Sir Ferdinando, 226, 232, 305, 311-12
Gosnold, Bartholomew, 225-6, 228
Graham, Border tribe, 8, 16, 26, 27-8
Grave, 384, 407
Gravelines, battle of, 273, 277-8
Green, Philip, Borderer, 13-14
Greenland, 165, 193, 195-6
Greenwich, 168, 193, 339-40, 398; —, Treaty of, 377-9, 398
Grenville family, 40-1; —, Captain, 41; —, John, 41, 222; —, Sir Richard, 43, 66, 257, 339; — and American colonisation, 6, 40-1, 206, 214-18, 221, 269; — at Flores, 51, 289, 299-301; — and the Armada, 269, 270, 279; — and *Terra Australis*, 160-1, 181-2; —, William, 40
Grey, Border family, 14-15; —, Sir Edward, 14; — Lionel, 14-15; —, Arthur, Lord Grey de Wilton, 123, 333, 338

Groningen, 401, 402
Guiana, 41, 221-5, 226, 236
Guinea coast, 39, 164, 166, 172-4, 259
Gunpowder Plot, 85, 86
Gwydir, 60, 61, 68, 71, 73, 74
Gwynne, Roger, Welsh Jesuit, 86

Haarlem, 345-6
Hakluyt, Richard, the elder, 206, 207, 209-10; —, Richard the younger, 159, 160, 161-2, 175, 188, 198, 201, 206-11, 215, 224, 226, 227, 232, 235
Hampshire, 356, 358, 359-60, 361
Hanseatic ports, 287, 290-1
Harcourt, Robert, 225
Hariot, Thomas, 160, 208, 215-16
Hastings, Lady Mary, 171
Hatton, Sir Christopher, 77, 159, 244, 368
Haverfordwest, 64, 82
Havre, 335-6, 338
Hawkins family, 39-40, 161; —, Sir John, 207, 257, 325, 326; — and the Armada, 263, 268, 276; — and the Navy, 251-5, 265, 271, 282, 299; — in the West Indies, 39-40, 174-7, 200, 233, 290, 301; —, Sir Richard, 183, 190, 253; —, William, 181, 274; —, Captain William, 188, 203; —, 'Old' William, 39, 166, 190
Henry V, 162; Henry VII, 35, 46-9, 55, 68, 158, 165, 347; Henry VIII, 4, 5, 25, 36, 45, 48, 50, 163, 165, 166, 167, 331, 348; — and Ireland, 91-7, 129; — and the Navy, 249-50; — and Wales, 52-3, 81
Henry II, King of France, 4, 330-1, 334; Henry III, —, 289, 377; Henry IV, —, 240, 289, 299, 304, 379, 396-8, 407; —, as King of Navarre, 256, 259
Henry the Navigator, Prince, 162-3
Herbert family, 45, 50, 56, 58, 62, 63, 77; —, George, 50, 83; —, of Cherbury, Lord, 50, 61, 62, 82-3; —, Sir William, 50, 87; *and v.* Pembroke
Herefordshire, 357
Herle, William, 349, 352
Hertfordshire, 356-7, 358
Hexham abbey, 11
Hicks, Captain, Cornish pirate, 64
Holinshed, Raphael, 367
Holland, 376, 382, 393
Holywell, 82
Hooker, John, 219
Horne, Robert, Dean of Durham, 11
Howard, of Effingham, Lord, Lord High Admiral, 268-9, 271-9, 282-3, 305, 309-10, 364; —, Lord Thomas, 276,

443

Index

Lodge, Thomas, 235
Loftus, Adam, Archbishop of Dublin, 98, 111, 120-1, 122, 424; — family, 121
Lok, Michael, 194, 220
London, 4, 51, 52, 59, 97, 127, 199, 200, 230, 279, 296-7, 304, 314, 325, 326, 356, 359, 361, 362-3, 403, 404, 407, 408; — Musters, 365-6; —, St. Paul's, 279, 388; Tower of —, 20, 22, 38, 43, 44, 112, 336, 363, 431
Lope de Vega, 178, 268
Lough Foyle, 422, 425, 430
Louth, County, 98
Lucy, Sir Thomas, 367
Ludlow, 67-8, 81
Luttrell, Sir John, 173

Maas, River, 380, 384, 400; Maastricht, 375
MacCarthy, Irish sept, 112; —, Florence, 112, 427, 429-30
Macdonald, Scottish clan, 4, 97, 110-11, 113-16; Macdonell in Ireland, 114-115; Sorley Boy —, 97, 110, 114-15
Macgillapatrick, Irish chief, 107
Macleod, Scottish clan, 4
Madison, Captain, 230
Madrid, 268, 288, 393
Magellan, Fernando, 183; — Straits, 159, 183, 189, 235
Magrath, Myler, Archbishop of Cashel, 87, 124
Maguire, Irish chief, 97, 153
Malaya, 199, 200
Malines, 351, 377
Manteo, American Indian, 214, 217-18
Margate, 279, 363, 405
Marlborough, John Churchill, Duke of, 245
Marnix, Philip, Lord of, 377
Marqués, Pedro Menéndez, 221, 289, 319
Mary I, 38, 39, 50, 129, 159, 173, 248, 249, 329, 330-1; Mary of Guise, Regent of Scotland, 331, 333-4; Mary, Queen of Scots, 29, 30, 255, 321, 330-1, 334, 338
Mathew family, 63
Maurice, of Orange, Prince, 382, 393-4, 399, 400-2, 406-7, 408-10, 413
Maurice family, of Clennenau, 54; —, Sir William, 54, 64-5
Meath, diocese, 117, 118, 119, 121
Medina Sidonia, Alonso, Duke of, 184, 267-8, 274-8, 281, 306-10, 311, 372
Mediterranean, the, 169, 197, 198, 248, 249-50, 281, 320

Melvill, James, Scottish minister, 12, 23
Mendoza, Bernardino de, Spanish ambassador, 211, 388
Menéndez, Pedro, colonial governor, 164, 175
Merriman, Captain, 115
Meteren, Emanuel van, 400
Meynartson, Dutch commissary, 413
Meyrick, Andrew, 189; —, Sir Gelly, 76, 87
Mexico, 163, 175-6
Middelburg, 349
Middleton family, 52, 59; —, Sir Hugh, 52; —, Marmaduke, Bishop of David's, 79-80; —, Sir Thomas, 52, 297; —, Captain William, 51
Mildenhall, John, 203
Milford Haven, 33, 64
Moluccas, the, 162, 163, 186, 187, 202
Monaghan, County, 155; —, fort, 422
Mondragón, Spanish commander, 340, 343
Monmouthshire, 56
Mons, 344-5
Monson, Sir William, 316, 320
Montague, Lord, 362
Montaigne, Michel de, 3, 173, 174, 212, 234
Montgomery, Mrs., 155
More, Sir Thomas, *Utopia*, 166, 234
Morgan, Hugh, 49; — of Llantarnam, 81; —, Sir Matthew, 87, 305, 345; —, Rees, 80; —, Sir Thomas, 51, 340, 342, 345, 352, 353, 363, 395; —, Walter, 344-5; William, Bishop of St. Asaph ,73-5, 78, 79, 82; —, William, of Pen-y-coed, 139
Morley, Lord, 361-2
Morocco, 167, 172-4, 310
Morpeth, 12, 13, 14
Morton, Earl of, Regent of Scotland, 10
Moryson, Fynes, 428-9, 437; —, Sir Richard, 156
Moscow, 168-9, 170-1
Mount's Bay, 33, 39, 41, 176, 258
Mountjoy, 7th Lord, 192, 428; —, Charles Blount, 8th Lord, 94, 123, 126, 153, 270, 370-1, 402, 416-17, 424, 427-37; —, character of, 428-9
Munster, 86, 99, 103, 107, 137, 138, 146-8, 149, 150, 392, 417, 426, 430-6; —, Plantation of, 141-4, 430; — Rebellion (1598), 144, 425, 427, 430
Muscovy Company, 137, 168, 187, 191, 201, 227
Musgrave, Sir Simon, 15; —, Thomas, 15
Musters, County, 354-61

445

Index

THE END